Michael D. Murphy

CULTURAL ANTHROPOLOGY
A Contemporary Perspective

CULTURAL ANTHROPOLOGY
A Contemporary Perspective

Roger M. Keesing
Australian National University

HOLT, RINEHART AND WINSTON
New York   Chicago   San Francisco   Atlanta
Dallas   Montreal   Toronto   London   Sydney

Library of Congress Cataloging in Publication Data

Keesing, Roger M.   1935-
    Cultural anthropology: a contemporary perspective

    1.   Anthropology.   I.   Title.
GN25.K43   301.2   75-41354
ISBN 0–03–089424–7

Parts of this book appeared in a different form in *New Perspectives in Cultural Anthropology* by Roger M. Keesing and Felix M. Keesing, copyright © 1971 by Holt, Rinehart and Winston, Inc. The 1971 title was based on *Cultural Anthropology: The Science of Custom,* copyright © 1958 by Felix M. Keesing.

The author wishes to thank copyright holders for their kind permission to reproduce the following:

Figure 2.1 from S. L. Washburn and Ruth Moore, *Ape into Man: A Study of Human Evolution* (Boston: Little, Brown and Company, 1974), adapted from J. T. Robinson, "Adaptive Radiation in the Australopithecines and the Origin of Man," Viking Fund Publication in Anthropology No. 36, *African Ecology and Human Evolution,* edited by F. Clark Howell and François Bourlière, by permission of Aldine Publishing Company. Copyright by Wenner-Gren Foundation for Anthropological Research.

Figure 2.2 from J. E. Pfeiffer, *The Emergence of Man.* Revised and enlarged ed. Copyright © 1972 by Harper & Row, Publishers. By permission of the publishers.

Figures 2.3 and 2.5 from François Bordes, *The Old Stone Age.* Translation copyright © George Weiden-feld & Nicolson Limited 1968. Used with permission of McGraw-Hill Book Company and Weidenfeld & Nicolson.

Figure 5.1 from L. R. Binford and S. Binford, *New Perspectives in Archaeology.* (Chicago: Aldine Publishing Company). Copyright © 1968 by Wenner-Gren Foundation for Anthropological Research.

Figures 6.1, 7.1, 7.2, 7.3, 7.4, and 7.5 from Chester S. Chard, *Man in Prehistory.* 2d. ed. Copyright © 1969, 1975 by McGraw-Hill, Inc. Used with permission of McGraw-Hill Book Company.

Figures 13.2 and 13.5 from Roger M. Keesing, *Kin Groups and Social Structure.* Copyright © 1975 by Holt, Rinehart and Winston, Inc. By permission of the publishers.

Extract from Napoleon A. Chagnon, *Yǫnomamö: The Fierce People.* Copyright © 1968 by Holt, Rinehart and Winston, Inc. By permission of the publishers.

PREFACE

What began as a major revision of *New Perspectives in Cultural Anthropology* has become a quite different book and, in fact, a new book. The remaining elements of my father's *Cultural Anthropology* are gone; and so is much of the framework on which I had built.

Readers who know *New Perspectives* will see that the new book takes a less eclectic and synoptic stance. I try still to give an up-to-date overview of the discipline that challenges students by leading them to frontiers of exploration and controversy. But I take here a critical stance, theoretically and in places politically, toward much conventional anthropological thinking and practice. I focus more centrally on the wider issues of the world of the seventies that give meaning and urgency to what anthropologists do and know—to the transformation of the Third World, to the ecological crisis, racism, sexism, and neocolonialism. This changed focus is not simply a matter of "relevance." It reflects both a transformed political awareness and a realization that the anthropological paradigm in which I was raised intellectually has, in its relativism and its stress on cultural integration and uniqueness, generated mystification and myopia as well as understanding.

The book is not simple. I do not pretend that we have adequate answers to the big and urgent questions that must ultimately motivate our specialized research. Students deserve more than a compilation of what we think we know about kinship terms, chiefdoms, age grades, totemism, and the rest. I ask big questions and point toward emerging answers.

There are many substantial changes in the book at every level—from more serious and less sketchy discussions of biological evolution and culture history to more adequate treatment of human ecology, social stratification, urban anthropology, the anthropology of women, and other subjects. I have sought to render some chapters less complex and opaque, notably those on language and kinship. In view of the roughly doubled length and the availability of good discussions of the discipline and its historical development, I have eliminated the long appendix sections on these topics. I have tried to eliminate the inadvertent sexism in the use of language and in content that pervaded *New Perspectives,* without being awkward or obtrusive (the reader will seldom find "man" here in the generic sense, for example).

In avoiding talking down to student readers, whose intelligence is too often insulted by the tone of texts, I hope I have also created a useful guide which scholars in other disciplines can use to explore an unfamiliar field.

The revision has benefited at every stage from the counsel and concern of David P. Boynton and George D. Spindler. Helpful comments on the revision have been contributed by F. Aguilera, Frank Bessac, Stephen Boggs, Robert Carmack, Mina Caulfield, Richard Davis, Derek Freeman, Beatrice Gardner, John Grinder, William Haviland, Herbert Lewis, Bridget O'Laughlin, Peter Reynolds, Herbert Schwartz, George D. Spindler, Louise Spindler, Annette Weiner, and many student users.

I am indebted to Françoise Bartlett and Ruth Stark of Holt, Rinehart and Winston for superb editorial assistance, and to the latter and particularly to Judith Wilson for devoted efforts to find photographs that usefully illustrate the text (and do not merely decorate it). Many friends and colleagues have contributed photographic illustrations.

Shelley Schreiner has shared the challenge of rethinking and reworking at every stage; my deepest debts, intellectual and personal, are to her.

R. M. K.

Canberra, Australia
January 1976

CONTENTS

PART 4   ANTHROPOLOGY AND THE PRESENT   427

CASES

THE ANTHROPOLOGICAL APPROACH

1

The journey into anthropology can well begin with a parable—one that happens to be true. A Bulgarian woman was serving dinner to a group of her American husband's friends, including an Asian student. After her guests had cleaned their plates, she asked if any would like a second helping: a Bulgarian hostess who let a guest go hungry would be disgraced. The Asian student accepted a second helping, and then a third—as the hostess anxiously prepared another batch in the kitchen. Finally, in the midst of his fourth helping, the Asian student slumped to the floor; but better that, in his country, than to insult his hostess by refusing food that had been offered.

In a world suddenly made small, this is too true a parable of the human condition. For humans have spent the vast span of their time on earth separated into small groups, each with its own language, its own view of the world, its own body of customs, its own premises. Now these differences divide peoples and generate suffering and conflict at a time when members of the human community

need desperately to understand one another and to join in a common enterprise. Yet if these gulfs between ways of life keep peoples apart, they also illuminate human nature and the customs and beliefs we ourselves take for granted.

These patterns of assumption, perception, and custom that divide Egyptians and Chinese, that divide Americans from both, and each of us from Australian Aborigines or African tribesmen, are the focus of cultural anthropology. By viewing ways of life comparatively, across the widest reaches of time and space, the anthropologist seeks to distinguish what derives from being human from what derives from being born into a particular group of humans in a particular time and place. Anthropology is a study of universalities and uniqueness; a study of startling contrast and surprising similarity; a study of meaning and logic in what seems bizarre. It is a study of ourselves, as reflected in the mirror of ways of life far different from our own.

Humans are at once animals and trans-

1

formed beings. They build on biological foundations a scaffolding of meanings and conventions that are their own creations and that can vary enormously and be tinkered with endlessly. Humans do not discover their world; they *create* it. They populate it with beings and forces they cannot see, and believe to be eternally true and right the rules, conventions, and meanings they themselves create and are constantly changing.

Humans, in short, are peculiar beasts. And we are prone to misunderstand our nature because we confuse what is to be human with what it is to be our particular kind of human, living in our world of custom and belief. We project our own world onto other people's worlds, and inevitably we distort and misunderstand theirs. The best corrective we have—as a strategy of seeing other ways of life from the inside, of seeing ourselves from the outside, and of seeing our common humanity through it all—is to study ways of life as different from ours as possible. That challenge has carried cultural anthropologists to remote jungles and deserts in search of new vantage points from which to view other peoples, ourselves, and the human condition.

In a modern world flawed by oppression, suffering, and conflict and threatened with global ecological disaster, knowledge about human differences and human nature is not simply a source of understanding. Such knowledge can guide the way to new human possibility—to action, to change, to deepened humanity, to survival.

1.
Anthropology as a Field of Knowledge

"Anthropology" means "human study." But obviously anthropologists are not the only scholars concerned with human beings: so are specialists on Beethoven, Euripides, the Oedipus complex, and the Boer War. Nor do anthropologists study only human beings; some spend their time crashing through African thickets in pursuit of fuzzy primates.

In a large anthropology department, it would not be strange to find a human biologist specializing in the fossil bones of early man; an archaeologist excavating ancient communities in the Middle East; a linguist analyzing the structure of West African languages; a folklorist studying Eskimo mythology; a specialist in kinship and marriage among Burmese tribesmen; and an expert on Mexican-American farm laborers in California. Each of them would probably have a Ph.D. in anthropology.

What do these different kinds of anthropologists have in common? What makes anthropologists different from sociologists, psychologists, linguists, or historians? To sort out what anthropology is, what anthropologists do, and how things got that way is by no means simple.

That anthropology includes specialists in human biology—in evolution, in race, in primate behavior—as well as specialists in diverse facets of society and culture is partly a peculiar turn of academic history. The *physical anthropologist,* or human biologist, has for decades stood quite apart from colleagues concerned with cultural behavior. His or her interests were highly technical; the closest colleagues were anatomists or biologists. The Eskimo myth expert probably had to memorize details about the teeth of fossil apes in order to obtain an academic union card, but once his Ph.D. was in hand he quickly brushed the teeth out of his mind. Yet as we will soon see, the wide gulf between the physical anthropologist and his colleagues in "cultural anthropology" has recently been bridged in many places.

What physical anthropologists do, and why, will be considered briefly in Chapters 2, 3, and 4. Subsequent chapters will be concerned with "cultural anthropology." In sketching the field of anthropology in the paragraphs to follow, we will focus on our Middle Eastern archaeologist, African linguist, Eskimo folklorist, Burmese kinship specialist, and their colleagues, and in sorting them out describe the subfields of cultural anthropology and the common ground that unites them.

One major subfield of cultural anthropology is *prehistoric archaeology* or *prehistory*. Popular stereotypes of the archaeologist digging in ancient ruins are quite misleading. Unlike classical archaeologists, prehistorians study peoples without written records. Their attempts to reconstruct ancient ways of life take them through old rubbish heaps more often than temples, using atomic age scientific methods to find clues to the past. Moreover, increasingly their investigations have been linked theoretically with anthropological studies of living peoples.

The *anthropological linguist* may be particularly interested in the structural design of languages or in historical relationships between them. Such a scholar usually has a particular interest in unwritten languages and a special concern with the relation of language to other aspects of culture; but the strongest professional ties are likely to be with other linguists (who in different universities may occupy various niches).

The anthropological study of folklore and mythology is less clearly a special subfield, and we will not treat it as such. Again, however, our expert on Eskimo myths would have common interests with fellow-anthropologists as well as with folklorists in other disciplines.

"Cultural anthropology" is usually used to label a narrower field concerned with the study of human customs: that is, the comparative study of cultures and societies. "Comparative" in this sense implies a focus on ways of life that to other social scientists are exotic—on peoples of Africa, Asia, the Pacific, and Indians of the Americas—especially what used to be called "primitive" peoples. (The term "primitive," though it was intended anthropologically to refer only to a relatively simple technology, has such negative connotations that it has generally been abandoned; at this stage, we will for brevity's sake refer to such small-scale societies as "tribal.")

But one can study human cultures in very different ways. For years anthropologists, originally attached more to museums than universities, looked mainly at the natural history of tribal peoples, at the historical connections between them (an enterprise obviously closely linked to that of the prehistorians). Such study of culture history is often called *ethnology*.

In recent decades, anthropologists have concentrated not on tracing historical connections between peoples but on searching for scientific generalizations about human social behavior and cultures. *Social anthropology* has replaced ethnology as the core area of cultural anthropology. The social anthropologist continues the traditional focus on tribal and other non-Western peoples, though increasingly he or she may study complex urban societies as well. Anthropologists are also allied with social scientists in other disciplines in seeking to throw scientific light on human social life.

The relationships among these subfields of anthropology are set out schematically in Figure 1.1. Note that "cultural anthropology" is used in both a broad and narrow sense.

What unites these subfields of cultural anthropology? Anthropology—unlike economics or history or sociology or psychology—began with a concern (both scientific and antiquarian) with the tribal peoples discovered along the frontiers of European expansion. From the beginning, anthropologists studying myths or marriage customs or languages were concerned with the "primitive," the remote, the exotic. When they were accorded a niche in the halls of academia,

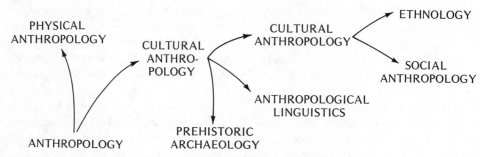

Figure 1.1   The subfields of anthropology.

they became the specialists in tribal life, in small-scale societies where change was slow, customs were relatively uniform, and technology was limited. Their role among the academic disciplines has always been broadly comparative. They have sought out the widest ranges of human experience in other times and places. And they have challenged their academic colleagues who would generalize too glibly from Western experience to talk of "economic man," "the human mind," or "the processes of history."

Anthropologists have long since broadened their interests away from tribal peoples to study peasants and urbanites and to examine the changes that have swept the non-Western world. So it is no longer true that anthropologists deal with different phenomena than sociologists or psychologists or political scientists (who themselves have increasingly broadened their domain of research to the Third World). But as we will see, the anthropologists' ways of looking at the phenomena of the modern world remain at least partly distinctive: their scientific "world view," their ways of tackling problems, and their research methods mainly developed in the study of small-scale tribal societies.

Though the members of our imaginary anthropology department (or its real-world counterparts) are a diverse group, they share a bond of common interest and training that gives anthropology a unity which might at first glance seem a myth. Though the cultural anthropologists may no longer remember much about ape teeth, most of them know a good deal about human biology, human evolution, and the behavior of our primate relatives. The African language specialist could probably talk intelligently about marriage systems in Burma, and would share with colleagues who specialize in Burmese and Eskimos many ideas about how to study farm workers in California anthropologically. Whatever the historical roots of anthropology's unity, the result has been profoundly important. The anthropologist, commanding a great range of evidence on human social behavior in the widest reaches of time and space, and *Homo sapiens'* biological heritage, is uniquely equipped to generalize about human nature, human differences, and human possibilities.

2.
Cultural Anthropology and Science

For modern Americans the "scientific" mode of approaching the world is treated with a special reverence and accorded great prestige. Science has taken us to the moon; it has given our species technological domination of the planet and insights into the nature of the universe and the biology of life.

The social sciences—psychology, political science, economics, sociology, social anthropolgy, and other allied disciplines—have felt a strong need to be "scientific." On the one hand, there is the prestige that derives from being a science, and there is an array of methods and models that have proven so powerful in exploring the natural world that they invite application to the study of human behavior and social life. On the other hand, as has been observed so many times as now to be trite, human abilities to understand, control, and predict human behavior and to grapple with problems of war, hostility, ignorance, and poverty have been outstripped by technology. We have the means to destroy human social life but lack the wisdom to direct its course.

Are the social sciences, and specifically anthropology, entitled to wear that sacred mantle of "science"? To answer this question we need first to consider what we mean by science.

What Is Science?

It seems most useful to define science roughly as a search for an orderly framework for explanation of events through systematic observation and/or experimentation. The special character of a scientific framework in the natural sciences is a systematic organization such that:

1. A class of events for which explanation is sought is defined.
2. A set of publicly specifiable, controlled procedures of observation, experimentation, and inference defined.
3. The theoretical statements (that is, the proposed scientific generalizations, laws, hypotheses) are specified in such a way that their relationship to the events is clear; hence their adequacy in accounting for the events can be tested. More simply, scientific statements must be related to observable events in such a way that they could be disproved on the basis of further evidence.
4. Scientific statements must ultimately be tied down as systematically as possible to the known and most basic laws of physics and chemistry.

This classical view of natural science remains broadly acceptable today. But our conception of what these provisions actually entail has shifted markedly in the last 50 years.

First, quantum physics posed some deep paradoxes regarding the observable and the observer. Even in subatomic physics the process of observing irrevocably changes the events being observed. Moreover, though events at one level are determinate (in the classical sense of causality), the events at a lower level are indeterminate except in some aggregate statistical sense. The behavior of each atom, or each subatomic particle, follows the laws of physics but cannot be predicted from them. Thus an older emphasis on "objectivity" and "prediction" has had to be scrapped or given new form.

Second, the process of scientific inference is by no means systematically based on a chain leading from observations to theories. Such works as James Watson's *The Double Helix* (1968) make clear that leaps of guesswork and intuition are needed to find a "right answer." The great biologist Paul Weiss once remarked that "nobody who followed the scientific method ever discovered anything interesting." Yet it remains true that once an answer is found, its "rightness" must be subject to possible disproof on the basis of further evidence.

Third, as Thomas Kuhn's *The Structure of Scientific Revolutions* (1970) makes vividly clear, a particular science at a particular stage works within a framework of assumptions: about what events are to be explained, about what would constitute an explanation, about how observation should proceed and how it should be tied to theories. Such a framework is called a paradigm. A major scientific breakthrough characteristically comes from pulling down such a framework and establishing a new one, not simply from making a new discovery. Yet as Popper (1972) and others have argued, this does not mean that paradigms are purely relative and noncumulative: some paradigms work better than others, and scientific knowledge cumulates as partial paradigms are joined together into more powerful and general ones.

Fourth, modern natural science increasingly is forced to deal with webs of explanation which are only indirectly testable and to postulate entities which are only indirectly observable. Thus subatomic physicists postulate the existence of particles they cannot observe in order to explain their measurements; cosmologists spin theories of the origin of the universe that become more or less plausible on the basis of astrophysical evidence but remain untestable; and astronomers devise more or less plausible explanations of quasars, the mysterious sources of radiation in distant space. Natural science today is much more a business of hypothetical entities and plausible guesses than it used to be.

Finally, the emergence since World War II of the sciences of *information*—of cybernetics, broadly defined—has given science a whole new side. These sciences deal not with things but with *differences*. They are concerned with form, pattern, and the organization of information (as Bateson (1973a), puts it, with "differences that make a difference"). They are only secondarily concerned with substances, causes, energy, and the like.

Is Anthropology Scientific?

What does all this have to do with anthropology and whether anthropology and the other social sciences are really "scientific"? There is, first, an important doubt whether humans trying to understand other humans can or should even try to be "scientific" about it. As European philosophers have pointed out, minds trying to understand other minds, conscious organisms observing conscious organisms, creatures with *moral* (that is, ethical/evaluative) systems studying creatures with (often different) moral systems can hardly begin to be objective. Physicists observing the statistical effects of unseen particles are processing their observations in mammalian brains subject to the foibles of psychology; but they come closer to objectivity than anthropologists observing Brazilian Indians. Though physicists disrupt the particles by observing their effects, they can control for this disruption; but the Brazilian Indians are *conscious* of being observed and may manage their outward behavior so as to create desired impressions (the anthropologist from an alien culture may not get the intended impression in any case). Moreover, our cultural values (for example, prudishness) and psychological orientations predispose us to see and record selectively (Devereux 1967). At best, minds meeting other minds involve a process of *intersubjectivity* that can too easily be spuriously glossed over and objectified.

Social scientists have sought very hard to be "scientific," to objectify and quantify. Ironically, in their concern with experimental rigor, systematic inference, laboratories, prediction, measurement, and so on, they have very often been emulating—even parodying—latter nineteenth-century natural science. As La Barre puts it, the social scientist has been "the invisible man desperately trying not to be seen seeing other men. . . . Fatuously 'experimental'-manipulative social scientists have lacked both the humility and the wit to recognize that they are feeding . . . man-contaminated data into their 'Truth Machines'" (La Barre 1967:viii).

Anthropologists have been less preoccupied with being scientific than most of their colleagues in psychology, sociology, and political science, and by and large this has probably been a blessing. Anthropologists have had to struggle with the problems of intersubjectivity as they have worked across gulfs of cultural differences: being unable to use tests, questionnaires, polls, experiments, and the like, in human communities where they were guests and where Western instruments of "objectivity" were obviously inappropriate, anthropologists have fallen back on human powers to learn, understand, and communicate. They have avoided many of the devices that spuriously objectify human encounters because they simply could not use them.

In any case, anthropologists have often dealt with phenomena for which classical scientific methods were clearly inappropriate. Trying to understand the symbolism and meaning of a myth or a ritual is not like predicting who will win an election or testing experimentally how a rat learns or how a freshman psychology student can be tricked. There is nothing to measure, count, or predict. The task is much more like that of trying to interpret *Hamlet.* One cannot dig up, measure, and test Shakespeare to find out whether one's interpretation is "true" and everybody else's is wrong. Rather, the interpretation can be "tested" only in terms of its plausibility in showing hitherto unperceived connections and meanings and its generalizability in illuminating other literary works in parallel fashion.

But the modern developments in science we noted—as in astronomical interpretation of quasars—have brought natural science rather closer to anthropological interpretation than one might think. An American astronomer at Cal Tech and a British astronomer at Jodrell Bank may have competing theories, but all either can do is try to find evidence that would make his or her interpretation more plausible than the other's. That partly closes the gulf between scientific theories and interpretations of literature or myths. Moreover, physicists dealing with the fundamentals of matter and energy now struggle with such deep and fundamental paradoxes of observation and indeterminacy and unobservability that their enterprise is pervaded by mystical faith and wonderment as well as methodological rigor. The point is not that anthropologists should glorify their reliance on insight and intuition and their leaps of faith, but rather that their dilemmas are more broadly shared than they often realize. (Anthropologists tend to be somewhat defensive about their imprecise methodology, subject as they are to the derision of their more "scientific" social science colleagues down the hall.)

A final point needs to be made about the relationship between anthropology and the modern natural sciences. The emergence of formal sciences of information that deal with form, pattern, relationship, and "programs" or algorithms in biological and man-made systems has important anthropological implications. As Bateson (1972a) has pointed out, the more "scientific" social sciences, in quest of methodological and formal models, have looked mainly to the physical sciences that deal with matter and energy. But that is probably the wrong place to look. For the emerging sciences of information deal with the organization of programs or algorithms and the transmission of information. And human knowledge—the knowledge of Bulgarian housewives and Brazilian Indians—falls into this broad class of biological information systems and is subject to their laws.

Consider the algorithms a spider acquires (as genetic information) whereby it spins webs. Webs are spun in a repeated design, created in a series of steps, yet adapted to different physical arrangements of leaves and branches the spider encounters. The web-building "program," though physically coded in the spider's cells, could be translated (if we knew enough to do so) into a mathematical model or a computer program.

Unlike the spider, the Bulgarian housewife acquires her "programs" for cooking dinner and serving second and third helpings by cultural learning. Brazilian Indians learn their "programs" for reckoning kinship or hunting monkeys. But as organized systems of information these programs are subject to the same laws as those for building spider webs. Moreover, just as we cannot yet learn about programs for web-building by analyzing spider cells electromicroscopically, we cannot learn about Brazilian hunting or kinship programs by neurophysiological investigation. The best we can presently do, in each case, is observe the events—spiders spinning webs over and over, Brazilians hunting or reckoning kinship (or talking about doing so)—and build the best and most systematic models we can of what they would have to "know" to do what they do.

We will suggest in a number of places in this book that the development of cybernetics offers hope that anthropology can increasingly be integrated with a formal theoretical science—a formal biology, if you like—of complex systems.

If all this does not provide a simple answer to whether social anthropology is "scientific"—or can be or should be—it throws useful light on the question itself. The anthropologist is trying to make sense of phenomena that, in scientific terms, are extraordinarily complicated. Like the astronomer, the anthropologist cannot do very much to experiment with the things he or she is studying. The human brain is a natural system of fantastic and mystifying complexity. And the social behavior of human beings is the product of so many intertwined variables that the narrow crystal focus of science seems scarcely adequate to this

challenge, though some hope lies in the emergence of interdisciplinary sciences of complex systems.

The anthropologist faces the problems of observer distortion in particularly drastic form, since he or she must try to communicate and understand across wide cultural gulfs. But facing these problems enables the anthropologist to see vividly how many of the devices used by colleagues in other social science disciplines to objectify the encounter between observer and observed depend on humans sharing the same implicit conceptual scheme. It allows the anthropologist to see that these devices often produce "data" that is spuriously objective and misleadingly precise. Being "scientific" (and hence impersonal, objective, experimental, and number-minded) can in cultural terms be seen as a special and peculiar preoccupation of ours, a modern substitute for the mystical powers of magic.

The anthropologist has no similarly elaborate bag of methodological devices to depersonalize and objectify the encounter with other human beings. In a sense, one has only a common humanity. To see what anthropologists do, and can do, with it we must turn to a mode of exploration that is peculiarly anthropological.

3.
Fieldwork

Fieldwork, the extended study of a community and its way of life, is in many ways the core experience of anthropology. First, of course, it is the source of information and generalizations the anthropologist brings home. The articles and books he or she writes distill out the essentials of accumulated knowledge and refer ultimately to particular experiences with particular people. "Bridewealth among the Agawaga is paid to the bride's father, who keeps the largest share and divides the rest among his close lineage kin," writes the anthropologist. The reasons for saying so are the events surrounding the eight marriages that occurred in the Agawaga village where the anthropologist lived, plus questioning and records of remembered past marriages. Such documentation of a way of life is called *ethnography.*

But fieldwork is more than that. For the anthropologist, fieldwork has been a kind of vision quest. By immersing oneself in another way of life, one comes to view oneself, one's own way of life, and humanity in a new perspective. Fieldwork is a profound experience, uncomfortable and sometimes shattering, but richly rewarding as well.

What does fieldwork actually entail? That depends in part on where the anthropologist goes to study. In the 1920s and 1930s, when the colonial frontiers were teeming with "primitives" and the ranks of anthropologists were thin, fieldwork usually meant going into an isolated tribal society armed with notebooks, camera, and quinine and setting up a residence in a native village for a year or longer. By the time an anthropologist arrived on the scene there were usually colonial administrators collecting taxes and imposing peace, and there were trade stores and missionaries. But the ethnographer set up housekeeping with the locals and did his or her best to ignore these intrusive influences. Since World War II, with new nations emerging on these frontiers and the rapid transformation of primitives into peasants, peddlers, and parliamentarians, fieldwork is increasingly done in less isolated settings. An Anatolian or Mexican village, an African port town, a Haitian market town, or an American ghetto may be the setting for fieldwork, as the world changes, the pressures for direct relevance to human problems increase, and the ranks of anthropologists expand.

Whether the setting is city, town, village, or jungle hut, the mode of anthropological research is in many important respects the same. Most essentially, it entails a *deep immersion* into the life of a people. Instead of studying large samples of people, the anthropologist enters as fully as possible into the everyday life of a small group of human beings. They become a microcosm of the whole. One learns their language and tries to learn their mode of life. One learns by participant observation, by living as well as viewing the new patterns of life. Successful fieldwork is seldom possible in a period much shorter than a year, especially where a new language and culture must be learned—ideally it is a good deal longer.

The ethnographer brings to the task techniques of mapping and census taking and skills of interviewing and observation. But one's position is radically different from that of political scientist or economist or sociologist colleagues studying events in their own society. The fieldworker's place and task are in many ways more like those of an infant. Like an infant, the anthropologist does not understand the noises, the visual images, the smells that carry rich meanings for the people being studied. One's learning must be of the same magnitude, and one's involvement correspondingly deep. As ethnographer, you typically cannot administer questionnaires at the outset to find out about the world you have entered, for many of the reasons an infant cannot: you do not know what the questions are that have answers and would have no medium for asking them. Time, deep involvement, a lot of guessing, a lot of practice, and a lot of mistakes enable you to begin to make sense of the scenes and events of this new cultural world.

But the anthropologist is not an infant, and that makes the task harder as well as easier. Unlike an infant, the fieldworker has self-sufficiency (though not always much in a jungle or desert) and can often use an interpreter to find out something about what is going on. The difficulty is that the anthropologist, unlike the infant, already knows a native language and set of patterns for thinking, perceiving, and acting. Instead of filling in an open framework with the design of one's people, as an infant does, the anthropologist must organize knowledge in terms of an existing design and interpret new experiences in terms of familiar ones. This renders the fieldworker's learning slower and harder (consider how much harder it is for an *adult* to learn a new language), and it inevitably distorts his or her perception.

Through all this, the anthropologist goes through routines of "gathering data"—taking a census, recording genealogies, learning about the local cast of characters, and querying informants about matters of customs and belief. What goes into his or her notebooks comes mainly from such routines. As we will see, marked advances have been made in recent years in minimizing the distorting effect of the ethnographer's own conceptual scheme and in analyzing another way of life in terms of the categories and premises of the people being studied. But as we learn more about learning, it seems increasingly likely that much of what the ethnographer learns never goes into the notebooks: it is in the realm that for lack of a better term we can call the "unconscious"—a knowledge of scenes and people and sounds and smells that cannot be captured in the written word.

What informants can tell the ethnographer about their customs may be a similarly inaccurate and partial rendering of what they see, do, think, and feel. Sometimes their reports are distorted by the intent to deceive or by linguistic misunderstanding. In any case, what people tell the ethnographer about their way of life must be cross-checked, substantiated, and filled out by detailed records of actual events and transactions. A modern anthropological study is a far cry from the older style where one simply said "descent is patrilineal" and left it at that. Detailed statistical tables,

and often maps and genealogies, enable the author's colleagues to reconstruct the network of people and events from which generalizations were worked out.

Recording the way of life of a small-scale and relatively self-contained society posed (or seemed to pose) few problems of sampling. The community in which the ethnographer lived, a village or hamlet, gave a reasonable sample of the way of life of the whole tribe, and within it customs and beliefs were shared by all or most people.

More detailed observation, more careful derivation of ethnographic generalizations from actual events, more concern with statistical patterns, and use of a wider range of informants have made it clear that things were never this simple. Ideal standards are more uniform than patterns of actual behavior. When deeply probed, the ideational worlds of different individuals in a tribal society show wide variation. And most anthropologists for years paid more attention to adult men than to adult women or children. Moreover, few anthropologists are actually well trained or highly skilled in detailed behavioral observation, and close study of the actual behavior and emotional states of people as they enact customs has barely begun.

The problem of sampling has become much more acute in larger-scale, more complex societies. Cultural diversity, large populations, social stratification, and rapid change have made fieldwork in large-scale modern societies, whether in the Third World or the West, a complicated business in which more concern with sampling, statistics, and methodological precision is needed. We will return in later chapters to problems of inference and evidence.

The anthropologist in the field, though concerned with methodological rigor, is above all in an intensely human situation where all of his or her insight, intuition, and empathy must be brought to bear.

As a vision quest, the anthropologist's path has different stages and different experiences for each fieldworker. "Culture shock"—the initial impact of radically different settings and customs—is common. So too are waves of despair where rejection, hostility, and incomprehensibility close in on all sides.

Consider the encounter from the other side. A people's life is interrupted by a strange foreigner, often with a family, who moves into the community, bringing all manner of new and strange things. This person seldom fits any of the kinds of foreigners the people have learned to deal with—missionaries, traders, government officers, politicians, or whatever. He or she is insatiably curious about things private, sacred, and personal, for reasons and motives that are incomprehensible. The person must be accorded a role of some sort; his or her clumsy efforts to speak properly, bad manners, and intrusions into daily life must be tolerated. All this attention may be flattering, but it may breed suspicion, hostility, and jealousy. In a less isolated and more sophisticated community, "being studied" may smack of condescension and may offend pride, not arouse it.

On the anthropologist's side, ethical problems loom large. Should one try to protect the identity of the community and its people by disguising names and places? Can one intervene in matters of custom and health? Can one betray the confidence of one's informants in some grave violation of the law?

And how deeply can one really penetrate into another way of life? Sitting in a Solomon Island mountain hamlet chewing betel with my friends, and bantering in their language, I feel a oneness with them, a bond of common humanity and shared experience. But can they feel that with me? Can I be more than a visiting curiosity and celebrity, a rich white man who will soon go back to his world?

Such are the challenges, the frustrations, the doubts, and the insights of the anthropol-ogist in fieldwork. From this experience, this immersion in another cultural world, one may return to write a book and to impress one's colleagues with learned jargon. But whatever the course of one's vision quest, the world will never look the same.

The return to the simplicity of a tribal or peasant way of life, intensely personal and devoid of hardware, has a strong appeal. Anthropologists have usually championed a somewhat romanticized view of "their people" and have stalwartly defended the value and even the nobility of tribal life. The popularized return of the "noble savage" in American folk culture of the late 1960s—as an ideological counter to the alienation, impersonality, and frenzy of modern life—has left anthropologists in a curious position. They find themselves pointing out that tribal peoples can be nasty too, that the foibles of human nature and the arbitrariness and non-sensicality of cultural conventions know no geographical boundaries.

And "primitive" peoples often *are* nasty, if we are prepared to think a bit about what "nastiness" can mean in this context. When peoples whose cultural conventions are very different encounter one another, the deportment of one people can be wicked, noble, nasty, uncouth, violent, sullen, silly, hilarious, or immoral from the standpoint of the other people. Looking relativistically, we can hardly dismiss another people as "nasty"—only as different. Yet such an ethical relativism is ultimately hard to live with. Those who might be prepared to accept cannibalism on the Amazon as a wholesome and nutritious custom are unlikely to be so generous about genocide as a Nazi custom or *apartheid* as a South African one. And if we are prepared to seek panhuman standards of ethics and values, we will find societies where aggression or morbid suspicion has gotten out of reasonable control—where people fall further short of the highest human aspirations in some respect than the rest of us. "Nastiness" is the wrong word here, but anthropologists sometimes encounter "noble savages" whom even they find it hard to like very much. Those who would romanticize fieldwork and the simple life can find a sobering note in a recent account by anthropologist Napoleon Chagnon of his fieldwork among the Yąnomamö of South America:

We arrived at the village . . . and docked the boat along the muddy bank. . . . It was hot and muggy, and my clothing was soaked with perspiration. It clung uncomfortably to my body, as it did thereafter for the remainder of the work. The small biting gnats were out in astronomical numbers, for it was the beginning of the dry season. My face and hands were swollen from the venom of their numerous stings. In just a few moments I was to meet my first Yąnomamö, my first primitive man. . . .

The entrance to the village was covered over with brush and dry palm leaves. We pushed them aside to expose the low opening to the village. The excitement of meeting my first Indians was almost unbearable as I duck-waddled through the low passage into the village clearing.

I looked up and gasped when I saw a dozen burly, naked, filthy, hideous men staring at us down the shaft of their drawn arrows! Immense wads of green tobacco were stuck between their lower teeth and lips making them look even more hideous, and strands of dark green slime dripped or hung from their noses. We arrived at the village while the men were blowing a hallucinogenic drug up their noses. One of the side effects of the drug is a runny nose. The mucus is always saturated with the green powder and the Indians usually let it run freely from their nostrils. My next discovery was that there were a dozen or so vicious, underfed dogs snapping at my legs, circling me as if I were going to be their next meal. I just stood there holding my notebook, helpless and pathetic. Then the stench of the decaying vegetation and filth struck me and I almost got sick. I was horrified. What sort of welcome was this for the person who

came here to live with you and learn your way of life, to become friends with you? They put their weapons down when they recognized Barker [a missionary] and returned to their chanting, keeping a nervous eye on the village entrances.

We had arrived just after a serious fight. Seven women had been abducted the day before by a neighboring group, and the local men and their guests had just that morning recovered five of them in a brutal club fight that nearly ended in a shooting war. The abductors, angry because they lost five of the seven captives, vowed to raid the Bisaasi-teri. When we arrived and entered the village unexpectedly, the Indians feared that we were the raiders. On several occasions during the next two hours the men in the village jumped to their feet, armed themselves, and waited nervously for the noise outside the village to be identified. . . .

I had not eaten all day, I was soaking wet from perspiration, the gnats were biting me, and I was covered with red pigment, the result of a dozen or so complete examinations I had been given by as many burly Indians. These examinations capped an otherwise grim day. The Indians would blow their noses into their hands, flick as much of the mucus off that would separate in a snap of the wrist, wipe the residue into their hair, and then carefully examine my face, arms, legs, hair, and the contents of my pockets. . . .

So much for my discovery that primitive man is not the picture of nobility and sanitation I had conceived him to be. I soon discovered that it was an enormously time-consuming task to maintain my own body in the manner to which it had grown accustomed in the relatively antiseptic environment of the northern United States. Either I could be relatively well fed and relatively comfortable in a fresh change of clothes and do very little fieldwork, or I could do considerably more fieldwork and be less well fed and less comfortable.

Eating three meals a day was out of the question. I solved the problem by eating a single meal that could be prepared in a single container, or, at most, in two containers, washed my dishes only when there were no clean ones left, using cold river water, and wore each change of clothing at least a week to cut down on my laundry problem, a courageous undertaking in the tropics. I was also less concerned about sharing my provisions with the rats, insects, Indians, and the elements, thereby eliminating the need for my complicated storage process. I was able to last most of the day on *café con leche,* heavily sugared espresso coffee diluted about five to one with hot milk. I would prepare this in the evening and store it in a thermos. Frequently, my single meal was no more complicated than a can of sardines and a package of crackers. But at least two or three times a week I would do something sophisticated, like make oatmeal or boil rice and add a can of tuna fish or tomato paste to it. . . .

Meals were a problem in another way. Food sharing is important to the Yąnomamö in the context of displaying friendship. "I am hungry," is almost a form of greeting with them. I could not possibly have brought enough food with me to feed the entire village, yet they seemed not to understand this. All they could see was that I did not share my food with them at each and every meal. . . .

Despite the fact that most of them knew I would not share my food with them at their request, some of them always showed up at my hut during mealtime. I gradually became accustomed to this and learned to ignore their persistent demands while I ate. Some of them would get angry because I failed to give in, but most of them accepted it as just a peculiarity of the subhuman foreigner. When I did give in, my hut quickly filled with Indians, each demanding a sample of the food that I had given one of them. If I did not give all a share, I was that much more despicable in their eyes. . . .

The thing that bothered me most was the incessant, impassioned, and aggressive demands the Indians made. It would become so unbearable that I would have to lock myself in my hut every once in a while just to escape from it: privacy is one of Western culture's greatest achievements. But I did not want privacy for its own sake; rather, I simply had to get away from the begging. Day and night for the entire time I lived with the Yąnomamö I was plagued by such demands as: "Give me a knife, I am poor!"; "If you don't take me with you on your next trip to Widokaiya-teri I'll chip a hole in your canoe!". . . I was bombarded by such demands day after day, months on end, until I could not bear to see an Indian.

It was not as difficult to become calloused to the incessant begging as it was to ignore the sense of urgency, the impassioned tone of voice, or the intimidation and aggression with which the demands were made. It was likewise difficult to adjust to the fact that the Yąnomamö refused to accept "no" for an answer until or unless it seethed with passion and intimidation—which it did after six months. Giving in to a demand always established a new threshold; the next demand would be a bigger item or favor, and the anger of the Indians even greater if the demand was not met. I soon learned that I had to become very much like the Yąnomamö to be able to get along with them on their terms: sly, aggressive, and intimidating.

Had I failed to adjust in this fashion I would have lost six months of supplies to them in a single day or would have spent most of my time ferrying them around in my canoe or hunting for them. As it was, I did spend a considerable amount of time doing these things and did succumb to their outrageous demands for axes and matches at least at first. More importantly, had I failed to demonstrate that I could not be pushed around beyond a certain point, I would have been the subject of far more ridicule, theft, and practical jokes than was the actual case. In short, I had to acquire a certain proficiency in their kind of interpersonal politics and to learn how to imply subtly that certain potentially undesirable consequences might follow if they did such and such to me. They do this to each other in order to establish precisely the point at which they cannot goad an individual any further without precipitating retaliation. As soon as I caught on to this and realized that much of their aggression was stimulated by their desire to discover my flash point, I got along much better with them and regained some lost ground. It was sort of like a political game that everyone played, but one in which each individual sooner or later had to display some sign that his bluffs and implied threats could be backed up. I suspect that the frequency of wife beating is a component of this syndrome, since men can display their ferocity and show others that they are capable of violence. Beating a wife with a club is considered to be the acceptable way of displaying ferocity and one that does not expose the male to much danger. The important thing is that the man has displayed his potential for violence and the implication is that other men better treat him with respect and caution. (Chagnon 1968a:4—9)

Tribal peoples, as they are encountered by the field anthropologist and as we will see them in the chapters to follow, are neither noble nor debased, neither childlike savages nor elemental humans unsullied by the ills of civilization: they are simply human. That means that however limited their hardware, however unencumbered and unharried their modes of life, they live enmeshed in a web of conventions that are their own creation: they strive and compete for absurd goals; they set standards they cannot reach, devise rules they do not follow; they play the roles the culture lays down, voice sentiments they do not feel. These creatures of cultural convention are the Elemental Humans.

AN EVOLUTIONARY PERSPECTIVE

Human Biology and the Growth of Culture

Part **1**

The separation of the social sciences from the biological sciences has largely isolated students of human social life from a central source of insight: evolutionary biology. Now that the evolution of *Homo sapiens* and the behavioral heritage of our primate cousins are coming so much more clearly into view, anthropology is almost uniquely favored in having one foot in biology and the other in social science. The ability to see humans both as biological organisms and creatures of culture, to see the cultural and the biological as interacting and complementary, and to see humans in ecosystems as well as social systems gives anthropologists a broad evolutionary perspective on the human condition.

Part 1 will draw upon evolutionary biology, primate studies, the fossil record of human development, and archaeological records of the past to open up such a broadened perspective. In Chapter 2 we will look at the course of human evolution. In Chapter 3 we will examine the evidence from ethology and other sources on the evolution of human behavior. In Chapter 4 we will draw on this knowledge of evolutionary process to consider human differences, between individuals and between groups. Then, in Chapters 5, 6, and 7, we will look at the evolution of cultures, from early hunting and gathering populations through the dawn of food producing and the rise of urban centers in the ancient world.

HUMAN EVOLUTION

2

Homo sapiens is a peculiar kind of primate. Paradoxically, we can understand this peculiarity only in the light of our primate heritage. Scientists have known for more than a century that humans are products of biological evolution, a single strand in a web of nature. But students of culture have stressed how humans are different and unique, with our abilities to cumulate experience and communicate symbolically enabling us to transcend our animal past. Thus it was the task of the physical anthropologist to tell us how early ape became human and the task of the cultural anthropologist to explore humans as transformed beings.

We now have important new evidence on the social life of living primates, on the human past, and on the biological roots of behavior. More important, our perspectives have changed. We have come to stress continuities, not radical differences, and this has given us clearer insights into what is shared, how we became human, and how we are distinctive. Here we will sketch, necessarily very briefly, the evolutionary heritage of *H. sapiens,* the relationships between human and animal behavior, and the biological bases of human variation.

4.
The Processes of Evolution

"We are no longer concerned with *whether* man evolved, because we know he did. We are still very much concerned with *how* he evolved, with what is most characteristically human about him and how those characteristics arose." So writes the great American biologist George Gaylord Simpson (1966:10), who has played a central role in the last thirty years in defining the synthetic theory of evolution dominant in modern biology.

Before looking at human evolution, it is worth reviewing quickly the central tenets of that theory and the important new developments brought about by the recent burgeoning of molecular genetics.

Evolution is a process that operates on *populations*. Any species, viewed in genetic terms, consists of a pool of genetic diversity. How this diversity is perpetuated and created has only recently become clear through breakthroughs in molecular biology. Evolution occurs through adaptation of a population to an ecological niche by the process of *natural selection*. Natural selection is not characteristically a "survival of the fittest" struggle in which the less fit fall by the wayside. It is a statistical process in which the genetic diversity within the population is channeled through differential reproduction; gene frequencies change through time. The genetic combinations that produce more viable adult forms are statistically favored in this weighted dice game; those that produce less viable adult forms are statistically weeded out. As environments gradually change, the genetic pool of the population changes in a direction *adaptive* to the new environment. Adaptation through natural selection is the key in evolution. But the game is statistical; the unit is the population-in-environment, not the individual.

Adaptive radiation is a recurrent evolutionary process: populations separate and become different through adaptation to different environmental niches. Thus birds have, by adaptive radiation over a vast time span, diversified into thousands of species fitting into a myriad of environmental niches opened by the possibility of flight. So too have fishes, exploiting the many niches of the oceans, rivers, and lakes. Thus the evolution of the major biological forms, including the mammals, over vast periods of time forms a broadly branching tree structure.

In the process of adaptation, the usual course is one of *specialization*. A species becomes specially adapted to an *ecological niche:* that is, to a habitat, to a food supply, to other species in the ecosystem (for example, to particular predators against which it evolves a defense). Extreme examples are the forms of mimicry where, for example, a butterfly evolves a design on its wings that simulates the eyes of a predator, or a harmless insect evolves a resemblance to a poisonous one. Evolution thus operates not solely on populations but on *ecological systems* within which various populations are components. In this process of adaptation of species to an ecosystem (which includes other species), some organisms specialize less and evolve more *generalized* modes of competing and surviving. In being generalized, in having flexible adaptive traits, lies long-run evolutionary advantage. Thus warm-bloodedness, the internal temperature-regulating system of mammals, enables forms to diversify into and survive in a range of environments. Climatic or other ecological shifts are more likely to extinguish a more specialized organism than a more generalized one. Since no two species can for long occupy the same ecological niche, the evolutionary process involves competition between species (as well as within species). Being generalized and efficient increases the chances of a life form surviving over long time spans.

In the synthetic theory of evolution, natural selection is not the only process of change, though it is by far the most important one. Sexual selection, where differential probabilities of mating are affected by sexual displays and the like, has been recognized for a century (Darwin 1871), but is belatedly receiving fresh attention (Campbell 1972). *Genetic drift,* a statistical pattern of random change (not necessarily adaptive) culminating in shifts in a gene pool, has long been known; but in earlier population genetics it was seen as a process that operates markedly only under special conditions (especially in small populations, as in the "founder" process where a population passes through a "genetic bottle-neck"). For example, if an island is occupied by a few rats in the bottom of a canoe, the genetic pool from which the new rat population is drawn is a very limited sampling from the parent population. As we will see, genetic drift has taken on new significance with very recent developments in molecular biology.

A major emphasis in the evolutionary biology of the 1950s and 1960s was an emphasis on the evolution of behavior patterns. As ethologists began to map in detail the behavior of animal species, the need to develop behavioral genetics became clear. For selection operates not on genes but on organisms, which are the complex outcome of interacting genes and environment in the developmental process of maturation. Selection operates on *organisms behaving,* on animals that *do* things more or less effectively. It has become clear that the evolutionary process works in a very complicated way. Though it is individual genes that are shuffled statistically in sexual reproduction, it is constellations of interacting genes that govern behavior patterns and hence must be modified *as complexes* by natural selection. Being taller may have enabled some ancestral giraffes to reach leaves better. But this does not simply cause genes that make giraffes taller to be favored. For one thing, being taller and still a viable organism requires corresponding complicated changes in the circulatory and nervous systems of a giraffe, and thus ramify through the whole genetic design of the organism. When we come to complex behavior patterns, such as the migration of birds that navigate thousands of miles, the interconnection of behavioral and genetic change must be incredibly complicated and intricate. It is clear that we cannot understand such processes in terms of linear cause and effect. Such changes must require complex cybernetic webs of connection, processes of feedback in which patterns of genetic change and the constellations of behavior to which they give rise are geared together. Our understanding of these processes is still far from complete, and in some ways is still rudimentary.

With the revolution of molecular biology, we have come to understand a great deal about that miraculous process of genetic coding and replication, through the nucleic acids DNA and RNA, that makes possible the specification of genetic instructions on a molecular level and their accurate transmission through heredity. We also see the process of *muta-tion:* the introduction of new genetic patterns into a gene pool through errors in the copying process. This is a crucial mechanism in evolutionary change. Most mutations are selectively disadvantageous—often lethal. But the continual appearance of new genetic potential in a population not only produces stunted, deformed, and nonviable organisms (leading to the disappearance of the mutant genes); it also produces the rare combination of adaptive new characteristics that leads to the incorporation of the new genetic possibility into the gene pool, and to adaptive change in the population. New genetic recombinations, created by the statistical reshuffling of genetic diversity within a gene pool, continually open new possibilities for evolutionary change. This process may be as important as genetic mutation in opening new paths for adaptive change.

Recent controversies in evolutionary biology have centered around discoveries that at the molecular level genetic changes seem, in many cases at least, not to go in the directional spurts that natural selection would seem to imply. Studies of amino acids, of DNA, and of immunochemistry seem to be showing instead a more or less constant, cumulative change—seemingly, a biochemical and genetic process of *drift.* The implications for the dominant synthetic theory of evolution which we have summarized are now being hotly debated (King and Jukes 1969; LeCam *et al.* 1972). For the moment, however, it seems possible to conclude that "although some aspects of molecular evolution may proceed in a nonadaptive manner, the evolution of behavioral complexes is controlled by natural selection" (Washburn 1972:353).

The complex branchings of the tree of life have been charted through the years mainly through study of the fossil record of ancient organisms. Fossils, mineral-preserved remains of animals and plants of the past, are stratified in geological deposits. From them a record of evolution has been reconstructed and correlated with shifts and upheavals in land masses, and changes in climate. The evolution of life forms and the shifting environments in which they lived have been progressively deciphered in the strata of cliffs and river canyons, in deserts that were once oceans or jungles, and in the upheavals, sinkings, and incisions of geologic time. Though the levels of biological and geological change have mainly been only roughly dated, often only in relative (not absolute) terms, recent scientific technology has given new precision to the dating process. Atomic scientists, studying the rates of radioactive decay (and hence chemical transformation) in various natural substances—such as the transformation of radioactive potassium into argon gas in rock—have given relatively accurate ways of measuring the absolute age of geological levels, and hence of the life forms whose fossil traces are found in them.

Comparative study of living forms provides a cross-section of the evolutionary time span and is therefore another important source of evidence about connections in the past. Thus comparative anatomy and comparative study of living forms help to reveal the evolutionary lines and branchings that lie behind them. It was Darwin's studies of finches and other forms found in the Galapagos Islands of the Pacific Ocean that gave him the crucial original insights into the web of evolution that connects all life.

Molecular biology has given exciting new evidence on the evolutionary tree of life. By studying protein chemistry and other biochemical similarities and differences, modern molecular biologists and immunochemists have begun to provide a clear and compelling new confirmation of evolutionary connections. The broad evolutionary connections reconstructed from the fossil record and study of living forms are confirmed beyond the slightest doubt by the molecular evidence now emerging. As we will see, the fine-grained evidence on closely related species— in particular *Homo sapiens* and our primate relatives—and particularly the effort to use biochemical "clocks" to date the evolutionary separation of related forms are still in a stage of development and controversy.

We know that evolution occurred. We know that humans are connected to this web of evolution and have very close primate relatives. We understand in general if not yet in full detail how evolution works. The evidence is increasingly rich, though so complex it is still difficult to read.

Our concern is with how *H. sapiens* evolved. And since we are shortly to shift our attention to human cultures and social life, we will be particularly concerned with the biological heritage that defines the givens of human nature, the givens of our social life on which humans build their cultural worlds. We will look first at the emerging record that gives partial answers to Simpson's questions: "*how* [man] evolved, . . . what is most characteristically human about him and how those characteristics arose" (1966:10). Having seen the evidence on how and when man evolved from a primate ancestor, we will return to look at the behavior of our living primate relatives for further insights into our primateness and our humanity.

5.

Hominid Evolution and the Emergence of *Homo Sapiens*

Our Primate Heritage

Before sketching what is known about how *H. sapiens* evolved, some cautions are in order. First, this is a time of exploding knowledge. What scientists now know is so rich and diverse that to begin to look at the details— for example, of the environments in which our ancestors lived and the climatic shifts that helped shape their movements and evolutionary development—would require volumes. A number of excellent sources are available for the interested reader to explore further (see Suggestions for Further Reading).

Second, the explosion in our knowledge, from the fossil record and biochemistry, means that what one now writes is out of date before it is printed. Thus the latest announcements of fossil finds, if treated with some skepticism and caution, will augment the picture sketched here. This said, let us turn to our fossilized ancestors.

H. sapiens is a mammal. Like other mammals, humans bear live young nourished before birth by a placenta. We are warm-blooded. We share a general skeletal design with bears, giraffes, and whales. We also share with them many details of body chemistry.

H. sapiens is a special kind of mammal, a *primate*. The earliest primates were tiny, unimpressive creatures that coexisted with the dinosaurs, but being more generalized, survived the demise of those large-scale reptiles. The earliest known ancestral primates, fossil *prosimians* ("pre-monkeys"), some 65 million years old, resembled small rats. They probably ate mainly insects and got about mostly at night while the great reptiles slept.

The evolutionary success of the early primates began in the trees, leading to a series of adaptations on which human evolution has built. A precarious life in a world of branches and leaves far above the ground put a premium on holding on and letting go, hence the gradual evolution of a versatile manipulating and grasping hand. Vision improved, especially night vision, and with it came expansion in the still-tiny visual cortex of the brain. Proliferating and diversifying, the prosimians, small and unspectacular but efficient denizens of the forest, prospered for millions of years.

Monkeys then proliferated, beginning about 35 million years ago, advancing primate possibility to a new level. Monkeys rely much more heavily on vision and less on smell than their ancestors. Their eyes had moved around to the front, giving efficient stereoscopic vision; color vision had developed. Monkeys thus saw a world of things, of objects rather than patterns and movements. With this new visual richness came a marked expansion of the brain cortex, especially those areas needed for experiencing and manipulating the world.

At the same time that monkeys were developing and proliferating in the forests, a new form of primate first appeared on the evolutionary scene: the ape. If we can judge by the meager fossil record, the early apes were more diverse, probably even more successful and numerous, than the early monkeys. The earliest apes were small and were distinguished from monkeys by a characteristic tooth pattern. The earliest ancestral ape that seems a solid candidate as a human ancestor is a fossil form that lived some 28 million years ago in the tropical rain forests of what is now Egypt. This ape, *Aegyptopithecus,* probably lived both in the trees and on the ground and was probably mainly a fruit eater (Simons 1972; Pilbeam 1972).

Geological disruptions and a downward

shift in temperatures, beginning some 25 million years ago, brought changes to the tropical forest mantle that had cloaked much of Africa and Eurasia. Grasslands, or savannas, opened like lakes, then like seas, dividing the thick forest. And where the fingers of grassland penetrated the forest margins, new settings for evolution were created.

The apes of this Miocene geological period were larger, and larger-brained, than *Aegyptopithecus*. They constituted a cluster of at least three species, collectively classed as members of the genus *Dryopithecus*. There is a good possibility that the divergence between chimps and gorillas, and between them and our ancestors, extends back in time to these Miocene forms (perhaps 15 million years or more); but as we will soon see, there is sharp disagreement among the experts.

The Miocene apes from which the hominids, or manlike primates, probably split (leading to modern man) were very likely arboreal, weighing some 30 to 50 pounds, with fore and hind limbs of about the same length and short stout bodies. They probably were fruit eaters and spent most of their time in and around the trees (Pilbeam 1972:48).

But the branching off of the hominid line involved a new mode of adaptation—an exploration and exploitation of the forest fringe and adjacent grasslands. The shift from trees to grasslands, and the consequent shift of diet from fruits to seeds and other vegetable foods, apparently began a process of major change in teeth and chewing apparatus and in a body that became adapted to life on the ground.

By the end of the Miocene and the early Pliocene period, some 14 million to 10 million years ago, at least two lineages of primates had begun to explore this new open-country environment and had become adapted to a changed diet. One was a very large ground-dwelling ape with massive jaws and cheek teeth, but without the large incisors and formi-

dable canine teeth of the living great apes, the gorilla, chimpanzee, and orangutan. The descendants of these giant apes survived in China until within the last million years, where they may well have been killed off by early men. (Some scholars have suggested that some survivors are alive and well and living in the Himalayas.) These giant apes are unlikely candidates as early hominids and therefore as human ancestors.

Another primate of the early Pliocene (14 to 10 million years ago) may well have been an ancestral hominid. This primate, *Ramapithecus,* was widespread in a belt across Africa and South Asia, a belt that was tropical and forested but apparently included open grasslands along river margins. That *Ramapithecus* was a human ancestor, one we can probably class as an early hominid, seems very likely on the basis of the fossil evidence of jaws and teeth. Whereas an ape's jaw and palate form a long "U" shape, the human palate forms a curved "V." Moreover, the teeth, with small incisors and canines, point in a human direction.

Though *Ramapithecus* was probably predominantly a forest-living arboreal animal adapted to overhead swinging by the arms, it apparently foraged extensively on the ground, probably getting about bipedally much of the time. Recent evidence suggests that human bipedalism developed not from knuckle-walking, as Washburn had suggested, but from overhead arm swinging (Oxnard 1969). Washburn had further suggested that the reduction of canine teeth among ground-dwelling early hominids was part of a complex involving tool use and upright locomotion: as primates developed the use of tools, they developed upright bipedal locomotion to free the hands for use in bashing predators or prey; and these new defenses made formidable canines unnecessary. But this hypothesized complex has been falling into separate elements. It seems much more likely now that overhead arm-swinging had preadapted the Miocene apes for upright locomotion when they descended from the trees and began to explore and forage on the ground. The reduction of the canines and modification of incisor and jaw seem to be an adaptation to eating grasses and other terrestrial foods (C. Jolly 1970). The fact that the giant apes of India and China underwent a parallel tooth and jaw modification as terrestrial foragers strengthens the case. Effective tool using apparently came a good deal later among hominids. If *Ramapithecus* is indeed an early hominid, then the hominid pattern probably evolved not on open savanna grasslands but along the forest margins.

Another line of argument would eject *Ramapithecus'* skeleton from the ancestral closet and keep the line leading to man and the great apes—chimps and gorillas—together much longer (perhaps until the last five million years). The argument has come mainly not from fossil primates and their evolution but rather from biochemistry. The question at issue is how closely we are related to the great apes and how much time would be required for this degree of biochemical differentiation. Wilson and Sarich (1969), working with immunological techniques to compare the protein chemistry of primates and other mammals, have found that the biochemistry of gorilla, chimp, and man are very, very similar, though both differ markedly from monkeys. They have sought to work out a protein "time clock," based on the assumption that at the molecular level change takes place at a constant rate through time (regardless of the species or the lifespan of the organism). According to their calculations, the split between humans and the great apes was as late as 4 million years ago, and probably not earlier than 8 million years ago.

The debate between fossil experts such as Pilbeam and Simons and biochemists is given some latitude for disagreement because the fossil record becomes essentially blank during the period 10 million to 5 million years ago. If *Ramapithecus* was not a hominid, then the biochemical evidence is given some leeway. It seems increasingly likely, however, that the assumptions of the protein "time clock" are wrong. (As Kohne (1970) has pointed out, if the longer lifespan and hence generation spacing of the great apes and humans are taken into account, the biochemical similarity between humans and chimpanzees becomes fully compatible with the early separation of the lineages the fossil evidence suggests; and there are other grounds for doubting the biochemical model of constant, nonadaptive change.)

While the question remains open, the fossil evidence seems increasingly compelling and the biochemical evidence increasingly doubtful. For one thing, when the hominid line pops clearly into view some 5.5 million years ago, the lineage has evolved far in a human direction, sharply different from the great apes. It seems most unlikely that these striking differences in body, teeth, and skull could have evolved in a scant 2 or 3 million years.

Let us look now at these distinctively humanlike forms, the now-famous *australopithecines*.

The Australopithecines

The discovery of the australopithecine fossils and their decipherment is one of the most fascinating detective, and even adventure, stories in science, and it is still unfolding. However, I cannot pause here to tell it but only to summarize a kind of composite picture of present evidence, which will inevitably be out of date by the time it is printed.

Australopithecines comprise a range of hominids that inhabited Africa, perhaps other areas, over a vast time span of perhaps four million years—from roughly five million to

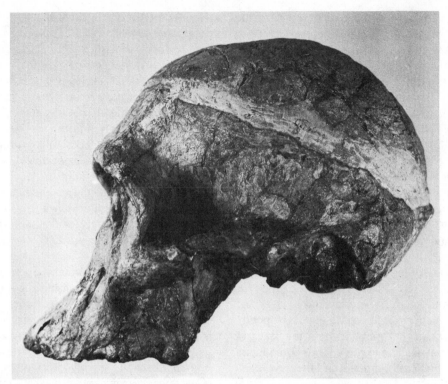

The skull of *Australopithecus africanus* found at Sterkfontein. (Courtesy of R. Broom and J. T. Robinson.)

roughly one million years ago. Evidence for the earliest datings is meager: a jaw fragment and tooth dated at 5.5 million years, a part of an arm bone some 4.5 million years old. Recent finds at Omo include teeth almost four million years old: by then early australopithecines were clearly on the scene.

Over this vast period of time the australopithecines changed and branched. The earliest forms were small (60—90 pounds) and gracile, or delicate in bone structure. Some later forms were larger and more powerful. Yet the larger, later forms led to an evolutionary dead end. At some time around two million years ago, or even two and a half, the lighter and more delicate australopithecine form (known as *Australopithecus africanus*) gradually evolved into more manlike forms.

For more than a million years the larger, more powerful australopithecines coexisted with their cousins who were slowly evolving in a human direction; and then they died out, apparently beaten out by their nimbler-witted, though barely human, rivals.

Things are not quite that simple. The gracile *A. africanus* was known from early remains from South Africa, where there later turned up a larger and more robust form christened *A. robustus* (almost 120 pounds, and at five feet a foot taller than *africanus*). The two, especially the gracile form, could not be effectively dated, though it was disturbingly clear that *robustus*, the more primitive looking, lived later or survived longer.

The spectacular discoveries by the Leakeys at Olduvai Gorge in Tanzania turned up an even larger and more massive, though still small by human standards, australopithecine, known as *boisei;* it resembles a superrobust *robustus.* The Leakeys also turned up a form they proclaimed to be the first man, *Homo habilis.* Some others would see in *habilis* a form transitional between the early gracile *africanus* forms and the first men. The datings of 1.7 million years came at the time as a scientific blockbuster, for if this was not necessarily the first man (and most scholars now admit *habilis* grudgingly to our genus), it was at the very edge of humanity. The new finds from Omo in Ethiopia and Lake Rudolf in Kenya pushed the date even further back and shed additional light on the situation. There is evidence that the heavy *boisei* forms lived in this part of Africa, changing little, from 3.7 million to 1 million years ago. Teeth and skull suggest that they may have been vegetarians and may thus have not competed directly with the gracile australopithecines that were evolving in this period in a human direction. There is also evidence from Omo of early forms like the South African *africanus* with a range of from 3 million to 1.8 million years. Finally came Richard Leakey's discovery of a form that seems to be closely akin to his parents' *H. habilis*—what has been called "late-gracile-into-*Homo*" as a way of avoiding quibbling about admission to the human genus. The probable age of a jaw fragment Richard Leakey discovered in 1971, and identified as *Homo,* is 2.6 million years. That begins to overlap in time with some of the late gracile australopithecine teeth found at Omo. Finally, there are hints that late australopithecine forms akin to *H. habilis*—though perhaps later—may have spread to (or evolved separately in) South Asia. One of the old "Java Man" finds, thought to be more recent, looks disturbingly like the African forms. And there, awaiting new discoveries and further debates, the matter stands.

New datings of the South African finds support an emerging general interpretation that from a small, relatively lightly built australopithecine of some 4 to 3 million years ago two lineages branched. One, lighter and gracile, had by 2.5 million years ago—at least in East Africa—begun to evolve markedly in a human direction, and hence to have reached the borderline of human status. The other lineage was larger, more robust, but presumably less intelligent; and eventually, after hundreds of thousands of years of coexistence with the gracile forms, it became extinct. But within that general framework there is room for endless complications and speculations—and occasionally a new find (such as Richard Leakey's 1972 discovery near Lake Rudolf of the 2.7 million-year-old Skull 1470) upsets existing interpretations. This looks disturbingly like a robust *boisei* australopithecine that had evolved in a human direction—and was using tools.

Through this quick sketch of fossil evidence, two big questions have gone unanswered. What were our australopithecine ancestors like physically? And more important, how did they live?

It used to be said in popularizations that australopithecines had the bodies of humans but the heads and faces of apes that had veered in a human direction. Yet it was not quite that simple. The australopithecines had become efficient bipeds. They stood upright, though they probably ran more efficiently than they walked. The australopithecine pelvis had come much but not all of the way to modern man as an efficient structure for bipedal locomotion (Zihlman and Hunter 1975). There is some evidence, however, that hand and arm structures may not have fully evolved in the human direction; thumbs were small, fingers massive, and arms probably longer and more massive than in most reconstructions.

The head and face did have an ape-man look—but how much ape and how much man depends in part on whether one chooses the smaller but more manlike *africanus* or the more brutish *robustus* and *boisei*. It also depends on whether the artist imagining the creature covering the bones is inclined toward the hairy and simian or the clean-shaven and humanoid. The australopithecine thus imagined could blend scarcely noticed into either a chimpanzee band or a nudist colony. As physical anthropology becomes more sophisticated, even here there is less room for speculation and artistic license than there used to be. Experts now think that the long body hair of our primate ancestors and living cousins would have been maladaptive once hominids moved into the grassy plains: a fur coat is too hot for a strenuous life of running after and away from quadrupedal neighbors on the hot savanna. At some early point, probably by australopithecine time, body hair became much less prominent (though our human fuzz remains) and sweat glands proliferated as an adaptive cooling device. By this point our hominid ancestors may have had hairy chins, but it is not likely that they had hairy foreheads. They might not fit unnoticed in a nudist colony, but they were far removed from shaggy simian mien. But we had best peel back to the bones.

The *africanus* forms have prominent brow ridges but relatively high and rounded cranial vaults (Figure 2.1). The most robust forms had heavier brow ridges, more massive facial structure, and a midline crest on the skull (like that of the gorilla) to which heavy muscles were attached. Where *africanus* had only moderately flaring malars (cheekbones), those of the more robust australopithecines were wide and more apelike and were matched by massive jaws.

The cranial capacity of the gracile australopitehcines, an index of brain size (but only indirectly of brain power), was around 450 cc—roughly a third of that of modern man and not substantially larger than that of chimpanzees (which average slightly less than 400 cc). The bigger australopithecines had somewhat larger brains, pushing the average to slightly over 500 cc (Figure 2.2).

Jaws and teeth, though far from human, clearly represent substantial change in that direction. Gone are large canines and the U-shaped palate of the ape. Instead the molars are large, the teeth adapted for new diet and changing facial structure, in which the forward projecting lower face, the old primate muzzle, was less prominent. The robust australopithecines had particularly large cheek teeth, and the massive facial architecture probably represents a buttressing of powerful jaws and big molars—an adaptation to a specialized diet.

What is more important to us than the way australopithecines looked is the way they *lived*. Here the problem of reconstructing is more subtle and complicated than hanging flesh and fuzz on bare bones. Much of our

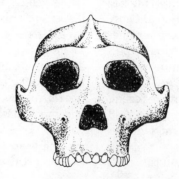

Figure 2.1 The reconstructed skulls of *Australopithecus africanus (left)* and *Australopithecus robustus (right)*. (From Washburn and Moore 1974:163.)

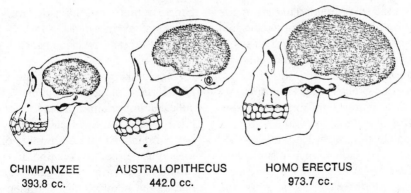

CHIMPANZEE   AUSTRALOPITHECUS   HOMO ERECTUS
393.8 cc.   442.0 cc.   973.7 cc.

Figure 2.2   Average cranial capacities of hominids, indicating more than doubling of brain size from *Australopithecus* to *Homo erectus* (chimpanzee cranial capacity included for comparison). (From Pfeiffer 1972:119.)

evidence comes from the amazingly rich record of tools, food remains, and even living sites accumulated by the Leakeys and others in recent years and from reconstructions of the savanna environment. But here the evidence that has survived for two million years must be filled in by informed guesses about the more perishable elements of australopithecine life. Another body of evidence from which we can extrapolate is the increasingly rich record of the behavior of our primate cousins and of other African animals, hunters and hunted. We can make informed guesses, from studying chimpanzees and gorillas in the wild, about the behavior patterns of the ancestor we shared with them; we can then project from that reconstructed behavior baseline a series of transformations leading to humans. By studying savanna-dwelling baboons and the variation in baboon behavior in different environments, we can get clues about how new environments shaped the social life of early hominids. We will look in detail at the behavior of our primate cousins in Chapter 3. We can learn much about hunting from studying the behavior of carnivores, their prey, and the predators that share their kills. From such inference and extrapolation can build a partial and fairly sound picture of

how the australopithecines lived. (From this point we will be mainly concerned with the gracile forms we presume were our ancestors, and with the late forms that shade into *H. habilis,* and not with the apparently more clodlike *boisei* forms that coexisted with them and were apparently eventually beaten out by them.)

The australopithecines lived mainly in fairly rich environments along ancient lakes and rivers, in grassy savannas with forest margins often near. This was an ideal setting for the evolution of an all-around scrounging pattern: gathering of wild roots, seeds, reeds, fruits, and other vegetable foods; collecting of eggs, reptiles, snails, large insects, tortoises, the young of nesting birds and burrowing animals; hunting of rodents, other small animals, and birds; raiding of the kill of larger carnivores; and increasingly, hunting of larger animals. The pattern of increased hunting of larger animals, larger brains, and better tools as the australopithecines grade toward the human genus in the last two and a half million years, is unmistakable. The tools and other leavings painstakingly analyzed by Mary Leakey at Olduvai are rich and diverse beyond the wildest imaginings of scientists 20 years ago. *Australopithecus* had long been thought to be too small-brained to have made effective tools. Yet not simply crude rocks that came to hand but carefully worked arrays of tools have emerged in late-australopithecine *H. habilis* remains at Olduvai, more than two million years old. Similar tools are turning up at Lake Rudolf almost a million years older. By two million years ago, the Olduvai hominids were living in campsites: Mary Leakey has found there evidence of an ancient living floor with an arc-shaped pile of rock that may have served as a windbreak. The animals the inhabitants were eating included giraffes, hippos, antelopes, and elephants: things had gone fairly far beyond collecting lizards.

In the two-million-year-old layers at Olduvai, a complex of tools that archaeologists have called Oldowan emerges. These are mainly chopping tools which are simple and roughly worked (though the impression of crudeness is partly due to the roughness of the stone materials early hominids in Africa used, in contrast to flints and other stones that fracture with sharp precision). Typical early Oldowan choppers are about the size of a tennis ball or smaller, but special-purpose tools such as what seem to be engraving-gouging tools, scrapers, and quadrilateral chisellike tools are also found. Bone tools also appear in some sites. Extrapolating from chimpanzee tool use (see §7)[1] and other indirect evidence, we can presume that australopithecines used branches and other perishable objects as clubs, projectiles, and instruments of aggressive display. Rocks were apparently extensively used as missiles in the hunt.

All of this evidence points to hunting of large animals as a crucial training ground for the business of being human: the pursuit served as a strong selective force for brainpower, a challenge to the toolmaker, and a shaping force for social organization. Over the

period of time from the early gracile australopithecines to *H. habilis,* early hominids had become hunters and had reached the dawn of humanity.

Toolmaking—especially the creation of specialized tool types by planned stages—is a critically important application of emerging intelligence, and a selective force for bigger, better brains. Organized hunting of large animals requires communication. Even the most rudimentary form of language would have helped the early hominids to plan and act in concert; their brainpower seems scarcely adequate for much more, though *H. habilis'* tool kit might presage or reflect a simple "word kit" with sounds for things and places (see §10). Hunting also requires a tightly structured group, systematic sharing, and other activities that begin to mark hominids as human.

We can presume (see §6 and §8) that the early hominids lived in small bands. Early australopithecines, living primarily by gathering plant foods and catching small animals, probably formed small bands—10 to 20 might be a reasonable guess, though smaller subgroups might have split off to forage together. The organized hunting of two million years ago would seem to require larger groups: catching an elephant or hippo takes considerable manpower, and consuming it is a business for a substantial group. On the basis of ethnographic research among the modern bushmen, Richard Lee estimates that "an elephant . . . would provide . . . something on the order of 1200 man-days of meat [which] would feed 400 people for three days" (Lee 1968b:345).

"The minimum number of adults necessary to separate an individual [elephant] from an angry and protective herd, surround and dispatch it, and then fight off competing predators" is substantial, though we cannot precisely estimate it (DeVore 1968b:349). This is not to say that the hominids of two million

---

[1]The symbol § refers to consecutive numbered main headings, 1 to 81, throughout the book.

years ago lived permanently in bands of 40 or 50 or more. That probably is too large. Large kills were probably relatively rare. Perhaps sometimes smaller groups coalesced to hunt and share the kill, although that would imply substantial communication, planning, and even the dawn of politics on a scale that may have come only later.

It seems fairly clear that a sexual division of labor had developed, with adult males hunting and females, juveniles, and children gathering wild foods. Sexual specialization is physically manifest in the fossil record: males were larger, stronger, faster. Females, with pelvic structures a compromise between efficient locomotion and bearing of large-brained infants, were bound closer to home by physique as well as children dependent for a longer and longer period. There probably was a home base, at least for the later-australopithecine *H. habilis* forms; for specialization in hunting and gathering implies a rendezvous, a home base to come back to with the day's yield of food. The division of labor and home base also imply that weak, sick, or injured animals could be taken care of, not simply left behind to die.

With the sexual division of labor had probably come the beginnings of a protohuman family: a pair bond between adult male and female, as well as a maternal bond to her young. This is a question to which we will return in §8.

Beyond this, inferences about social organization become increasingly precarious. Observations of modern carnivores show that hunters minimize dominance and hierarchical structure, while the hunted need it to survive. How, as hominids became increasingly dependent on hunting, did the presumed dominance of their primitive ancestors become transformed? One expert, David Pilbeam (1972), argues that pair bonding between male and female and the first glimmerings of language were involved: nonaggressive behavior could become valued. Others see language as coming much later, but view the emergence of a protofamily as crucial in the evolution of a hunting society where males cooperated instead of staking aggressive claims to status and its benefits.

It is worth remembering too that the early hominids were hunted as well as hunters. But presumably the tight cooperation that made collective hunting possible could be used for collective defense against carnivorous neighbors. Though the early australopithecines may well have slept in trees at night for safety, the living sites of 2 million years ago suggest nights spent on home ground, not in a branch office.

The record of how the early hominids lived is far from full, but it is surprisingly rich. From it we get an overall picture, if not a detailed one. In the four million years when small bands of australopithecines roamed the savannas of Africa, they lived as bipeds in a world of quadrupeds. Not spectacularly large or fast or strong, they were adaptable and increasingly clever. Very gradually they extended the equipment conferred by biology with learned skills, organization, tools, and accumulated knowledge—with the dawning of *culture*. By the time *H. habilis* came on the scene, these protohumans were formidable and efficient predators on the African landscape. The stage was set for the emergence of a new and yet more impressive and formidable human ancestor.

The First Human

About 1.3 million years ago, in one or several parts of the world, a more clearly humanlike form evolved. *Homo erectus* was a highly successful and adaptable creature who was to flourish in Africa, Asia, and Europe for more than a million years.

The earliest well-dated find of *H. erectus* comes from Olduvai. But *H. erectus* may have been evolving across a broad zone of tropical savanna from East Africa into Asia. (Here our perspective may be excessively narrow because recent fossil finds come mainly from East Africa.) Though their precise origin and spread remain unclear, a series of remarkable discoveries has given us increasingly vivid insights into *H. erectus'* mode of life.

H. erectus had a body so much like that of modern humans—judging by the less than complete fossil evidence—that it is almost indistinguishable anatomically from modern man. The bones were thicker and heavier than those of most moderns, the muscle attachments geared to powerful limbs. It is above the neck, in skull, face, and jaw, that *H. erectus,* though definitely human, still showed the mark of hominid forebears: a low, sloping forehead, thick, heavy brow ridges, and a massive jaw. In its long time span, the *H. erectus* lineage changed in the direction of *H. sapiens,* with a higher-domed skull to accommodate an expanding brain and smaller jaws as the diet came to include food that was softer and more easily chewed. The cranial capacity of *H. erectus* varied widely both within populations and across time. The small and early forms show a cranial capacity from 750 cc; the large-brained

individuals of later populations had cranial capacities above 1000 cc, within the range of modern *H. sapiens.*

It is *H. erectus'* brain that commands our attention, because what he did with it took him far in the direction of the Paleolithic hunters of the last 100,000 years—much farther than anyone would have suspected even a decade ago. A series of spectacular discoveries has impressively augmented our knowledge of how these first humans lived and hence of how modern *H. sapiens* evolved.

The most spectacular find was at Terra Amata in Nice, France: an ancient campsite where some 400,000 years ago *H. erectus* bands came to camp over a period of many years. Due to the amazing richness of the finds, the painstaking effort of revealing and reconstructing this record before a new apartment house sealed the Terra Amata site forever, and some good luck, we have a vivid picture of how these early humans lived during their visits and what their environment was like. On a beach and adjacent dune, *H. erectus* bands had built huts and used them as a base for hunting and collecting shellfish and vegetable foods. Apparently they came seasonally, when game animals—red deer, extinct elephants, wild boar, ibex, rhinoceros, and wild ox—were abundant on the nearby

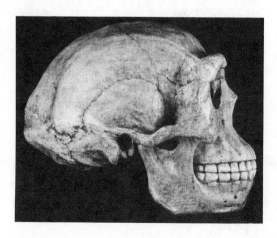

Homo erectus, reconstruction of a skull from Choukoutien. (Courtesy of the American Museum of Natural History.)

flood plain. For these early humans were above all hunters: that is what shaped their lives and sharpened their developing brains. With these new abilities and the new brain-power and organization, they made effective tools of stone and bone; cooked their food with fires that served also for warmth and protection; built huts and windbreaks; used animal hides for sitting and sleeping; and apparently used bowls for collecting, storing, or cooking.

From other sites we get further views on the way of life of those early hunters. From two sites in Spain, Torralba and Ambrona, we find detailed evidence of *H. erectus* hunters cooperating in a hunt of huge elephants, driving them by fire and careful strategy into a bog where they were trapped, killed, and butchered. We are not certain about the dating, but these spectacular hunts probably occurred almost 400,000 years ago. Armed with fire-hardened spears, bone daggers, and stone weapons, and using fire and impressive brainpower and organization, these early humans were formidable predators—the most effective hunting animals the world had known, though they were slow afoot and without great strength or powerful fangs. Their brains were their strength; brains evolved to meet the challenge of organized hunting.

From Olorgesaille in Kenya, another vista of man as hunter was revealed. Here *H. erectus* had staged a carefully planned slaughter of a large troop of baboons—apparently by ambushing these large and powerful animals (the males of this extinct species were as big as a man) at night and clubbing and stoning them to death. A great array of weaponry, the stones brought from 20 miles away, was assembled for this surprise attack, in which more than 60 baboons were killed and butchered.

The Choukoutien caves near Peking, excavated in the 1930s, yielded rich evidence

of *H. erectus'* long tenancy. Alternating with these early humans were other occupants—saber-toothed tigers and cave bears—that competed for the same apartments. Humans gained firm possession of the great caves only when they acquired the use of fire. Fire enabled these early cave dwellers to cook, to fight off fierce predators, and to live in cave depths and harsher climates. It also enabled them to harden wooden and bone tools and weapons. The early humans of Choukoutien were, like their counterparts in Europe and Africa, successful hunters of game animals—sheep, buffalo, horses, pigs, and deer.

These *H. erectus* sites have led experts to emphasize the way hunting shaped the evolution of the human brain and social organization. It is worth underlining another implication of these sites—the emergence of a *home base,* of hearth and home around which the life of the group could revolve. Australopithecine bands had probably moved and foraged together, though hunting implies that males of a band probably moved off, then rejoined the group. They had probably developed at least temporary and shifting camp sites that served as short-run home bases. With the emergence of *H. erectus'* more stable home base, a more systematic division of labor became possible. Young, old, injured, or sick could remain at the home base, pursuing domestic tasks or ones that can be done in place, such as toolmaking. Male members of the band could hunt, carry heavy loads, and do other arduous tasks; female members could forage for wild vegetable foods and small game. With a home base, mobility in hunting can increase: the territory that can be exploited can be larger. The band's mobility would not be constrained by the pace of young children and the need to carry them and domestic possessions; only nursing infants need be carried by their mothers on foraging ventures. Fire not only helped to render a home base secure; as a source of warmth it was a focal point; as a source of light it created an island of culture in the nocturnal seas of nature's darkness.

We can infer as well from these *H. erectus* sites a fairly effective means of communicating information about plans, things, and events. That ability, one our primate relatives do not possess, marks the beginning of *language*. The full development of human language is probably quite recent (§10). Perhaps *H. erectus* could use only fairly simple grammars, with words for things and places. Even a language of limited scope would have given these early humans enormous adaptive advantages—and would have exerted further pressures toward the evolution of human intelligence.

The tools of bone, wood, and stone found in *H. erectus'* habitations mark considerable advances in technology. But the advance in stoneworking is staggeringly slow. Oldowan-type tool kits (which date back to *H. habilis*)—heavy chopping tools and a variety of small scrapers, engravers, and notched tools—are found in early *H. erectus* sites in Africa and at two early sites in Europe. They prevailed in China, India, Java, and elsewhere in Southeast Asia until about 100,000 years ago. About 600,000 years ago there appears in the strata of Oldowan a different tool type known as a hand axe. These hand axes, with associated tools, define a tool-working tradition known as Acheulian (Figure 2.3). The majority of the European sites (including Terra Amata and Torralba-Ambrona) have yielded Acheulian tools—hand axes (probably actually used for skinning and slicing meat), cleavers, blades, borers, scrapers, engraving tools, and various kinds of notched tools. Acheulian tool working, while more diverse and sophisticated than the early "hand-axe" stereotypes suggested, was relatively crude and limited, and it lasted a very long time. Not until the last

100,000 years did Acheulian tool working give way to a more sophisticated stone tool kit.

The Emergence of *H. sapiens*

H. erectus successfully exploited a wide area of the globe. Bands were most heavily concentrated in grassland areas where game animals abounded, and their ebb and flow followed the movements of migratory game.

At one or several places, large-brained late *H. erectus* evolved into early *H. sapiens*. Just where and when we may well never know, for this is a time when the four great glacial advances of the Pleistocene period were underway (Günz, Mindel, Riss, and Würm), grinding to oblivion most of the fossils that might otherwise have survived in Europe and northern Asia (Figure 2.4).

Numerous theories about the "ice age" have been advanced and debated. We still are not certain what caused these periods of glaciation or whether they are over. Apparently the first glaciation had seen the first *H. erectus* migrations northward from Africa (the earliest-known European sites are in southern France, at Vallonet and Escale caves, some 750,000 to 1 million years old). After an intervening interglacial stage, there was a second great glacial advance, during which the Torralba-Ambrona hunters had lived, some 400,-000 years ago.

In the following second interglacial period, the glacial retreat warmed England to the point where rhinoceroses grazed along the Thames. ("As far as the weather is concerned, that was the time to be in England" (Pfeiffer 1969:153)). Important evidence of the transition to *H. sapiens* comes from Swancombe, near London, where the back portion of a skull turned up (in three installments, found over a period of 20 years). Here, some 250,000 years ago, lived early

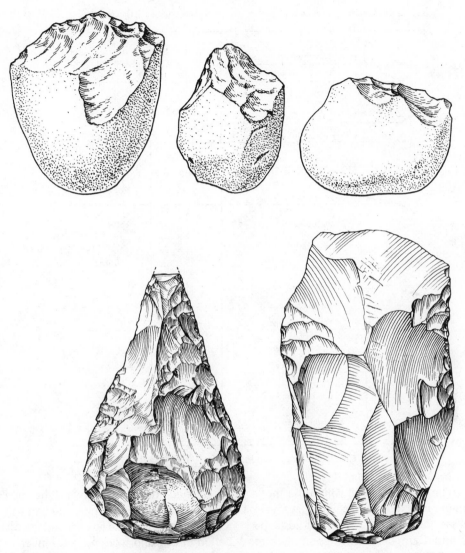

Figure 2.3   Pebble choppers from Olduvai Gorge *(top left* and *center)* and from Grotte du Vallonet *(top right).* Acheulean handax *(bottom left)* and cleaver *(bottom right).* (From Bordes 1968.)

humans that had—with large brain cases— taken a big leap in the direction of *H. sapiens.* Whether they had gotten there, or only part way, cannot be clearly inferred: it is time for a fourth installment, so we can tell what they looked like from the front.

From roughly the same interglacial period,

we have portions of another fossil skull from Steinheim in western Germany. The Steinheim skull includes face and upper jaw, and those are more primitive looking than the back of the skull, suggesting that in western Europe at this stage there was, as one might expect, a form transitional to fully modern *H.*

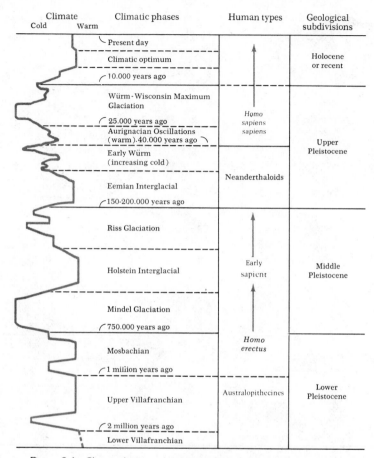

Climate Cold Warm	Climatic phases	Human types	Geological subdivisions
	Present day		Holocene or recent
	Climatic optimum		
	10.000 years ago		
	Würm-Wisconsin Maximum Glaciation		
	25.000 years ago	Homo sapiens sapiens	
	Aurignacian Oscillations (warm).40.000 years ago		Upper Pleistocene
	Early Würm (increasing cold)	Neanderthaloids	
	Eemian Interglacial		
	150-200.000 years ago		
	Riss Glaciation		
	Holstein Interglacial	Early sapient	Middle Pleistocene
	Mindel Glaciation		
	750.000 years ago		
	Mosbachian	Homo erectus	
	1 million years ago		
	Upper Villafranchian	Australopithecines	Lower Pleistocene
	2 million years ago		
	Lower Villafranchian		

Figure 2.4   Climatic history of the Pleistocene. (From Chard 1975:78.)

sapiens. The brain was well within the modern human range, but the face and jaws were not yet as modernized. Statistical tests by Weiner and Campbell, using computers to analyze evolutionary distance between skull types, suggest that these forms, though transitional, merit classification as *H. sapiens* (Campbell 1963). A late *H. erectus* or borderlike *sapiens* skull fragment found at Vértesszöllös, Hungary, is older than Swanscombe or Steinheim, yet points strongly in their direction. Further finds at this important site may give clearer clues to where, when, and how *H. sapiens* evolved from advanced

H. erectus, and carried forward the still flickering but brightening flame of human culture.

The humans of the late second interglacial period in England were no great inventors in the tool department: their surviving hardware is still Acheulian, like that of their *H. erectus* predecessors. But their warm interglacial haven in England was becoming cooler; another glaciation was beginning to grind down from the north.

The third great glacial advance, the Riss, put the survival skills of retreating early humans to a severe test. Bringing grinding sheets of ice into northern Europe, changing forests to grasslands and tundra from which game animals migrated to the south, bringing eternal cold, lowering the sea and scouring the land, the Riss glacial epoch not only challenged survival skills but helped to transform early man biologically and culturally. Selective pressures for intelligence, and the application of intelligence to adapt culturally to precarious and changing environments, gave a strong push in the direction of modern *H. sapiens.*

Our evidence of humans during the Riss glacial period, which gripped the earth for more than 100,000 years, has been scanty. But in 1971 French archaeologists, the DeLumleys, discovered in a cave in the foothills of the Pyrenees the remains of a band of early humans weathering out the eternal winter. About 200,000 years ago they lived in a spacious cave overlooking a river and gorge, bleak but abundant with game. Many tools, mostly flakes, give some evidence of a hunting way of life; and most important, a crushed skull of a young man and two jaws (that resemble the Swanscombe and Steinheim fragments) give a glimpse of the early humans who used the tools. The massive brow ridges, receding forehead, and forward-jutting face of the Tautavel skull are clearly transitional between *H. erectus* and the Neanderthals who were to appear on the scene. *Homo* had, as the Swanscombe and Steinheim fragments suggested, become an incipient sapient.

Another set of clues, about 150,000 years old, come from Lazaret in southern France. There the DeLumleys found another cave site where, inside the cave, hunters had erected tents made out of animal hides, probably to keep the wind out and the drips off. In these tent sites they found remarkable evidence of what looks ritual or magical: a wolf skull behind the portal of each tent.

Beyond this meager evidence of emerging

H. sapiens—increasingly wise and doing his best to come in from the cold—we have found only stone tools. We are lucky to have glimpsed in these recent discoveries of human populations in the Riss glacial epoch the ways of life that preserved a foothold in southern Europe.

Around 125,000 years ago the retreat of the Riss glaciation ushered in a warmer period that was to last about 50,000 years. Seas rose and forests and the game that lived in them returned to northern Europe. Fragmentary human fossils, notably from Fontéchevade in southern France (about 110,000 years old), show that another more modern form of man was emerging from the transitional forms from Tautavel, Swanscombe, and Steinheim.

The Neanderthals

By the midpoint of the warm period, about 100,000 years ago, *H. sapiens* had evolved into the forms known as Neanderthal. These Neanderthals had large brains, equal to those of modern man; but the jaws were still massive, the face thrust out, brows still massive, and forehead sloping.

The Neanderthals have been much maligned and much misunderstood. Being discovered when evolution was still popularly viewed as heresy, they bore the brunt of caricature and distortion—either as apes or freaks but not as ancestors. Moreover, the skeletons discovered earliest were, as we will see, a specialized and extreme form. And one specimen on whose remains a widely influential reconstruction of a stooping, brutish cave man was based turns out to have been bent with arthritis.

Our evidence on the Neanderthals is now rich. It includes the remains of hundreds of individuals, including substantial samples of local populations, covering about 60,000 years. It also includes excavation of diverse living sites across varied environments in many parts of the world.

With this new evidence we see the Neanderthals as almost certainly the ancestors of modern *H. sapiens;* they turn out to be roughly what we could expect. Despite great energy and scholarship invested to show that the evolutionary line to modern man passes around but not through the Neanderthals, they seem now to constitute a critical stage in the emergence of modern humans. Most scholars have taken Neanderthal skeletons out of the closet and into the family gallery.

The early Neanderthals continued to make hand axes, continuing Acheulian patterns; but the tools were becoming more diverse and more specialized. Hand axes and other tools were carefully finished and detailed. Here the high intelligence of the Neanderthals, as indirectly reflected in brain size, gave more range for experimenting and perfecting, and for communicating about technology. Although the ability of Neanderthals to vocalize distinct vowel sounds may have been limited, fairly efficient forms of language must have been present (see §10). This undoubtedly helped to create and maintain a high minimum standard of intelligence and to accumulate local cultural traditions and spread them.

About 75,000 years ago the gradual onset of another glacial period in Europe brought cooler climates and turned woodlands into tundras. At this stage, a major advance in stone toolmaking occurred. Fine flake tools had been made by Neanderthals by knocking two or three finished flakes off a preshaped core of stone (a technique known as Levalloisian). The later Neanderthals now carried this technique a long step forward by preparing a disc-shaped nodule, then knocking off flakes with hammer blows toward the center of the disc until the core was almost gone. The fine flakes were then retouched into specialized tools. This first step in the direction of assem-

bly line production enabled humans to make many tools easily and quickly and brought about a new era of specialized tool kits. More than 60 distinct tool types, specialized for scraping, cutting, gouging, piercing, and other tasks, have been distinguished by experts. These new tool kits, known as Mousterian, gave humans impressive new extensions of hand and arm, impressive new ways to convert natural objects into cultural "things" (Figure 2.5) (we will return to these technologies in §15).

From 75,000 to 40,000 years ago Neanderthals spread into and adapted to a wide range of environments, from northern steppes and snowy valleys to near-desert and tropical rain forest margins. Regional specialization is noteworthy—a florescence of woodworking in the tropics, virtuosity in making warm clothes from hides in the cold north. In deserts, ostrich egg shells may have been used to carry water. In late Neanderthal times hunting had in some regions become highly specialized. The makers of a particular Mousterian tool kit in Europe seem to have become the world's finest judges of horseflesh: they seldom hunted anything else. If wild horses couldn't make you go out for dinner, you went hungry.

After long years when the brutish Neanderthal countenance (partly based on bad reconstructions) led us to think of them as primitive clods, we have in recent decades had remarkable glimpses of their humanity. Neanderthals, or many of them, buried their dead and often placed offerings in graves: in one cave site in Iraq remains of flowers were found in a burial. The sprinkling of ochre and the apparently ritual placement of cave-bear skulls in one site and mountain goat skulls in another seem to point clearly to developed religious ideas. There is also evidence that the Neanderthals cared for the elderly and the sick.

Things were not all sweetness and light.

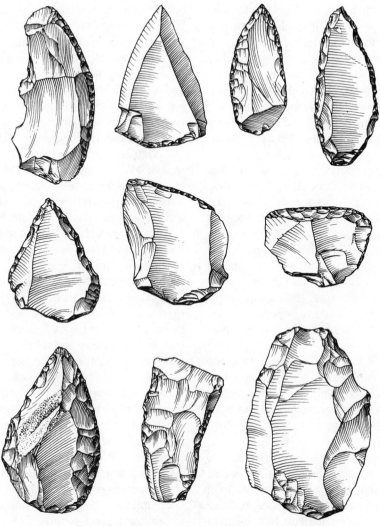

Figure 2.5   Mousterian tool kits. (From Bordes 1968:99.)

Neanderthal remains give clear evidence that humans killed one another. They also almost certainly ate one another: the mutilated remains of 20 bodies that had apparently provided a feast were found at Krapina in Yugoslavia; and at Hortus in France, charred and shattered human bones were thrown into the garbage along with animal bones. The discovery in Europe and Asia of Neanderthal skeletons minus the skulls, and especially of a skull (with the opening in the base enlarged to extract the brain) deep in a cave grotto, ringed with stones, seems to point to a widespread cult of ritual headhunting.

The late Neanderthals of glacial Europe developed relatively specialized physical forms, apparently in adaptation to extreme cold. The nose was broadened, the face more projected, brow ridges were more massive, and the brain case moved down and back, with corresponding shifts in the condyles that support the head. All of these features probably adapted the Neanderthal "design" to preheat icy air during respiration and buffer the brain from cold. These "classic" Neanderthals were the ones on which older stereotypes were based. Contemporaneous with them, in warmer parts of the world, were more generalized and less "brutish" Neanderthals.

How do Neanderthals relate to modern man? Many theorists through the years have seen the Neanderthal as an offshoot of the line leading to man—a population that was an evolutionary dead end, being abruptly replaced by modern man. H. sapiens, in the form of Cro-Magnon men who succeeded Neanderthals in Europe, had in this view evolved somewhere else. By conquest or competition, these modern populations displaced the Neanderthals and sometimes interbred with them.

Support for this view seemed to come from the populations of Mount Carmel in Palestine, where a range of forms, some clearly Neanderthal and some more like modern men, was seen as evidence of hybridization.

This theory is still tenable but increasingly precarious. A range of compelling arguments against it is marshaled by Brose and Wolpoff (1971). They point out that statistically, there are many reasons to view late Neanderthals as biologically transitional to modern man. Moreover, an alleged sharp break between the Mousterian tools of Neanderthals and those of the modern H. sapiens who succeeded them in the Upper Paleolithic (used to support theories of invasion and displacement) does not bear close examination. Many late Neanderthal sites in Europe, Africa, and the Near East show a continuity in tool types: the blade and other tools (for example, bone tools) long viewed as distinctive of Upper Paleolithic (that is, modern) populations

occurred in Neanderthal sites, though with lesser frequency.

The most compelling argument for viewing Neanderthals as our ancestors is that although they have turned up across a vast area of the world, no trace has been found of any other H. sapiens population contemporaneous with the Neanderthals that was developing into modern humans.

What led to the evolution of modern H. sapiens? We are not sure. The Mount Carmel fossils are now viewed by many scholars as a transitional population; some early and rugged H. sapiens of near modern type, not yet precisely dated, have turned up in eastern and southern Africa; and there seems to be a continuous line in Southeast Asia leading from Neanderthal to near-modern forms.

Loring Brace, an advocate of Neanderthals-as-our-ancestors, stresses the importance of Neanderthal teeth as gripping tools—built-in pliers or vises. These functions, he believes, were important in shaping the Neanderthal design of face and head. With better stone technology these pliers were increasingly superseded (or vises were no longer virtues). This, Brace feels, could have contributed to the transformation of Neanderthal facial architecture into that of modern H. s. sapiens. As we will see, there is some recent—though controversial—evidence that the Neanderthal vocal tract was a limited instrument for making distinct vowel sounds. This has led to a suggestion by Pilbeam: evolution of the vocal tract that made fully human speech possible would have raised and transformed the pharynx, shortened the skull base, and changed the facial design in a modern direction. Moreover, more efficient speech would have had such adaptive value that a rapid evolutionary burst seems highly plausible. It is possible that some other complex of selective pressures gave the Neanderthal skull its special shape, and that the relaxation of these pressures, due to ecological and/or cultural changes, led to the transformation of Neanderthals into modern humans.

Whether modern man evolved from Neanderthal forms in one or several regions or across the whole range of Neanderthal habitats is not clear. The evidence, meager for the crucial period, would seem to point toward the evolution of modern humans in many places (though not necessarily independently; by this time, contacts between groups were widespread, and adaptive changes could have spread rapidly). If we view the Neanderthal skull design as a complex in which a modern-sized human brain was packaged in a distinctive way, built around teeth and vocal tract and held in a kind of dynamic balance, then rapid parallel evolution in widely separated populations becomes plausible. Once the factors—whatever they were—that held the design in balance were shifted by biological and/or cultural advance, then the whole design could shift into a new kind of balance—that of modern *H. s. sapiens*.

However, in parts of Africa and Southeast Asia, populations apparently descended from the older Neanderthal populations of the areas retained physically archaic features well into the period when fully modern populations had emerged in other regions; presumably with greater mobility and hybridization, these "archaic" populations were eventually absorbed.

When populations with a developed Upper Paleolithic technology appear on the archaeological scene, they, the Cro-Magnon men who did cave paintings and hunted woolly mammoths, were biologically modern. We had arrived, for better or worse. What we made of it belongs mainly in the realm of culture, not biology; we will sketch the subsequent unfolding in Chapters 5, 6, and 7. In Chapter 4, we will glimpse the microevolution of modern populations, the biology of race and human variability. Before we look at the biology of modern human populations, another kind of look at the evolutionary past is in order. We have looked at the evolution of human anatomy. It is time to look more closely at the evolution of human *behavior*.

HUMANS AND OTHER PRIMATES
The Evolution of Behavior

3

Until the 1960s, most cultural anthropologists dealt with humans in biological perspective by stressing how different and unique we are and how our ability to use language and cumulate custom set us apart from other animals. After 15 years of rethinking, humans look no less remarkable, and in sum perhaps no less unique, in the animal kingdom; but anthropologists have come to look at the human animal in a very different way.

Human behavior was contrasted, in the older studies, with the social life of insects, the instinctive behavior of animals, with their limited reliance on learning, and the behavior of trained animals like dogs and parrots as manipulated by humans themselves. What little we knew about behavior of other primates came mainly from zoos and laboratories.

Across the animal world our understanding of behavior patterns has now been advanced dramatically. Ethologists like Lorenz and Tinbergen have documented the "innate releasing mechanisms" whereby birds, fishes, and other organisms are programmed to respond to environmental stimuli, and have studied animal communication. The evolution of behavior patterns as well as physical structures has become a central concern. As we begin to see how complicated are the genetic templates for behavior and how they interact with environmental stimuli, simple distinctions between "instinct" and "learning" are no longer adequate.

With these new ways of looking at the world of nature have come new perspectives on humans. We are looking for continuities with our animal past, not simply contrasts. Central in this enterprise has been systematic study of our closest animal relatives in their natural habitats. Rich evidence is being built up on the social life of many primate species.

Particularly fascinating are behavioral studies of chimpanzees and gorillas, our closest animal kin, and studies of the baboons that, like early hominids, live on the ground in open grasslands—and whose ancestors shared these environments with australopithecines. Having derived riches beyond expectation from studying primate behavior in natural settings, scientists are intensifying laboratory studies as well, to probe the implications of what they have observed in the wild, and the results have often been startling. The literature on primate behavior is vast, detailed, and intricate. We need not be concerned here with primate behavior for its own sake; we are interested in what primate studies tell us about human behavior and how it evolved.

What can these studies tell us about the nature of *Homo sapiens?* Like cultural anthropology itself, primate behavior studies give no immediate, easy, and unequivocal answers about the extent and nature of human aggression, about how the incest taboo or language or the family originated, about how central sexuality is in human biology and psychology. But they allow us to say much more, and speculate much better, than we could without them.

Studying the range of variation in primate behavior enables us to reconstruct with fair confidence a number of things about the behavior of the ancient primates from which we and modern apes are descended. Examining *H. sapiens* and the fossil record of human development in the light of that primate pattern, we can make fairly good guesses about how and why humans changed in adapting to a mode of life as hunter and gatherer, a mode which our ancestors maintained relatively unchanged for hundreds of thousands of years. We can also speculate about how the biological heritage of humans equipped them for those spectacular leaps of technology whereby human life has been transformed in

the last 10,000 years. And we can ask how a biological and psychological nature adaptive to life in small-scale societies serves us in a radically refashioned modern world.

We assume throughout this discussion that almost no interesting elements of human behavior are entirely and directly determined by biological programming; they represent the interaction of biological programs and social—hence cultural—experience. Similarly, most nonhuman primate behavior patterns represent the interaction of genetic programs and social learning, though the mix between the two has shifted markedly in the course of human evolution. By the same token, human cultures are less arbitrary, less variable than anthropologists used to imagine: the creations of culture are constrained by and bound to biological templates (Freeman 1969). In no realm of human behavior has cultural creativity had free rein.

In the pages that follow, we will look at a number of facets of primate behavior—social structure, sexuality, play, communication, and the like, and we will use the evidence to make inferences about the emergence of human behavior. At the end, we will be able to reflect both on the distinctiveness of human culture and on the evolutionary continuities that bind humans to their animal cousins.

6.
Primate Social Organization

All known nonhuman primates (we will call them primates for short) live in groups, often called bands or troops. These groups characteristically have a home range. Looking across the whole primate order, we see wide variation in the size and composition of social groups. In some monkeys and among the gibbons, a female, her mate, and their young comprise a simple, stable group; among macaques and many other monkeys, the group consists of multiple males and females without stable heterosexual bonds, and numbers sometimes run into several score. Most primate species live in more or less closed groups of between 10 and 80 animals. This spectrum of variation is examined in detail in recent publications (Chance and Jolly 1970; Jay 1968b; Kummer 1971; A. Jolly 1972). For our purposes, a narrower focus is useful. We will look most closely at the social behavior of our closest relatives, the great apes. The rich documentation of chimpanzee behavior is especially valuable. We will pay secondary attention to baboon behavior: first, because many baboons are, like our australopithecine ancestors, savanna dwellers; second, because they pose some important and instructive contrasts with chimpanzees and gorillas; and third, because they show striking variation between species in different environments.

Baboons

Let us look first at the cynocephalus baboons, one of two main classes of baboons. These baboons are predominantly savanna dwellers, living largely on the ground but dependent on trees for safety and sleeping.

Cynocephalus baboons live in highly stable groups averaging from 40 to 80 individuals. Groups keep apart from each other on their daily ranges, with their daily movements carrying them several miles; their home ranges typically comprise an area of some 10 to 15 square miles.

Males are formidable animals, averaging about 75 pounds and armed with vicious canine teeth. Females are less than half that size. On the open savanna lands where their daily scrounging expeditions take them, flight to the trees is often impossible. Their defense is a rigid and tightly organized social group in which the strong adult males protect females, infants, and juveniles.

Dominance is extreme. The fully adult males, one to six to a group, are at the top of the social ladder. The most dominant males—and rank is clearly established—have exclusive access to females at the height of sexual receptivity—hence they do the reproducing, with the adaptive benefit that entails. They also preempt shady sitting places and desirable food, and they are groomed by "fol-

Male juvenile cynocephalus baboons chasing one another while an adult male watches. Note the savanna setting. (Courtesy of Irven DeVore/Anthro-Photo.)

lowers." The dominance of highest-ranking males is established by physical combat, but once established, it is seldom challenged. Physical dominance over females and juveniles, however, is sternly enforced with bites and brute force. Interestingly, dominance is not defined strictly by individual combat or strength: coalitions reinforce positions of individuals. Females, to a minimal degree, also form dominance hierarchies.

Mothers and their infants form an important subunit of the group. We will see that this mother-young bond is basic in primate social organization. In the savanna baboons, infants are a focus of group interest as well—other females and males hold and care for the infant. Juvenile females and males play defined but different parts in the social life of the group. These roles are shaped partly by physical differences. Females mature much faster, so that adult females outnumber adult males, and young males must survive on the periphery as they mature, gain strength, and eventually join the Establishment if they can. The sexual drives of adult males are strong and continuous. Females are sexually active only during estrus periods, and as we have seen, access to them is tightly restricted.

As in other primate species, baboons grow up and spend their lives within the same group. Since individual animals know one another well, actual contests for dominance are minimized; usually a gesture or mild threat is enough to reinforce an established pattern of relationship. The relatively long period of maturation means that an animal learns much of what it has to know from observing and participating in a group. We have come to see vividly, in primate behavior studies, the importance of learning in the adaptation of local groups. As we will see more dramatically with chimpanzees, play and imitation are crucial processes in the acquisition of adult skills.

Hamadryas baboons, a species closely related to the cynocephalus baboons, living in Ethiopian deserts, show a fascinating pattern of contrasts in social organization. Like most primate species, the cynocephalus baboons have no social groupings larger than the band, and apart from the always-important mother-infant units, they are not divided into subgroups. The hamadryas baboons, apparently in adaptation to an arid environment without the protection of sleeping trees, have evolved both larger and smaller social groupings (Kummer 1968, 1971).

Hamadryas baboons sleep on exposed cliffs in large troops of from somewhat less than a hundred to several hundred. During the day, however, the troops separate into a larger number of one-male groups. A mature adult male is likely to have about four females in his group. The females are forced by physical coercion to follow him; they groom him and mate with him when they are in estrus. A young male initiates one of these groups by forcing a juvenile female to follow him, usually before she is sexually mature, though sexual maturation is earlier in this species.

Not all animals belong to one-male groups. Some old or immature males remain on the periphery, and juveniles move freely

A hamadryas baboon male and his female sitting on their customary sleeping ledge. The male is threatening a neighboring family group. (Courtesy of Hans Kummer.)

within the group in play and foraging. But adult females are kept rigidly within their groups, and adult males interact in few settings. There are no dominance hierarchies between males: each is king of his little castle.

If the troop is large, it segments—in daily foraging columns and in large-scale fights—into smaller bands of from 20 to 90 animals (apparently the equivalent of the cynocephalus baboon groups). These are made up of a cluster of one-male groups. In contexts involving band movement or collective defense, however, one or several old males recurrently take the lead. The composition of these bands is apparently more constant than the composition of the troops; a band may join another troop temporarily at a different sleeping cliff. The entire troop acts as a unit only in the sense of mutual protection at night and in a collective departure on the day's foraging, during which bands split off and then may spread out to forage in one-male groups.

This remarkable multilevel social organization appears to be an adaptation of the baboon behavioral repertoire to a different, and demanding, physical environment (Kummer 1971).

Further insights into the antecedents of human social behavior have come from Thelma Rowell's studies of cynocephalus baboons in woodlands rather than savannas. Rowell found that the rigid structure and dominance hierarchies of the grassland baboons were much less striking among forest baboons (Rowell 1966). They live in rather flexible multimale groups, and almost all males change troops in their lifetimes. It is the adult females and their offspring that maintain group continuity. Dominance hierarchies and male aggression are much less striking than among savanna baboons. A number of experts believe that baboons originally evolved as woodland animals and that the

savanna adaptations, like those of the hamadryas baboons, are specializations for life in a new habitat.

Chimpanzees and Gorillas

The social organization of chimpanzees presents striking contrasts to that of the baboons, especially the savanna baboons. Where rigid structure enables savanna baboons to survive in groups where they would otherwise be at the mercy of predators, chimpanzees are marked by flexibility and the lack of rigid organization.

There is no stable, discrete social group among chimpanzees: individuals move about freely, though they characteristically form loosely structured small bands. These bands in turn may aggregate into larger groupings. "Chimpanzees . . . live in an open society. . . . The parties of a wide area meet and recombine in a constant process of reorganization. This seems to be an ecologically ideal fusion-fission system, providing group sizes and compositions for every conceivable context" (Kummer 1971:90—91).

Chimpanzee bands may, at different times, comprise (1) adult males only; (2) mothers and offspring, sometimes with a few other females; (3) adults and adolescents of both sexes, but not mothers with infants; and (4) representatives of all categories. In the course of a day, bands of one kind or another may branch off, then coalesce, then split again on other lines. The continuities in such a shifting scene partly reflect relatively permanent association of a population with a home range, though individuals forage in a wide area.

There are dominance hierarchies among individual animals, but they are not asserted with the rigidity and violence observed among baboons. Dominance and submission behavior, such as physical cuffing and quasi-sexual presenting of the rump by the submitting animal, is matched—and often followed—by comforting, touching, reassurance behavior (van Lawick-Goodall 1968b). Violent fights are rare.

The affective communication (that is, the expression of emotional states) constantly going on between chimpanzees suggests a major theme in their social organization: close interindividual (one is tempted to say "interpersonal") bonds of *friendship* keep animals together and seem to underlie the formation and continuity of social groups. Mother-infant ties are close, and the dependency of infants is much more prolonged than among baboons. There is no separation between chimp mother and infant for four to six months, in contrast to one month for baboons. Juveniles are nursed for four to five years, may share their mother's nest for another three years, and are dependent until about age eight. Bonds that begin to look like kinship are beginning to emerge: an elderly mother was accompanied and groomed by her adult sons; and "brother-sister" and "brother-brother" bonds may last into (or perhaps through) adulthood.

The long period of dependence reflects the great importance of social learning among chimpanzees. We will see that tool-using is an important adaptation. We are beginning to realize how much of chimpanzee behavior is learned through participation in a social group, thus at least protocultural. "Non-human primates learn, but they do not teach" (Pfeiffer 1972:312); they learn by imitating, trying, playing. The play of juvenile chimpanzees is strikingly similar to that of humans. Kortlandt (1973:13) vividly describes how he observed wild chimpanzees in the Congo from a vantage point where he could also see a tribal hamlet where children were continually playing:

While watching my chimps, I could always hear the hullabaloo of the children. The chimp youngsters played almost exactly the same games as the human ones—running around, doing gymnastics, mock-fighting, playing tag and king-of-the-castle, dangling on low branches . . .

Jay (1968a:501) has noted:

That an animal practices in play the skills and activities he needs when grown is of tremendous evolutionary importance. . . . Surely it is more than a coincidence that the nonhuman primate taxonomically closest to man . . . is also the most manipulative, exploratory, and similar to man in play. The range of variation in play form and games among chimpanzees is second only to man.

Though information on the gorilla is less rich, these near-relatives also closely resemble humans in their play. This description from Schaller's field notebooks on the mountain gorilla will strike a familiar note in a retired babysitter or playground watcher:

A juvenile and a 1¾-year old infant sit about four feet apart. Suddenly the juvenile twists around and grabs the infant, which rushes away hotly pursued by the juvenile. The juvenile catches the infant and covers it with his body, propped on elbows and knees. Twisting and turning, struggling and kicking, more and more the infant emerges from beneath the juvenile. Freedom gained, the infant grabs an herb stalk at one end and the juvenile snatches the other end. They pull in opposite directions; the juvenile yanks hard and the infant is jerked forward. They then sit facing each other, mouths open, and swing their arms at each other and grapple slowly. Another juvenile comes dashing up, and in passing swipes at the juvenile and all three disappear running into the undergrowth (Schaller 1963).

The importance of sex in the social organization of baboons is clearly evident. For chimpanzees, matters are not so clear. Chimpanzees tend to be casual about sex as about most other things. Though dominance is clearly important, it is not usually invoked to exclude sexual access to females. Van Lawick-Goodall once observed seven males, including an adolescent, waiting their turn to mount a receptive female.

As with other nonhuman primates, chimpanzees females are sexually receptive only during estrus. But during sexually receptive periods, females are not always besieged with eager partners; in fact, copulation is not the frequent event it is among baboons. Van Lawick-Goodall observed 213 actual or attempted copulations in a year of observation. Males took the initiative 176 times, and their overtures were accepted about 80 percent of the time.

On . . . 10 occasions the males "gave up" and after shaking branches in the direction of the females moved away. . . . On 37 occasions females solicited males. Typically, the female approached to within six feet, flattened herself in front of the male with her limbs flexed, and looked back at him over her shoulder. Five times the . . . soliciting females were ignored. (van Lawick-Goodall 1968b:361)

Chimpanzee sexuality, while clearly an important force in social organization, scarcely seems the primal drive Freudians postulate for humans. Copulation is one element in the complex of bonds between individuals. Fondling and inspecting of the genitals and other expressions of diffuse sexuality serve to assert and maintain the closeness between animals; but sex for its own sake hardly seems to be what keeps them together. Among gorillas, sexual expression seems less central, and copulation is apparently rather rare. Schaller (1963) observed copulation only twice in 13 months of observation.

Our data on the social organization of gorillas is much less detailed than our evidence on chimpanzees.

Mountain gorillas have been observed most commonly in groups of 5 to 30 individuals, though groups as small as 2 have been observed. All groups contain at least one large, mature male and one or more females and their young. The larger groups contain other males, but they are usually peripheral and often drift out of the group; in any case, one male is dominant (Schaller 1963).

Difficulties of observation have so far made it hard to determine whether there is more flexibility in group membership than meets the eye or to find long-term continuities in mother-child and sibling-sibling behavior. Gorilla social structure is highly cohesive. Groups adhere to limited ranges, but they lack marked territoriality and share overlapping range areas. We may hope that from continuing studies by Dian Fossey, who has managed to achieve closer contacts with gorillas than did Schaller in his pioneering research, we will get a rich and detailed picture of gorilla social life.

It is worth observing that the gorilla of Hollywood scriptwriters—the ultimate Brute —is a myth. Actually, gorillas are gentle and unaggressive animals. When cornered by dogs when defending their young, they will attack, as early explorers discovered; but the normal response to danger is a bluff charge, with fearsome chest-beating and tooth-rattling but no actual attack. Having made his aggressive display and given his group a chance to retreat, the dominant male will, if the observer stands his ground with shaking knees, in effect shrug and walk away.

The recurrent themes in primate social organization—social groups occupying home ranges; internal structuring based on age, sex, and dominance; importance of the mother-infant unit; and the increasing length of dependence and importance of learning and play—provide vivid evidence on the social behavior of our primate ancestors and important clues about how hominid behavior evolved. Before drawing these clues together and making inferences from them, we need to look at another source of insights: the ecology of primates.

7.
Primates in Ecological Perspective

Kummer (1971) has recently synthesized persuasively our evidence on primate behavior from an ecological point of view. To try to cover the same ground would be presumptuous and unnecessary. Rather, a series of observations directly relevant to the evolution of human behavior can be drawn.

1. Territoriality and group size and structure are modes of adaptation to food resources. The size of a home range, the degree to which its borders are closed or open, and the size and internal structure of the group are geared to the distribution of food, the availability of watering and sleeping places, the homogeneity of the environment, the nature of predators, and other ecological factors.

Unlike humans, nonhuman primates lead a hand-to-mouth existence, neither storing nor accumulating nor sharing food. Day to day each animal requires the food and water to stay alive. The aged, ill, or injured must be left to die. The size of the group, its spatial distribution, and its composition must provide for safety from predators, but most of all they must render efficient the business of finding food every day. The way primate groups move in space, the way they defend their territories or permit penetration of their home ranges, the way they communicate, all relate directly to the food quest. The contrast between cynocephalus and hamadryas baboon social organization shows how the same basic behavioral repertoire may be transformed in adaptation to contrasting environments.

2. Among the apes, and especially chimpanzees, tool-using is an important element in adaptive behavior—one of many forms of learned behavior that enable a population to exploit their environment efficiently.

The significance of tool-using by animals has been much debated. Consider the following examples of tool-using from the animal world: an otter using a stone brought from the ocean bottom to crack open mollusc shells; a baboon using branches to pry rocks up and get larvae from underneath; a chimpanzee using twigs to fish termites from a nest; a gorilla waving branches to frighten away an anthropologist.

Hall (1963:131 ff.) emphasizes that tool-using as an adaptation for food-getting, nest-building, or the like, may not be a great evolutionary advance, but simply another way of doing a specialized job. Most animals that use tools do so only to obtain food. Furthermore, the use of branches or stones for aggressive displays (which occur mainly in apes, seldom in monkeys) is not necessarily a close approximation to man's use of clubs or stones as hunting or defensive weapons. But recent studies of chimpanzees show that their tool-using goes much further in a human direction than Hall had thought (Figure 3.1).

Chimpanzees use probes of various sorts to extract termites from their nests. Often the instruments must be carefully adapted to the task at hand. One population of chimpanzees also has been observed to fashion leaf sponges to extract rainwater from the crotch of a tree—apparently a case of local innovation, since chimpanzees in other areas use their hands. Other chimpanzees have been observed in the wild to crack hard fruits with stones, use twigs to scrape honey from combs, and use branches and other objects as projectiles. Innovations in a particular band spread within the group and beyond. Studies of the great apes in the wild bring them dra-

Figure 3.1   A wild chimpanzee uses a grass stem to fish termites from a nest. (After a photograph by Baron Hugo van Lawick)

matically into a realm long thought to be exclusively human. Chimpanzees *make* tools, albeit simple ones; their use must be *learned* as part of a group tradition; and their elaborations are by no means limited to the modes of food-getting or threat that Hall had discussed.

Primates in their natural environments, impressive as their toolmaking and tool-using may be, undoubtedly do not use their potential brainpower to the fullest. Here, as with the symbol-manipulating we will shortly see, primates can be pushed further by patient laboratory experimentation. An impressive recent example in the realm of toolmaking was Richard Wright's success in teaching a five-year-old zoo orangutan named Abang to make flint tools. Abang learned from demonstration—all in a little more than three hours—how to use a hammerstone to break a chunk of flint, select a sharp-edged flake, and use it to cut a string to open a box containing fruit.

Striking evidence of local learning among monkeys comes from Koshima Island in Japan, where a group of macaques has been intensively studied by primatologists. Feeding sweet potatoes on the Koshima beach to the forest-dwelling macaques led to an impressive innovation: a two-year-old female discovered how to wash the sand from her potato in a brook. Within five years all but the oldest adults were washing their sweet potatoes. Learning of the new technique passed along lines of closest social ties, between siblings and mother and child. Old conservatives, as conservatives will, continued to grit their teeth.

3. Within a given species or group, behavioral patterns and group organization may be adjusted to the demands of an environment. Thus the chimpanzees studied by Itani and his colleagues have been observed, when crossing open country between tropical forests, to form tightly knit groups in defensive formation. On reaching the safety of the forest, the ranks dissolved again (Itani and Suzuki 1967). As we have noted, baboons in the forests of Uganda have a less tightly structured social organization, less marked by dominance and defensive solidarity among males, than those living in more dangerous savanna country (Rowell 1966).

4. Studies of primates and other animals in their natural settings have given us a new view of relations between species. Characteristically, there is remarkably little interaction between different species of animals in the

Learning in monkeys: A young Japanese macaque learns potato washing from its mother. (Courtesy of M. Kawai.)

wild, apart from the dramas of hunter and hunted. Modern studies show that different animal species in the wild mingle surprisingly freely. It is common around a water hole to see antelope, zebras, warthogs, baboons, giraffes, elephants, and even lions intermingling, seemingly oblivious of one another. Animals spaced out and in flight are very often fleeing the hairless ground-dwelling bipedal primate who for more than a million years has probably been the most dangerous predatory animal in Africa. We have also seen how animals of different species, including primates, may be symbiotically related. Baboons and gazelles may feed together, intermingled; the baboons see better while the gazelles smell and hear better. Together they are hard for a predator to surprise.

5. In chimpanzees, an important though relatively rare activity is *hunting*. Chimpanzees cooperate to hunt, going after arboreal monkeys, young baboons, and other small animals. When they hunt and kill, their usual easygoing demeanor is transformed into what almost can be read as "blood lust." Episodes of killing apparently go in bursts, with an apparent meat-eating craze catching hold, then dwindling. It is interesting and important that when chimpanzees hunt they sometimes display *sharing* behavior; at times this amounts to begging or collective tearing of the carcass, but at other times it seems almost ritualized. Here as elsewhere, chimpanzees give us little glimpses of our ancestors and of ourselves (see Teleki 1973).

8.
The Evolution of Hominid Social Organization

These sources of evidence about our primate ancestors help us to speculate productively about how our hominid ancestors evolved behaviorally in a human direction.

The most dramatic transformation of primate society was the development of a pair

Meat eating by chimpanzees: *(left)* A meat sharing cluster of four adult chimpanzees. Male in left foreground is accepting a sliver of baboon carcass from "owner," in right foreground. *(right)* An adult male prepares to eat his share of a young baboon killed and divided. (Courtesy of Geza Teleki.)

bond: the association of male mate with mother and offspring. The human family represents a major new evolutionary development. Geared to the beginning of the family was a change in the sexuality of hominid females. They became sexually receptive more or less continually, with the menstrual cycle as a modification of the estrus cycle. One clue about the development of this primal family may lie in the increasing importance of cultural learning, and its concomitant, the prolonging of infantile dependency. The juvenile chimp remains dependent in some respects for several years and has a great deal to learn. The hominid infant had more and more to learn over a longer time span, and a stable familial base that included a protector and provider was an important adaptation.

The appearance of a "provider" itself marked a crucially important change. Providing implies *sharing,* and a division of labor in which male and female play complementary roles. Perhaps the development of hunting was the crucial element here. From a primate ancestor who hunted occasionally (and perhaps shared meat but not vegetable foods, as chimpanzees do) evolved australopithecines that hunted regularly and increasingly well. With a home base—and the family and division of labor imply hearth and home, however transitory—males could specialize in hunting. Sexual dimorphism, with males stronger and faster, was not only adaptive to hunters but necessary, since bearing large-brained offspring constrained the evolution of the hominid female pelvis.

From a primal family, with a regularly associated male, could evolve wider patterns of kinship within the group. We have noted the beginnings in chimpanzees of mother-child and sibling bonds lasting into later life. The father was woven into this design at some stage as protector and provider, and an important new element was introduced. The *incest taboo* prohibiting mating within the family group underlay the formation of human society. As we will see in §48, the incest taboo, universal in human societies though culturally variable in its range of extension beyond the nuclear family, has posed a central challenge to theorists of kinship. At some stage, perhaps with *H. erectus,* mating and the formation of pair bonds *between* bands rather than within them would have led further in the direction of early human society.

Kinship is often taken by anthropologists to be a realm of cultural convention resting only indirectly on the framework of biology (see Chapter 13). The importance of the *primary bond* between mother and infant, with deep physiological roots, places this assumption in a new light (Freeman 1974). In the first year of life a neonate develops deep, though always ambivalent, attachment to the person, normally the mother, who has provided basic care. The emotional roots of mother-child bonding—and the deep-seated ambivalence to the provider/withholder of gratification—may, as Freeman suggests, provide the basic template for kinship bonds as they form more widely (see also Bowlby 1969). Note the importance here of the old primate mother-child unit. Freeman suggests that the primary bond had strong adaptive value in the evolution of hominid behavior, as defense against predation as infantile dependence was prolonged.

Many pieces remain to be fitted into this puzzle, and many inferences will remain speculative. Yet an increasingly vivid picture of primate social life has given us strong indirect evidence about the primate precursors of the hominids and has made possible increasingly strong inferences about the evolutionary pressures and processes whereby hominids became human.

9.

Territoriality, Aggression, and Human Nature

Are we by nature aggressive killers? Are our hands stained with blood as an hereditary curse we cannot wash off?

Popular writers such as Robert Ardrey and Konrad Lorenz have argued that our hominid heritage predisposes us to aggression, which we can perhaps channel but not eliminate. They see in present-day wars a re-enactment of primal aggressive urges. Others (see Montagu 1972) have argued that "aggression" comprises a diverse collection of culturally patterned behaviors, and that both harmony and aggression are shaped by culture, not biology.

Both positions, baldly argued, are wrong. We know from detailed biological research that there are specific brain mechanisms through which aggression is triggered, in the form of rage, violence, or threat. This is not to say that we have *drives* for aggression, only that there are evolutionarily old mechanisms in the limbic system of the brain, which in humans, as in other mammals, provide the *circuitry* through which aggression is triggered.

What triggers aggression in man? Herein lies the difficult part. One of the fascinating mysteries of man is the way evolutionarily old and new systems of the brain are interwoven: the way the evolutionarily old limbic system, part of our mammalian heritage, and the higher cortical system we use to build a world of symbols are interrelated. Mammalian rage can be generated not only by physical threat or aggression but by verbal taunt or insulting gesture. We are the only animals that kill one another for peace.

Being mammals, our aggressiveness is affected by biochemical and genetic factors, by surging hormones as well as stirring martial music. But the argument that warfare, particularly in modern man, is a release of aggressive violence is much too simple. Humans have shown in many times and places that *when cultural controls break down* they can go into a frenzy of blood lust; such violence is well documented by Freeman (1964). In the midst of war, some individuals may derive deep biological satisfactions from violence and killing. But the symbolic element, the institutional framework, the cultural patterning, make human warfare a much more complex phenomenon than the prophets of aggression suggest. We will reflect on these complexities in §63. To say that the mass killings of Vietnam reflect blood lust is far too simple: for every small-scale My Lai massacre there were pilots impersonally pushing buttons or locking on radar tracks, able to carry out such missions because the random killing was psychologically denied, the massacre impersonalized, the humanity of the unseen victims swept from the conscious mind.

In the course of evolution, as we became more efficient tool and symbol users and hence more effective killers, many of the old mechanisms of physical aggression and agonistic display disappeared: erectile hair, massive canine teeth, and the like. With our cultural efficiency in killing, we evolved complex brain circuits that serve to control and deflect aggression. Humans control their rage, binding their aggressiveness into institutional webs. We are never more human than when we express our aggression with words, not blows. Humans lost many of the primate mechanisms of aggression in the course of their evolution; they replaced them with sharp tongues.

Are we then aggressive killers by nature or not? If we want from anthropology a clearcut and simple answer, we must be disappointed. It is as foolhardy to deny the biological bases of human aggression as it is to deny the complex cultural control and patterning of aggression. The emerging answers are complicated and require us to try to unravel the interweaving of old and new, biological and symbolic, individual and institutional. We are just beginning to learn to do that. Our usual modes of theorizing and explaining push us toward being too simple, toward seeing one side of a multifaceted reality. This theme is one we will encounter again in the pages to follow. Instead of asking for simple answers, we humans need, if we are to understand our world and to survive as a species, better ways of understanding complexity.

10.
Primate Communication and the Evolution of Language

Observers of chimpanzees in the wild have commented on the din they produce—crashing, screeching, making vocal noises amazing in volume and variety. They and other nonhuman primates communicate vocally and by gesture and expression, with a richness equaled in few if any other animals.

Students of primate communication have noted that we are prone to misunderstand the primates' modes of exchanging messages. We want to know what a particular sound or gesture "means." But actually primate communication seldom conveys information about "the world." Rather, primates mainly communicate about their own internal emotional and physical states and about their relationships with one another.

Primates do not usually send signals one at a time, so that a particular noise denotes anger, a particular gesture denotes affection, and so on. Rather, the same signal or message is communicated in many modes simultaneously—by vocalization, gesture, touch, smell, and facial expression. The same vocal sound may carry quite different messages,

depending on the other signals that accompany it and on the social and environmental context. We should remember that most communications take place within groups of animals that know one another well. Signaling *between* groups tends to be simpler and more direct, as when bands of foraging chimpanzees signal one another's approach with loud noises from afar to divert the other group from a collision course.

Chimpanzee communication in the wild is—as with other facets of chimpanzee behavior—a particularly valuable source of insights. To pose some contrasts between human and chimpanzee communication, let us return to the scene where the primatologist Kortlandt was observing wild chimpanzees at the forest margin from a vantage point that also overlooked a Congolese village. The play of the juvenile chimps looked remarkably similar to the play of the children in the distance, but all the games of tag, mock fighting, and the like, took place "without a single sound."

Social intercourse in the chimpanzee group was achieved chiefly by silent facial expression, arm and hand gestures, and bodily postures. From time to time, however, some of the adults . . . would burst out in a deafening pandemonium of hoots, screams, and yells, . . . the accompaniment of their brief intimidation displays and sexual riotings. The human adults in the village, on the other hand, . . . were sitting quietly . . . talking. (Kortlandt 1973:13)

The richness of gestural codes in chimpanzees is only beginning to be comprehended. "So complex and so delicate is this language of gesture in the chimpanzee that it cannot be said to be less evolved than our own" (Campbell 1970; see van Lawick-Goodall 1968). Primate bases for much of the human gestural repertoire can be seen in chimpanzee communication:

Much of our gestural repertoire has been inherited from our ancestors. Chimps embrace each other in greeting; they reassure by touching each other; they seek reassurance by stretching out the hands, palm up, waiting to be touched by the other's hand. . . . Chimps greet with a kiss, probably a ritualized form of offering food. (Eibl-Eibesfeldt 1968:484)

We will return to the nature of nonverbal communication in man, its evolutionary and cultural components, in §28 and will note Eibl-Eibesfeldt's recent research in this realm.

Chimpanzees do not have language. Why not? To answer that, we need to know something more about language, about humans, and about chimpanzees. We can then begin to understand how our capacity for language may have evolved.

In Chapter 9, we will look at our burgeoning but still only partial understanding of the fantastically complicated and intricate system that is language. At this stage we can build in part on what we all know about language from talking and listening. To that we need to add a few points concerning what makes language special.

A most important property of human language is that we talk about *things* in the world; we have *names* for things. Using these labels, we are able to make *propositions* about the world. To do this we do not depend on those things being perceptually present. Animals communicate about the world only through their responses to phenomena that are perceptually there, for example, a threatening predator, an approaching band, the presence of food. They cannot communicate about things absent or imagined, and as Bateson (1972a) points out, they cannot express negatives.

The labels languages attach to perceptual classes of things are characteristically arbitrary. There is no resemblance between the sound we write as "cow" and the class of animals we label with that sound; the sound could equally well refer not to four-legged beasts with udders but to butterflies, houses,

or celestial bodies. Language is coded *noniconically:* the sign is not modeled on the thing it stands for. To use Holloway's (1969:395) phrase, language entails "the imposition of arbitrary form upon the environment." (As we will see, nonlinguistic communication, in animals and to a substantial degree in man, is mainly coded *iconically:* the snarl is modeled on actual attack, the beckoning hand follows the desired path of direction, and so on.)

The differences between language and the codes of animal communications go beyond this ability to symbolize, to communicate about things with arbitrary, noniconic signs. Only language rests squarely on social learning. Only language has a "duality of patterning" so that smaller building blocks (sounds) are combined into meaningful larger blocks (words) that can in turn be constructed into sentences. Humans thus use *sequences of signs* in a way no animals do in the wild. The duality of language patterning makes possible another crucial and distinguishing feature of human communication: its *productivity.* From a set of elements, speakers *create* messages, messages that may be new and unique, yet are implied in the code.

For each of these "design features" (Hockett 1960) distinctive of human language, we can find fuzzy borderline cases or partial instances in the animal world. Moreover, as with every major evolutionary advance, the gap between nonlanguage and language must have been spanned by a gradation of transitional forms. Yet, despite these continuities, language as a total system is quite unlike the communication system of other animals and represents a major new evolutionary plateau.

Why do chimpanzees not have language? We used to assume that their brains were incapable of manipulating symbols, as humans can do with their highly evolved and expanded brain cortex. Chimpanzees clearly could make vocal noises handily enough; the

Chimpanzee potentialities: What further surprises will these close relatives provide? The infant chimpanzee Nim being reared in a human family. (Courtesy of Herbert Terrace.)

ties of a chimpanzee named Sarah. Premack and his associates gradually taught Sarah to use different shapes and colors of plastic to represent objects ("apple"), acts ("give"), and names of researchers. Placing these plastic signs—which had become symbols for Sarah—in nonarbitrary order ("Mary give apple") on a magnetic language board, the chimpanzee learned to build "sentences" and answer questions involving abstract ideas (color, shape, size). Further experimentation with chimpanzees is probing their ability to learn and expand upon man-made codes, and possibly even to teach these codes to other chimpanzees. Such experiments that push to surprising limits the symbol-manipulating powers of chimpanzees are of course a far cry from human language. A human creates and teaches; the chimpanzee learns and expands. Symbolic codes are human, not animal, creations. We should not, as Washburn

deficiency, we assumed, was in their brain-power.

Anthropologists and psychologists have been startled by the success of several researchers in the last several years in teaching chimpanzees to manipulate symbols. The Gardners, a husband and wife team at Nevada, taught the chimp Washoe to use deaf-mute sign language; and with a nonvocal symbol system Washoe was able not only to use labels for things but to build gestural "sentences" ("drink sweet please hurry"; "out open please hurry"). Washoe's accomplishments were achieved partly because of an insightful strategy: while she was being reared, the humans with her used only sign language, never speech (Gardner and Gardner 1969, 1971).

Psychologist David Premack took a different tack in developing the symbolic capabili-

The chimpanzee Lana using an electronic device to manipulate symbols syntactically. (Courtesy of the Yerkes Regional Primate Research Center, Emory University.)

(1973) points out, be so surprised that chimpanzees can manipulate *concepts* so as to communicate with humans (when humans teach them an adequate physical representation): they presumably are thinking and acting in terms of such a conceptual scheme, using brain equipment they largely share with us. The error that had misled anthropologists was assuming that manipulating concepts in logical sequences, and using language, are essentially similar or imply one another. The special system that is *language* is something quite different and specialized, a system that evolved in hominids not only long after our ancestral line had split from that of chimpanzees but perhaps long after the hominid brain had undergone a major expansion. "The uniqueness of the human brain, and of the sound code communication system which it makes possible, evolved millions of years after the separation of the lineages leading to apes and man" (Washburn 1973:18).

What are the special characteristics of the human brain structure? One element in the shift to man was an increase in absolute brain size, as we noted in §3. But size alone does not account for a change; some dwarfs have brains the weight of a chimp's and only one third the weight of a normal adult human's brain yet fully possess human linguistic competence.

Human language depends on some specialized developments in the cerebral cortex. One is *lateralization,* or the existence of two complementary cerebral hemispheres. One side, normally the left, is the specialized center of linguistic competence and of many of the operations of logic and analytical thought; the other side, normally the right hemisphere, appears to be central in some modes of relational, intuitive, mystical, Gestalt—the right words are hard to find—thought and perception. The implications of laterality and of contrasting conceptual and perceptual modes are

being explored by neurophysiologists such as Sperry (1974) (see also Dimond 1972; Dimond and Beaumont 1974; Gazzaniga 1970).

In the left cerebral hemisphere are three small areas of the brain critically important for normal linguistic performance. Though the details need not concern us, injury to any of these three areas produces some form of speech impairment. One of these areas has been important in debate about the evolution of language: it is a kind of switching center where "cross-modal transfers" are achieved. A message from the visual system is correlated with a message from the auditory or tactile system: we can see a cup and feel its shape, see a ball bounce and hear the noise it makes (recall the slight cognitive jarring that results

Seeing and using symbols: Koko, a young gorilla studied by Penny Patterson, makes her hand sign for "toothbrush" to herself when she turns to a picture of one in a magazine advertisement. Some anthropologists have argued that being able to "see" photographs depends on cultural learning. Primate behavior studies have cast much anthropological theorizing in doubt. (Photograph by R. P. Cohn, courtesy of P. Patterson.)

when, due to distance, we see visual evidence of percussion well before the sound reaches us, such as the puff of a starter's gun at a track meet).

Geschwind (1967, 1970) and others have argued that nonhuman primates do not have the needed brain circuits to achieve cross-modal transfer, which would be required for naming and symbol manipulation to take place. But recent evidence, including laboratory studies, field observation, and the symbolic achievements of Washoe and Sarah, suggest that among the great apes these capacities are at least partly developed. A suggestive clue is the way a chimpanzee can use a grass stalk to get termites from a nest, while his baboon neighbor watches over his shoulder but cannot learn to fish for termites himself.

Chimpanzees apparently have evolved substantial powers of concept manipulation, partly due to an increasing transfer of operations from the evolutionarily ancient limbic system of the brain (which controls most communications in nonhuman primates and other mammals, as well as the basic drives of sex, hunger, thirst, and reproduction) to the expanded cerebral cortex. In man the cerebral cortex is further greatly expanded, specialized into complementary hemispheres with new neural mechanisms and circuitry into a system for learning, using language, and building a world of symbols that is distinctively human.

A final clue we need in order to speculate intelligently about the evolution of language has already been noted in passing. Lieberman, Crelin, and their associates have studied the evolution of the vocal chamber, especially the pharynx. Tracing the development of these instruments for vocalization, they reconstructed the equipment of *H. erectus* and Neanderthals, and compared it with that of monkeys, chimpanzees, and modern humans. Sophisticated computer computa-

tions were used to reconstruct the range of vocal sounds that could be produced and distinguished. These workers concluded (Lieberman, Crelin, and Klatt 1972; Lieberman and Crelin 1971) that the equipment to differentiate efficiently the vowel sounds central in human speech evolved very recently. *H. erectus,* like a newborn human baby, would have been able to differentiate and control only very limited patterns of sound. Even the Neanderthals, with brains equivalent in size to modern man's, had limited vocal apparatus that would have made the possible repertoire of sound quite limited and the production of speech slow and inefficient by our standards. However, these findings and interpretations have recently been questioned by several specialists. If further evidence sustains the original findings, the evolution of fully modern linguistic capabilities will have to be placed quite late in time—perhaps with modern *H. sapiens* in the last 50,000 years.

How then might language have evolved?

Recall the time scale and the path of hominid evolution as set out in § 5: the long period of australopithecine development; the transition to humanity *(H. habilis)*; *H. erectus* and his spread as big-game hunter and gatherer; the evolution of *H. sapiens;* the emergence of and Neanderthals about 100,000 years ago, and the ascendancy of modern *H. s. sapiens* about 40,000 years ago.

The emergence of *H. erectus* was clearly associated with the accelerated use of tools; and *H. erectus* populations, with their large-scale hunts and home bases, must have had some means of communicating that enabled them to plan and organize. That meant a major advance in communication beyond the australopithecine level must have begun to take place between two and one million years ago. The evolution of *H. sapiens,* particularly with the emergence of the Neanderthals, apparently reflected another advance in communication. Yet if Lieberman and Crelin are right, fully human speech did not develop until modern man replaced the Neanderthals. At the moment, this must remain an open question. It seems likely on other grounds that Neanderthals communicated linguistically rather well, though perhaps not with the acoustical virtuosity of modern humans.

One crucial point of current speculation and controversy, as we will see in Chapters 9 and 11, is the extent to which human capacities to learn language—and hence to some degree the basic grammatical structure of language—are genetically programmed. Some theorists believe that because of the dramatic ease and speed with which children learn languages, and because all languages have marked similarities in structure, our linguistic capacities must rest heavily on innate programming. Others would agree that linguistic capacities rest on innate mental abilities, but feel that these are not specifically *linguistic* patterns but more general ways of organizing concepts. "The evolutionary capacity for syntax may have its roots in much broader aspects of mammalian behavior than has been previously recognized" (Peters 1972). Other theorists, following Piaget, would reject the importance of genetic programming of linguistic capacities, believing instead that the human infant begins with a more or less blank slate. To the extent linguistic abilities reflect genetically programmed systems, we must account for, and estimate the time period of, that evolution. If genetic programming of linguistic capacities is not a major factor, we would have to account for the deep structural similarity of human languages by positing a fairly recent common historical origin—though this still would not account for the miraculous speed and ease with which young children learn language.

The unfolding pattern of linguistic competence in a young child suggested to Lancaster (1968) that early humans may have had a similarly simple grammar. By the age of about two, all children go through a stage during which they use only two grammatical classes of words—a so-called pivot class of commonly used all-purpose grammatical words for acts and relations and an open class of words for things. (The actual words that serve as pivot or open words for a particular child vary widely; a particular child's pivot words may include what for adults are nouns or adjectives). At this stage, the child manages with this simple grammar—plus gesture—to communicate remarkably well about his or her world to a sibling or to mother. Lancaster speculates that ontogeny may reflect phylogeny here—that is, that the earliest forms of hominid language (perhaps in *H. erectus*) may have been similarly simple in grammatical structure. If the "words" used were shared by a local population, a powerful though simple addition to hominid behavior would have been possible.

A few pivot words suggesting major activities such as hunting and a few others indicating relative nearness in space and time, in combination with a small vocabulary of object names, could have had enormous adaptive significance. (Lancaster 1968:456)

The recent evidence on what chimpanzees can do with symbol manipulation and a simple "syntax" of symbols, and on the limitations of the vocal equipment of nonhuman primates, hominids, and early humans, has suggested another possibility (not necessarily contradictory) to Gordon Hewes (1973): the earliest forms of language may not have been *vocal.* Early humans may have developed simple *gestures,* perhaps at first strictly iconic, to express names for things and for acts and relations. (Note that the *syntax* of gestures, their combination to make simple propositions, could have involved at first a simple grammar of the sort Lancaster suggests, though perhaps with three or more "grammatical" classes of gestures.) According to this theory, only much later, probably with the Neanderthals, did vocalizations become associated with and eventually replace the gestural symbols. The efficiency of this new system could then have accounted for the rapid evolutionary and cultural burst of modern humans on the scene. This theory would account for the gradual evolution and partial genetic programming of increasingly complex "syntactic" patterns of thought. In a rapid late evolutionary burst, the capacities for vocalizing signals and the special structural features of language would have evolved in the last 50,000 years.

This theory has attracted a good deal of support. Some scholars object that gestural communication is primarily organized in the evolutionarily ancient limbic system, while Hewes' theory requires that that system be transformed so that gestures are assigned arbitrary meanings in the newly burgeoning brain cortex. However, the same transformation must in any case be postulated for the development of vocal language. The vocalizations of nonhuman primates and many human vocalizations are controlled by the limbic system. In monkeys electrical stimulation through implanted electrodes can be used to trigger cries of fear or rage (see Ploog 1970). Whether vocalization was the original medium of language or a late transformation of it, there clearly has been a shift from limbic to cortical control.

In contrast to the limbic-emotional system of monkeys, the human language system is dependent on the cortex of the dominant hemisphere. The reason that chimpanzees cannot learn to speak is that they do not have the necessary neurological base to learn. The reason that humans can learn to talk so easily is that an extensive biological base has evolved which makes this learning so easy that it is almost inevitable. (Washburn 1973:129)

We probably will never know the details of how language evolved, but exploration from several directions has grealy reduced the dimensions of our ignorance. Perhaps the most important implication, especially for our understanding of human social life, is that the processes of thinking, of using concepts, are separate from the labelings of language and much older. "Symbolic behavior in general has nothing to do with language, but is a normal function of the mammalian brain" (Washburn 1973:130). Thinking and speaking, ideas and words, can no longer be seen as two sides of the same coin. Verbal language as we know it is an evolutionary new, though vastly intricate and powerful, system for expressing conceptual relationships. It has enabled humans to create more subtle and complex conceptual systems—as witness logic and mathematics; but it builds on evolutionarily older patterns of conceptual thought.

11.
Culture and Biology: An Interactionist View

The sketch just given of nonhuman primate behavior and the evolution of man reflects my conviction, based on recent research, that man's primate heritage has shaped human nature to a far greater degree than an earlier generation of anthropologists believed. To sum up why and how, and what this means for our understanding of human societies, it is worth posing two old questions anthropologists thought they had answered long ago.

First, how is human culture unique, and how sharply does it distinguish us from other animals? And second, how important are cultural factors, relative to biological ones, in shaping human behavior?

Does human culture—our accumulated symbolic heritage based on social learning—make us unique in the animal kingdom? We used to be sure that only humans had culture and that culture was what made us human. Now things are not that simple.

There is a conceptual problem that needs to be dealt with at the outset. In the process of biological evolution there can be, in a sense, no sharp and sudden break, no emergence in a single organism or a single generation of a radically new mode of organization. Evolutionary change is gradual and continuous. It reflects changes in statistical frequencies within populations rather than sudden new patterns. Though individual mutations have an immediate and all-or-none character, the wider patterns of change they may contribute to are complex and gradual.

In that sense, the idea of an ape without culture giving birth to a human with culture, or of the transition taking place in one or a few generations, is biologically untenable. There must have been "protohumans" with "protoculture" even if the end result of that evolutionary sequence was a radically new mode of organization. An argument that distant ancestors of whales and porpoises could not swim very well is irrelevant to the question of whether present marine mammals represent a radical evolutionary change.

The question must be whether, through infinitesimal cumulative changes, hominids evolved the capacity for a radically different mode of organization represented in *H. sapiens,* and whether that new mode can usefully be characterized by the term "culture." So laid out, it is plain that the question could be argued forever without being resolved. The position we take depends on how we define "radically different" and "culture."

If we look carefully at the evidence, how we answer the question hardly matters. Humans *do* have a new mode of organization, but it is no longer easy to state briefly where that newness lies. Chimpanzees have used their tools to knock down the material props of our distinctiveness and their learning to undermine ours. Humans' new modes of organizing and manipulating experience build on and through language. They are made

possible by a vast increase in brainpower, making possible what Holloway (1969) calls "the imposition of arbitrary form upon the environment": humans create, through symbols, a thought world of their own. Yet this new mode of integration builds on evolutionary old elements, and there is no reason to assume smugly that man represents its ultimate possible expression.

The path to that integration was gradual, leading through "protoculture" and "protolanguage." Chimpanzees are turning out to be farther along that path than we had long thought, but the path has led—as did life on land, or in the air, at earlier evolutionary stages—to whole new modes of existence. If the continuities along this path rule out overly simple generalizations about "culture," *H. sapiens* still appear as a new and radically transformed primate. Insisting on principle that humans were qualitatively different has been poor science and has deprived us of the insights of evolutionary biology. *H. sapiens* as transformed ape is more comprehensible and no less wondrous than he was as disembodied creature of culture.

How important are biological factors in shaping human social behavior? How plastic is the human infant to the shaping of cultural experience? And how widely diverse have human cultures been in different times and places?

Our attention to primate social behavior reflects a conviction that biology shapes human behavior to a greater degree than most anthropologists 20 years ago were prepared to accept. Striking advances in biochemistry, genetics, and neurophysiology have begun to reveal the incredible complexities of the biological mechanisms of heredity, learning, and thinking. The human infant is by no means as plastic, as subject to radically variable cultural shaping, as many scholars had believed. What is learned and learnable, even language itself, is probably guided by genetic templates to a greater extent than most cultural anthropologists had thought possible.

A recurrent theme in this book is that the seemingly endless diversity in cultures has been overemphasized. Variations in cultures *as systems of socially shared and transmitted knowledge* (see §23) may be more shallow than deep, more a diversity of content than variation in form and structure. To the degree this turns out to be the case, the universals of form and structure presumably largely reflect constraints of biology.

Does this mean that human behavior is essentially similar in all times and places? That a biologically laid down "human nature" shows through clearly beneath the overlay of culture? Not at all. It means that the tremendous diversity anthropologists have been cataloguing for a century has to be put in a wider evolutionary framework. Viewed in that framework, cultures *are* extraordinarily variable, and human infants *are* amazingly plastic.

Through cultural learning an infant can become a Yąnomamö tribesman, Zulu warrior, Hopi Indian farmer, Mexican peasant, or Manhattan apartment dweller. Biological "givens" such as the drives of hunger, thirst, and sex are endlessly refashioned and rearranged by cultural conventions. Hunger will serve to illustrate. It can be "normal" in different societies to eat one meal a day, or two, or three, or more—and that determines when a person gets hungry. It also determines what he gets hungry for. Rotten grubs at 4 in the afternoon are no more and no less "natural" than ham and eggs in the morning. Even in the transformation of a genetic design laid down at the moment of conception into a living human being, through growth and maturation, cultural and environmental influences loom large. Thus children of Japanese

immigrants to the United State are significantly taller than their parents, and the "overbite" in the mouths of most of us is apparently an adaptation in the maturation process of eating soft foods. Eskimos who chew corn flakes and not blubber develop a similar overbite. Culture fashions, from our genetically laid down potential, what we become. Only by knowing the vast range of ways cultures can fill in the openings left by nature can we see in perspective the possibility that the shape of the openings may be less flexible than we had thought.

Moreover, to argue that culture is more important than biology, or to argue the reverse in some form, misses the central point. What permits human adaptation is the *system* of *biology-plus-culture*. Our biological programming has evolved to enable us to survive, and for human society to be possible. In evolutionary terms, the special genius of *H. sapiens* that has given them ascendancy over the planet was leaving the cultural half of the combination biology-plus-culture open and undefined. It could develop and change to fit environmental pressure and the opportunities that opened up for new ways of life and new niches. To argue over which components of the system are most important is to misunderstand what systems are and what humans are.

We cannot begin to understand how different are human ways of life, what human nature is, or what human life could be without looking carefully at the range of human experience in jungle hamlet, desert camp, and peasant village as well as in modern city. Anthropology offers no easy answers about human nature and human possibility. But with a uniquely broad perspective on the varieties of cultural experience, and with foundations in both the biological and social sciences, it equips us to ask such questions wisely and well.

THE BIOLOGY OF HUMAN DIFFERENCES

4

Neither scientists nor lay persons have ever been able to view the nature of human differences as a biological question. The matter has always been taken as a social or political or moral question, and biological perspectives have been distorted or ignored.

This is true not only of racists, who have used, misused, and ignored biology to advance political ends and justify privilege and oppression. It is also true of liberals and humanists, anthropologists and others, who in their zeal to combat racism and sexism have often been very bad biologists.

This chapter outlines some biological perspectives on human differences, between individuals, between populations ("races"), and between men and women. At the end, some social and moral implications can be drawn on racism and other forms of oppression based on human differences. We will return to these issues in Part 4.

12.
Processes of Microevolution: Populations, Races, and Variability

To view differences within and between human populations from a biological perspective is difficult. It helps to review the mechanisms and processes of microevolution, and the technical concepts needed to understand variability within species, without talking about humans at all. Our sketch of the evolutionary processes whereby a species becomes internally differentiated will, for the sake of the necessary objectivity, deal not with humans but with birds.

Populations

A species does not consist of "types" but rather of *populations*. Let us take as the simplest case a species of mountain birds inhabiting a Pacific island. For many thousands of years the population has been cut off from the related birds of the same genus on surrounding islands. The birds of our island comprise a breeding population, isolated geographically and genetically from their cousins on the next island. The genes statistically represented in our bird population comprise a gene pool. Within this gene pool are marked ranges of individual variability—in size, color, and also in the genetically programmed details of mating or nest-building behavior. Sexual reproduction is a mechanism for reshuffling genetic possibility, creating new combinations of this genetic variability. If a population is to survive over long time spans as part of a complex ecosystem, which includes predators and food supplies, this variability and the process of reshuffling and recombination are vital. Male and female of the same species often differ in bodily form and often coloration, a phenomenon known as *sexual dimorphism.* Often birds within the same population exhibit two or more alternative shapes, colors, or designs of the same bodily system, just as Englishmen differ in eye color, hair form, or blood types—a phenomenon known as *polymorphism.* Where biologists find such a polymorphism, they infer that it is maintained in statistical balance by natural selection: the alternative genes, in statistical combination, confer some adaptive advantages that would be lost if one or the other set of alternative genes disappeared.

How does change take place? How did the species on the different islands become different? First, there is the possibility that originally the birds that established the population on one island represented, by chance sampling, a rather different batch of genetic potential than the birds that established the population on another island—even though these original "founding" birds were of the same species and represented a chance dipping out from the same gene pool. Particu-

larly in the early stages in the population of a new island, when numbers were small, the chance patterns of genetic combination in mating would have led to a statistical increase in some genes and a decrease in others—a process called *genetic drift.* Genetic drift is statistical change in the gene pool over time due to random chance in reproduction.

A gene pool is also continually affected by mutations, or chance errors in the genetic process due to copying "mistakes" in genetic coding. Most mutant genes are maladaptive, often lethal, because they introduce a design error incompatible with the workings of the organism. If a mutant gene fits into the overall design to produce an organism that still "works" (and that is not very likely), the chances are still slight that the new form will work better than the existing forms.

An ecosystem poses a range of survival challenges. These challenges place pressures that act statistically on the gene pool: individual organisms that represent efficient combinations of the genetic possibility in the gene pool, in terms of these challenges, have a slightly greater probability of reproducing. Thus the genes they carry are favored in the genetic game of natural selection. R. L. Gregory (1970:76) vividly builds on this analogy of evolution as a statistical game—in this case chess:

Evolution, we may say, is a continual sacrifice of individuals to gain information from each loss. . . . Individual games are lost. From the point of view of Natural Selection, individual lives appear quite trivial. All that matters is the circumstances of their ending and how far this adds to the pool of genetic information.

The rare mutant gene that contributes to a modified design that works—and works *better*—can become established and can spread. The combination of natural selection and drift leads to changes in the gene pool that eventually (when the population is isolated, as on our island) lead to speciation. What had been the same species through time becomes different subspecies, then eventually different species. As different species, the birds from the two islands would be reproductively isolated so that they could not interbreed, or could not if they mated produce viable offspring. Moreover, due to evolutionary changes in behavior patterns, they might through time come to adapt ecologically in somewhat different ways: to feed on different insects, or in different ways, or to inhabit different types of forests. They would fit into somewhat different ecological niches.

The operation of selection in the diversification and evolution of birds calls for a closer look. Note that though coloration may confer protection through camouflage, birds are often brightly colored. That it is so often the male that is brightly colored suggests that this is often due to sexual selection in the evolution of mating displays. Display behavior and other elements of being conspicuous (or noisy) may contribute to the spatial dispersion of population (Wynne-Edwards 1962). So too do patterns of courtship, nest-building, and other facets of mating and territoriality.

The case of our hypothetical bird population living on different islands is relatively simple. More often, animal forms live on major continents where geographical boundaries between regions are not so sharp and dramatic. Yet different species of sparrows or squirrels or trout may have developed in different regions of the same continent.

The critical factor here is that the breeding populations, hence the gene pools, must have been separated in some way during the period of speciation. Haffer (1969) has studied the speciation of Amazonian birds, where numerous species and subspecies of the same genus occur in different regions of this vast rain forest. How did speciation take place? Haffer hypothesizes that during the climatic fluctuations of the Pleistocene, marked

changes in humidity took place that periodically transformed the rain forest. In dry periods, the forest shrank into areas separated from one another by savannas. In these forest refuges previously united populations were divided, and over long periods, they diverged evolutionarily into subspecies or separate species through natural selection. When more humid climatic periods again joined the rain forest, the result depended on the degree and nature of speciation. Where speciation was complete, the populations could not interbreed. But since through the evolution of different behavior patterns the populations had come to exploit somewhat different ecological niches, *sympatry* was possible along the contact zones; that is, the two populations could occupy overlapping zones because they were not in direct competition. In other populations, speciation had gone far but not all the way: interbreeding was impossible, hence the species were taxonomically separate. But because they were competing for the same ecological niche, there was no geographical overlap, what is called *competitive exclusion*. In other cases, subspeciation resulted in some genetic incompatibility between populations, but some hybridization occurred in the contact zones. Where speciation had not gone this far, hybridization may have led to more or less complete merging of the gene pools so that the populations fused.

When populations within the species are partly isolated by geographical barriers, so that mating across the mountain range or across the plain occurs with much lower frequency than mating on each side of the "barrier," rather different phenomena occur. Mating between the local populations relatively isolated by geography results in *gene flow* between the local gene pools. Speciation does not occur, but the statistical frequencies of genes in the partly separated gene pools diverge. Thus local populations may come to have somewhat different coloring, somewhat different bird songs, and other genetically shaped variations, that is, they become *polytypic*. Where barriers between populations are less clearcut, but some geographical variations in gene frequencies have become established, the populations may grade relatively continuously into one another. For example, at one end of an area, genetic pattern A_1 may occur with 75 percent frequency and pattern A_2 with 25 percent frequency. At the other end of the area, A_2 may occur with 75 percent frequency and A_1 with 25 percent frequency. In the middle zone, the percentages gradually change, forming a statistical gradation known as a *genetic cline*. This situation characteristically results when the cluster of genes involved are adaptive to some environmental condition, for example, temperature or rainfall, that has a continuous range of variation.

Note that there can be a hierarchical structure of local populations: the birds of one valley may be somewhat different from the birds of the next valley (in the statistical frequency of genes and hence coloration or size). But the birds of the two valleys between which mating occurs along a contact zone, may represent together a single population in comparison to the birds of the same species that occupy a different complex of valleys several hundred miles away. Because genetic isolation of these areas has never been complete, or because it is too recent for speciation to have gone very far, the birds of these two valley systems all comprise a single subspecies. These regional populations in turn constitute a single unit in comparison to another subspecies on the other side of the continent that is similarly made up of relatively separate regional and local populations.

"Race"

The term "race," if it means anything at all in population biology, refers to geographically distinct populations. But the geographi-

cal levels of population, in this model of subspecies, fall into a hierarchical series. The local breeding population constitutes one level (that is, the distinctive birds of a relatively isolated valley). Those of a local region (for example, a complex of adjacent valleys partly separated by mountains) constitute a higher geographical level of population, and those of a major zone or continent constitute yet another level. Which one is a "race"? The term unfortunately has been used ambiguously. One can adopt the convention that the breeding population is a "local race," while higher levels are "geographical races" of larger or smaller scale. But the ambiguity remains and has led many or most population geneticists to abandon the term in favor of more precise alternatives.

Variability

When we refer to individual organisms, the coded information transmitted by heredity is the organism's *genotype*. The physical form that results from the interaction of the genetic information with environmental influences in the maturation process is the *phenotype*. Note that it is easier to observe size, shape, and color of living organisms—to count and measure phenotypes—than it is to analyze the genetic patterns that underlie them. Yet since the science of population genetics, and its mathematical models, deal with *genes,* the investigator wants if possible to study the genetics of variation, not simply count heads and measure tails.

A local breeding population does not contribute a "type." Rather, it constitutes a reservoir of genetic diversity. In such phenotypic characteristics as skin color, hair form, or stature, individuals vary along a continuous range. At the genetic level the genes for eye color, blood groups, and many other characteristics represent two or more alternative genes at the same locus. The statistical frequency of such alternative patterns in a population is almost always held in balance by some complex of selective forces.

The emphasis on natural selection is important. As we will shortly see, it has been argued that in many species, including *Homo sapiens,* the selective pressures that shape statistical frequencies of alternative genes are not neatly grouped in geographical areas. Therefore the subspecies model, emphasizing local isolation and regional differentiation rather than continuous gradients of selective forces (and hence of statistical frequencies of the genetic complexes they hold in balance), may not be appropriate.

Armed with this model of how birds evolve into diverse forms, and the doubts that go with it, let us turn now to human microevolution.

13.
Human Differences: Populations and "Races"

Physical anthropologists differ from the outset in applying the models of population genetics to the recent evolution of man. A crucial first question is how old might be the genetic diversification of modern human populations. Carleton Coon (1962), in a much-criticized study of race, argued for great time depth. In his view the line between *Homo erectus* and *Homo sapiens* was crossed independently at several different times and places, and these different crossings led by different paths to the major races of modern man. Coon added some racist touches—he saw the Caucasoids as being the first across and helping their less fortunate distant cousins along—and a storm of controversy was stirred. Subsequent theorists have mainly assumed that modern races reflect differentiation since the evolutionary emergence of modern man, that is, within the last 35,000 to 40,000 years. Recently Sarich (1971) has pulled together the arguments for

the diversification of modern races being much older: he believes the time depth is not otherwise adequate to account for the degree of racial differentiation. (It is ironic that it is Sarich who feels that a span of four to five million years is enough time for humans and chimpanzees to have evolved from a common ancestor.)

Neanderthals were essentially fully modern except for certain features of cranial and jaw architecture. As Loring Brace argues, this complex of features seems to represent an adaptation to the conditions of Neanderthal existence—perhaps to using teeth and jaws as tools. If so, when these conditions of life changed as new technology developed and spread around the world, the selective pressures maintaining this Neanderthal complex of features would have been relaxed; and this could have transformed populations in many parts of the world in a similar direction. If this view is correct, then modern human populations may have evolved from Neanderthal populations in different regions.

We know that by 40,000 years ago fully modern populations were in Australia and Borneo; no datings in Africa or Eurasia are that early, though they will probably turn up.

Experts who believe that the "subspecies" or regional microevolutionary model applies to humans as well as birds would see the breeding populations of early humans as small, but as overlapping across broad geographical regions or even continents. Thus forested sub-Saharan Africa, Australia, the Mediterranean region, the tundra of Northeast Asia, tropical Southeast Asia, and other areas relatively isolated ecologically and geographically by oceans, deserts, mountains, or climatic break lines would have provided settings across which interbreeding local bands were linked like chain mail.

The relative role of adaptation and genetic drift due to isolation has been much debated. Twenty-five years ago, the operation of drift on small, geographically separated early human populations was assumed by many scholars to be the primary force of differentiation. Now the emphasis is much more strongly on local evolution due to adaptation and natural selection. Though natural selection may not be the only process involved, since sexual and other cultural selective pressures undoubtedly operate as well, experts are increasingly wary of assuming that any polymorphisms in human populations—for example, eye color, blood type, or straight or curly hair—are selectively neutral.

The applicability of the "subspecies" models of population differentiation (the one we illustrated for birds) to early human populations has recently been seriously questioned by a number of scholars (see Alland 1973). First, as we will see, the growing realization that selective pressures rather than sheer reproductive isolation shape frequencies within a gene pool makes the application of the hierarchical geographical model suspect within population genetics, unless it can be shown that the distribution of selective pressures is similarly discontinuous and regionally clustered. (The applicability of the geographical subspecies model to such diverse organisms as frogs, butterflies, zebras, stone martens, and wolves has recently been challenged.)

Second, while the boundaries between local breeding populations are determined, for birds or zebras, by the ability to mate and reproduce (hence depend on geographical propinquity, genetic compatibility, and behavioral compatibility), the boundaries between human populations are and have probably always been substantially defined in cultural terms. A group may consider the group across the valley who speak a strange language and wear their hair in a peculiar style to be suitable enemies, but not possible marriage partners.

Third, culturally transmitted patterns can rapidly change the behavior of human popu-

lations and so change the operation of selective pressures on them. Thus selective pressure for powerful plierlike jaws can relax quickly when new and better tools are developed, and pressures of climate can relax quickly with control of fire or wearing of clothing. Moreover, such technological innovations can and apparently did spread quickly and more or less independently of the exchange of genes between contiguous populations.

The most serious doubts concerning the applicability of the geographical subspeciation model have to do with the way selective pressures operate on populations. Do these pressures cluster geographically so that a complex of pressures shapes a complex of interrelated adaptive responses within a geographical area? Perhaps, in some cases and for some characteristics. But such scholars as Brace (1964), Livingstone (1964), and Hiernaux (1964) have challenged whether this is the general case—and hence whether the model of geographical subspeciation, applied to humans, is useful. The thrust of this argument has been usefully summarized by Alland (1973).

These scholars argue that the more usual case if one analyzes the statistical frequencies of genetic characteristics or such phenotypic patterns as skin color, hair form, tooth size, or facial morphology is a continuous, *clinal* distribution, not a local clustering of selective forces. If we look at the distribution of skin color among human populations (as they apparently were before recent migrations muddled the picture), we find a distribution that corresponds fairly directly with distance from the equator and hence exposure to solar radiation. If we examine hair form, we find thickly curled hair to be a probable protection against solar heat rather than against harmful solar rays—hence it correlates partly, but not directly, with skin color. For more simple genetic complexes we can study gene frequencies, not simply their phenotypic outcomes, and similar continuous clines of shifting frequency are characteristic. Thus, for example, the gene controlling the abnormal hemoglobin of sickle-cell anemia, a major problem among black Americans, is held in a dynamic balance in West Africa because in its *heterozygous* form—that is, where one parent contributes the sickling gene and the other parent a normal gene—the child develops some resistance to fulciparum malaria. But an individual who is homozygous for the sickle cell trait—who receives a double dose of the sickle gene, one from each parent—will suffer from a usually fatal anemia. Hence the frequency of the sickle gene in West African populations apparently varies clinally according to distributions of malaria and the severity of local malaria strains (Livingstone 1958). Blood group frequencies are affected by disease, and probably also by so-far unknown biochemical factors, perhaps associated with diet.

The point is that if each of the myriad genetic complexes that occur with different frequencies in local and regional populations has its own distinctive distribution pattern, corresponding to the distribution of particular selective pressures; and if many or most of these selective pressures shift clinally without sharp break lines or discrete regional clustering, then we create more confusion than clarity by using the geographical subspeciation model to classify human populations.

Thus, Brace (1964), Livingstone (1964), Alland (1973), and others would argue that to describe the major "racial stocks" of human beings on the basis of a supposedly interconnected complex of physical traits is not only socially insidious. It also obscures our understanding of the complex processes of adaptation that have affected gene frequencies in particular populations by defining "types" for which there is no explanation other than supposed past geographical separation.

If we come back to geography and call someone a "Negro" whose ancestors came from sub-Saharan Africa, we find ourselves with a highly diverse collection of people that do not fall into neat local populations. Rather, external trim—hair form or skin color—and blood chemistry have their own highly complex patterns and clines of microvariation. At no level from local populations to larger regions or continents does one find the clusters of associated "traits" that would make classification into geographical races useful or meaningful (Hiernaux 1968).

All we find is some evidence of what we know on other grounds: that American Indians *did* come from Asia (though in how many waves of migration we do not know), that large populations of sub-Saharan Africa evolved in broadly similar environments (and that many of them spread from a narrower region), and so on. We know that with the vast increase in world populations in the last 10,000 and especially 5000 years, some regions have been centers of population explosion and spread. In some cases, such regional populations had gone through intensive selective pressures, so that features of their external trim that represent regional evolutionary adaptations have spread far beyond the regions where they initially occurred. The flaring malars, or cheekbones, and epicanthic eyefolds that occur with high frequency in modern Chinese, Japanese, and Mongol populations may well have evolved in one or more regions of Northeast Asia in adaptation to intense cold. And with the explosion of populations following the subsequent domestication of animals and development of agriculture, these features may have spread widely in East Asia.

Those who would reject racial typologies of modern populations argue that these classifications do nothing to clarify the highly complicated questions of how such human variations evolved and what sorts of continuing evolutionary pressures affect their course. Did such regional evolutionary pressures affect the exterior trim of populations that were relatively isolated, in breeding terms, from one another? Or did the illusion of isolation result from the operation of some complexes of selective pressures, for example, of climate, disease, or diet, within discrete geographical regions? Are the distributions of a particular phenotypic pattern, and the genes that control it, marked by a gradual cline (for example, adaptations to solar radiation) or a sharp break line (for example, because a subsistence food or an insect that is a disease vector survives only within certain altitude ranges)?

The simplistic typologies that most classifications of race impose do nothing to answer these crucial questions. By assuming that isolation of regional populations occurred for long periods of the remote past (an assumption probably true only in a few special cases, such as with Australian Aborigines and Khoisan or Hottentot peoples of South Africa), and by searching for broad typological common denominators rather than examining the dynamics of adaptation and diversity, racial typologies have probably impeded our understanding of the human past and of human differences.

With the realization that microevolution through natural selection is so important, and that it is still going on, physical anthropologists have increasingly narrowed their focus to microevolution in smaller areas. Great schemes for classifying races and tracing their connections in the distant past have receded. Local studies of microvariation have been aided by computer techniques for estimating biological distances between populations. A typical modern strategy would be to pull together a wide range of interdisciplinary evidence about the differences—physical, genetic, linguistic, and cultural—between local populations in order to trace their probable connectedness in the fairly recent past

(see, for example, Howells 1966). Interdisciplinary studies, for example, by Neel and his colleagues of the population genetics of the Yąnomamö (our slime-dripping, wife-beating friends in Chapter 1) and their neighbors have further brought to light the interplay between biological and cultural factors in the diversification of local populations. Modern physical anthropologists increasingly are concerned with the effects of cultural practices having to do with mating, settlement patterns, child care, diet, fighting, and disease on microevolution. These and other cultural factors crucially affect gene flow, the size of the breeding population, and hence the degree of local diversity in population.

What, then, of all the talk about "race"? Biologically, it is highly dubious whether the term serves to divide human populations—at whatever geographical level (for example, from "Congo pygmies" to "Negroes")—in a way that illuminates genetics, adaptation, or past evolutionary processes and historical population movements. Alland (1973) gives a detailed summary and interpretation of the evidence for this. The term "race," applied to human populations, is essentially sociological, cultural, and political, not biological. Unless a convincing body of evidence is produced to show that the differentiation of early populations of modern humans took place through geographical isolation or through regional complexes of selective pressures, and such evidence does not seem to be forthcoming, then racial classifications will continue to be dangerous scientific rationalizations for old stereotypes.

There is in *any* human population a great range of diversity in biochemistry, physiological factors (such as metabolic rates, brain wave rhythms), cognitive capacities, emotional dispositions, and the like, as well as in size, appearance, strength, body build, and other gross physical features. Every human population contains a reservoir of diverse genetic potentiality and includes individuals differing in abilities ranging from musical talent to speed afoot to abstract reasoning ability and a vast number of other capacities. These abilities in turn represent the interaction of highly complicated genetic systems with environmental factors, including nutrition, cultural patterning of physical activity, and learning. This diversity within each population is maintained by sexual reproduction—that genetic trick of reshuffling that permits the survival and adaptation of populations. The genetics underlying abstract reasoning abilities, verbal facility, memory, kinesthetic imagery, and other aspects of "intelligence" are complicated and little understood. Thus to sort out individuals within a population on any one-dimensional scale of intelligence or other abilities (even if it is done by having them perform a task appropriate to the culture they share) vastly and dangerously oversimplifies the diverse genetic and environmental components that are being "measured." To rank individuals according to their performance on tasks not part of their normal cultural repertoire adds dangerous new muddles.

If *individuals within populations* represent a range of diversity in cognitive capacities and the physical bases of "personality," might different *populations* differ in the statistical distribution of their capacities and predispositions? Here politics has inevitably intruded on science. It is poor biology to insist categorically—as many physical anthropologists have—that all human populations represent the same range of variation in these "mental" respects though they demonstrably differ in physical characteristics. There is no reason to *assume* that the distributions are identical.

Nor can we assume categorically that differences in cultural patterns—for example, between the "aggressive" Yąnomamö of South America and the "gentle" Bushmen of South Africa—do not in part reflect statistical differences in the genetic templates of person-

ality. In fact, natural selection could have militated for gentleness in remnant populations of hunters and gatherers surrounded by more powerful food producers, where submission to neighboring peoples was a prerequisite for survival; the process could also have selected for aggressiveness where peoples were competing violently with neighbors for resources, territory, and mates. The difficulty in finding out is partly that we do not know well the genetic bases for such personality factors; partly that the personality factors are overlain by cultural differences (for the cultures involved are clearly adaptive to such exigencies of survival); and partly that fear of racist interpretations has impeded such research.

But here it must be insisted that if frequencies of the genes that shape the multiple facets of cognitive ability, temperament, or the like, differ among populations, this is almost certainly true only at the level of local breeding populations (hence narrowly local genetic isolates), not the broad continental "races" whose superiority or inferiority racists want to demonstrate.

Accepting the *possibility,* so far undemonstrated, that local breeding populations differ in the frequencies of the genetic complexes underlying personality and the many facets of "intelligence," let us examine one by one the flaws in the racist argument that different treatment of "Negroes" or other "races" educationally, socially, or legally is biologically justified.

First, as we have seen, the lumping of major "races" as "Negroid" or "Caucasoid" or whatever seems to be biologically meaningless. There is no reason to believe that the peoples of sub-Saharan Africa, for example, have constituted a geographical breeding isolate of the kind that could lead dark-skinned Nilotic populations of the Sudan, West African horticulturalists, or East African pastoralists to share significant genetic patterns underlying personality or cognition or have similar distributions of gene frequencies in these respects (see Hiernaux 1968).

Second, to lump the great diversity of human cognitive capacities, which includes many components, into the single variable "intelligence" is an insidious and gross error. If different local populations represented different statistical distributions of these components, we might expect to find, if we randomly selected 500 individuals from six different sample populations, that in one population there are a few more potential gifted mathematicians, in another a few more potential gifted musicians, in another a few more potential great orators, in another a few more potential poets. To suppose that in one population would be concentrated the highest frequency of individuals with different kinds of cognitive gifts is biologically foolish. But if the various component capacities are collapsed into a single measure of "intelligence," that illusion can be spuriously created. (It is equally spurious to assume that the realization of talents within a particular cultural tradition can be taken as an index of genetic potential; we do not know how many potential Einsteins or Mozarts have spent their lives herding cows or washing dishes.)

The illusion of measuring intelligence is fostered, of course, when the creators of the measuring device are those who presume their genetic superiority, for the "test" they create is in subtle or even blatant ways based on their own culture and alien to the experience of the populations being tested. As Geertz (n.d.) has shown, even the most basic assumptions about the world of common sense experience are patterned by cultures in different ways. To construct a "culture-free" measure of cognitive capacities is virtually impossible. Australian Aborigines or Nilotic cattle herders would doubtless construct tests of mental abilities that would confound American suburban children.

The highly diverse genotypes in any population, in the realm of both mental and physical capacities, represent *potentialities*. All humans are probably operating far below the possible limitations of their capacities to reason, to create, and to remember. Cultural experience fosters particular complexes of skills—in finding direction, in remembering by rote, in solving particular kinds of problems or recognizing particular kinds of patterns. It is possible that thousands of years of selective pressure have selected for extremely high visual acuity, pattern-recognizing facility and direction-finding capacity among hunting and gathering peoples (notably, Australian Aborigines) and perhaps for storage of information in memory in nonliterate societies. Relaxation of these selective pressures through the technology of food-producing and of writing may perhaps have led to reduced biological potentialities, in terms of frequencies within populations. But it is equally possible that these potentialities remain latent, in differential degree, within technologically advanced populations; perhaps we ourselves could develop them to equal, though individually different, degree if we were raised as infants in societies in which these skills were fostered culturally.

Other factors may affect the realization of genetic potentialities. Some are biological: marginal protein intake or other malnourishment undoubtedly affects brain development in maturation and hence precludes realization of full intellectual potential, just as it affects realization of physical potential; many populations surviving at the margins of protein deficiency show dramatic increases in stature and strength with improved diet. Other factors are sociological: opportunities to realize genetic potentials in the cognitive realm have been relatively closed to women, despite their equal intellectual endowments, in almost all societies; and in complex societies, such opportunities have characteristically been closed to ethnic minorities in varying degree and to nonelite social classes. (The rationalization of systems of class oppression on grounds that the lower classes are genetically inferior is very old. The Jensens and Shockleys of the world are the latest in a long lineage who would try to rationalize class privilege on biological grounds.)

Having demonstrated the "superior intelligence" of their own kind by oversimplification and sleight of hand, racist investigators have often pointed to the impressive achievements of "Caucasians" in the realms of "culture"—literature, art, philosophy—and technology as a demonstration of these genetic gifts in action. The "superior civilization" that is supposed to show that Northern Europeans are genetically superior is mainly a cumulation of elements borrowed from "inferior" peoples—Middle Eastern, Chinese, African, and others. Moreover, the "superiority" supposed to be manifest in genetic patterns thousands of years old has somehow appeared only in the last few centuries. If we had observed the "races" in 1000 B.C. or A.D. 800, the "superior" Northern Europeans would have seemed a sorry and backward lot in comparison to their "genetically underprivileged" contemporaries in other parts of the world. If this way of discovering the relative genetic gifts of human groups were valid—and it doubtless is not—a neutral "judge" would very probably infer that Chinese are much better endowed genetically than the Northern Europeans. How silly as well as dangerous are the racist conclusions that different human groups merit separate and unequal treatment, and how founded they are on oppression, not science, becomes apparent if one suggests that Chinese should receive better schooling than Caucasians so as to realize their superior gifts.

That then leads to the most flagrant, and fatal, error in the logic of racist argument, for the distributions of the diverse component elements of intelligence within any population

represent great ranges of individual variation. The range of variation *within* all human populations in the genetic distribution of these potentialities greatly exceeds any possible variation *between* populations; and the ranges of variation in different populations, if they differed, would largely overlap.

The challenge, which no society has met fully and well, is to create a way to foster the diverse gifts distributed randomly within every population so that each individual can achieve maximal realization of his or her potential. Individual self-realization and collective good must somehow be articulated and balanced. Any social system that sorts individuals into categories based on sex, skin color, social class, or cultural background so as to lock individual realization within socially or politically defined boxes and to open opportunities to some that are denied to others is insidious. And to misuse the biology of human diversity to justify such compartmentalization is a gross distortion of science.

14.
Male and Female in Biological Perspective

A lively area of research and political controversy in the last few years has been the differences between the sexes. Are sex differences, and male and female roles, largely the products of cultural experience or of biological design? Any simple answer would be wrong.

Many feminists who are committed to redefining sex roles in modern societies, and hence to the conviction that male and female are what a culture makes them, have gone back for support to Margaret Mead's classic *Sex and Temperament in Three Primitive Societies* (1935). Mead argued that sex roles are mainly a matter of cultural definition. Thus the tribal Mountain Arapesh of New Guinea, through child-rearing practices and patterns of cultural experience, assumed male and female roles that are in many ways the direct reverse of our own: women were aggressive, dominant; men were submissive, gentle, passive. Yet there is strong evidence that there was considerable observer bias in this and other studies of the period. Recent fine-grained studies of child-rearing, adolescence, and adult behavior using modern recording technology and informed by ethological perspectives have yielded sharply contrasting interpretations (see, for example, Freeman 1974; Blurton-Jones 1972; Mc Grew 1972). Later Mead offered a less extreme interpretation of sex differences, though her explanation of universals in female-male differences was psychoanalytic (1949).

If we look at humans in evolutionary perspective, it would indeed be surprising if the *sexual dimorphism*—or female-male morphological differences—so striking in nonhuman primates had so nearly disappeared in humans that females and males grew up to be what their cultures made them. In all human populations, *statistically* (and that word is crucial) males are larger, stronger, and faster running. The reasons why they should be so become obvious if we reflect about the last two or three million years of evolution, when human survival almost certainly depended on a sharp division of labor by sex. Females are probably equipped hormonally and in genetically laid down behavioral dispositions to nurture and care for infants as well as to bear them (Freedman 1968, 1974). The statistical ranges of behavioral predispostions of male and female infants seem to be rather different, though how different remains to be clarified by research (see, for example, Diamond 1965; Freedman 1968). Here, as with race, political pressures cloud research and interpretations of research. Freedman's assessment will probably turn out to be sound:

There can be little doubt that human dimorphism follows the general mammalian trend and that it shares similar functions. Thus when we find little boys less passive, more negativistic, more aggressive, more rivalrous, or more investigative than little girls, we probably have our mammalian-primate ancestry to thank and not some proposed libidinal stage nor some makeshift social force. . . . Of course . . . cultural institutions . . . support and differentially shape such biological trends. (Freedman 1968:268)

Extreme proponents of human ethology go much too far in arguing the radical biological contrast between the sexes and the immutability of sex roles. Thus the assumption that men must be dominant, that women are biologically incapable of political leadership and coalition (see, for example, Tiger 1969), has rightly received a broadside attack from feminist critics.

If male and female infants tend statistically to be programmed to respond rather differently to culturally patterned experiences, that does not mean that sex roles are immutable; nor does it mean that cultural transformations and reinforcements of biological differences are not centrally important and often socially insidious; sugar and spice, frilly dresses, and assumed incompetence conspire to turn girls into what they are supposed to be. And it in no way justifies sexist oppression or prevents liberation from it. The massive elaboration of the human brain cortex gives women and men equally a fantastic symbolic power to learn, to think, to change, to build new worlds. With birth control, modern medicine, genetics, and other developments humans have transformed and transcended a host of biological constraints.

Moreover, statistical differences in the behavioral predispositions of human females and males hide wide individual variations, and hence there is broad overlap between the sexes. It seems clear that in temperamental predisposition many female infants are "less passive, more negativistic, more aggressive, more rivalrous, or more investigative" than many male infants. In a nonsexist, nonracist society in which alternative paths of life are open to individuals on the basis of potential and interest rather than social stereotype, oppressive channeling of both female and male could be transcended.

Sex differences—what they have been and what they can be—illustrate the possibility of a balanced view of culture and biology. Such a view sees the human infant neither as raw stuff to be shaped by the impress of endlessly diverse cultural possibility nor as a genetically predetermined primate superficially clad in many-colored human raiment.

THE GROWTH OF CULTURE
Paleolithic Peoples

In the following three chapters, we will outline the evolution of cultural systems that transformed hunters and gatherers into cultivators and herders, and then some of them into peasants and city dwellers. The spread of new technologies and new modes of organization in the Old and New Worlds will be briefly traced, and we will assess the way these advances reshaped the primitive world.

We will examine briefly in these chapters the major interpretations and explanations of cultural development—of the food-producing and urban "revolutions" and other transformations. Later, in Chapter 12, drawing on these sketches of unfolding human history, we will consider more generally the mechanisms of cultural change and the major theories of cultural development. Finally, in Part IV, we will look at the traumatic effects on the Third World of the expansion of the West, and the emergence of a world society.

Here we will first briefly consider the strat-

egies and methods of archaeology, the detective work whereby the processes of cultural development are reconstructed from clues in the leavings of the past. We will then rejoin the unfolding development of culture where we left it in Chapter 2, viewing humans in Old and New Worlds as Paleolithic hunters and gatherers. Then in §17, we will look at those hunters and gatherers that have survived into modern times—in whose ways of life anthropologists have increasingly sought to find windows to the past.

15.
Archaeologists: Detectives of the Past

For many people the stereotype of an archaeologist is a rather quaint type at the bottom of a precisely dug pit brushing off potsherds with a whisk broom, oblivious to the world beyond his hole. For others, the stereotype is an eccentric professor excavating Greek temples or Egyptian tombs; but that is a *classical* archaeologist, not the prehistorian who is our concern.

The stereotypic pot-sorting scholar who couldn't see the trees from his hole, not to mention the forest, was not always far from the truth 20 years ago. But the new generation of archaeologists are a different and formidable breed who refuse to be content to describe and classify the leavings of the past and reconstruct detailed regional sequences. They are determined to see past ways-of-life-in-environments as *systems,* to theorize about processes of cultural change, to seek to reconstruct social life and even thought worlds as well as material leavings.

The theory-minded archaeologist begins with severe disadvantages, since the evidence is usually meager and hard to interpret. And the nature of the evidence one has to work with predisposes one to focus on the material rather than the ideational side of human life. The aspect of culture that can best be reconstructed is the mode of adaptation to the physical environment—tools, settlement patterns, subsistence economy. Of the rich dimensions of human thought and creativity one can at best find a few leavings in the form of pottery decorations, carvings, rock paintings, and the like.

Even here, however, theoretically minded archaeologists are looking for new ways to reconstruct social arrangements and ideational worlds in the leavings of the past. The "new archaeologist" is likely to use deductive strategies to explore nonmaterial facets of a past way of life. Given what we know about primitive religions or kinship systems, one asks, what kinds of clues might such systems in the past have left, and where might a detective best look for them?

The same deductive strategies are applied in other phases of archaeological research. Instead of discovering an old living site and analyzing the clues found there to reconstruct

the mode of life of its inhabitants, the archaeologist might better begin by examining an ecosystem. Theories about how humans adapt to an environment and how it shapes their social lives should point to where key settlements would have been and what sorts of evidence might illuminate past life in this setting. By using theory to guide the search for evidence, archaeologists can test the theories; and the sites studied become, by their nature, pieces in a wider puzzle.

Richard Gould, an archaeologist, has recently spent many months living with a remote group of Australian Aborigines little affected by European contact. By observing how they live, how they make and use tools, how they know and exploit their environment, Gould has been able to resolve a number of mysteries about the archaeology of prehistoric Aboriginal settlements. There is also a growing rapprochement with ethnography as a source of evidence. A number of archaeologists concerned with theory have done field research with Australian Aborigines, Eskimos, and other contemporary hunter-gatherers and have excavated recent settlements to learn better how to read the evidence of the past.

The archaeologist of the 1970s has at his or her command an increasingly powerful set of technical means for interpreting evidence and for finding clues in rocks or pollen that would in years past have been hidden.

For the last 20 years archaeologists have relied heavily on radiocarbon dating of sites and artifacts, using atomic age physics to estimate absolute dates. Earlier, careful stratigraphic techniques and paleontological evidence were used to work out *relative* chronological sequences, but absolute dates were rarely possible. In recent years atomic age technology has given archaeologists sophisticated new means of dating; potassium-argon dating of rocks, archaeomagnetic dating of fired clay, fission-track dating of rock and pottery, thermoluminescence dating of pottery, and obsidian-hydration dating of stone tools (Michels 1972a). Through pollen analysis and other technical processes, often calling on scientific laboratories and colleagues in various fields, the modern archaeologist can often put together evidence incomparably richer than that available to his predecessors.

Compared to the evidence available to the social anthropologist doing fieldwork, archaeological evidence is inevitably limited, partial, and one-sided. But as archaeologists have become theorists concerned with cultural dynamics, they too enjoy some major advantages. Social anthropologists do fieldwork for a year or two, characteristically in societies whose history is unknown or only partially known. It is therefore not surprising that their theories have tended to be timeless, to portray small-scale societies in stable equilibrium, and to focus on structure rather than process. Social anthropological theory is plagued, as we will see, by problems of chicken-or-egg circularity. The theory-minded archaeologist can see in the record, however sparse, long-range continuities, which can be read as processes covering many decades or centuries. He can seek to learn how cultures change, how settlement and subsistence patterns are adapted to shifting climate or technological developments or demographic trends, how trading patterns or political systems are related to ecological systems, and so on. Potentially, he can help to resolve chicken-or-egg questions by finding either eggshells or chickens in the earliest layers.

What is most important anthropologically about the new approaches to archaeology is that social anthropologists and prehistorians have begun to work together, to maximize the advantages of each perspective and to exchange insights. Just as the physical anthropologist—long a creature apart from his colleagues in cultural anthropology—increasingly becomes a key contributor to a common enterprise, so the archaeologist and social anthropologist have begun to go beyond the pleasantries—or formalities or hostilities—of being in the same university department and have begun seriously to learn from one another. The archaeologist up from the hole and the social anthropologist standing back away from the village that was a microcosm have begun to see and share broader perspectives on the human condition. The unity of the different subfields of anthropology, preserved at some cost through the years and often more a myth than a reality, has now begun to gain critical substance and importance.

16.
Late Paleolithic Cultures

In Chapter 2, we looked at the cultural leavings of the Neanderthals—the Mousterian tools, the evidence of burials and rituals, the hunting of large animals and of one another. We left the story of unfolding human cultures with the emergence of modern *Homo sapiens* and with the beginning of the Upper Paleolithic (the end of the Old Stone Age) cultures.

Let us begin with a paradoxical situation: Vast amounts of research and analytical skill have been invested in studying the Upper Paleolithic cultures of western Europe, especially in southern France; yet despite a wealth of data, our knowledge of these cultures remains limited, and our knowledge of how, where, and why they evolved is meager.

Sackett (1968), Binford (1968), and others have recently noted that the problem is only partly that many pieces of a large-scale puzzle are missing. More seriously, traditional archaeological approaches focusing on tools and on the efflorescence of cave art fail to see these cultures as adaptive systems, as total ways-of-life-in-environments.

The more basic questions of Upper Paleolithic life remain unanswered and, in fact, seldom asked. For example, what precisely were the subsistence techniques of Upper Paleolithic foragers, what population sizes and densities might they support, and with what kinds of settlement patterns were they associated? . . . Do the successive Upper Paleolithic artifact complexes [endlessly classified by specialists] refer to distinct types of economic and social organization, or do they merely reflect stylistic variations within a single cultural tradition? (Sackett 1968:65)

Our glimpse of Upper Paleolithic cultures can well begin with an overview. Some 35,-000—40,000 years ago, the diverse Mousterian stoneworking traditions were succeeded by a series of distinct and more advanced toolmaking techniques, with many regional variants, in a Europe dominated by the fluctuations of the latter part of the Würm glaciation and in the Near East. In this period, anatomically modern populations—the famous Cro-Magnons—appear on the scene. Just how these relatively diverse hunting and gathering cultures are related to one another is not yet clear, but "all of these cultures appear to be historically related by their common possession of distinctive stone-tool industries that are usually dominated by advanced blade technologies" (Sackett 1968:62). The high population density, at least in a belt across the middle latitudes of Europe, was made possible by an abundance of large-game animals and technological advance.

Here Upper Paleolithic societies seem to have achieved levels of economic success and cultural complexity that were not to recur until Neolithic times in the Old World and that have been rivaled among historic hunters and gatherers perhaps only by such groups as the maritime cultures of the Pacific Northwest Coast. (Sackett 1968:62)

How these cultures entered the European scene and how their bearers were related to the Neanderthals they succeeded have been matters of much controversy. Whether modern populations evolved from Neanderthals at all has been much argued; and if they did, most scholars have assumed that this did not happen in western Europe—hence that the "classic" Neanderthals of Europe were evicted or exterminated by biologically modern populations bringing new cultures. "Beginning some 35,000 years ago new peoples with new ideas and new ideas for living displaced and eventually replaced antecedent Neanderthal peoples and their Mousterian ways of life" (Howell 1969:xxi).

But even this local replacement is in doubt. Brose and Wolpoff (1971) assemble a broad range of evidence showing cultural continuities between Mousterian and Upper Paleolithic cultures. They argue that modern populations evolved in Europe, and perhaps elsewhere as well, in association with late Mousterian technology and that the Upper Paleolithic cultures subsequently diversified from a Mousterian base. Bordes, the leading modern expert on Paleolithic tool industries, would not balk at such an interpretation:

In western Europe, there is no difficulty in tracing back the origin of the Perigordian [the earliest Upper Paleolithic culture] to the Mousterian. . . . Now the human type of the Lower Perigordian . . . was a man of modern type even if he showed some primitive characteristics. It is impossible to make him into an invader bringing with him a Lower Perigordian culture, for . . . this culture is unknown outside western Europe. . . . It is much more probable that one is a descendant of the other. (Bordes 1968:220)

The nature and sequence of Upper Paleolithic cultures has probably been somewhat distorted by a primary focus through the years on western Europe, especially the Dordogne area of southwestern France. The cultural traditions documented for this rich and carefully studied region have been taken as a standard against which central and eastern Europe, and even the Near East and northern Asia, have been compared. The Dordogne was undoubtedly rich ecologically and culturally, but in this respect it may have been one area of several—the others being less well studied or well preserved. Had some other region served as the standard, the details of the Upper Paleolithic might seem rather different.

The major cultures of the Upper Paleolithic as reconstructed for the Dordogne, and their rough time scale, are set out in Figure 5.1. The Lower Perigordian, as noted by Bordes, shows strong continuities with one of the regional Mousterian cultural traditions. The Lower Perigordian (also called Chatelperronian) is marked by tool industries that include numerous and varied scrapers, Mousterian points, and—distinctively new—pointed blades with curved backs extensively retouched. What evidence we have of dwelling sites, mainly cave shelters and extensive open-air settlements, also shows strong continuities with Mousterian ways of life.

The succeeding Aurignacian stage of west European Upper Paleolithic culture represents more of a break with the past and may well have been imported, perhaps from the

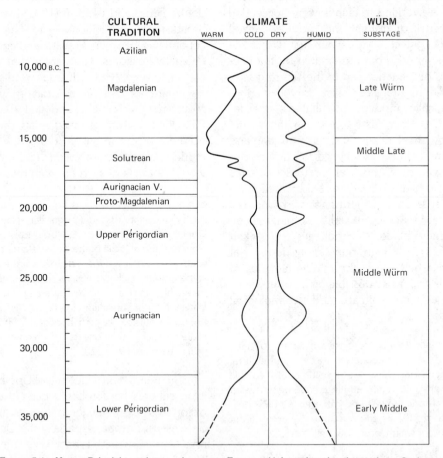

Figure 5.1   Upper Paleolithic cultures of western Europe. (Adapted and redrawn from Sackett 1968.)

Near East, though it too shows continuities with one of the Mousterian cultural complexes. The tools are quite distinctive: fine-blade types, burins, or gravers, special end scrapers retouched with fine flaking. There are more bone implements than in earlier tool complexes. The Aurignacians and Perigordians co-existed in different local areas at some periods (though keep in mind that we do not know who "they" were in terms of language or customs).

The bearers of the Solutrean toolmaking culture emerged on the scene some 18,000 years ago. This was a period of superb stoneworking, in which beautiful blades were made. The late Solutrean bifacial "laurel-leaf" shaped points require finely controlled flaking, achieved by delicate and controlled pressure rather than percussion (Figure 5.2). The Solutrean was a regional efflorescence, not found outside of Europe west of the Rhone River of France.

Magdalenian cultures were marked by less impressive stonework, but by an efflorescence of bone tools—harpoons, toggles, points, smoothing tools, and the like. Many

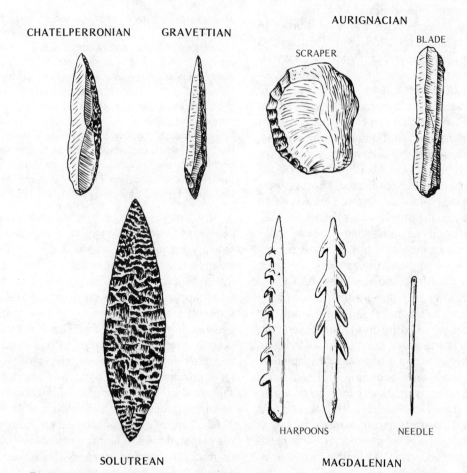

CHATELPERRONIAN   GRAVETTIAN

AURIGNACIAN

SCRAPER   BLADE

SOLUTREAN

MAGDALENIAN

HARPOONS   NEEDLE

Figure 5.2 Typical artifacts of the Upper Paleolithic. Chatelperronian and Gravettian points; Aurignacian pressure flaking and blades; Solutrean laurel-leaf point; Magdalenian bonework.

scholars have noted the apparent parallels in adaptation between these Magdalenian cultures of a cold and snowy late glacial Europe and the cultures of Eskimos and other modern circumpolar hunters and gatherers.

For the rest of Europe and Asia, the data are less rich. From the Soviet Union, however, a body of evidence is accumulating that gives new perspectives on the mosaic of regional sequences and general technological progression of the Upper Paleolithic. "[The Russian] Upper Paleolithic is extremely rich, diversified and original. It seems certain that different cultures must have coexisted, and that in most cases this Paleolithic does not fit into the framework of the west European industries" (Bordes 1968:185). Through this diversity, however, emerges a general progression of increasingly efficient technology and of adaptation to the vicissitudes of glacial advance and retreat. Evidence of the Upper Paleolithic for the Near East is not yet easily interpreted, but affinities with Europe, especially with the Aurignacian, suggest that considerable movements of ideas or populations between the Near East and Europe were taking place. More needs to be known about ecology and the movements of game animals, as well as about similarities between tools, before we can make better sense of cultural connections in these areas. The evidence from North Africa and northeast Asia is still too limited to permit more than a cataloging of regional variations on familiar themes.

What we need for the Upper Paleolithic, as Sackett's remarks quoted earlier indicate, is a better view of the systemics of adaptation, of the subsistence economy and settlement pattern from which we can extrapolate to social organization and even to ideology. Attention by artists and humanists, as well as prehistorians, to the spectacular cave paintings of some Upper Paleolithic peoples, notably Magdalenians, has given important insights into hunting and possible religious

ideas; but the wide gap between toolmaking and artistic efflorescence needs to be closed.

In hunting the usually plentiful game animals of late "Ice Age" Europe—reindeer, mammoths, bison, and horses—Upper Paleolithic peoples achieved a rich standard of living and high population densities, at least in ecologically favored zones. The European environment in this period was ideal for cultural elaboration by hunting-gathering peoples. Not only herbivorous game animals but birds and fish abounded in an environment of wind-swept plateaus, sheltered valleys, rivers, and streams.

Though serious gaps and ambiguities remain in our knowledge of . . . technology, especially with regard to perishable manufactures and in specific areas such as food storage and preservation, their extant artifacts and pictorial art suggest that Upper Paleolithic man possessed almost the entire range of techniques and equipment found among historic hunters and gatherers . . . [including] the specialized technology required for intensive semi-Arctic land and riverine exploitation such as tailored skin clothing, refined missile systems involving the throwing board and bow and arrow, and fishing harpoons, leisters, and gorges. (Sackett 1968:64)

The magnificent cave art of the Upper Paleolithic poses challenges of interpretation and a continuing fascination. Cave art was mainly limited to a small region in France and Spain (Figures 5.3 and 5.4). Cave paintings reflect apparent religious concern and a close symbiosis, symbolic as well as pragmatic, between hunter and hunted. That Paleolithic peoples may have used the natural species and their relationships as symbolic vehicles for expressing their own social relationships is suggested by modern studies of hunting and gathering peoples (see §17, and Lévi-Strauss 1962). Fertility rites, initiation ceremonies, ritual preparations for the hunt may have been dramatically enacted deep in the flickering caverns painted by these first moderns. Some cave art, at least, "was intended to enliven

Figure 5.3   Bison pierced by weapons. Niaux cave in the Pyrenees, a Magdalenian site. (After Cartailhac and Breuil.)

Figure 5.4   Engraving of a mammoth. One of fourteen in Grotte des Combarelles, a Magdalenian site. (After Capitan and Breuil.)

and brighten domestic activities'' (Ucko and Rosenfeld 1967; see also Leroi-Gourhan 1968). And some art seems to have been created for interior decoration. In the art of the late Paleolithic, Marshack (1964, 1972) sees evidence of early calendric reckoning and a concern with seasonal rituals and an elaborate mythology. While the evidence for such inferences about the ideational worlds of Paleolithic hunters is precariously thin, scholar and layman alike are struck by their kinship with these people of the ancient past, these first moderns.

Paleolithic hunters not only developed a mosaic of regional cultures across Europe and Asia and into parts of Africa. They were the first settlers in vast new regions that had never before seen human occupation: the Americas and Australia and the islands that were joined to it in glacial times.

How far back in time the first humans crossed the Bering Strait from Siberia into North America has been fiercely argued for years. Keeping early humans out of the New World was a matter of strenuous commitment for some scholars—and almost a life work for one or two. Since the advent of accurate dating methods it has been incontrovertibly evident that early hunters (the Folsom hunt-

ers of New Mexico and others) were in the Americas by 12,000 years ago. But suggestions and scattered clues that the earliest Americans arrived thousands of years earlier than that have been met by many with skepticism and critical efforts at refutation.

We now have a fairly clear picture of the environmental sequences of glaciation and warming that would have made migrations possible or impossible, and we also have a fairly accurate timetable. The Bering Strait was bridged by a land corridor for two periods when glaciation reduced world-wide sea levels: the first, between 36,000 and 32,000 years ago and the second, from 28,000 to 13,000 years ago. The latter period is not all that meets the eye as a possible period for migration: about 20,000 years ago, glaciation closed the valley of the MacKenzie River, which earlier had provided a corridor and through which ancestors of the Folsom and other big game hunters later migrated south in search of game.

But were they the first Americans? Had there been others ahead of them in an early period (20,000—28,000; 32,000—36,000?) when the way was open?

We are not yet certain, but clues of an earlier wave of migration have been turning up at an accelerating pace. Alway the evidence seems not quite certain, but can so many clues be explained away?

Burned bones of dwarf mammoths on an island off southern California have been dated at 29,000 years. Were the animals burned by humans? Artifacts and mammoth bones from central Mexico seem to date from 22,000 years or slightly more; a skull from near Los Angeles is dated at 23,000 years ago; and a caribou bone scraper with a man-made edge found in the Canadian Yukon yielded a date of 27,000 years, according to recent tests. Finally, from the Ayacucho Valley in Peru comes evidence of early humans dated at about 20,000 years (MacNeish 1971). Though individual datings can be doubted, a picture of earlier hunting populations in the New World some 25,000 years ago, perhaps earlier, is increasingly coming into focus.

Of these earliest Americans, if they are not figments of a fallible technology, we know very little. MacNeish (1971) provocatively suggests continuities between the early American finds and archaeological complexes in eastern Asia. The Yukon finds at Old Crow (28,000—23,000 years old) and some other early tools from Friesenhahn Cave, Texas, and Hue Yatlaco, Mexico, suggest kinship with a flake and bone tool tradition known from China and dated at some 50,000—30,000 years. Other Mexican finds (23,000—22,000 years) and Peruvian strata (14,000—12,500 years) suggest a relationship to a blade, burin, and leaf-point tradition dated at 30,000—16,000 years in the USSR. But the oldest Peruvian tools are crude core choppers, which suggest affinities with an ancient core-tool tradition in Asia over 50,000 years old. MacNeish anticipates that evidence of a very early migration, perhaps more than 40,000 years ago, may yet turn up in North America. Controversial crude chopperlike stones, perhaps the work of humans, have been found in the southern California desert,

in alluvial levels estimated at more than 50,000 years by geologists. Yet given the apparent timetable for the evolution of modern *H. s. sapiens,* this seems earlier than we could reasonably expect on the basis of present knowledge. But perhaps not.

Turning from such speculations to the big-game hunters of 12,000—10,000 years ago, we are on much firmer ground. The most famous sites came from the Southwest, especially from New Mexico. But we now have evidence of large populations ranging from the east coast to the west coast of North America, as far north as Alaska and as far south as Mexico. One of the two characteristic blade types, the Clovis point, has been found in every one of the U.S. mainland states.

The Clovis sites, dating from about 11,500 years, show these early Americans to have been specialists in hunting large animals, especially mammoths. In a country teeming with game, including the now-extinct mammoth, mastodon, camel, giant ground sloth, and saber-toothed cat, skilled Upper Paleolithic hunters apparently found a big-game hunter's paradise. Most of the Clovis finds were kill sites or campsites. The handsome points used to kill large animals may have been used on lances or spears—used for thrusting or throwing, perhaps with an atlatl, or spear thrower. To kill mammoths requires teamwork and leadership as well as bravery, but this had been part of the hunting heritage brought from Upper Paleolithic Europe, a heritage going back to *H. erectus* hunters at Torralba and Ambrona in Spain, a third of a million years earlier.

The Clovis points give way in the archaeological record to somewhat different blades known as Folsom points. These are smaller than the Clovis blades and fluted along most of their length. These in turn were replaced by unfluted points called Plano points.

It is foolish to think about a new "kind" of people every time new hunting blades appear archaeologically. But there is an important change evident by 10,000 years ago in the ecosystem and thus in human subsistence. The mammoths were dwindling, and the users of Folsom and Plano points increasingly turned to the great herds of bison. The Folsom-using hunters killed a large bison, now extinct, in great numbers—probably often for hides, not meat. Folsom-users surrounded these large bison in drives; the later Plano-using hunters went after a smaller species of bison, familiar from the Western frontier, driving them over cliffs in great numbers or trapping them in ravines. This implies either wanton slaughter or the coalescence of several groups, or both. It is estimated that 60,000 pounds of meat were butchered at one Plano site: 150 people would have been unable to carry away even a third of the meat.

Could human hunters have contributed substantially to the extermination of big-game animals and other distinctive fauna of the Americas? To those who have seen in the American Indian a great and wise ecologist with reverence for nature and its harmonies, the thought that he exterminated many animal species is uncomfortable. Yet more than 100 species became extinct during the brief efflorescence of massive big-game hunting in North America. Prehistoric overkill looms large (Martin and Wright 1967), though others such as Butzer (1971) argue that with the passing of the Pleistocene many of these animal populations were in precarious straits for natural reasons. But the post-Pleistocene Americas provide a continuum from snowy forest to grassy plains, deserts, and tropical jungles. If the animals were not hunted out, why did they not continue to migrate to follow a changing climate?

These evolving big-game hunting cultures are lumped together as *Lithic*. They represent a fairly brief specialized exploiting of unusually abundant big game, a way of life probably centered initially on the Great Plains and spreading into other environments where the big-game animals could be found. We do not know how important gathering of wild foods was to these Lithic peoples, but the specialization of their tools suggests that vegetables were not a mainstay of their diet.

This specialization was dependent on an abundance of game, and with a drier climate in the Plains it could not endure. Overlapping the later phases of the Lithic, beginning around 10,000 years ago and extending in some areas until the arrival of Europeans, emerged other ways of life classed as Archaic. These Archaic cultures were regionally specialized and diverse, but everywhere they showed an expanded tool kit and an exploitation of the range of wild vegetable foods, marine resources, and small game afforded by diverse environments. In the Western Great Basin, seeds, wild nuts, and small game were gathered by mobile families; basketry, fire drills, bow and arrow, and wooden-handled flint knives were among the items in an expanded tool kit.

In the Eastern Woodlands, a mixed economy of fishing, hunting, and gathering permitted larger social groups and more dense and stable settlement. Bone and antler tools were common, mortars were used to pound wild vegetable foods, and diverse stone tools were used. Here, settled populations of early Indians were adjusting to the balance, seasonal rhythms, and diversity of environments so as to find a stable and productive ecological adaptation. On the Northwest Coast, specialized food collecting, especially salmon fishing, permitted a rich elaboration of culture and large, stable populations.

In marginal environments such as the Great Basin and the subarctic, these adaptations and the Archaic endured for several thousand years, in some cases into the historic period, or ethnographic present (so that we find the Basin Shoshoni [see Case 1, p. 90], the Naskapi, and others carrying on a hunting and gathering way of life in historic times). In other regions, where ecological possibility was greater, agricultural innovations spreading from Mexico were to transform Archaic ways of life. In the circumpolar regions, Eskimo groups have spread in recent millennia, elaborating a highly specialized hunting way of life.

Early Indians in Central and South America were following related progressions of adaptive diversity and expanding technology (though especially for South America, regional sequences are known in comparable detail only for a few areas, notably in Peru). In parts of *Mesoamerica* (the region from central Mexico to tropical Guatemala, Honduras, and beyond) and vast areas of South America, tropical rain forest provided new niches in which hunting and gathering ways of life diversified; again, as in North America, the spread of agriculture transformed the ways of life except in the most remote and difficult environments, leaving remnant hunters and gatherers in arid northern deserts, a few areas of tropical rain forest, and the icy southern tip of South America.

Paleolithic peoples in Africa are so far not well known. Upper Paleolithic traditions are found in various parts of North Africa, such as the Capsian culture of Tunisia and the Dabban industry of Cyrenaica, which may be as old as 30,000 years. Hunters and gatherers apparently diversified into many environments, tropical and savanna, in sub-Saharan Africa. Their toolmaking traditions are coming to light in Congo forests, Angola (with its Lupemban chisels, adzes, planes, scrapers, and blades, including delicate leaf points), and other areas. Here again, more complex and balanced ecological adaptations were gradually worked out, such as the Ishango cultures of the Congo, beginning perhaps 9,000 to 10,000 years ago. Here a settled community on the shores of Lake Edward exploited a rich environment by hunting hippopotamus, antelope, buffalo, pig, and one

another, and by fishing. Pounding stones suggest that vegetable foods were also extensively used; harpoons and spears reflect complex hunting technology. Moreover, a bone handle with a fragment of quartz fixed in its head is marked in an elaborate pattern of notches that may represent a complex arithmetical system (de Heinzelin 1962). As in the Americas, the spread of agriculture—in sub-Saharan Africa relatively recently—transformed or obliterated hunting and gathering ways of life except in isolated areas such as the Congo rain forest and the Kalahari Desert, where Pygmies and Bushmen moved onto marginal environments and retained hunting and gathering ways of life into the modern period.

In Asia, the Upper Paleolithic turns up in widespread areas: in Japan (connected to Asia in the Pleistocene), in China, in India, and out into what is now the Malaysian zone and Australia, again by way of land bridges. From Java, from the great Niah cave in northern Borneo, and from the Philippines come remains of Upper Paleolithic toolworking. The Borneo cave yields a skull and flake tool with a controversial dating of 40,000 years and documented levels of Paleolithic traditions from 30,000 to 18,000 B.C. In this period, it appears that early populations moved out across small gaps of water onto a continental shelf later cut off as Australia and New Guinea. Australian archaeology is still in its early stages, but it is clear that humans have been on the Australian continent for at least 30,000 years and probably 40,000. A similar antiquity, of some 30,000 years, is probable for the peopling of tropical New Guinea, which provided niches for human adaptation markedly different from the arid deserts of much of Australia. Parts of Australia, and adjacent Tasmania, were temperate and ecologically rich; and parts were tropical: here our perspectives are distorted by early genocide and the spread of diseases that eliminated Aborigines from all areas desirable to Europeans.

The survival of Aboriginal ways of life in arid and remote parts of Australia affords a remarkable vista on the Paleolithic past, as we will see—for agriculture reached and transformed the peoples of New Guinea, but not the Australian Aborigines. Pockets of hunting and gathering remain in remote areas of thick rain forest and on isolated islands in south Asia, in India's tribal pockets, among Negritos of Malaya and the Philippines, in the Andaman Islands in the Bay of Bengal, and in a few other areas. Again, these peoples give us some insights into the Paleolithic past.

Having glimpsed the course and spread of Paleolithic cultures in the Old and New Worlds, let us return to western Europe at that period, some 12,000 to 10,000 years ago, when the last glacial retreat brought about the transformation of the big-game hunting cultures along with the end of the special ecological conditions that made them possible.

During the Upper Magdalenian, the density of population was relatively high in France. . . . The end of the glacial times was fatal to this striking human expansion. The disappearance of the cold fauna and the replacement of the steppe, rich in game, by forests was followed by demographic recession and the breaking of the Upper Paleolithic cultures. (de Sonneville-Bordes 1963:354)

A variety of local adaptations were worked out, based on the exploitation of aquatic resources (fish and shellfish) and wild fowl and on gathering and hunting of small animals. Extremely small geometric flint tools, called microliths, and the bow and arrow were characteristic. Note that this course in some ways parallels the development of diverse and balanced Archaic cultures in North America after the specialized big-game hunting of the Lithic, and that it involves relatively sedentary patterns of settlement and balanced and diverse resource exploitation. But partly because of the traditional mystique of big-game hunting and the efflorescence of cave art, these more balanced, diverse, and

sophisticated technologies and more stable and settled modes of life have been viewed by most scholars (such as de Sonneville-Bordes 1963) as a recession and degeneration, not an advance. The Mesolithic has been viewed as a poor way station between the late Paleolithic and the next cultural great leap forward, the advent of agriculture.

Yet as L. R. Binford (1968) points out, in some ways these post-Pleistocene adaptations represent cultural advance. By concentrating populations in zones where rivers and shorelines permitted rich subsistence economies and sedentary residence, these ways of life probably promoted population expansion. Binford hypothesizes that population increase, and a subsequent spilling over of population into adjacent frontier regions, may have created pressures encouraging new innovations in technology, and hence created conditions that fostered steps toward agriculture.

This account takes us to the dawn of agriculture, on which volumes have been written and controversy has centered. We will return in Chapter 6 to these transformations of technology, their spread, and the new ways of life they made possible. First, we will look briefly at the hunting and gathering peoples of modern times—the ethnographic present—and see what light they may shed on human life in the vast period when subsistence was based on hunting and gathering.

17.
Modern Hunters and Gatherers

One of the major anthropological developments of the last decade has been a surge of interest in hunting and gathering peoples. For more than 99 percent of the human time span, our ancestors lived in small bands as hunters and gatherers. How hunters and gatherers lived and how human nature is biologically adapted to hunting and gathering modes of subsistence and social grouping have become central questions. Three important collections of papers in the last decade (Lee and DeVore 1968a; Damas 1969; Bicchieri 1972) have pulled together the evidence on hunters and gatherers of modern times and their implications.

Before looking at the hunters and gatherers of the ethnographic present and trying to generalize about economy, social organization, politics, and the like, it is important to begin with a question. How much can such evidence tell us about human life in the ancient past and about human nature? With what confidence can we extrapolate from the present to the past?

Some reservations are in order. First, the technologies of modern hunters and gatherers incorporate quite recent advances.

In the last few thousand years before agriculture, both hunting and gathering became much more complex. This final adaptation, including the use of products of river and sea and the grinding and cooking of otherwise inedible seeds and nuts, was worldwide, laid the basis for the discovery of agriculture, and was much more effective and diversified than the previously existing hunting and gathering adaptations. (Washburn and Lancaster 1968:295)

Except to some extent in Australia, modern hunters and gatherers had access to fairly recent complexes of technological advance. In some cases, as in marginal societies of tropical South America, modern hunting and gathering peoples may previously have had agriculture and lost or abandoned this technology. The same may be true for the much advertised Tasaday, the "lost tribe" of Philippine hunters and gatherers recently found in the interior of Mindanao, whose close linguistic relatives cultivate subsistence crops.

Second, the marginal environments in which modern hunters and gatherers have survived hardly give an adequate view of hunting and gathering ways of life in the much richer environments of Paleolithic Europe or the early savannas of Africa where hominids evolved. Even for Australia, our stereotypes are based on remote deserts, not on the temperate and well-watered forests of the east coast.

We must not model our thinking about the Paleolithic world on the world as we know it today. . . . The Paleolithic world [was] . . . swarming with game. The zones in which the last tribes of hunters and gatherers have taken refuge today only serve to put wrong ideas in our heads. (Bordes 1968:235)

Nor can the residual hunters and gatherers, and their social and political relations, necessarily instruct us well about social organization in a world in which all peoples were hunters and gatherers. Even before Europeans arrived on the scene, most of these peoples were in a sense refugees who had retreated into remote areas to maintain older styles of life as best they could. And very often that meant a kind of political servitude to dominant cultivators in surrounding regions, and often a symbiosis with them, with the hunters and gatherers clearly subordinate. The fabled gentleness and harmony of the Bushmen, Congo Pygmies, and others may in part have been a cultural, and even psychobiological, adaptation to survival in marginal subservience. In Aboriginal Australia, where hunters and gatherers lived in a world of hunters and gatherers, political relations look rather different; and in an Upper Paleolithic hunting camp, Neanderthal cave, or *H. erectus* band things may have been radically different.

Finally, the surviving hunters and gatherers have been further transformed by colonialism and its aftermath: attempted genocide, the coming of missionaries, introduced diseases, introduced technology, and ecological disruption. (To this list we might add the impact of anthropological fieldwork—often by substantial teams—perhaps for some hunters and gatherers the latest indignity to which they have had to submit; we will return to this question in Chapter 25.) The patterns of social organization we find now may not accurately reflect modes of life of even 100 years ago, not to mention 100,000.

All that said, we still have much to learn from modern hunters and gatherers.

Ecology of Hunters and Gatherers

First, let us look at the ecological adaptation of modern hunters and gatherers and extrapolate cautiously into the past. A number of generalizations are possible:

1. A wide range of technological skills and tools are used to exploit local environments. Microadaptation is rich and diverse, and

Australian Aboriginal technology: A woman dips water into a wooden bowl. (Courtesy of C. P. Mountford and the State Library of South Australia.)

many of these skills and techniques would be hard or impossible to read from the archaeological record. Hunting weapons include bows and arrows, slings, traps, snares, spears and spear throwers, blowguns, boomerangs, and bolas (ropes with weights in which a running animal's legs become entangled). Poisons are often used on projectile points. Great skill in tracking, driving, pursuing, and trapping game is evident from many areas.

A wide range of containers—bamboo tubes, animal skins, ostrich eggs—for carrying liquids and cooking are used in different hunting and gathering societies.

Fire is produced by friction in various ways: the fire drill, operated by hand or with a bow to turn the drill; the fire plow, or stick pushed in a groove; or the fire saw, a stick drawn back and forth across a piece of wood. Yet apparently in at least one isolated pocket, the Andaman Islands, hunting and gathering peoples lost the ability to produce fires, hence

Australian Aboriginal technology: A hunter edge-grinds an ax head. (Courtesy of R. Edwards.)

Australian Aboriginal technology: Fire making. (Courtesy of R. Edwards.)

A Pygmy net-hunter prepares his trap. (Courtesy of The American Museum of Natural History.)

had to keep them lit. Keeping the home fires burning can be a problem if home is where you happen to hang your dilly bag.

2. Despite our probable preconceptions about the hardships of survival in a hunting and gathering way of life, the food quest seems not to be a constant and exhausting business. For hunting and gathering bands, unable to do very much to control their natural world, the *possibilities* of material comfort and accumulation are quite limited. And given these limits to the feasible goals of life, hunters and gatherers seem to have a surprisingly easy time of it, and to have considerable time for leisure and relaxation. Considering the implications of detailed evidence on the subsistence of the !Kung Bushmen of southern Africa, and similar findings from other hunters and gatherers, Sahlins (1972:1—2) dubbed the hunting and gathering band as "the first affluent society."

An affluent society is one where all the people's material wants are easily satisfied. To assert that the hunters are affluent is to deny . . . that the human condition [must keep] man the prisoner at hard labor of a perpetual disparity between his unlimited wants and his insufficient means. . . .

There is [instead] a road to affluence, departing from premises . . . that human wants are finite and few, and technical means unchanging but on the whole adequate. Adopting the Zen strategy, a people can enjoy an unparalleled material plenty.

3. The *efficiency* of labor invested in terms of the return on energy expended is very low (R. Lee 1969; Kemp 1971). But to use such a measure, like inflicting the concept of gross national product on the Third World, may insidiously impose alien criteria from an industrialized capitalist society. We need at least to remember—as if we should need reminding in the midst of plastic, smog, and energy crises—that technological advance may bring an erosion of the human spirit.

4. The idea of "man the hunter" is misleading as well as chauvinistic. Modern studies of Australians, Bushmen, and Pygmies have revealed how central in their survival is the collecting of vegetable foods by women.

Australian Aboriginal technology: Trimming the edge of a digging stick. (Courtesy of R. Edwards.)

!Kung woman carrying child as she gathers food. (Courtesy of Lorna Marshall.)

Hunting—dramatic, collective, ritually central, and, when successful, punctuating the daily routine—is easily overemphasized. Modern evidence reveals that among such hunters and gatherers as the Bushmen, roots, fruits, nuts, seeds, berries, and other vegetable foods collected by women provide the staple base needed for survival (Lee 1969). Game, to be sure, provides the times of plenty and contributes crucially to the diet; but man as hunter, bereft of great speed or a keen sense of smell and dependent on limited weapons, is hard pressed in what for any carnivore is a difficult game of chance. Only in unusual ecological circumstances was a specialized dependence on hunting or fishing possible—as among the Eskimos, some

Northwest Coast peoples, or in the past, the Clovis or Magdalenian big-game hunters.

5. *Sharing* is a major theme in the use of resources. It exists in relations between bands, where access to water is granted when needed and hunting territories are not jealously guarded. It prevails within the bands, where "generalized reciprocity" (Sahlins 1965) entails sharing of meat and other foods beyond the bounds of individual families. The openness, communal spirit, and free sharing of resources by such peoples as the Tasaday and Pygmies have probably been exaggerated: they have become a kind of ideological foil, noble savages in their idyllic primitive Eden. But the contrast with, say, peasant villagers is indeed striking.

What about the effects of humans on ecosystems? At the hunting and gathering technological level, they were much less dramatic than they became with the advent of agriculture. Humans as hunters and gatherers played a role as simply another species within the ecological system, locked in a complex network of interdependence. Populations were small and scattered. Human modes of social life, populations, and distributions of population were geared to the animal and plant species which provided subsistence. Hunters and gatherers doubtless in the short run produced many ecological "runaways" by hunting out particular animals or changing migration patterns. But the imbalances humans created in the long run limited and controlled their numbers and ways of life, creating new equilibrium. As hunters (and prey) among hunters, and as gatherers competing with herbivores for wild foods, humans were inextricably bound in a web of nature. When technology transformed them into a new and far more numerous kind of being, their influence on ecosystems became profound and disruptive.

Social and Political Organization

The "classic" model of the social organization of hunters and gatherers is the *patrilocal band*. In this social arrangement the men of a band would form the political core; men would spend their lives hunting in the territory where they grew up. Daughters, however, would leave the band at marriage (a rule of *exogamy*, or marrying outside one's own group; see §48). Thus wives would come into the band at marriage, leaving their childhood home territory. This would mean changing their foraging grounds, but that would seem less precarious as a mode of ecological adaptation than having young men move to a new hunting territory. Such a mode of organization may have deep roots in the human and even hominid past—though as noted in §8 we do not know at what stage a rule of exogamy linked bands together. Such patrilocal bands were seen as characteristic of Australian Aborigines and many other hunters and gatherers. In Australia and some other areas, marriage rules went far beyond a rule of outmarriage to posit complex rules for the exchange of women between bands. Lévi-Strauss (1949) has argued that such "alliance systems" are ancient and basic—a possibility to which we will return in §48.

Sparse and scattered resources in some ecological settings made fairly stable and concentrated bands maladaptive. In such marginal areas, nuclear families might disperse for all or part of the year. The Basin Shoshoni, survivors of the desert mode of Archaic adaptation in North America, are a striking example.

Case 1: Shoshoni Social Organization

The Shoshoni Indians of Nevada, and other Shoshonean-speaking peoples of the Great Basin of western United States (Ute and Paiute), had an extremely simple and fragmented social organization. classed by Steward (1955b) as a "family level of socio-cultural integration."

The Shoshoni environment was extremely arid, harsh, diversified, and unpredictable. It included desert and near-desert, lakes and streams, high pine forests, and a range of intermediate settings at different elevations. Winter was cold and severe, summer hot and dry. The sparse food resources, mainly rabbits and other small game, and even more important, pine nuts and other wild vegetable foods, were scattered and unpredictable.

In such a setting, human settlement was sparse—one person to every 5, 10, or even 50 or 100 square miles. Mobility was necessary, so that no permanent settlements were possible, and only tiny groups could make ends meet in the business of subsistence.

The Shoshoni and their neighbors developed an adaptation whereby a nuclear family (an individual set of parents and their offspring) or a polygynous family (a man, his several wives, and their offspring) lived alone for most of the year—perhaps 80 percent of the time. They moved in pursuit of food, following the seasons. Only when resources such as fish or pine nuts were temporarily abundant did several families live together. In winter, they sometimes camped together, living largely on whatever dried nuts and seeds they had been able to store. At other times, they joined together in communal hunts for rabbits or antelope. Such gatherings were times for dancing and collective religious rites.

Since families were exogamous, spouses had to come from outside. Characteristically, however, marriage alliances would be worked out between two families, so that when a young man from one family married a young woman from another, the younger children of the two families would also marry when the time came. When a man took two or more wives, they were supposed to be sisters. If a spouse died, his or her surviving sibling was supposed, if possible, to marry the widow or widower. The several families united by such marriages would usually be the ones that coordinated their movements so as to group together seasonally when resources permitted (Steward 1938, 1955b).

A number of modern studies of hunters and gatherers in Australia, North America, and Africa have cast doubt that the classic patrilocal band model may be too simple. Bands tend to be diverse and heterogeneous, there is considerable mobility and individual and subgroup shifting from band to band, and bands hunt extensively on one another's territory. Even out-marriage is often less neat than in the classic model. The !Kung Bushmen illustrate some aspects of this flexibility and diversity.

Case 2: !Kung Bushmen Social Organization

The !Kung Bushmen are hunters and gatherers living in the forbidding Kalahari Desert of southern Africa. The arid environment permits survival only in small, scattered bands. Bushmen bands, ranging in size from about 20 to 60, are spread over some 10,000 square miles; the total population is only about 1000.

Each band has a territory. Within a territory, rights to gather wild vegetable foods, the everyday staples on which existence depends, are limited to band members. Water is another scarce good, and each band has primary rights to the waterhole or holes on which they depend (though outsiders may use the water with permission). Hunters of large animals may cross into the territories of other bands quite freely in pursuit of game. If a band's waterhole goes dry, its component families move temporarily to live with other bands where they have relatives.

Each band is made up of a cluster of families. Some are nuclear families, with all members related to one another by bonds of kinship. However, some families are augmented by the presence of one or more married children and their families. Other families are polygynous: a man has two or more wives.

Bands are not exogamous by rule. Marriage is forbidden within the nuclear family, between certain close kin, and between a man and a girl whose name is the same as his mother's (there is only a limited set of names for men and women, transmitted along family lines; name sharing is taken to imply distant kinship). Some marriages do take place within a band. When a man takes his first wife, he goes to reside with his bride's

A Bushmen band. (Courtesy of The American Museum of Natural History.)

father until two or three children have been born. During this time he contributes his labor to the relatives of the bride—doing bride service— adding to the larder of his father-in-law and his band). Since marriage often takes place well before the bride reaches puberty, this may cover a span of 8 or 10 years, during which the husband is absent from his band. After that, the husband may take his wife and children back to his father's band or may choose to remain with his wife's people.

Each band has a headman chosen by consensus. He has formal authority over the disposition of a band's resources and its movements; but his political powers are in fact quite limited. Group action is usually based on consensus of its members. In some ways the headman's stewardship is symbolic. His *de facto* power depends on his personal skills at leading, organizing, planning, and maintaining internal harmony. Headship of the band passes through family lines, from a headman to his oldest son.

Internal conflicts, as between a headman and his younger brother or another kinsman, are resolved either by the dissident member moving to another band where he has relatives or by the splitting off of the dissident faction to form a new band. Affines, persons related to the band by marriage, may join a band and enjoy equal rights with persons born into the band, but these rights lapse if they leave. The rights of a person born into the band to live in band territory and share in its resources remain even though he or she may live elsewhere; the option to return remains open (Marshall 1959, 1960, 1965).

Whether such flexibility and diversity were characteristic of hunters and gatherers in the Upper Paleolithic, or even in the recent past, has been hotly debated. Some experts urge that this flexibility represents an effective mode of ecological adaptation and political relations and therefore is old and basic; others counter that it is a recent by-product of colonialism and intrusion by the external world.

The political organization of hunting and gathering societies runs a wide gamut. Where the environment was rich and the population relatively large and sedentary, a degree of political centralization far beyond that of recently studied, marginal hunters and gatherers is revealed in the early records. Even bearing in mind the tendency to promote leaders met along early colonial frontiers into "kings" and "chiefs," one is struck by early accounts of leadership in lush southeastern Australia. A party of early colonists near what is now Melbourne "were met by a number of natives who, on a shot being fired over their heads, 'ran a small distance but soon approached again with the king, who wore a very elaborate turban crown and was always carried on the shoulders of the men" (Howitt 1904 quoting Shillinglaw 1870). Elaborate hierarchical structures involving clan chiefs, formal clan and tribal councils, and tribal paramount chiefs are reliably reported.

Among the surviving marginal hunters and gatherers, with smaller, often scattered, populations and often forced subservience to surrounding peoples, political leadership tends to be much less formal and stratified, based primarily on personal powers—whether of hunting, ritual, peace-keeping, oratory, or general leadership—and carried out by egalitarian decision-making or consensual support. The Bushman case is a typical example.

Fighting within and between groups was undoubtedly more widespread and often more violent than recent stereotypes of the primitive Eden imply. In the surge of literature on hunters and gatherers in the 1960s, conflict and warfare were often underplayed. The bashed skulls and charred bones of Neanderthal sites, records of warfare among Australian Aborigines, and similar clues from the recent and more remote past should make us wary of projecting too much peace and harmony into our conceptions of human life during the distant Paleolithic past. We will return to the questions of warfare and the maintenance of internal order in Chapters 17 and 18.

Religion and World View

In Chapter 19, we will look at religion and world view among "primitive" peoples, including hunting and gathering peoples. Here our brief concern is evolutionary; we can pause only for the most general observations.

The religious systems of hunters and gatherers, diverse though they are, are characterized by a *oneness with nature.* In a world you cannot control, a natural balance you must study and adjust to, a human environment dominated by climate, the cycling of the days and the years, your kinship with nature is compelling and sacred. It may be expressed in mystical personification of natural forces (animatism) or by belief in supernatural beings (animism); by belief in a divine creator; or by conceptualizing relations between social groups in terms of relations between animals, birds, or natural forces (totemism; see §65). Colin Turnbull's picture of the African Pygmies of the Ituri forest—the immediacy and vividness of their perceptions of the natural world, the intimacy of their knowledge of it, and their mystical oneness with the spirit of the forest—gives a compelling sense of humans *in nature,* not against it.

In evolutionary perspective, what do religions do for humans as hunters and gatherers? Some theorists suggest that religious practices may have ecologically adaptive functions of which those who practice them are unaware: thus it has been suggested that divination by scapulimancy (cracks on animal shoulder blades) among some North American hunters may have served as a kind of primitive randomizing device for finding game. By steering hunters randomly in a new direction each time, the patterns of cracks may have kept them from hunting out the animals of particular areas (Moore 1957). And it has been suggested that sexual license at rituals among Baja California Indians may have served to articulate a cycle of human reproduction with seasonal variations in food

In a world of material simplicity, Australian Aborigines have reached profound philosophical depths. Here a Central Australian holds a firestick for warmth. (Courtesy of C. P. Mountford and the State Library of South Australia.)

Australian Aboriginal religion is rich in symbolism and in relating the visible present to the mystical dreamtime of the past. (Courtesy of C. P. Mountford.)

supply (Aschmann 1959). But for hunting and gathering peoples, as for other humans, religion meets other crucially human but more subtle needs. Religious beliefs (as Freeman (1968) vividly argues) project human psychic conflicts onto the cosmos; they answer questionings, give a fabric of meaning and legitimacy to human action; and they create human order out of death, uncertainty, and randomness. Moreover, religion may help to buffer humans from themselves—to constrain cleverness and purposive action with wisdom and faith, to control a dangerously shortsighted rationality. If to be coldly rational and pragmatic is to be sane, then man is "the only animal that needs to be insane to survive" (Coon 1971:388; see also Rappaport 1971b; Bateson 1972a). Religion may be both the inevitable product of the human superbrain and a protection from its excesses. We will return to these questions in §37 and §63.

The recent snowballing concern with hunters and gatherers reflects not only scientific curiosity and specialization. It reflects as well a growing realization of how precarious is our own future, of how strange and frightening and potentially catastrophic is the new wave of life that is sweeping us along. With our evolutionary perspectives on the human condition, we begin now to perceive that a hunting and gathering way of life is what we are biologically adapted to: a small-scale life of close, face-to-face communal relations, oneness with each other and the world of nature. The vast, alien, crowded, plastic world we have created exacts a great cost, even as it opens new vistas of understanding, control, and possibility. A search for control led humans at the dawn of food-producing away from the balances of the past; it is urgent and appropriate that we now look back to that past as best we can in search of wisdom. The revolution in our thinking about progress and primitivism is vividly underlined in the words of a distinguished geneticist:

The intellectual arrogance created by our small scientific successes must now be replaced by a profound humility based on the new knowledge of how complex is the system of which we are a part. . . . I find much of relevance to contemporary problems in my field, human genetics, in our studies of primitive man. . . . In the most sophisticated way we can summon, we must return to the awe, and even fear, in which primitive man held the mysterious world about him, and like him we must strive to live in harmony with the biosphere. (Neel 1970)

THE GROWTH OF CULTURE

Food-Producing and the Tribal World

6

The origin of food-producing—cultivation of plants and domestication of animals—has been tirelessly explored archaeologically and endlessly debated theoretically. Though the sequences of what happened are emerging fairly clearly, how and why they happened is by no means certain.

Why all this attention to food-producing? One reason is that food-producing led to profound transformations of society; it greatly expanded human population and revolutionized ways of life on every continent but Australia. A second reason is that food-producing, like urbanization, has posed a critical challenge to theoretical explanation, to our understanding of how and why cultures change.

In §18, we will sketch the beginnings of food-producing in the Old and New Worlds. In §19, we will trace the waves of change these new technologies sent sweeping through the primitive world. In §20, we will look at the diversity of the tribal societies Europeans found during the age of exploration and discovery as representing "adaptive radiation" into diverse ecological niches; and we will look more closely at shifting cultivation and pastoralism as modes of adaptation.

Before turning to the end of the Paleolithic and the dawn of agriculture, a word on terminology is in order. Food-producing levels of technology are conventionally classed as *Neolithic,* or New Stone Age. It is true that new modes of stone tool-making marked by polished and ground tools came into use at this stage. But far more important changes of technology and social life were taking place as well: classing this cultural stage on the basis of stone tools is like calling the last 25 years "the Age of Plastic"—not wrong, but not very enlightening. "Neolithic" will be used often in the pages to follow, but it will refer to whole technological complexes of which stone tools are but one element.

18.

The Evolution of Food-Producing

First, we will look at the Near East; then we can turn to the Americas and Asia to trace the independent emergence of food-producing.

The Near East

In the late stages of the Upper Paleolithic, hunting and gathering peoples had developed diversified, broad spectrum patterns of food gathering—collecting fish, crabs, molluscs, birds, small game, and in some places perhaps cereal grasses.

Until the period 10,000—8000 B.C., such an advanced hunting and gathering pattern prevailed in the Near East. Prefiguring the changes to come were several early developments in technology that were to prove important in food production. One was development of ground-stone technology, used in making stone implements for grinding. Another was the development of storage pits and other means of preserving or processing wild vegetable foods. It should be noted that gathering of a broad spectrum of wild foods, along with hunting of larger animals (increasingly focused on single species), may have contributed to a more complex division of labor.

At the end of the Pleistocene, climates changed in the Near East. Oak woodlands expanded across upland areas that had previously been dry, creating a zone of optimum wild resources—including edible nuts, fruits, and wild cereal grasses. Seasonal climatic changes promoted intensive collecting for a short period of the year and long storage of wild vegetable foods. The changes in the environment reduced the diversity of wild plants, including grains; it also promoted the spread of herd animals—sheep, goats, gazelles, and orager.

This environmental richness promoted increasingly sedentary residence in larger communities. By the ninth millennium B.C., gathering of wild grains, in areas where dense stands were present, had led to substantial semisedentary settlements in areas such as Palestine (the Levant) and Syria. It seems increasingly likely that it was not in these ecologically rich areas that wild grains were first cultivated but around the less favored margins. Population increases in the ecologically favored zones may have spilled out into the surrounding marginal areas, where they would then have intruded on the subsistence economies of more nomadic peoples. The pressure for subsistence could have provided the stimulus to extend the wild grains to the less favored environments or artificially create more dense stands of grain. This hypothesis, advanced by Binford (1968), has been discussed by Flannery (1969) and Meyers (1971). Another suggestion, advanced by Flannery, is that mobile food collectors, moving from one resource zone to another, may have spread and propagated wild grains beyond their normal habitats.

Thus arises the more general question that has focused interest on the origin of food-producing: Why do people change their subsistence economy? Climatic change is often invoked, but that explanation seldom stands up to critical examination and is too simplistic. Is it the pressure to support an increasing population, the impetus of threatened famine? This is unlikely. Studies of humans and animals show that population stabilizes by natural (or cultural) means far below the carrying capacity of the ecosystem. Do humans have some natural urge to tinker with subsistence, to improve technology, to exploit more and more efficiently an environment they know well? As we have seen, modern hunters and gatherers hardly show such urges. Besides, this is a nonexplanation. (It is reminiscent of Molière's doctoral candidate, who when asked why opium makes people sleep, explained to his examiners that "there is in it a dormitive principle." Is there in humans a progressive principle?) Humans, Binford argues, tinker with changes in their subsistence when the systemic balance of culture-in-ecosystem is disrupted—perhaps by climatic change, but more likely by intrusive competition in a marginal zone.

The precise sequence of how and where the first grains were intentionally sown or the first animals domesticated will probably never be known. But in the Levant, the Zagros Mountains, and Anatolia, at roughly the same time (8000—6000 B.C.) and apparently in rather similar ecological situations, grains such as emmer wheat and barley began to be cultivated; and sheep, goats, and pigs were domesticated (Figure 6.1). At first, this was no striking and revolutionary change. Gathering of wild grains, nuts, wild legumes, hunting of wild cattle, goats, and other hoofed animals, and eating of fish, molluscs, birds, and the like, continued. Thus in the Bus Mordeh dry-farming era, an early level identified by prehistorians at Ali Kosh in Iran (7500—6750 B.C.), cultivated cereals constituted only about one third of plant foods, and domestic sheep and goats contributed only about one third of the meat consumed.

Most of the total weight of meat and plant foods of this period came from wild resources. . . . There is no reason to believe that the early "food-producers" were significantly better nourished than their "food-collecting" ancestors. Nor was their subsistence base necessarily more "reliable." (Flannery 1969:63—64)

Apparently the unpredictability of seasons played a part in domestication of animals: grain surpluses of an abundant crop could be "stored" and in a sense invested by feeding them to sheep and goats, which could be traded (or consumed) in lean years.

Archaeological and ethnographic evidence suggests that plant cultivation and animal herding, far from being two separate subsistence activities, are interrelated in ways which help "bank" surpluses and even out the erratic fluctuations of the Near Eastern environment. (Flannery 1969:69)

This dry-farming complex had by 6000 B.C. generated substantial new developments in technology, social organization, and mode of life. By this time pottery had come on the scene and was being used for containers and cooking vessels. The settled communities, clusters of houses made from sun-dried brick, still depended on stone tools and on many things made with them. Pottery developed rapidly, and local patterns of manufacture and decoration flourished and spread. To illustrate, by around 6000 B.C. at Catal Hüyük in southern Anatolia, a settlement some 32 acres in area reveals a large and stable population. Cultivated cereals included barley, einkorn, emmer, and wheat (early versions of modern cereal crops). Sheep, goats, and dogs were domesticated. Yet wild oxen, wild pigs, and red deer were hunted to augment the diet. The inhabitants lived in rectangular houses separated by courtyards. Houses were rebuilt many times over long periods. Access to houses was through openings in the roofs. Flint, greenstone, and obsidian polished tools were used, in addition to those of antler and bone. Woolen textiles were used for clothing and apparently for wall hangings. Reliefs and paintings richly decorated some rooms, suggesting family shrines. Carved figures of bulls, rams, and leopards suggest elaborate symbolic systems.

By this time, humans had irreversibly changed the ecological balance in the Near East. Wild legumes had been displaced, environments changed, animal populations disrupted. These disruptions were accelerated when the beginnings of irrigation, around 5000 B.C., further changed the face and bal-

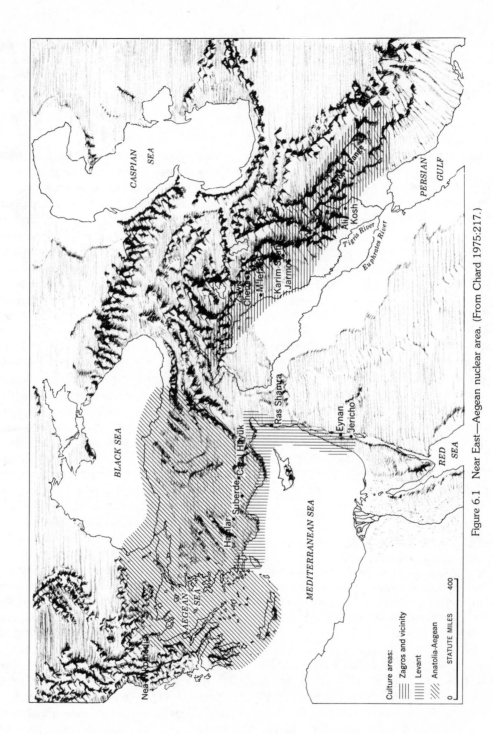

Figure 6.1 Near East—Aegean nuclear area. (From Chard 1975:217.)

ances of the land. Significantly—in view of Binford's hypotheses about subsistence changes—irrigation seems not to have taken place first in the ecologically favored uplands where population density was greatest, but in the dry and marginal lowland steppes, notably the Khuzistan steppe of Iran. With irrigation, the balance of ecological favor and population concentration shifted toward the lowlands; there, civilization was to emerge. We will leave Near Eastern civilizations waiting in the wings until the next chapter and trace the emergence of food-producing in the New World and then in East Asia and elsewhere.

The New World

The independent origin of major complexes of food-producing in the New World has for years posed a major challenge to prehistorians viewing the sweep of cultural development. How similar and parallel were the sequences and processes? And how can theories explain their differences?

The European adventurers who reached the New World in the 16th century encountered a series of cultures almost as advanced (except in metallurgy and pyrotechnics) and quite as barbarous as their own. Indeed, some of the civilizations from Mexico to Peru possessed a larger variety of domesticated plants than did their European conquerors and had made agricultural advances far beyond those of the Old World. (MacNeish 1964:259)

A major area where New World peoples domesticated plants is the region known as Mesoamerica (see p. 84). Here a crucial range of plants was domesticated that transformed ways of life in Mesoamerica and North America—principally *maize* (corn), and secondarily beans, squash, chilies, and other cultigens.

In the period from 8000 to 5000 B.C., in the relatively marginal upland valleys of Oaxaca and Tehuacán (and doubtless in other areas of southern highland Mexico), hunters and gatherers were subsisting on a wide range of plants and animals: wild cacti and the maguey or century plant (which must be baked for several days to make it edible); tree pods, nuts, fruits, and wild grasses, including the precursors of maize; and deer, rabbits, and diverse small game.

From 5000 B.C. onward at Tehuacán, and somewhat later in Oaxaca, maize, beans, and squash were domesticated. Though beans and squash seem to have been domesticated first, maize is so central to New World food-producing that it has been a focus of attention and fantastic detective work by plant geneticists—notably Paul Mangelsdorf—and archaeologists. Maize has been traced back step by step to the wild form, with the cob no bigger than a cigarette filter.

The transformation of subsistence in these high Mesoamerican valleys was fairly slow. In the early period of domestication, prior to 3500 B.C. at Tehuacán, only some 10 percent of the subsistence diet came from cultivated plants though the list of new cultigens expanded rapidly to include chili peppers and various new species of squash and beans. (The complex of maize-beans-squash-chili provides the basis of Mesoamerican subsistence into the present; and it fits together in an important way—the amino acids and other biochemical elements of the plants mutually complement one another.)

By about 3400 B.C. at Tehuacán, small pit-house villages appear as the first fixed settlements. In the next several centuries, domesticated dogs appear and domesticated plants increase to make up some 30 percent of the diet. About 2300 B.C., pottery-making began and more advanced hybrid forms of maize were cultivated.

Thereafter, with the Formative Period (1500—200 B.C.), the pace of cultural development quickened. Larger, sedentary communities, increased population, and the development of ceremonialism mark the early

Formative. At this stage, focus begins to shift to ecologically more favored zones, such as the great Valley of Mexico and Oaxaca, which in succeeding centuries would be centers for the rise of civilization. After 850 B.C., irrigation had begun in the river valleys, population was rising sharply at Tehuacán, and the rise of Olmec culture on the coast near Vera Cruz was reflected in the beginnings of temple mounds. Civilization was on its way.

Apparently South America had at least one, and probably two, independent centers of plant domestication. Cultivation of squash, beans, and gourds began in the coastal valleys of Peru as early as 5200 B.C., though these were only a minor augmentation of a diverse subsistence economy in which aquatic resources such as shellfish, fish, snails, and riverine crustaceans were central. Cotton was also an early domesticate, perhaps used along with gourds in the technology of fishing. By 2500—2000 B.C., agriculture had assumed a somewhat greater importance, especially in interior areas where river valleys provided rich floodlands. By 1900 to 1750 B.C., Peruvian coastal villages and interior settlements show considerable population increase and expanded use of a range of plants, including chilies, cotton, squash, and lima beans. By 750 B.C., maize had arrived in Peru, presumably from Mesoamerica. Moreover, new plant domesticates turn up, apparently from outside, that represent a different and important mode of cultivation.

The plants we have considered so far are propagated by seeds. The new cultigens, apparently domesticated in one or more other parts of South America, involved *root* propagation; the tubers were eaten. These included potatoes, sweet potatoes, and manioc (cassava). The latter seem to have been domesticated somewhere in the margins of tropical South America, along with sweet potatoes, guavas, peanuts, cashews, and pineapples. Other Andean cultigens, though precise origins are unknown, include potatoes and tomatoes. Domestication of animals, which never got very far in the Americas, was limited to dogs, turkeys, guinea pigs, and those New World relatives of the camel, llamas and guanacos.

Archaeologists continue to debate the models that can best account for changes in subsistence through the course of centuries. And they continue to debate whether parallel processes took place in different Old and New World areas. The issues are not yet clear; but as evidence improves and theories are refined, social anthropologists can well watch and enrich their understanding of cultural process.

One thing is by now clear. Peoples with a mixed hunting and gathering economy and intimate knowledge of their environment had the potential means to domesticate the plants they gathered. Manipulating seeds—which sprouted around settlements, often in rubbish heaps—could easily lead to small experiments in cultivation, at first minor extensions of natural propagation and minor contributions to the diet. Domestication of plants thus could take place in a number of different areas. Why humans tinkered where and when they did apparently reflected ecological and demographic pressures. But archaeologists inevitably seek explanations external to human social and ideational worlds; and that may be only one side of the process. We will return to these questions in Chapter 12.

East Asia

Did plant domestication take place in Old World areas other than the Near East? Yes, and apparently even earlier, if somewhat controversial datings from Spirit Cave in Thailand hold up. There, seeds of peas, beans, and water chestnuts have been dated as early as 9700 B.C.: the world's first farmers may well have lived in Southeast Asia. Other surprisingly early dates, as old as 8000 B.C., have come from recent excavations in Taiwan. In any case, the full development of the Southeast Asian Neolithic produced a complex of crops (rice, taro, and the yam, a starchy tuber unrelated to the sweet potato) and domesticated animals (pigs and chickens) that was to be crucial in the spread of the Neolithic into tropical regions of the Old World.

The beginnings of agriculture in China, coming well after the early agricultural sequences of the Near East, have long been assumed to reflect the spread of ideas, if not of crops. On the loess plateau (composed of fine, deep, wind-blown sediment) of north-central China, archaeologists have excavated remains of a way of life, called Yangshao, not yet firmly dated but probably earlier than 3000 B.C., where early farmers lived in settled villages. They cultivated millet, farmed intensively (though without irrigation), made pottery, and raised pigs. The Near Eastern staple crops do not turn up in China until somewhat later. A strong case can now be made for China as the center for domestication not only of millet but also of rice, sorghum, and hemp, all of which appear to be represented in some of the early sites. India may also have been an area of early plant domestication, but this is not yet clear.

The Near Eastern crops spread early to the Indus Valley of Northern India and to the Nile Valley. (It is probably no coincidence that these rich, fertile areas were not the original spawning grounds for agriculture and assumed central importance only with the beginnings of substantial irrigation and waterworks; so too with the rich river valleys of China.) The Ethiopian area seems to have been another area of domestication, though the Near East may have served as stimulus: millet and sorghum may have been domesticated separately there, as well as barley, coffee, and lotus. Whether sub-Saharan Africa produced an independent early complex of tropical domesticates, including yams, has been much debated. At this stage, new domesticates were being added in Europe and elsewhere, and new ideas were ramifying around the primitive world in a way that makes origins often almost impossible to trace.

19.
The Spread of Food-Producing in the Primitive World

The rapid growth of population and food production in major river valleys of the Old World—the Tigris and Euphrates, the Nile, the Indus, the Yellow River—and an accompanying transformation of societies into complex urban civilizations were to come quickly. So too was the rise of impressive New World civilizations in Mesoamerica and Peru. But outside the nuclear areas where civilization was emerging, the hunters and gatherers scattered through Old and New Worlds were being engulfed or swept along by the waves of Neolithic culture. Here we will briefly look at the spread of Neolithic ways of life that produced the "primitive world" European "discoverers" were later to encounter in Africa, in parts of southern Asia, in the Pacific, and in much of North America and large parts of South America.

For this is the realm of "primitive tribes," where so many of the ways of life that fill the pages of anthropology books were recorded. And though they were often depicted by explorers, and are still popularly depicted by the media, as representing survivals from the ancient past, that is hardly true. Tribal peoples—with a food-producing technology, lacking complex central governments—have not been that way "since time immemorial." In the total span of human experience, they represent a recent burst of new cultural possibility into a wide range of ecological niches: a kind of adaptive radiation that has produced the diverse ways of life of tribal peoples.

The progression of new cultural systems has produced many major centers—of political and economic power, new ideas, new social forms, and new technologies—and hundreds of minor ones, spreading, dissolving, obliterating one another. The disruptions were least drastic, least rapid, around the margins; as we have seen, at the farthest margins, small pockets of hunters and gatherers remained until the age of discovery and beyond. But for most of the non-Western world, a neat division of the map into "culture areas" or patchworks of tribes is misleading. The appropriate image, if we must have images, is more like the splashing of raindrops onto a window, with new drops spreading over old ones and creating new patterns. The pattern that Europeans found was often obliterated, or swept into the corners; or it was frozen by colonial administrations.

Southeast Asia and the Pacific

In Southeast Asia, the Neolithic complex of rice, yam, and taro cultivation, and developed seagoing technology, spread from China some 3000—2500 years B.C. Java, Sumatra, the Celebes, Borneo, the Philippines, and Taiwan were settled by mobile Neolithic cultivators and fishing peoples speaking Austronesian languages, replacing or assimilating hunters and gathérers. Later waves of cultural influence, Hindu and Islamic, were to transform Java, Sumatra, and more remote Indonesia; Islam reached the southern part of the Philippines and the margins of Borneo. Meanwhile Austronesian-speaking Neolithic seafarers settled the large island of Malagasy (Madagascar) off the coast of Africa.

Neolithic seafarers also moved outward into the Pacific. Agriculture had reached the hunters and gatherers in New Guinea several

thousand years before Austronesian seafarers moved past the vast island and through the Melanesian islands. Austronesian speakers, ancestors of modern Polynesians, had penetrated these islands and reached Fiji well before the beginning of the Christian era. Melanesia itself—the Bismarck Archipelago, the Solomons, the New Hebrides—constitutes a mosaic of variation, from complex cultural and linguistic borrowings and interbreeding between Austronesians and the expanding descendants of the hunters and gatherers who had settled New Guinea thousands of years before. From Fiji and then Tonga the ancestral Polynesians spread by superb navigation and chance drift voyaging to the far reaches of a vast triangle of islands—to Easter Island near South America, to Hawaii, and to New Zealand, with its great glaciers. The tiny islands of Micronesia, with a total land area the size of Rhode Island scattered over an ocean the size of the United States, were settled by Austronesian speakers from the central Pacific and from islands of Southeast Asia (perhaps Taiwan, perhaps the Philippines, perhaps both).

What is important for the moment is the span of time involved. The diverse forms of social organization Europeans encountered had not been there for many thousands of years. In most cases, they had only been there for several centuries, and these centuries were not times of stable isolation. Rather, such peoples as the Tongans of Polynesia and the Yapese of Micronesia were in the process of engulfing their neighbors with empires and exacting tribute.

The subsistence economies of these Pacific islanders are based on crops that had come from the Southeast Asian Neolithic complex—especially yams, taro, and breadfruit, with domestic pigs, dogs, and fowl. The peoples of the Malaysian zone mainly concentrated on shifting cultivation of dry or hill rice. However, in some areas of the mainland and

Neolithic technology opened the resources of the oceans: A Kwaio tribesman (Solomon Islands) uses a four-cornered lift net to catch small fish channeled toward his platform by coconut-frond weirs. (Photograph by the author.)

on some islands of Southeast Asia, irrigated rice, often grown on elaborate man-made terrace systems, made possible greater population concentrations. We will glimpse the social implications of these subsistence modes, in different environments, in §20. These Malaysian peoples acquired in many areas the technologies of ironsmithing, spread from Asia; iron tools were a valuable asset in cultivating rain forest environments.

South and Central Asia

In India and adjacent south Asian areas, the rise of great civilizations obliterated tribal ways of life except in the margins, in the mountain forests of the Himalayan foothills, Burma, and Indochina. In some of these regions, tribal peoples have preserved their traditional ways of life until modern times. (The Montagnards of Vietnam, decimated by recent war, are a tragic example.) Some of

the "tribal" peoples in India and Southeast Asia are not simply remnant groups that have survived in the margins: rather, they have been kept in marginal subservience to serve the needs of rulers as elephant catchers, or to provide honey, spices, or other forest products to settled peoples.[1]

In the arid zones of the Near East and across central Asian steppes and north Asian tundra, it was not domesticated plants but domesticated animals that made possible new adaptations. In an arid mountain belt across south-central Asia, from near the Mediterranean to the Himalayas, herding of sheep, goats, and later camels made possible mobile pastoral ways of life—another offshoot of the early Near Eastern food-producing pattern. These pastoral adaptations, often requiring seasonal migration, or *transhumance,* permitted continuing occupation of zones in Iran

[1]An observation for which I am indebted to Surajit Sinha.

and Afghanistan that had become too dry for agriculture.

Domestication of the horse, probably in central Eurasia around 2000 B.C., opened new possibilities for successful adaptation to the vast grassy steppes of central Asia. The mobile horse nomads of the steppes appear in the literature of subsequent centuries as the scourges of settled peoples: the Scythians, the Hyksos, the Huns, the Mongols, and so on.

Historically, pastoralism represents an offshoot of the mixed agriculture and herding complexes of the Middle Eastern Neolithic— an offshoot in the opposite direction from the complex of tropical shifting cultivation, in adaptation to dry grasslands.

The fully nomadic peoples like the Mongols ironically represent not an independence from settled agricultural communities but a kind of symbiotic interdependence with them. The horsemen who were the scourge of Egypt, of medieval Europe, and of China depended on settled communities for many of the products they needed to survive. In turn, the herds of the nomads contributed centrally to the economy of settled groups during the periods of peace. Nomadic life offered an escape from poverty for peoples on the margins; yet in times of drought the settled communities provided a refuge for nomads.

In the Arctic, reindeer have for centuries lived in close association with the humans who herded them—Lapps, Tungus, Chuckchi, and others. Reindeer may have been domesticated under the example of horse domestication, but some experts think the stimulus may have gone the other way, that reindeer herding may be very ancient.

Africa

The Saharan belt of Africa, especially its southern margins, was relatively well watered several millennia before the Christian era. In some regions, a seminomadic way of life based on herding of cattle, apparently independently domesticated in Africa, was flourishing as early as 4500 B.C. We have seen that to the east, in or near Ethiopia, millet and barley were being cultivated not long afterward, and probably again these crops were domesticated locally.

By 1000 B.C. or earlier, a complex of Neolithic cultivation using root crops and grains was widespread in West Africa. Whether this West African Neolithic complex involved independent domestication of yams and perhaps other root crops, or whether this tropical farming complex reflects only the spread (through Malagasy and an East African "corridor") of Southeast Asian Neolithic crops, has been much debated.

The introduction of ironsmithing from the north set the stage for the explosive expansion of West African farmers, speaking Bantu and related languages, across southern Africa. This expansion seems to have occurred within the last 2000 years.

The farmers of tropical forest regions of sub-Saharan Africa are shifting cultivators, growing yams, millet, sorghum, and other crops. Where ecological circumstances permit, farming is more intensive; use of plows and hoes, in lieu of digging sticks, and in some areas irrigation systems, support larger populations and relatively dense and permanent settlements. In modern times, the old complex of domesticated plants has been augmented by maize, peanuts, and manioc.

A second great complex, cattle herding, spread through Central and East Africa. This area had apparently been occupied mainly by Hamitic peoples, light-skinned like the Amharic peoples dominant in modern Ethiopia. The Nilotic and East African cattle complexes, with elaborate modes of social organization and ecological specialization, have been much studied anthropologically. These adaptations were made possible by grassy savanna lands in much of East Africa. Their spread has been constrained not only by the range of potential environments but also by distributions of cattle disease, such as trypanosomiasis, spread by the tsetse fly, and rinderpest.

Africa represents a complex cultural layer cake that shows the result of relative proximity and close contact with the early centers of civilization. Though we have seen that there are a few surviving remnants of hunting and gathering ways of life, food-producing spread early into most areas. As the case of ironworking illustrates, subsequent technologies and new ideas followed close behind: the plow; writing; trade in gold, ivory, and slaves; and institutions of centralized political power. Thus kingdoms, not tribal (stateless) societies, held sway in much of sub-Saharan Africa. The southward spread of Coptic Christianity (the ancient Christian Church of Egypt) and subsequently of Islam represent further waves of cultural influence: the latter is still transforming black Africa. Moreover, the explosive expansion of Bantu speakers resulted in the obliteration or absorption of many tribal peoples and the formation of complicated "composite" kingdoms (see, for example, Case 56, Chapter 17).

African adaptations of Neolithic and post-Neolithic innovations usefully underline once more the error in projecting great stability and vast age to the tribal world. The peoples Europeans found in "Darkest Africa" had not remained the same "since time immemorial." Over long periods of time Africa emerges as a swirling, moving scene with populations shifting, splitting, conquering, and mixing. Cultural intrusion and domination are old, not new, in Africa; in the southern half of Africa, Europeans are but the most recent intruders.

The Americas

In the New World, the spread of food-producing followed rather different patterns. Cultivation of maize, squash, and other plants was diffused into the eastern United States.

But the relatively rich subsistence economies of the Archaic peoples of the Eastern Woodlands were not transformed overnight by food-producing. The adoption of agriculture in North America was a gradual process. Experts disagree about the importance of agriculture among such peoples as the Hopewell mound builders, who remained well into the Christian era. However, well before Europeans arrived, southeastern North America produced an efflorescence of centralized political systems (for example, the Natchez [see Case 50, Chapter 16] and the Creek Confederacy) and elaborate religious systems that clearly are derivative from the flowering of civilization in Mesoamerica.

In the Southwest, maize cultivation early made possible sedentary ways of life, again influenced by Mesoamerica. Such cultural sequences as the Anasazi and Hohokam have been reconstructed with painstaking detail by American archaeologists. Here for many centuries the sedentary horticulturalists of cliff dwellings and later Pueblos constituted islands beset by surrounding predatory hunters and gatherers. The survival of these Pueblo islands in the even more stormy seas of modern times is eloquent testimony to their strength and cultural integrity, to the human capacity to endure. We have belatedly begun to try to learn from their wisdom as we have visibly begun to sink.

Though agricultural innovations could have taken hold along the west coast of North America, they did not. Again, Archaic patterns of subsistence—shellfish, fish, and acorns in California, salmon fishing in the Northwest Coast—permitted sedentary ways of life by substantial populations. This usefully serves as a reminder that students of cultural development need theories not only to explain why experimentation with the natural environment led to food-producing only in some times and places and not in others; but also to explain why, given access to new technologies that could transform the subsistence economy, people may enthusiastically adopt, casually dabble with, or completely ignore the new possibilities.

With the introduction of the horse, the Great Plains, teeming with bison, were to become a center of cultural efflorescence again almost 10,000 years after the Clovis hunters. Earlier anthropologists assumed that horses were introduced at the time of the first Spanish expeditions; it now seems likely that Indians did not acquire horses until considerably later, making all the more remarkable the flowering of Plains cultures known from the history of the West. The buffalo hunters of the Plains moved in from several directions. Some, such as the Cheyenne, derive from the southeast or northeast, from sedentary maize-cultivating peoples. Others derive from the Archaic hunters and gatherers in the West. The rapid emergence of classic Plains horse cultures in only a century or two—the Cheyenne, Comanche, Sioux, Blackfeet, Kiowa, and the rest—again usefully reminds us how dynamic cultures can be, how rapidly new possibilities can transform old ways of life.

In South America, agricultural ways of life spread early through Andean regions along the Pacific coast. The sweet potato-based subsistence of the Aymara of Bolivia is one of many regional variants. In lowland South America, old hunting and gathering ways of life were in varying degree transformed by the domestication of tropical root crops, notably manioc. The traditional systems of lowland South America, especially in areas relatively exposed to Europeans, are hard to reconstruct because of the incredible genocide of the early colonial period and the extermination of vast numbers more through introduced diseases. The extermination of Brazilian Indians—and only remnant survivors remain—still continues with the government permitting ethnocide and at times genocide in the name of progress.

Horticulture had become important in the Amazonian lowlands by 1000 B.C. But in rain forest environments, the advantages of sedentary life and concentrated populations were balanced against the advantages of dispersal and mobility in exploiting the diverse environment. A mosaic of local balances between food collecting and food-producing evolved in lowland South America. These were in some areas affected by the rise of the great Inca state; marginal tribes seem to have been woven into the design of empire. With the destruction of that empire, some marginal groups such as the much-debated Siriono of Bolivia seem to have become attenuated remnants of a richer past.

The spread of food-producing into the world of hunters and gatherers was, as this world-wide sketch suggests, sometimes revolutionary, but often simply evolutionary—modifying gradually what had been there before. Food-producing did greatly expand populations, opening marginal grassland, rain forest, and island environments to substantial settlement. Levels of settlement size and sociopolitical organization rarely achieved by food-gathering peoples were made possible. By a kind of adaptive radiation, new systems of organization and regional diversity were explored. This range of alternative paths of life explored by tribal peoples becomes for us, beset by crises of survival, a vital resource—a source of wisdom and perspective on what humans can be. These experiments in human possibility had not run their course when European expansion destroyed or transformed them. So we should not accord to these tribal ways of life a spurious permanence or stability in an imagined distant past, but should see them as a fairly recent phase in a dynamic unfolding of adaptive possibility. The urban African acquiring a transistor radio is playing out the latest phase in a drama of innovation, change, and adaptation that was going on at Olduvai Gorge 2 million years ago, a drama that later saw his own ancestors adopting agriculture some 30 centuries ago and iron tools some 20 centuries ago.

20.
Neolithic Modes of Adaptation: Shifting Cultivation and Pastoralism

The many modes of adaptation worked out by tribal food producers represent a vast mosaic of variation. We will glimpse some of the many tribal ways of life in Chapters 13 to 20.

Two important offshoots of the mixed economies of the early Neolithic—shifting cultivation and pastoralism—will be briefly examined, and several illuminating case examples will be set out. The nature of shifting cultivation and pastoralism as *adaptive systems* will be our primary concern. We will have a first look at ecosystems, technology, and the organization of production in small-scale societies. We will also begin to raise questions about cultural process: about how cultures change, and why they take the forms they do—questions to which we will return in Chapter 12. In asking how ecosystems shape the lives of tribal peoples, we will also want to look at the other side, to ask about the impact of tribal peoples on ecosystems.

Shifting Cultivation

Early agriculture on and around the fertile hilly flanks of the Middle East, and later in rich river lands, had involved an artificial extension of the environments where the plants had grown in the wild. When humans in the tropical rain forests of Africa, Mesoamerica, Southeast Asia, and the Pacific developed modes of cultivation, their challenge was much more difficult. Though plants suited to tropical climates were domesticated, especially in Southeast Asia, the task of creating an environment where these plants could grow was by no means easy.

We think of a tropical rain forest as a lush and fertile place. But this is seldom true, except where volcanic soil creates a rich environment. More commonly, tropical soils are infertile. Under the towering forest canopy, primary rain forest is by no means the lush tangle of vegetation of Hollywood's stereotype. Not enough sunlight penetrates to support thick undergrowth, except where rivers or other openings break the canopy. What fertility there is comes from the thick layer of decaying vegetation fallen from above. When the giant forest trees are cleared—an immense task with stone adzes and fire—the ground is opened for planting yams, taro, maize, dry rice, and manioc. Burning the leaves and branches accumulated in clearing the area temporarily enriches the soil. But then the problems set in. Torrential rains and hot sun leach out the nutrients quickly and can laterize the soil into infertile crusts. By the time a crop has been harvested, the soil is often exhausted. After a second crop, if one is possible at all, the soil is likely to be useless for cultivation. (Meanwhile, hungry insects and birds from the surrounding forest have done their best to harvest the crops ahead of the humans who planted them.)

The solution worked out by Neolithic peoples in the tropics was a system known as *shifting* or *swidden cultivation*. Any family or kin group must have considerably more land than is needed for gardens at any time. As a crop is harvested in one garden, a new garden is cleared and planted. The old garden is allowed to lie fallow, and secondary growth of grasses, bushes, and then forest covers it. At some optimum point—often 10 to 20 years if land is sufficient—a balance is struck between renewed fertility of the land and the difficulty of clearing it again for a new garden.

Usually the ground is worked only by simple digging sticks, often improvised and at best hardened by fire. Technically, such cultivation without the use of the plow is called horticulture rather than agriculture. Polished stone axes and adzes, the original cutting and felling tools of Neolithic peoples, were supplanted by iron in Africa and Southeast Asia, reducing the labor investment of felling and fencing and making it more feasible to clear virgin forest where it was available.

Many European observers have commented on the wastefulness of shifting cultivation. They were misled by the seeming lushness and fertility of tropical rain forests and by their mistaken assumption that land lying fallow is wasted and that more intensive agriculture would support larger, more sedentary populations with a higher standard of living. But in fact, shifting cultivation usually is a highly effective and balanced ecological adaptation; and efforts to introduce intensive agriculture in tropical forest have usually been disastrous. *Balance* is a crucially important element in swidden horticulture:

In ecological terms, the most distinctive positive characteristic of swidden agriculture . . . is that it is integrated into and, when genuinely adaptive maintains the general structure of, the preexisting natural ecosystem. . . . Any form of agriculture represents an effort to alter a given ecosystem in such a way as to increase the flow of energy to man: but a wet-rice terrace accomplishes this through a bold reworking of the natural landscape; a swidden through a canny imitation of it. (Geertz 1963:16)

As we have seen, the major corps used in shifting cultivation represent a combination of root crops (yams, taro, manioc, and sweet potatoes), seed crops (dry rice, maize), and tree crops (bananas, breadfruit). Especially in Southeast Asia and the Pacific, domestic pigs are often raised; and where possible, aquatic resources and small game augment a monotonously starchy diet deficient in protein. The swiddens of Neolithic horticulturalists usually contain not only the staple crops but also a wide range of supplementary cultigens, including bananas, leafy greens, squashes, beans, sugarcane, and the like. Thus in a single three-acre swidden among the Hanunóo of Philippines, Conklin (1957) recorded more than 40 species of plants under cultivation at once. (The Hanunóo have separate labels for more than 400 cultivated plants.)

The nature of swidden horticulture as a mode of adaptation is well illustrated by the Tsembaga Maring of New Guinea.

Case 3: The Ecology of Tsembaga Maring Subsistence

The Maring are a tribal people living in two large river valleys, the Simbai and Jimi, of mountainous highland New Guinea. There are about 20 local groups of Maring speakers, varying in size from a little over 100 to 900. We are fortunate that three detailed studies of Maring ecology have been carried out in different local groups, by Rappaport (1967, 1968, 1971c), Clarke (1971), and the Vaydas (n.d.), giving us unusually rich information. Here we will examine the Tsembaga Maring, a local group of 200 studied by Rappaport.

The Tsembaga are shifting horticulturalists. Though their steep valley habitat rises in less than three miles from the Simbai River (2200 feet) to a mountain ridge of 7200 feet (a territory of 3.2 square miles), only the slopes from the river to about 5000 feet can be effectively cultivated. About 1000 acres of this sloping land were used as gardens or were lying fallow. Forty-six acres had been planted during the year of study; about 100 acres (10 percent of the total garden land) were in gardens that year, since some gardens are used for two years or longer. Rappaport believes that the potential carrying capacity of the land might be about 200 persons per square mile of arable land; the actual density was 124.

Horticulture provides 99 percent of the everyday Tsembaga diet. But they also eat wild pigs, marsupials, reptiles, and grubs from the surrounding forest. A typical garden contains not only the standing staples, sweet potatoes and taro, but also other starchy crops such as yams, manioc, and bananas; and a wide range of legumes, leafy greens, and other vegetables, plus sugarcane. The intricate intermingling of garden crops, as Geertz (1963) suggested, creates a kind of miniature garden version of a tropical rain forest.

Building a garden involves first clearing secondary forest. Men and women begin by clearing undergrowth (now with machetes, previously with stone adzes; see Salisbury (1962) for evidence on a similar technological transition elsewhere in New Guinea). After about two weeks, men fell most of the trees; they leave the largest ones stripped but standing. Clearing, Rappaport estimates, requires more than two and a half times as much energy investment per acre as felling the trees. The gardens are then fenced to keep out wild and domestic pigs—an incentive to cluster gar-

Tsembaga maring cultivations: *(left)* A new garden is planted; *(right)* a mature garden from which taro and sweet potatoes have been harvested. (Courtesy of Roy Rappaport.)

dens together to minimize fencing. This chore requires somewhat less than half the energy investment per acre of the initial clearing, and again is done by men. One or several months later, when the garden litter is dried, it is stacked and burned, and the garden is weeded; this work is divided between women and men. Preparing the garden requires a relatively brief investment of work, but keeping it weeded over the months that the crops are maturing requires sustained effort—more than three times the total energy of initial clearance. Harvesting and hauling crops are also demanding, though visibly rewarding, tasks. Rappaport estimates that about 300,000 calories per acre are invested in gardening, and that about 5 million calories of food per acre are harvested—somewhat more than 16 to 1 as a return on energy invested. Rappaport (1971c) estimates that in a more typical year when residences were scattered through the gardens, the yield ratio would probably be around 20 to 1. This ratio is more than double the return on subsistence energy invested by the hunting and gathering !Kung Bushmen of southern Africa (R. Lee 1969; Harris 1971; cf. Kemp 1971 for the Eskimo): evidence of the progressively more efficient investment of energy made possible by human technological advance.

A factor in gardening strategies is the number of domestic pigs to be fed. Tsembaga pig husbandry runs in cycles. When a family is feeding only one or two pigs, one major garden at middle altitude, sufficient to feed the animals and their owners, is cultivated. When the number of pigs is increased, a garden containing mainly sweet potatoes (fed to the pigs as well as eaten by humans) is cultivated high on the slopes above 4500 feet; and a second, lower-altitude garden is planted with mainly taro and yams. We will see in Chapter 12 (Case 14) how this cycle of pig husbandry is geared to Tsembaga religious ritual and politics.

The Tsembaga live in a relatively harmonious balance with their natural environment, though data from other Maring areas suggest that the stability of the Tsembaga may be overemphasized. The Tsembaga undoubtedly observe destructive changes in their environment and may alter their strategies accordingly; and the ecosystem itself is to a substantial degree self-corrective. "Information feedback from the environment is sensitive and rapid in small autonomous ecological systems, and such systems are likely to be rapidly self-correcting" (Rappaport 1971c:355).

But what prevents the Tsembaga population from expanding to exceed the carrying capacity of the land? What prevents the progressive deterioration of the environment due to disruption by humans? We know that for many areas of highland New Guinea, such disruption has been considerable: thousands of acres of forest have—after being cleared for gardens or burned for hunting—reverted not to secondary forest but to rank, tangled sword-edged imperata grasses that render the land economically useless.

If population remains in balance, if the ecosystem remains in equilibrium, could these conditions be achieved by the social and cultural institutions—even the religious beliefs—of the human population?

Betty Meggers, analyzing in ecological perspective the ways of life of South American Amazonian jungle peoples, clearly thinks so:

The pattern of culture that arose in Amazonia is almost as remarkable an adaptive configuration as the rain forest vegetation. Warfare provides excitement and a means of acquiring prestige, but also helps to prevent population increase. Sorcery not only explains the occurrence of death in a culture ignorant of germs and infection, but inhibits expansion of community size. (1971:159)

Whether analysis begins with religious practices, social organization, or some other sector of a cultural complex, explanation of the content and role of the elements involved will inevitably reveal functional relationships with other categories of behavior that are adaptive. (1971:43)

We will return to the question—a central one in the theoretical debates of modern anthropology—in Chapter 12. There we will look in detail at Rappaport's sophisticated

and persuasive argument that Tsembaga Maring culture—its religious rites as well as its social organization and economy—represents an intricate and balanced adaptive system that adjusts Maring life to the exigencies of their difficult environment.

But how do adaptive beliefs evolve, and not maladaptive ones? Rappaport concedes that the mechanisms whereby adaptive beliefs and ritual practices are selectively favored and maladaptive ones weeded out are not yet clear. And he concedes that religions may sometimes be maladaptive or neutral: we have to trace the "circuits" of the system to find out. We will return in Chapters 12 and 19 to the question of how cultures change and of how adaptation shapes this process.

Are tribal peoples always in equilibrium with the ecosystems of which they are a part? The way in which tribal peoples can be a disruptive force, and can culturally create environmental imbalance, is vividly illustrated by the Iban of Borneo (who also illustrate one mode of the dry rice cultivation characteristic of much of Southeast Asia).

Case 4: Iban Agriculture

Iban communities consist of long houses, the component apartments of which are occupied by separate families. We will trace this pattern of family organization in Case 31. Here the system of cultivating dry rice will give important ecological insights.

An Iban "tribe" is a population occupying a series of long-house communities in a single river system. Marriage normally takes place only within a tribe; head-hunting is directed outside. The tribes are not permanently settled, however. The Iban have proliferated and greatly expanded their territory in historic times—moving steadily into the vast virgin forests of the Baleh region and displacing alien tribes that stood in their way with "fierce attacks."

The "rich, untouched vegetation" of the Baleh was, to the Iban, the most inviting of prizes, and their desire to exploit it was the overruling incentive of their advance and an important motive in prompting their fierce attacks on alien tribes that stood in the way. Head-hunting and a craving for virgin land went hand in hand. (Freeman 1955:111)

The desire for virgin land expresses a knowledge of the rich subsistence it provides. In prayers, the Iban ask for

Land that is fat, fat in deep layers, Luxuriant land, land that is fruitful, Soil soft and fecund, land richly fertile (Freeman 1955:115).

An Iban swidden: This steep hillside, cleared and burned, will be planted with rice and harvested. If it is planted with a second crop, severe erosion and deforestation may result. (Courtesy of Hedda Morrison.)

By cultivating virgin forest—feasible with their homemade iron tools—the Iban secure rights over the secondary forest that is created. But the drive is not only to secure land, where "land is wealth" (Freeman 1955:115), but to keep pressing onward, with an "insatiable appetite."

Iban fell virgin forest, clear, and burn in ways not dissimilar to Tsembaga practices. But growing dry rice imposes a seasonality, in which planting, weeding, harvest, and threshing of the rice structure the annual round of life. This round can be ecologically balanced, if the scrub vegetation *(krukoh)* that grows in old gardens is allowed to return to secondary forest and lie fallow. But Iban prefer to maximize short-term rewards, not long-term balance. Their more usual strategy is to cut and clear the *krukoh* scrub vegetation and to plant a second year's rice crop in the same garden. This makes weeding, burning, and other tasks easier; and it yields a maximum return, since the second year's crop is often better than the first. But the two-year cycle leaves the land plundered, and the family carves deeper into the virgin forest again—leaving erosion, deforestation, and ecological devastation in their wake.

> The reason for this overcultivation . . . [includes] an historically rooted conviction that there are always other forests to conquer, a warrior's view of natural resources as plunder to be exploited, a large village settlement pattern which makes shifting between plots a more than usually onerous task, and, perhaps, a superior indifference toward agricultural proficiency. (Geertz 1963:16)

The Iban case—if we look at it from the standpoint of the neighboring peoples being decimated by head-hunting and driven from their territories—illustrates another facet of adaptation in the world of Neolithic tribesmen. The neighboring humans constitute part of a people's environment.

The Yąnomamö of Venezuela, whom we met in Chapter 1, provide a further illustration. Chagnon shows that Yąnomamö warfare, characterized by stealthy, brief raids, is not aimed at territorial expansion. The function of the hostility and militant ideology seems to be "to preserve the sovereignty of independent villages in a milieu of chronic warfare" (Chagnon 1968b:336). That is, villages preserve their autonomy by mutual antagonism. But note also that there is a danger of circularity in such "explanations": if villages raid one another, it is "adaptive" to maintain a hostile stance; but it would be rather more "adaptive" not to raid one another at all (see Hallpike 1973). We will return to such problems of circularity.

The ecological imperialism and historic movement of the Iban give another important insight. We must be wary of *assuming* that ecological equilibrium prevails in a tribal society, and then trying to find out what preserves it. The equilibrium we think we see may be an illusion created by a short period of observation and the artificial stability of colonial administrations. The Iban case should also make us wary of assuming that tribesmen have some mystical reverence for Nature, some balanced world view we have lost. For people who practice agriculture, land becomes a *thing*—something humans own, something they control and manipulate to human ends; and it ceases, often, to be a

A Yanomamö chest-pounding duel: Physical violence is culturally fostered among these South American forest tribesmen. These duels are used to settle grudges "peacefully," to avoid bloody warfare. (Courtesy of N. A. Chagnon.)

surface they share with fellow animals and plants.

All tribesmen were in part conservationists, consciously or unconsciously; but they were also to some degree plunderers and manipulators, constrained in their ecological disruptions by their limited technology, not their reverence for nature. Where the balance lay for a particular culture (or a particular individual) varied a good deal. We can well gain ecological wisdom from studying the world view and folk wisdom of tribal people. But our images of tribal ways of life should be tempered by remembering the Iban. My own are tempered by memories of long hours spent walking through rain forest with Kwaio tribesmen in the Solomon Islands of Melanesia, many of whom slashed constantly and randomly at the vegetation along the paths with their machetes—for whatever psychic

satisfactions cutting greenery affords. It is tempered as well by my knowledge of the way Solomon Islanders quickly hunted wild pigs to extinction when they obtained firearms, and dynamited the fish in their lagoons.

Pastoral Adaptations

Pastoralism is a second classic mode of food-producing adaptation. The herding of cattle—or camels, reindeer, sheep, and other animals—takes many forms, yet a general contrast with agriculture emerges. Neolithic cultivation creates miniature environments in which domesticated plants can thrive. But the technology of tribal peoples enables them to exert little control over the environments needed by large domestic animals. Patterns of rainfall and vegetation and the mobility and requirements of the animals largely structure modes of pastoral adaptation. Pastoralists are in some places fully nomadic, moving continually to follow resources; in others, they migrate seasonally to fit into an ecological cycle (seasonal transhumance). Pastoralists may have fixed territories and permanent bases, or groups may move freely over large territories.

Two great regional complexes of pastoralism were worked out in the Old World. One has been in a great belt across central Asia and north Africa, the other in sub-Saharan Africa. In the Asian complex, there is a wide range of variation—as wide as the contrast in environments: from arid deserts to grassy steppes. The nomads of the Asian steppes, with their fleet horses and mobile camps, their subsistence heavily based on mare's milk and other animal products, ranged over vast areas. Occasionally, when such leaders as Attila (406—453), Genghis Khan (1162—1227) and Tamerlane (Timur; 1336—1405) crystallized the dispersed hordes, the horse nomads became the scourge of the sedentary peoples at the margins of the steppes. Less specialized are the many pastoralists who herd those old human companions, sheep and goats. The Basseri nomads of southern Iran illustrate one such mode of adaptation.

Case 5: Basseri Nomads of Southern Iran

The Basseri of southern Iran are a tribe of tent-dwelling nomads numbering some 16,000. They migrate seasonally through a strip of land some 300 miles long, an area of about 2000 square miles. Some of the villagers through whose areas the Basseri move claim a common origin with the nomads; the mosaic of languages and cultures of agricultural villagers and nomads is quite complicated.

The seasonal migration pattern is shaped by the physical environment. There is winter snow in the northern mountains, a well-watered middle region around 5000 feet elevation (where most of the agriculturalists are settled), and lower pasture land to the south that becomes arid in summer. Each of the nomadic tribes of South Iran has its own traditional migration pattern.

The Basseri economy rests squarely on their large herds of sheep and goats. Milk, meat, wool, and hides come from these herds and can be traded with villagers to meet other needs. Transportation is provided by horses, donkeys, and camels. Sheep's and goats' milk are mixed at the time of milking, and soured; sour milk, junket, and cheese are the primary foods. During the summer, when pastures are rich, the Basseri remain temporarily settled. Food surpluses are built up, in the form of cheese and meat on the hoof, that provide subsistence in the leaner winter months. The Basseri also eat agricultural products. Most are obtained by trade, but the Basseri grow some wheat at their summer camps. Hunting and collecting contribute minimally to the economy.

The mobility of the Basseri is reflected in the realm of social organization. Family groups, conceived as "tents," are the main units of production and consumption. These tent groups, represented by their male heads, hold full rights over property and sometimes act as independent political units. All of the property of a tent group—tents, bedding, cooking equipment—must be moved, along with the herds, when the group migrates. An average family would have 6–12 donkeys and somewhat less than 100 sheep and goats. In winter, the families separate into small clusters of 2–5 tents, associated as herding units. The rest of the year, larger camps of 10–40 tents move together. Members of these camps comprise solidary communities; but because of their mobile patterns, quarreling may lead to temporary or even permanent fission. (There are higher levels of political organization and centralized leadership as well, but these need not concern us at this stage. We will return to the nature of political organization in small-scale societies in Chapter 17.)

The African complex of pastoralism is based on cattle herding. The symbiosis between humans and cattle, and the symbolic elaborations of the "cattle complex," have been a focus of anthropological interest. These elaborations are carried to most remarkable lengths in East Africa. The Karimojong of Uganda provide a vivid illustration.

Case 6: Karimojong Pastoralism

The Karimojong comprise some 60,000 pastoralists occupying about 4000 square miles of semiarid plain in northeastern Uganda. The position of cattle among the Karimojong is best introduced by their ethnographers, the Dyson-Hudsons:

> Cattle are property, and accordingly they represent variable degrees of wealth, of social status and of community influence. They are a man's legacy to his sons. They can be exchanged to symbolize formal contracts of friendship and mutual assistance. The transfer of cattle from the groom's family to the bride's is needed to validate a marriage. The sacrifice of cattle is a vital feature of religious observances. The focus of Karimojong aspirations is the acquisition of cattle, and disputed cattle ownership is at the root of most Karimojong quarrels. Cattle are considered proper objects of man's affection, and this conviction is an integral part of each man's life cycle. (1969:359)

Yet first and foremost cattle provide subsistence, by transforming the energy stored in the grasses, herbs, and shrubs of a difficult environment.

Blood and milk products, not meat, provide the primary subsistence. Cattle are bled once every three to five months. Cows are milked morning and night; ghee (butter and curdled milk) can be stored and is centrally important in the diet. Milk, often mixed with blood, provides the main diet, especially for the men who move with the herds.

Cultivation of sorghum provides secondary subsistence. Women, based in the permanent settlements in the center of Karimojong land, do the cultivation, while men follow the sparse rainfall to find grazing lands. Cultivation and collecting of wild foods provide important daily subsistence for the women, and also give some insurance-in-diversity in a harsh environment where droughts and cattle diseases pose a recurring threat. Cattle are slaughtered rarely, mainly for initiations and sacrifices; and those are mainly performed when drought forces reductions in the herd.

With a limited technology that precludes bringing food or water to their herds, or storing most foods, the Karimojong must follow strategies that minimize risk in a harsh and unpredictable environment as well as maximize subsistence production. Rather than modifying their environ-

East African pastoralists. Samburu men with their cattle. (Courtesy of Department of Information, Kenya.)

ment, the Karimojong must adapt their lives to it; but in doing so, they build a rich world of cultural symbols and social arrangements (see, for example, the account of Karimojong age-sets in Case 42, Chapter 14).

Can we usefully view the cultures of East African pastoralists as adaptive systems? As Gulliver's (1965) comparison of Jie of Uganda and the Turkana of Kenya shows, that leads part—but not all—of the way toward anthropological understanding.

Case 7: The Jie and the Turkana

The Jie of Uganda and the Turkana of Kenya are two of a cluster of tribes very closely related culturally and linguistically. The Turkana split off and migrated several centuries ago into a larger but much more arid and barren region. Gulliver (1965) documents the close similarities between Jie and Turkana in the cultural principles governing property rights, livestock, and family structure. In their more densely populated, more fertile setting, Jie maintain permanent settlements and aggregate into fairly stable large groups. Though there are no formal property restrictions on where one's cattle can graze, mobility is limited and the population is fairly stable. Among the Turkana, living in a marginal desert environment, camels and goats play a major part as well as cattle. Settlements are constantly moved, there are no permanent points of reference, families act as isolated units, and alliances are temporary. Here an ecological setting limits and shapes the way a cultural pattern can unfold. On the one hand, social organization has undergone major changes in this adaptation to a new environment. On the other, had Turkana entered this new environment with different concepts of rights over animals and territory and different principles of kinship, their adaptations to the new setting would have taken different forms.

These sketches of subsistence and ecology in several of the hundreds of tribal societies, and of the processes of adaptive diversification that have shaped their ways of life, will give some sense of the mosaic of variation that was the tribal world. That world constitutes a crucial source of wisdom about human possibility and human nature. In the eight chapters of Part 3, we will examine this mosaic of diversity more closely—looking at kinship, economics, political processes, law and religion in the broadest possible comparative perspective.

We need first to sharpen our theoretical tools, by learning more about culture, about society, and about language: that will be the major challenge of Part 2.

But first, we will turn to the rise of civilization, and the evolution of urban life.

THE GROWTH OF CULTURE
Urbanization and the Rise of Civilization

The waves of change that food-producing technology sent sweeping across the Old World had not yet washed across its further margins by the time new turbulences began to transform the Near East. This time it was not the mountains but the great river valleys that were the settings for new transformations of society.

The development of urban ways of life, and the rise of civilization, represented both evolution and revolution: evolution in that—like the emergence of agriculture—they occurred by gradual increment, not dramatic shift; and revolution in that—like food-producing—urban civilization moved societies to a whole new scale and mode of life. Urbanism—life in towns and cities—was generally a concomitant of the emergence of civilizations, or written traditions within class-stratified societies (though, as we will see, civilizations rarely emerged where there were no cities).

In subsequent centuries and millennia, urban civilizations were to evolve in five other centers, largely independently: in Egypt, India, China, Mesoamerica, and Peru. These several paths to urban life followed somewhat parallel courses; and by tracing parallels and divergences between these courses, many scholars have hoped to sort essentials from inessentials, to infer causal connections and recurrent patterns, and hence to discover basic processes of societal evolution.

The rise of urban civilizations not only dramatically changed human life in the great river valleys where urban centers developed. It radically transformed the village farmers at their margins: they became *peasants,* pieces in a wider design, supplying food to the elites and craft specialists in the towns. And the great cultural traditions, the priestly religions and philosophies and literatures that developed in the centers of civilization, penetrated into many parts of the tribal world. Islamic, Hindu, Aztec, and other civilized traditions

121

gave tribal peoples new conceptions of the cosmos and of themselves.

In the sections to follow, we will briefly trace the emergence of urban civilization and the efforts of scholars to distill out general theoretical models. And we will examine the transformations of communities in the hinterlands and on the tribal margins of the civilized world.

21.
Courses Toward Urban Life

The Near East

As village farming ways of life developed across a broad belt of the Near East, the alluvial river valleys were, in the early stages, peripheral. The lower valley of the Tigris-Euphrates was a maze of channels, lagoons, and canebrakes, alternately flooded and arid and with soils rendered infertile by alkaline deposits: hardly an auspicious setting for early farmers.

In this setting the first ventures in irrigation were begun in the Ubaid period, beginning around 4750 B.C. and lasting until 3500 B.C. (Figure 7.1). Waterworks—for irrigation, drainage of swamps, and control of floodwaters—were used to transform the environment; and the organization they demanded was one element in the transformation of the social order that was to come. Perhaps religion was an important shaping force, in the absence of central political organization; the earliest Ubaid structure, at Eridu, is a shrine.

Though early agriculture and irrigation were limited in scale, population clearly increased markedly, and agricultural surpluses supported craft specialists, workers, priests, and merchants. This made possible the construction of increasingly elaborate temples and the conduct of extensive trade. In the late Ubaid period, which lasted until 3500 B.C., a greatly increased population and the expan-

sion of irrigated lands are reflected in elaborate public works and in territorial expansion across the whole alluvial plain of Mesopotamia or Sumer. But there were still no cities: the people remained village farmers. The elaborate temples were probably centers for the redistribution of agricultural surpluses, trade of raw materials and specialized goods, and the planning, construction, and maintenance of waterworks.

By the end of the succeeding Uruk period, around 3200 B.C., rapid changes were ramifying through the social order and urbanization was in full swing. At this stage, true cities (such as Ur), monumental temples, an extensive specialized labor force supported by food surpluses produced in the surrounding hinterlands, elaborate commerce, and the beginnings of written records attest to a dramatic cumulative change in the social order. The development of writing, apparently initially an elaboration of the bookkeeping of commerce, has often been taken as the hallmark of civilization. The latter Uruk period was at best proto-literate. With these elements of emerging civilization came other concomitants: depictions of war chariots show that wars of conquest, and probably slavery, had entered the scene.

The succeeding Early Dynastic period, from 2900 to 2400 B.C., was marked by the emergence of despotic kingship. Though organized state religion remained important, secular rulers had replaced priests as focal points of power and the accumulation and redistribution of wealth. That military force was a central instrument of this power is clear from walls and fortifications. The technology of war was reinforced by early bronze metalworking.

Egypt

In Egypt, village farming had developed as part of a North African complex only indirectly derivative from the early agricultural

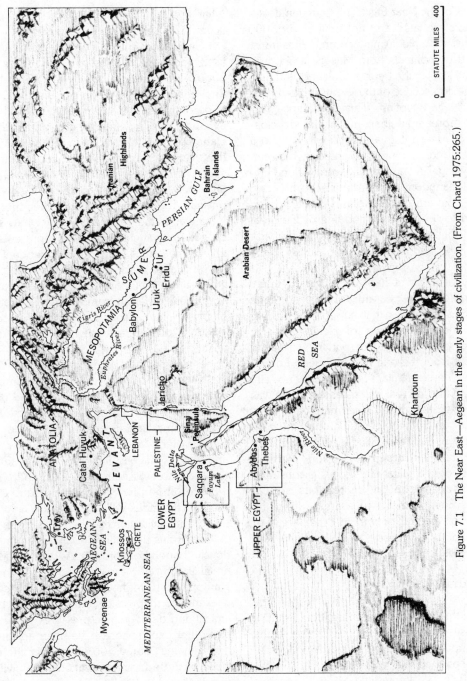

Figure 7.1 The Near East—Aegean in the early stages of civilization. (From Chard 1975:265.)

systems of the Near East. The Egyptian developments are later; and not until about 3000 B.C. were simple farming communities transformed by contacts from Mesopotamia, perhaps by sea via the Persian Gulf and Red Sea. But the florescence of these outside ideas was distinctively Egyptian. This florescence was much more rapid than the earlier development of Mesopotamian civilization. Within a few centuries, perhaps generations, the scattered villages along the Nile were welded into a single kingdom under a pharaoh, the living god. A pattern of cosmic and human order, geared to the seasonal flooding of the great river, was established that was to persist with remarkable conservatism for some 2500 years.

Dynastic Egypt had a totalitarian central government. Its peasantry produced large economic surpluses that supported a lavish court and new classes of clerks, artisans, priests, and officials. This pattern was quite different from the one that had been unfolding in Mesopotamia. There were no city states, in fact, no real urban centers; there was no large-scale industry or commerce or middle class. Everything focused around the god-king: Egypt has been called a court civilization rather than an urban civilization. Perhaps because of its totalitarian rigidity, its conservatism, its centralization of religious secular power, Egypt did not profoundly affect the course of cultural growth in other areas or itself explore new modes of political and economic possibility.

India

On the Indian subcontinent, the formative processes that gave rise to civilization in the great Indus River Valley—what is now Pakistan—spanned the period of roughly 4000 to 2000 B.C. We know little of this Formative period, though village farming communities in what are now Baluchistan and Afghanistan seem likely centers of development.

Civilization emerged in the Indus Valley itself about 2300 B.C. and continued until about 1750 B.C. (Figure 7.2). The best-known sites are the urban centers of Mohenjo-daro and Harappa. These are laid out with avenues in a rectangular grid and with an elaborate matrix of drains and sewers. Citadels, central granaries, and palaces point to strong central government, though the balance between secular and religious power is unclear. It is also unclear whether the vast triangular area of the Indus Valley where similar cultural patterns prevailed represented a unified state or a series of independent city states. Stamp seals, mainly representing animals, are accompanied by a pictographic script quite different from the writing systems of Mesopotamia and Egypt. There is some evidence that literacy may have been quite widespread.

The agricultural economy was relatively similar to that of the Near Eastern complex, with wheat, barley, sesame, peas, and dates as principal food crops, and cotton used for fiber. Domesticated animals included old Near Eastern favorites, but also sebu cattle and water buffaloes. The evidence of subsistence economy, and nature of art and polity, point toward an independent course to civilization in the Indus Valley, not simply a derivative of the civilizations of the Near East.

The Indus civilizations disappeared mysteriously though not abruptly. As with the Mayan civilization of Mesoamerica, the decline of Harappa and Mohenjo-daro has posed a challenge to theorists of cultural process: ecological and demographic pressures, invasion, and other explanations have been advanced and debated. Some 500 years after the collapse of these Indus civilizations, the civilization that was to become the historic heritage of India developed in the Ganges Valley to

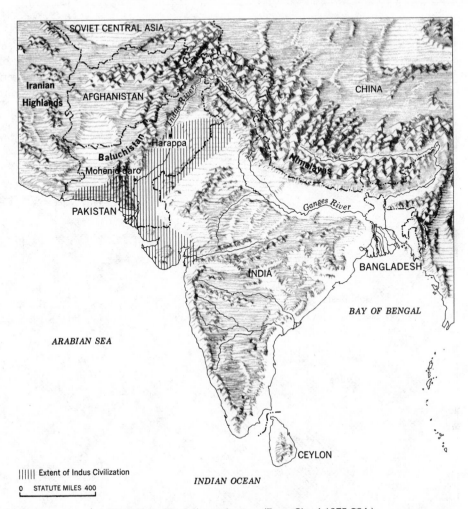

Figure 7.2   The Indus civilization. (From Chard 1975:284.)

the southeast; but that represents a fusion of Persian and eventually Islamic and other influences, as in later periods the streams of civilization flowed into one another and changed each other's courses.

China

In China, the early Yangshao villagers were superseded in the Yellow River Basin by those of the Lungshan period. Larger, more permanent villages, often with earthen walls, point to more intensive farming, though there were no dramatic changes in subsistence economy. There is indirect evidence of social stratification, craft specialization, and the existence of administrators and priests; but each village apparently remained separate and independent. The cereal cultivation of the Yellow River Basin apparently supplanted root crop cultivation across most of what is now China.

In the Yellow River Basin, an incomplete archaeological record does not show yet how Lungshan village farmers were transformed into an urban civilized society. But by 1500 B.C. the Bronze Age Shang Dynasty (Figure 7.3) manifested the full range of elements that mark Old World civilizations; writing, calendrics, bronze metallurgy, a royal establishment, temples, social classes, militarism, trade, and urban centers economically

Figure 7.3   Early Chinese civilization. (From Chard 1975:293.)

dependent on agricultural surpluses from the hinterlands. The pattern was not quite urban in the sense of Ur in Mesopotamia or Mohenjo-daro in the Indus Valley. The walled city centers were originally occupied by an aristocracy, and the bulk of the population lived almost as suburban villagers. But in the course of time, the walls came to incorporate more, including the quarters of craft specialists. The subsistence economy remained essentially Neolithic, with no signs of irrigation. Only the tight administrative structure, apparently some sort of feudal hierarchy with a theocratic king at its apex, enabled the mobilization of agricultural surpluses necessary for civilization to flower.

Though some elements may have diffused from the West, the pattern is distinctively Chinese. Moreover, unlike the florescences of Mesopotamia, Egypt, and the Indus Valley—where civilization ultimately withered and died—the line of Chinese civilization continues essentially unbroken into the twentieth century. Older theorists viewed civilization in China, because it emerged later than in the Near East, as a secondary elaboration of imported patterns. But such theories reflect our own historical parochialism and the false sense of cultural superiority of the age of imperialism.

Mesoamerica

In the New World, the course of civilization ran separately, but again with some striking parallels. The rise of civilization in Mesoamerica has been the focus of concerted archaeological attention for decades, and there is a vast technical literature. We can only sketch a few highlights.

Whether the rise of civilization in the New World was affected by developments in the Old World has been debated for decades. A recent summary of the evidence that might point to significant contact can be found in Riley, Kelley, Pennington, and Rands (1971). But the differences between Old World and New, the limited scope and depth of any influences there may have been, are as striking as the parallels.

The rise of civilization in Mesoamerica began in an unlikely enough setting: a swampy coastal rain forest area near Vera Cruz, Mexico, where Olmec culture emerged as early as 1200 B.C. Writing, the intricate calendric system that was a hallmark of Mesoamerican civilization, and monumental architecture begin with the Olmec. A religious cult, based on a supernatural jaguar-human, seems to have been a driving force; the impact of Olmec religion is reflected in art, cosmology, and calendrics in other early Mesoamerican centers such as Monte Alban in Oaxaca and the Valley of Mexico (Figure 7.4). Though its seminal influence is compelling, neither the processes that generated Olmec civilization nor the reasons for its collapse around 200 B.C. are fully clear. However, recent theorists of cultural process have stressed the importance of high agricultural productivity—despite the absence of irrigation—and trade in the emergence of a non-egalitarian society in the Olmec region.

The locus of cultural development was soon to shift to the great highland valleys of Mexico and Oaxaca, where ecological conditions were ripe for the development of irrigation and the evolution of complex states. Before we turn to these highland valleys, our focus will shift to the south—to the famous Mayan civilization. Though in technology, in subsistence, and in state organization the Maya were surpassed by other American civilizations, in the realms of art and science they represent one of the great peaks of human achievement.

The Formative period of Mayan civilization, spanning the period from 300 B.C. to A.D. 300, was a time of architectural elaboration of ceremonial centers, with a number of

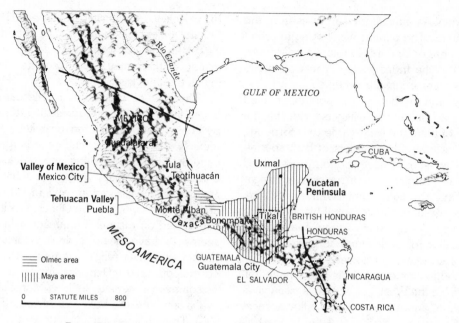

Figure 7.4   Mesoamerican civilizations. (Adapted from Chard 1975:303.)

distinctively Mayan elements such as corbelled vaulting. In this and the succeeding Classic period, the Maya worked out a special elaboration of the Mesoamerican pattern that had taken shape with the Olmec: hieroglyphic writing, calendrics, and ceremonial centers with their pyramids and monumental temples; and a cosmology, mediated by priests and specialists, that included a pantheon of Feathered Serpent, rain god, and other deities. The older picture of Mayan society as a peaceful and harmonious theocracy within which priestly learning, astronomy, and art could flourish has been tempered somewhat in recent years. New evidence suggests that the Maya may have had a highly stratified society ruled by an hereditary aristocracy maintained by suppression and conquest.

Mayan society was in the early stages sustained on an agricultural base of shifting maize cultivation, but in later stages the Maya relied on tree culture, ridged fields, and inten-sive use of marine resources to sustain more concentrated populations. Whether the collapse of Mayan Classic civilization in about A.D. 900 was primarily due to the disintegration of the subsistence base, to external conquest by the militaristic societies gathering momentum to the northwest, or to internal collapse or overthrow of the power structure has been hotly debated; experts remain divided.

To the northwest, in the great Valley of Mexico and in Oaxaca, a course toward urban life continued. Most recent assessments of the evidence strengthen the probability that irrigation systems, under pressure of population increases, were a crucially important factor in the rise of urban centers. The great city of Teotihuacan in the Valley of Mexico covered at its height some eight square miles and had a population of perhaps 100,000. Here, from A.D. 250 to 650, lay the center of power of a region that extended from what is now

Guadalajara as far southeast as Guatemala. The military power and organizational efficiency of this empire ruled through garrison centers has led to comparison with the Romans (even as the Mayans have been called the "Greeks" of Mesoamerica).

Teotihuacan was ruled by an elite aristocracy, though again the balance between theocratic and secular power is difficult to reconstruct. Great markets, specialist artisans, and of course the peasants, bureaucrats, and soldiers that sustained the empire, were elements in the increasingly complex social mosaic. Price (1973) summarizes the evidence that Teotihuacan may have been sustained, and its sociopolitical organization partly shaped, by an irrigation system that greatly expanded productivity in an arid zone.

Teotihuacan declined from its peak around A.D. 500, from some combination of internal, ecological, and external erosions of power and stability. Collapse was marked by the looting and burning of Teotihuacan around 750, but external invasion was, as with the Roman Empire, more symptom than cause of collapse. Pressures by migratory raiders from the north and west may, in the centuries of strength, have helped to maintain power and order.

From succeeding periods of militarism emerged the Toltecs, with their capital at Tula, and then the Mexica, or Aztecs, with their great city of Tenochtitlan. The Aztecs had created a powerful empire that had spread a new cultural order far to the north and south. The florescence of Aztec culture is richly documented in the records of the Spanish conquest. Yet the power of the Aztec empire was not, apparently, fully secure. Despite a complex and in some ways egalitarian social structure, the Aztecs were militarist expansionists who exacted harsh tribute and sacrificed thousands of captives in their ritual blood baths. That Cortes' tiny column was able to overthrow a powerful empire and capture a great city was due in part to the rise in revolt of peoples the Aztecs had held in the bondage of empire.

The ascendancy of the Aztecs partly reflects advances in subsistence production. *Chinampas,* gardens created from the lagoon, were richly fertile and permitted continuous intensive cultivation with high yield; these supported a large urban population in Tenochtitlan.

Peru

In the central Andes of South America, civilization seemed to have emerged centuries later than in Mesoamerica; hence influence from the latter was seen as a probable catalyst. But the apparent point of Mesoamerican influence, seen in the Chavin culture of the highlands, dates no earlier than 1000 B.C.; and recent excavations at Kotosh in the highlands of Peru reveal elaborate masonry temple structures and other signs of emerging civilization that seem to be older than Olmec sites, probably dating to 2000 B.C.

The temple centers of Chavin times reflect the elaboration of a cult in which the jaguar predominated; theocratic control seems likely, but no major shift toward urbanization seems to have occurred. The agricultural base reflects both South American domesticates from highlands and lowlands and maize varieties that seem to be derived from Mexico. The period after Chavin culture faded, the centuries spanning the beginning of the Christian era, was marked by elaboration of irrigation and terrace cultivation and by a concomitant increase in population and settlement size. During the Classic period in Peru, from A.D. 250 to 750, tightly organized states formed and aggressively expanded, waterworks and temple complexes were elaborated, metallurgy was advanced, and various regional art styles flowered. In the following three centuries, a cultural uniformity emerges, perhaps reflecting military expansion and incorporation of regional cultures.

By A.D. 1300, urban centers had emerged along the coast (Figure 7.5). The Chimu kingdom, centered around its exten-

sive capital of Chan-Chan, achieved impressive centralized control, political organization, and public works, including highways and large waterworks for irrigation. In the highlands, meanwhile, a new political force had been emerging: the Inca. From the first dynasty in A.D. 1200, the Inca had expand-

Figure 7.5   Andean civilizations. (From Chard 1975:321.)

ed, and by the fifteenth century had built a tightly organized totalitarian state which controlled a vast area—a state that was to be abruptly confronted and destroyed by the Spaniards under Pizarro.

Interpreting the Rise of Urban Civilizations

From these six "pristine" cases where civilization emerged more or less independently, many scholars have sought to derive general theories. Pioneers such as Wittfogel (1955) and Steward (1949, 1955a, 1960) and more recently scholars such as Adams (1966), Sanders and Price (1968), Trigger (1972), and Krader (1968) have sought to distill general from particular, primary from secondary, cause from effect. The picture is still not clear, and increasingly scholars are wise enough not to expect it to be simple—not to expect the same sequences and the same mechanisms operating in all times and places.

If we look carefully at the details of the "pristine" cases and those derived from them, we are led to be cautious: urbanization (as a mode of spatial organization) varies partly independently of the state (as a mode of social and political organization); and each varies partly independently of civilization (as a mode of cultural elaboration).

Anthropological studies of the origins of urban life have been bedevilled by an undue preoccupation with unilineal evolution and evolutionary typology. Anthropologists . . . have attempted to discover a single process that would explain the development of all complex societies. . . .

The shortcomings of a unilineal approach have not been significantly overcome by token efforts to attribute the origins of civilizations to a limited range of casual factors, such as irrigation for some and trade for others. . . : It is clear, for example,

that while the state is a necessary concomitant of urban life, many states have existed without cities. (Trigger 1972:575—576)

From the sequences we have outlined, some general patterns do emerge. It is worth drawing them together.

1. Early in the shift toward state society and urbanization, populations increased markedly. This process reflects increased agricultural productivity; and often, but not always, it reflects new technological developments, notably irrigation.
2. Increasing populations usually clustered together into larger communities—into towns and eventually cities.
3. Kinship-based and egalitarian social groupings were superseded in importance by emerging *classes,* with power and wealth becoming concentrated in fewer hands. Social stratification increased in inequality, and rigidity.
4. Centralized political authorities emerged. Just how and why must be examined for each area, and the process is not clearly understood. Control of waterworks, redistribution of specialized resources, military operations—all were important in giving rise to central political power, but their balance is not clear.
5. Increased specialization in the division of labor, and the rise of full-time craftsmen, created a greater economic interdependence of populations; concomitantly, food surpluses were produced by and exacted from surrounding rural populations.
6. The urban centers became hubs for radiating systems of political and economic integration. Thus, for instance, specialized resources from different regions could pass into the center and be redistributed.
7. Technological and scientific advance (metallurgy, monumental building, astronomy) and cultural advances (writing, art) were usually achieved, made possible by full-time specialization.
8. Priesthoods, religious cults, and theocratic

organization were characteristic themes in the early stages of civilization and state organization; and early cities often grew up around temple centers.

9. A shift toward militarism and expansionism, toward the incorporation of state religion into expansionist totalitarian society, commonly followed more theocratic states.

For each of these features, some partial exception can be found. Yet the unfolding of these complexes of urbanism, sociopolitical centralization and complex differentiation, and civilization clearly reflects functional interconnectedness.

In good American fashion, we want to know what caused what. Did irrigation cause political centralization? Did population increase cause urbanization? For cultural "evolution," as for biological evolution, that is not the way things are connected in the world: a "domino" theory of change will not do. These are the wrong questions to ask.

Rather, we need a more complex cybernetic model that sees multiple interconnectedness. Societies are like ecosystems. A bit of DDT here and there or a few chemicals will affect the ecology of a lake in ways more complex than we can yet trace. We can well ask what triggers sequences of change, what upsets the established systemic balance of village farming communities in the Yellow River or the coasts of Vera Cruz; but changes once set in motion produce changes which produce changes. Technology, sociopolitical organization, religion, all are interwoven, and in change, they remain interconnected as the design of each is transformed.

But which are prime movers? Which change first? Adams (1966) argues against giving primary weight to ecological and economic factors; he sees changes in the social order as more important in transforming economy than the reverse. Sanders and Price (1968), interpreting the Mesoamerican sequences, argue that ecological factors—especially demographic expansion due to the transformation of subsistence economy—are much more central than Adams had thought. Their interpretation, however, is far from simplistic; it suggests the complexity of interplay between technology, its demographic consequences, and the social ramifications of these. More recently, Price (1973) has assessed the status of Karl Wittfogel's theory of "hydraulic civilizations," where the need to direct and manage construction and control of waterworks led to the development of "Oriental despotism" (Wittfogel 1955). Finding increasingly rich evidence that in some areas complexity and the development of extensive irrigation did go hand in hand, she nonetheless urges against simplistic interpretation:

The which-came-first question is . . . sterile . . . , a pseudo-problem. It is our contention that the expansion of a productive system based on hydraulic agriculture and the attendant social complexity are related in a positive feedback system of cause and effect that is essentially self-reinforcing and self-intensifying. (Price 1973:235)

Even this more sophisticated model of change should not, as Trigger warns (1972), blind us to the extensive variations, multiple patterns, and divergent sequences. When an archaeologist runs into an irrigation canal he should try not to get carried away. Price (1973:243) agrees that "both centralization of authority and internal social differentiation may be responses to a number of different empirical factors." How paths to urban life and state society have been traversed in different times and places, and how diverse or parallel are their courses, will become more clear only when we have much better evidence and more powerful models for interpreting the leavings of the past.

22.

Civilization: Spread and Consequence

From the major centers of civilization spread influences that created numerous secondary centers, and transformed the farming communities of many parts of the world.

The rise of civilization in the Near East and Egypt and its elaboration in Anatolia (the Hittites), the Aegean (the Minoans), and so on, sent shock waves into the hinterlands of Europe, central Asia, and Africa. However, recent evidence suggests that scholars may have been premature in attributing such developments as the megaliths or giant stone blocks in France and Stonehenge in England to influence from the Mediterranean civilizations. New adjustments in radiocarbon dating make it seem likely that some of the European developments may actually have preceded the Mediterranean ones (Renfrew 1973). The famous "astronomical computer" interpretation of Stonehenge (Hawkins 1964) highlights a growing realization that sophisticated advancements in civilization may in some areas have been achieved independently in agrarian societies. Even where early influences from the outside clearly provided a catalyst, the transformation of previously tribal societies into small and even large states often produced distinctive and remarkable cultural elaborations. The early states of black Africa are a good case in point.

To trace the spread of civilization into tribal regions of the world in any detail would require a whole book. Especially where great world religions—notably Hinduism, Buddhism, and Islam—took root in formerly remote agrarian societies, local elaborations and regional histories are complex and fascinating. In Indonesia, for example, Hindu, and later, Islamic, religions blended with old regional cultures to produce a fascinating mosaic, and a historic sequence of kingdoms and empires in miniature. The Indonesian island of Bali, with its blend of traditional, Hindu, and Islamic elements into a unique and fascinating way of life, has long commanded anthropological interest. Similarly, Buddhism in Ceylon—grafted into an old South Indian social system which is itself transformed by Hindu ideologies of caste and religion, and with ancient animistic elements—has produced a fascinating cultural composite. So too in marginal India, in Burma, in Thailand, in Tibet have the great civilizations taken local root and flowered in distinctive ways.

Anthropologists studying in many areas of the world—whether in remote Afghanistan or village India or Indochina or Muslim Mindanao in the Philippines—find themselves in communities that are not without history, not self-contained culturally, not independent Neolithic ventures in human possibility. These peoples follow—in local ways with old local roots—ideologies and religions first elaborated thousands of miles away by other peoples with very different cultures.

Especially where the community an anthropologist studies is part of a wider society that has a literate stream of historical, philosophical, and religious thought, one may talk of a "Great Tradition" and "Little Tradition" (the latter, the local pattern of custom and belief of local area and community). We will turn in Chapter 23 to the articulation of Great and Little Traditions and to the problems of understanding the cultural whole from close-up views of its fragmented local elements.

When urban centers began to crystallize, with their priests, bureaucrats, craftsmen, and privileged elite, the life of the farmer in his rural village was forever transformed. Whether particular urbanites specialized in producing mystical revelations, ornamentation for the homes of the rich, or bureaucratic order and confusion, their products could not be eaten. Their food had to come from rural farmers, in the form of taxes, tribute, spoils, or market goods. And the farmer was thus no longer merely self-sufficient, no longer in charge of his own destiny: he had become a peasant.

Peasants, who have been carrying on life at the periphery of urban centers since the rise of early civilizations—but whose ways of life were not exotic and romantic enought to capture the attention of Enlightenment philosophers or early anthropologists questing for "primitives"—have belatedly commanded attention. "The peasant is an immemorial figure on the world social landscape, but anthropology noticed him only recently" (Geertz 1962:1). In the 1950s and 1960s, peasants have received much attention, as we will see in Chapter 22. Peasants have come to center stage in anthropology, to take their place with tribesmen, who increasingly are themselves donning peasant garb. (The next transformation of consciousness is beginning; we are on the verge of noticing that their wives have been standing next to them all along.)

At this stage, our evolutionary sketch of human biology and the growth of culture has brought us toward the present. We will turn shortly to a comparative view of the ways of life humans explored in tribal societies, ways that are our major source in understanding human diversity. But first, we need to refine our ways of looking at humans, their ideas, and their groups.

CULTURE, SOCIETY, AND THE INDIVIDUAL

Part 2

The processes whereby hominids became human, and whereby their cultural patterns developed and diversified, have been sketched. But before we can wisely interpret these diverse cultural ways to arrive at some heightened conception of the human condition, or turn with greater insight to the dilemmas of the latter twentieth century, we need better tools for thinking.

A fairly general understanding of what culture and society are has sufficed so far in setting out how humans evolved and how their ways of life developed. We now need to sharpen these tools of understanding. We need, in short, the outlines of a theory for understanding humans-in-groups.

In the next five chapters, we will examine and use anthropology's conceptual tool kit. In doing so, we will equip ourselves to think about tribal peoples in broad comparative perspective and to reflect wisely on the challenges and problems of the present.

CULTURE AND PEOPLE
Some Basic Concepts

8

We have talked in preceding chapters about the evolution of culture: about the emergence of cultural man from protocultural hominid and about the development and diversification of the ways of life of hunter-gatherer, tribesman, urban artisan, and peasant. In the process, we have talked about the organization of society and how it has progressively been transferred.

We have reached a state now where greater precision is needed if understanding is to deepen. We need to know more clearly what social scientists mean by "culture" and "society," and how the two are related. In this chapter and the next four, a way of thinking about individuals and groups, ideas and meanings, and stability and change will be developed. This way of thinking can then be brought to bear on tribal and modern societies, in broadest comparative perspective, in hopes of obtaining some clear vision of what humans are and can be.

Anthropologists, like other social scientists, are far from agreement on how best to conceptualize the complex facets of social life. The way of thinking about culture, society, and the individual that we will sketch here builds on a substantial consensus about general principles among such recent theorists as Geertz, Lévi-Strauss, and Goodenough. We will also glimpse in passing several issues, more philosophical than substantive, that divide these scholars. This theoretical approach views the realm of ideas, the force of symbols, as centrally important in shaping human behavior—not simply as secondary reflections of the material conditions of social life. The reader should be forewarned that not all anthropologists agree with this view (see, for example, Harris 1971). Alternative theories will be noted in Chapter 12. But to give them equal stress would leave us with all-purpose conceptual tools that do not do any jobs very well.

23.
The Anthropological Concept of Culture

The anthropological concept of culture has been one of the most important and influential ideas in twentieth-century thought. Usage of the term "culture" adopted by nineteenth-century anthropologists has spread to other fields of thought with profound impact, and it is now commonplace for humanists and other social scientists to speak, say, of "Japanese culture."

Yet, paradoxically, the notion of culture implied in such usages has proven too broad and too blunt for carving out the essential elements in human behavior. The reaction of some scholars has been to abandon the term as a central conceptual tool; the response of others has been to sharpen and narrow the instrument to render it more precise.

"Culture" in the usage of anthropology does not, of course, mean cultivation in the arts and social graces. It refers, rather, to learned, accumulated experience. A culture—say, Japanese culture—refers to those socially transmitted patterns for behavior characteristic of a particular social group.

Anthropologists have not been totally precise, or totally consistent, in their usages of this crucial concept. Some representative attempts at definition reveal different facets of culture:

That complex whole which includes knowledge, belief, art, morals, law, custom, and any other capabilities and habits acquired by man as a member of society. (Tylor 1871)

The sum total of knowledge, attitudes and habitual behavior patterns shared and transmitted by the members of a particular society. (Linton 1940)

[All the] historically created designs for living, explicit and implicit, rational, irrational, and nonrational, which exist at any given time as potential guides for the behavior of man. (Kluckhohn and Kelly 1945)

The mass of learned and transmitted motor reactions, habits, techniques, ideas, and values—and the behavior they induce. (Kroeber 1948)

The man-made part of the environment. (Herskovits 1955)

Patterns, explicit and implicit, of and for behavior acquired and transmitted by symbols, constituting the distinctive achievement of human groups, including their embodiments in artifacts. (Kroeber and Kluckhohn 1952)

Goodenough (1957, 1961) has recently argued that most such definitions and usages have blurred a crucial distinction between patterns *for* behavior and patterns *of* behavior. In fact, Goodenough says, anthropologists have been talking about two quite different orders of things when they have used the term "culture"—and too often they have moved back and forth between the two sorts of meanings. First, "culture" has been used to refer to the "pattern of life within a community—the regularly recurring activities and material and social arrangements" characteristic of a particular human group (Goodenough 1961:521). In this sense, "culture" has referred to the realm of observable phenomena, of things and events "out there" in the world. Second, "culture" has been used to refer to the organized system of knowledge and belief whereby a people structure their experience and perceptions, formulate acts, and choose between alternatives. This sense of "culture" refers to the realm of ideas.

When archaeologists talk about the culture of an early Near Eastern farming community as an adaptive system, they are using the concept in its first sense. It is the way-of-life-in-ecosystem characteristic of a particular people: "Culture is all those means whose forms are not under genetic control which serve to adjust individuals and groups within their ecological communities" (Binford

1968:323). We will, when the need arises, use the cumbersome term *sociocultural system* to refer to the pattern of residence, resource exploitation, and so on, characteristic of a people. We need a narrower sense of "culture" as an *ideational* system.

We will use "culture" to refer to systems of shared ideas, to the conceptual designs, the shared systems of meaning, that underlie the ways in which a people live. Culture, so defined, refers to what humans *learn,* not what they do and make. As Goodenough (1961:522) expresses it, this knowledge provides "standards for deciding what is, . . . for deciding what can be, . . . for deciding how one *feels* about it, . . . for deciding what to do about it, and . . . for deciding how to go about doing it."

This ideational notion of culture is not radically new. For example, Kluckhohn and Kelly's 1945 definition of culture in terms of "designs for living" follows a similar course. Nor is it without philosophical problems. There are many who shrink from postulating such "mentalistic" entities. Yet there is a strong and powerful precedent, as we will see, from the study of language. Linguists have made impressive advances by distinguishing language, as a conceptual code, from speech, the overt behavior based on that code. As in any question of scientific conceptualization, the ultimate test of a definition or distinction lies in what you can do with it. It is too early to be sure that an ideational concept of culture will in the long run be a valuable and workable analytical tool; but at present it is clearing promising paths into little-charted territory.

An initial difficulty in the study of culture is that we are not in the habit of analyzing cultural patterns, and seldom are we even aware of them. It is as though we—or the people of any other society—grow up perceiving the world through glasses with distorting lenses. The things, events, and relationships we assume to be "out there" are in fact filtered through this perceptual screen. The first reaction, inevitably, on encountering people who wear a different kind of glasses is to dismiss their behavior as strange or wrong. To view other peoples' ways of life in terms of our own cultural glasses is called *ethnocentrism.* Becoming conscious of, and analytic about, our own cultural glasses is a painful business. We do best by learning about other people's glasses. Although we can never take our glasses off to find out what the world is "really like," or try looking through anyone else's without ours on as well, we can at least learn a good deal about our own prescription.

With some mental effort we can begin to become conscious of the codes that normally lie hidden beneath our everyday behavior. Consider the mental operations you perform when you go into an unfamiliar supermarket with a shopping list. You have a generalized mental guide to the sections a supermarket will have: one with fresh fruits and vegetables, one with bread, one with fresh meats, one with ice creams and frozen desserts, and so on. On the shelves somewhere will be spices; and somewhere among the canned fruits and vegetables one is likely to find canned juices. So a first challenge in an unfamiliar supermarket is to orient yourself, perhaps simply by traversing the aisles with your shopping cart, picking out the items you are looking for as you pass them. In all this, you are matching your set of mental categories, your generalized mental guidebook, against the one actually used in laying out this supermarket.[1]

But when your first pass through is finished, you are likely still to have some items on your list: perhaps the yogurt, which was not next to the milk where you expected to find it, and the Worcestershire sauce, which was not next to the ketchup, where you

---

[1] Large supermarket chains have systematic designs, aimed not at your convenience but at your money.

looked. You look at their list of categories on the wall, if there is one, comparing their scheme with yours and wondering how they are classifying the items you are looking for. And then there is the chop suey or enchillada sauce, which must be in some exotic food section you haven't found. . . .

In all this, you are drawing on a vastly intricate system of knowledge that is stored in your brain but is only partly accessible to your consciousness. The knowledge in your mental guidebook is not quite like that of any other shopper. But your knowledge and theirs are sufficiently similar that you avoid bumping into one another most of the time, and you avoid violating implicit codes of physical intimacy, eye contact, and orientation in space—as well as eventually finding the groceries you are looking for.

When it comes to going through a queue at the checkout stand, another set of implicit codes comes into play. And finally, your transaction with the cashier involves a complex set of shared understandings. (You can perceive such implicit rules more vividly if you deliberately break them and watch the reactions: try putting pebbles down on the checkstand counter instead of money, or bargain with the cashier by offering 50 cents for a 79 cent tube of toothpaste.)

Consider another set of American codes in action. Smith, a junior executive, comes into the office of Jones, his senior boss. Smith is a young man on his way up, and plays golf with Jones on Saturday. He refers to "Mr. Jones" to the secretary, but once inside Jones' office he addresses his boss as "Ed"—therby affirming their close personal relationship.

Smith may well shift to "Mr. Jones" if the secretary comes into the office, then back to "Ed." Now Roberts, another junior executive equivalent in rank to Smith, comes in. But he does not play golf with Jones or see him socially, and does not address him by his first name. At this point, with Roberts addressing the boss as "Mr. Jones," Smith may either shift to "Mr. Jones" or keep calling the boss "Ed." So intricate are these normally unconscious codes, yet so well understood by all, that Roberts, Jones, and Smith all know precisely what Smith is communicating by making either choice: either formality and equal status with Roberts (by "Mr. Jones") or competitive advantage and "oneupmanship" (by "Ed").

Project from these examples to the vast body of other shared understandings we need in order to eat in a restaurant, drive in traffic, or play a game of tennis—and what the anthropologist means by culture will begin to come into view.

Culture consists not of things and events that we can observe, count, and measure: it consists of shared ideas and meanings. Clifford Geertz, borrowing from the philosopher Gilbert Ryle, provides an interesting example. Consider a wink and an involuntary eye twitch. As physical behaviors, they may be identical: measuring them will not distinguish the two. One is a signal, in a code of meanings Americans share (but which presumably would be unintelligible to Eskimos or Australian Aborigines); the other is not. Even more subtle meaning is conveyed by a second winker who derides the first for winking badly by producing a burlesque, intentionally inept, wink (Geertz 1973a:6—7). Only in a universe of shared meaning do physical sounds and events become intelligible and convey information.

Recall the episode of the Bulgarian hostess feeding her Asian guest into oblivion, with which the book began. A Bulgarian hostess serving a second or third helping is not part of Bulgarian culture; but the conceptual principles that lie behind her acts, the patterns of meaning that make them intelligible, are. Bulgarian culture is something learned, something in the minds of Bulgarians, and thus it cannot be studied or observed directly. Nor could our Bulgarian woman tell us all the premises and principles on which her behavior is based. Many are as hidden from her perception as they are from ours.

When we say that Bulgarian culture is an ideational system, that it is manifest in the minds of Bulgarians, we raise a thorny philosophical issue. Does that mean that a culture is ultimately a psychological system that exists in individual minds? Is Bulgarian culture "in the heads" of individual Bulgarians? Does Bulgarian culture consist of some common denominator of what individual Bulgarians know?

Goodenough would say that it does—and many of his colleagues would agree. But that gets us into sticky philosophical questions. Geertz argues that cultural meanings are public, and transcend their realization in individual minds. A code for communicating exists in a sense that goes beyond any individual's knowledge of it. A Beethoven quartet exists in a sense that transcends individuals knowing it, performing it, or printing the score.

Yet to describe a shared code of meanings and behaviors as transcending individual minds has its dangers as well. For cultures are the cumulative creations of human individuals; cultures, as systems of communication, are shaped and constrained by how individuals learn, think, and understand—hence by structures of mind and brain. And not all individuals share identical conceptions of their culture. Here the example of the Beethoven quartet may mislead us, because as a written composition it has a standard and enduring formal pattern regardless of who knows or performs it. But for several hundred thousand years before the invention of writing, human cultures existed only in varying, changing, and partial realizations in the minds of individuals; and that has been true of music and oral literature, as well as agricultural knowledge and gestural codes such as winking. Diversity

of cultural codes, alternative forms of knowledge and belief, may well be necessary if adaptive change is to occur; and though Beethoven quartets do not change, cultures do.

In one sense Geertz is right: meanings that are shared and public by that fact transcend private worlds of thought and belief. From the perspective of any individual actor on the social stage, the play exists above and beyond his playing of his part. There is a kind of collective magic whereby shared beliefs and symbols have life of their own, whereby shared consciousness transcends individuals' experience. Why a shared understanding between two human beings is more than the sum of its two parts is a basic riddle, perhaps *the* basic riddle, of human social life. After centuries of Western social thought, it remains mysterious.

Why worry about culture at all, if it leads us into a never-never land of unobservables and shadowy mentalistic formulations? Some scholars believe that anthropologists should focus on *behavior,* on things observable and measurable, and leave "the mind" to philosophers.

A number of major issues are at stake here, and philosophers of science are far from agreed on them. Some who are prepared to talk about culture in this ideational sense regard it simply as a hypothetical abstraction that makes sense of what people are observed to do and say. There is then no sense asking whether such a construct is "true" or "real"—only whether or not it works. If we are of another persuasion, cultural codes "really exist," and if we are clever and patient enough we can find out what they are like.

To clarify the issues, we must be clear what we mean by saying that a culture—say, Hopi Indian culture—is an *abstraction*. First of all, a culture is a *composite*. No single Hopi knows all aspects of the way of life of his or her people, because each person participates in only some segments of the network that is Hopi society. Specialists in ritual or technology will know elements of their culture that others will not; men and women will know different segments of their cultural code. The anthropological description of Hopi culture puts together into a composite these various segments of the code.

Second, a culture is a generalization. No two Hopi will have precisely the same knowledge of their way of life, so what we describe as common to all of them is in one sense a kind of common denominator, more general—and thus abstract—than the detailed variants of each Hopi.

But a culture is more than a mere common denominator, since it is an idealized standard version of the composite cultural knowledge of individuals, a version in some respects different from any individual's. Anthropologists, of course, have no magical way of getting inside Hopi heads to discover what individuals know, believe, and assume about their world; but then individual Hopi Indians cannot do that with one another. They, like the anthropologist, can only infer what other people know and think from what they say and do.

Hopi culture—or particularly the culture of a large-scale complex society such as Japan—is an abstraction in a third sense. Some elements of the code will be shared by all or most Japanese, and enable farmers to interact with city dwellers and tradesmen to interact with executives. Other elements will be common to farmers, or to particular kinds of farmers, or to farmers in a particular community. Furthermore, a farmer and a businessman in a particular community will share some elements of the code that neither shares with his counterparts in neighboring communities. A view of culture as an ideational code enables the anthropologist to deal effectively with such variations, much as a linguist does

in dealing with dialects. One can, where relevant, distinguish the "subcultures" of particular social strata, occupational groups, or localities. These naturally account in greater detail for events on this limited scale, just as a study of some regional dialect accounts in some detail for pronunciation, idioms, and vocabulary in the particular area. Where one's concern is more general, one can speak of the common code of which these are variant versions—the Japanese language, or Japanese culture. In each case, it is concern with some particular problem or phenomenon, on a particular scale, that determines which level of the code one describes.

Still, one might object, why do we have to talk about this shadowy hypothetical entity culture, which by definition we can never observe or record? Why can one not simply study acts and events in a social system without invoking a metaphysical entity like culture? This, surely, marks the way toward a precise science of human behavior. Or does it?

There are compelling reasons why we cannot understand human behavior without postulating an ideational code beneath it. We can measure to our hearts' content without capturing the meanings of wink and burlesqued wink and distinguishing them from twitch. The most compelling reasons to interpret social action in terms of ideational codes, not simply to analyze the stream of behavior, come from the study of language. We will see in the next chapter that much of what we perceive in the world, and cloak with meaning, is not in the physical world at all. We put it there, in our "mind's eye."

Before we refine and deepen our understanding of culture in the next four chapters, we need to add other tools to our conceptual inventory; we need to see how culture relates to society, and how cultural structure and social structure are interwoven.

24.
The Relation of Culture to Society

If an ideational concept of culture is to help us make clearer sense of human life, we need to counterbalance it with a clear notion of what society and social system mean.

We cannot talk about Hopi Indians as members of a culture. They are members of a *population* distinct from surrounding populations in a number of ways: they live in separate communities, speak a common language, share the same body of customs, and interact with one another more closely and more often (at least in aboriginal times) than with outsiders. Hopi Indians share or participate in a culture. They are *members of a society*.

A society is a population distinguished in such ways—usually by territorial separation and a shared language and culture—from those around it. Just as a culture is an abstraction, so is a society. For Hopi society is an enduring aggregate that remains despite the birth and death of individual members.

A society is a special kind of *social system*. A social system is an aggregate of people who recurrently interact with one another. It can be as small as a family; it can be a dormitory or a factory; or it can be an entire society. A social system is such an aggregate of people viewed through a special kind of analytical lens: it is seen as having a *social structure,* as comprising a set of positions connected by recurrent patterns of interaction.

As Geertz puts it, culture is "an ordered system of meaning and of symbols, in terms of which social interaction takes place"; and a social system is "the pattern of social interaction itself."

On the [cultural] level there is the framework of beliefs, expressive symbols, and values in terms of which individuals define their world, express their feelings, and make their judgments; on the [social] level there is the ongoing process of interactive behavior, whose persistent form we call social structure. Culture is the fabric of meaning in terms of which human beings interpret their experience and guide their action; social structure is the form that action takes, the actually existing network of social relations. Culture and social structure are then but different abstractions from the same phenomena. (1957:33—34)

Social structure—or, as some would call it, social organization—is an abstraction from patterns of actual behaviors and events—a web of relationships; culture refers to systems of ideas (but of course we can only infer these from behaviors and events). In §38 we will return to the relationship between social and cultural facets of human life.

Here an analogy may make the contrast more clear. Imagine that, as an experiment, we set eight chairs in a circle. Four chairs are black, four are white, and the chairs are numbered, as in Figure 8.1. We give each of the eight participants an instruction that tells what

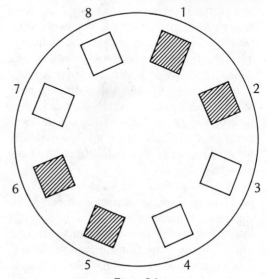

Figure 8.1.

kind of chair to sit in and what to do while sitting in it.

A. White Even-Numbered Chair: Try to impress the person two seats to your right with your knowledge of music, poetry, or art.

B. White Odd-Numbered Chair: Disagree with everything the person on your left says.

C. Black Even-Numbered Chair: The person two seats to your left may not know what he is talking about, but flatter him along and agree with whatever he says.

D. Black Odd-Numbered Chair: Try to change the topic of conversation.

When we turn our eight participants loose, the results can be at least roughly anticipated (hopefully the chairs will not be used as weapons). However, there are two quite different kinds of generalizations that we can make about the results of the experiment. First, we can look at the patterns of interaction that take place. It is immediately clear that the occupants of chairs 1 to 4 and 5 to 8 form two largely separate social systems (however small scale). Only the occupants of chairs 1 and 5 would intrude into both sides. (Had our instruction to them been to change the topic of conversation to their left, the two groups would have been fully separate.) The flow of interaction, of agreement and disagreement, would crystallize in particular patterns (even in repetitions of the same experiment), even though the actual conversations would vary widely. We could sort out *roles* and social positions; and abstracting from these patterns, we could describe the social structure of our experimental groups.

A second mode of description would simply be to say that the instructions specified the rules of the game; and that the patterns of interaction represented expressions of a set of "rules" about what to do in what positions. The *instructions* would constitute the special culture of the group. Further, we could note that if we increased the number of chairs or shifted the arrangement of colors, while keeping the instructions the same, the social structure would change while the culture remained the same.

Neither mode of analysis is intrinsically better than the other. Each illuminates some facets of the same events. As long as the cultural "rules of the game" are appropriate to deal with the kinds of social arrangements and situations people encounter—as they are in the isolated tribal groups where anthropologists devised their conceptual tools—a description of cultural structure often makes more clear sense of what happens than a description of social structure. Sociologists, on the other hand, have emphasized descriptions of social structure: partly because in studying their own society they can take cultural principles for granted, and partly because in complex modern societies ordered social life goes on despite great diversity in cultural codes. In fact, what we badly need, and are exploring, are ways to show both facets, and their interrelationship, at once. For especially in a world of rapid change, the cultural order and patterns of social organization slip far out of fit with one another. We will see in §78 Geertz's analysis of such a case, where he usefully underlines the inadequacies of describing either the social order or the cultural order without showing the interplay between them.

The challenge of interpreting the interplay between social system and patterns of culture is vividly expressed by another leading theorist, Victor Turner, in his reflections of Mukanda, an initiation ritual of the Ndembu of Zambia:

A simile that occurred to me likened the cultural structure of Mukanda to a musical score, and its performers to an orchestra. I wanted to find some way of expressing and analyzing the dynamic interdependence of score and orchestra manifested in the unique performance. Furthermore, I wanted to find a theoretical framework which would have enabled me to understand why it was that certain persons and sections of the orchestra were obviously out of sympathy with the conductor or with one another, though all were obviously skilled musicians, and well rehearsed in the details of the score. Neither the properties of the orchestra qua social group, nor the properties of the score, taken in isolation from one another seemed able to account fully for the observed behavior, the hesitancies in certain passages, the lapses in rapport between conductor and strings, or the exchanged grimaces and sympathetic smiles between performers. (Turner 1968a:135—136)

The quest for a way of understanding the interplay between orchestra and score—between social system and culture—so as to give a wider understanding of social processes has been a major theme in recent anthropology.

To deepen our understanding of how cultural knowledge is structured, and how human behavior can best be understood, it is useful to turn at this stage to the study of language: for linguists, exploring the fantastically complex knowledge that underlies our everyday abilities to speak and understand, have learned much that can guide us.

LANGUAGE AND COMMUNICATION

9

Human uniqueness in the animal kingdom, as we have seen, arises largely from our capacity to build and manipulate symbols. It is language that allows humans to transcend many of the limitations imposed by biology, to build cultural models of their world and transmit them across generations.

To learn about humans and their nature, we must learn about language. This is not simply because language is what makes our culture possible and what makes us unique in nature. Language is also the keystone of culture itself: a largely unconscious but highly complex system of "rules" and designs whereby knowledge about the world and principles for action are coded. It is also the best explored and mapped segment of culture, and hence provides a set of crucial clues about how humans think and perceive and how what they know and believe is ordered.

Yet for all the recent efforts to analyze how humans speak and understand speech, much remains mysterious and obscure; and the mysteries about language may tell us as much about humans as do theories of grammar.

When we talk to one another, we accomplish a commonplace miracle: commonplace because we do it so effortlessly and so often; miraculous because *how* we do it remains largely a mystery, despite a profusion of recent research.

Consider a few facets of what we do in speaking to and understanding one another.

First, we do not simply produce and understand sentences we have heard before. We *create* sentences we have never heard, many of which have never been used by anyone before.

Second, deciphering the meaning of sentences we hear—something we accomplish almost instantly—is an immensely complex analytical feat. Consider these two English sentences:

Time flies like an arrow.
Fruit flies like bananas.

Despite the contrived outward similarities between the two, we can almost instantly perceive the radically different patterns of meaning they convey.

Third, though the actual sounds of speech are unbroken, continuous sequences, we hear them as strings of distinct "blocks" of sound. And though no two repetitions of the same word or sentence are acoustically the same, we perceive them as if they were.

Fourth, when we listen to speech sounds, we do not simply select from these sounds the elements and features that are relevant and discard the rest. We create the sentences we hear out of imperfect sequences of sounds that are often incomplete or partly garbled. The listener reconstitutes the design of the sentence in his mind, even though he must fill in the missing pieces; and he can do that only by perceiving its structure.

Finally, one's knowledge of one's language is almost entirely hidden from consciousness.

These facets of speaking and understanding profoundly shape the way linguists approach language. If linguists are to grasp and analyze how humans achieve the commonplace miracle of speaking and understanding speech, they must probe beneath outward, observable behavior. They must postulate, for the speaker and listener, a code the communicants share. Without postulating such an underlying code or theory in the minds of their subjects, linguists could analyze what speakers *did* say—but they could not account for what they *could* say. They could not account for the way a speaker creates sentences, many of which he or she has never heard; they could not account for our ability to decode complicated sentences so as to grasp their meaning; and they could not account for the way one creates a sentence design in one's mind out of the muddled and often incomplete sounds one hears.

Every child learning his or her language must likewise use a limited and imperfect sample of the speech of the adults he grows up with to arrive at a "theory" (hidden from his consciousness) of the code they are using. It is this theory, more or less shared by all speakers of a language, that linguists seek to describe. The contrast between actual speaking and the underlying code was first clearly drawn by de Saussure (1916) in a distinction between *le parole* ("speech") and *la langue* ("language"): the first, actual speech behavior; the second, the code underlying it. More recently, Noam Chomsky has phrased this as a contrast between *performance* and *competence*.

Competence is the knowledge of the language (which by definition the linguist can never observe directly) an idealized speaker-hearer—that is, one who knows the language completely—draws on to produce sentences and understand them. Performance is actual speech behavior, with its pauses, "hemming and hawing," false starts, ungrammatical utterances, and endless variability. Here we will refer to this contrast as that between competence and performance; or, more generally, simply as the contrast between *language* (the conceptual code) and *speech* (its manifestation in actual behavior and sound).

Note at this stage that our distinction between language and speech parallels the one we drew in the last chapter between culture and behavior. Linguistic competence can be seen as one element of "cultural competence." To those who would argue (of speaking or other social behavior) that we should concentrate on observable behavior, and not postulate slippery and metaphysical-sounding mental codes as lying behind acts, the evidence from language is devastating (Chomsky 1959).

The new linguistics of the 1960s and 1970s, generally known as *transformational linguistics,* has been revolutionary in its goals and in the understanding of linguistic structure that it has opened. For linguists have taken up the challenge of describing formally—in explicit rules and symbols—how linguistic competence is organized. From their mappings, we have begun to see a magnificently complex design underlying the seeming diversity of languages.

The new linguistics is complicated, formal, forbidding. But a simplified model of what linguists are discovering has exciting implications for understanding other realms of human behavior, and well rewards the time spent in decipherment.

To go beyond a simplified model here would convey the impression that linguists know more, and are more in agreement, about the structure of language and the process of speaking than is the case. The mysteries of speaking—a commonplace miracle that most of us take for granted—loom large despite impressive progress. Before we look in broad outline at language structure, a recent semiserious remark by a linguist exploring the frontier will give useful caution: "The life expectancy of a theory in linguistics is seventeen minutes, except late on Friday afternoons." A more serious assessment of where we stand in understanding language will usefully introduce our sketch of what has been learned so far:

Transformational work in grammar has revealed the vastness, intricacy, and underlying obscurity of the system involved . . . [and] the primitiveness and semi-contentlessness of any so far worked out conception of grammar. . . .

We can . . . see with increasing clarity the quite incredible scope of human grammar and correspondingly the limitations of any set of principles that can be posited today to reconstruct this system. (Postal 1972)

25.
The Structure of Language

In the years since Noam Chomsky burst on the linguistic world with his book *Syntactic Structures* (1957), wrecking old theories and launching a new one, linguistics has moved to the forefront of scientific concern. Computer scientists, mathematicians, psychologists, neurologists, and many others have been drawn to the study of language; ranks of linguists have proliferated and new journals have flourished. How languages are organized, how children acquire linguistic competence, how the brain processes speech, have become burning issues on the frontiers of science. Linguistics is no longer an arcane concern of strange academics who mumble in Tibetan and endlessly tinker with obscure grammatical crossword puzzles.

Anthropologists used to be among the rare few who were interested in these crossword puzzles (one or two could even mumble back in Tibetan). Yet now that linguistics has become a burgeoning international scientific concern, anthropologists have mainly lost touch with this area of study; many seem not to have noticed that a revolution has taken place.

Linguists are not trying to understand everything about language. Because the problems and mysteries are so vast, they have narrowed their goals a good deal. What they are attempting to do is understand the chain of operations that connect the sounds of sentences with their meanings. These operations can be conceived as mental operations if we take into account two things: (1) linguists have no direct access to what goes on in people's minds and therefore can only build formal models or analogues of what *might* go on; and (2) in actually speaking and understanding language, users may use many shortcuts, canned sequences, and so on— that is a matter of performance.

A language can be thought of as comprising a potentially infinite number of sentences.[1] Each sentence consists of a sequence of sounds, and it expresses a proposition (makes a statement, poses a question, and so on). That is, it expresses a *meaning*, a set of relationships. For example, "John hit the ball" proposes a relationship between subject—John—and object—ball. What linguists are trying to do can be conceived the following way. Imagine that the *sound sequences* grammatically possible in a language are put in pile A and all the meanings or propositions they express are put in a separate pile B. The task linguists have set for themselves is to write a set of formal rules—a *grammar*—that accomplishes the following things:

1. Connects each sound sequence in set A with the matching meaning or proposition in set B.
2. Makes fully explicit each successive logical step required to convert a sound sequence progressively into its corresponding meaning (or vice versa, to convert a meaning into a corresponding sound sequence; the rules can be thought of as working in either direction). That is, the connection between each member of set A and the corresponding member of set B must be fully specified in explicit formal rules, so that no intervening intuitive jumps are needed. It is these jumps that the linguist seeks to understand.
3. Finally, the rules must account for why most conceivable combinations of the sounds and

words in a language do not correspond to *any* member of set B: they are meaningless or ungrammatical, as with our "Running dog brown the is."

This phrasing enables us to see more clearly that some members of set A can be paired with two or more different members of set B; that is, their meanings are ambiguous. "Flying airplanes can be dangerous" can warn us either against piloting airplanes or against getting in the way of them. "Susan took John's coat off" can mean either that Susan took John's coat off John or that she took it off herself. "Sam almost killed Pete" may mean that Pete was gravely wounded or that Pete was narrowly missed. Notice also that two or more sentences can express the same meaning (so that two or more members of set A correspond to one member of set B): "Cannibals ate John" = "John was eaten by cannibals."

As we have noted, a grammar, while accounting for all the sentences that are linguistically possible, also filters out and rejects sentences that are linguistically impossible. Some are discarded because they don't follow grammatical rules; others, because the meanings they express are internally contradictory (such as Chomsky's famous "Colorless ideas sleep furiously"). Sometimes the line is hard to draw: "My goldfish, who believes that I'm a fool, enjoys tormenting me" is ungrammatical unless you have certain beliefs about the mental powers of goldfish; but most speakers would accept the sentence if you plugged in "cat" instead of "goldfish" (Lakoff 1971:332).

This emphasis on whether sentences are grammatical, and on what sentences mean, has an interesting methodological implication: it forces the linguist to rely very heavily on native speakers' *intuitions about sentences*. They cannot simply observe speech behavior.

---

[1]However, the grammatically possible sentences represent only a tiny fraction of the possible arrangements of the words of the language. "Running dog brown the is" is not an English sentence.

This quest for a formal grammar of linguistic competence is much more limited than trying to understand how speakers speak and how hearers hear. These are questions of performance. It is assumed that speakers and hearers *draw on* or *apply* their competence, their knowledge of the language, in some way. But they doubtless use many shortcuts, probabilistic strategies, and canned phrases in speech behavior; they use many nonlinguistic cues, such as facial expression and tone of voice, and they are affected by nonlinguistic factors such as memory capacity and extraneous noise. Linguists assume that the grammatical knowledge they seek to describe will form part of an ultimate theory of linguistic performance.

Linguists have often been misunderstood as trying to write rules describing the ways speakers "generate" sentences. Though the term "generative grammar" has been used to describe the new linguistics, what a grammar "generates" is the relationship between paired patterns of meaning and sound. This new linguistics pioneered by Chomsky is most often called "transformational" (though like "generative," that label is increasingly misleading, as we will see).

It might seem most logical, in looking at the chain that connects the sound pattern of sentences with their meanings, to start at one end or the other. It turns out to be easiest for us to begin where Chomsky did: in the middle.

Syntax

Transformational linguistics has given a new look to an idea that dates back to the rationalist philosophers of the Enlightenment: that the grammatical design of a sentence has an outer face and an inner face. The outer face is the sequence of words (and wordlike fragments, such as "-ing"):

John was eaten by cannibals.
John was drunk by midnight.

The inner face is the pattern of logical relations the sentence expresses, through which its meaning is interpreted. When we hear sentences, we almost instantly and quite unconsciously decode the outer sequences into the underlying structures: only a contrived twister like "fruit flies like bananas" or an ambiguous sentence like "Flying airplanes can be dangerous" makes us partly aware of our decoding operations.

How a language relates the inner faces, or *deep structures,* of sentences to their outer faces, or *surface structures,* is called *syntax.* (Note that surface structures are not the sound sequences of set A (see above), but rather strings of words and wordlike elements that are converted into sequences of sounds by the rules of *phonology.* As we will soon see, the relationship between the deep structures of sentences and the structures of meaning (set B, above) is a matter of much present debate.) After 15 years of detailed study of syntax, especially the syntax of English, many elements and principles remain unclear; the deeper we probe, the more complexities we find.

A simple sentence expressing a proposition—"John hit the ball"—poses no great analytical problems. The sentence consists of a subject (a noun phrase, in this case, simply "John") and a verb phrase (in this case, the verb "hit" and its object, "the ball," another noun phrase). Note that "The ball was hit by John," a passive construction, expresses an equivalent meaning. "The ball hit John" expresses a very different proposition. (A few of the subtleties of language begin to emerge even in such a simple example: note that the verb "hit" has a different implication if the subject is animate (John) than if it is inanimate (a ball).)

But consider the decoding operation required in a more complex sentence:

Because the boy had been talking to the old lady he met at the laundry he got home late and was scolded.

Here a series of propositions is made:

1. The boy talked to a lady.
2. The lady is old.
3. The boy met the lady at the laundry.
4. The boy got home late.
5. (Someone) scolded the boy.

Moreover, a series of logical relationships between these propositions is proposed. (4 occurred because of 1; 5 occurred because of 4; they occurred temporally in the sequence 2, 3, 1, 4, 5.) How what amount to five sentences or propositions are articulated together to express the appropriate relationships between each poses staggering analytical and logical problems. Transformational linguistics represents a frontal assault on such complexities of syntax—complexities the brains of native speakers deal with almost instantly, effortlessly, and unconsciously.

The rules of syntax can be thought of as a set of logical operations for taking simple logical relationships between subject, verb, and object and embedding, joining, editing, and rearranging these elements into strings of words. In the complex sentence above, "Because" serves to embed the clause "the boy had been talking to the old lady" and specifies that "he got home late" as a result. The "and" before "he was scolded" serves to conjoin "he got home late" and "he was scolded" and to imply that the second was a result of the first.

These syntactic rules prune out redundant words ("he" serves through the rest of the sentence to designate "the boy"; the someone who scolded the boy is unspecified; the lady the boy was talking to is the lady he met at the laundry); they embed and conjoin sentences; they rearrange word order ("someone scolded the boy" > "(he) was scolded"); and they add such outward trim as marking past tenses.

Such rules for rearranging, editing, and connecting have been called *tranformational* rules. These rules successively transform a set of propositions (such as those of 1—5 in the complex sentence above) into a complex sequence of clauses and phrases; hence they successively connect the underlying deep structures of sentences with surface structure strings. The operation of such a sequence of transformational rules to connect inner and outer faces of a sentence is called a *derivation*. In the last several years, linguists have sought to find more formally powerful ways of phrasing these derivational rules that not only account more efficiently for this chain of connections but show how and why nonsentences are filtered out as ungrammatical.

In recent years, linguists have discovered that the apparent great diversity of languages lies in their special transformational rules. The surface structure representations of sentences in different languages are very different—in word order, verb systems, gender, and so on—as learners of foreign languages know only too well. But the further linguists have penetrated into the deep structures of the world's myriad languages, the more languages seem to share a common design. And that has led to new excitement on the linguistic frontier. If the deep structures of diverse languages are formally similar, can it be that we are probing the basic logic of human thinking? Is the structure being uncovered the very structure of the mind?

So far not much has been said about what deep structures are like; there have been only vague references to "underlying logical structure," and so on. That is not completely accidental, because funny things are happening at the inner face of sentences. A few years ago, linguists assumed that deep structures, like surface structures, consisted of basic parts of speech—nouns, verbs, adjectives, and so on; but they were related in simple skeletal sentence designs that were rearranged and fleshed out by transformational rules. But the deeper linguists have probed in recent years, the less sentencelike are the underlying patterns of syntax they have been led to infer. The parts of speech seem to be secondary derivations from more abstract categories; thus the latest interpretations (by such pioneers as Lakoff, McCawley, and Bach) suggest that nouns, verbs, and adjectives are all derived from a single abstract category of "contentives." Moreover, these abstract deep structures correspond very closely to the formal structures of symbolic logic. McCawley thus argues that George Boole's classic 1854 book, *The Laws of Thought,* in which he formalized symbolic logic "to investigate the fundamental laws of those operations of the mind by which reasoning is performed . . . and . . . to collect . . . some probable intimations concerning the nature and constitution of the human mind" was closer to the mark than has been recognized. McCawley and Lakoff have seen in the deep structure of language a universal "natural logic"—a challenging development for anthropological students of human nature and human diversity.

Phonology

Phonology is the study of how languages convert the surface syntactic structure of sentences into acoustic patterns, or sequences of sounds. Phonology is a crucial facet of language for anthropologists, because it has provided several important analogies and models—some of which anthropologists must now discard.

The best place to start in understanding how sentence designs are cloaked with sound is with the noise-producing equipment humans can use to transmit linguistic signals. The mouth is a sound chamber. To differentiate signals, sounds of different acoustical frequencies must be produced. By moving the tongue and lips, causing the vocal cords to vibrate or not, opening or closing the nasal passages, and obstructing the flow of air through the chamber in different ways, a speaker can produce distinctive patterns of sound.

The vocal cords, which act as resonators, are turned on when we speak normally and turned off when we whisper. But even in normal speaking they go on and off. They are vibrated for a "d" and are not vibrated for a "t" (which is otherwise formed in the same way). That is, "d" is *voiced* (as in "din") and "t" is *unvoiced* (as in "tin"). The same contrast is used to differentiate "goal" from "coal", "zoo" from "sue," "bin" from "pin," and "van" from "fan."

The nasal passage, which acts as an auxiliary resonating chamber, can be opened or closed, allowing us to distinguish "m" from "b" ("mat" versus "bat"), "n" from "d" ("not" versus "dot"), and "ng" from "g" ("tang" versus "tag").

Vowels are produced by passing air through the vocal chamber. They are distinguished from one another by the movement of the tongue in two dimensions—up and down and front and back. They can also be distinguished as rounded (with the lips rounded, as in "o" and "u") and unrounded. Each form of articulation concentrates sound in a particular frequency range.

Consonants impede the flow of air by breaking it (stops, like "t" and "d") or impeding it so as to produce sounds through turbulence (fricatives, like "s" and "th"). These sounds are technically defined by the point of articulation—bilabial (with the lips), or dental, or alveolar (with the palate, behind the teeth), or velar (with the back of the palate, as in "k" and "g"), or some combination (such as labiodental, with lips and teeth, as with "f").

To understand how phonological systems work, we must keep foremost in mind that what matters most is not what sounds are used in language. What matters are *contrasts between sounds*. For actual sounds vary continuously, blending imperceptibly into one another. Yet we treat sounds as though they fell into neat, separate compartments. We apparently do so on the basis of *distinctive features*. Distinctive features are either-or contrasts: voiced or unvoiced, nasal or non-nasal, high or low, tense or lax, aspirated (with a puff of air, as with "p" in "pin") or unaspirated, stop or fricative, and so on. Roman Jakobson, Morris Halle, and others have argued that distinctive features are always binary (either-or). There apparently is a large set of distinctive features that is universally used or drawn upon in different languages. That is, each language uses a subset of the full set of possible distinctive features; some features are used in all or almost all languages. By the intersection of a set of distinctive features, the "sound compartments" of a particular language are uniquely defined. Each contrast between "words" (except two words that are phonetically identical, *homonyms*, like "pair" and "pear") reflects at least one contrasting feature.

For years linguists have treated these separate compartments of sound, known as *phonemes*, as the elementary units of a language. They were, for any particular language, like a chemist's table of elements: from them were put together, according to that language's special rules of combination, the compounds that carried meaning. Linguists worked out "discovery procedures" for beginning on a new language (where one could never tell what contrasts between sounds would turn out to be distinctive) and finding out what phonemes were its basic elements. One

began with a *phonetic* transcription that could distinguish all the contrasts in sound that might make a difference. Then one winnowed out all those contrasts that turned out not to matter, thus moving to a *phonemic* transcription.

If there was any solidly established linguistic principle, it was the central importance of phonemes. Anthropologists looked enviously at these units the linguists had found, as they rummaged through the messy data of cultures looking for equally neat, separate compartments that expressed the uniqueness of a particular way of life. As we will see, American anthropologists have borrowed heavily in recent years from this mode of linguistic analysis—seeking ways to discover the unique structure of a culture and the features it treats as distinctive in carving up the world of experience (§29).

Yet modern transformational linguistics places the phoneme in jeopardy as a central unit of language. What had been treated as a separate, and primary, *level* of language is now seen as a stage in a process, connected to syntactic rules in complicated linkages.

Rather than treating phonemes as a separate level, one can regard the surface structure representation of sentences as containing packages of information about sound. This information apparently is coded in terms of distinctive features, but not strictly speaking in terms of phonemes. The phonological rules of a language fill in a great deal of the necessary information about the sounds of words on the basis of regularities in sound patterns. Thus if the second sound in a word (say, "stack") is an unvoiced stop, the information that the first sound is also unvoiced is redundant in English; there is a quite regular rule in English that any fricative at the beginning of a word, followed by an unvoiced stop, must be unvoiced. A cycle of such rules fill in all predictable blanks.

Other phonological rules shift, delete, and

rearrange patterns of sound and assign stress patterns. Such rules deal with the syntactic structure of the string of words, not the individual words themselves. Thus the word "stack" is pronounced differently in "Put it on the stack behind the barn" and "Shall I put it on the stack?" This difference is determined by the syntactic design of the sentence: the intonation contours would be the same if we substituted "box" for "stack" in each sentence. Still other phonological rules assign sound patterns to grammatical markers like PAST and PLURAL. English phonogical rules for pluralization, for example, must assign a voice fricative to "beds," an unvoiced fricative to "ships," and a vowel and fricative to "horses."

Precisely how phonological rules work is still a matter of exploration and controversy. Some transformational linguists would retain phonemes as underlying units whose realization depends on cycles of rules. Others would eliminate them entirely from grammatical description. Here, as elsewhere in linguistics, what had in the 1950s been accepted as solidly established theory is open to reexploration, controversy, and rethinking (see Brame 1972; Anderson 1975).

Semantics

How words carry meaning and how sentences express meaningful messages by stating propositions, asking questions, and giving commands are the central problems of *semantics*. Semantics, in brief, is the study of meaning: an enterprise now being pursued by linguists, philosophers, anthropologists, psychologists, and others.

How words carry meaning and how sentences encode messages are rather different, though related, questions. Progress has been made on both fronts.

It is assumed that we each have some kind of mental dictionary, a *lexicon*. In it we some-

how must store our knowledge of what words mean, of how they fit into grammatical designs, and of their sound patterns. But here again, linguists have encountered unexpected complexities; and the further they probe, the more complicated matters get.

The meanings of words are shaped by contexts, and many words fall into *sets*. For example, "sister" or "cousin" in English is definable in terms of the whole cluster of words for kinds of relatives: their meanings can best be specified in terms of *contrasts with one another*. The same is true of words for directions (north, south, east, west), colors, cooking (fry, bake, and so on). Linguists and anthropologists are probing how words fall into domains or fields and how their contrasting meanings can be defined. A hope has been that the meanings could, like the sound compartments of a language, be defined in terms of intersecting distinctive features. Thus *componential analysis* seeks to define a set of words that contrast with one another (a contrast set) in terms of a set of intersecting features. Thus we might define "chair," "stool," and "bench" in terms of three dimensions—seating capacity, padding, and backrest.

A. Seating Capacity
  A_1 single
  A_2 multiple   "chair"[2] A_1C_1
B. Padding
  B_1 upholstered   "stool" A_1C_2
  B_2 bare   "couch" A_2B_1
C. Backrest
  C_1 present
  C_2 absent   "bench" A_2B_2

There are a number of problems in such an approach. First, the choice of dimensions is often quite arbitrary, so there are often

[2]Of course, at a more specific level (what ethnographic semanticists call a lower level of contrast), we distinguish armchairs, overstuffed chairs, rocking chairs, and other kinds of chairs.

dozens of possible solutions. Many English speakers probably use shape (round versus square) to distinguish stools from benches and chairs. Especially in dealing with another culture, there is little assurance that the analyst's distinctive features mean anything to the people he or she is studying. No convincing sets of universal semantic features (like those of phonology) have been advanced; and since there are a great many things in the world people could treat as distinctive, in contrast to the few ways they can make noises, perhaps we should expect universal semantic features to operate only in the most physiologically or physically restricted areas like color perception or the reckoning of kinship.

Second, a distinctive-feature approach classes things by what they are not, paying most attention to semantic *boundaries*. Yet increasing evidence suggests that we class things by what they are, not simply by the outer boundaries of categories. It is impossible to produce an intuitively convincing distinctive-feature definition of a weed (in contrast to a flower), a dog, or a chair (in contrast to the other objects in the room). The intersection of features seems far too simple a model to deal with the human ability to *recognize patterns*. We instantly perceive the *relations between* a great many features as forming a coherent and recognizable pattern. Thus we perceive a pattern of "dogness," whether the dog is large or small, black or white, barks or does not, wags tail or has none, has four legs visible or none, and so on. Moreover, for some words there seem to be focal meanings: weediest weeds, reddest reds, even perhaps chairiest chairs (Rosch 1974).

Here students of semantics are facing a problem that pervades the study of language and of culture more generally. Our methods for analyzing structure are most efficient in dealing with phenomena in sequences of steps—in treating features, rules, or processes one at a time. Yet human equipment for perceiving and thinking seems to operate in terms of simultaneous *relationships between* features as patterns. An analogy may be useful. When a witness sees a bank robber, he or she perceives the robber's face and appearance as total patterns of features. Yet when a police artist tries to draw a composite picture of the robber, the witness must pick out nose, eyebrows, mouth, chin, and so on, one after another. Recognizing meanings probably depends partly on the same kinds of mental processes as recognizing faces; yet linguists and anthropologists are forced to pull features apart, as do the witness and police artist, and treat them one at a time.

These problems also confront semanticists as they seek to account for the way the same word has different senses in different contests, and the way it enters different domains. Thus gardens flower, and so do civilizations; the blood that is thicker than water is different from the blood people sacrifice for their country or the blood you wipe from a cut; and what makes your blood boil is different from what makes water on the stove boil. To sort out and define the different senses of "flower," "blood," and "boil" here is far from easy. The different senses of a word often have no common denominator, only a "family resemblance"—that is what metaphors are all about.

The same kind of problem may underlie many of the difficulties in formalizing a grammar in sequences of rules. The way we actually create and understand sentences may depend on perceiving total patterns, as well as performing sequences of analytical steps. This may partly account for a gulf between a transformational grammar of language competence and the psychological processes of speaking and understanding that are beginning to emerge in psycholinguistic research.

Such a contrast between psychological processes and our formal models may also underlie the difficulties on another side of semantic theory—how the meanings of individual words are shaped and transformed by the syntactic design of the sentence in which they occur. For the meaning of a sentence is not simply the summing up of the meanings of the individual words in it—a problem those who have sought to devise ways of translating Russian and Chinese by machine are grimly aware of.

Linguists have sought ways of combining the meanings of individual words in the lexicon with the syntactic deep structures of sentences in such a way that the meanings of the sentences as such could be derived. In Chomsky's formulations of the mid-1960s, a special class of semantic rules, called *projection rules,* was posited to bridge the gulf between the deep structure of a sentence and the meaning it expressed. With further probings of syntactic structure, in the newer approach of *generative semantics,* the deep structures have become deeper and more abstract. Lakoff, McCawley, Ross, Postal, and other linguists of the frontier now argue that the deep structure of a sentence *is* its semantic representation. But there are many remaining mysteries concerning how sentences convey meanings.

Surveying the complexities, mysteries, and controversies of the linguistic frontier from the perspective of anthropology, one is led not only to awe about the vast intricacy of the mind but also to a feeling that our language faculties must depend on a mental calculus that is somehow simpler and more powerful than the formal models linguists are using.

26.
Language: The Implications for Anthropology

It is worth stepping back from this brief look at the complexities of linguistic analysis to reflect on some implications for anthropology. In the process, we will glimpse some further aspects of language—for example, how children learn language—that have important anthropological implications.

Language and Perception

When you hear someone speaking, you are performing an act of *creation:* you are hearing a sentence only parts of which are "out there" in the form of sound waves. You segment, punctuate, interpret, fill in missing elements. You impose discontinuity and contrast, and hence order and structure, on the continuous, messy stream of sound.

That we create the structure of the sentences we hear has helped students of human behavior reach a broader insight: that the world of things and events we experience is not given to us by our sensory receptors, as images on the retina (or sounds or smells); we *create* that world. On the basis of "internal models of reality," models built in our minds, we create the things and events we see.

Man does not see [in] the way he thinks he sees. Instead of a passive-receptive act in which scenes . . . are simply recorded . . . the act of perceiving is one in which man is totally involved and in which he participates actively, screening and structuring. . . . The visual process is therefore *active and creative* (Hall 1972:54).

The visual perceptual system . . . "reads" from optical images non-optical properties of surrounding objects. For example, we "see" that a table is solid, hard, easily scratched. It is these non-optical physical properties which are important. . . .

The perceptual system "infers" the existence of optically hidden features. We "see" the legs of the table, though hidden. (Gregory 1970:77)

Perception . . . does not mediate behavior directly from current sensory information, but always via internal models of reality—which themselves reflect the redundancies in space and time of the external world. (Gregory 1969:239)

It is the anthropologist's special insight that these internal models we use to create a world of perceived things and events are largely learned and largely cultural. What we see is what we, through cultural experience, have learned to see. I became vividly aware of this on many occasions when I was walking with Solomon Islands tribesmen through a rain forest that to me was an unbroken and undifferentiated sea of green. One of them would suddenly scramble far off the path to retrieve a sprig of betel pepper from high in a tree, or some other culturally important "thing," that to me was just part of the background. But similarly, many things struck me as strange and hence worth noting that to my hosts were so taken for granted as not to be consciously noted. A Solomon Islander in New York City would similarly be in a different world of perception than a Manhattan native. (We need not rove so widely to realize how the perceived world depends on who is "seeing" it: to most of us, the works inside a TV set are a meaningless tangle; to a TV repairman they are a familiar tracery of connections.)

Some anthropologists, notably the great French scholar Claude Lévi-Strauss (whose work we will encounter in the chapters to follow), have seen this imposition of cultural form on the world of nature as the essence of our humanness. Lévi-Strauss views this process of categorizing and conceptualizing as akin to the way binary contrasts are used in the sound systems of language (recall that the voiced versus voiceless binary opposition is used to distinguish "bin" from "pin," "zoo" from "sue," and so on). Through such binary oppositions, cultural order is cooked up from the raw stuff of experience.

Language Acquisition and Cultural Acquisition

How children acquire language has become a focal area of recent research, spurred by developments in both linguistics and cognitive psychology. There are several amazing facets of a child's acquisition of his or her native language.

1. It takes place amazingly rapidly, with the major burst coming between two and three and a half years.
2. It apparently follows generally uniform stages of unfolding development for all normal children in all societies.
3. It is based on a very partial, limited, fragmented, and usually poor sample of adult speech; that is, the child builds an amazingly good and systematic theory of the language incredibly quickly with only limited and rough evidence to build with.
4. Acquiring linguistic competence seems largely unrelated to intelligence and other patterns of cognitive skill.
5. The rapid burst of language acquisition is demonstrably tied to sequences of biological maturation.

All this has led Chomsky to conclude that children begin the process of language acquisition with a big head-start: he believes that a universal grammatical system is biologically programmed in the brain. The child knows language, but not *a language*. Exposure to a sample of adult speech enables the child—once biological maturation activates the necessary neural circuitry—to acquire quickly the special transformational and phonological rules of his or her native language. The child is programmed to build the right kinds of theories with great efficiency. The difficulty of learning a second language in adolescence and afterwards comes partly from code interference, but probably more seriously from deactivation of the neural circuitry for efficient language learning—for some of us, probably more drastically than for others.

Chomsky further concludes that this linguistic faculty is specialized and quite independent from other cognitive faculties for learning, problem-solving, and so on. All children of anywhere near normal intelligence acquire language seemingly almost automatically, regardless of their struggles and differential abilities in acquiring other skills.

This view seems biologically plausible. Consider the fact that the communicative codes of other animals are mainly coded genetically in quite fine detail, though augmentation by learning is often required. Evolution is capable of generating species-specific codes (though language is, as we have seen, unique in being *symbolic*—humans in different times and places have obviously invented different labels for the "things" in their worlds); and the evolutionary time span of hominids and early humans would probably be long enough for the grammatical structures to evolve gradually (even though full developed vocal language, and the systems of transformational rules that make natural languages so flexible and rich, are probably more recent; recall §10).

Though Chomsky's view may be biologically plausible, it may not be right; at least, it may well be overstated. From various cognitive psychologists, notable Piaget and his associates, have come two main thrusts of criticism:

1. Linguistic competence may be closely related to other kinds of cognitive competence. Thus a child may use the same general cognitive strategies—ways of building theories about the world—to learn about his or her language and to learn about the social environment, to build theories about family relationships, physical objects, causality, and so on.

2. These genetic programs for building theories need not be as detailed as the theories they produce. As Piaget has argued, a very complex system can develop from the cyclical operation of relatively simple organizing principles. In developmental biology, the same thing seems to be true. An acorn does not contain the design of a complete oak tree, but rather the information needed for an oak tree to build itself, given the needed environment and the shaping forces of gravity, photosynthesis, and

so on. "It is much simpler to specify how to form a complex organism than to specify the organism itself" (Wolpert 1968:125).

The right answer probably lies somewhere between Chomsky's view and Piaget's; just where it lies is still a mystery, though new evidence should enable researchers to narrow the possibilities greatly in the next few years.

Linguistic Universals and Cultural Universals

Just where the right answer turns out to lie will have very fundamental implications for anthropology. How closely related is language to other realms of cultural knowledge? How do children acquire their competence in nonlinguistic culture? Could there be important cultural universals hidden beneath surface diversity? Could universal modes of logic and thought, universal organizations of knowledge, be based heavily on genetic programming?

Twenty years ago, most linguists believed that each language was unique, that it represented a separate way of organizing experience, a separate universe of linguistic elements (phonemes, words, parts of speech), and of rules for putting them together. A child had to begin with no foreknowledge of this unique code used by the people he or she was born in the midst of. One began with a blank slate.

Most anthropologists, at least until the last several years, began with a similar assumption that each culture is unique—a distinctive system of "things," customs, ways of thinking, values, providing a distinctive view of the world. The child, then, similarly was seen as beginning with a largely blank mental slate that had to be filled in with the special conventions of the culture into which he or she had been born.

With the emergence of a universal grammar beneath the special transformational patterns of different languages, the diversity of languages has taken on a very different look. Just how extensive is the universal core of languages, and how detailed is the universal pattern, are not yet fully clear. But with extensive transformational studies of American Indian, Australian Aboriginal, New Guinean, and other "exotic" languages in the last several years,[3] and with deeper probings of deep structure by the generative semanticists, the nature of linguistic universals is becoming more clear. It is no longer true that linguistic universals are based on English, or on English and Russian, though anthropologists' reports of exotic languages do provide occasional frustrations for the linguistic theorist:

That properties and events have mental powers might seem to be an impossible belief, not a strange one. . . . However, Kenneth Hale informs me that, among the Papagos, events are assumed to have minds (whatever that might mean), and that sentences like "My birth enjoys tormenting me" would be perfectly normal. I leave such matters to the anthropologists. (Lakoff 1971:322)

Whether language universals point toward other universals of culture is at present an open question. The middle and outer sections of the chain of the linguistic rules connecting meanings with sounds—its transformational and phonological rules—are probably largely unconnected with other operations of the mind. It makes sense to view them as an input-output "device," a *transducer* that takes messages in one medium (sound) and translates them into meaning-carrying sequences of symbols (the deep structure of

[3]An important development here is training of native speakers of some of these exotic languages, such as Navaho, Maori (New Zealand Polynesian), and Kachin (Burma) as linguistic theorists. Because of its emphasis on intuitions about sentences, transformational analysis works best, and penetrates deepest, when the linguist is a native speaker of the language he or she is studying.

sentences). But at the inner face of sentences, language and thought become fused: the world of meanings is the world of cultural knowledge, in all its richness. The natural logic of propositions that are encoded into speech is the logic of thinking (though not necessarily the *only* logic of thinking, as we will see). And here the possibility that universal principles for organizing knowledge, universal modes of perceiving and thinking, underlie the diversity of cultural content now looms large.

Moreover, we can well pose the question that Chomsky poses for language: could an infant learn a culture if he or she began with a blank slate, with no genetically programmed "knowledge" of what kind of world it was, of how it should be responded to, and of how to construct and organize theories of a particular cultural milieu? Here we as yet have almost no answers. Piaget has for years argued that armed with a fairly simple strategy for building theories, children progressively put together theories, then reorganize them at a higher and more sophisticated level: cultural knowledge unfolds in stages. But as with language, the genetic programming may well be much more extensive than Piaget believes. Biological maturation may activate detailed programs that, interacting with cultural experience, enable the child to create progressively more complex models of the world. These questions remain almost completely open at present—central though they are to understanding how humans become human and to interpreting the diverse cultural worlds humans have created. We will return to them.

Language, Culture, and World View

Anthropologists in the 1940s and 1950s were very much concerned with "language and culture." Does a people's language shape their ways of thinking and perceiving?

Is a people's world view encoded in their language and structured by its unique grammar?

At the turn of the century, von Humboldt hypothesized that the unique design of each language encoded a distinctive view of the world. This idea was elaborated in the 1920s by the brilliant anthropologist Edward Sapir, who argued that "the worlds in which different societies live are distinct worlds, not merely the same world with different labels attached." He advanced the view that language patterns are centrally important in structuring these distinct cultural worlds. This idea was carried further by Sapir's student Benjamin Lee Whorf, an insurance executive for whom linguistics was an avocation. Whorf produced a series of papers based mainly on his research on the Hopi Indian language (published in Whorf 1956). He argued that the European languages embody not only ways of speaking about the world; they embody as well a *model of* that world. Contrasting "Standard Average European" with Hopi, he sought to show how our ideas of "thingness" are shaped by the grammatical treatment of nouns, and how our model of time as past, present, and future—ticking past like an endless belt—reflects the tense system of our language structure. Hopi concepts of time and space, as built into their language structure, represent a different model of the universe: a model, Whorf argues, that should make the theory of relativity more intuitively meaningful to a Hopi than to a European.

This powerful and plausible hypothesis has been pursued by other writers as well, notably Dorothy Lee. She drew on data from the Wintu Indian language of California and the Trobriand language of Melanesia to distinguish between "lineal and non-lineal codifications of reality" and other linguistically structured contrasts in world view (see §65, especially Case 77).

The hypothesis has been tested extensive-

ly, yet the results have consistently been ambiguous. This is partly because, like a jellyfish, it is hard to get hold of—you grab it and it slithers somewhere else. Does Whorf mean that it is the grammatical framework that structures thought? How can you find out, because both are in the realm of ideas which is by definition unobservable? You can get at language structure only through speech and can get at thought only through speech (or introspection). This imposes both a circularity and a consistent impression that the "test" is missing Whorf's point. The hypothesis remains largely impregnable because it has been untestable (see Fishman 1960; Black 1959).

The Whorfian hypothesis has been eroded more by the shifting tides of intellectual fashion and the waves of linguistic theory than by empirical disproof. The Whorfian thesis is a somewhat ethereal expression of a conviction that languages and cultures are unique. If our focus is on how different peoples are, how diverse their conceptual worlds and how variable their cultures, then the Whorfian thesis is both an expression and a partial explanation of that diversity.

Yet in recent years both anthropologists and linguists, having taken for granted a great variation in the content of custom and the details of language, have focused increasingly on how similar are languages and cultures. A quest for universals and similarities in basic design and underlying structure became in the latter 1960s both fashionable and theoretically necessary. Transformational linguists, as we have seen, argue that the deepest structures of syntax and the basic linguistic design are the same in all languages, and that the kinds of linguistic features Whorf used to illustrate the contrasts between European and Hopi reflect differences in surface structure. They imply differences not in thought but in ways of expressing the same thoughts. If this were not so, it would seem impossible to move between different linguistic codes the way some bilinguals can—as with the simultaneous translation used in the United Nations.

Further erosion has come from evidence and increasing conviction that thinking and manipulating language are not ultimately the same thing. To interpret Whorf as trying to find *correlations* between linguistic structures and modes of thinking is inevitably misleading; rather, he saw linguistic categories and classes as the units or vehicles of thinking itself. Since these linguistic elements are organized into grammatical systems, so the organization of thought must inevitably mirror this structure. Yet the basic assumption that the elements of perception and thought *are* the elements of language now seems tenuous and misleading at best. We should not reject Whorf's ideas out of hand. They are exciting partial truths, and they make us vividly aware of variability on a level where many do not expect it. Linguists of the frontier would mainly agree that "the categories and distinctions inextricably interwoven in the fabric of the language system . . . [introduce] unconscious or preperceptual distortion" (Grinder and Elgin 1973:8), that they set up a filter between a human being and the world he or she perceives. But the distortions now seem less deep, less pervasive, and less binding than they did in Whorf's day.

Refinements in cultural theory have further recast questions about language and culture. For if language is the conceptual code underlying speech, and culture is the conceptual code underlying social behavior, language clearly is *part of* culture. One can now ask in what ways language is similar to, different from, or a source of clues about, the *rest* of culture.

When we talk about "a language" or "a culture," we confront the difficulty we can call code variability. Your theory for speaking English (as well as the way you actually speak, which is not the same thing) is different from everyone else's. Your theory for shaking hands—how, when, and with whom—is not the same as everyone else's. Furthermore, there are things you probably do not know about electrical wiring, pole vaulting, and nuclear physics that are part of our language and culture. How, then, can we speak of "the English language" or "American culture" as a common code? The same problem confronts us when we talk of Hopi Indian language or Hopi culture.

Linguists manage the problem by talking about *dialects* (of regions and social classes) and finally *idiolects,* the special versions of a language characteristic of each speaker. For most purposes, it has been useful to focus on the common features of the code that all speakers share and to ignore dialect and idiolect variations. "English" (or "German") is thus an abstract model of what is common to its speakers, though it may not correspond to all versions. It is also a composite, since it includes the special vocabularies of electrician, pole vaulter, physicist. In addition, the edges of "French" and "German" are not sharp. French blends into Italian, and German into Dutch, along country borders. But linguists have found it conceptually useful to ignore the "marginal speaker" most of the time.

For many purposes the cultural anthropologist can usefully follow the simplifying assumptions linguists make about code variability. One can speak of Hopi culture, ignoring code variation and messy cultural borders and lumping together the knowledge of Hopi wife, Hopi artisan, and Hopi priest. But there are problems lurking here, as we will see in the chapters to follow.

An important approach to the borders between language and the rest of culture has come in recent years from American anthropologists much influenced by linguistics (notably Goodenough, Frake, and Conklin). The world of things and events, through the eyes of another people, is most clearly mirrored in the categories of their language. How a people class animals, birds, plants, or winds may be quite different from the way we do it. Thus the Kwaio of the Solomon Islands label fresh water as one substance, salt water as another; they place birds and bats in one category, in contrast to moths, butterflies, and the like; they class fish and marine mammals together; and they label with a single term most colors we could call blue and black. Are they bad primitive "scientists"? Not at all. Rather, just as a language can use different kinds of sound contrasts (nasalized versus non-nasalized, rounded versus unrounded), so a culture can use different features to distinguish between categories. It is not that our categories are right and theirs wrong—the Kwaio simply use different contrasts to carve up the world. What looks like bad science may reflect failure of the Western observer to understand another people's underlying premises about classifying. Upon discovering in an ornithology book that the large green parrot and the large yellow and blue parrot which Kwaio label with different words are in fact male and female of the same species, I confronted my Kwaio friends. "Of course," they shrugged, wondering why I didn't know that all along. Even the notion of what labels are about may have special cultural overtones. Raymond Firth, a distinguished New Zealand anthropologist who studied the tiny, isolated Polynesian island of Tikopia, tells of how he once accompanied some Tikopians to another island. Trying to find out whether his friends had categories for the birds on this island, Firth asked them, "Do those birds have names?" "Yes, they have names, but we don't know them."

Systems of folk classification are often highly complicated and elaborated. Conklin (1962), for example, found that the Hanunóo of the Philippines have more than 1800 distinct "species" labels for the plants in their environment, while Western botanists class them into less than 1300 species. Though people elaborate folk taxonomies in focal areas of cultural importance (so that Eskimos can make very fine distinctions about snow and snow conditions), they also endlessly classify phenomena that are of very little concern in their daily lives. Humans, apparently, are incurable and compulsive classifiers (Lévi-Strauss 1962; see §65).

Study of such folk conceptual systems has come to be called *ethnoscience*. The hope of such studies is that we can penetrate the conceptual world of a people through analysis of their linguistic categories. This has spurred greater interest in semantics among anthropologists, who have been in the forefront in the development of componential analysis (p. 154).

Most research in ethnoscience has been predicated on assumptions that the thought world of each people is unique—assumptions drawn from an older pretransformational linguistics—and has been aimed at formally describing that uniqueness. Some researchers, building on a view of culture as a cognitive system, as "what one must know in order to generate culturally acceptable acts and utterances appropriate to a given socio-ecological context" (Frake 1962b:39), have sought to formalize this knowledge as a "cultural grammar." We will look at this enterprise in the next chapter. We will see that it rests in substantial measure on a now-outmoded linguistics; and we will consider both the advantages and the dangers of using the structure of language as a model for studying other realms of culture (see Keesing 1972a). We will also see that the growing interest in linguistic universals has begun to take hold in the anthropological study of semantics.

Here we can conclude a first look at language and culture by summing up some implications of linguistics for the anthropological study of culture:

1. A distinction between ideational code

and its enactment in behavior, such as we drew in defining "culture," finds strong support in linguistics. The linguists' distinction between language and speech has proven so powerful conceptually that we can make a similar distinction between culture and social behavior with considerable confidence.

2. We will need to study the cultural code—even though it cannot be directly observed—and not simply the patterning of behavior, because

a. Codes are finite, while behavior is creative and potentially infinite in variability. Without a code theory we cannot account for the creativity of behavior, for what may happen next as well as what has already happened.

b. Codes have sharp edges and neat rules, while behavior has fuzzy edges and only statistical regularities. Without knowing the code we cannot tell which things, acts, and events a people treat as the same and which they treat as different. The psychological code imposes sharp edges and even creates perceptual patterns that do not exist "out there."

3. The "rules" of cultural codes, like the rules of language, are mainly unconscious. At least we cannot assume that people will be able to tell us what their "rules" are. The ideologies and rules of thumb people talk about may or may not correspond to the rules they use to operate in the world.

4. The overall design of all cultures, like the design of all languages, is likely to be similar. We know little so far about what that structure is like, but the design of the whole code or of large segments of it may be somewhat similar to the design of the segment linguists have explored. We can expect cultures to vary greatly in content and particular rules—though we might hope for such things as universal distinctive features.

5. The general outlines of cultural designs may be partly shaped by genetic programming and neurophysiological structure.

6. We can use linguistic variability as a guide for studying code variability in cultures. At times we can assume Hopi culture is a single system, ignoring variation and fuzzy boundaries. At other times we can use the equivalent of dialect and idiolect to talk about the special code variants of subgroups *(subculture)* or of individuals *(personal culture)*.

7. The transformationalist emphasis on syntax, on how the elements of language structure are built into larger designs, can usefully point our attention toward the "syntactic" rules for constructing behavioral sequences. We continually produce behavior sequences, as well as sentences, that we have never experienced before, building new combinations of familiar elements. Where most attention in symbolic anthropology has been directed to the "phonology" of concepts and categories, anthropologists can well now begin to explore the "syntax" of action.

8. Finally, transformational linguistics has all but demolished the hope for systematic *discovery procedures,* ways of going from the observable "facts" (what people say and do) to a theory of the ideational code that underlies "facts" without making leaps of guesswork and intuition. The emphasis has shifted from how systematically we arrived at a theory to whether or not it *works.* (As we noted in §2, such a shift in emphasis pervades the modern natural sciences as well.)

27.
Sociolinguistics and the Ethnography of Communication

A number of anthropologists in recent years have become concerned with the study of language in its social context.

Linguists have made simplifying assumptions that the anthropologist often cannot afford to follow. A linguist searching for a universal design of languages, of which French, Chinese, and Hopi are all expressions, can well afford to ignore the differences between the grammars of two different

Frenchmen. But many of the anthropologist's problems lie on precisely this level. Not only are there diverse versions of French or Hopi culture; we all have code *repertoires,* and we can move from one to another (colloquial to formal, for instance). This all means that code variability and what it communicates *are part of the code.* Finally, the linguistic competence of different people in the same society is clearly not the same, in terms of the wider social and cultural setting—as witness the child from an American ghetto whose dialect and limited code repertoire restrict his or her social opportunity. All this suggests that understanding of code variability, in linguistic and cultural terms, will be a major challenge in the years to come.

Here, the studies of the American linguist William Labov (1970b, 1972) have been particularly interesting and important. Labov urges that detailed study of code variation and of language in its social context are theoretically necessary as well as practically important: "Linguistic theory can no more ignore the social behavior of speakers of a language than chemical theory can ignore the observed properties of the elements" (Labov 1970a:85).

Labov and his associates have focused particular attention on Black English.

Case 8: The Structure of Black English

A number of educators have regarded the speech patterns of ghetto Black schoolchildren as a debased, impoverished, and ruleless form of communication, "as if the children had no language at all. The language of culturally deprived children . . . is not merely an underdeveloped version of Standard English, but is a basically nonlogical mode of expressive behavior" (Bereiter et al. 1966:112–113). Such utterances as "They mine" or "Me got juice" are offered as illustration. Disastrously poor results on standard tests of verbal ability have been used to conclude either that a culturally impoverished environment or genetic inadequacies in the capacity for logical thinking—or both—are responsible.

But Labov has carefully applied the methods of modern linguistics to the speech of poor urban black children—testing the hypothesis that their speech is not defective but, like Chaucerian English, based on somewhat different grammatical and phonological rules. The results strikingly bear out the hypothesis. Sentences such as "I ax Alvin do he know how to play basketball" (or "They mine") turn out to be governed by systematic rules, often rules that differ only slightly from those of Standard English.

For example, in Standard English a rule of negative concord applies to one indefinite before the verb: "Nobody knows anything." In Black English, negative concord is obligatory to all indefinites within the clause ("Nobody knows nothin'") and may be added to preverbal position in the following clauses: "Nobody didn't know he didn't" = Standard English "Nobody knew he did." Such rules are straightforward, regular, and standard.

The social, educational, and psychological consequences for a black child faced with a strange dialect whites speak and he or she does not—if the teacher and others regard Black English as ruleless subhuman babbling—are disastrous. The challenge educationally is to add Standard English to the repertoire of speakers of Black English so that they acquire the options of breaking out of oppressive systems of social stratification and opening educational and economic doors—*not* to replace a defective way of speaking with a correct one.

The conclusions of Arthur Jensen and others that Black English reflects cognitive inferiority not only constitute racist oppression but they betray linguistic ignorance. The grammatical rules of Black English, Labov observes, do not reflect differences in "fundamental predicates of the logical system." Most of them represent not radical contrasts with the rules of Standard English, but rather "extensions and restrictions of certain formal rules, and different choices of redundant elements" (Labov 1970b:147).

Viewing Black English as an impoverished and defective way of speaking disguises another interesting fact. When the Creoles of the Caribbean and the fringing regions (including coastal areas of the American South) are compared with one another, with the Gullah dialects of the Carolina coast, and with various dialects of Black English, a number of positive similarities emerge. These common patterns remain hidden when each is compared to a dominant and socially elite language and judged defective. The common features of New World Black dialects almost certainly trace back to West African languages, perhaps through the medium of a *lingua franca,* or common language, used in the slave trade (see §72, Chapter 21).

Other anthropologists and linguists, notably Dell Hymes and his students, have examined the way language is used in different societies, how speaking is embedded in a social matrix and culturally defined. Studying the ethnography of speaking has turned up fascinating variations in both tribal and modern societies.

Particularly interesting have been patterns of code variability in non-Western settings. Three examples will illustrate. To use the Javanese language in a particular situation, a speaker must choose one of three levels or styles of speech—a "lowest" (and most rough and informal), a "highest" (or most formal and elegant), or a middle level. There are also ways to make the lowest style even lower and the highest even higher. What levels a speaker of Javanese knows will depend on his social class, but each speaker will have some repertoire to choose from. His choice depends not only on his status but also on that of the person spoken to, the relationship between them, and the situation. A single sentence illustrated by Geertz (1960)—"Are you going to eat rice and cassava now?"—is so completely transformed when spoken on different levels in Javanese that only one word, the one for "cassava," is the same on both the highest and lowest levels. Even more radical code switching occurs in Paraguay. Guarani, an Indian language, has remained the dominant language of the people. Yet Spanish is the official language and is used in government, schools, and commerce, and more than half of the Paraguayans are bilingual in Spanish and Guarani. They use Spanish in formal social relationships, official business, and to express respect; they use Guarani with friends and relatives, in making love, and in talking with status inferiors (Rubin 1968).

The assumption that one language code corresponds to one culture and one cultural code corresponds to one social system has been a convenient simplification. But studies of multiple codes among Indians in the northern Amazon show even more dramatically that it is an assumption we will have to abandon. Here more than 25 "tribes" speak distinct languages, though many aspects of culture are uniform through the area. However, since a man "belongs to" his father's tribe but must take a wife from a different tribe, his mother and his father come from tribes speaking different languages. An individual normally knows both his father's language and his mother's language, and most individuals learn two to three other languages as well. The social organization is based on assumptions of code diversity (Sorensen 1967).

28.
Communication: A Wider Perspective

A social world in which people communicate with one another only through language would be colorless and flat—like a place where people could exchange only typed messages with others they could not see. It is what we "say" to one another by physical appearance, expressions, gestures, tone of voice, and the way we arrange ourselves in space that adds rich dimensions to human social life. We not only send "linguistic messages" to one another but we also exchange information about our internal states (what "mood" we are in), about our relationships to one another (are we hostile or friendly?), and about the way our linguistic messages or acts are to be interpreted (are we joking, serious,

playing, or fighting?). Such nonlinguistic communication is the very fabric of social life.

Here, recall the discussion in §10 of the evolution of language. Linguistic signs impose "arbitrary form upon the environment" (Holloway 1969:395). They are *noniconic,* they are not modeled on the phenomena they label. Linguistic messages are *digital,* depending on the presence or absence, not the magnitude, of the component elements. Linguistically, a sentence is the same sentence whether it is whispered or shouted. It becomes a different sentence only when one or more relevant features are removed, added, or changed, as when a singular noun is pluralized.

But the total *message* we communicate to the listener by a whispered utterance is likely to be quite different from that communicated by the same sentence spoken or shouted. We, like chimpanzees, send a great amount of nonlinguistic information by means of vocalization—by volume, intonation, tone of voice. A whispered sentence, and the spatial closeness of speaker and hearer that usually goes with it, communicate something about the relationship between speaker and hearer, and their relationship to others who are present. Recall that this is what animals communicate about most often: their relationships to one another and their emotional states.

And this is a crucial point. Two different mechanisms, and to some extent even different regions of the brain—one evolutionarily old and basic to animal communication, the other evolutionarily recent and elaborated only in humans—are interwoven in the process of everyday message exchange between human beings. Language has not *replaced* older mechanisms; it has been added to and interlinked with them. How this has developed and why, and how these systems are interconnected, remain mysterious. The evolutionary implications of these coordinate human communications systems have been provocatively explored by Bateson:

If . . . verbal language were in any sense an evolutionary replacement of [nonverbal] communication . . . we would expect the old, preponderantly iconic systems to have undergone conspicuous decay. Clearly they have not. . . . This separate burgeoning evolution [of nonverbal communication] alongside the evolution of verbal language indicates that our iconic communication serves functions totally different from those of language and . . . performs functions which verbal language is unsuited to perform. . . .

It seems that the discourse of nonverbal communications is . . . concerned with matters of relationship—love, hate, respect, fear, dependency, etc.— . . . and that the nature of human society is such that falsification of the discourse rapidly becomes pathogenic. From an adaptive point of view, it is therefore important that this discourse be carried on by techniques which are relatively unconscious and only imperfectly subject to voluntary control. (1968:614—615)

Many aspects of human nonlinguistic communication have biological foundations; but while these are genetically transmitted, they are overlain with cultural learning. This is one reason why human nonlinguistic communication is so difficult to study. The people being studied cannot talk about this kind of communication well; neither can the observer, even if he or she grasps the patterns involved. Moreover, in this little-understood interweaving of cultural learning and biological programming we are prone to overemphasize one or the other.

Thus ethologists like Eibl-Eibesfeldt (1975) look at human expressions and gestures for evolutionarily old and biologically laid down patterns. But the evidence so far is meager, and there is great temptation for a biologist to use it selectively. Anthropologists like Birdwhistell (1970) have gone too far in the other direction, in stressing culturally patterned variation in nonlinguistic communication. Here the complex interplay of the old and the new, the biological and the cultural, will have to be unraveled in the years to come.

Among the most sophisticated attempts to sort out the interplay of genetically laid down and culturally learned patterns have been the studies of the psychologist Paul Ekman and his associates, some of them anthropologists. Ekman, like Eibl-Eibesfeldt, has worked extensively in non-Western settings; both have spent long periods filming New Guinea tribesmen. Ekman's group has concentrated on facial expression (Ekman 1973). They see the repertoire of facial expression—of anger, disgust, pain, surprise, doubt—as basically programmed genetically and produced spontaneously and unconsciously. But they see a wide range of culturally shaped cues as *triggering* the facial expression of emotion. (A Kwaio tribesman from the Solomon Islands to whom you say "your tooth" may kill you for a deadly insult; and proffered a spider, he may look hungry and not horrified.) Moreover, these facial expressions may in social situations be controlled by "display rules" or social conventions: stoicism despite pain, a poker face or bravado despite anxiety (hence, stereotypes of the "inscrutable Chinese," and so on). The same is probably true of some other realms of nonlinguistic communication, such as tone of voice.

Gestures are another matter. The code of gestures is to a substantial degree based directly on cultural conventions, and is consciously used to convey information—a wink, a shake or nod of the head, a beckoning of the hand. Gestures—Ekman and his associates would rather call them emblems—are thus a sort of extension or annex of spoken language (recall from §10 Hewes' argument that codes of gestures may in fact be ancestral to verbal language). In contrast to gesture, we

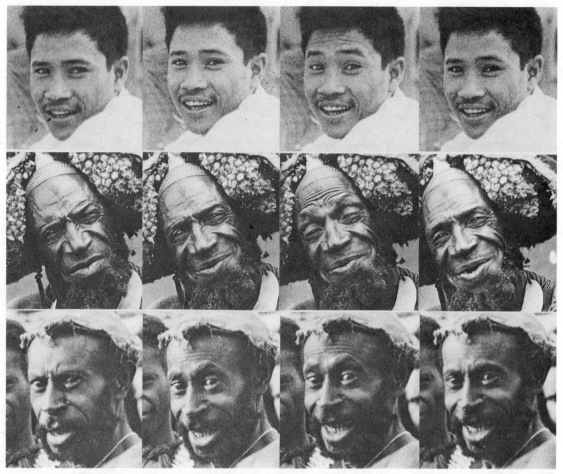

The eyebrow flash in three different cultures: A panhuman phylogenetic pattern? (From I. Eibl-Eibesfeldt, *Ethology: The Biology of Behavior,* 2d ed. Copyright © 1970, 1975 by Holt, Rinehart and Winston. By permission of the publisher.)

communicate subtly and unconsciously to one another by posture and bodily orientation, as popular books about "body language" have made many of us aware (see Scheflen 1973).

Hall (1966), in his study of the way cultures use physical space to communicate about social relationships, brings to consciousness many patterns we normally take for granted. Americans surround themselves with a kind of envelope of private space, a sort of invisible plastic bag. This space is normally inviolate in our everyday interaction. Try, for instance, in talking to people, to move gradually closer and closer to them; you will find them retreating to preserve their envelopes intact. Only in a few contexts, such as lovemaking and contact sports, do we invade one another's envelopes. Even in a crowded bus or subway, when our envelopes get all squished together, we go to considerable lengths to affirm to one another that we are not really invading private space; we depersonalize the close physical encounters by staring into space, reading tabloid newspapers, and so on.

Many of the messages we exchange tell us how other messages are to be interpreted—whether they are "true," "serious," "joking" "threatening," and so on. Bateson (1955) calls these messages about messages *metacommunication.* By metacommunication, we put "frames" around messages that tell others how to interpret them: "You old son of a bitch" may be dire insult or friendly camaraderie among age-mates. We had best be careful to make that clear ("Smile when you say that . . .").

Bateson has argued that such framing, evolutionarily at least as old as mammalian play, reaches new and important complexity in human communication (Bateson 1955). Paradoxes in which the framing messages contradict the messages within the frame are basic to this process. Animals biting one another but at the same time framing or labeling it as "just play" show the simplest form of such contradiction: the bite is not what it seems to be. But in man, art, fantasy, symbolism, and ritual develop these paradoxes more fully. Consider the multiple frames of metacommunication in an Ingmar Bergman film. The events on the screen are not going on in the world, but are projected film images—a first-order fiction all movies share. But unlike the newsreel that may have preceded it, the Bergman film is "fictional" in a second-order sense. Yet the scenes portrayed in the film are not simply what they seem to be: the clock on which the camera lingered may be a metaphor of time, or of impending death. Several further layerings of symbolism, each involving new frames and further paradoxes, may exist. And finally, there is a framing so that trying to interpret the symbolism becomes a game between Bergman and the viewer, a game that continues among the viewers when the lights go on and the other frames are dissolved.

Much of the richness of cultural structure lies in such framing of contexts. Our ability to participate in the events of our cultural world and understand what is going on depends not so much on knowing what will happen next— we often do not know that—as on knowing the right frames. The ethnographer living temporarily in a different cultural world has gone only half the way when he or she understands a strange language and strange customs. The harder half is knowing when to laugh. And if the fieldworker learns that and the other framings of the culture, you are not likely to read about them in his or her book. Like the wings of a butterfly, they yield better to poetry than to science.

The difficulties of describing contexts and nonlinguistic communications may reflect a more general problem, one about which Bateson (1972b) has recently reflected. It now seems likely that many cultural patterns are coded and processed in evolutionarily old structures of the brain, and in the right cerebral hemisphere (§10) where patterns of thought quite different from and complementary to those of logical thought and language are localized. These patterns are generally inaccessible to consciousness, and they may well turn out not to be describable in language, based as it is on a qualitatively different kind of coding. Bateson's explorations suggest that these deep and unconscious codings of culture deal not with things but with *relationships,* not with content but with pattern. Such codings of pattern and relationship not only underlie human nonlinguistic communication; they may well also be reflected in many other facets of human behavior. The foundations of art—templates of symmetry and pattern, of rhythm and harmony, the bases of poetry and music and metaphor— may lie in realms of mind and brain that are relatively inaccessible to systematic analysis and relatively impervious to logical dissection and formal description:

[The] algorithms of the unconscious are coded and organized in a manner totally different from the algorithms of language. And since a great deal of conscious thought is structured in terms of the logics of language, the algorithms of the unconscious are doubly inaccessible. It is not only that the conscious mind has no access to this material. . . . There is [also] a formidable problem of translation. (Bateson 1972b:139)

We will return to these deep problems and paradoxes at the end of Chapter 20.

It is far from clear, at this stage, that the formal languages of mathematics and logic are even adequate to describe the algorithms of *language,* especially the *use* of language. Rather than discovering the structure of language from mathematical formulations (which was Chomsky's early strategy), linguists and other explorers of mind may increasingly have to invent new mathematical systems to replicate our ways of thinking and perceiving.

This underlines the emergence, across the frontiers of science, of new ways of exploring complex systems. We noted earlier that the genetically coded information in an acorn poses problems akin to the organization and acquisition of language. It is striking that developmental biologists are beginning to talk about their problems in ways explicitly similar to those being used by linguists:

We assume that an organism at any particular instance of its development can be represented by a finite string of symbols. . . . The problem then becomes to find "grammatical" rules, which will transform the strings in such a way that the sequence of strings produced by repeatedly applying the rule will reflect the biological development. . . . (Herman and Walker 1972:343)

In neurophysiology, in artificial intelligence (the creation of logical blueprints for automata or robots), and in related fields a uniform cybernetic language for describing complex systems—in terms of grammars, feedback, information, hierarchical and heterarchical organization—is beginning to pay important scientific dividends.

This in turn begins to lay the foundations for a general theory of communication, or *semiotics.* Such a general theory had first been envisioned by de Saussure in 1916; but it now seems that a general science of communication could unite the study of biological and social systems in a way de Saussure could scarcely have imagined:

It is amply clear even now that the genetic code must be regarded as the most fundamental of all semiotic networks and therefore as the prototype for all other signalling systems used by animals, including man. From this point of view, molecules that are quantum systems, acting as stable physical information carriers, zoosemiotic [animal communication] systems, and, finally, cultural systems, comprehending language, constitute a natural sequel of stages of ever more complex energy levels in a single universal evolution. It is possible therefore to describe language as well as living systems from a unified cybernetic standpoint. While this is perhaps no more than a useful analogy at present, hopefully providing insight if not yet new information, a mutual appreciation of genetics, animal communication studies, and linguistics may lead to a full understanding of the dynamics of semiosis, and this may, in the last analysis, turn out to be no less than the definition of life. (Sebeok 1968:12)

Here we have wandered beyond the frontiers of the known. As we examine human social systems and ideational worlds in comparative perspective in later chapters, we will stay within the frontiers most of the time; to do otherwise would obscure the many insights and findings anthropology can reveal. But we will venture to the frontiers when it is important to do so—when to stay within the bounds of present knowledge would disguise the fact that what anthropologists know and understand about human behavior shrinks in comparison to what they do not know. But here we can take some comfort from the fact that scientific advance characteristically comes from asking harder and bigger questions, and thus discovering the limitations of knowledge and the depths of mystery that lie beyond.

THE STRUCTURE OF CULTURES

10

Cultural anthropology is a study of human differences, seen against a background of what is shared. But how different are humans in different times and places, how diverse are their ways of life? Modern anthropology presents us with a paradox: Each culture, as an ideational system, is a unique set of concepts, categories, and rules. Yet at the same time, a common design underlying that uniqueness is beginning to emerge. Moreover, similarities in social arrangements and customs in widely separated parts of the tribal world lead specialists to hope that regularities and even "laws," or similar sequences of cause and effect, will emerge from this seeming diversity.

Anthropology, then, is both a study of uniqueness and a search for regularity. We will focus in this chapter on the nature of cultural variability, touching on its moral implications. We will consider the quest for a common underlying design, and we will examine the search for cross-cultural regularities.

29.
Cultural Uniqueness and the Search for Universals

In what ways are cultures unique? Is each culture a distinct universe of categories, meanings, and values that must be understood only in its own terms? Or is there some common design that underlies the apparent diversity?

Such questions have been muddled by the confusion Goodenough (1961) noted (see §23) between culture as an ideational system and culture as the "pattern of life within a community." Clearly, asking whether a people's ideational world is unique and must be understood in terms of its own categories and inner logic is not the same as asking whether the way a people organize social groups or gain their livelihood is unique.

Here we will continue to treat cultures as

ideational systems. In asking about the uniqueness of cultures, we are thus asking about the way *knowledge* is organized by different peoples. We are asking about the structure of their models of the world, their principles for choosing, acting, and communicating. When we have occasion to deal with ways-of-life-of-communities-in-ecosystems, we will use the cumbersome term *sociocultural systems* (the cumbersomeness of the term is useful: it reminds us that it is a hybrid of cultural patterns and their social realizations). Later in this section, and in §31, we will examine the search for regularities in modes of social groupings and processes, economic activities, and other facets of the "patterns of life" worked out in different times and places.

The questions, though different, are not unrelated. Ideational systems must, of course, be compatible with the needs of subsistence and must produce workable social arrangements in ecosystems if they are to endure.

The position that the conceptual world of each people is unique and can be understood only in its own terms has been an important force in recent American anthropology. This position, as we saw in §26, derives largely from the theoretical foundations of pretransformational American linguistics (see Keesing 1972a). Each language was viewed as a separate universe of categories and principles of arrangement. Thus the parts of speech and grammatical principles of each language had to be worked out afresh. Central here was the notion that the phonemes of a language (§25) represented its unique way of carving up distinctive blocks of sound. In fact, the label introduced by the linguist Pike (1967) for analysis of an ideational code in terms of its own distinctions and categories is *emic*— from "phon*emic*" (description of a language in terms of its distinctive system of phonemes). An emic analysis of behavior takes an actor's eye view and analyzes the stream of events in terms of its internal structure. Pike contrasted this with *etic*[1] analysis, where the observer uses a descriptive notation derived from comparative study and describes the behavior from this external perspective. (The two are not incompatible, but can be used at different stages for different purposes: to arrive at an emic analysis, one must begin with an etic description.)

Ironically, at the same time in the latter 1950s when these ideas about language were diffusing into American cultural anthropology and providing models for analyzing cultural diversity, the transformationalist revolution was gathering momentum in linguistics. And as we saw in Chapter 9, transformational linguistics has cast aside the dogma that each language is a unique conceptual universe. Its quest is for a general and universal design of which each language is a variant form. Each language must be described in terms of the theory of that design—though by studying different languages we will enrich our general theory. At the deeper levels of structure, languages are very much alike. Their differences are relatively superficial, differences of content but not structure, of details but not general principles. Furthermore, as we have seen, many transformationalists argue that the outlines of this design must be innately laid down.

The similarity of languages at the deepest levels of syntactic structure, and in general organizational principles, underlies considerable diversity in semantics, phonology, and transformational rules. It is quite possible, for other areas of culture, that great diversity (and hence, in some sense, "uniqueness") of *content* fills in an organizational framework that is universal. Hence both the arguments for uniqueness and for a universal design of cultures might, in different senses, be valid. It is

---

[1] From phon*etic*—the notation a linguist uses to record the sounds of an unfamiliar language.

also possible that language is a highly specialized subsystem locked, as it were, in a separate corner of the mind; and that in other realms of culture diversity runs rampant and uniqueness holds sway.

Those who have argued that cultures as ideational systems must be analyzed in terms of their own internal order have pointed to the content, not the overall structure, of cultural codes, illustrated below.

Case 9: Hanunóo Color Terms

In his study of the way the Hanunóo of the Philippines conceptualize and deal with the plant world, Harold Conklin (1955) was led to explore the way they classified colors. Other investigators using standard color chips had found considerable differences between the way we divide the color spectrum and the ways used by many non-Western peoples. But what Conklin found was more interesting. The whole Hanunóo system for classification turned out to be quite unlike ours; moreover, the "domain," or realm, that was being classified seemed rather different from our notion of color. One distinction crucial in classifying Hanunóo "colors" turned out to be whether the object was wet and lush or dry. Can we legitimately call these "colors" at all?

Such studies seemed to show not only that peoples vary in the particular categories and features they use to classify their universe, but that the domains, or large segments into which they divide the world of experience, might well not be the same as ours. It is not simply that their categories for classifying birds or plants or directions or colors or supernaturals are different from ours. How can we even be sure that the very concept of bird or direction or color is part of their ideational world as well as of ours?

Case 10: Trukese Residence Rules

Two different anthropologists, doing a census of the same tiny Pacific island, in the Micronesian lagoon of Truk, several years apart, classified the same households very differently in terms of an anthropological scheme for recording postmarital residence, or where husband and wife reside after marriage. How could this be? How could the same household be "patrilocal" when studied by one able anthropologist and "matrilocal" when studied by another? One of them, Ward Goodenough, concluded that the problem lay in the very notion that another culture can be classified in terms of such a preconceived scheme. In fact the Trukese perceive a set of alternatives for choosing a place of residence quite different from those in the anthropological scheme. To understand their choices, one had to understand how they conceived the alternatives, and which choices they perceived as different and which as the same. Otherwise, the anthropological scheme was wedging the distinctively shaped pegs of Trukese culture into a standard set of round and square holes (Goodenough 1956).

Such substantive diversity, uniqueness of content, is by this time well documented. At the same time, the range of variation is turning out to be a good deal less wide than we thought it might be. The same domains are turning up in different cultures, and the diversity of semantic categories in at least some domains is turning out to be a good deal less extreme than one might have expected.

Anthropologists may have exaggerated diversity because of the methods they have been using. Recall our illustrative attempt to define "chair," "stool," and "bench" by the intersection of distinctive features (§25). By this method, any object one sits on either is a chair or is not: there can be no degrees of "chairness." If we applied this method to the Kwaio of the Solomon Islands, who use a single term for fishes and porpoises, or for birds and bats, we would have to say that their conceptual scheme is quite unlike ours and treats different features as distinctive. If the *boundaries* of categories are unique in each culture, the conceptual worlds are unique.

But are they? If we instead conceive of a word as having one or more partly overlapping cores of meaning from which concentric circles of extended meaning, metaphor, and doubtful application extend outward, we see a different possibility. The cores may be much more similar in different cultures, at least in some domains, than the way they extend out toward the boundaries. Occasionally, the Kwaio contrast "real fish" with porpoises or contrast "real birds" with bats, which are classed by the same term. The possibility that such cores of meaning are more similar than comparison of category boundaries would

suggest has not yet been systematically explored, but this now appears to be the case with ways of classifying colors (Berlin and Kay 1969; see Conklin 1973) and kinds of relatives (Lounsbury 1964; Scheffler 1972b).

Formal organizing principles are a different matter. Even those who have argued most strongly for uniqueness, for example, have seen in *taxonomies* a universal mode of classifying things in the world. The problem here is that we do not yet know enough about the brain, about thinking, about the organization of knowledge, and about perception to draw the outlines of a universal design. An ideational approach to culture is badly in need of what is beginning to emerge in linguistics—a general theory. We are still in the stage of examining fragments and classifying bits and pieces. We do not yet have a framework to fit them into.

We do know a good deal about what humans sharing a cultural code are able to *do*. And that implies that cultural knowledge includes at least the following:

1. Principles for assigning patterns in the perceptual world—things, people, events, processes, and contexts—to *categories*. (There is growing evidence that these categories of thinking are not all labeled in language.)

2. Basic premises about interrelatedness of things and events: ideas of causality, rules of logic and inference, concepts of time and space, and so on; and basic cosmological and ontological premises about what orders of existence or categories of being there are, what kind of a universe this is, and so on.

3. Knowledge about the interrelations of particular things and events, based on these premises:

propositions that parallel our sciences of botany, zoology, astronomy, and so on.

4. Conceptions of desirable goals or states of affairs; and hence standards for choosing among alternatives, and ideal general standards against which specific alternative courses of action are judged.

5. Techniques and strategies for dealing with the environment, physical and social, in such a way as to maximize these goal states—what Spindler (1974) calls *instrumental linkages*.

6. A very broad category of norms that tell us how to act appropriately in particular situations: who should do what, when, and how. (These include standards for responding to breaches of the normative code by others.)

7. Rules for encoding and decoding linguistic and nonlinguistic messages.

But the essence of the problem is the *formal structure* of these segments of knowledge—how they are put together and how they are processed in human thought. Our list tells nothing about this structure.

It seems probable that there are different levels of arrangement: from the deepest levels of unconscious premises and abstract relational principles that could not be verbalized, to the normative principles we do not habitually verbalize but can often conjure to consciousness, to our ideologies. These ideologies may have little relation to the implicit codes humans actually follow, but it is characteristic of these strange animals that they will fight and die for them.

Several conceptual and methodological pitfalls wait to trap us if we seek to map cultures as ideational systems. Geertz (1973b) warns that analyzing cultures as cognitive systems of individual actors is a dangerous reduction: it describes what is shared and is in a sense public—a system of symbols and meanings—as if it were individual and private. Recall his example of the Beethoven quartet (§23) which transcends any individual's knowledge of it. Yet Geertz' alternative approach carries us dangerously close to "reification": cultures are not that neatly shared—unlike a Beethoven quartet, different individuals know different versions and different pieces. But Geertz' warnings usefully remind us that an anthropologist's description of a culture—like a linguist's description of a language—presents an idealized composite not represented in the mind of any native actor; they also remind us that for each actor the cultural system of the society is also in a sense external:

From the point of view of any particular individual, [cultural] symbols are largely given. He finds them already current in the community when he is born, and they remain, with some additions, subtractions, and partial alterations he may or may not have had a hand in, in circulation there after he dies. While he lives he uses them, or some of them . . . to put a construction upon the events through which he lives. (Geertz 1966c:57)

Once we see that a composite cultural description is the anthropologist's creation, transcending the cognitive world of individuals, we are partly freed from worrying morbidly whether what one writes has "psychological validity," whether it represents what is really "in the heads" of native actors. The anthropologist is trying to create a framework for interpretation of another people's world.

But there is another danger: of neatening up the internal organization of a culture, overemphasizing its integration. Geertz has argued (as we will see in §69) that cultures are not fully integrated, fully consistent; they incorporate discontinuities as well as logical connections, contradictions as well as consistencies. In building a composite conception of a culture as an ideational system, one is prone to exaggerate the neatness with which its elements fit together. We will return to this question in Chapter 20.

Finally, there is the danger of assuming that a single mode of analysis will be appropriate to the different subsystems of a culture. The most obvious danger is taking language—the best-mapped segment—as a guide for the rest and uncritically borrowing models from the linguists. This is partly because the anthropologist's problems center on what the linguist takes as given, the system of knowledge, belief, assumption, and conventions that produces particular ideas at particular times. The anthropologist is concerned with social contexts, with a world of cultural meanings, with "things to say" more than with devices for turning them into sounds. This is not to say that the processes whereby we organize and formulate ideas are unrelated to the processes whereby we turn them into patterns of sound. (And increasingly, they come tangent at the inner face of sentences, the deepest deep structures of language.) But *how* they are related is a matter for exploration, not simple assumption. Moreover, as we saw in §28, there are realms of culture—nonlinguistic communication, patterns of art, music, dance, dream, mysticism—that probably are coded and organized in ways very different from the organization of language. We will return to these questions in §69, after glimpsing customs and beliefs in broad comparative perspective.

Seeking to find out how cultures as ideational systems are organized, and whether universal structures underlie cultural diversity, inevitably leads one to ask what constraints limit and shape cultural designs. Are cultural universals, whatever they turn out to be, shaped by genetic programming? If so, how detailed is this programming? Nobody yet knows.

Whatever the overall framework of cultural knowledge and thinking and however channeled by genetic programming, humans in different times and places have filled in this framework with an extraordinary range of concepts, beliefs, and rules. The French anthropologist Claude Lévi-Strauss has

shown with particular vividness how the human mind operates on the raw materials of experience to produce endlessly elaborated conceptual schemes (§69).

Despite this diversity, human cultures and sociocultural systems have more in common than a universal organizing blueprint. They have more in common partly because humans live in a world that has many common features—whether people are in snow, desert, or rain forest, in the mountainous interior of a continent or on a tiny oceanic atoll—day and night, stars, a lunar cycle, shadows, wind and rain, birth, death, and regeneration; partly because their constitution and biological drives are the same; partly because the constants of mating, birth, infancy, growth, and eventual death provide the framework for life everywhere; and partly because all people live in a universe where life is fragile and most events are beyond human control. All these things make the *contents* of cultural codes far more similar than they might be. Cultures represent varying ways of doing, and thinking about, the same things.

Further limitations on variation in cultural codes come from the exigencies of life in organized societies. Many of the forms of social arrangement or custom humans *could* think of simply would not work. Many they have devised probably have not survived—not necessarily because the tribe died out in a struggle for existence but because the system changed into something more viable.

To what degree there are substantive universals—universals of content as well as of organization—in culture and patterns of social life, and what they might be, are old anthropological questions. Those who have sought to find a set of categories or compartments that *every* culture fills in have been hoping to be able to convert tens of thousands of pages about disparate customs into a framework for comparison. They have also hoped to reveal more clearly the limits of human variability and the organizational and operational challenges that confront every society.

Some scholars have sifted carefully through masses of data looking for features all societies share. Others have worked from the top down, seeking to find a series of problems that every society faces—some resulting from the biological nature of *Homo sapiens;* some from psychological, intellectual, and perceptual processes; some from constants in the life cycle; and some from organizational problems of perpetuating the group, socializing its young, controlling internal conflict, and the like.

Some quests for cultural universals have emphasized biological and psychological "needs" (Malinowski 1944). Others have emphasized the "functional prerequisites" of ordered social life (Aberle et al. 1950). Clyde Kluckhohn, in an important evaluation of the question of universals (1953), gives balanced emphasis to biological, ecological, and sociological pressures that limit human variability. Murdock's 1945 study of cultural universals consists mainly of an empirical sorting through vast ranges of ethnographic evidence in search of minimal common denominators—the incest taboo, marriage, some way of disposing of the dead, and so on. The categories that result are useful for some comparative purposes as a set of pigeonholes into which cultural details can be put and from which they can be retrieved when needed.

Geertz argues that reducing the rich diversity of human experience to common denominators yields vacuous general categories that hide rather than illuminate human nature:

If one defines religion generally . . . —as man's most fundamental orientation to reality, for example—then . . . that orientation . . . [becomes devoid of] content. . . .

What composes the most fundamental orientation to reality among the . . . Aztecs, lifting pulsing

hearts torn live from the chests of human sacrifices toward the heavens, is not what comprises it among the stolid Zuni, dancing their great mass supplications to the benevolent gods of rain.

To get down to less abstract levels and assert, as Kluckhohn did, that a concept of the afterlife is universal . . . one has to define it in . . . terms . . . so general . . . that whatever force it seems to have virtually evaporates. . . . Is it in grasping such general facts [as] that man has everywhere had some sort of "religion" or in grasping the richness of . . . Balinese trance or Indian ritualism, Aztec human sacrifice or Zuni rain dancing that we [best] grasp . . . what it is to be . . . human? (Geertz 1966c:40—43)

The skeletal design of our biological nature, and the universal givens of life cycle and experienced world, do not make humans what they are: they become human by learning rich, diverse, and in some sense unique cultural ways of living in particular times and places. It is the seemingly paradoxical counterpoint of diversity and uniformity, cultural nature and human nature, one world and many, that we will seek to trace and understand in Part 3.

30.
Cultural Diversity and Cultural Relativism

The diversity of humans' modes of thought and belief, and the variety of custom and world view, have led to a troubling realization. What according to our values and moral standards is evil or forbidden or unthinkable may be treated by another people as valuable and right. Thus a South American people may practice cannibalism or raid their neighbors to collect their heads; or they may kill infants to limit population or placate their ancestors. On what moral grounds can we condemn their acts? How can we impose our standards on their world? For if they had our technological power, they might with equal validity condemn and suppress those customs and beliefs of ours that violated their standards.

The concept of cultural relativism, and particularly of ethical relativism—which posits that each way of life can be evaluated only according to its own standards of right and wrong—has profoundly affected American anthropology. Its most articulate spokesman was Melville Herskovits, who referred to cultural relativism as a "tough-minded philosophy." He argued that it underlined the "dignity inherent in every body of custom," and met a "need for tolerance of conventions" different from our own (1951, 1955, 1972).

Critics have risen against this position, both in philosophy and anthropology. Some have argued that ultimate values and general ethical commitments are very similar in different cultures and have sought a kind of universal common denominator of ethical codes.

The extent to which this argument is true is open to considerable debate. But does it matter? Let us step back and view humanity in global perspective, seeing humans as able to imagine a better world than they have managed to create, to conceive lofty and noble standards they can reach for but seldom attain. Does a vision of the desirable have to have been glimpsed and sought in every pocket of the tribal world for it to be a worthwhile and philosophically defensible goal for mankind? Are the wisdom of sages, prophets, and philosophers and mankind's highest aspirations and greatest insights to be thus canceled out in favor of common denominators?

Moreover, cultural relativism leads us into moral impotence in a world where few are prepared to foresake the right to judge. Genocide, racism, and wars of oppression have been and are the "custom" of millions of people, yet even the advocate of cultural relativism in the abstract is unlikely to withhold judgment about them.

Here then lies a dilemma. For much of the conflict and injustice in the modern world has been caused precisely by the powerful seeking to impose their values and ideologies on one another and on the weak—to spread their particular vision of the good life. How then can we transcend ethical relativism without committing the obverse, ethical imperialism?

There is no simple answer. Many anthropologists would urge that cultural relativism is not a position one can ultimately live with—but that it is a position one needs to pass through in search of a clearer vision. By wandering in a desert of relativism, one can sort the profound from the trivial, examine one's motives and conscience and one's customs and beliefs. Like all vision quests, it can be lonely and dangerous; but it can lead to heightened perceptions of ourselves, of what it is to be human, and of what humans could be if they would. In a world where people foist their political dogmas and religious faiths on one another, where modern ideological inquisitions save souls by dispatching them with flame and lead, we sorely need such wisdom.

A major step in this direction is to understand how *different* peoples are and in what ways. In the chapters to follow, we will glimpse the branching paths of human possibility that have been explored by peoples in different times and places. The reader should then be able to reflect on these troubling moral issues with greater insight.

31.
Methods of Cross-Cultural Study

Scholars have sought for many years to discover regularities and patterns across the range of human cultures. Many have hoped to read, from such patterns of association or covariation, sequences of development or chains of cause and effect.

In a classic 1889 paper, Sir Edward Tylor

proposed that by examining correlations between forms of descent or kinship and forms of marriage, one could discover complexes of custom that fit together and thus infer sequences in the development of social institutions. Though here, as so often, Tylor showed visionary brilliance, those who sought to follow his lead ran into difficulty. As reports on primitive custom came in from all over the world and began to pile up, the task of pulling related observations from the library and rendering them comparable became almost insurmountable for any single scholar.

A major assault on this problem came from the Yale Institute of Human Relations, beginning in 1937. G. P. Murdock and his associates worked out a system whereby materials from a great many world cultures could be reproduced verbatim and organized according to a standard indexing code. This enterprise, known as the Human Relations Area File (HRAF), is now shared by a number of American universities that have full sets of the data.

These files have been in turn put to use for cross-cultural reference by various scholars, as with studies of social structure by Murdock (1949) and of sex and reproduction by Ford (1945).

A typical user of the file arrives at a hypothesis, on some theoretical grounds, that cultures with characteristic A will tend to have custom X, while cultures without A will not have X. If A and X are related in some obvious way (if A is square-shaped houses and X is square-shaped roofs) their association will be uninteresting. If A is a way of disciplining children and X is a type of magic, a kind of art style, or a legal system, a demonstration that they are associated lends support to the theory that led to the prediction.

The user goes to the file and rates all societies, or a sample of them, in which A and X or their absence are relevant features—or ideally the user has several other people rate

the cultures so as to minimize the chance that the evidence will be read in a biased way. The investigator then builds a matrix table that shows the distribution of A and X, where $\overline{A}$ is "not A" and $\overline{X}$ is "not X."

	X	$\overline{X}$
A	14	7
$\overline{A}$	7	21

Of 49 societies in the sample, 21 had characteristic A and 28 did not; 14 of those with A also had custom X, while 7 did not. On the other hand, most of those societies without A did not have X. This seems a convincing indication that A and X go together. But just *how* convincing? We need a way of knowing how often patterns like this would appear purely by chance, even if A and X were completely unrelated. This is partly a matter of the sample size. An identical proportion would be represented if the table read

$$\frac{2 \mid 1}{1 \mid 3},$$

yet this could happen very easily if the first seven were pulled randomly out of a hat. If the sample were 10 times as large,

$$\frac{140 \mid 70}{70 \mid 210},$$

it would be all the more convincing. Statistical measures are used to give a *significance level* for such a pattern—telling us how convincing the association is by showing how improbable the purely chance occurrence of such a pattern would be if the variables were unrelated.

This method has been used in recent years to study a bewildering variety of hypotheses—about the relation between child-rearing techniques and religious beliefs, love magic, witchcraft, menstrual taboos, initiation rites, and a host of other things; about the relation of social structure to religious beliefs, art styles, childhood games, and the like; the relation of subsistence economy to everything from sleeping arrangements to stature and mythology.

Useful as the Human Relations Area Files have been, it takes time, resources, and human judgment to use them, and so far they include only a limited sample of world societies. To broaden the sample and take advantage of developing electronic data processing systems, Murdock (1957) published a "World Ethnographic Sample," which scored 565 societies according to 15 criteria (dealing with mode of subsistence, forms of kinship grouping, and so on). The results, tabulated in columns, could be analyzed by computers, by factor analysis (a means of clustering together a set of variables correlated with one another), or other means.

In his journal *Ethnology,* Murdock has expanded this sample and refined his coding system, so that by 1967 the societies in his published *Ethnographic Atlas* totaled almost 1200. The coding categories cover such items as subsistence economy, kinship groups, high gods, games, division of labor, social stratification, and house types. The coding is designed for punch cards, so the variables can be easily processed by computers.

The many recent comparative studies using these larger coded samples include two massive attempts to "correlate everything with everything" and find out what variables were associated to a statistically significant degree. Thus Coult and Habenstein (1965) used a computer to test all possible correlations between Murdock's variables and mark those that were statistically significant. Textor (1967), in an even more massive summary, built by computer all the fourfold tables possible in cross-correlation of 526 variables, for 400 societies, and weeded out by hand and computer the statistically insignificant and

spurious associations. What remains is a massive source of hypotheses to be tested by more intensive means.

Further attempts to reduce or analyze the complexities and obscurities of such "random search" statistical summaries have come from factor analyses by such scholars as Driver and Schuessler and methodological assessments like that of Köbben (1967). Driver and Schuessler (1967) strikingly reveal how seeming world-wide correlations may hold well on some continents and only slightly if at all on others. Murdock's expanded new sample should yield valuable new insights on this and other comparative problems.

Cross-cultural studies, and what they have and have not accomplished, are reviewed and summarized by Naroll (1970). Naroll and Cohen have further edited a massive handbook of anthropological method (1970) where cross-cultural methods are discussed in a series of papers by leading comparativists.

The cross-cultural method is fraught with difficulty. First there is what has come to be known as "Galton's problem"—the fact that some cases included in a sample may not in fact be independent but may reflect a common historical origin for the pattern in question. Various sophisticated techniques have been proposed for circumventing this danger. But the whole problem of what is an independent observation and what is a representative sample clouds the application and validity of simple statistical methods (see Barnes 1972).

Second, correlations do not show cause and effect, yet most scholars are trying to read such directionality into their findings. If A and X tend to go together, it may be because A causes X or because X causes A. But it can also be because a third and undiscovered factor causes both A and X. Actually, it can be argued that our very notions of linear causality are biases of our own culture and that in nature things do not happen that way. We should expect to encounter complex cybernetic systems, where causality connects elements in intricate networks, so that a change affects the whole system.

Third, because of the uniqueness of cultures, coding them in terms of standard categories inevitably distorts their structure. Classifying descent and residence in a society is easy if the ethnographer simply says "residence is patrilocal" or "there are six patrilineal clans." If the ethnographer gives pages and pages of statistics and cultural detail, it is often apparent that none of the coding categories really fits. The more we know, the harder it may be to reduce rich cultural detail into holes in punch cards.

Fourth, there are serious problems in the sample—any sample—given the quite simple statistical methods used in most cross-cultural studies. As Barnes (1971) points out, what the boundaries of "a culture" are, how many people are supposed to share "a culture," and for what time span, are problems that have been given insufficient attention in cross-cultural studies.

All anthropologists recognize that errors and distortions are introduced in cross-cultural studies. But those who believe in cross-cultural methods feel that the errors will cancel out and that, if anything, empirically valid patterns will be disguised, not magnified, by them (Köbben 1967). Many of those who do not believe in such methods think that the errors are cumulative and that the whole notion of cultures having or not having a standard set of features like a catalog of spare parts is fundamentally wrong. They believe that revealing cross-cultural comparison will come from study in depth of a few well-chosen cases, not massive but superficial statistical studies. Yet even most critics of large-scale statistical comparisons regard them as useful sources of hypotheses for more intensive study.

In Chapter 12, we will sketch a model of social and cultural change that will illuminate the possibilities and problems of comparing different ways of life to discover why they assume particular forms in particular times and places. First, we need to look at another crucially important aspect of people-in-groups: the place of *individuals,* and how they are shaped by, and shape, the cultural world in which they grow up.

CULTURE AND
THE INDIVIDUAL

11

A New Guinea tribesman, gravely examining the inkblot patterns on a Rorschach plate proffered by an anthropologist, describes what he sees in them: a swirl of moving birds, bats, and mythical creatures of the forest where he lives. His fellow villagers also saw swirling animals and beings in the plates.

The way these New Guineans respond to these plates—not just *what* they see, but the *way* they perceive and report their responses—can be scored by a clinical psychologist, using standardized principles of interpretation. What if the New Guineans' responses are ones that, if an American had produced them, would indicate severe psychological imbalance?

Perhaps the tribesmen are expressing a personality pattern similar to the American's, but the kinds of pathological childhood experiences that engendered the personality of the American are standardized in the child-rearing practices of the New Guineans. Hence

what is abnormal in the United States is normal in this New Guinea tribe. Furthermore, it is possible that the tribe's beliefs in dangerous ancestral ghosts, their male cult of mysterious flutes and rites forbidden to women, and the ordeals by which boys are initiated into the cult are projections of the psychological stresses and conflicts these childhood experiences produce.

Such lines of interpretation build on a series of assumptions—about cultures, about social life, about the depths of the human mind, about the instruments of testing. In the 1940s and 1950s such possibilities were explored by many American anthropologists. "Culture and personality" became a major subfield of the discipline. Spurred by efforts in World War II to delineate the "national character" of enemies and allies, methods for probing personality in other cultures proliferated and were refined.

In recent years interest in such problems

has waned. New conceptions of culture, new focal points of interest in psychology, and the frustrations and circularities of assaulting such major questions head on have shifted attention elsewhere. Smaller, more manageable questions have continued to command attention—questions about learning, about cross-cultural variations in cognitive styles and skills, about psychological abnormality in non-Western societies, about how the genetic diversity and psychological differences within a population are channeled by its culture, about the effects on personality of drastic culture change. There have now been, in the early 1970s, signs of a renewed attack on larger questions, though in more sophisticated ways that avoid some of the circularities, and the assumptions of personality standardization, that plagued past research.

Asking, though briefly, about the relationship between the psychological worlds of individuals and the cultural knowledge they share will give us a clearer conception of how ways of life shape and are shaped by the human individuals who live them.

32.
Culture and Personality: Conceptual Problems

A culture, as we have used the concept, is a picture of the ideational world of a people built up as a composite by the anthropologist. The anthropologist builds that composite by studying the knowledge, beliefs, values, and goals of individuals. Though we know that the thought world of each of them is different from every other's, the ethnographer seeks to discover that knowledge they must broadly share in order to communicate. This focus on what is shared rather than what is distinctive of each individual is useful to an anthropologist trying to make sense of what people are doing. It is a way of summing up what they know and do, what makes their world different.

But that raises the danger that we will be trapped into talking about culture as if it were some thing *outside* the minds of individuals, and that we will see it as shaping personality, thwarting drives, and causing behavior, as if it were an external force.

"Much of the literature in anthropology has perpetuated the myth that *culture uses man*" (Spradley 1972b:30). What a particular Eskimo does is not shaped by Eskimo culture as an external force—though it is partly shaped by the individual's conception of what other Eskimos do and of the system of customs they are following. If Eskimo culture shapes an Eskimo's behavior, it shapes it in and through his mind.

But there is also a danger in saying that culture simply *is* the psychological world of the individual. The Eskimo's behavior expresses emotions and drives, not simply "rules" and programs, and we do not want to call these part of his or her culture. Moreover, much of what he knows about his world concerns his family, his neighbors, his dogs, the most comfortable place to sit, and the most rewarding place to hunt. His knowledge is of specific, individual, unique people, places, and things of his familiar life space, as well as general principles, rules, and categories.

An Eskimo's *cultural* knowledge is only one segment of what he knows: a theory of what kind of world he lives in and what fellow Eskimos do (and should do), believe, and mean. Moreover, he himself may well consciously perceive "the system" as external: he has some free rein to try to beat it, join it, or change it.

An infant arrives in a social world that already exists, with rules, customs, and meanings that must be learned; in that sense too, then, the culture is external and prior to each child acquiring it. Yet the culture in another sense exists only as the sum of its realizations in individual minds at a particular time.

How to sort out the shared cultural code from the dynamics of individual personality and life experience has led through the years to circularity and methodological and conceptual headaches. Some progress is being made in this sorting. But further progress—mainly a deepened understanding of how cognitive, emotional, and motivational strands are interwoven in mind and brain, and of how a child learns and what capacities the child brings to this task—is needed before the sorting can be more than provisional.

Despite the difficulties, research in the last several decades has built up a substantial body of evidence on the interweaving of cultural patterns and the psychology of individuals. These can be set out as a series of propositions with which most workers in the field would agree, even though they disagree in matters of shading, emphasis, conceptualization, and explanation.

33.
Culture and the Individual: Substantive Findings and Explorations

1. Through childhood experience, each individual builds up a conceptual system, a theory, of what kind of world he or she lives in and how humans act and should act. These theories about the stage on which human life is set and the ways for humans to act are partly shared with other members of one's society, partly melded of unique experience and the particularities of each individual's niche in life.

2. Each of us has a sense of identity, a conception of one's self and one's place in the world. This sense of personal identity is culturally shaped to some degree, yet it varies widely among individuals in ways that reflect genetic differences in temperament and endowment and the particularities of experience and life situation. (Thus the self-conception of orphan or last-born child or member of pariah caste may be negatively shaped by the niche society affords.)

3. In any population, individuals vary greatly in the genetic templates underlying personality. These differences are not yet well understood, but they include differences in various sorts of cognitive capacities, in metabolism, and seemingly in hard-to-define inclinations to be gregarious, introverted, and so on. Childhood experiences, which are far from standardized in any society, reshape and build on these varying biological templates and fill them in with emotional coloring and the content of cultural learning. This process generates the diverse personalities of a society. We will see shortly how crucial is the sorting out and channeling of such individual diversity into the role system of the society.

4. Even cognitive patterns, the versions of cultural knowledge individuals learn, need not be standardized. They need only be *congruent,* so they fit together. Any society's members have varying rules and principles, alternative ways of doing things. Wallace (1970) has shown how people's expectations can still be borne out and communication maintained amid such diversity in cultural codes. It will be suggested in the next chapter that a reservoir of such code diversity within a society may be necessary, as is biological diversity, if adaptive change is to be possible.

5. Childhood experience molds and channels the emotional and motivational organization of each individual's personality in more or less parallel ways. Here the conceptual line between each individual's version of the culture and other elements of personality becomes difficult and messy. If individuals grow up in an African or Melanesian society where sorcery is culturally defined as the

cause of every death, and where neighbors are culturally defined as the people most likely to cause one's death, people are likely to have fears and suspicions that would be abnormal and paranoid in our society. The extent to which such emotional orientations are standardized, and the extent to which they can best be thought of as cognitive or as expressions of personality dynamics, have been much debated. Here the intricate interweaving between what an individual has learned about the world and biologically rooted drives and motives has been hard to sort out. That one gets hungry is predictably human; whether you get hungry for a ham sandwich at noon or grubs in mid-afternoon depends on where you happened to grow up. That one has sexual desires is biologically predictable; but what partner one finds desirable and how and where erotic gratification is managed depends substantially on cultural learning. So too with angers, fears, and joys: what we respond to and how we respond are culturally patterned, though the wellsprings of these emotions lie deep in the evolutionarily ancient limbic system of the brain.

Each society provides, through its social organization and child-rearing customs, settings in which learning takes place. Much research on culture and the individual has focused on how the world is learned, not simply on what is learned about it. These more or less standardized experiences shape personality. How often and under what circumstances an infant is fed or bathed, how it is held, how and when it is disciplined, or the age and circumstances of weaning vary widely and are usually subject to fairly clear cultural conventions (see, for example, Whiting 1963). Though there is much variation in individual experience, based on the nature of social and emotional relations within the family, position in a sibling set, particularities of life history, and biological predispositions, some degree of cultural patterning and channeling—though not *standardization*—of personality is created.

6. Personality patterns and styles of emotional expression may often reflect genetic and biochemical factors, for example, dietary deficiencies, interacting with cultural learning and individual experience. It has been suggested that a culturally patterned form of collective hysteria (*amok* in Malay, *latah* in the Arctic, the Windigo psychosis among the Ojibwa Indians) might reflect a chemical imbalance—such as calcium deficiency—as well as a set of cultural expectations about what to perceive and how to respond, though evidence is inconclusive (Wallace 1960; Foulks 1972). Similarly, culturally patterned aggression, seemingly endemic in some societies, may also reflect biochemical deficiencies as well as cultural learning.

Cross-cultural studies of mental illness and forms of trance, vision, hysteria, possession, and other culturally defined forms of illness and abnormal or extranormal behavior have suggested the complex interplay of genetic, environmental, and learned components. Sorting out these elements is enormously difficult.

Case 11: Qolla Aggression

The Qolla of the South American Andes, and other Aymara-speaking Indians, have been described by many observers for more than a century as highly aggressive, hostile, violent, treacherous—the list of derogatory adjectives goes on. Various observers have attributed the social and psychological turbulence of the Aymara to their harsh high-altitude environment, impoverished existence, and cruel domination by Indian and then Spanish and mestizo ruling classes.

Bolton regards these interpretations as only partial: they do not account for individual variations in aggressiveness among the Qolla, for the mechanisms whereby social and psychological stress is translated into aggressive behavior, and for the quite different behavior exhibited by other populations subject to seemingly similar pressures. There must be a missing element, and a way to break out of the circularity of explanation.

Bolton hypothesized that high altitude and poor diet place many individuals far below the optimal levels of blood sugar (glucose), though individual biochemistry and diet lead to different degrees of such hypoglycemia. Drawing on extensive neurophysiological and biochemical evidence, Bolton suggests that moderate hypoglycemia may activate aggressive response patterns in the neural system so that individuals so affected are prone to excitability and violence and are easily triggered off by normally innocuous stimuli of everyday social life. Bolton tested blood sugar levels of Qolla men, and, independently, had Qolla rate one another on a four-point scale of aggressiveness. In the sample, Bolton's hunch was strikingly supported: of the 13 men ranked by the Qolla as highly aggressive, 11 showed moderate blood sugar deficiency, while one was normal and one was low. Among the 13 at the low end of the aggressiveness scale, 8 had normal blood sugar, 3 had moderate deficiency, and 2 had a severe deficiency (Bolton had hypothesized that a severe deficiency would lead to low energy and hence perhaps would limit aggressiveness).

The sample is fairly small, the measurements inevitably less than ideal, and biological knowledge of the mechanisms involved still unfortunately somewhat limited. But this example does suggest that there is a physiological link in a complex web of variables—involving diet, altitude, and social stress—that makes the Qolla vulnerable to interpersonal conflict and socially and psychologically disruptive bursts of hostility (Bolton 1973).

In some cases, cultures define special roles for biologically abnormal individuals. Edgerton (1964) has shown that the substantial proportion of humans born with some form of intersexuality (hermaphrodites) can be accorded quite different social niches. We Americans want to know whether an intersex individual is "really" male or female, and do our best to alter surgically or at least disguise a condition incompatible with our social categories and role system. The Navaho Indians treat intersex individuals as special, sacred, and valuable—the source of benefit and wealth for those not divinely blessed in this way (Edgerton 1964). As Geertz (n.d.) observes, "intersexuality is more than an empirical surprise; it is a cultural challenge"—a challenge cultures meet in diverse ways, depending on their view of the nature of the universe, their conceptions of culture, nature, male and female, and on the system of social roles into which the "abnormal" can be fitted.

Even schizophrenics and others so mentally disturbed as to have no place in our society but a mental hospital may find productive and crucially important niches as shamans, seers, visionaries (Silverman 1967). Whether the talk of the schizophrenic, divorced from the realities of the physical world, comes from a disordered mind or a divine source is something our cultures tell us. Whether a schizophrenic ends up as a mental patient or a religious prophet depends on the circumstances of time and place and his or her talents in selling a unique vision of self and of the world to other people.

7. Cultural experience also selects from the repertoire of potential cognitive skills, reinforcing and developing some in culturally distinctive ways, leaving others relatively undeveloped. Thus Micronesian seafarers who navigate by stars and tides, or African Bushmen or Australian Aborigines tracking game, or Polynesians reciting vastly long genealogies, or Balinese in trances or Plains Indians on vision quests, all are using special culturally fostered skills. These skills are not shared equally by all: every society has its experts and its clods, whatever the skill in question. Differences in cognitive style have been extensively studied cross-culturally in recent years—though as with projective tests of personality, difficulties of rapport and cultural bias in the test instruments make findings difficult to interpret (see Cole and Scribner 1974).

8. In situations of rapid change, individuals must find paths of life in a world where cultural patterns do not fit, where old rules cannot apply, old standards are inappropriate, old satisfactions are blocked. Yet some deep cultural orientations and some elements of personality seem to endure, sometimes over generations, despite great changes in the outward mode of life. The Spindlers' recent work on cultural transmission and cultural change seems particularly illuminating (see G. D. Spindler 1973; Spindler and Spindler 1971). They view individual adaptation to cultural change in terms of cognitive perceptions and strategies, but place these in a wider context of a world that is forcing a subordinate group to accommodate to new and oppressive situations and alternatives (see Chapter 21). In the Spindlers' formulation, a culture consists in part of *instrumental linkages,* behavioral strategies that lead to culturally valued goals. Each individual must work out a kind of mental map of the ways to find one's way through the mazes of life. Each such map must recognize that there are alternative goals, paths, and strategies, must accommodate the conflicts between them, and hence must give the individual a measure of control over his or her life.

In situations of rapid culture change, traditional ways through the maze may no longer be possible; new goals emerge, and paths to

A Micronesian navigator, his cognitive skills fostered by study of the stars and detailed knowledge and experience of currents, winds, and tiny islands (Teruo of Puluwat, Central Carolines). (Courtesy of David Lewis.)

A Micronesian master navigator teaches apprentices the star compass with pebbles, on Puluwat, Central Caroline Islands. (Photograph by P. J. Silverman. From T. Gladwin, *East Is a Big Bird*. By permission of Harvard University Press.)

them may be glimpsed but not fully open. Individuals may become partly bicultural, may draw on old values and virtues to validate new strategies, and so on. Or two ways of life may be compartmentalized so an individual moves between them. This requires a complex cognitive reorganization in which individuals reformulate their models of the world and their strategies for coping with it and finding paths through it.

We will return to psychological adaptations to drastic change in §76.

In all this, we see a growing emphasis on *cognition*—on how humans organize their knowledge of the world, not simply how their emotions and motives are culturally channeled.

We need to balance this emphasis on cognition by looking at the beginnings of a resurgent interest in the organization of emotion, in the classic concerns of psychoanalysis as given new life and new light by ethology and modern psychobiology.

We will then return to a predominantly cognitive concern as we ask how a culture is learned. A child's acquisition of cultural competence has—like the formation and dynamics of personality—been illuminated by advances in other fields. What had been a relatively sterile and unproductive field of study has been given new light and new excitement.

34.
Personality in Evolutionary Perspective

The most influential stream of thought in modern personality research has been psychoanalytic theory—the work of Freud and such scholars as Jung, Abraham, Ferenczi, Fenichel, Hartmann, Klein, Winnicott, Anna Freud, Horney, Sullivan, Fromm, and Erikson.

Since the first two decades of this century anthropologists have had a continuing dialogue with psychoanalysts, through such figures as Kroeber, Linton, Mead, Kluckhohn, LaBarre, Leach, and Fortes. The anthropological side of these dialogues has ranged from sympathetic borrowing to critical skepticism. A few scholars whose primary training or commitment was in psychoanalysis, notably Roheim, Kardiner, and Erikson, have worked directly with anthropological materials.

One element in this dialogue has been to ask whether psychoanalytic theories of the unconscious could illuminate custom, belief, and behavior in non-Western societies. Might the supernatural spirits of a tribal people represent projections of parental figures, hence of the conflicts of primary experience? Such questions, to which we will shortly return, have been a continuing theme in psychoanalytically oriented anthropology.

Another element has been the effort to broaden psychoanalytic theory, rendering it less culture-bound. Could the repression of overt sexuality by the Viennese bourgeoisie whom he treated have misled Freud into overly limited models of the unconscious? Bronislaw Malinowski's early clash with Ernest Jones about the Oedipus complex (Malinowski 1927) has been followed by many efforts to generalize psychoanalytic theory in the light of cultural variation. Did the hostility of father and infant son, and rivalry over the mother's sexuality, which Freud viewed as central in human psychology everywhere, take the same form, and have the same importance, where—as in the Trobriand Islands—a boy's maternal uncle, not his father, was the stern disciplinarian?

Anthropological interest in psychoanalysis

had often been limited by a relatively narrow concern with social relations and how societies worked. And after a burst of interest in "depth psychology" in American culture and personality research, there was widespread disillusionment with the apparent chicken-or-egg circularities of interpretation and the lack of firm evidence on the processes of mind. A very large proportion of modern anthropologists are relatively untrained in, skeptical about, and generally uninterested in psychoanalysis and other related theories of personality.

Some scholars, such as George Devereux and Weston LaBarre, stuck to their psychoanalytic orientations through the years, and they have been joined by others[1] who have been drawn into psychoanalytic theory after more conventional social anthropological training. There are now signs of a resurgence in the continuous but long-attenuated stream of psychoanalytic anthropology; and there are strong signs that this resurgence will now yield much deeper insights than have yet been possible.

It would be premature even to sketch the shape of a more powerful and anthropologically useful theory of the unconscious mind. But drawing on the evidence from Chapter 3, we can at least examine why deepened understanding is becoming possible, and can glimpse some partial outlines of an emerging theory.

A theory of the human unconscious and its relationship to the cultural products of mind can now become biologically grounded in a way that has never before been possible. It is not that Freud was uninterested in biology: he was first a neurophysiologist and always an explorer of the biological roots of human mental life. But unfortunately, in Freud's day almost nothing was known about

[1]Such as T. O. Beidelman, Paul Bohannan, A. L. Epstein, and Derek Freeman.

human evolution, about the evolution of behavior, about the behavior of primates and other mammals in natural settings, and about the brain. Freudian theory, seeking to be a biological theory of the mind, had to be created virtually in a biological vacuum.

Freud, in the absence of an adequate knowledge of animal behavior and its evolution, drew on inference and on clinical data: he saw animals as driven by biological urges to eat and to reproduce, and thus to the killing and combat of hunting and mating. Since humans are animals, such biological urges must lie deep in the brain and be overlain by the mechanisms of conscious mind. Cultural learning must provide the controls whereby the animal nature of man is kept within bounds and bonds, for without cultural controls our drives of sex, hunger, and aggression would break loose and ordered social life would be impossible. But our true animal nature and the wellsprings of our psychic and hence physical energy lie beneath these conscious overlays.

Human mental life is therefore a continuing dynamic of conflict and control, of channeled expression, redirection, and repression of basic instinctual urges and energies. Cultural control and hence social life exact a severe cost in anxiety, conflict, and often neurosis. The normal processes of the psyche—of dreams and other fantasy, of symbolizing, of everyday social interaction—express the blockage, redirection, and disguised expression of the energies of our natural life forces. Since we are unable, due to cultural convention, to deal directly and consciously with the sexual and aggressive drives so central in unconscious mind, we repress, we sublimate, we disguise in symbols, we deny, we redirect. Though the costs of psychic health are severe and are manifest in neurosis or at worst in psychosis, these processes of fantasy and repression also underlie the cultural creations of art and religion.

This seems now not to be all wrong, but to be partly wrong. In the light of modern ethology, it substantially distorts our animal nature.

First, all mammals are, in varying degree, *social* animals. They are biologically programmed not simply to satisfy individual urges, but to live in groups—and this is vividly true of the higher primates, as we saw in Chapter 3. The behavior patterns that are transmitted biologically and shaped by evolution are orchestrated so as to produce group behaviors that are adaptive.

The model of conscious mind superimposed on primal nature is partly supported by modern knowledge of the brain in evolutionary perspective, but it is too simple. The evolutionarily ancient limbic system of the brain is geared to survival and reproduction, and it is the neural source of surges of rage and other emotions. In the course of mammalian evolution it has not been superseded and eliminated, but with the development of the mammalian neocortex, it has been connected into a more complicated system where the old limbic system continues to serve the basic demands of survival (McLean 1964, 1968, 1969, 1970).

In humans, the further elaboration of the neocortex made possible a vast new power of symbolic thought as well as language. The synthesis of old and new regions of the brain is far from fully harmonious; and it is possible on neural and behavioral grounds to support Freud's view that our cortical symbolic systems are the servants of the limbic system, not the reverse. Humans are never more human than when they create intricate webs of symbolic rationalization for their "gut"—that is, limbic—emotions.

But that is only part of the picture. In mammalian and hominid evolution, limbic system and neocortex *have been evolving together as a system*—a system that must be adaptive if species are to survive. Humans, in evolving massive cortical capacities for problem-solving and symbolic elaboration, have also evolved a complex circuitry that connects with older parts of the brain. Cortical control of limbic processes is a product of evolutionary selection, not a cultural imposition on our biological nature. *It is our biological nature to be cultural.*

Thus the modern neurosciences point to serious inadequacies in Freudian and other psychoanalytic conceptions of consciousness and unconscious. Mind and brain are staggeringly complex. No dichotomy of the Freudian sort between unconscious and conscious, or between primary and secondary process, or any other *stratigraphic* theory of mind that sees "levels" as deeper and shallower can be adequate. The structures of the brain whereby left and right cerebral hemispheres are complementary—the left normally performing predominantly linguistic, logical, and sequential operations and the right performing primarily holistic, integrative operations— render any stratigraphic conception of mind inadequate. So too do the results of brain damage, which point to different brain locations and different processing and organization of the programs for language, for dealing with the natural environment, and for dealing with the social environment. For example, some brain-damaged patients are severely handicapped in their social relations due to an inability to "read" the responses and moods of others, yet can read newspapers or perform manual operations unimpaired; in other cases patients' social relations are unimpaired but their ability to "read" and manipulate the physical environment is severely impaired by brain damage. In one celebrated case, a Soviet composer totally lost the powers of language due to massive brain damage, but continued to compose music. Conscious and unconscious need now be viewed as an extreme oversimplification of a vastly complex system we are only beginning to understand.

The very notion that cognitive programs and the forces of motivation are separate, however complicated, will no longer do. As Bateson (1972b) argues, the forces of motivation are not simply surges of psychic energy, but complicated neurally coded programs. And as the neurophysiologist Karl Pribram has suggested (1967, 1971), these motivational programs and the largely learned programs for dealing with the world in culturally appropriate ways are much more closely interconnected than Freud could have suspected.

What we urgently need is a model of what psychoanalysts call conscious and unconscious that is squarely built on modern evolutionary biology and the neurosciences. If that means scrapping substantial elements of psychoanalytic theory, then these elements must go.

Fortunately, however, modern clinical explorers of the human psyche have been dealing with and theorizing about real and crucial manifestations of a human mind much more complicated than the early investigators could have imagined. The challenge is not to deny or abandon what has been found, but to place it into a progressively more powerful framework of biological understanding—a challenge Freud himself would have been the first to pursue had he lived to see the efflorescence of ethology and the neurosciences.

Moreover, probing the neural bases of behavior and the structures of mind no longer need rely on the great leaps of faith that were required in psychoanalytic explorations of the psychic depths. Interpreting dreams or myths is still a subtle and difficult matter; though we know a good deal about the neural bases of memory and symbolization, there is much more that remains mysterious. But for many aspects of behavior the gap between biology and mental activities has been closed considerably. Rage, trance states, fear, and even love have been greatly illuminated by modern biologically grounded behavior theory. Asking about the depths of mind is now a scientific challenge where the controls of experimental biology and the insights of clinical and symbolic interpretation can be complementary and mutually illuminating.

If the innately programmed elements of human behavior are not simply an ancient residue of our distant animal past, but have evolved as adaptations to the conditions of hominid social life, then we can build here on the knowledge described in Chapters 2 and 3. What are these special conditions and how might they fit into the findings of psychoanalysis?

Two critical developments in hominid social life were the prolonged dependency of human infants and the continuous pair relationship between mates that constitutes the basis of the family and hence of human social life. These developments render biologically plausible a major finding of the psychoanalyst John Bowlby and its extension by other researchers. Bowlby (1969) and his colleagues have discovered that human infants are programmed to form a deep biopsychological *bond* with the adult, normally the mother, who provides close and continuous nurturance between the ages of approximately three and seven months. This *primary bond* is a psychologically compelling deep attachment human infants are biologically geared to form, which then becomes a kind of template for other subsequent emotional social relationships.

Though the primary bond is normally with the mother, cultural conventions can modify its nature considerably. In European upper classes a nanny assumed this nurturant role. (Winston Churchill's lifelong bond with his nanny Mrs. Everest, and his distant though adoring relationship with his mother, is a vivid illustration.[2]) The circumstances of life history

may render this relationship diffuse if a child has multiple nurturant adults in the crucial period. But anthropological material on this matter must be treated with caution: Freeman's (1974) data from Samoa, where the presence of many nurturant aunts and other relatives was supposed to render the attachment of a child diffuse, compellingly show that the primary bond was with one person, usually the mother. The emotional *content* of the primary bond varies considerably according to the nature of the particular life experience. Undoubtedly it always is ambivalent, entailing both love and hostility: for the nurturant person inevitably both gratifies and frustrates the infant's physical and emotional needs.

The biological program to form this primary bond must have an important adaptive function. Presumably it lays the biopsychological foundation for the long dependent relationship of the child and helps to preserve safety and thus survival. But it is also noteworthy that the primary bond apparently provides a model or template for the close emotional relationships a person enters into with other members of the group (especially kin— see §40). It also appears to provide an emotional template for the pair-bonding relationship whereby man and woman create the setting for bearing their children.[3] The varying emotional content of the primary bond from individual to individual presumably partly accounts for the tone of adult social relationships.

Traditional psychoanalytic theory grasped part of this phenomenon in its central emphasis on the Oedipal relationship that emerges in a subsequent developmental stage. The always-secondary attention paid to the cir-

---

[2]The example is taken from Freeman (1974). George Devereux (personal communication) notes that upperclass Hungarian mothers carefully hide the identity of peasant nannies from their children so as to try to curtail such bonds, presumably at great psychological cost.

[3]Derek Freeman (personal communication), drawing on considerable evidence, argues that falling in love is an unconscious reactivation of the primary bond. Whatever the cultural rules for marriage, impassioned lovers find one another—at least sometimes—in every society and often risk death to be together.

cumstances of female infants and the psychology of women in psychoanalytic (as well as anthropological) theory has led to some distortion in this regard (see Chodorow 1974; Mitchell 1974). An infant girl's primary bond to her mother is, as Freudians perceived, partly transferred to her father—hence the Electra complex. That is, the emotional relationship of the primary bond is transferred to the male parent and "sexualized."[4]

The psychoanalytic focus on male infants—and only negatively on female infants[5]—led to limited understanding of the psychological orientation of women as derived from this "primal" situation. The close bond between mother and daughter, marked by unbroken continuities, and its importance are discussed by Chodorow (1974) in a paper to which we will return in §72. Psychoanalysts have paid much more attention to the Oedipal father-son relationship, where father is punitive and threatening, both as disciplinarian and as sexual rival vis-à-vis mother.

The broadened view anthropologists get of the familial situation in comparative perspective has led Fortes (1974), Devereux (1953), and others to see the threat and ambivalence of parent-child relations from the standpoint of the parents as well as the children. Humans, foreseeing their own demise, can hardly avoid seeing in their children their eventual successors, survivors, and replacements. Culturally patterned ambivalence and tension is a common theme (Fortes 1974). Here the evidence from anthropology is particularly vivid: conflicts and emotional dramas that are probably universal in human experience, yet in our society may be openly acted out only by psychiatric patients, may in other societies become a focus of ritual practice and cultural convention. As Fortes (1974:93) has observed, "What may appear as idiosyncratic or even bizarre individual responses . . . in one culture will be embodied in public and normal custom in some other culture."

[4]It is this transferred complex that, if Freeman is right, is reactivated when a girl falls in love.
[5]As in the literature on penis envy.

Case 12: The First-Born among the Tallensi

Among the Tallensi, a tribal people of Ghana, descent and inheritance pass from father to son. (We will view the Tallensi households of father and multiple wives in Case 39, Chapter 14.)

The Tallensi strikingly dramatize and ritualize the tensions between parents and the children who will replace them. The focus of customary observance is the first-born son, who culturally bears the brunt of ambivalence of a father toward being supplanted by his sons.

It is important, first, that the Tallensi marry and have children—in fact, a man must have a son if he is to attain fulfillment psychologically and culturally. Children are desired and sought; without a male heir one cannot become an ancestor and hence be assured of a permanent place in the Tallensi cosmos.

Tallensi consider the crowning glory, indeed the only worthwhile object of life, to be assurance of leaving descendants, ideally in the male line. . . . To have lived successfully one must die with the hope of achieving ancestorhood and that is possible only if one leaves male descendants. (Fortes 1974:84)

A first-born Tallensi son is ritually shown the inside of his father's granary for the first time, as part of the funeral ceremony. (Courtesy of Meyer Fortes.)

But it is the first-born son, and secondarily the first-born daughter, whose birth signals the end of the uphill path of a person's life and the beginning of the downhill path leading to senility and death (the Tallensi are not really anxious to hurry into ancestorhood). From the age of five or six, the first-born son may not eat from the same dish as his father, may not wear his father's cap or tunic, carry his quiver, or use his bow; and he may not look into his father's granary. After the first-born son reaches adolescence he and his father may not meet in the entrance to the house compound. Parallel taboos restrict the relations of a first-born daughter with her mother, with the mother's storage pot being forbidden to the daughter.

When the parents die the replacement by the first-born children is ritually dramatized. First-born son and first-born daughter take the lead in the mortuary rites: the son puts on his dead father's cap and tunic. An elder holding the dead man's bow leads the son to the forbidden granary and guides him inside. And only when his father is dead does the son assume full ritual maturity and make sacrifices—especially to his dead father, as mediator between those still living and more remote ancestors.

Some elements in the ritual symbolism are fairly transparent—the phallic bow, explicitly a cultural symbol of manhood, the granary as repository of seed and fertility. But more important are the ways in which the taboos and rites dramatize changes of status built into the human life cycle and give them cultural expression (the transition to the status of parenthood, the founding of a sibling group in which the oldest assume responsibility); and even more important are the ways in which these rites and restrictions express psychological ambivalence and hostility along socially channeled paths. All parents in all societies are ambivalent toward the children that drain their energies and will eventually replace them; inevitably they feel hostility and resentment as well as love and attachment. In all societies, these negative feelings must be transcended: a society where parents were encouraged to kill or desert their children (except under the very special exigencies of culturally enjoined infanticide) or simply not to have any could hardly be well equipped for long-term survival. But the ambivalence can be dramatized in ritual avoidance and taboo, and thus to some extent stripped of guilt and relieved of tension. Among the Tallensi, the making of first-born son and daughter so directly into symbolic replacements focuses and at the same time de-fuses the hostility of parents and the thwarted rivalry (for example, the Oedipal conflict) of children. The cultural creation of ancestors at the same time denies the finality of death and the loss of loved ones.

Freud, in his famous but now scientifically outmoded essay "Totem and Taboo," conjectured that the beginning of human society came when a band of protohumans enacted a drama of "primal parricide." The young males were dominated by the powerful old male, who claimed all the females. "One day" the young males rose up together and killed the senior male, their father. They ate him and gained access to the females—but then, in a flood of guilt, renounced the females and venerated the slain father in symbolic form as totem. This is a handy story for explaining the incest taboo, with its great emotional power, and also the origin of totemism (§17, p. 85). The guilt of rivalry and parricide was seen by Freud as a persistent central theme in the human unconscious. The insights of "Totem and Taboo" need not be totally discarded, but they must be placed in a radically different framework: the primal parricide emerges as a kind of parable of the father-son-mother psychic drama of conflict, sexual rivalry, and eventual replacement rather than as a contribution to hominid ethology.

Freeman (1967:30) has argued that "the essential elements of the Oedipal situation—the sexual drive, dominance, aggression, and fear—are phylogenetically given, and . . . are basic to the nature of the human animal and to human behavior in all known kinds of family or procreative groups."

We can see another broad social theme. Men are born of women; whatever political control they gain and whatever symbolic elaborations they build, they cannot acquire or control the power to create life. Moreover, they are born into the women's realm; and if the male realm is sharply separated, boys must be pulled over to the men's side. There is considerable anthropological evidence that male envy of female reproductive powers is a central though covert symbolic theme in a great many societies. Male initiations, secret cults, and other elaborations may partly represent male compensations for their ultimate inadequacy: their inability to create life or even to control reproductive powers (Ardener 1972; Ortner 1974). We will return to this theme in Chapters 19 and 24.

If religious institutions or rites may in part be expressions of psychological conflicts, is it possible that deities or other supernaturals are psychological projections? Is a punishing deity a psychological projection of a disciplining father? The psychoanalyst Abram Kardiner, the psychoanalytic anthropologist Geza Roheim, and others have long argued that supernaturals are indeed creations of projection and relations with them, in propitiation or expiation, reenact or express conflicts or guilt toward parental figures. We will shortly see Derek Freeman's interpretation of the thunder god among Malay tribes as a projected father figure.

Many, perhaps most, anthropologists would reject such interpretations. The private and personal fantasy of an individual may be subject to interpretation in terms of individual psychological experience, many would say, but beliefs and rites that are shared and public cannot be interpreted in terms of the individual psyche. Many would cite Émile Durkheim's dictum that shared patterns of culture—"collective representations"—cannot be accounted for through the psychology of individuals. The converse has been forcefully argued by LaBarre (1970), Devereux (1975), and others. Belief systems, bodies of myth, and ritual sequences all have histories in time and space. The illusion that they do not derives from the anthropological study of societies for which there are no historic records. A particular myth or ritual procedure has a history that can have begun only as a private fantasy which was socially communicated. Each modification in retelling, or borrowing of a myth, or alteration of a rite is similarly the product of individual minds.

To become shared and hence part of the culture, a religious or ritual element must be socially communicated and must be accepted by others. These characteristics, LaBarre and Devereux argue, distinguish a private fantasy that serves only the private psychological needs of its creator from the private fantasy that strikes a responsive chord in others and that draws on psychological experience shared with others as well as on a cultural repertoire of symbolic elements.

The process whereby one person's dream becomes a society's myth, and one person's private compulsion becomes a society's ritual,

is little understood. A culture apparently includes a body of symbolic material—a lexicon of symbolic building blocks—out of which myths and rites are constructed and modified; it may also include unconscious "grammars" for tale telling (Colby 1973), myth-making (Lévi-Strauss 1969a, 1969b, 1971, 1973), and ritual-creating.

These elements presumably represent cultural elaborations of universal processes of mind (to some extent, so do "grammars" of dream-making, which largely draw on the same stock of symbols). The creation or modification of rites or myths may be somewhat more culturally channeled and formally structured than many of the creations of private fantasy; but they are ultimately created or modified by individual minds and become shared or borrowed from the neighbors only if they are psychologically meaningful to other people.

What about the stock of symbols? Freud's work suggests universal themes in symbolism, and anthropologists of both Freudian and non-Freudian bent have similarly noted recurrent themes. But the contrast between scholars who interpret these in terms of individual psychodynamics and those who (following Durkheim) interpret them as collective representations is wide. The contrast is vividly illustrated by Needham's interpretation of a peculiar Southeast Asian rite and Freeman's psychoanalytic counter-interpretation:

Case 13: Blood and Thunder in Malaya and Borneo

Rodney Needham (1964) noted a series of striking parallels in specific rites and beliefs between two groups of Southeast Asian hunters and gatherers who apparently have no historical connection. The forest Negritos of Malaya, the Semang and their neighbors, are widely reported to propitiate a thunder god, Karei, who visits punishment—notably in the form of thunder—when certain taboos are violated. Thunder is not mere noise, but an awesome and dangerous force to rain forest nomads. Karei sends thunder when the living commit tabooed acts, including incest but also such strange acts as burning leeches or mocking animals (by calling them names, for example). When Karei visits thunder upon the Semang they make a curious blood sacrifice: a person cuts his or her own leg, mixes the blood with water, and throws it up as an offering to Karei.

All this would be curious but not problematic except that Needham observed a remarkable set of parallel beliefs and rites among the Penan of far-off Borneo, apparently unrelated historically to the Semang. The Penan similarly propitiate a thunder god. This god, as in Malaya, visits thunder upon the living to punish their transgression of ritual prohibitions. In a thunderstorm the Penan similarly take blood from leg or foot, mix it with water, and throw it as an offering to the thunder god. And finally, the ritual prohibitions enforced by the thunder god include burning of leeches and mockery of animals.

How asks Needham, can we account for such specific parallels in rite and belief? He points out flaws in the assumption that what is biologically laid down is universally human but what is cultural is purely arbitrary and highly variable from group to group. For there are, he argues, natural or seemingly archetypal symbols—blood, fire, tree, stone, and so on—that are so widely used that they seem almost to be part of the universal mental equipment of human beings (even though there is no reason to think that they are programmed biologically).

Certain things in nature seem to exert an effect on the human mind, conducing to symbolic forms of the most general, and even universal, kind. They seem . . . to make a primordial impress on the unconscious mind of man as a natural species. (Needham 1964:283–284)

But that, unfortunately, does not explain the specific parallels whereby, unlike their neighbors, the Malay Negritos and the Penan make blood sacrifices from their legs to expiate the burning of leeches and the mockery of animals.

Derek Freeman (1968) takes Needham's challenge to explain both universal themes and the remarkable parallels in specific details of ritual and belief. The point, he argues, is not that "things" make an impress on the human mind, but rather that the human mind projects human motives, feelings, and qualities onto inanimate objects and natural forces. What accounts for these projections? The search for meaning in exotic symbols, beliefs, and rites requires probing psychological depths: "Much cultural behavior, if it is to be understood, has to be deciphered—just like a dream" (Freeman 1968:358). Freeman turns to psychoanalytic understandings of projection and fantasy to interpret the ethnographic evidence.

What is Karei, the thunder god, and his mate Manoid? Freeman argues that they are projections of parental figures. The punishing, cruel gods do not necessarily reflect the psychological experience of actual aggression of parents toward the children. Rather, as the psychoanalyst Melanie Klein (1950; Klein and Riviere 1937) has argued, a child's aggressive, destructive feelings toward the parents, laden with guilt and anxiety, are projected upon the parents (or, as in the case of the thunder god, on symbolic parent figures). "Looked at scientifically, the thunder-god becomes a kind of projective screen on which are displayed the aggressive fantasies and impulses of humans—as well as their fears" (Freeman 1968:362).

Freeman goes on to point out the widespread symbolic connection, both clinical and ethnographic, between thunder and lightning and oral aggression (the child's oral aggression projected upon the parents). Thus Karei, the Semang thunder god, sucks fruits that are formed from the blood sacrifice of humans (hence, according to Freeman, the blood-sucking leech is symbolically associated with bloodthirsty deity). But thunder and lightning also symbolize phallic aggression and the generative powers of the parental figure. Freeman (1968:371) pauses to push Frazer's 12-volume exploration of "the Golden Bough" (1890) a notch further: "the mistletoe like the lightning flash from which it sprang is a symbolic representation of the generative and phallic power of the father-god in the form of semen." The symbolic association of the leech, as devouring worm, with the father-god is doubly appropriate because of its phallic qualities.[6]

If avoiding burning leeches makes symbolic sense, we still are left to wonder why the Semang (and like them, the Penan) cut their legs to make blood sacrifice to the thunder god when a thunderstorm approaches. Why the cutting of oneself? Why the leg? And why the offering of head hair as well, which Needham describes for the Penan?

The self-mutilation, Freeman believes, is the redirection onto the self of aggression in the face of dominance and fear—a behavioral complex that goes far back into our primate past. But why the leg and hair? Because, Freeman argues, they are so commonly, perhaps universally, symbols of the genitals, and of sexuality. Cutting the leg, or cutting the hair, is symbolic castration[7]—and thus an act of submission to the feared father figure.

Freeman ends with an interpretation of the prohibitions by Karei and his Borneo counterpart against the mockery of animals. He notes that the animals involved are either symbolically phallic or regarded as lecherous because of their overt sexuality (monkeys, dogs). He suggests that the mockery symbolically expresses aggressive feelings against the father's genitals or against the envied sexual behavior of the parents. He ends by pointing out that mockery is very often an expression of envy, and

---

[6]Here the convergence of psychoanalytic and neurophysiological evidence begins to provide a solid foundation for symbolic interpretations: "The close neural organization of oral and genital functions in . . . the limbic brain is presumably due to the olfactory sense that, dating far back in evolution, plays an important role in both feeding and mating" (McLean 1968:28—30).

[7]Castration in psychoanalytic theory need not imply literal castration, but rather grievous and painful bodily damage and hence loss of part of oneself; castration serves as the extreme expression of the emotional complex associated with fear of such pain and loss. Here, as elsewhere, much misunderstanding of psychoanalysis derives from too literal an interpretation of technical terms.

interprets ritually expressed mockery of men by women as disguised penis envy. This theme of sexual conflict enables us to relate Freeman's interpretations to more general issues we have raised. We have noted that male envy of the reproductive powers of women is a parallel theme, so that both may be represented in rites of sexual antagonism. Among such peoples as the Mehinacu of Brazil, such antagonism is dramatized both in men's secret cults and in women's ritual responses to male bravado. Mehinacu women, in one rite, throw garbage and filth upon the men.

Are such psychoanalytic interpretations farfetched? If one is unfamiliar with or skeptical of psychoanalytic interpretations, perhaps so. But then one must come up with equally compelling alternative interpretations of such exotic customs and practices, and also of genital mutilation, self-torture, and other seemingly bizarre behaviors—and one must explain the very real emotions of fear, anxiety, aggression, or transcendent euphoria that so often accompany them. (It will not do to point out that such emotions are often feigned and enacted in perfunctory fashion: for many actors in ritual dramas, they are deep and real. If they were not, presumably the dramas would lose their meaning and wither away.)

Psychoanalysts have increasingly interpreted the sexual symbolism of fantasy material as referring not simply to genital sexuality but more broadly to creative, generative powers. Thus the phallus or sex act may not be the ultimate or primary referent of a symbol but part of a spectrum of meaning: physical sex can stand for fertility as well as the reverse. This points toward a broader and more anthropological theory of symbolism than Freud grappled with in his early work with patients whose sexuality was severely repressed. As we will see, Bateson (1972b) would go further, and would say that the symbolic designs of unconscious mind are not about "things" like sex or fertility or death at all: they are about *relationships* of symmetrical conflict, dominance, dependency, and the like, which can be expressed in terms of sex,

fertility, death, or whatever (1972b). Bateson is perhaps going too far in an intellectualist direction. His view does not seem to account for the compelling emotional power of symbols, but it is a useful corrective to notions of the surging unconscious mind.

Bateson goes on to speculate on the evolutionary functions of the multiple species of the unconscious—art, ritual, myth, dream. He speculates that human intelligence, though it has proved fantastically powerful in manipulating the physical world, has fragmented and segmented experience. Ritual, myth, and art—the realms where the processes of unconscious mind hold sway—reconstitute wholes out of dissected parts, propose integration and pattern, rejoin mind and body.[8]

The answers have barely begun to emerge. But we can at least take a new look at the relevance of psychoanalytic interpretations to anthropology with some firm starting points that were not clear a generation ago. Whatever the unconscious turns out to represent in terms of the fantastic intricacies of mind and brain—and it seems to lump together several quite different regions of brain and processes of mind—it is a product

---

[8]Here we may not simply be mentally unchaining the passions of our animal past. In the light of recent research on lateral complementarity of brain hemispheres, we may be putting the right, usually subordinate, hemisphere in charge of operations: an effect also accomplished by meditation, psychedelics, and other means (see Ornstein 1973).

of natural selection in hominid evolution. Our innately programmed behavioral patterns are not survivals from a presocial animal past; they are adaptations to human social life.

The primary bond, the programmed psychosocial responses to the family situation, have evolved not through the superimposition of culture on our animal nature but as part of a nature that is and must be biocultural. And the interplay between those realms of mind psychoanalysts have called the conscious and the unconscious is vastly more intricate than one could have imagined 50 years ago, yet is the very essence of our humanity.

35.
Learning a Culture

If anthropologists knew how a child learned his or her culture, their problem would mainly be solved. For to know this, they would have to understand the nature of an infant, its biological capacities, modes of perception, and predispositions. They would have to know the design of the brain and whatever program was laid down genetically to be filled in by the content of learning. They would have to know the extent of biological diversity. They would have to know what it is that is learned, in a social setting, that fills in these biological outlines and capacities with the content of cultures.

We know none of these things. Each frontier is still being reconnoitered, and progress on most fronts has been limited. What we can say so far about learning a culture reflects the continuing mysteries humans pose.

A human infant is, we know, an incredibly complicated pattern of biological systems and capacities, many of which are activated long before birth. But it is also like a seed that must be implanted in the soil of social experience if it is to grow into a human being.

Humans differ from their primate cousins in the degree and duration of their helplessness. Without nurturing over a period of years, a human infant cannot survive. Psychological bonding, as we have seen, is presumably an adaptation to this biological dependence. During this long dependence, the child must learn the rich complexity of a way of life. This learning is mediated by the symbolic system he or she must learn: the child acquires a code of linguistic symbols and meanings, which in turn provides a medium for learning, a means of instruction and reinforcement.

An infant is faced with the challenge of extracting regularities of pattern from the "blooming buzzing confusion"—the noises, visual images, and tactile experiences of the world "out there." Just how an infant proceeds to build a model of the cultural and social world is little understood because the infant's mind has been a sealed "black box" inaccessible to the investigator. Yet through modern studies, we are acquiring in a number of fields new and revealing insights into the process of cultural acquisition. In developmental psycholinguistics, in cognitive development studies, in formal study of grammars, the range of possibilities is being progressively narrowed.

As we saw in §26, it now seems likely that the mind of the infant is much less a blank slate than earlier theorists had believed. The illusion of the blank slate derives mostly from a maturation process in which neural circuitry in the brain and other physical connections progressively take full form in the early years of life, activating genetically programmed behavioral patterns and potentials not displayed by the newborn infant. Thus the activation of infant smiling responses, of maternal bonding responses, and of language acquisition patterns are spaced out progressively over the first two years.

However, it is still not clear how detailed are the genetically programmed templates for behavior: the slate is clearly not as blank as scholars used to believe, but we do not yet know how much of what information is written on it. Universals of language have led Chomsky (§26) to assume that infants are born with a detailed genetic program for language acquisition. Piaget and his associates, in contrast, believe that the complex repertoire of cognitive skills, the logical thinking of "mature intelligence," represents the cumulative results of the infant's starting with very simple interactions with the environment and progressively building up a more and more complex system of thought. Piaget (1970:719—720) rejects the notion that there is "a hereditary program underlying the development of human intelligence: there are no 'innate ideas.' Even logic is not innate." Maturation, he says, does not activate programs for cognitive development, but opens "new possibilities for development [by] giving access to structure which could not be evolved before these possibilities were offered."

Yet it seems likely that Piaget has seriously underestimated the genetic and neurophysiological structuring of intelligence, though his work in tracing and comparing the developing structures of intelligence will be of lasting value.

It is clear from modern linguistics, at least, that the human infant must be a theory builder of remarkable capacity. From a limited and imperfect sample of the possible events in a cultural universe, he or she must *create a theory* of the rules, programs, and logic of which this sample was an expression. The child must continually test and refine elements in this theory. For what social life requires is not an enactment of "canned" sequences one has learned and stored. Rather, one must produce sequences one has never observed, but which are implied by one's theory. The situations of social life are ever-changing and often unique. Just as they call for linguistic utterances that the speaker has never heard but which his grammatical theory defines as possible and meaningful, so they call for other behavioral responses that are new to one's experience but culturally "grammatical." Whether the human infant could be such a powerful theory builder without considerable biological preprogramming of how to process "evidence" and how to organize knowledge seems highly improbable. Given the universality of of preprogramming in the animal world, it would be surprising indeed if the human infant had to begin to decipher, entirely from scratch, what kind of world he or she lived in.

An emerging intellectual climate which stresses similarities between natural systems of all kinds, biological and social, which assumes that biological and psychocultural are ultimately two sides of the same coin, and which seeks universals rather than insisting on uniqueness and relativism makes it possible and urgent to ask such questions, whatever the answers turn out to be.

Peoples vary in the extent to which cultural routines are taught by verbal instruction rather than observation. Clearly, bodies of specialized knowledge like music, mythology, and mathematics are transmitted largely through language. Yet there are great areas of culture to be learned of which neither adults nor learners are fully conscious and which neither can talk about very well. The codes of gesture, posture, and facial expression, the shared knowledge we use to communicate about moods, contexts, status, and the like, are mainly learned by observation, not instruction. One's self-conception or sense of personal identity is probably mainly derived from such implicit learning. A person matches and manipulates the private world he or she has learned but cannot verbalize against a background of the public and ideal virtues, standards, and images espoused by the society; and a sense of one's worth, one's life, and one's place emerges.

The emphasis on early childhood experience in culture and personality research has diverted attention from later learning. What we learn about ourselves, about our way of life, and about our relations to one another is not only learned in infancy. In preadolescence, adolescence, and adulthood crucial learning of cultural patterns and of self-identity is taking place.

Later learning does not simply add new content to the learner's psychological world: it changes the *structure* of that world. One comes to see oneself in relation to the world in new ways. Moving away from home, having one's first sexual experience, going to college—such transitions do not simply add new elements to a person's life; they can serve to reconstitute a "new" person, changed in his or her relationship to the world. The importance of initiation rites in cultural learning lies not only in what the initiate is taught about being a man or a woman and on what mysteries are revealed. By dramatically changing one's status, initiation also transforms one's *relationship* to the ways of one's people. It gives the initiate a new perspective on the games of life.

Such a focus on the learning task of the individual can shed a new light on child-rearing practices in different societies. It seems reasonably likely that (1) human infants are exceedingly complex and intricately programmed learning "devices"; (2) the bulk of this programming, and many of the crucial patterns that are learned, are stored deep in unconsciousness; and (3) humans build, on the higher levels of consciousness, ideologies, conscious routines of ritual or etiquette, ideal norms, and rules of thumb that only partly correspond to the underlying unconscious knowledge that actually guides behavior. If

this is so, then a people's child-rearing customs and patterns not only organize the contexts where learning takes place but they also represent that people's ideologies and theories about what children are like and how they learn. Those theories may well have little to do with what and how children actually do learn. It is conceivable that cultural learning takes place not so much through the child-rearing practices of a society as *in spite of them.*

36. Personality and Role System

Though every normal individual in a society acquires a competence to enact the basic patterns of his or her culture, we now see that there are considerable variations in temperament and abilities in every generation. This leads to a recurring organizational problem: individuals will be differentially suited to play the various roles that must be filled in a society.

The problem varies in shape and magnitude according to the scale and complexity of the society. Recall that the differentiation of political and economic roles increases markedly as we move from band societies to tribes, to chiefdoms, and to states. Social theorists have characterized this span in terms of a shifting emphasis from ascribed status, where roles are fixed by birth, in simpler societies to achieved status in more complex societies. But that is too simple for our purposes. Take the political leader, for example, on whom a group's very survival may depend. In band societies the leader, however restricted his powers, is likely to be a man who earned by deed the respect and loyalty of his fellow band members. The Melanesian Big Man (§61) is likewise suited by talent and temperament to enact that role—or he would not be in it. But in a hereditary aristocracy where the oldest son of a king or chief succeeds him, the successor may very well be unsuited in personality and ability to perform the job that is his by right.

Elites manage, by direct and subtle means, to perpetuate themselves. Yet the rigidity of the systems for securing rights across generations restricts the mobility of the genetic hand dealt in each generation. Genetic chance has repeatedly defied the efforts devoted to instilling the values, skills, and knowledge appropriate to a rightful successor's role. A bevy of councilors, ministers, priests, and others have historically buffered kings and other hereditary leaders—so that the succession of an inept or young heir to high office is not disastrous. The high places that slaves and eunuchs have often occupied in court circles reflect two related advantages: their social mobility to rise to heights of achievement without threatening the formal status of others and their lack of descendants, so they can found no rival dynasty or faction.

The role system of a society does not simply constrain the psychological drives and strivings of individuals: it provides avenues for satisfying them. Thus the Melanesian feast-giving entrepreneur is driven by motives to achieve and acquire status and power: his culture defines what the game is, what the goals are, and creates a role for the best players. The differential distribution of the genetic capacities or potentials for various styles of achievement is a critical resource for any society. The schizophrenic as shaman, and the intersexual as bringer of spiritual blessing, reflect outer limits on a general and essential process whereby humans build on

the diversity that is dealt as genetic hand in every population.

Our focus on uniformity of personality and on the plasticity rather than the genetic templates of human nature has kept such problems in the background. In much older culture and personality research, one inferred a society's basic "personality type" by observing culturally standardized ways of behaving, and then "discovered" that this was a culture which people with that personality would fit into nicely. How diverse resources of temperament and ability were distributed into social niches was seldom asked. Yet examination of the channels of access and assignment into the role system of a society—how those people become butchers, bakers, candlestick makers, priests, and premiers who are reasonably suited by personality and abilities to perform these roles—is an important problem on which we need more evidence. At this point we must post a sign, "unexplored territory," and go on.

This brief survey of the relationship between biology and experience, between the individual and the collective, must suffice for the moment. But we will return at several points in the chapters to follow, particularly in §63, Chapter 20, and §71, to the relationship between individual experience and shared cultural patterns.

At this stage, we need to tie together our knowledge of human cultures in evolutionary perspective, as laid out in Part 2, and our knowledge of cultural and social theory as given in Part 3, in order to explore how a particular way of life in a particular setting develops and changes.

HOW CULTURES CHANGE

12

In recent decades, anthropologists have returned to questions about how ways of life evolve and diversify—questions that dominated nineteenth-century anthropology, but had long lain fallow. In seeking models of sociocultural development, anthropologists have extended biological thinking into the realm of culture, have added new ideas of their own, and have belatedly rediscovered some old and important ideas that have long been part of Western thought.

Here we will sketch the outlines of a model of how people's ways of life develop and change. Our concern will be primarily with how this process operates when the neighboring peoples are roughly the same in scale and technological power. We glimpsed in §21 and §22 how, with the emergence of preindustrial states in the ancient world, surrounding peoples were caught up in wider systems of domination and exploitation. In Part 4, we will examine the consequences of the Western expansion that engulfed the tribal societies and civilizations of the non-Western world.

37.
Cultural Change: Adaptation and Dialectic

Today, it is compellingly clear that human societies—most dramatically, our own—are subject to the laws of evolution. The behavior of a species must be adapted to its ecosystem if it is to survive. That modern industrialized societies have radically transformed the earth as ecosystem does not—we now see, perhaps too late—allow them to transcend the laws of evolution: humans are confronted with these laws on a vast new scale.

Cultural anthropologists used to ask whether analogies exist between the ways cultures develop and change and the processes of biological evolution (§4). It is now clear that that was the wrong question. The laws of evolution operate on the behavior of populations in ecosystems. These laws are indifferent to whether the individual organisms acquired these ways of behaving from their genes or from listening to their mothers. Cultural learning completes the open-ended potentials specified in human genes. Selection operates on the combination culture-plus-biology-in-societies-in-ecosystems.

Man is an animal and, like all other animals, must maintain an adaptive relationship with his surroundings in order to survive. Although he achieves this adaptation principally through the medium of culture, the process is guided by the same rules of natural selection that govern biological adaptation. (Meggers 1971:4)

To ask how human ways of life are shaped by evolutionary processes—by selection, by drift, and so on—leads us, of course, to ask about the distinctive characteristics of humans as cultural animals. As we noted in Part 1, it is the special talent of *Homo sapiens* as super-brained creatures of language and culture to adapt to an extraordinary range of environments: only humans can be exclusively either carnivores or herbivores, can live in broiling desert or arctic tundra, on land or sea. Modern humans even manage to fly south for the winter.

In the pages to follow, we shall ask how sociocultural systems evolve. Though the work of a number of theorists will be touched on, no effort will be made to trace systematically competing theories of cultural development. Rather, we will sketch a composite model of sociocultural change that can guide understanding in the chapters to follow. There are still too many unknowns to fill in details of the model with certainty: the main areas of controversy and doubt will be noted.

A crucial starting point is that it is not

cultures that evolve. "Cultures, unlike human populations, are not fed upon by predators, limited by food supplies, or debilitated by disease" (Vayda and Rappaport 1968:494). We have defined a culture as a system of more or less shared ideational designs for living characteristic of a particular people. These ideational designs are only one set of elements shaping the behavior of a population in an ecosystem; it is on these *behavior patterns* that evolutionary processes operate. We are not asking, then, how cultures evolve but *how sociocultural systems-in-environments evolve.*

When we place the behavior of human populations in this broadened biological perspective, we risk a misunderstanding. It is true that human populations are ultimately subject to the biological laws that affect any animal population: they must reproduce in adequate numbers and not produce irreversible degradation of their ecosystem.

But this is not to say that the process of change in the cultural (that is, learned) components of human behavior is the same as (or parallel or analogous to) the process of natural selection that shapes the genetic information in a population. Woodpeckers cannot decide not to peck holes in trees. If their feeding patterns degraded the vegetable components of their ecosystem, their population would be affected accordingly—and their genes would change only by an indirect process of gradual adaptation. A people can change their customs: they can prohibit hunting a totem animal or decide not to build nuclear power plants. The *consequences* of such changes are subject to biological laws, but the *processes* of change are quite different.

A culture, then, is adaptive only in a limited sense. It must, in interaction with the givens of human biology, with human psychology, and with social process produce behavior patterns viable in a particular environment. In the pages to follow, we will explore how these processes operate.

In Chapters 5, 6, and 7, we noted that new developments in technology and transformations in the nature and scale of social and political organization were intertwined. We saw that between hunting and gathering peoples and tribal food producers, and between the latter and civilized urbanites, are broad gulfs in both the efficiency with which the investment of human energy yields a return and in the scale and complexity of social life. Over a broad span, technology has clearly evolved in the direction of greater power and control, a process comparable in some ways to the evolution of the major orders of life: amphibians, reptiles, birds, mammals. This "upward"—in the sense of complexity, scale, and thermodynamic efficiency—evolutionary path has been explored extensively by Leslie White, an American anthropologist who with stubborn conviction maintained a focus on cultural evolution through years when such studies were harshly dismissed by his colleagues.

Most cultural anthropologists (in the narrow sense that contrasts them with prehistorians) concerned with cultures as adaptive systems have focused not on this broad sweep of technological advance and its social concomitants, but on the *diversification* of tribal ways of life in different settings—with what Sahlins (1960) likens to adaptive radiation in biological evolution. They have seen different settings for tribal life as ecological niches in which diverse ways of life have evolved through adaptation.

We will be primarily concerned here with these processes of microvariation and adaptation. But this perspective will have to be broadened by the insights of modern theory-minded prehistorians. Archaeologists are increasingly concerned with the same ques-

tions of cultural process, but their data give them a longer and vitally important time perspective. Seeing sequences of cultural change over a span of centuries, not over a year or two of fieldwork, prehistorians can make no assumptions that the way of life whose leavings they find at a particular level represented a stable equilibrium, an adaptive balance. If they find long-term stability, that demands theoretical explanation; if they find gradual unfolding or rapid bursts of change, these too demand explanation. One of the recurrent sins of social anthropologists is to extrapolate from short observation by inferring that "the system" is in stable equilibrium across the span of generations—or was until Europeans muddled things up. Their archaeologist colleagues know better. And these colleagues are increasingly seeking theories of how sociocultural systems evolve. (They in turn urgently need to draw on the specialized knowledge of ethnographers who study live humans, in all their wondrous complexity; and increasingly are doing so.)

Let us, then, return to the question: How do sociocultural systems-in-environments evolve?

A major mode of interpretation in modern cultural anthropology, as advanced in somewhat different forms by such theorists as Steward, Sahlins, and Service, and given recent comprehensive statement by Marvin Harris, gives an unequivocal answer: they are primarily adaptations to the material circumstances of human life.

Steward (1955b) postulated that there is a core area of culture that is particularly responsive to ecological adaptation: the division of labor, the size and stability of local groups and their distribution in space, residence rules. Adjustments to ecological pressures directly affected these core elements of social structure; thus, the seasonality of climate, availability of water, or fertility of the soil would shape how many people could live in settlements, how permanent these could be, how they would be scattered, and how the population would organize their productive efforts. These influences on social structure then ramified through a culture so as to promote changes in realms only secondarily related to ecology— in cosmological ideas, patterns of political succession, art, and the like.

Subsequent theorists of cultural adaptation follow Steward in viewing subsistence technology and production and the social organization whereby foods and other scarce material goods are produced, controlled, and distributed as the core areas of culture where selective pressures are most direct. A people's world view or religious ritual is likely to be indirectly if not directly related to the material conditions of life, but it is a people's philosophy that is to be explained in terms of their economic life, not the reverse. Such an approach has been called *cultural materialism* by Harris (1968). Its analytical strategy is to expect that

Similar technologies applied to similar environments tend to produce similar arrangements of labor in production and distribution, and . . . these

in turn call forth similar kinds of social groupings, which justify and coordinate their activities by means of similar systems of values and beliefs. (Harris 1968:4)

Such a strategy allows room for cases where an ideology—say, Islam imported into the Philippines or sub-Saharan Africa—produces change in social organization, and for the particularities of history and cultural distinctiveness.

Steward's model of sociocultural adaptation, according religious beliefs and customs a secondary and peripheral role, has been considerably modified by subsequent students of ecological adaptation. If we take a thoroughgoing evolutionary view, we must leave open the possibility that religious beliefs and other symbolic systems may have directly adaptive functions: for these beliefs result in *behavior,* and behavior (even avoiding work on the Sabbath) has ecological consequences.

The most sophisticated exploration of the complex web of connections among belief, behavior, and ecosystems has been Roy Rappaport's analysis of the Tsembaga Maring of New Guinea, whose system of swidden horticulture we viewed in Chapter 6 (Case 3).

Case 14: Tsembaga Culture as an Adaptive System

Rappaport (1967, 1968) begins by noting the role of pig raising in Tsembaga life. Normally, when few pigs are being raised, pigs root freely in the day and return to the owners' houses at night to be fed the substandard sweet potatoes. The pigs are then sacrificed to ancestors at times of intergroup fighting or illness. Rappaport notes that these sacrifices have physiologically adaptive consequences, even though the participants are presumably unaware of them. When a pig is sacrificed to ancestors to cure a patient's illness, the patient (as well as his immediate kin) receives high-quality protein badly needed at a time of physical stress (where the normal diet is marginally protein deficient). So too do the warriors when a sacrifice is made before a fight.

More interesting in their ecological ramifications are the elaborate ritual cycles that bring the number of pigs far above the normal level.

Maring local groups live in alternating states of hostility and peace. When warfare breaks out between groups, usually ones occupying adjoining territory, the fighting may continue sporadically for weeks. Often it is more or less balanced, and there is no decisive victory. But sometimes one of the groups is routed. The survivors take refuge with relatives in other groups; their houses, gardens, and pigs are destroyed. But the territory laid waste cannot at that stage be occupied by the victors; it is still guarded by the ancestors of the vanquished.

When hostilities end, a group that has not been driven from its territory performs a ritual in which a *rumbim*, a sacred shrub, is ritually planted. All their pigs, other than juveniles, are killed and dedicated to the ancestors. Most of the pork goes to allies from surrounding groups who took part in the fighting. Stringent taboos in force during hostilities are partially lifted, but material and spiritual debts to allies and ancestors remain unpaid. This state of debt and danger—though of formal truce—remains until the *rumbim* can be ritually uprooted and a pig festival *(kaiko)* can be staged. And that takes a great many pigs. It takes time and great effort to raise large herds, perhaps 5 or 10 years.

As the pig herd builds up, the burden of feeding them requires great expansion of gardens and major investment of effort. The Tsembaga herd of 169 animals Rappaport recorded just before their *kaiko* pig festival was

Tsembaga Maring magic: Objects to be used in the purification of the dance ground are bespelled. The stake is to pierce corruption, the cordyline-leaf broom is to sweep it away. (Courtesy of Roy Rappaport.)

A visiting group charges onto the Tsembaga maring dance ground. (Courtesy of Roy Rappaport.)

getting 54 percent of the sweet potatoes harvested and 82 percent of the manioc. The gardens were 36.1 percent larger before the pig festival than they were afterwards.

Pressure to uproot the *rumbim* and slaughter the pigs predictably comes from the women on whose shoulders rests most of the burden of feeding expanding herds. It also comes from quarreling and often violence triggered by pigs breaking into gardens; to minimize this, the settlement pattern becomes increasingly dispersed.

The *kaiko* festival begins with planting of stakes at the boundary. If a vanquished and dispersed neighboring group have remained elsewhere as refugees, and have not been strong enough in the intervening years to reoccupy their territory and plant their own *rumbim,* the victors may at this stage extend their boundaries to incorporate the conquered territory: since no *rumbim* has been planted there, the territory is officially unoccupied. Moreover, the participation by the vanquished in the ritual life of the group where they have taken refuge—especially in planting *rumbim* elsewhere—moves their own ancestors and their own group affiliation to those territories.

When the *rumbim* is uprooted, many pigs (in the case observed, 32 out of 169) are slaughtered and distributed to allies and in-laws in other groups. The *kaiko* continues for about a year. During this time, the host group entertains neighboring friendly groups from time to time, and dancing and food distributions take place. Rappaport speculates that these dances function as "courtship displays," as in animals; but more important, by bringing together the potential allies of a group, they serve to display to the outside world (like a modern political conference of allied nations) the strength of a potential coalition in the event of war. Rappaport notes that invitations to dance are extended by individuals, recruiting relatives, in-laws, and friends in other groups, along the same lines as invitations to fight:

> Dancing and fighting are regarded as in some sense equivalent. Their equivalence is expressed in the similarity of some pre-fight or pre-dance rituals, and the Maring say that those who come to dance come to fight. The size of a visiting dancing contingent is consequently taken [by the group and its potential enemies] as a measure of the size of the contingent of warriors whose assistance may be expected in the next round of warfare. (Rappaport 1967:196)

After a night of dancing, the participants trade: the *kaiko* thus provides a setting for peaceful exchange of scarce goods, including salt and stone tools as well as symbolic wealth.

The *kaiko* concludes with major sacrifices of the remaining adult pigs, which are distributed to members of other local groups following lines of kinship and alliance. An estimated two to three thousand Maring in seventeen local groups received pork from the Tsembaga *kaiko* distribution Rappaport observed. This was also an occasion for the distribution of wealth between groups in connection with marriage transactions.

When the *kaiko* festival is concluded, fighting could break out again. And usually it did. But a second ritual cycle could eventually be performed if peace was preserved that long; and then the two local groups that had been warring were supposed to be permanently at peace.

Rappaport believes that the ritual cycles of the Maring have a number of consequences, of which the participants are not aware, that help to preserve the balance of the ecosystem, maintain ordered relations between local groups, redistribute land resources in relation to population, and distribute resources— including traded scarce goods and badly needed animal protein.

Ritual cycles . . . play an important part in regulating the relations of these groups with both the non-human components of their immediate environments and the human components of their less immediate environments. (Rappaport 1967:182).

In later analyses, Rappaport has extended this model by tracing the cybernetic interconnections[1] between Tsembaga culture and

[1]Cybernetic interconnections are loops or circuits in an information system through which messages are transmitted—a process called *feedback*. A simple physical example of *negative feedback*—that is, feedback that preserves the stable balance of the system—is a thermostat. As the temperature goes down, the thermostat activates a heating system; as the heat rises, the thermostat shuts it off. But a cybernetic system need not be mechanical—a tightrope walker's pole operates as a circuit that maintains balance through negative feedback. Cybernetic systems may also include *positive feedback* circuits: more of A produces more of B which in turn produces more of A—an armaments race is a dramatic example (see Gregory Bateson's paper "Cybernetic Explanation" in Bateson 1972a).

ecosystem. He has looked in detail at cosmology—the classes of spirits the Maring believe to exist and play a part in human affairs. And he notes not only adaptive value in some of these beliefs, but even a kind of parallel between the world as conceived in supernatural terms and the ecosystem. "The behavior of certain spirits, who the Tsembaga say occupy the lower portion of their territory, and the consequences of their behavior, correspond closely to that of the anopheles mosquito whom the Tsembaga do not understand to be a malaria vector" (Rappaport 1970:49). But such parallelism is not necessary for the cultural beliefs to have adaptive cybernetic consequences—that is, to trigger and channel "messages" through the "circuits" of the system of humans-in-environment so as to correct imbalances in the system.

Rappaport's view of humans-in-environment as an incredibly complex network of circuits through which information passes, a network that includes cultural beliefs and their consequences as well as ecological events, is boldly innovative and at first hard to grasp. It leads him to see ritual operating as a "homeostat" (like a heating thermostat), and as a "transducer" (converting complex information about the number of pigs, state of human relations, preparedness for war, or strength of allies into a simple binary or "yes-no" signal the neighbors can easily "read": the *rumbim* is uprooted). It leads him to speculate that *sanctity,* the unquestioned ultimate truth of religious belief, may have a major adaptive significance in human life. Our elevation of science and rationality, our loss of ultimate faith, may be more directly related to our ecological crisis than most have realized (Rappaport 1970, 1971a, b).

But can systems of cultural belief be adaptive rather than maladaptive, if these beliefs lack empirical foundations? Scientific accuracy of a cosmological belief is not the crucial

matter—only "whether or not it elicits behavior contributing to the well-being of the actors and to the maintenance of the ecosystem of which they are parts" (Rappaport 1971d:261). Accurate, naturalistic (that is, scientific) explanation may even have negative survival value in the long run:

It is by no means certain that the representations of nature provided us by science are more adaptive or functional than those images of the world, inhabited by spirits whom men respect, that guide the action of the Maring and other "primitives." Indeed they may be less so, for to drape nature in supernatural veils is perhaps to provide her with some protection against human parochialism and destruction. (Rappaport 1971d:262)

Rappaport's model, distinguishing between a people's conceptual system (their "cognized model" of their world) and their behavior, is in some ways more sophisticated than Harris'. Harris (1968:16) adopts a clumsy conceptualization of culture that includes too much—that treats cultures as "behavior patterns associated with particular groups of people," so that a culture becomes "a people's 'way of life.'" The way members of a group live and the system of knowledge they use to guide their lives are not the same; to merge them muddles our understanding of change at the outset.

Interpretations similar to Rappaport's have been advanced about the way beliefs in the pollutedness of women—especially in New Guinea and elsewhere in Melanesia—may serve ecologically adaptive ends. In many New Guinea societies, relations between the sexes are sharply polarized. Men's and women's domains are widely separated: men stage dramatic rituals, often have initiation rites, organize for war and ceremonial trade from which women are excluded; women work in the gardens, raise pigs their menfolk will use for prestige and social advancement, do domestic chores, and bear and raise children. So polarized are relations between the sexes in many New Guinea societies that men and women occupy separate houses and have sexual relations infrequently in an atmosphere of tension and danger. In some of them, as we will soon see, male homosexuality is institutionalized and further polarizes the sexes. Often, but not always, polarization of the sexes is expressed in terms of a belief that women's bodily functions are polluting.

If we take an evolutionary view, it is not the beliefs but their behavioral consequences that are adaptive or maladaptive.

A belief that women are polluting and that male and female are radically different and antagonistic may have the consequence that husband and wife avoid intercourse until a baby is weaned, after two years or more. The cultural explanation may be that semen and mother's milk must be kept separate: but by spacing childbirth the adaptive consequences may include insuring maximum protein for infants in a society subsisting dangerously close to the margins of protein deficiency (Whiting 1964).

Lindenbaum (1972) and others have also viewed pollution taboos as, among other things, symbolic means of regulating population. Lindenbaum notes that pollution taboos and the accompanying sexual polarization are most commonly found where population pressures are extreme, as among the Enga of Highland New Guinea. Sexual antagonism is found in other New Guinea societies such as the Fore where populations are low and precarious, but its expression takes different forms, reflecting the fragility of social arrangements and the dangers from without (Lindenbaum 1972, n.d.). The forms of sexual antagonism and polarization found under conditions of population pressure, manifest in fear of pollution, serve as "a form of ideologi-

cal birth control" (Lindenbaum 1972:148). Lindenbaum's analyses make clear the interconnection between a people's dimly or obliquely perceived ecological problems and the symbolic expressions and solutions they devise. She illustrates how ritual symbols may be used to make ecological and political statements and reflect people's perceptions of their demographic situation.

This mode of cultural interpretation— seeing beliefs and practices as shaped and pruned by ecological adaptation—is undoubtedly partly correct. But here it is the "partly" that needs underscoring. Such a mode of interpretation has an inherent plausibility, and hence a seductiveness, that makes it dangerous unless the needed grain of salt is thrown in.

A first major problem is assuming stable equilibrium and effective adaptation where it may not exist. The people the anthropologist studies may in fact be quite badly adapted to their environment, and thus ill-nourished and threatened by demographic decline.

Let us look again at the Maring of New Guinea studied by Rappaport. Rappaport has plausibly argued (see Cases 3 and 14) that the ritual cycle of pigs, sacrifice, and peace making preserves a balance with the natural environment and hence that rites and beliefs serve adaptive ends. But are Maring local groups really that well adapted to their environment? Recent studies in the same area by Georgeda Buchbinder (1973) and William Clarke (1971) suggest that they may not be. Buchbinder's demographic and nutritional study of the Maring shows that they are threatened by demographic decline. Moreover, the subsistence they extract from their relatively infertile environment may be much less adequate than Rappaport believes. Buchbinder's data suggest that a diet marginally deficient in protein and drastically deficient in iodine may have severe consequences for

Maring health and reproduction. Female fertility seems to be curtailed by dietary deficiencies; the onset of menstruation, in particular, seems to be long delayed. The Maring may in fact be clinging as best they can to survival in a difficult environment. But this can by no means be comfortably assumed.

Nor can we comfortably and easily assess the success of a cultural adaptation, except perhaps in a very long-range sense. The very power to expand, to displace neighboring peoples, may often be an expression of a cultural instability and disequilibrium, often one that contains the seeds of its own destruction.

Cultural adaptationists have often erroneously implicitly equated evolutionary success with equilibrium: an assumption that breaks down when one looks at the archaeological record, at histories of empire, at biological evolution, or—in the tribal world—at "predatory expansion" by such people as the Iban of Borneo (Case 4).

Another case from New Guinea will illustrate the complexity of interpreting success or adaptiveness in the realm of culture.

Case 15: The Marind Anim

The Marind Anim of the southern coast of New Guinea had a remarkable culture that had apparently been going through an efflorescence—in the sense of artistic creativity and collective ritual and also in the sense of expansion at the expense of neighboring peoples—in the century or more before European contact.

Marind Anim culture centered around cults of male homosexuality, ritual license, and head-hunting. Marind Anim boys were led into a set of initiatory grades, where they were introduced to an orgiastic cult of sodomy, sustained by the cultural dogma that semen is essential to growth.

The elaborate ceremonial cycle was built around the male fiction of sexual supremacy and independence, but involved ritual intercourse with women in what amounted to gang rape: the semen was collected and mixed with food or used in ritual decoration. Van Baal's interpretation bears on issues we will touch on in subsequent sections and hence is worth quoting:

The great secret is that the venerated power [of male potency and hence of males in general] is not really as powerful as it pretended to be. The source of all life, sperma, is effective only. . . if produced in copulation. These self-sufficient males need the females and they know it. . . . In secret in the celebration of the rites, they will allow their dependence and immediately afterwards they go out head-hunting. It is as if by that time their rage has mounted to such a pitch that they have to find an outlet for it. (1966:949)

Marriage begins with such a gang rape of the bride by the husband's kin group; and this is repeated with young married women, at a cost of their physical suffering—a cost that is validated by the cultural dogma of

Marind-Anim: *(top)* A man is given an elaborate hair-do; *(left)* a warrior in full regalia; and *(right)* men's house. (Photographs courtesy of Koninklijk Institut V/D Tropen, Amsterdam.)

fertility, where the mingled sperm of the men of the community is supposed to sustain fertility. Though there is little data on marital inter-course, it is clear that homosexuality remains a central theme in most married men's lives.

The cultural concern with fertility was not without substance, since infertility was very high (subsequently exacerbated by venereal disease) and the population was threatened with demographic collapse. A South Pacific Commission demographic study concluded that the custom of collective sexual assault—in part, a cultural response to infertility—was in fact a major factor in perpetuating and worsening that problem.

Yet even though Marind Anim sexual practices did not provide demographically for reproduction of the population, this was a center of efflorescence in ceremonialism, art, and myth. Moreover, the Marind Anim sustained successfully an expansionist "foreign policy" that decimated marginal tribes in head-hunting. The power of the Marind Anim was sustained by rich sago resources that permitted large populations to concentrate in sedentary villages.

But what about demographic decline? Apparently in the period for which evidence can be pieced together, the Marind Anim maintained their population by capturing children in their head-hunting raids. They literally drained the reproductive capacities of neighboring peoples to support a predatory and expansionist "foreign policy" and an orgiastic life-style. (Van Baal 1966)

This practice in turn underlines the long-range imbalance of Marind Anim adaptation. As in imperialist Europe, prosperity at home was sustained by exploitation and murder abroad; and the expansiveness and success were inevitably limited. This pattern of Marind Anim adaptation probably had not been maintained for very long; and had Europeans not intruded, it would probably have collapsed.

This might serve as a parable of the expansion of the West, and of our technological expansion, "progress" and power at the expense of balance. But it further reveals the oversimplification and danger of assuming that the customs of a tribal people are ecologically adaptive, as products of natural selection.

The Marind Anim case illustrates another problem in the rather narrow adaptationist view of many cultural ecologists. The anthropologist in the field, working in a single village or cluster of settlements and taking this area as a microcosm of a culture and a society, has often gotten too limited a view in space as well as in time. The ecosystem approach to human populations can probably be most productive if we do not simply consider (as Rappaport does for the Tsembaga Maring) how a particular local group or even a tribal group is adapted to its environment; but rather if we see a series of contiguous (or interpenetrating) human populations as constituting "cultural species" within a wider ecosystem. Thus, the Marind Anim and their neighbors would constitute a regional system, as would the peoples of the Melanesian Massim, the islands off eastern New Guinea, who trade valuables around a large ring of islands (see Case 45). The Maring and neighboring peoples, the Iban of Borneo and their neighbors (whose heads they hunted and whose land they invaded; see Case 4), the fierce South American Yąnomamö and their cultural relatives would be seen as constituting regional mosaics whose populations, boundaries, resources, and strength *might* be in stable equilibrium, but might be highly unstable and imbalanced in the direction of absorption, conquest, extinction, and so on. Each people would to some extent be competing for land and resources (see Vayda 1961; Sahlins 1961) and hence be more or less successful. But their relationship might also be complementary and symbiotic—as with the Basseri pastoralists of southern Iran (Case 5) and the peoples of Swat, northern Pakistan, whose interpenetration in complementary ecological niches in the same region has been brilliantly analyzed by Barth (1956).

A further difficulty in a narrow ecological adaptationist view of cultures is that just as the human mind can invent strange rites, beliefs, and customs, so the anthropological imagination can conjure up an ecological explanation for even the strangest cultural practices.

To *assume* that rites or beliefs have adaptive consequences thus imposes a dangerous circularity in anthropological investigation. Given a strange and seemingly arbitrary detail of custom, some adaptive consequence can be found. One is reminded of a similar early enthusiasm in biology:

Naturalists, surveying the variety of plant and animal structures, performed prodigies of explaining them as evolutionary adaptations. There was, for example, an artist named Thayer, who, while doing some excellent pioneer work in pointing out the protective value of coloration, went so far as to maintain that flamboyant flamingos chastely blended into their surroundings—which he proved by painting these spectacularly colored birds against an equally spectacular sunset. (Where the birds stood during the remaining twelve hours of daylight the artist failed to indicate.) (Hardin 1959:259)

One anthropological equivalent of flamingo painting has been to argue that headhunting raids or diseases are adaptive because they limit population: these partial truths, carried to their logical conclusion, suggest that a society best solves its population problem by becoming extinct. To see details of custom as handy ecological devices can lead the analyst into excessive Panglossian zeal: the custom of the Kaulong and Sengseng of Melanesia where a woman is expected to be strangled by a kinsman when her husband dies may indeed regulate population; but so do typhoid epidemics, napalm attacks, and mass murders.

These difficulties in a narrowly adaptationist view of culture suggest that we need to look very carefully at the mechanisms whereby adaptation is supposed to operate.

If a people's culture complements and completes the open-ended programming of biology with a set of customs specially adaptive to their particular environment and the technology at their disposal, there must be two processes at work:

First, some mechanism must be producing a stream of customs, beliefs, and practices some of which may turn out to be adaptive to the ecosystem of which they are a part.

Second, some mechanism must be weeding out or changing those customs, beliefs, and practices that are not adaptive and favoring the accumulation of ones that have adaptive consequences. The first mechanism must be some kind of cultural analogue of genetic mutation; the second must be a process of natural selection. We will perceive strengths, but also weaknesses, in the cultural adaptationist model if we look carefully at both mechanisms.

The human ability to perceive practical problems and solve them, an ability made possible by the *Homo sapiens* super-brain, clearly provides part of the first mechanism. While mutations are blind, human problem-solving is not: if water is dripping down a human back, its owner will devise some shelter; if plants do not grow as well on steep slopes as they did in a previous level environment, farmers experiment with new techniques until they find ones that work. If the new techniques require larger work groups than the old ones did, farmers recruit the needed personnel, and eventually cultural rules are created that rationalize the new arrangement. This is one way that humans achieve adaptive social and cultural systems, and do so faster and more flexibly than other organisms can evolve adaptive behavior patterns genetically.

That cultural rules and principles are adjusted to fit patterns of changing practice raises an important point about sociocultural change. As Wallace (1970) and others have argued, members of a society have quite diverse conceptualizations of their culture—of what the system is and should be. Just as a reservoir of genetic diversity is crucial in biological selection, so this diversity in individual versions of cultural codes may be adaptively crucial. Cultural change probably does not take place so much through collective decisions to change the rules of the game as it does through gradual shifts in the distribution of alternative versions of the rules. These shifting balances in the ideational realm channel shifting patterns of behavior, and vice versa, in a continuing dialectic.

It is clear, however, that cultures are not simply pragmatic solutions to problems. The adaptive (or maladaptive) consequences of many beliefs and customs are not perceived by the people who follow them. Not knowing that mosquitoes transmit malaria, people attribute sickness to ancestral spirits and sacrifice pigs to them; whether their ritual response is adaptive or not is beyond their view. Here, where people are not solving their ecological problems directly (where, as Rappaport puts it, the "cognized model" of the actors is scientifically incorrect), some process would have to be operating whereby customs with maladaptive consequences were abandoned and customs with adaptive consequences were reinforced and retained.

But how do new nonempirical beliefs and customs emerge, which can then be weeded out by evolutionary selection? How and why do humans create a stream of nonempirical

beliefs and customs some of which are potentially adaptive? In various times and places, peoples have created and institutionalized a bewildering variety of nonempirical customs and beliefs: mother-in-law taboos, filing of front teeth to stubs, beliefs in sorcery and garden magic and flying witches, in the pollutedness of women, in thunder as a threatening deity, customs of circumcision or ritual cannibalism, elaborate conceptualizations of the cosmos, bodies of myth. If cultural adaptationists such as Rappaport are right in seeing such nonempirical practices as adaptive, then the process of symbolic elaboration must represent a crucial mechanism in the evolution of sociocultural systems.

But the mind, it would seem, has its own laws, or so Lévi-Strauss (1962) would have us believe. Rappaport tells us that the Tsembaga Maring massed dancers communicate about the strength and readiness of a kin group, and as a courtship display to potential mates. The important thing is to dance or not to dance (and how many people do it). Whether the dancers go clockwise or counterclockwise, in the center of the settlement or in a dance ground away from it, wearing white feathers or green leaves, presumably does not matter ecologically. Yet it is precisely such details of symbolic arrangement that distinguish the creations of the mind. The mind, as it were, spins out symbolic elaborations only partly constrained by adaptation and material existence.

To the extent they have ecological consequences at all, need these symbolic elaborations have *adaptive* consequences? May some elements of a people's beliefs and customs be selectively neutral? May some in fact be maladaptive? It is here that the circularity of interpretations which *assume* customs serve adaptive ends (if they have any practical consequences at all) has been most dangerous.

If this were so, there would have to

be some efficient selective mechanism leading to the abandonment of nonempirical practices that were (unbeknown to those who followed them) maladaptive; and hence, positively selecting those customs that happened to be adaptive. How efficient are such weeding and pruning mechanisms? And thus, how comfortably can we assume that the ritual we observe or the belief we encounter is not ecologically maladaptive?

What selective pressures eliminate ritual rules that lead to malnutrition or illness, beliefs that inefficiently disperse population, or social customs that reduce subsistence production? Or, asked another way, how much leeway does a population have to pursue practices that are either adaptively neutral or ecologically disadvantageous?

Presumably, people living in a rich environment have more leeway than people living in a marginal and difficult environment. The Paleolithic hunters of southern France could probably have had a great range of social arrangements and cosmological beliefs and still have enjoyed plenty of meat; Eskimos or Bushmen presumably have much less leeway. And all societies must avoid cataclysmic population increase.[2]

There are, in the anthropological literature, hundreds of customs reported that are probably in some degree maladaptive ecologically, yet are still followed. Since our examples of adaptive ritual practices have come from New Guinea, a rather dramatically maladaptive one from another New Guinea society will serve to illustrate the point.

[2]Few populations, human or animal, actually expand so that they approach the carrying capacity of the environment; various mechanisms—including the disease-carrying microorganisms of the ecosystem—tend to maintain populations in relative balance. In human populations, customs such as infanticide, warfare, and child spacing through abstinence undoubtedly contribute to this balance.

Case 16: *Kuru* and Its Consequences

Among the New Guinea Fore, about 1 percent of the population, mainly women, died annually from an inevitably fatal degenerative disease of the nervous system called *kuru*. The consequences demographically were catastrophic: a sex ratio imbalanced in favor of males by as much as three to one in some areas and a declining and fragile population structure.

The Fore explain *kuru* as caused by sorcery. Not only did *kuru* generate a rather frantic system of marriage and social organization, because of the imbalanced sex ratio and frequent death of wives and mothers; when a group's women died of *kuru* the men were likely to make war on their neighbors to avenge sorcery, further disrupting the social order and decimating population.

Yet recent study has shown that *kuru* is a disease caused by a virus that attacks the central nervous system after a long incubation period. The virus, which concentrates in the brain tissues of the victim, was transmitted by a special Fore custom: Fore women and children ritually ate the bodies of their own dead relatives, including their brains. Only by eating the brain of a victim can a person become a future victim.

The colonial administration, by prohibiting cannibalism, has broken

The fatal outcome of *kuru:* A Fore girl in the terminal stage of the disease. (Photograph courtesy of D. G. Gajdusek. In *Tropical Neurology* by John D. Spillane, ed. By permission of Oxford University Press.)

the cycle: fewer Fore die each year, after the disease has lain latent. But the point is that natural selection did not weed out a desperately maladaptive ritual practice. Natural selection does not automatically eliminate customs that have harmful consequences: *human beings must change them.* And since people most often do not consciously perceive directly the ecological consequences of their customs, the process of their consciously changing the customs into more adaptive ones is haphazard at best. Lindenbaum (1972:251) suggests that, ironically, Fore ritual cannibalism may be a symbolic attempt at self-regeneration in a society whose members perceive the threat of depopulation.

The Fore case, one might object, is atypical. It is possible that *kuru,* and the ritual cannibalism that transmits it, are relatively recent among the Fore. Eventually, by trial and error, they might have abandoned the practice of ritual cannibalism and broken the cycle themselves. But the response in the meantime—building an elaborate and further maladaptive theory of sorcery to explain the disease—is itself revealing. It lends weight to Lindenbaum's hypothesis that rituals are partly symbolic statements about the body politic and a people's perceived demographic situation. (We will see in §63 Mary Douglas' further argument of this point in connection with pollution practices and other ritual treatment of the body and its substances.) But it hardly lends confidence to the notion of efficient pruning mechanisms chopping out maladaptive customs or of humans inadvertently and fortuitously creating only adaptive ones.

It does reinforce, however, the notion that within regional ecosystems, populations, and hence their cultures, are to substantial degree in competition. While all populations probably have a complex tangle of adaptive, partly maladaptive, drastically maladaptive, and adaptively neutral customs, the organizational, economic, and demographic success of different populations will vary—and with this differential success, culture-bearing populations will spread, contract, dwindle, conquer, or be absorbed. The Fore were probably doomed to absorption by their neighbors, whose less maladaptive culture the survivors would eventually have adopted.

The most urgent point—one that could be illustrated with scores of less dramatic cases—is that a great many societies practice rituals, follow customs, and hold beliefs that have harmful or at best neutral ecological or demographic consequences. And they do so with a persistent faith and commitment to the ways of the past that is as characteristically human

as flexibility and pragmatism. The garden magician uttering spells over crops is carrying on in the style of his ancestors despite the fact that empirically the spells have no effect and ecologically his energy might be better spent making a better fence or digging drainage ditches.

The magician, like the Fore theory of sorcery, illustrates another oversimplification in the cultural adaptationist view. One set of the givens to which cultures must adapt comes not from the external environment, but from the processes of the human psyche. The mind imposes demands of its own. In the face of anxiety, uncertainty, and tragedy, the mind demands explanation and security, and projects fantasy. Garden magic may, as Malinowski argued, be psychologically adaptive rather than ecologically adaptive; so too may be a theory of illness, even when it has disruptive social consequences. The psychodynamics of the unconscious may loom large here: early childhood fears, desires, and fantasies projected upon the cosmos, not ecological adaptation, may create and shape a people's supernaturals and their ritual acts (here recall the Semang thunder god, Case 12). It is important to see the human brain in evolu-

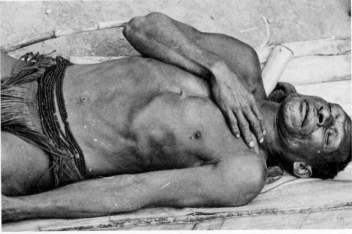

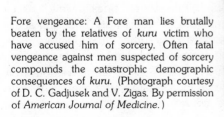

Fore vengeance: A Fore man lies brutally beaten by the relatives of *kuru* victim who have accused him of sorcery. Often fatal vengeance against men suspected of sorcery compounds the catastrophic demographic consequences of *kuru*. (Photograph courtesy of D. C. Gadjusek and V. Zigas. By permission of *American Journal of Medicine*.)

Solomon Islands' Magic: Does it serve adaptive ends? A Siuai magician (Bougainville Island) rides atop an enormous slit drum to lighten the load magically. (Photograph courtesy of D. L. Oliver.)

tionary perspective. It evolved primarily as a fantastically powerful device for communicating symbolically, for conceptualizing the world and solving the practical problems that the world posed. Yet humans with their super-brains are also driven by fears, inflamed by aggressive angers, haunted by doubts, and puzzled by unknowns; and the brains that produce solutions to problems also spin out webs of fantasy and explanation. That these symbolic webs do not always usefully serve ecological ends makes them no less importantly human.

The relationship between cultural creativity and ecological channeling is best seen not simply as a limiting of possibility but as a two-way pattern of interaction. Human beings have a remarkable capacity to prefer as their staple food the one that happens to grow best or be easiest to catch in their environment. But they also will take a useless plant and invest it with rich symbolic significance that "adaptation" can scarcely account for. The problem is to keep both sides in view—to see humans both as pragmatists, choosing adaptive paths, and as symbol manipulators, elaborating complex, rich, and variable codes.

Much remains to be learned about how cultures as ideational systems change. Whether the course of cultural change is partly based on the unfolding or progressive development of a particular people's conceptual system—whether a system of ideas partly determines its own path of change—is a question that strikes horror in the heart of a fervent materialist. Yet there is much to be learned from studying linguistic change; and much more must be discovered about the structure of cultures as ideational systems before we can wisely either dismiss the question or begin to answer it.

The cultural adaptationist model, especially as conceptualized by Harris, is overly simple in another respect. By failing to distingush precisely between a people's culture as ideational system and the patterns of social relations in which they engage, Harris is led to overlook the way change can be generated within the social system as well as in its adaptation to the environment. Here Harris parts company with "dialectical materialists"—that is, with Marxists.

Marxists view the process of production, and the material conditions of human life, as providing the foundations on which institutional and ideological superstructures are built. But in no sense does this imply a materialist reductionism in which social institutions or ideologies are mere reflections of or adaptations to material circumstances (which Marxists dismiss as "vulgar materialism"; *see* Friedman 1974 and Godelier 1974). Rather, the relationship between the economic substructure and ideational system and social structures is immensely complicated, involving a network of interconnections that must be traced in each case.

Moreover, conceiving societies and their cultures as nicely integrated and well adapted ignores the pervasive contradictions in their structure. The conflicts and contradictions that generate change, in Marxist interpretations, are most clearly represented in the relationship between social classes. Marx was pri-marily concerned with understanding the nature and historical emergence of nineteenth-century European capitalist society, with its sharp polarization of bourgeoisie and proletariat, and with the possibilities of its revolutionary transformation. But a model of social change through the internal dialectics within a society may well, as Marxists have argued, have a more general applicability.

Anthropologists drawing inspiration from Marx are beginning to generalize these models of social change so they can illuminate the workings of preindustrial societies, including tribal societies. We will return shortly, in Chapter 16, to the nature of social classes in comparative perspective.

Here it can be noted that even in societies where developed social classes do not exist, people fall into contrasting social niches and have different rights, different spheres of life, different rewards, and different interests. Even when this division is at its simplest, it contrasts young people and adults, mature adults with elders, men and women—and often, nobles and commoners, rich and poor, and so on. And conflicts and contradictions, and relations of exploitation and conflict, are to greater or lesser extent manifest in every society, however small scale and simple.

Such a perspective leads us to see that a society and a culture are never unitary and neatly integrated—they always represent some composite of conflicting perspectives and conflicting interests. It will not do, then, to say that a culture evolves as an adaptive system: the rites and ideology of a people may be substantially created, transmitted, controlled, and imposed by the male elders who constitute a small segment of the population.

A Marxist model, modified and generalized to fit small-scale societies, enables us to see ideologies as created not by a society but by those groups or segments or classes in a society that secure the power to create them and impose them. Pollution taboos, sexual polarization, and an ideology that rationalizes the economic and political subordination of women may be less a means of ideological birth control that regulates population than an instrument of male domination. (We will return to these questions, notably in §63.)

One crucial difference between biological evolution and sociocultural change which emerges clearly in Marxist theory is that humans have, or can have, a consciousness of their position and the consequences of their actions that other animals do not. In the Marxist model of change, this consciousness becomes an agent of change.

In a tribal society, "class" consciousness of men or women, of young and old, may be diffuse and partial. A people may opaquely perceive their way of life and their demographic state in relation to those of their neighbors (as Lindenbaum suggests). But fairly drastic shifts in the balance of power between men and women (as in the transformation of a system where descent is traced through men into one where descent is traced through women), or in the balance of power between young and old (for example, where warrior age grades assume substantial power, as among the Zulu of South Africa or the Masai of East Africa) may result not simply from gradual evolution but from a heightening of consciousness and an assertion of collective power perhaps catalyzed by a single leader or a single group. In a colonial situation, such heightened consciousness may produce revolutionary struggle or millenarian cults, as we will see in Chapter 21.

That humans are conscious of their state and the consequences of their acts entails another difference between sociocultural change and biological evolution. Social systems can be viewed in *moral* terms; biological systems cannot. Humans oppress one another, but it is absurd to talk about spiders oppressing their mates or predators oppressing their prey.

What is called for is a much more powerful and less simplistic model of social change than has yet been achieved. The notions Rappaport borrows from systems theory point in the right direction: systems theory and cybernetics give us the needed language and mathematics for talking about complex circuits and interconnections. But a more sophisticated model will have to suspend assumptions about equilibrium and integration, and add Marxist-derived insights, if it is to enable us to analyze with the needed precision how and why societies and cultures change.

It is not yet possible to build a comprehensive model of sociocultural change that reveals the precise interconnection of ecological, economic, ideational, psychological, and social factors. But our expansion of the cultural materialist position as illuminated by Marxism and systems theory here provides a framework within which the crucial questions can be strategically asked, if not yet firmly answered. In Part 4, we will examine the more drastic and cataclysmic course of change when a technologically more powerful civilization swept across and engulfed the world of tribal societies and the states of Africa and the Americas.

Anthropological interest in how tribal societies and preindustrial states have developed and changed was for years quite limited. But in the last 25 years anthropologists have been increasingly dissatisfied with static, timeless models of how societies *work*. The perspectives on history and process made possible by modern archaeology are partly responsible; and so too are the dramatic transformations of formerly tribal societies that have gone on as anthropologists watched. Studies of process and development, not simply static reconstructions of an imagined past equilibrium, are demanded. Finally, the growing awareness of our own ecological crisis has sent us belatedly back to the tribal world in search of wisdom about living with nature, instead of hammering it into our own design.

In all this, anthropologists are learning to see familiar scenes of the tribal world in new and more penetrating ways. And they have begun to rediscover, and give their own special stamp to, the theoretical issues that social philosophers have been debating since Marx, since Hobbes, and even since Plato.

THE LEGACY OF
TRIBAL PEOPLES

Part

There are two compelling reasons to study anthropology. The most direct is to understand more wisely, and hence to act more effectively in, the world of the 1970s. Colonialism and its aftermath, struggles for cultural identity and revolution, the search for world ecological survival, efforts to build a new social order—all can be illuminated in important ways by anthropology. These themes are central to Part 4.

But to illuminate the problems of the present in terms of anthropology requires that we draw on the legacy of the past. Thus the second, related, reason to study anthropology is to learn about human diversity. Why does it matter that an African tribe had a peculiar mode of reckoning descent, trading valuables, maintaining law and order, or conceptualizing the cosmos? It matters for several reasons.

The alternative paths of life explored by different peoples become crucial human resources as we search for ways to reorganize our lives so as to survive as a species. Anthropologists have been entrusted by the peoples they have studied—who often now are listening to transistor radios and voting in national elections—with the accumulated wisdom of their past. This is not simply a matter of preserving human natural history, of recording "endangered and vanishing cultural species." It is more urgently a matter of learning about cultural possibility, about myriad natural experiments in being human, about the outer limits of human nature. Whether humans must be motivated primarily by individual self-interest, as in capitalist rhetoric, or can be motivated by collective obligation, as in socialist rhetoric, is best not left to political ideologists, but studied in the alternative ways humans have organized their lives. Whether some proposed utopian mode of raising children will produce neurosis or social solidarity can well be asked in the light of the ways of raising children that have been explored and have survived the test of generations.

By asking about cultural diversity—and about possible universal patterns beneath diversity—we learn important things about the challenge of building pluralistic societies in the latter twentieth century. Here is a challenge that faces not only the giant states of East and West, but also the Third World societies of Africa, Asia, and Latin America.

Cultural diversity is also an important source of insights about our own society and culture. Many things we take for granted about the social and natural world, about human nature, and about time, space, and causality are not givens of universal human experience. As we saw in §26, the world we perceive is a world we create in our minds, and many elements of this world are based on cultural learning in particular times and places. In this challenge of understanding ourselves, the perceptions of us and our way of life by Third World scholars increasingly become important sources of insight and perspective. (They also become sources of insight about the consequences and costs of advanced technology and affluence to Third World peoples who now face urgent and agonizing choices about Westernization and "development.")

Part 3 will look at the alternative ways peoples in tribal societies have organized their social groupings, economic systems, and political institutions, and have spun the gossamer fabrics of religion and ritual. But the reader should be forewarned that these facets of tribal ways of life do not fit as neatly into separate compartments as do the institutions of complex societies. When a Melanesian in the Trobriand Islands presents a large part of his yam crop to his sister's husband, it is at once a social obligation, an economic transaction, a political act, and a ritual observance. He lives in a society without a government,[1] without law courts and legal contracts, without prices and money, without churches. When, in the chapters to follow, we look at "political systems" or "kinship systems" or "religions," we often will simply be seeing the same events from different directions.

---

[1] Other than, in modern times, a colonial one and now a national one.

KINSHIP, DESCENT, AND SOCIAL STRUCTURE

13

A starting point in understanding and mapping other ways of life is to find out about the cast of characters—what kinds of people there are and how they are organized into social groups and networks. Exploring *social organization* in non-Western societies has been a major challenge to social anthropology.

The most complicated, fascinating, and important modes of social grouping in tribal societies are based on kinship—on ties with blood relatives, in-laws, and ancestors. Thus for decades the anthropological study of social organization has been above all the study of systems of kinship, marriage and descent. Yet other modes of social groupings are woven into the designs of social life in jungle as well as city; and in modern complex societies they come increasingly to the fore.

In this chapter and the next, which are closely tied together and complementary, we

will look at the social organization of tribal societies. We will glimpse continuities as well—back to the social organization of hunting and gathering peoples and forward to complex modern societies. Exploring the organization and structure of social groups in small-scale societies, especially groupings based on kinship, will lead us past esoteric Inner Mysteries—for this is a forbiddingly specialized and technical field. It will also provide a framework of the social groupings of tribal societies that we will need in subsequent chapters to understand economic, political, and legal processes.

We will begin by setting out some useful guides for thinking about human social life, building on foundations laid in Chapter 8. Then, in this chapter, we will look briefly at the way social categories based on age and sex, and on kinship and descent, structure tribal social life. In Chapter 14 our exploration of social organization moves on to marriage and family structure as well as patterns of formal and informal social relations in small-scale societies.

38.
Social Organization: Some First Principles

When anthropologists talk about "social organization" or "social structure," they often mean by that a set of problems centering around kinship in a broad sense. Biological facts of sex, infantile dependence, and the life cycle impose broad constraints on human life in all times and places. On this biological framework, human societies have worked out principles of mating, family structure, and relatedness by birth, descent, and marriage that vary from one to another far less than they might. Study of these principles has been a central theme in anthropology since the latter nineteenth century; and the puzzles they pose have by no means yet been solved. Social organization is, as we have noted, not simply a matter of kinship; rather, it has to do with all the modes of organizing social groupings that bind people together and make ordered social life possible.

Fortunately, some basic ways of thinking about people and groups are as useful when we focus on U.S. suburbia as when we look at the complicated kinship groupings and age grades of a Brazilian Indian tribe. A key here is to distinguish, as we did in §24, between two facets of human social life, the cultural and the social.

To study social organization, it is often said, one begins with *social relationships*. But what is a social relationship? If we take two people, A and B, we can see two sides or facets to their "relationship." First, there are the ways they interact, the things they do and say in their dealings with one another. But there are also their *ideas about* their relationship, their conceptions of one another, the understandings and strategies and expectations that guide their behavior.

Both patterns of behavior and conceptual systems have "structure," in the sense that they are not helter-skelter or random. But they are different *kinds* of structure. Imagine an intersection governed by traffic lights. If we observed it for a while, we could record the "behavior" of the cars in terms of the density of traffic in various directions at various times and the number of cars that stop, go through, and slow down, according to sequences of changing lights. From these records would crystallize patterns of regularity, the "social structure" of the intersection. We would probably find the social structure of a North American intersection quite different from a South American one. But alternatively, we could describe the principles for making decisions used by drivers when they cross the intersection—not only the laws that are written down, but the unwritten "rules" about honking horns and going through while the lights are changing. These rules also have a structure, but it is quite different from the patterns of traffic flow—it is structure of organized *knowledge*.

In tribal settings before European intrusion, the situations a person encountered in life usually corresponded fairly neatly to the guides for action his or her culture laid down—though as we will see, some lack of "fit" is basic to human life. In times of rapid social change, these gulfs between the way the world is and the cultural guides for living in it become increasingly wide. Thus driving "rules" in a Latin American country can lead to chaos if the number of cars is quadrupled and freeways and cloverleafs are introduced. The Brazilian Indian from the savannas of Matto Grosso would hardly be equipped to cope with downtown São Paolo. We need to perceive and study the structure of both social and cultural orders if we are to understand process and change and to see how individuals, finding paths through the maze of life, are connected in wider networks.

Here and in the chapters that follow, this distinction between the cultural (ideas, categories, and "rules") and the social (people, acts, events, and groups) will be centrally important. It enables us to see at the outset a contrast between *cultural categories* and *social groups*. A cultural category is a set of entities in the world—people, things, events, supernaturals—that are classed as similar for some purposes, because they have in common one or more culturally relevant attributes. Thus trees, weeds, bachelors, and left-handed baseball pitchers are categories in our culture. As categories, they exist only in human minds. Note also that not all categories have one-word labels in our language. Nor are they sets of entities we keep in separate "chunks" in our mental schemas. Rather, they are sets we *draw mental lines around* in particular contexts. Women who wear size 7 dresses comprise a relevant category in only a very few contexts (mainly for people who make or sell dresses, while they happen to be at work). Thus any single entity can be classed, in varying contexts, as belonging to dozens of different cultural categories. A category of human beings, grouped conceptually because of some socially relevant features they share (like men or warriors or descendants of ancestor X), we can call a *social category.*

A *social group,* on the other hand, consists of actual warm-blooded human beings who recurrently interact in an interconnected set of roles—that is, positions or capacities. Thus groups can be distinguished from forms of aggregation, such as crowds or gatherings, whose interaction is temporary and limited. Members of a social group need not all interact face to face, though such *primary groups* are common in the small-scale communities anthropologists usually study. What defines a

group is its internal organization, the connection of its members in a set of interconnected roles. Thus the stockholders of General Motors comprise a *secondary group.* Although most of its members do not interact with one another, they are bound into a group through their relationships with the management.

Who belongs to a group is seldom neatly defined by some cultural principle such as being descended from the same ancestor or being the right age or social class. Such membership in a social category usually defines *eligibility* to be a member of a group. Whether an eligible person actually takes part in a group is likely to depend on the circumstances of life history, on economic interests and resources, on personal choice.

To illustrate some basic points about categories and groups, we will look at a hypothetical example from our own society—one that parallels closely the kinship-based categories and groups of tribal societies.

Imagine that three generations ago, in a New England community, 10 men founded a music festival which has taken place ever since. Priority for tickets to the festival now goes to the festival Patrons, who comprise all those descendants of the 10 founders who take part in meetings and maintain an active interest. Many of the descendants *eligible* to be Patrons have, of course, moved away and lost touch. But if they ever moved back, they could become active again, and if they happened to visit on the day of a performance, a good seat would always be found for them. At any performance, there will also be persons in the audience who come as guests of Patrons or who are simply filling in the remaining seats.

What sorts of social units have we here? First, all descendants of the founders, whether Patrons or those who have moved away or lost interest, form a *social category.* Their descent status makes them eligible to activate a set of rights if they can and wish. Second, those descendants who are Patrons comprise a *corporate group,* which ultimately controls the activities of the festival—and whose members enjoy the attendant privileges, though they may well not turn up at a particular performance. Finally, the audience actually attending a performance comprises a *gathering.* But if they gathered in some more organized fashion to perform a common task—to erect a new stage, for example—we could call the mixed bunch who actually came an *action group* or *task group.* The anthropological literature is full of confusions about "clans" and "moieties" and "lineages" and "kindreds" where these distinctions between groups and categories, corporations and action groups, have been blurred or overlooked.

Before we turn to the fascinating complexities of kinship organization in tribal societies, we will look briefly at the way categories based on sex and the life cycle create a framework for social life.

39.
Sex and the Life Cycle in Tribal Social Organization

The differences between male and female provide an important axis of cultural partition in every society. Obviously, no society consisting only of males or only of females could exist across generations. But given the fact that only a limited amount of sperm must cross the division between the sexes (recall here the homosexually preoccupied Marind Anim of New Guinea), humans have had considerable latitude in the way they have defined the place of women and men and the appropriate relationship between them.

How much power men and women have, and how their status and worth are culturally defined, is not, as we have seen, simply a matter of a particular people's symbolic imag-

ination. On the one hand, the productive (and reproductive) powers of women and men must be organized in such a way that in a particular environment, and with a particular technology, people feed themselves, avoid disease, and bear and raise children relatively successfully. Ways of life where these needs are met inefficiently, compared to the neighbors, are unlikely to survive in the long run. Moreover, the power and status of men and women are defined by continual negotiation and political and economic conflict. To see such customs as simply alternative cultural possibilities, as two generations of American anthropologists were inclined to do, will no longer suffice.

We glimpsed in §37 societies where the roles of men and women are sharply polarized, and particularly where taboos define women as polluted and polluting. We will return to such polarization of the sexes in Chapter 19 and again in Chapter 24. In other societies, as we will shortly see, women have considerable political and economic power, and this is reflected in their higher symbolic status. The Hopi, whose matrilineal descent system we look at in this chapter, are an important example. In other tribal societies, such as some Philippines societies, the gulf between the sexes is relatively deemphasized. The Isneg of the Luzon mountains serve to illustrate. Not only are men and women accorded relatively equivalent legal status, and given equal weight in tracing relations of kinship. In addition, many of the specialist roles in Isneg society, notably religious roles, are open to or conventionally filled by women; seeresses and priestesses play an important part in Isneg religion.

The division of a society into male or female realms combines with physical maturation to create a series of social compartments. The human life cycle, like sexual differences, allows considerable leeway for cultural definition—differences in where the compartments are divided, in how high and impenetrable are the walls between them, and in the role accorded to people in each compartment.

Let us consider first the constraints. Infantile dependency, bonding, and the need for enculturation during maturation must always be culturally provided for. Very young children, not yet toilet trained, weaned, or able to understand the cultural conventions of adults, must be suckled and nurtured, taught and ushered into their adult world. Since child care is in all known societies primarily a responsibility of women, the association of women with dependent children in turn has limited the other roles that have been accorded to women.

The course of maturation, the development of secondary sexual characteristics, and the strong sex drives of adolescence must be culturally managed. That women's prime child-bearing years cover roughly a 20-year period requires that whatever social stability is to be created for the rearing of dependent children be crystallized most strongly in the period following adolescence and prior to middle age. And societies must come to terms with the fact that physical strength reaches its height in young adulthood, remains for some 20 or 25 years, and then begins to ebb markedly. The course of senescence, where the powers of mature adulthood slip away, gradually leads—if the aging survive that long—to a dependence like that of the child.

These universals of the life cycle impose fairly marked constraints on cultural possibility. (There is undoubtedly a considerable gap between the outer limits of human possibility, the range of organizationally and ecologically viable and psychologically feasible ways of life humans *could* live in successfully, and the cultures humans have actually *evolved*. It is a useful exercise to try to design societies that could exist but do not: useful partly because it raises important questions about the limits of human nature and partly because we desparately need to explore new social possibilities.)

In societies where men's and women's spheres of life substantially overlap and are not sharply polarized, childhood is likely to be a fairly relaxed period in which the skills and duties of adulthood are gradually acquired.

Adolescence is probably always a transitional stage between the dependency of childhood and the responsibility of adulthood. Where relations between the sexes are not polarized, this is often a period of quite casual sexual adventuring, as in some Polynesian societies. A striking example is provided by the Trobriand Islanders of Melanesia, who became a classic anthropological case from Bronislaw Malinowski's famous early studies. Our introduction to the Trobrianders will begin with their attitude toward sex as one of the good things in life, but we will encounter many other aspects of their fascinating social and economic life and cultural structure in the pages to follow.

Case 17: Premarital Sex in the Trobriands

Young people in the Trobriand Islands of Melanesia are encouraged to indulge in sexual play in childhood and to begin sexual intercourse when that seems the thing to do. For girls that is very early indeed—when they are 6 to 8 years old, according to Malinowski (1929:75). For boys intercourse begins, he says, at age 10 to 12. In earliest adolescence sexuality is free but very casual. By the mid-teens Trobriand couples begin to pair off and to form more serious liaisons. Eventually one of these continues into a serious tie leading to marriage.

Adolescents organize outings and trips that widen their range of sexual adventurings and add spice to sexual affairs close to home, especially during periods of intense sexuality that are geared to the seasonal gardening cycle (see Cases 44 and 75).

However, contrary to popular stereotypes, such a free attitude toward sex is far from universal in the tribal world. Particularly where male and female realms are sharply separate and women are defined as polluting, sexual relations may be strained and premarital relationships marked by prudishness and rigid prohibition. A striking example are the people of Wogeo Island, off New Guinea. As part of a complex of pollution taboos in which the sexes are sharply polarized, and in which men incise their penises to let blood in explicit imitation of menstruation, premarital sex is prohibited and adult sexual relations are apparently strained and marked by great anxiety on the part of men over the dangers of pollution.

In societies where adult male and female compartments are walled off from one another and sharply contrasted, maturation is likely to be a culturally drastic transition, especially for boys. Men may live in a sacred realm of men's houses, cults, and so on—or in a world of warfare or high finance—while women stay in the home, performing the tasks of child support and everyday subsistence. For a girl the transition to adulthood entails physical maturation and a change from being daughter to being wife and mother, but she remains in the female realm. An infant boy, however, inevitably starts on the female side, so that to become a man requires a major transition.

One way this transition can be managed is to begin introducing young boys into the men's sphere of life early but sporadically, so that the transition to manhood is long and gradual. Males learn early that they are men

and that this makes a difference, with that difference becoming fully important as they mature physically and socially.

A more drastic solution is to leave young boys basically in the women's sphere of life through childhood. Then, at some point, which need not closely match physiological puberty, they are dramatically removed from daily life, subjected to some physical or ritual ordeal—often circumcision—and then incorporated into the adult men's compartment. Less commonly in such societies, girls undergo a similar ritual transition from girlhood to womanhood.

Such rites marking the transition from one social category to another have been made famous by Van Gennep (1909) as *rites of passage*. The transition is ritually expressed, first, by removing the subject from the old category; placing him or her in an external, suspended state, cut off from regular contact; and finally, ritually reincorporating the initiate in a new category. Since others must establish a new set of relations with the initiate, this is enhanced by the sequence of disappearance-reappearance—a kind of rebirth in the new state.

Transitions between age categories need not correspond to stages of physical maturation. In any case, only the onset of menstruation for girls takes place at a precise time: the development of secondary sexual characteristics of puberty is spread over a period of years. Those societies that pass members through age categories individually are more likely to gear transitions to physical development, though external factors like the first successful hunt may define the transition points. Societies that initiate young people collectively in a large and elaborate production may do so at intervals of several years, producing a wide age spread among initiates. (We will glimpse complex systems of age sets in §51).

As physical powers of adulthood fade away, financial and political powers characteristically begin to dwindle as well. In many societies, however, elders continue to play a dominant political role, or at least to command the sacred knowledge on which human well-being depends. Meillasoux (1960) and others have addressed the questions of how and why physically weak and economically dependent elders in Africa can accumulate and maintain great power. Like elders everywhere, they rely heavily on the myth that wisdom accumulates with age (see Terray 1972:128 ff.).

In a kinship-oriented society the role of the elderly apparently never entails the insecurity and alienation from family that have developed in our own society as a result of shrinking kinship ties, economic pressures, the isolation and mobility of nuclear families, and the population explosion in the ranks of the elderly due to medical advances. Another more subtle element here is our changed world view—where time now stretches into the future and where progress and directional change move us inexorably away from the past. What we experience are *new* events, not the same patterns coming up again. In thinking of movement in straight lines, we have lost track of circles and cycles. Tribal peoples, living in a world of continuities with the past, a world of repeated cyclings rather than of progressive change, usually perceive old age in a very different way than we do. The child who cares for an aged and helpless parent is simply following a cycle where those who gave nurturance in helpless infancy are becoming helpless themselves (though recall from the Tallensi first-born, Case 12, the inev-

itable ambivalence in both directions regarding this cycling).

Biologically, death may end the life cycle abruptly and with finality. But in many societies death does not remove actors from the social scene—it moves them into a new role.

The nature of ancestors and the way in which they enter human life will be touched upon in Chapter 19. Here we need to keep in mind that a people's social world need not include only the actors we can see and hear. A whole range of "religious customs" like sacrifice may be puzzling if we think of the supernatural as radically separate from the natural, but quite intelligible if we see these events as communications and transactions with classes of social actors that are beyond our field of view.

The social categories defined by sex and age provide a general framework of "kinds of people" in a small-scale society. But how one relates to particular people in these categories—which ones are friends, which are enemies, which are close, and which are distant—characteristically depends on a cross-cutting and crucially important system of *kinship*.

40.
Kinship in Tribal Societies

It is hard for us to understand a way of life where relationships with people are preeminently relationships with relatives. In many societies, all members of the community trace connections of blood or marriage with one another; in some places, a person is either your relative or your enemy. And such systems have probably prevailed through most of the human time span on earth.

Study of the forms of social arrangement built around kinship has been a dominant theme in anthropology for almost a century. Almost all the leading figures in anthropological theory have participated at one time or another in debates about kinship, and a very extensive body of technical literature continues to expand. Even those who are not specialists in this area must lead their readers through the intricacies of kinship—in a jargon incomprehensible to the uninitiated—in describing life in a small-scale society. We will not attempt here to cover all the technical concepts and controversies, though the reader who makes his way through the pages that follow will be well on his way toward understanding more technical works in the field (Keesing 1975 seeks to take the interested anthropological initiate further into the cult of kinship mysteries).

Before we begin, it will be rewarding to ask why anthropologists have worried so much for so long about the intricacies of kinship.

Kinship as the Basic Idiom of Social Relations

In the societies anthropologists usually study, one has to make sense of kinship to make sense of anything else. Even where people in a nonliterate society are competing for economic advantage or political power, they are likely to talk about what they are doing in terms of kinship. Moreover, kinship ties serve as models or templates for relationships to nonrelatives and often to deities. Relationships of "fictive kinship"—such as our godparents and the much more important *compadrazgo,* or ritual co-parenthood of Latin America (Case 91, Chapter 22), are modeled on blood ties. In many places supernaturals are metaphorically treated like fathers.

The anthropologist who studies a tribal community can anticipate that people do not always live up to the ideal standards of behavior between relatives, and that they act toward one another in many roles other than those based on blood relationship. Yet a first challenge is to sort out the cast of characters,

and it has usually been useful to begin with complex webs of connection by blood and marriage. Having done so, one can proceed to decipher the complex social processes carried out in this idiom and perceive how kinship serves as a basic model for relating to other people. The anthropologist often finds that he or she must be assigned a place, albeit fictional, in this scheme of kinship, in order to take part in the life of the community.

Kinship as a Focal Point of Values

Obligations between relatives are viewed as morally binding, and their fulfillment ranks high among the paramount virtues of a tribal people. If we think back to our primate ancestry, and the transformations of social organization that opened the path to human society, the reasons for this system begin to emerge.

What three major transformations made human social life possible? First, the continuing association of a male—"the father"—with the primate nuclear group of mother and offspring. Second, the prohibition of mating within this enlarged nuclear group—the incest taboo. And, finally, the systematic *sharing* of food and other scarce resources, both within and between these nuclear groups.

Kinship systems build on the close biopsychological bonding between an infant and the adult, normally mother, who provides closest nurturance in the first year of life (Freeman 1974). They build outward on the complex of relationships between father and mother, between parents and children, and between siblings, and extend them out to and beyond members of a local band. The obligations of kinship have a central symbolic significance we can understand in the light of these three hominid transformations. They symbolize, for humans as hunters or tribesmen, the collective as opposed to the individual, social obligation rather than self-gratification; and they symbolize the cultural in contrast to the biological. As we will see, the rule that one must marry someone outside one's own band creates and symbolically marks interdependence between groups, making possible the organization of a wider society. In the light of our primate heritage, it is not surprising that kinship has been central in the thought worlds of tribal peoples, as expression and symbol of what makes humans human. Moreover, if, as Freeman (1974) suggests, kinship is an extension and a sort of reenactment of the primary bond so central in the emotional life of each of us, it is doubly intelligible that emotionally blood is so much thicker than water.

Limited Variation in Kinship Systems

Let us look at a third and major reason for our attention to kinship in comparative studies. Many areas of culture have an extremely wide variation in different societies: house shapes, art forms, methods for disposing of the dead, modes of dress, and so on. The variations are as wide as physical and environmental possibility, and human imagination, permit. (Though we will see in §68 and §69 how even here the human mind imposes its own constraints on cultural possibility.) Yet far less variation occurs in the realm of kinship. We find over and over again variations on the same themes, different combinations of familiar elements. This should not surprise us. Even human imagination can devise only so many ways of assigning parentage, tracing descent, classifying relatives, transmitting rights across generations, forming groups, and regulating mating. Given the common elements of human biology we sketched in Part 1, the range of possibility is distinctly limited.

It is good intellectual exercise, and a rewarding challenge, to try to devise ways humans could have solved these biological problems without assigning parentage to children, without using some form of marriage to make these assignments (thereby creating family units), and without building from such parent-child-marriage links a network of kinship connections. Yet although in some ways societies have approached these limits, all known societies have some form of marriage and attribute some importance to kinship. Once these commitments have been made, the range of possibilities is greatly narrowed.

It is worth looking briefly at some of the outer limits of variation at this point. By approaching the subject of kinship with some classic natural experiments in the possibilities of human life, we will get a first glimpse of the fascination of kinship systems, and a reminder that we can understand them only by breaking out of our assumptions about what is "natural" and viewing them in terms of their own logic.

Case 18: Banaro Social Structure

The Banaro of New Guinea live in villages that are divided into two "halves," and everyone belongs to one side or the other. A child belongs to the side of his father; but this is also the side of his mother, because a man must marry a girl from his own side. But if each side is self-contained, how are the two sides bound up together into a single society? Because every man has an "opposite number" on the other side, and to pass through the various stages of life he is dependent on this opposite number. If we look at a man we will call A, and his opposite number B (who is not related by blood or marriage, since all A's kinsmen are on his own side), we see this dependence most clearly when A's son marries. It is B, not the groom, who sexually initiates the bride—on an altar and disguised as a "goblin." B then has regular sexual relations with the bride until she has her first child; only then is A's son permitted to live with her. The first child is the "child of the goblin" and has a special (but not kinship) relation to B's side (Thurnwald 1916).

Case 19: Nayar Taravad and Marriage

Among the Nayar castes of South India, the basic social group, the taravad, was composed of men and women descended in the female line from a common ancestress. Children become members of their mother's taravad, not their father's. In fact, the only "marriage" in anything like our sense was a religious ritual before the "bride" reached puberty. After that a woman had many lovers who simply visited her; the presumed father of a child had only the most minimal ritual attachment to the child (Gough, in Schneider and Gough 1961).

Case 20: Nuer "Ghost Marriage"

Two unusual forms of marriage among the Nuer, pastoralists of the Sudan, will illustrate other possibilities. A widow ideally marries the brother or another close relative of her dead husband; or she may simply take lovers. The socially defined father of any children she bears is the dead first husband (what has been called "ghost marriage"). In another form, an old and important woman may "marry" a girl. The woman finances marriage transactions as if she were a man. The young woman then bears children by lovers, and the old woman is treated (for purposes of inheritance and the like) as their "father" (Evans-Pritchard 1951).

Case 21: Toda "Fatherhood"

Another possible system for marriage and assigning parenthood is found among the Toda of India. One woman ideally has several husbands—in many cases, brothers. How, then, for social purposes, to decide which one is the father of a child? By a ritual "presenting of the bow," which determines the father of this and subsequent children until it is another husband's turn. If the man who has last gone through this ritual dies, and until another husband does so, any children born are considered those of the dead man (Rivers 1902).

Case 22: Father and Mother in Mota

Another possibility, from Mota in the South Pacific Banks Islands, is the validation of fatherhood by the payment of an expensive midwife's fee. If the father is unable to make his payment, another man can do so; and this man then assumes the role of father to the child. In such a case, the woman who bore the child no longer raises it; the wife of the man who paid the midwifery fee assumes this role (Codrington 1891).

Mota provides another interesting variant as well; a man is expected to marry the widow of his maternal uncle.

Case 23: The *Ghotul* of the Muria

The Muria of India have worked out an intriguing way of handling the problems of sex and marriage. Boys and girls spend their adolescence living together in coeducational "dormitories" called *ghotul*. The aim is free sexual relations between all dormitory-mates, and any regular pairing off is discouraged. In some dormitories no couple is allowed to sleep together for more than two nights in succession. Yet the marriage rules specify that a boy must marry a girl from a different dormitory (Elwin 1968).

These variations, though revealing and intriguing, still remain within fairly narrow limits. Other social experiments, consciously constructed in some utopian spirit, have gone farther in transcending the limits of kinship, marriage, and the family—as with Israeli *kibbutzim* or modern American communes.

Recently, talking with a group of Kwaio friends in their Solomon Island mountain settlement, I was led to an interesting insight into kinship systems of tribal peoples. During a betel-chewing break in which we had been discussing the "strange" customs of the neighboring tribes, I led the discussion further afield: I told them about Nuer "ghost marriage," Mota motherhood, and a series of other "strange" kinship practices of the tribal world. For each case the Kwaio immediately perceived the social logic and gave me a neat "structural analysis"—even though the system of descent or marriage was in some cases very different from their own. This suggests that tribal peoples in different places share certain premises about social groups and their relationships that we, in modern industrialized societies, no longer share with them. Part of the challenge in studying the "curious" customs of "primitive" peoples is to find these general social logics according to which such customs make sense.

Despite the range of variation we have glimpsed, remarkably similar modes of kinship organization turn up across the ethnographic world. Thus the same mode of classifying relatives or organizing groups through common descent may turn up, without historical connection, in Africa, the South Pacific, and aboriginal North America. One of the challenges in the study of kinship is to seek out the way elements of kinship organization interlock as systems, so that the same clusters of elements may develop in different times and places.

Kinship, like chess, provides endless fascination for the specialist and an aura of mystery, unintelligibility, and triviality to the outsider. Yet there is a practical urgency to understand at least the outlines of non-Western modes of kinship organization. In a world where more and more people are seeking to operate in, and change, societies quite different from their own, ignorance of these outlines can be disastrous. In such cross-cultural encounters one must try to perceive forms of kinship, descent, and marriage quite different from one's own in terms of their structure and logic. Common sense, being cultural sense, can be a poor guide indeed in another cultural world. Those who have condemned bride price as degrading to women; those who have forced "natural" laws of inheritance on peoples who pass property to their sisters' children and not their own; those who are bewildered or morally outraged by marriage customs or forms of the family very different from their own—all face frustration in trying to change what they do not understand, and cause disruption, bewilderment, and even disaster for the people whose ways of life they seek to transform.

41.
What Is Kinship?

Kinship, to us, intuitively refers to "blood relationships." Our relatives are those connected to us by bonds of "blood." Our in-laws, to be sure, are related by marriage and not blood—and so are some of our aunts and uncles. But it is successive links between parents and children that are the essential strands of kinship.

Is this true in other societies? Consider the Toda or Nuer, where the child's socially recognized father may be a dead man—or, with the Nuer, a woman. And how can we talk about "blood" relationship between father and child, or mother and child, in cultures that have quite different theories or metaphors about the connection between parent and child? In some, the mother is thought to contribute no substance to the child, but only to provide a container for its growth. The Lakher of Burma, for example, believe that two children with the same mother and different fathers are not relatives at all.

Moreover, the Trobriand Islanders of Melanesia and some tribes of Australian Aborigines staunchly deny that copulation between father and mother is the cause of pregnancy—hence seemingly denying the father a physical connection to the child. One of the several theories of procreation advanced by the Trobrianders is that women are impregnated by ancestors while wading in the lagoon—which apparently leaves their spirits undampened. There has been much debate for years about this "ignorance" of paternity: whether it is a matter of theological dogma, like Christian virgin birth, whether it reflects a radically different theory of "causality," and so on.

But, at least, such variations must lead us at the outset to be wary of assuming that kinship is simply a matter of "blood relationship." It is safest to broaden our scope considerably to say that relations of kinship are connections *modeled on* those conceived to exist between a father and child and between a mother and child. In a particular culture these connections may be viewed as the same for father and mother (as with our "blood" relations) or as different—based on metaphors of seed and soil, of bone and flesh, of substance and container, or whatever. Moreover, "modeled on" leaves room for those cases like Mota, Nuer, and Toda where a socially defined parent is known not to have actually fathered or borne the child. (Adoptive parenthood in our society and many others would similarly be modeled on "natural" parenthood.)

We conceive kinship relations, based on "blood," to be natural and immutable; they entail diffuse obligations of solidarity (what Fortes calls the "axiom of amity"). They contrast with relationships "in-law"—that is, contingent and legal relations established by the marriage contract. Schneider (1972) and others have argued that this symbolic system is only indirectly related to sex and reproduction, and that other peoples may have quite different conceptualizations of the realm of kinship similarly related only indirectly to perceived relations of biological parenthood.

But the contrast in this realm seems less wide than it might be. However a people conceptualize the biological connection between presumed father and child and between mother and child, it is this relationship—inalienable and deep—that is always or almost always the basis of kinship bonds. And even where the *contributions* of father and mother are thought to be different, these bonds of kinship are extended, in almost all societies, through both father and mother as though they were equivalent. We are sometimes misled, as with the Mota midwife fee or the Nuer woman-woman marriage, because parents characteristically occupy several different roles toward their children. And some of these roles, such as having custody, caring for and nurturing the child, or being socially recognized in terms of descent or inheritance, may be contingent on the natural parents being married or on some legal *validation* of the connection of parenthood.

In-laws are technically classed as *affines*. Relationships with them are called *affinal*.[1]

Tracing kin relations out through father and mother creates networks of kinship ties (Figure 13.1). Such kinship relations are classed as *bilateral,* or *consanguineal.* The greater importance of these networks of kinship ties in tribal societies has been underlined already. But the ways tribal peoples use networks of kinship very often parallel the ways we use them. Our ties with relatives appear most clearly on special occasions like Christmas or birthdays, when presents or cards are given or exchanged, and especially on the major events in our lives—our christening or Bar Mitzvah, our wedding, our funeral.

So too in tribal societies the ties of kinship between individuals come out most dramatically in the focal points of a person's life—birth, initiation, feasts, marriage, death. The action group that mobilizes around a person

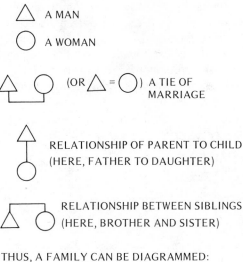

THUS, A FAMILY CAN BE DIAGRAMMED:

Figure 13.1. Anthropological conventions for diagramming kinship relations.

[1]Usually, as in our system, the spouses of aunts and uncles are not classed as affines, but are classed with blood relatives (see Keesing 1975:43—45).

in support, celebration, or mourning is in almost all societies crystallized from networks of the individual's relatives and affines. Where these relatives, or some close circle of them, are conceptually recognized as a special cultural category, the category has a special anthropological label: it is called a *kindred* or *personal kindred*. An idealized kindred is diagrammed in Figure 13.2.

The descending arrows in Figure 13.2 indicate that the descendants of siblings of grandparents (or of great grandparents and more distant relatives) may be included for some purposes within a kindred category. Since in real life families often include many siblings, not simply two, the actual kindred of a tribesman or tribeswoman may include dozens of relatives. The number who actually participate in kindred-based action groups may be much smaller—since many potential members live far away, have competing obligations, belong to the opposite political faction, and so on.

Kindreds cannot serve as the basis of ongoing corporations; the groups crystallized from them are always temporary and mobi-

lized in particular situations (as at a wedding or christening or funeral in our society). The reason is that each individual has a unique circle of relatives, and any person belongs to many such circles, not one. Your Uncle George is also someone else's father, another person's brother, still another person's cousin. George can act in each of these capacities on different occasions, but he cannot act in all of them all the time. If you decide to get married on the day Uncle George's oldest son graduates, he is likely to miss your wedding.

Kinship ties in a tribal society play a part in many spheres of life where they are no longer important to most of us. The people who live in a community, the people who work together, the people who compete and quarrel are, as we will see, mainly relatives. Before we can understand how kinship shapes social groups in tribal societies, or look at an old preoccupation of social anthropologists, the way kinds of relatives are classified with "kinship terms," we must examine some organizational problems in tribal societies and see ways in which kinship is used to solve them.

42.
Descent Systems

The basic elements of kinship organization apparently were part of a cultural heritage built up during millennia when humans were hunters and gatherers. First and most basic was the tracing of kinship networks between individuals. Second, there was a system of *band* organization in which mobile local groups exploited territories. Third, there was the *incest taboo* (which we will consider shortly) prohibiting marriage with close kin; and probably in at least many cases, its extension into a rule that a mate had to be found in a different band. The latter meant that a wide range of any person's relatives, through his mother, his grandmothers, and others, were

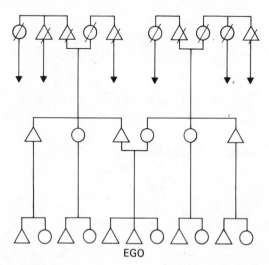

EGO

Figure 13.2. A personal kindred. (From Keesing 1975:15.) The diagonal slash indicates "deceased."

in other bands—and that helped to bind bands together in peaceful political relations.

These heritages from the long human past as hunters and gatherers provided crucial elements for the solution of a series of organizational problems that began to confront peoples much more seriously with the advent of food producing. These problems emerged as humans were able to live in larger, more stable groups, and as land became a crucial "thing," a means of growing food or feeding herds—not simply a territorial surface to hunt and gather on.

1. How will stable, strong local groups be formed, capable of acting as independent political units, in the absence of any central government?
2. How will the relation of people to land be defined? With Neolithic food producing, land tenure is no longer a matter of hunting territories. The soil itself has become vital to life; and Neolithic technology is usually incompatible with a fixed relationship between individuals and small partitioned tracts of land.
3. How will the relationships of people to land and other resources be maintained across generations, and how will they be adjusted to demographic fluctuations?
4. How will an individual have rights, safety, and allies in local groups other than his own?
5. How will political relations between local groups be maintained without a central government? And when feuding or warfare between groups begin, how can it be controlled?

The seeds of a solution, flexible and adaptive, lay in the band organization of hunters and gatherers. If a bandlike local group could become more solidary, if its members could collectively hold title to land, and if ties of intermarriage and kinship could weave together members of different bands, a workable and neat solution to these problems would seem to have been available.

What was needed was a way to convert bands, with political rights over territories, into land-owning *corporations,* or corporate groups. A corporation, in the tribal world as in the business world (and as with the patrons of our hypothetical music festival), is a group of people who together *act as a single legal individual.* In the tribal world a group usually acts corporately with regard to an estate in land. Characteristically, a corporation has a name or some other symbolic expression of the way it acts as a legal individual, an undifferentiated unit, vis-à-vis outsiders—however differentiated its members may be from one another seen from inside the group. Seen from outside, in an important sense the members are all one.

A corporation can meet the five major organizational problems of the tribal world. Its members can collectively hold title to land and other property. They can exploit their resources by cooperative labor (even though members may garden in smaller family units and may own the actual garden plots, as opposed to the land, separately). Corporations can, in their status as legal individuals, be unified political forces; they can conduct litigation and make treaties, conduct feuds and wars, and enter into contracts. And they are stable, since the corporation continues despite the death and replacement of individual members.

But how are such corporations to be formed and defined in the tribal world? Could it be achieved by simply conceptualizing the local band group or territorial unit as a corporation? Perhaps. But in the tribal world, a conceptual innovation was worked out that tied together the local solidarity of a territorial group with the symbolic solidarity of shared kinship.

The crucial conceptual innovation worked out in the tribal world was to define a social category not with reference to a living person but with reference to an *ancestor*—that is, with a rule of *descent.*

If we define rights over a territory with

reference to an ancestor 3 or 5 or 10 genera-tions back—who founded or owned or con-quered the territory—then we can neatly relate the people descended from that ances-tor to the territory. But organizationally, this by itself will not suffice. From the standpoint of any particular ancestor, he has too many descendants. From the standpoint of any liv-ing individual, he or she has too many ances-tors—8 great grandparents, 16 great-great grandparents, and so on. If the individual had rights over the territories of each, the result would be unworkable organization in which practically everyone had rights practically everywhere.

A further principle is needed, a principle that limits and excludes. The simplest way is to define only a few of the descendants of a founding ancestor as having rights over the territory and to exclude the rest. The most common principle of descent is *patrilineal,* or *agnatic.* In Figure 13.3, A shows how descent is traced patrilineally through a line of men; B shows an idealized and simplified patrilineal descent category. Note that women, as well as men, are members of a patrilineal descent

category, but only men transmit this member-ship to their children.

An apparent mirror image is *matrilineal,* or *uterine,* descent, where descent is traced through a line of women (Figure 13.4). As we will see, organizationally matrilineal descent is by no means the neat mirror image of patrilineal descent it appears to be on the diagrams.

These rules of descent serve to define corporate descent groups that can effectively solve the organizational problems of tribal societies we have noted. Consider a rule of patrilineal descent, combined, as it usually is, with a rule of *exogamy,* requiring that mar-riage take place between men and women of different bands. The patrilineal descendants of the founder of a territory can be organized as a corporate group sharing rights to the territory. This means that problem (1), mem-bership in local groups, is solved. Problem (2), the relation of people to territories, is solved. Problem (3), how rights are trans-ferred and maintained across generations, is solved by the perpetual corporation and the rule of descent. Problem (4), how individuals

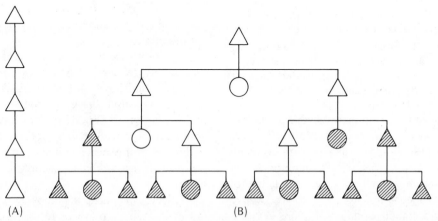

(A)   (B)

Figure 13.3.   Patrilineal descent: Figure A shows how descent is traced through a line of men. Figure B shows a descent category formed by patrilineal descent. It is simplified in that, in the real world, families are not all composed of two brothers and a sister. Living members of the descent category are indicated by hatching.

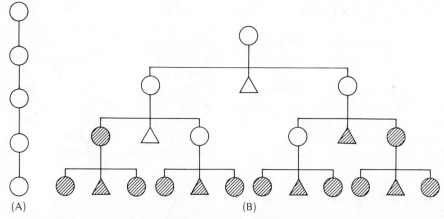

Figure 13.4.   Matrilineal descent: Figure A shows how descent is traced through a line of women. Figure B shows a descent category formed by matrilineal descent. Living members of the descent category are indicated by hatching.

can have ties to other groups and territories, is solved by the rule of exogamy—for a person will have outside allies in mother's group, father's mother's group, and so on. Problem (5), how political relations between groups can be maintained, can be at least partly solved by using these ties of intermarriage, and common descent from more distant ancestors, as bases for alliances.

But the overall solution is not that simple, as we will see. Moreover, some cautions are needed at the outset. First, patrilineal or matrilineal descent from the founding ancestor does not usually make a person a member of a descent corporation, an actual social group. In most societies using these organizational principles, being descended in the correct line *entitles* a person to be a member of a descent corporation: that is, patrilineal or matrilineal descent defines a category of persons entitled to be members. Whether they actually *are* members depends on the circumstances of life history and often on individual strategy and choice. In this respect, descent groups are like the corporation controlling our New England music festival: not all those eli-

gible to be members actually are members. Moreover, in many such societies, many people actually act as members of descent corporations even though they do not have the proper descent "credentials." This gap between descent entitlement and corporation membership—between being in a cultural category and being in a social group—is often important in making such forms of organization flexible and adaptive.

Second, once we perceive this gulf between descent entitlement and corporation membership, we can understand another mode of forming descent corporations. This is to say that *all* descendants of a founding ancestor, through any combination of male and female links, comprise a descent category. Such a nonexclusive mode of tracing descent is called *cognatic descent*. As we noted earlier, an individual then belongs to many cognatic descent categories. The organizational problem is then to use patterns of residential history, strategy, and choice to narrow any particular individual's corporation membership down to a single group, despite his eligibility and secondary interests in the other groups and territories from whose founders he can trace cognatic descent.

Third, chains of descent often serve to define rules and rights other than corporation membership. Thus, succession to a position or office might be determined by descent in the male line; or individually owned property might be inherited in the female line. Some anthropologists would not want to call this descent. But in any case, descent *cate-* *gories*—patrilineal, matrilineal, or cognatic— may be accorded cultural relevance even where no corporate groups are involved.

Finally, this enables us to understand how, in a single society, different modes of tracing descent may be used for different purposes. Thus we must be wary of talking about a *society* as "patrilineal" or "matrilineal," as many anthropologists have done for typological classification or shorthand reference.

Case 24: The Tallensi of Ghana

The Tallensi of Ghana, whose system of restrictions involving first-born children we examined in Case 12, have a complicated social and ritual organization in which patrilineal descent is central (Fortes 1945, 1949). Thus corporate groups of Tallensi society are composed of persons patrilineally descended from a common ancestor. The Tallensi so empha-

A Tallensi lineage sacrifice. The Baobab tree is a shrine to lineage ancestors. Here pots of beer are assembled; they will be used for ritual libations, then shared by those present—who include both lineage members and cognatic descendants of the ancestors. (Courtesy of Meyer Fortes.)

size patrilineal descent that they have often been cited as a classic example of a "patrilineal society."

Yet Tallensi individuals are bound together by complex webs of kinship on the maternal as well as paternal side. A man sacrifices to the spirits of his mother and close maternal relatives, as well as to those on his father's side.

Furthermore, a Tallensi individual does not only have an interest in his father's corporate descent group; he also has secondary interests in his mother's group, his father's mother's group, and others to which he is more distantly related through a female link. When members of a patrilineal descent group sacrifice to their ancestors, any descendant through female as well as male links is entitled to partake of the sacrificial meal. Moreover, not only are members of a patrilineal descent group forbidden to marry one another, as in many such systems; but any man or woman who are descended from the same ancestor by any chain of male or female links are forbidden to marry. Such patterns, it has recently been argued, show that Tallensi may conceptualize their relatedness in terms of cognatic descent, as well as patrilineal descent and bilateral kinship (Keesing 1970).

Finally, the Tallensi also attribute importance to relationship in the female line. Thus two persons who are descended, even distantly, through a chain of female links from a pair of sisters are conceived to have special and close ties; and witchcraft powers are specifically believed to be passed through such lines of matrilineal connection.

Here, then, in a single society seemingly dominated by patrilineal descent, we find—used in different ways for different purposes—the three major modes of conceptualizing descent, as well as widespread webs of bilateral kinship.

Patrilineal Descent Systems

There are several reasons why it is useful to begin a brief look at descent systems in tribal societies by looking first at those based on patrilineal descent. Though sexism has been a continuing pressure in anthropology, that is not the main reason why patrilineal systems are taken as the more general case and matrilineal systems are viewed in terms of them. There are good reasons for doing so.

First, there is a matter of evolutionary priority. Despite the recent revival of mythical schemes where descent was traced through women in the ancient past, there is not a shred of evidence that matrilineal systems are old: the ones we know from the tribal past are almost all specialized adaptations to sedentary agriculture, and hence quite recent. Some kind of patrilineally based organization is almost certainly older. There may well have been a time in the early hominid past when mother-child relations were conceptualized in some way that did not involve a pair-bonded mate; but that we will never know, and it is very definitely not the same thing as matrilineal descent. Second, patrilineal forms of social organization are much more widespread and more common—roughly three times as common—as matrilineal forms. Third, matrilineal systems are subject to fairly severe structural constraints, so that the range of organizational possibility is considerably narrower. It is more strategically useful to identify these constraints in terms of the wider range of variation in patrilineal systems.

However, as we will see, there has been considerable sexist slanting in the interpretation of tribal social systems, and we can well be on the lookout for it in anthropological interpretations of other societies. Even where ethnographers have been women, they have often been led—by training or because of a role defined by men of the society they studied—to look at the social world from a male point of view.

It is hard for students who live in Western industrialized societies, in urban settings, and whose closest social ties are to friends and neighbors, not relatives, to visualize social life in a tribal society: where the scale of community is drastically reduced and where kinship and descent define where you live and how you relate to the people in your social world. It is useful to many people to introduce unfamiliar modes of organizing social relations by phrasing them in more familiar terms: to describe a hypothetical descent system in terms with which the Western reader is familiar. Having viewed an idealized imaginary system in these terms, we will command a model against which to contrast the many forms found in the real world. The imaginary society is here given English labels for people and places; but its counterparts in the real world are tribal societies—in Africa, Asia, the Americas, and the Pacific.

Imagine a town of some 10,000—20,000 people, composed of six districts. Each district is made up of some five or ten small neighborhoods. All of the people in the town have one of a dozen names—Smith, Jones, Brown, and so on. (Those who find these names too WASPish can substitute others: they have the advantage of being short and familiar.) Children, as in our society, have the

same last name as their father. No two people with the same last name are supposed to marry.

In a particular *neighborhood,* the houses and land on a particular street are all owned by people with one name. Let us narrow our focus to the Smiths living on Elm Street (Figure 13.5). All of them are descended from Sam Smith, the grandfather of the oldest men now living. They own their Elm Street land collectively. Each Smith has a separate household for his family, though families assist one another in their work.

John Smith, one of the older men, acts as spokesman for these Elm Street Smiths in business and property matters and leads them at religious services in the shrine at his house. One of the peculiarities of the legal system is that should one of the Elm Street Smiths get married, injure someone, or commit a crime, all of the Elm Street Smiths join together to bear the costs, or are all held accountable. To an outsider, one Elm Street Smith is as good as another. Note that it is only the Smith men, their wives (who are not Smiths), and their unmarried children who live on Elm Street. The married daughters of Smiths have gone to live with their husbands.

On the next street lives a group of Joneses, and on the other side a group of Browns. But within this neighborhood, there are six other streets of Smiths. All of these Smiths are descended from a common great-great-grandfather; and they recognize this common descent (from George Smith) at a neighborhood Smith church. There George Smith is buried, and there they occasionally gather for collective rites. The neighborhood Joneses, Browns, and others also have their own churches. The people with a common name and a common church own only church property collectively, and although they do a few nonreligious activities together, they are not a tight little group like the Elm Street Smiths.

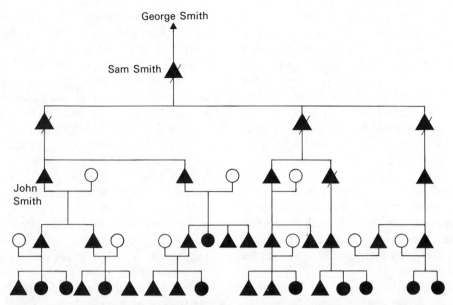

Figure 13.5.   The Elm Street Smiths: The hypothetical genealogy shows the men, women, and children living on Elm Street. Note that most grown Smith women have married out, and non-Smith women have married in. (From Keesing 1975:29)

All of the Smiths within the district seldom see one another, except at a yearly religious outing, but they have a general feeling of unity based on the common descent they trace from a Smith ancestor seven generations ago.

Finally, all Smiths in the *town* believe that they are descended from a founding Smith, though they do not know how they are related. They have a few common religious symbols, but have no further social unity. Recall that no two Smiths—however remotely related—are ideally supposed to marry. In fact, Smiths from different districts rarely do marry, despite some disapproval. But marriage between two Smiths in the same district is regarded as very wrong, and marriage between Smiths in the same neighborhood would be strictly prohibited.

In everyday circumstances the Smiths on Elm Street are a separate corporation and deal with other Smiths, even those in the same neighborhood church, as they would

with anyone else. But if the Elm Street Smiths quarrel with Browns on a nearby street, or another neighborhood, matters can escalate so that the Elm Street Smiths are joined by some or all Smiths of the neighborhood and the Browns are backed by other Browns. But such alliances, which may sometimes unite Smiths of the same *district* (but different neighborhoods), are temporary and limited to the particular dispute at hand. When things are settled—and this often comes from the arbitration of Smiths whose mothers are Browns and Browns whose mothers are Smiths—these alliances dissolve.

There are many variations on this pattern in the tribal world, and we will glimpse a few of them. First, some important features of patrilineal descent systems can be illustrated in terms of the Smiths and Joneses, and some needed technical terms defined.

First, note that the Elm Street Smiths are related by common descent; but so too are all the Smiths in the neighborhood, all the

Smiths in the district, and—according to tradition—all the Smiths in town. That is, descent categories can be formed at higher and higher levels, with more and more remote "apical" ancestors serving as the point of reference. But note that the Elm Street Smiths form a *descent group,* while all the Smiths in town form only a descent category. The Smiths on Elm Street form a solid little local corporation, with collective property, collective legal responsibility, and so on. The Smiths in the neighborhood form a group too, but the things they do and own as a group are much less important. The more inclusive descent categories serve to define limits of exogamy and provide the bases for political alliances.

Such descent groups and categories, based on descent from more and more remote ancestors, are called *segmentary.* A look at a wider hypothetical genealogy of Smiths will illustrate (Figure 13.6).

Such systems are called segmentary because they are divided at each level into segments (the descendants of Sam, Joe, and Ed Smith; and, as higher-order segments, the descendants of George and Fred Smith). Their genealogical structure is hierarchical. But this view of them one gets at any time is "frozen," like one frame of a movie film. To understand how such a system works, and how groups form and change, we must look at it in terms of processes in time. Consider the Elm Street Smiths, a group based on common descent from grandfather Sam Smith. If we visited Elm Street three generations later, Sam Smith would be a great-great-grandfather, and far too many Smiths would be descended from him to live on Elm Street. How then can the system work?

It works because what looks at any single point in time as though it were a stable and permanent arrangement of people, territories, and genealogical connections is in fact only a temporary crystallization. Over longer periods new groups are forming and old ones are

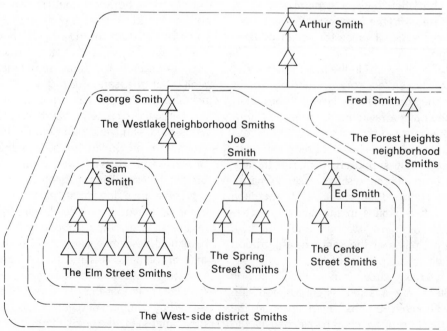

Figure 13.6. The genealogy of the Smith lineages. (From Keesing 1975:30)

dying out. When we look three generations later, John Smith, who was *leader* of the Smiths before, may now be treated as the *founder* of the Elm Street Smiths, who now will include his descendants but not those of the other men who lived with John Smith on Elm Street (see Figure 13.5). Some of John Smith's brothers and cousins may by this time have no living descendants; others may have had only daughters, or granddaughters, who married and left. The descendants of others may have proliferated, but moved elsewhere to found new corporations, often due to internal quarrels or feuding. After the span of three generations, what had been a Jones Street may now be a Smith Street. All the Browns in the whole neighborhood may now have disappeared.

Another important feature of such a system of patrilineal descent groupings is that for any particular corporation and territory—say the Elm Street Smiths—there are actually two partly overlapping categories of membership. First, there are all those men, women, and children whose fathers were Elm Street Smiths, and hence are members of the corporation by birth. But not all of them live there. The adult Elm Street Smith women have

mainly left to live with their husbands, and hence are scattered around other streets and neighborhoods. Second, there is the group of persons actually living on Elm Street: Smith men, their wives (who are not Smiths), and their children. The *descent group,* which is only partly localized, and the *local group,* which is only partly based on descent, are usually both important in different contexts— and it is dangerously easy to get them confused.

Finally, two technical terms are needed. A *lineage* is a descent group consisting of people patrilineally or matrilineally descended from a known ancestor through a series of links they can trace. When descent is in the male line (as with Smiths and Joneses), we can call these "patrilineages." When descent is in the female line, we speak of "matrilineages." A larger descent category like all the Smiths in the town, who believe they are descended from a common ancestor but do not know the actual connections, is called a *clan.*

The tribal world contains many fascinating variations on the "typical" system of segmentary patrilineages illustrated by the Smiths and Joneses.

Case 25: Segmentary Lineages among the Tiv

Among the Tiv of Nigeria, the whole population of some 800,000 traces descent by traditional genealogical links from a single founding ancestor. Moreover, each level of the segmentary hierarchy corresponds to a separate territorial segment. It is as though instead of Smith lineages being scattered around a neighborhood also occupied by Joneses, Browns, and others, a whole neighborhood was made up of Smiths, and a whole district was made up of Smiths, Browns, and Joneses, all of whom traced common descent from the same distant ancestor, and so on. Figure 13.7 illustrates this mode of segmentary organization among the Tiv.

In this and other real segmentary patrilineage systems, the people do not, of course, live in a town, but are scattered over large areas. The tribal equivalent of Elm Street

occupied by a corporate patrilineage is likely to be a territory of several square miles, with the people clustered in villages, hamlets, or scattered homesteads.

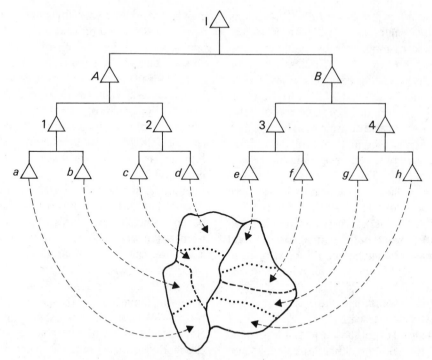

Figure 13.7. Segmentary organization among the Tiv: Note here how the geographical distribution of lineages corresponds to their genealogical relationships. (From P. Bohannon 1954 by permission of the International African Institute)

In segmentary systems, the genealogical relations between segments may provide an idiom in which the political relations between segments are expressed and the results of conflict are rationalized. The intertwining of patrilineal descent with politics is explored in §61. There the political process of a segmentary system similar in some ways to the Tiv (the Nuer, Case 52) and the intertwining of patrilineal descent groups with a centralized kingship (the Bunyoro, Case 56) are illustrated. These will provide the reader with further substantive background in the way tribal Smiths and Joneses actually operate.

How big the local corporations—the equivalents of Elm Street Smiths—are is an important axis of variation: they may consist of 20 or 30 individuals or several hundred. Systems also vary in the depth of segmentary hierarchies. The Tiv, all tracing descent from a single ancestor, illustrate one extreme. At the other extreme, local lineages like the Elm Street Smiths may trace no higher-level connections of common descent with one another.

The relative importance of descent groups, including out-marrying sisters, and descent-based local groups, excluding sisters and including wives, also varies. At one extreme are systems where the wife loses all legal interests in her patrilineage of birth and acquires full interests in the corporation into which she marries. Among the early Romans, when a girl married she was ritually removed from her lineage and was ritually introduced into her husband's lineage—even acquiring a new set of ancestors, those of her husband. The husband's legal rights over her then replaced those of her father (Fustel de Cou-langes 1864). In some other systems, ties to the husband are very weak, marriage is frag-ile, and the wife retains full legal interests in the lineage of her birth. The logical extreme of this (though there descent is matrilineal) is the system among the Nayar of South India (Case 19), where marriage scarcely exists at all and the residential groups comprise broth-ers and sisters. Usually a balance is struck between the strength of a woman's ties to her brother and the lineage of her birth and her ties to her husband and his group.

Even if we look only at male members, not the in-and out-marrying women, the cor-respondence between membership in a descent category and membership in a local group is sometimes far less neat than our example of Smiths and Joneses suggests. This is where our distinction between categories and groups—between those *entitled* to rights in a corporation and those who actually exer-cise them—is badly needed. In many "patri-lineal" systems, notably those in the highlands of New Guinea, a very large proportion of men (sometimes more than half) are not liv-ing in the territory to which they have rights through patrilineal descent. Instead, they are scattered around, some living in their moth-ers' territories, others in their fathers' mothers' territories, and so on. Some of a person's legal rights and ritual relationships may be based squarely on patrilineal descent, so that a person retains them no matter where he or she lives, but these then have no direct corre-spondence with local groupings.

The same lack of neat correspondence between local groupings and the scheme of patrilineal descent emphasized in the "official charter" occurs in some African societies, like the Nuer, who seem on the surface to be very much like the Smiths and Joneses, and who conceive their political relationships in terms of patrilineal descent (see Case 52).

Our quick look at patrilineal modes of solving the organizational problems of tribal societies can well end on this note of disorder, this lack of neat correspondence between the formal model of descent and the realities of who actually lives where and does what with whom. Recall how patrilineal descent seemed a beautiful formal solution to the five organi-zational problems laid out at the beginning of this section. But there are hidden difficulties. One was at the end of challenge (3): " . . . how can they be adjusted to the demographic fluctuations whereby some groups proliferate and others dwindle?" A second was hidden in (5): "how will political relations between groups be maintained . . . ?" Without a cen-tral grovernment, the system must adjust to the shifting tides of warfare, power, and feud-ing.

These problems prevent any unilineal descent system from being as neat and stable as its formal blueprint. There *must* be flexibili-ty to accommodate demographic shifts, adapt human groupings in the resources and pres-sures of an ecosystem, follow the tides of politics, and allow room for the strivings and foibles of human individuals. The question is not, as some have posed it, whether a society is "neat" or "messy"—for all social life is a layer cake of order and disorder. It is, rather, by what mechanisms are flexibility and adap-tibility maintained and how are they justified, ignored, rationalized, or disguised ideolog-ically?

Matrilineal Descent as an Organizing Principle

Matrilineal descent, the tracing of descent ties from an ancestress through a line of daughters, is much less commonly used than patrilineal descent in solving the organization-al problems of tribal societies.

Matrilineal descent systems were badly slighted anthropologically for many years. When in the late 1950s and early 1960s they began to receive their due, they were still seen in terms of male-oriented premises. These premises are not—as some anthropologists would have it—radically incorrect. (It does not in the long run advance liberation in a sexist society to depict other societies as less sexist than they actually were.) But the conventional anthropological premises about matrilineal systems, as summarized by Richards (1950) and Schneider (1961), do introduce a subtle interpretive bias. Let us begin by making these premises explicit, and then reflect on their possible biases in terms of substantive evidence.

1. There is no such thing as a matriarchy. In no known society have women held the key political power.

2. In a matrilineal society, it is thus always the case that the major political power of a descent corporation is in the hands of men: they comprise or control the "board of directors" of the corporation.

3. Therefore matrilineal systems cannot be in any simple sense the mirror images of patrilineal systems. If men control political power in each, there is an asymmetrical relationship between the two forms.

4. Because men control key political power in a matrilineal system, it is misleading to speak of descent as passing from mother to daughter; instead, one can better think of descent as passing from a woman's brother to her son (Fortes 1959a).

We will look shortly at some of the cases where male dominance was greatly tempered, if men were indeed dominant at all.

As D. Schneider (1961), drawing insights from Richards (1950), points out, matrilineal descent entails internal strains and potential conflicts. In a patrilineal system both political direction and replacement of members are managed through men. A patrilineal corporation can lose control of its women when they marry out; they are not structurally crucial,

because a corporation's men provide leadership and also provide children who will succeed them and perpetuate the corporation. In a matrilineal system, however, the corporation, given a rule of exogamy, faces a structural problem. If it is the male members who go to live with their wives, then they are dispersed, and the "board of directors" is scattered away from the corporation "headquarters." If instead it is the women who marry out, leaving the men on their lineage land, then the corporation must somehow retain control over—and "get back"—the children of these women who are the corporation members of the next generation.

This situation in turn generates what Richards (1950) has called "the matrilineal puzzle." A woman's ties to her husband are potentially at odds with her ties to her brother; and if the corporation is to endure and be strong, her ties to her brother must prevail over those to her husband at the crucial times. It is her brother who must keep primary control over her children. Her sons must be her brother's heirs. In such a situation of structural conflict, marriage is almost inevitably fragile. Divorce rates are likely to be high.

In a matrilineal society, the pattern of postmarital residence is important. One possible pattern, called uxorilocal residence, is for a husband to come and live with his wife in her corporation's place. If this pattern is repeated in each generation, the localized group will consist of a set of matrilineally related women, the husbands of those women that are still married, and unmarried children of lineage women, plus lineage men who are not at that stage married and who have come back to home base (most often, after divorce or between marriages).

In such societies, women often exercise strong power in lineage matters. However, the corporation is hard-pressed to maintain its strength if all or most of its adult men have scattered. Most often, the potential problem is largely avoided, because in such societies the population is clustered into sizable communities, and in any single community, several different matrilineages or matrilineal clans are clustered together. "Marrying out" may mean moving across the plaza or a few hundred yards away. The men are thus not "scattered" in the way a diagram might suggest and are close enough at hand to take an active part in corporation affairs. The Hopi Indians of Arizona will serve to illustrate this pattern of uxorilocal residence.

Case 26: The Hopi Indians

The pueblo-dwelling Hopi Indians have a highly intricate social and ceremonial organization. The major groupings are exogamous matrilineal clans, each tracing relationship to a particular animal, plant, or natural phenomenon. These clans are land-owning corporations. They are also central in the elaborate ceremonial cycles, in which each has a special part to play and a special set of ritual paraphernalia.

These clans are segmented into unnamed matrilineages, localized in sections of the pueblo. The core of these local groupings is a line of matrilineally related women. A Hopi man joins his wife's household—and she can send him packing any time she pleases. A typical household consists of an older woman and her husband, if she still has one; her daughters and their husbands and children; and her unmarried sons. Note that the husbands are outsiders and that the senior woman's grown sons have married and moved elsewhere. Thus, while the lineage retains effective control over its women and their children, the adult men are scattered as outsiders in their wives' households. Women have considerable power in the public realm and preeminent power in the domestic sphere.

The system hangs together partly because of a complicated series of cross-cutting memberships and ritual obligations in other kinds of groups not based on descent. But it also works because men, by marrying girls of the same community where they and their fellow clan members live (which they can do because a number of clans are represented in a pueblo), manage to remain near their "real home" and to participate collectively in their clan's ceremonial activities and corporate affairs. Thus the male "board of directors" of a matrilineal corporation functions in important situations even though the men are scattered around the pueblo in their wives' households.

Where the rule that men are to marry out means much further out—that is, where corporation territories are more scattered—adjustments that keep at least the few lineage men most central to the corporation's "board of directors" at home may be possible. They may remain unmarried, get divorced, bring their wives "home" (in an alternative residence pattern), or otherwise manage to stay at or near corporation "headquarters."

Very probably Hopi women exercise more power than some anthropological theorists have conceded. So too did women among the Iroquois, and among some of the matrilineally organized peoples of the American southeast such as the Choctaw and Creek.

The Hopi residence pattern begins to suggest some of the constraints that limit the form and also the occurrence of matrilineal descent systems. Matrilineal descent groups characteristically are found in societies that:

1. are predominantly agricultural;
2. have sufficiently high agricultural productivity to permit the sedentary residence of substantial populations;
3. have a division of labor in which women perform many of the key agricultural tasks.[2]

Even in such societies, patrilineal or cognatic descent groups, rather than matrilineal ones, are quite common.

An alternative and important pattern of residence, in a matrilineal descent system, is to have corporation women go to live with their husbands, but somehow to get the children (at least the boys) back to their lineage territory, so the adult men of the corporation are grouped together. This pattern is technically called viri-avunculocal (husband's mother's brother) residence. The Trobriand Islanders of Melanesia provide a fascinating example.

[2]The Hopi, where agriculture is mainly in the hands of men, constitute an exception. See Schlegel (1973) and Udall (1969) for closer views of the role of Hopi women.

Case 27: The Trobriand Islanders

The Trobriand Islanders are a Melanesian people living near New Guinea, practicing shifting horticulture and living in villages scattered through rich garden lands of their large island. We will encounter them many times in Part 3. We have already glimpsed their free adolescent sexual lives.

The garden lands are divided into territories. Each territory contains sacred places from which, mythologically, its ancestress is supposed to have emerged. From her are descended, in the female line, the members of a *dala*. Since the precise genealogical links are not known but the groups are strongly corporate, *dala* are known to the Trobriand literature as *subclans*. A Trobriand subclan is a matrilineal descent group consisting of:

1. men related through their mothers, their mothers' mothers, their mothers' mothers' mothers, and so on;
2. the sisters of the men, and other women similarly related in the female line; and
3. the children of these women (but not the children of the men).

The genealogical structure of such a group is similar to that diagrammed in Figure 13.4B.

Who lives in a subclan's territory? A subclan is centered in a village, in its territory. Since the subclans are exogamous, husbands and wives do not belong to the same subclan. Who, then, stays in the subclan's village? Is it the women, who provide the continuity of descent and whose children provide the next generation of corporation members? Or is it the men, who control the "board of directors," and one of whom is its leader? Either the women or the men must marry out.

In the Trobriands, it is the women of the subclan who go away to live with their husbands. But, then, how do their sons end up in their own subclan villages and lands instead of in their fathers'? The answer is that during adolescence, a time when boys are freely drifting in and out of sexual liaisons and are relatively independent, a boy moves away from his parents' household and goes to the village of his own subclan. His sister remains attached to her father's household until she marries. Ideally, as a man's own sons leave him, his sisters' sons are moving in to join him.

The village, in this simplest case, thus consists of

1. adult men and young men of the subclan;
2. their wives, who belong to different subclans; and
3. the young children and unmarried daughters of men of the subclan.

A subclan is ranked as either "chiefly" or "commoner" (as we will see in Case 54). Within these ranks the actual prestige and power of subclans varies considerably. But whatever its status, the Trobriand subclan is a strong and enduring land-owning corporation, with strict rules of exogamy.

Each subclan is said to belong to one of four *clans*. The importance of these clans is obscure, but it is clear that they are social categories of subclans traditionally associated by matrilineal descent and having symbolic connections with certain bird and animal species. They are not corporate groups, and a single clan may include some of the highest-ranking and lowest-ranking subclans. The rule of subclan exogamy is extended in theory to all members of the same clan, but some marriages to clan members from other subclans do in fact take place. Sexual affairs between members of the same clan, but different subclans, are regarded as naughty but not outrageous.

The system as it has been outlined is simple and stable—one subclan owning one territory with one village in it, where male members and their families live. That relationship, validated by the myths of origin, implies great stability and permanence. In fact, the Trobriand dogma of procreation, which denies a role to the father, asserts that the children born of the subclan are a sort of reincarnation of the subclan's ancestors, thus underlining the continuity of the social order.

But as we saw in dealing with patrilineal descent groupings, the real social world of real people is always less neat and stable than that. Descent corporations do not stay the same size: proliferation, dwindling, and extinction of lineages require mechanisms for groups hiving off, collapsing, and taking over one another's lands. At any time, the interests, strategies, and alliances of individuals and groups, and the variations of demography, require that residence and affiliation be more flexible and variable than the dogma would have it.

In reality, if we could look at the Trobriand social scene over a period of a century or two (before the introduction of transistor radios), the identity and arrangement of subclans and their territories would almost certainly shift drastically over that time span. One mechanism whereby this occurs is the branching off of a segment of a proliferating (and usually, an important) subclan so that it attaches to the village and territory of another subclan. This can take place when a girl from subclan B marries an important man from subclan A, who then—to bolster his strength and prestige—gives his sons a foothold in the A village. The sisters' children and matrilineal descendants of these sons who stayed put then establish a branch of subclan B in the village of subclan A.

By this mechanism, many local segments of subclans are living in different territories from those where their ancestors are supposed to have emerged. Moreover, many villages are composed of two, three, or more subclan segments. Sometimes the attached "immigrant" subclan segments outrank and politically dominate the original "owners." This upsets our neat earlier equation: 1 village = 1 subclan. For one village can contain its original subclan plus segments of one or two other subclans. And conversely, segments of a single subclan may be attached in several different territories, so that the subclan segment, not the whole subclan, is the locally based corporate group. In fact, in many respects the village (when composed of two or more subclan segments) is as important as the subclan in Trobriand life (as we will see in Case 41).

A second adjustment of the Trobriand descent system to ecological pressures and the shifting complexities of social life concerns residence. On close examination, it turns out that a surprisingly large percentage of Trobriand men are not living in the village where their own subclan segment is based. Many are living in their fathers', fathers' mothers', or other villages. This does not mean that subclans as corporations are all mixed up—only that a man can be an active member of his corporation even if he happens to be living somewhere else (Powell 1960, 1969a).

Finally, the whims of demography are subject to human rearrangement, since a great many children are adopted into households other than those of their birth. This does not affect their subclan membership, but it shifts them into different households—often those of subclans other than father's or mother's—during their childhood.

Thus, as with patrilineal descent among the Smiths and Joneses, matrilineal descent in the Trobriands shapes strong corporate groups that solve many of the organizational problems of tribal life in this setting. By allowing flexibility, choice, and readjustment of living arrangements, it also permits effective adaptation to the changing pressures of an environment and the shifting tides of social life.

Near the Trobriands, on the Melanesian island of Dobu, an even more fascinating compromise of residence was adopted. Husband and wife alternated annually between residence in her matrilineage village (where he was a feared and insecure alien) and residence in his matrilineage village (where she was an outsider). Fortune's (1932a) description of the tensions involved is an anthropological classic.

In many societies with matrilineal descent groups, the wife goes to live with her husband, yet the husband lives in his father's place, not in his matrilineage territory. Such a pattern is called viri-patrilocal residence. If one traces out the implications of such a scheme, it would seem that lineages could not be localized. Neither the men nor the women of the corporation live together. Such systems, common in Melanesia and parts of Africa, are conventionally viewed as representing a late stage in the disintegration of a matrilineal system into a patrilineal or cognatic sys-

tem; the matrilineage is no longer a strong corporation, but a kind of remnant category or debating society. But some detailed studies have shown that lineages in such societies can be localized and powerful to a surprising degree, despite a residence rule that ostensibly prevents localization (see, for example, Kopytoff's (1964, 1965) analysis of the Suku of Zaire; see also Keesing 1975, Case 14).

Other Forms of Descent Organization

It is worth emphasizing that it is not a *society* that is matrilineally or patrilineally organized. Recall that two or more modes of descent may be relevant in different contexts in the same society. *Double descent*, where corporate patrilineal descent groups and corporate matrilineal descent groups occur in the same society, provides the most dramatic illustration.

Case 28: Double Descent Among the Yakö

The Yakö of Nigeria, living in large towns of as many as 11,000 people, are organized in a way very similar, at first glance, to our patrilineal Smiths and Joneses. A small patrilineal group, like the Elm Street Smiths, reside together in a compound. But whereas Smith streets were scattered among Jones and Brown streets, Yakö compounds are grouped together into a cluster, a large local patrilineage that corporately owns land. Finally, a series of patrilineage clusters are grouped together into a clan, occupying a single "district" of the town. This correspondence between territories and segmentary levels recalls the Tiv (Case 25). The clans are exogamous, so a Yakö man's wives (he often has several) come from other districts.

Yet at the same time, the Yakö trace matrilineal descent, and any Yakö belongs to his mother's matrilineal clan. Whereas the patrilineages are concerned with real estate and ritual involving lands and first fruits, the corporate matrilineal clans are concerned with movable property, with legal responsibility for their members and rights to payments for their death, and with ritual involving fertility spirits. Any Yakö belongs to both his or her father's patrilineage and mother's matrilineage.

Thus two different modes of corporate group organization, through patrilineal and matrilineal descent, fulfill complementary functions in different spheres of Yakö life. Since only full siblings normally belong to both the same patrilineage and the same matrilineal clan, people opposed in one situation may well be allies in another—hence helping to bind together the large Yakö communities (Forde 1950).

Kinship specialists have realized rather recently that *cognatic descent,* where any series of male or female links to the founding ancestor establishes descent entitlement, can also produce workable descent corporations. The problem is to narrow down, from the many groups where a person *could be* a member, the one where he actually *is* a member. Here a number of mechanisms are possible. One is to specify that a couple can live with either the husband's or the wife's group; but whichever they choose, their children belong to that group. Another is to give privileged status, among those persons eligible for membership, to those who trace descent in the male line. Thus, other things being equal,

a chain of affiliations with the father's group will be made, though some people in each generation will affiliate with their mother's group due to economic strategies or the circumstances of life history. A person seldom has as much freedom to choose or change his or her membership as the formal rules seem to imply. In practice, cognatic descent can produce corporations similar to those based on unilineal descent and be just as efficient organizationally. In a sense, the difference is that cognatic descent builds into the rules a great range of flexibility and then uses only a portion of that range, while unilineal descent gives little flexibility in the rules yet allows it, as needed, in some disguised form.

Case 29: Cognatic Descent Among the Kwaio

The Kwaio of the Solomon Islands of the western Pacific divide their mountainous terrain into dozens of small territories. Each is believed to have been founded by known ancestors some 9 to 12 generations ago. All cognatic descendants of the founding ancestor of a territory have rights to live there and use the land, and most of them raise pigs for sacrifice to the ancestors associated with that territory.

Yet a person obviously cannot live in, and have equally strong rights to, the many territories (often a dozen or more) to which he is related by cognatic descent. Usually he has a strongest affiliation to only one territory and to a descent group based there. Those who are affiliated with the descent group form the nucleus of the land-owning corporation; they are, so to speak, voting members with full rights. The other cognatic descendants, affiliated somewhere else, have secondary rights and lesser ritual interests.

How then does a person come to have a primary affiliation out of the large number of potential ones through his father and mother? In practice, he or she seldom affiliates with a descent group other than that of father or mother. But which? First, a person who is patrilineally descended from the founding ancestor of a territory is considered to have the strongest rights in the corporation and the greatest say in its ritual affairs. Second, a woman normally resides in her husband's territory, and a person usually affiliates with the group with which he or she grew up as a child. All of these factors combine so that most people affiliate with their fathers' descent groups, and, cumulatively, most descent groups are made up mostly of patrilineal descendants of the founding ancestor. Cognatic descendants then have a secondary interest in the corporation. Yet in every generation, due to the circumstances of life history, some people grow up with their maternal relatives and affiliate with the mother's descent group. As long as they maintain an active participation in the corporation, they are treated as full members.

However, many men do not live in the territory where they have primary interests. In fact, Kwaio residence is quite fluid, and many men live in four or five territories or more in the course of their lives. They take an active, though secondary, interest in the ritual and secular affairs of several different descent groups. Depending on the context of the moment, a member of group A and a member of group B may both be participating in the ritual affairs or feast of group C, in which both have secondary interests based on cognatic descent.

Here the interplay of cognatic descent and patrilineal descent, and the strategies of feasting and gardening and the circumstances of life history, produce solidly corporate yet flexible and adaptive descent groups (Keesing 1970).

Families, Kindreds, and Bilateral Organization

Descent-based corporations provide effective solutions to the organizational problems of tribal societies. Hunting and gathering peoples may conceive the relatedness of band members in their territory as based on descent (as with many Australian Aboriginal peoples); but the pressures toward corporate control of resources mainly arise with the advent of food production. With the urban revolution and advanced technologies, non-kinship forms of social groupings come to the fore, as we will see in Part 4. However, anthropologists working in peasant communities or even in urban settings often encounter important social groupings based on descent (Chapter 22).

Corporate groups based on descent turn out to be far from universal in the tribal world. There are other, equally adaptive solutions to the same problems. Many swidden horticulturists of Southeast Asia, in particular, and some pastoralists such as the Lapps, use bilateral kinship as the major principle of social organization. Thus in many parts of the Philippines, Borneo, and Indonesia, property is owned by family groups, and social structure is built up out of local groupings—families, settlements, and neighborhoods. Here, bilateral kinship assumes much of the "functional load" that is carried in other places by descent groups. Local groups are made up of consanguineal and affinal kin, and action groups are crystallized temporarily out of personal kindreds. Such systems are perfectly "workable," and we have at last begun to pay attention to how they work.

Case 30: The Subanun of the Philippines

The Subanun are swidden horticulturists scattered through the mountains of the Philippine island of Mindanao. They lack any formal political structure and are organized in no enduring kinship groups larger than the family. Yet they maintain complex networks of kinship relations and legal rights that weave families together. A family, consisting of parents and unmarried children, forms an independent corporation—owning property, sharing legal accountability, and producing and consuming its own subsistence crops.

Two families arrange a marriage between their children through prolonged legal negotiations. Until an agreed bridewealth payment is completed, the married couple must contribute labor to the bride's parents, but in marrying they leave the parental families and found a new independent corporation. The family corporation formed by a marriage, like a legal partnership, is dissolved by the death of either partner (or by divorce), and its property is divided. Surviving members or divorced partners—even a widow or widower with no unmarried children—form a new corporation, however fragmentary, that is economically self-reliant and legally independent. Only remarriage or adoption can incorporate survivors of a dissolved family into a new one. Once married, a Subanun can never return to his natal household. However, the contractual obligations between parental families that sponsored the marriage is strong and enduring: if one spouse dies, his or her household is legally obligated to supply another one if they can.

Marriage between close kin, even first cousins, is common. Given the independence of every family and the absence of larger corporate groupings, marriage of close kin entails few problems; every marriage is by its nature an "out-marriage." Each household lives in a separate clearing, as far from others as the arrangement of fields permits. Though 3 to 12 neighboring households comprise a dispersed "settlement," these alignments are only temporary. Any family is the center of a unique cluster of neighbors and kinsmen, bound first to the two families that sponsored its formation and later to the families with which it is contractually linked through marriage sponsorship. As the Subanun's ethnographer Frake observes,

Despite [the] network of formal and informal social ties among families, there have emerged no large, stable, discrete socio-political units. . . . The Subanun family [is] . . . largely a "sovereign nation." But . . . the Subanun family is not a descent group. Its corporate unity endures only as long as does the marriage tie of its founders. The continuity of Subanun society must be sought in the continuous process of corporate group formation and dissolution rather than in the permanency of the groups themselves. (1960:63)

Case 31: Iban Social Organization

The Iban of Borneo, whose expansionist shifting cultivation of dry rice we examined in Case 4, have a social organization apparently highly adaptive to their mode of life and ecosystem. Yet they, like many Southeast Asians, organize corporate groups without reference to unilineal descent, though in a very different way than the Subanun.

The Iban live in sizable communities, each one politically independent and occupying a defined territory. These communities include from as few as 30 to as many as 350 people. They are striking in that the inhabitants reside together in a single longhouse. The families in a longhouse are mainly cognatically related, but they do not comprise a corporate group. Their unity is expressed in ritual observances.

Each of the component families, *bilek* families, is strongly corporate. A *bilek* family is a separate economic unit, cultivating rice and other crops and owning heirloom property. It is also a separate ritual unit, performing its own rites and having a separate set of magical charms and ritual prohibitions. Each *bilek* family lives in an apartment in the longhouse.

A *bilek* family typically contains three generations: a pair of grandparents, a son or daughter and the spouse, and grandchildren. The *bilek* family continues (unlike the Subanun family) as a corporation across generations. The device whereby this is accomplished is simple: at least one son or daughter in each generation stays put, brings in a spouse, and perpetuates the corporation. The other children characteristically marry into other households. Fission of a *bilek* family can occur when two of the children marry and bring their spouses in; one of the married children can claim his or her (equal) share in the family estate and move the new nuclear family out to form a new corporation.

A marrying couple face a choice of whether to live with the bride's or groom's *bilek* group. That choice determines which family corporation

A newly built Iban longhouse surrounded by rice fields. (Courtesy of Hedda Morrison.)

An Iban family: Members of a *bilek* eat their midday meal. (Courtesy of Hedda Morrison.)

their children will belong to—hence Freeman's (1960:67) term *utrolateral* ("either side") *filiation*. Sons and daughters, in fact, stay in the family home at marriage with approximately equal frequency. They must marry an outsider, since *bilek* families are exogamous. However, any first cousins or other more distant relatives who are in different *bilek* families are allowed to marry. Marriage is very much a matter of personal choice, and after the early years of marriage divorce is rare.

Larger action groups are predominantly recruited from within the longhouse, according to the context of the moment. As among the Subanun, this recruitment is usually along *kindred* lines. The personal kindred is an important social category for the Iban, including a bilaterally expanding range of kin. In theory, it includes all an individual's known blood relatives; in practice, only fairly close kin are likely to be socially relevant. Kindreds, of course, overlap; they are not corporate groups. When life-cycle rites, feuds, or other intermittent events place a particular person on center stage, his or her kindred rally to provide the supporting cast (Freeman 1955, 1958, 1960).

It is well to end with a cautionary note. Descent groupings are obvious and easily recorded, and they lend themselves neatly to comparative schemes. Yet anthropologists may often have overestimated the impor-

tance of descent at the expense of more subtle principles of social grouping, which might emerge if they only looked for them. Focusing on descent categories, they have used great ingenuity to explain why people who are not patrilineally related to a place happen to be living there. But this may be to confuse figure and ground. We might do better to focus on local groups rather than descent categories, on the strategies of gardening, friendship, property interest, and the like, that lead people to live where they do. A people may talk about the cumulative outcomes of individual choices in terms of ideologies of descent even though "descent rules" actually have little to do with who decides to live where and do what. Descent may be, in some societies, more a way of thinking about local groups than of forming them.

43.
Descent Systems, Evolution, and Adaptation

Experts believe that matrilineal descent systems have arisen under a fairly limited set of circumstances: where subsistence is derived primarily from horticulture, where women play a central part in this subsistence production, and where ecological settings and technology permit the sedentary residence of substantial populations. Since these circumstances have developed mainly within the last five thousand years, we can presume that it is mainly within this period that such systems have developed and diversified (though some approximation to matrilineal descent had developed among hunters and gatherers in some ecologically rich areas of Australia.)

There might have been an early period in hominid social organization where mother-son units, rather than mates, constituted the nuclear units of society. But it seems a good deal more likely, in view of the apparent evolution of continuous sexual receptivity (in place of estrus cycling) in the period when a sexual division of labor for hunting and gathering was evolving, that pair-bonding is very old and occurred long before cultural symbol-

ization of kinship. If so, the supposed *de facto* "matrilineal" organization of early humans due to ignorance of paternity probably never existed (because a male mate was already part of a nuclear group when hominids began conceptualizing such arrangements). In any case, mother-child ties among the great apes and early hominids and matrilineal descent systems have only the most superficial similarities.

The wider prevalence of patrilineal descent systems suggests that they may be adaptive to a much wider range of ecological conditions. They are characteristic of nomadic pastoralists across most of Eurasia and of most African pastoralists (see, for example, Cases 5 and 6; for a recent discussion of social organization among pastoralists, see Rubel 1969 and Pastner 1971; the latter emphasizes, however, that within the patrilineal pattern everyday task and residential groups are characteristically bilateral and flexible). The dominant role of men in subsistence and their greater mobility, since women care for small children, are important factors (recall the Karimojong, Case 6, where women remain settled in camps and men move with their herds).

In predominantly horticultural societies where men play at least an equivalent role in production, and especially where population is not dense and sedentary, patrilineal descent systems are more likely to have evolved. But note that in a great many Southeast Asian societies, as in the Philippines (Case 30) and Borneo (Case 31), social organization is commonly based not on descent groups but on bilateral networks of kinship.

Cognatic descent has been viewed by Goodenough (1955) and others as an adaptation to land scarcity, since choices of descent group affiliation would tend to even out the balance between lands and population density, or to circumstances that require mobility or mobilization of shifting allegiances.

The dominant theory concerning the actual evolution of descent rules sees shifts in the division of labor, due to a change in technology or environment, as setting off a chain of adaptive responses: a change in the statistical pattern of residence (toward virilocal or uxorilocal) leading to changes in the composition of local groups, leading to a reconceptualization of descent.

But all this is too simple. As we saw in Chapter 12, ecological adaptation is important in shaping social organization and culture, but it does not operate mechanically. As I have argued (in Keesing 1975:140—143), the view of social structures as adjustments to an ecologically adaptive division of labor gives inadequate weight to power politics and ideologies. Ongoing negotiations and battles in the realm of sexual politics may be crucially important here. Whether descent is traced matrilineally or patrilineally may depend on the state of battle and on the relative power of men and women in defining a people's ideologies. The political power of men and women is undoubtedly closely related to their economic power; but that in turn is a matter of politics as well, not simply of human adaptation to an ecosystem. That in one society women have control over planting materials and the magical knowledge on which agriculture depends while in another society men have this control may reflect differences not in technology or environment, but in the histories of sexual politics. Such an interpretation allows room for the marked differences of social organization and cosmology among close cultural relatives living in substantially similar environments in Melanesia and other parts of the world (see Keesing 1975:139—140).

That there may be no perfect correlations, no simple explanations that are simply ecological, forearms us with caution and skepticism. The search for regularities, for correlations between modes of subsistence and modes of organizing and conceptualizing social units of production, goes on and illuminates both regional and global patterns of variation. The challenge is to incorporate these regularities—and the long-term perspectives opened up by theory-minded archaeologists—within an increasingly sophisticated theory of sociocultural change. In such a theory, adaptation and power politics, ecology and ideology, class interests and individual strategies, equilibrium and change must all be given appropriate weight. To show how they are interwoven, we will need to draw on the developing sciences and formal languages for dealing with systemic complexity, the models of systems theory and cybernetics.

44.
Kinship Terminology

The epitome of all that seems arcane and obscure in kinship studies, to the uninitiated, is the long preoccupation with kinship terminologies: the way people classify kinds of relatives.

Kinship terminologies are highly systematic and invite algebraic fun and games. They also invite comparison, since the same complex patterns are found on different continents. And for decades, they have promised to provide some kind of Rosetta Stone for understanding social organization, since they clearly represent some kind of mapping of the social world of a people. But we are not yet sure how to read them.

Our way of classifying kin as "uncles," "cousins," and so on, is not an immutable fact about the world. It is an arbitrary set of cultural conventions, and in fact a quite unusual one. It may seem obvious that a people should have words for "brother" and "sister" (different words from ours, to be sure, like the French *frère* and *soeur*). Yet such categories do not occur in more than 80 percent of the world languages.

First, a great many peoples place at least some of what we call "cousins" in the same categories as siblings. Thus, as we will see, one's father's brother's children may be classed with one's own brothers and sisters. But even ignoring these wider ranges of terms for siblings, we find seven major ways of classifying siblings, of which ours is but one. The most common form uses *relative sex* (whether the relative classified is the same sex as the speaker or the opposite sex) as the crucial criterion.

We need not delve here into the many forms of kinship classification and the long debates about how they map the social universe. But a very brief look at two Trobriand kinship terms will serve to illustrate the puzzle-like nature of kinship terminologies, the ways those of tribal peoples differ from ours, and two sharply opposed ways of interpreting them now in the forefront of social anthropology debate.

Even in societies with strong corporate descent groups, bilateral networks of kinship connect individuals in different corporations as well as within them. After nearly a century of serious study, it is not yet clear whether kinship terms in tribal societies are

1. basically ways of classifying relatives on the basis of *kinds of genealogical connections* between them and ego, the person doing the classifying (as in our society); or
2. basically ways of dividing up a person's social universe into major *"kinds" of people*—"kinds" that may well be based not on genealogical connections but on membership in corporate groups or local groups or even broad categories like "marriageable women."

Let us turn to the Trobriand kinship terms to illustrate. What we know about the meaning of these Trobriand words comes mainly from the famous Polish-born anthropologist Bronislaw Malinowski, who worked in the Trobriands during World War I. He gives us these meanings by listing the closest genealogical positions covered by each term. We will have to do the same.[3] But the proponents of the second position above object from the outset—for that presupposes that these words are used to classify genealogical connections, not "kinds" of people in the Trobriand social universe.

Term A: *tama*

Malinowski tells us that *tama* include a person's father, his father's brother (FB, for short), his father's sister's son (FZS for short, using Z for "sister" to distinguish it from "son"), and all of the members of the father's matrilineal clan in his own generation or lower generations. We look at two possible interpretations of the meaning of *tama,* based on the two theoretical positions sketched above.

Interpretation 1

Tama means, most centrally, "father." However, its meaning extends out to include other persons whose relationship is culturally similar to that of the father. These extensions are based on two principles that reflect equivalence or substitutability.

The first principle, very, very common in the tribal world, is that two siblings of the same sex are treated as equivalent in the reckoning of kinship. Thus, in Trobriand and hundreds of other tribal societies, FB = F,[4]

---

[3]We will also, for the sake of exposition, adopt the sexist convention of looking at kin terms from the point of view of a man (as ego, or the point of reference). But it is worth noting in passing that many conventional interpretations of kin terms don't work if viewed from the perspective of a woman speaker.

[4]Conventionally, in the analysis of kinship terms, the equals sign means "is classed with." That is, the two kinds of relatedness are labeled with a single word.

MZ = M, FFBS = F, and so on. The way the latter equivalence works will illustrate how distant collaterals (who would be cousins in our system) are classed with parents, siblings, or children. Note the logic of the following chain: FFB = FF, thus FFBS = FFS, which = FB, which = F. By the same principle, a man classes his brother's children with his own, and a woman classes her sister's children with her own.

The second rule of extension whereby *tama* are classed together occurs much less frequently, almost always in societies organized along matrilineal lines like the Trobriand Islanders. By this rule, a person's FZ is classed with FM in the reckoning of kinship. And when that is so, then the same equivalence looked at the other way around means that a woman's brother's child is classed with her son's child in the reckoning of kinship. Note that in a system of matrilineal corporations, a woman's brother and her son are members of her group, but their children are born into different groups. This rule is one variant of a principle of kinship classification known as *Crow* (after the Crow Indians).

This Crow principle leads to an equivalence between FZS = FMS = FB = F (which is why FZS is *tama*). As we will see, such chains of equivalence also class FZDS and other men in the father's subclan as *tama*.

Interpretation 2

All that is nonsense. The notion of "extension" from one's "real" father to other fathers simply superimposes our genealogical biases (and our feeling that father is different from uncles) on the Trobrianders. All *tama* are "real *tama*." In fact, what the word *tama* means is "domiciled man of my father's subclan hamlet." Father is one of these men, so is father's brother; but so too are a range of others whose genealogical relations to ego

vary widely. This is not to say that a Trobriander does not or cannot distinguish his mother's husband from other *tama*—simply that for purposes of this carving up of his social universe, they are the same "kind" of person.

Term B : *tabu*

The category *tabu* is "self-reciprocal," like our "cousin" (if you are my cousin, I am your cousin). It includes, first, both grandfathers and both grandmothers; FZ, FZD, FZDD: any man or woman of the grandparents' generation; any male or female ancestor; any woman of the father's, father's father's, or mother's father's clans. Reciprocally, it includes all grandchildren; a women's MBC (C is "children"), her MMBC, descendants, and so on.

Interpretation 1

The basic meaning of *tabu* is "grandparent" (and, reciprocally, "grandchild"). Extension to other men and women of the grandparents' generation, and to ancestors and descendants, reflects a general cultural equivalence based on their removal by age and generation from ego.

The other equivalences, of FZ, FZD, FZDD, and—reciprocally—of a woman's BC, MBC, and MMBC, reflect the Crow rule we have already encountered. That is, FZ is equivalent to FM, hence is a *tabu;* and by applying this rule repeatedly, FZDD = FMDD = FZD = FMD = FZ = FM (hence *tabu*). (The classing of FZDS as *tama* reflects a similar chain for a man.)

Interpretation 2

The Trobrianders are not concerned with long chains of genealogical connection, which they often do not know anyway; rather, they are concerned with kinds of people who play some similar part in their lives. *Tabu* are in fact classed together not because of some positive feature they share in common, but because, as ego passes through the various stages of the life cycle, they are distant and marginal to him—and in some respects dangerous. It is from this category of persons marginal to his life that he must find a wife, since girls in other categories are ruled out by the rules of exogamy.

Both sorts of interpretation have strong adherents at present. Position 1 was first advanced in the early 1960s by Floyd Lounsbury (1964, 1965; Scheffler 1972a) though it builds on some quite old principles of kinship analysis. It has attracted widespread support. Position 2 has been argued for some years by British social anthropologists, notably Edmund Leach (1959) and Rodney Needham (1971).

The strength of position 2 lies in an intuitive fit to the society involved. Each society's set of "relationship terms" is viewed as a unique conceptual universe, and it is explored and mapped in terms of the social groupings, categories, and distinctive customs of the people under study. (In the Trobriand case, however, recent evidence on the variability of residence patterns makes the "fit" less convincing.)

The strength of position 1 lies at the opposite pole in its generality of application (Scheffler 1971). Consider the Trobriand categories. Not only the two we explored but the whole range of others are almost precisely matched on the other side of the earth among the Cow Creek Seminole Indians of Florida. Yet Seminole social organization has almost none of the special features used by proponents of position 2 to account for the Trobriand categories. Using Lounsbury's equivalence rules, we find that many kinship terminologies from different continents fall into place as subvarieties of the same family, though there is no historical connection between them. On the debit side, some of the

equivalences the rules specify do not really make much intuitive sense. To many, the whole operation looks uncomfortably like Lounsbury's first oral description of it—"a trick that works."

The long-standing motivation behind studies of kinship terminologies has been that if we could find how they map the social universe of a people, we could acquire a key to comparative analysis. More recently, the formal symmetry and algebraic possibilities of kinship terminologies have made them a focal concern in ethnographic semantics or "ethnoscience." Formal analysis of kin terms has become, for many anthropologists, an end in itself. Attempts to use *componential analysis* in semantics have mainly dealt with kinship terms. (Recall the attempt in §25 to define "chair," "stool," and "bench" in terms of the intersection of distinctive features.) When componential analysis is used to define the meaning of a kinship term, such criteria as generation, sex, or relative age are used as distinctive features. Thus a kinship term Lounsbury would treat as having a primary meaning of "father" (with extensions to FB and more distant kin) might be componentially defined as "male + first-ascending-generation + father's-side." FB and FFMBDS thus fit the definition as neatly as father himself.

Unfortunately, analyzing kinship terms in only their genealogical senses, pulled out of social contexts, affords the analyst a spurious kind of freedom (see Keesing 1972b). It too easily becomes a kind of algebraic game, where solutions tell us very little either about the meanings of the terms to those who use them (in metaphorical and nongenealogical senses as well as genealogical ones) or about how words convey meanings (§26). Anthropological contributions to semantic theory have probably been blighted, not cultivated, by preoccupation with kin terms.

In looking at kinship terminologies we

have deviated slightly from the main course—to glimpse an area anthropologists have explored with fascination for decades. Our primary goal has been to see how kinship and descent intertwine in forming the fabric of social order in tribal societies. We are now prepared to trace out, in the next chapter, the bonds of marriage and family structure that stitch the fabric together.

But first, it is worth pausing briefly to assess the importance of kinship (and descent) in shaping social relations in tribal societies.

45.
Kinship and Social Relations

An earlier generation of ethnographers usually recorded the formal outlines of a society's "kinship system"—the kin terms, the residence rule, the rule of descent, the number and names of clans, rules of exogamy and forms of marriage, special rules of kinship avoidance, and such matters. When a finer-grained detail began to be recorded these ideal blueprints turned out to correspond only quite loosely to actual patterns of social relations. Local groups turned out not to be made up exclusively of lineal descendants, as rules of thumb would have it; "wrong marriages" were common, and postmarital residence often "violated" the "rule"; and kin competed and quarreled as the ideology insisted they should not.

What to do about this emerging gulf between what people actually do in a tribal society and the idealized version of their "kinship system" they presented to the ethnographer has been a major theme of modern social anthropology.

To some anthropologists, it seems best to focus on individual goals and strategies, and the way coalitions are formed to advance collective ends and manipulate power,

wealth, and status. The "rules" then show up as ideologies that are manipulated to advance political goals. When they are pulled out of these contexts and presented in codified form to the ethnographer, they not only give too neat a picture of "the system" (and hence create the illusion of a gulf between the rules and actual behavior). They also create a false picture of how rules operate: the rules are seen as moral dictates constraining behavior. Such critics as Leach (1961) and Barth (1966a) would argue that statements of the supposed "rules" in real social contexts are political acts; the ideologies are "epiphenomena," at once by-products and instruments of the processes of economics and politics.[5] Thus a Kwaio man (Case 29) may argue eloquently in the course of litigation that agnates have primary rights in a child custody case, citing the ideology of agnatic descent—and everyone understands that he is doing so because he and his allies are the child's agnates. The next day he may insist on receiving a share of sexual compensation for his sister's errant daughter—and may with equal vehemence cite the ideology of cognatic kinship. And it is the man opposing him in litigation (though in other settings they might be the best of friends) whom he eloquently addresses as "brother," where on other occasions their kinship relationship is not mentioned.

But there is another equally revealing approach to the apparent gulf between ideal rules and ideologies and what people actually do. The Kwaio, like other tribal peoples, do not expect one another to follow the "ideal" rules. But they do manage to understand, interpret, and even anticipate such acts as I

---

[5] A Marxist such as Asad (1972) would agree, but would argue that the insistence on *individualism* is itself a by-product of Western ideologies; he would want us to look more carefully at class interests, their economic roots, and their historic development. We will return to these issues.

have described. If they can do so, there must be some more subtle "code" of knowledge they share. A major theme in recent American social anthropology has been to probe beneath rules of thumb and ideal rules and categories to discover and describe as best possible this shared knowledge that makes communication and ordered social relations possible.

My efforts to describe such shared knowledge among the Kwaio vividly illustrate how "lineages" and other kin groupings have been given a false concreteness. In tribal societies, real warm bodies move from one social situation to another, as we do; and many of the things people do, places they go, and action groups they temporarily join have little or nothing to do with their membership in descent corporations.

Case 32: Kwaio "Descent Groups" and Social Relations

The Kwaio "descent system" is comprehensible only if we see how the role a person is enacting in a particular situation determines the part he or she will play, and how this may not neatly correspond with "membership" in a descent group.

One of my subjects is an agnate in descent group A and he is priest for the A's though he has not lived with them since infancy. He grew up and has always lived with his mother's kin, from descent group B. In the course of a mortuary feast our man was giving, a leader from group A approached from the left and presented him with a major valuable, which he accepted with his left hand. At the same moment, a man from B approached from the right and presented another valuable to him—which he accepted simultaneously with his right hand. Our subject was acting at the same moment as both an A and a B—and no one was confused. This is, of course, the limiting case where dual membership is expressed simultaneously. Yet in the course of a feast or marriage, an individual often acts as a member not only of more than one descent group, but of half a dozen other [descent categories]. Status in each case is clearly labeled, according to context. (Keesing 1968b:83)

Confusion and conflict of interest are avoided because ego's status is defined by context. One day ego behaves as a member of [group] A, another day he may behave as a member of B, C, or D. Descent-group membership does not, at most times, demand some exclusive allegiance, such as residence. It merely includes ego in a social category from which groups are crystallized in certain defined contexts. What is required to make such a system work is a situational sorting out, or clear labeling, of statuses, and a set of principles for making decisions in those situations where two allegiances conflict or where presence is required in two different places at once. (Keesing 1968b:83)

I have analyzed the action groups that crystallize in different settings—in feast-giving, in fighting, in ritual, and so on—as the enactment of different *roles*. A person acts as feast-giver one day, as member of fighting party the next. In both situations, which descent corporation he belongs to may partly account for his taking part, and for what he does with whom.

Yet the group that joins together to fight will predictably only partly overlap with the group that sponsored the feast; and neither will correspond neatly to the group that joins together in ritual, which most nearly corresponds to the Kwaio "descent group":

The category of persons whose primary descent affiliation is to a particular named territory (for example, "Kwangafi"), because they are agnatically descended from its founder, is relatively clear. But this category does not define a "localized descent group," since adult women are mainly scattered in their husbands' territories and some male members live in territories other than Kwangafi. "The Kwangafi people," in this neat sense of a descent category, are crystallized into a social group only in a few contexts, mainly involving ritual; they compose a dispersed ritual community, not a local group. On the other hand, in different contexts "The Kwangafi people" refers to the people domiciled in Kwangafi and their families; that is, it includes in-marrying wives not related to Kwangafi and excludes Kwangafi women living elsewhere. "The Kwangafi people" may refer also to a much wider category of all those people *cognatically* descended from the founders of Kwangafi who sacrifice to Kwangafi ancestors. In still other contexts, "The Kwangafi people" may refer to an action group temporarily crystallized around the men of Kwangafi for some purpose such as feuding or feasting; these may include a broad scattering of cognates, affines, neighbors, and political allies.

. . .[T]he component elements that contribute to being a "Kwangafi person" in different contexts (descent category membership, domicile, actual residence, sex, neighborhood cluster membership, etc.) can be analytically untangled. Distinguishing the different contexts where descent status is relevant and analyzing the roles involved enables us to make sense of much of the apparent flux of social interaction. One can anticipate fairly accurately, as Kwaio can, what group or category will comprise "The Kwangafi people" in a particular setting or event. (Keesing 1972b:23).

Such an approach leads us to look more carefully than we usually have, in studying tribal social organization, at the groups that form temporarily to make gardens together, hunt together, fetch water from the stream, or sti and gossip; and hence to give more adequate emphasis to the role of friendship and personal choice, as well as kinship or descent status, in the fabric of everyday social life among tribesmen. And that in turn helps us to understand more clearly the apparent gulf between kinship ideals and actual behavior. Kinship norms specify how people should or would behave to one another in a world where only kinship mattered. But actual kinsmen are also neighbors, business competitors, owners of adjacent gardens, and so on; and their quarreling and enmity characteristically derive from these relationships, as well as competition for inheritance, power in the family or lineage, and so on. Brothers should support one another. But the owner of a pig who eats your garden should pay damages. If the owner is your brother—and in small-scale tribal societies it is your kin who will most often be your neighbors and rivals—there is a gulf between the ensuing quarrel and ideal behavior between kin. This gulf does not mean that the norms or rules are wrong or unimportant, but that the world in which they are applied is complicated and human.

MARRIAGE, FAMILY, AND COMMUNITY

14

Here we will continue to explore the structure of tribal societies, looking first at marriage in comparative perspective and then at the family and community. As we see how descent corporations shape marriage and family organization, it will be clear why we have to approach the latter through this indirect route. This chapter, like the last, deals mainly with phenomena anthropologists lump broadly together as kinship.

46. Marriage in Comparative Perspective

Does marriage occur in all societies? Anthropologists trying to compare customs are always caught in a dilemma: how far to stretch the meaning of a term like "marriage" so that it covers customs quite different from ours without losing its shape altogether.

To understand marriage in comparative perspective, it is useful at the outset to recall three cases summarized briefly in the last chapter, and to look at several other cases:

1. The Nuer (Case 20), where a widow remarries her dead husband's close relative, but where their children are legally considered to be fathered by the dead first husband; and where an elderly woman of sufficient means can "marry" a girl, and then be legally defined as the father of the children the girl bears by her lovers. Evans-Pritchard (1951) further distinguishes all the forms of Nuer marriage (including the above), which are validated by transfer of cattle from the husband's lineage to the wife's lineage, from what he calls "concubinage," where sexual relations are permitted but the man acquires no legal rights over the woman and over children she bears by him.

2. The Toda (Case 21), where a group of men have a single wife; and where fatherhood is legally defined by ritual presentation of a bow by each of the husbands in sequence. The father of a child is the one who last presented the bow, even if he has since died. Among the

Iravas of southern India, a group of brothers apparently entered into marriage as a legal corporation, collectively taking a wife whose children were then defined as having a corporate father (Aiyappan 1945:98—103).

3. The Nayar (Case 19), where—to satisfy Hindu law—the girl is ritually married before menarche; but where, when she matures, she takes lovers as nocturnal visitors into the household she shares with her brothers and close matrilineal kin. Note, however, that the lovers must be socially recognized and approved by the men of the household, and that they formally acknowledge their paternity or possible paternity (a woman may have several lovers at once) of the child.

With several other cases, we will have a sufficiently broad perspective to understand the essentials and variations of marriage in the tribal world.

Case 33: The Okrika Ijo

The Okrika Ijo of the Nile Delta have two forms of marriage. In the first, the husband and his kin make a large payment to the wife's guardian; in the second, they make only a small payment. In the first case, the husband acquires proprietary rights over the wife and the children she bears by him (as with the Nuer marriages involving payment of cattle); in the latter, he acquires rights of sexual access, but her guardian retains legal rights over her and her children (Williamson 1962).

Case 34: *Mut'a* Marriage in the Middle East

Mut'a marriage in the Muslim Middle East is a contractual arrangement whereby a woman accompanies a man during a legally specified period while the man is making a pilgrimage or some other lengthy trip. The man pays the "wife" for her sexual services; but this is not simply a form of contractual prostitution, since children she bears from their "marriage" are considered to be among his legitimate heirs.

Case 35: Homosexual Marriage in Western Egypt

In the Siwah Oasis of western Egypt, all normal men and boys engage in homosexual relations. Homosexuality is openly discussed and socially approved. Until recently, marriages between men and boys were legally possible and were celebrated with great pomp; the marriage payments for a boy were sometimes as much as 15 times as great as the fixed payment for a woman (Cline 1936).

Some anthropologists, notably Gough (1959) and Goodenough (1970), have sought to find common denominators of marriage in different societies so as to distinguish essential features from inessential ones and to distinguish marriage from other forms of liaison that may be socially recognized. Others, such as Leach (1955, 1971), have stressed the diversity of marriage forms, the various elements involved—sexual, economic, legal, and political—and the futility of seeking a universal definition.

Given the evolutionary perspective we took in Part 1, it makes sense to begin with first principles that are rooted in human psychobiology as well as sociology and to work upwards.

First, there are psychobiological as well as social pressures that work toward the relatively stable pair-bonding of sexually mature male and female. There are also evolutionarily old pressures for male dominance and its expression in priority of sexual access to particular females. When humans contrive cultural conventions that place couples in continuous sexual relationships, and when control over these relationships is made a political and legal concern of the male partner and other males, they are obviously not enacting "private instincts"; but they are not creating totally arbitrary cultural rules either: they are swimming with, rather than against, the streams of human psychobiology. Humans have swum against these streams in some times and places, always with some difficulty.

There obviously are streams running in another direction that push humans into sexual adventuring with a variety of partners: social conventions in different times and places have accepted, channeled, or attempted to deny or to dam these streams.

Another deep current in human psychobiology, as yet not clearly understood (see §48), is that the relationship between brother and sister—between young people raised together—is in general antithetical to the pair-bond sexual relationship. This, too, has sometimes been overridden by cultural convention (§48). But there are apparently psychobiological as well as sociological reasons why the family one grows up in is not the setting for adult sexuality: why a woman characteristically has two distinct kinds of men in her life, brothers and lovers (and a man has two kinds of women, sisters and lovers).

Finally, the old primate unit of mother-plus-young remains an important building block of human social organization. Mothers visibly bear and suckle infants; fathers do not visibly father them. Defining fatherhood and its social and legal entailments has given different societies much room for variation.

Gough (1959) sees marriage as being, in all times and places, a customary transaction that serves to establish the legitimacy of newborn children as acceptable members of society. Goodenough (1970) tries to stay closer to the psychobiological pressures we have examined in trying to reach a universal definition:

Marriage [is] a transaction and resulting contract in which a person (male or female, corporate or individual, in person or by proxy) establishes a continuing claim to the right of sexual access to a woman—this right having priority over rights of sexual access others currently have or may subsequently acquire in relation to her (except in a similar transaction) until the contract resulting from the transaction is terminated—and in which the woman involved is eligible to bear children. (Goodenough 1970:12—13)

Goodenough's definition is broad enough to include both the ritual marriage of the sexually immature Nayar girl—who would be eligible to bear children if she could—and the later formal liaisons with her lovers. It can include Nuer "ghost-marriage" (the second mate is acting by proxy) and concubinage (which involves rights of priority in sexual access, though not proprietary rights; a similar distinction separates the two forms of Okrika Ijo marriage). It can include woman-woman marriage among the Nuer (and elsewhere, as in Dahomey; Herskovits 1938(1):319—322). Where marriage is between a man and a male transvestite socially accorded a female role (as with the Plains Indian *berdache*), Goodenough's definition can be stretched to fit; it probably does not fit the Siwah Oasis case or some marriages between male homosexuals in modern Western societies, though with some further stretching these patterns could be wedged in, since they are legally modeled on male-female marriages.

Goodenough's comparative analysis is useful not so much because it gives us a stretchable and serviceable definition (we could do without that), but because it relates variable cultural and social conventions to fundamentals of human psychology and biology.

Leach's and Goodenough's emphasis on variability is also important: we should not see marriage as serving a simple function. Marriage is crucial because it ties bundles of rights and relationships into one or several packages (for as we have seen, a society can have more than one form of marriage): it regulates sexual relations; defines the social position of individuals and their memberships in groups; establishes legal rights and interests; creates domestic economic units; relates individuals to kin groups other than their own; and serves as an instrument of political relations between individuals and groups.

All this said, we are in a position to understand why many of the marriage systems of the tribal world seem strange to us, why we are prone to misunderstand them. (We are also in a better position to see why my Kwaio friends were able to perceive the logic in Nuer, Mota, Trobriand, and other customs that seem strange to us.)

We can set out a series of general premises crucial to understanding marriage (and kinship) in the tribal world.

1. Marriage is characteristically not a relationship between individuals but a contract between groups (often, between corporations). The rela-tionship contractually established in the marriage may endure despite the death of one partner (or even of both).

2. Marriage entails a *transfer or flow of rights*. The exact set of rights passing from the wife's group to the husband's (or vice versa)—work services, sexual rights, rights over children, property, and so on—varies widely. But if we ask what rights are transferred, and assume that something tangible or intangible passes back in the other direction to balance the transaction, we are well on our way to understanding many otherwise peculiar-looking marriage systems.

3. Though marriage involves rights to priority of sexual access by the husband, it need not, as we have seen, be exercised directly or exclusively. (Hence woman-woman marriages, wife-lending, sanctioned love affairs, or alternative partners; in 63 percent of Murdock's (1949) sample societies, for example, sexual relations were permitted between a man and his wife's sister.)

4. Marriage need not be monogamous. More than one relationship of marriage can in many societies be contracted at once, and sometimes one contract can involve two or more wives or two or more husbands.

5. Marriage may be primarily an economic relationship or a political alliance rather than a sexual relationship.

6. The role of father is subject to wide variations. More precisely, the roles that for us coalesce—mother's husband, mother's sexual partner, legal father, presumed physical begetter—may be culturally separated out among different persons (recall that some of these might, as among Nuer or Dahomey, be women.)

The most crucial point in understanding marriage comparatively is to view it as a legal relationship and to sort out carefully who the parties are, what rights and what valuables are transferred, and how these are distributed and assigned, and what interests of individuals and groups are advanced by such contractual arrangements.

47.
Marriage: Contracts and Transactions

With this introduction, and with the case materials already presented, some of the major themes and variations in tribal marriage systems can be sorted out.

Let us look first at the flow of symbolically important valuables in marriage systems and the reciprocal transfer of rights.

Marriage Transactions and the Transfer of Rights

In a great many tribal societies, marriage is a contract between two lineages, or two families or two kindreds, whereby the groom's kin make a substantial payment of valuables to the bride's kin. These characteristically are goods laden with symbolic value—cattle, shell valuables, or ceremonial objects such as brass gongs, ivory tusks, dog's teeth, feathers, or whatever things a people invest with special nonutilitarian value. And the transfer of these symbolically laden valuables is characteristically publicly dramatized.

Seeing a young woman led off to her nuptial bed and a life of hard labor in exchange for a herd of smelly cows was more than many missionaries could bear, and such "degrading" customs were suppressed by missions or by colonial regimes in many areas. The term "bride price," with its connotation of a woman sold as chattel, was current.

Anthropologists have often used alternative terms such as "bridewealth" or "progeny price," which direct attention to the transfer of rights over a woman's children, not her body. Here we will use "bridewealth," even though no one term best fits all forms of marriage prestation. What matters is that in each case we sort out carefully who the par-

ties to the contract are, and most important, that we sort out what rights are transferred in the other direction. The most important usually turn out to be rights over the bride's children. If the parties to the contract are patrilineages, what the husband's lineage is "buying" is not so much the wife as her future children, as lineage members. But this is too simple, because bridewealth usually involves a transfer of other rights—to the wife's sexuality, to her work, and more generally to her presence, where her own relatives are compensated for losing her.

In some societies *bride service* is an alternative form to bridewealth. Here the groom or suitor resides with the girl's people and works for them for some specified period. This is often a way for a man of little means, who cannot afford bridewealth payments, to acquire a wife. An equivalent or alternative means of acquiring a wife "free," in some societies where bridewealth is usual, is permanent residence with the bride's kin. Here the children may even affiliate with their mother's people, not their father's. The Nuer form of concubinage, where the male partner acquires sexual rights but not proprietary rights over his mate and her children, and the cut-rate form of marriage among the Okrika Ijo (Case 33), represent other possibilities. In these cases, two bundles of rights are involved. In one form of liaison, they are tied together, in exchange for a large bridewealth payment; in the other form of liaison, only the lesser bundle involving sexual rights is transferred.

Bridewealth payments are most characteristic of patrilineal descent systems, where the husband's lineage is acquiring rights over children borne by a woman from another lineage. Here a symbolic element of exchange often is expressed as well: the cattle your brother received when you married a man from another lineage will serve to acquire a wife for him, so that bridewealth cattle become a token and symbol of the reciprocities of exchange. In that sense, they serve as a bridge between the systems such as our own where marriage is based on more or less free choice and the systems of systematic marital exchange between descent groups we will examine in §48.

Bridewealth is less commonly paid where descent is traced matrilineally. Here, the husband's lineage does not acquire rights over children. Such payment usually occurs where the husband's lineage compensates the wife's lineage for loss of her work services (and hence occurs when wives go to live with their husband's people.) Note that, as among the Subanun (Case 30), bridewealth contracts can be made between the *kindreds* of bride and groom—though then two clusters of individuals, not two corporations, are involved.

Why, then, the payment of *dowry* in Europe and many parts of Asia? This turns out not to be payment for a husband. Rather, it usually is a payoff to the out-marrying wife and her children for her share in the family estate, in societies where women and men share rights in property but women marry out and leave their estate. However, dowry can become entangled with concepts of rank, so that important families pair off in strategic alliances of property, and dowry becomes a demonstration of wealth to secure prestige.

Affinal Relations

A marriage contract, once concluded, does not then simply result in a couple living together in domestic bliss or squabbling. The corporations or alignments of kin—related as *affines*—that contracted the relationship continue to have important interests in and through the marriage.

The nature, centrality, and complexity of the affinal relationships between kin groups are vividly illustrated by the Trobriand Islanders, whose matrilineal descent system and kinship terminology we have already encountered.

Bridewealth: New Guinea Highlanders (Chimbu) of the groom's subclan present goldlip pearl shells to the bride's kin. (Courtesy of Australian News and Information Bureau.)

Case 36: Affinal Relations in the Trobriands

The most dramatic, and best-known, custom that binds affines together is called *urigubu*. The Trobrianders grow tremendous quantities of yams, root vegetables that can be stored for long periods after harvest. In fact, they grow far more than they need. Yet the husband and wife who produce the yams keep much less than half of their crop, the less desirable tubers, for their own use. The rest they give away in formal presentations.

But to whom? Ideally, the bulk goes from the producer to his sister's husband. Figure 14.1 illustrates this presentation. In one sense the presentation is from the man X to his sister Y and her children, who are members of his subclan (vertical hatching). However, recent evidence makes it clear that Trobrianders think of this primarily as an obligation of X to his sister's husband, Z, who is the head of household 1. A man also makes *urigubu* yam presentations to his mother and father, after he has left their household and gone to form one of his own in a different place.

Though these are the most common forms of *urigubu*, we know from new evidence that these obligations fall upon the subclan as a corporation, not just on individual households. It is the responsibility of men of the corporation to muster and assign resources so that proper amounts of *urigubu* yams go to the households of all of the subclan's married females. Each household in a subclan (say, household 2 in Figure 14.1) is assigned one other household (ideally, the household of X's sister, Y) for which to raise *urigubu* yams in a special garden. But X also will present a basket of yams to his other sisters and other close kin—presentations that, as we will soon see, are reciprocated.

The logic of this custom seemed well deciphered. The adult men lived on the corporation's property; the women through whom descent was traced never lived there, since they live with their fathers until marriage. *Urigubu* seemed to be, like dowry, a payoff to the out-marrying women in produce from the lands of their corporation. This interpretation is now

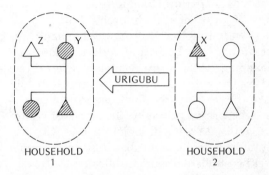

HOUSEHOLD
1

HOUSEHOLD
2

Figure 14.1. Urigubu presentation of yams in the Trobriands: This shows the most basic form of *urigubu*. However, X may also present *urigubu* yams to his mother and father, or to other women of his subclan and their husbands. Hatching indicates membership in the same subclan.

less satisfying. New evidence more clearly shows *urigubu* as a relationship between male affines (brothers-in-law), not between brothers and sisters. It also shows that because of deviations in the ideal patterns of residence, "most of the adult males who garden for [women of the subclan] do not reside in their sub-clan's villages, so that the *urigubu* they provide is not the produce of the land of their, and their sisters', own sub-clans" (Powell 1969b:581).

But with this new evidence has come a realization that subclans are linked together in complex webs of affinal alliance. A marriage is a political act, establishing a formal bond and contractual relationship between corporate subclans that lasts as long as the marriage; and the *urigubu* presentation annually reaffirms it.

Symbolically, the *urigubu* underlines both the unity of men of the corporation in meeting their obligations to affines and the unity of male and female corporation members. Moveover, there is an element of subordination implied in the *urigubu* presentations. Symbolically, they imply the dominance of the husband's subclan—hence, as we will see in Chapter 17, their easy conversion into a more formal tribute to the high-ranking sub-clan of the husband in a politically strategic marriage.

The large-scale and dramatic presentations of yams in the annual *urigubu* are countered by periodic reciprocation of valuables *(youlo)*. But these represent only one element of the complex webs of transactions and obligations that bind together the subclans and individuals in a Trobriand marriage. To understand what happens when, and after, a Trobriand girl marries, we have to think in terms of two different marriages and two affinal relations between subclans. Marriage 1 is her parents' marriage, which affinally links her mother's subclan, A, with her father's subclan, B. Then there is marriage 2, her own marriage to a man from subclan C, which affinally links her subclan A with subclan C. At the time of marriage 2, there are eight different presentations of food and valuables to and from the bride's kin. But curiously, most of them are between the C's and the B's; the A's stay mainly on the sidelines. The B's again play a central part when the daughter becomes pregnant. It is the women of the B's who make a pregnancy cloak, the B's who perform magic, the B's who are directly involved in the events of birth of the children, though these children are A's. If marriage 1 is ended by the death of the husband, his wife's relatives, the A's, must prepare the body and conduct mourning rituals; the dead man's subclansmen, the B's, must abstain from direct contact. If marriage 1 is ended by the wife's death, the A's must abstain and the affinally related B's take the lead. At the final mortuary rite, the dead spouse's subclan makes large presentations to the survivor's subclan, and the affinal relationship ends. As we will see in Case 45, Chapter 15, the role of women in these mortuary rites and distributions is much more important than Malinowski's published works indicated.

Why the B's should play a central part in the marriage of the A daughter to a C man, and in the death of an A wife, will have to remain a mystery for the moment. We need more pieces for the puzzle before we can solve it, and see a new side to *urigubu* presentations, in Case 72.

Our whole time perspective on marriage is likely to mislead us when we look at affinal rights and relationships in non-Western societies.

In tribal societies, marriage is a long drawn-out *process* that involves several transactions or stages. The relationships established in the marriage transaction may continue long after death of one or both parties. Thus among the Kwaio of the Solomon Islands (Cases 29 and 32), marriage entails an opening "down payment"; then a major feast, which may take place several months later, at which bridewealth is paid; and finally a third transaction where the bride's mother presents her with a married woman's pubic apron. Only then is the marriage physically consummated. And in some societies, marriage may become legally binding only after the first child has been conceived or born (compare the Banaro, Case 18).

The contract between husband's lineage and wife's lineage may endure even though either he or she dies. If he dies, rights over her sexuality and future children may remain with his lineage, so that the dead husband's brother or some other close kinsman replaces him as husband. This is known as the *levirate*. This is what happens in Nuer "ghost-marriage," except that the dead first husband is still classed as father of the children. If the wife dies, her lineage may be contractually obligated to ship over a replacement—her sister, her brother's daughter, or some other close relative. This is known as the *sororate*.

Even where a widow remarries a man not in her husband's lineage (usually implying an initial marital contract where her own relatives retained ultimate legal control over her), her

dead husband's lineage may have some "residual rights" and interests in her activities. Among the Kwaio of Melanesia, for instance, part of the bridewealth paid for a widow goes to her first husband's relatives.

The preference for a man to marry the widow of his maternal uncle in Mota (Case 22) is also worth mentioning, because it again illustrates our tendency to misunderstand other people's marital customs. Rather than being a bizarre custom, as felt by early observers, this is a quite sensible expression of a man's succession to the status and prop-

Kwaio bridewealth: Relatives of the groom assess the adequacy of strung shell valuables hung up at a wedding feast. (Photograph by the author.)

erty rights of his mother's brother (in a system, like the Trobriands, with matrilineal descent and Crow kinship terminology). In stepping into his uncle's shoes, he assumes the responsibility to take care of the uncle's widow (he also marries a younger girl who bears his own children).

Even after both husband and wife have died, the complex of obligations established in the marriage may endure. Among the Kwaio, the kinsmen who helped to finance a man's bridewealth payment are entitled to a major share of bridewealth when, years later, the daughters of the marriage they helped to finance are married.

Marriage Choice, Preference, and Obligation

Looking at marriage as a contractual relationship between groups helps to free us from our preoccupation with husband and wife. It is useful to ask, in this light, how far marriage in tribal societies is based on free choice by the marrying pair and how far it is constrained by rules and senior kin.

In some tribal societies, marriage is based on more or less free choice. But when substantial bridewealth is involved, a young man is likely not to have the means to finance his own marriage; hence, his personal fancies are likely to be subordinated to the wishes of his elders in choosing a politically and economically appropriate mate. (Colonialism, with its plantation systems and cash economies, has given young men in many tribal societies more power and leeway than they had in precolonial times.)

Choice of a marriage partner may be constrained not only by the politics of affinal alliance but by standards of appropriate or culturally valued marriage. Marriage to a girl in a particular kinship category may be strongly preferred, socially desirable, or a matter of legal right. Thus marriage with

mother's brother's daughter (MBD) or father's sister's daughter (FZD) or some relative may be the ideal form, with other arrangements permitted but less favored. Where this occurs, the preferred form may be a way of consolidating property or "getting around" the rule of descent or inheritance. When people say it is "best" for a person to marry a particular kind of relative, we can understand them only by asking, "'Best' for whom, when, and why?" (We will shortly see some systems where affinal alliance between particular kinds of relatives is enjoined, not simply encouraged.)

An important preferential form occurs among the Bedouin, other Middle Eastern Arabs, and some other Islamic peoples. This is parallel cousin marriage, where a man has rights to marry his *bint 'amm,* ideally, his father's brother's daughter (FBD). The structural causes and consequences of this peculiar form have been much debated. Marriage with father's brother's daughter implies lineage *endogamy* (in-marriage). That is, given a system of patrilineal descent, a man is expected to marry a girl in his own group. With generations of such in-marriage, the skeins of genealogical connection become highly complicated, and any two people can usually trace relationship through many pathways. Given a rule that patrilineal connections should be traced where possible, some anthropologists have argued that many people would end up marrying the "right" kind of girl even without that as a special preference. But this overlooks the *right* to marry FBD, and focuses on the marrying pair rather than their fathers. In a sense, FBD marriage represents a mode of exchange: brothers directly exchange their sons and daughters. In some of these societies, both men and women have property rights, and it has been argued that FBD marriage is a way of keeping property consolidated among close lineage members. The marriage preference also clearly reflects ideas about the ritual impurity of women, so that the relationship between and through two men contrasts with a relationship between or through a brother and a sister.

Marriage Stability and Divorce

The stability of marriage—how frequent divorce is and how it affects the transactions and other relations between husband's and wife's groups—is an important variable. In some societies, marriage is very fragile, and divorces are common. In others, most marriages are permanent. Americans concerned about mounting divorce rates are likely to seek in such variations some secret for reversing this trend. But since divorce in non-Western societies so often involves a contract between corporations, it is hard to understand through Western eyes.

An early line of explanation showed that when bridewealth is high (in terms of the economy in question), marriage tends to be stable; but when bridewealth is low, divorce is common. But that leads to what look like chicken-or-egg questions: Is marriage stable *because* of the high bridewealth costs, or can a society afford to have high bridewealth only if it has a stable form of marriage?

One line of approach is to look at the rule of descent. Because the husband-wife and brother-sister ties are in more direct opposition with matrilineal descent, it has been argued that marital instability is a concomitant of corporate matrilineal descent groups. A strong patrilineal descent system, it was argued, would be associated with stable marriage. But as we have already seen, what is really important is the relative strength of the brother-sister and husband-wife ties. When a girl's tie to her natal (birth) group is severed or greatly weakened when she marries, divorce is uncommon. When her affiliation to her natal group remains strong, she may enter into several successive marriages. This still

does not fully explain differential marriage stability in patrilineal descent systems, since it only pushes the question one step further back. But it correctly underlines the importance of looking carefully at the relative importance of those two overlapping groupings in a unilineal descent system—the lineage, composed of unilineally related brothers and sisters, and the local group, composed of unilineally related men (or more rarely women) and their *spouses.*

The causes of divorce in non-Western societies run the gamut from quarreling and failure to live up to expected roles (a lazy wife, an improvident husband) to infertility or adultery. Divorce may be highly formalized, or it may be just a matter of one partner ordering the other out or giving public notice that the union is over; a Hopi wife merely puts her husband's things outside her house door. More interesting to the social anthropologist is what happens to bridewealth payments, if any, and what becomes of the contract between kin groups in terms of rights over children, kinship relations, and so on. Sometimes all or some bridewealth must be returned, though this may depend on the cause of divorce, whether the woman has borne children, and so on.

This underlies the importance of tracing out how rights are distributed and transferred in a society. It is no accident that some of the great early amateur ethnographers were specialists in jurisprudence who set about to study patterns of rights while most anthropologists were still studying patterns of basket weaving.

Plural Marriage

The frequency of plural marriage (polygamy) in tribal societies has already been noted. The more common form is *polygyny,* or marriage of a man to two or more women. In some areas, polygyny is the normal marriage pattern, as in most of tribal Africa.

We will see in discussing family structure that polygynous families pose some difficult structural problems. We tend to misunderstand the workings, and the problems, of such systems by placing ourselves in the shoes of co-wife or husband—and hence imputing sexual jealousy and other notions of ours to them. Polygyny may be degrading to women in the eyes of a missionary, but what matters is whether it is degrading to the women who practice it. When a new wife means another worker to share the hard tasks of farming, a woman may encourage her husband to acquire one and may even take the lead in promoting a union.

Co-wives may be from different lineages, or they may be sisters (in what is called *sororal* polygyny). The latter, at least as a preferred form, avoids some of the conflicts that can disrupt polygynous families.

Polygyny may be practiced only by men of wealth or high rank or by most men in the society. If the latter seems to imply an unbalanced sex ratio, recall that the same end might be achieved by having girls marry at 15 and men at 35—which is roughly what happens in many polygynous societies. It may also result from differential mortality rates, as when some men are killed in warfare.

Conflicting interests of co-wives in the children each bears by a single father provide a major source of division, both within households and within patrilineages. The relations between half-siblings and the distribution of rights to each, in relation to their common father and different mothers, are always important in such systems. Lineage segmentation in a patrilineal system often takes place between half-brothers, with ties through the different mothers (and their lineages or ancestors) reflecting and symbolizing the contrasts between segments.

In a good many societies two or more men may share sexual access to one woman. These arrangements have been called *polyandry*. But it is a delicate problem of definition whether they involve plural *marriage* or simply the extension of sexual rights by the husband to other men (for various reasons in different societies). Only where fatherhood is assigned to two or more husbands (as among the Toda, Case 21), or is in some sense collective, does this actually involve plural marriage rather than extension of rights of sexual access. A common form of such plural mating involves a group of brothers (what has been called *fraternal* polyandry). Polyandry is often associated with population imbalance, produced in some places by female infanticide. It is *not* characteristically associated with matrilineal descent or an unusually high status of women.

The early evolutionary stage of "group marriage" or primitive promiscuity envisioned by earlier writers is a figment of Victorian imagination. The rare cases where two or more men cohabit with two or more women are extensions of plural mating—and they are complicated arrangements, not simple and free collective ventures.

Case 37: The Marquesans

The Polynesians of the Marquesas emphasize rights of a firstborn son and his aspirations to power and prestige. He often marries a woman of high rank, and, in order to recruit male followers, adds some of her lovers (younger brothers and men of lesser rank) as retainers (*pekio*) in his entourage. An important man may take a secondary wife as *pekio*, and she may add her lovers to the collection. That multiplies the ranks—and looks only secondarily like the "group marriage" imagined by early ethnologists (Otterbein 1963).

We have seen how, to understand marriage customs that seem strange or exotic at first glance, we must go beyond our own ethnocentric assumptions and search out their underlying logic. We ourselves, in narrowing marriage down to an intensive personal relationship between husband and wife on which the rearing of children and so much else depends, have placed a tremendous burden that human frailty very often cannot support. A return to the broader contractual relationships of tribal peoples would hardly be possible for us. But as the pressures of modern life rend more and more families apart, it is ironic to hear still about the "curious customs of the natives."

48.
Incest, Exogamy, and Alliance

A central question in social anthropology for decades has been why human societies prohibit matings between siblings, and between parents and children, as incestuous. Why are there *incest taboos?*

There have been partial exceptions. Brother-sister and father-daughter matings were apparently common, and accepted, in Ptolemaic and Roman Egypt; and among the Azande of Africa, some aristocrats are permitted to keep their daughters and sisters as mistresses, though they are not allowed to bear children. There are several cases of dynastic incest, where—as in ancient Egypt, Peru, and Hawaii—royal brothers and sisters, who approached the status of gods and goddesses, were mated to preserve the sacredness of a royal line.

Though some kind of incest taboo is universal, not even within the range of the immediate nuclear family are these taboos uniformly conceptualized or applied. Thus a Kachin tribesman of Burma cannot have sexual relations with his daughter or his sister because it is sinfully incestuous; but he cannot have sexual relations with his mother because that would be *adulterous*. And half-siblings with the same mother can apparently have sexual relations among the Lakher of Burma. Some societies define incest as a terrible sin that draws the most drastic punishment; others blithely declare that it is unthinkable or nonexistent.

Moreover, the extension of prohibited sex from the immediate family out to more distant relatives follows highly diverse genealogical paths. It may depend on degrees of cousinhood; but it may depend on lineality, so that sex relations within the lineage are defined as incestuous.

Thus, though the core of prohibited relatives—parents and children—is almost always the same, the extension of the taboo to wider categories of relatives takes many shapes.

Many theories, psychological, sociological, evolutionary, have been advanced to explain the universality of the incest taboo. The theory that humans raised together since infancy have less sexual attraction for one another has received recent support in Wolf's (1966, 1970) Chinese evidence, and for siblings, it is certainly a partial truth. But for parents and children, this explanation is less satisfying. What about the Oedipus and Electra complexes posited by the psychoanalysts? And why, if there is no desire, is it necessary to have such an emotionally charged rule? A number of early writers saw the incest taboo as a primitive device to prevent inbreeding. With the development of population genetics this theory was abandoned, and then revived again in more sophisticated form by a distinguished group of anthropologists (Aberle et al. 1963). The genetic foundations of this rethinking of the incest taboo have recently been challenged by Livingstone (1969). Other interpretations have focused on the divisive social and psychological consequences of mating within the family. Thus Malinowski contended that the roles of parents and children are incompatible socially and psychologically with the roles of sexual partners (an argument subsequently refined by the sociological theorist Talcott Parsons).

A number of theorists have sought ecological or demographic explanations of the incest taboo. One views protohuman "families" as unlikely to contain mates of appropriate age—hence the need to mate outside the group. But, again, why an emotionally charged rule to validate what people are doing anyway? More recently, it has been suggested that it would have been ecologically adaptive to protohuman hunters to bring in a new adult member from outside the group.

Our understanding of the incest taboo has been expanded by the recent observation that among chimpanzees ties between mother and son and between siblings remain strong through adulthood and that mother-son matings are avoided. The evolutionary and psychobiological roots of mother-son incest taboo—and probably, Oedipus complex as well—begin now to come into view. The early hominid family of mother and dependent young was expanded by two related evolutionary developments: a lengthening of the period of childhood dependence and the emergence of pair-bonding, associating a male to the primate nuclear group. We will probably never know whether the symmetrical prohibition of father-daughter mating

occurred long before the emergence of language and culture or only when protohumans began to elaborate symbolically on their behavior patterns. But the model of mother-son incest avoidance (and the probable psychological tensions involved) was there to be drawn upon in prohibiting father-daughter and brother-sister mating and in investing the whole complex with great symbolic import.

Other explanations of the incest taboo turn out not to explain the incest taboo at all, but they do illuminate the evolution of exogamy. In a characteristically brilliant early insight, Tylor suggested the social significance of exogamy:

Exogamy, enabling a growing tribe to keep itself compact by constant unions between its spreading clans, enables it to overmatch any number of small, intermarrying groups, isolated and helpless. Again and again in the world's history, savage tribes must have had plainly before their minds the simple practical alternative between marrying out and being killed out. (1889:267)

The evidence from hunting and gathering societies and from early human sites (such as Torralba, Ambrona, and Terra Amata) suggests that, at least by the time of *Homo erectus,* intermarriage between bands was binding them into wider networks within which regional cultures could evolve, networks that could provide the basis for temporary crystallization of larger groups. (We have seen how such crystallizations take place among modern hunters and gatherers, such as the Basin Shoshoni, Case 1.)

But Lévi-Strauss' (1949) argument that exogamy and the incest taboo developed as a single complex is very probably wrong. Lévi-Strauss argued that protohumans, living in bands within which they mated and raised their young, were self-sufficient. There was no basis for union of the bands into a wider society. The crucial step toward culture, and hence wider social integration, would have been a renunciation by the males of a band of their own females, so as to obtain as mates the females of other bands. Lévi-Strauss viewed this as a great social gamble, which, once it paid off and established bonds of exchange between bands, was the essential step toward human society. The incest taboo became The Rule symbolic of culture itself and the transition from natural to cultural order. It acquires a central fascination in human ideational and emotional worlds. Though he is probably wrong in linking the evolution of the incest taboo with the evolution of band exogamy, Lévi-Strauss is probably right in stressing (following Tylor and adding the insights of the great French sociologist Marcel Mauss) the symbolic and political importance of exogamy.

On this theory of exogamy and exchange, Lévi-Strauss has built a widely influential theory of marriage. Where most anthropologists had focused on descent and kinship, Lévi-Strauss focused on the exchange of women by groups of men as the essential element in social structure. Such systems of exchange are solutions to the "primal" problem of how to get women back from other groups in place of one's own, who are prohibited as mates. Kinship and descent systems, in Lévi-Strauss' view, are *primarily* devices for defining and regulating the nature of this exchange.

Lévi-Strauss argues that we are misled by the fact that for each of us there is a seemingly endless number of potential mates. For us the gamble imposed by a rule of out-marriage is a statistical one—we renounce our sisters and brothers and get a splendid selection in return. This is not necessarily the simplest or safest solution to guarantee the return of a spouse, particularly in the tiny societies characteristic of most human history.

What is simpler and safer, in a society of tiny scale, is to specify a rule for the *exchange of women with other groups*. Lévi-Strauss calls systems that specify a mode of exchange

of women among groups *elementary systems* of kinship. A society that simply specifies a range of prohibited spouses is a *complex system*.

Lévi-Strauss (1949) argues that though elementary systems are rare, they occur at the primitive margins of the tribal world and, in vestigial form, in the ancient systems of China and India. Thus they may once have been far more widespread, perhaps the characteristic forms of society until the last several thousand years. The simplest system for exchanging women is one where the whole tribe is divided into two exogamous descent categories (our side and their side, with one's side determined by either patrilineal or matrilineal descent). Such categories are called *moieties*. They represent the simplest form of what Lévi-Strauss calls *direct exchange (échange restreint)*: men of each side give their sisters to the other side and get wives in return. More complicated forms of direct exchange are found in Australia. Australian Aborigines, perhaps partly because they were unencumbered by a complex technology, worked out extraordinarily complicated systems to conceptualize their universe and social relationships. Not only was complexity an end in itself among these Stone Age mathematicians; they borrowed whole elaborations from their neighbors to keep up with the Joneses and superimposed them on their own systems, where they often fit quite badly. Thus you cannot try to decipher an Australian system with strong faith that there *is* an answer that works—Aborigines were quite adept at cheating when they found themselves checkmated (and hence unmated) by the rules of their own game.

One of the more simple and straightforward, though still controversial, Australian alliance systems will illustrate the fascinations and frustrations that have made trying to decipher Australian kinship a favorite anthropological game for almost a century.

Case 38: The Kariera of Australia

The Kariera were a hunting and gathering people, numbering about 750, living in a territory along the coast of northwestern Australia. The tribe, distinguished by minor differences in language and culture from its neighbors, comprised some 20 to 25 local groups. These local groups, of about 30 people each, are called hordes in the literature (Radcliffe-Brown 1913). They consisted of patrilineally related men, their wives (who, by the rule of exogamy, came from other groups), and their children. Each horde was tied to its territory through ritual association with its ancestors.

Each Kariera man or woman belonged to one of four named classes, known in the literature as sections: he or she was Karimera or Burung or Palyeri or Banaka. These four sections fit into the scheme of hordes in pairs. Roughly half of the Kariera hordes (and here it is easiest to think only of their male members) consist of Karimera and Burung men. Roughly half consist of Palyeri and Banaka men. These two "types" of hordes were arranged in roughly checkerboard fashion.

A man who is Karimera belongs to the same horde as his father. But his father, and the other male members of father's horde in father's generation, are Burung. Though father is Burung, grandfather and other men of his generation are Karimera. That is, this distinction between Karimera and Burung sections alternates between generations. The other "kind" of horde containing Banaka and Palyeri sections similarly alternates generations (Table 14.1).

TABLE 14.1   Kariera Hordes and Sections

	TYPE 1 HORDE	TYPE 2 HORDE
GENERATION LEVELS	Karimera	Palyeri
	Burung	Banaka
	Karimera	Palyeri
	Burung	Banaka
	Karimera	Palyeri

Note that the sections, unlike kinship terms, are absolute, not relative. If we look from the standpoint of a Karimera man, Palyeri men are in the same generation (or two removed) but in the other kind of horde; if we look from the standpoint of a Banaka man, Palyeri men are in the same kind of horde but in a different generation (one up or one down).

There are no terms designating the units Karimera + Burung or Palyeri + Banaka, though they are so easy to distinguish analytically as patrilineal moieties that many anthropologists have misleadingly done so. Nor are there terms for the two types of hordes, except that a man may distinguish between "my people" (his horde and those with the same sections) and "they people" (those with the other two sections) (Radcliffe-Brown 1913, 1951:39; Scheffler n.d.).

A man must marry a girl from the opposite kind of horde, but his own generation. Thus

Karimera	marries a Palyeri,	children are Burung
Burung	marries a Banaka,	children are Karimera
Palyeri	marries a Karimera,	children are Banaka
Banaka	marries a Burung,	children are Palyeri

The system of kinship classification reflects this division of the social universe, though just how has been hotly debated by specialists. All relatives are divided into two categories, *cross* and *parallel*. They are further distinguished by sex and generation. The kin term *nyuba* denotes "cross" relatives of opposite sex and own generation. These include a man's mother's brother's daughter, father's sister's daughter, mother's mother's brother's daughter's daughter, and a great many other cousins, second, third, fourth, fifth, and others more distant. For a Karimera man, any Palyeri girl (unless she is in the grandparent or grandchild generation) is his *nyuba;* and these are the only girls he can legitimately marry. These include his first cousins, and among the Kariera a young man has a legitimate first claim on the daughter of his maternal uncle. Sister exchange between two men of the appropriate sections is also a favored marriage arrangement.

It seems best to view the section system as a way some Australians invented, probably not very far in the tribal past, for conceptualizing complex kinship systems in simpler fashion. The alliance systems very probably are much older and were conceptualized, as in South India and Melanesia, in terms of kinship categories—though the elaboration of section systems and the further complicating of alliance systems may have gone hand in hand. Kinship terms and section labels work in quite different, though complementary, ways. The section terms simplify the system because to act appropriately to a person from another horde, perhaps a stranger, you do not have to know genealogical relatedness; you need only know what section he or she belongs to. For Australian tribesmen, who often spent part of their lives traveling on "walkabout" far from home, such a scheme was a great invention.

In more common Australian systems, notably the anthropologically famous Aranda system, the four sections are subdivided into eight; a man must marry a girl from one of them, who by the rules of the system can be no closer than a second cousin. Other systems, like the equally classic Murngin, are even more complicated and are fraught with internal inconsistency.

Specialists on Australian kinship are far from agreed that Lévi-Strauss' ingenious interpretation of these as symmetrical alliance systems fits the facts. A recent insight is that over much of Australia, marital alliance involved not the exchange of wives between local descent groups, but the exchange of mothers-in-law. A young girl (in an Aranda-type system) who is a young man's mother's mother's brother's daughter, or who is classed with her in the kinship terminology, is bestowed on him (by his and her elders) *as his mother-in-law.* From that time onward, there is an avoidance relationship between them; but the daughters she later bears when she marries become his wives (Shapiro 1970).

The great complexity of Australian kinship and marriage systems, and the way they have been borrowed piecemeal to keep up with the Joneses, and further elaborated in ways inconsistent with the system they have been grafted onto, should warn us against assuming that tribal cultures are stable, ancient, and internally well-integrated. As Barnes has commented:

Aborigines, like anthropologists, enjoy making systems . . . and it is easier in Arnhem Land, as elsewhere, to make a model in the mind than to persuade one's neighbors to abide by its rules through the generations. If, as Lévi-Strauss maintains, totems are good to think with [see §17 and §65], then equally subsections and kinship categories are good to play with. It seems likely that some Aborigines in northeastern Arnhem Land are still in a muddle about subsections and terminology, while others have a clear picture of how the system ought to work, as they see it. (1967:45—46)

Lévi-Strauss interpreted the Australian section systems, however complicated, as still symmetrical or "direct": the group yours gives wives to gives wives back to your own. Lévi-Strauss showed how an alternative form is possible, under a rule that your group gives its women to one set of groups and receives women from a different set of groups. Such a system of *indirect exchange (échange géneralisé),* Lévi-Strauss argues, risks more in the gamble of renouncing one's own women—but the rewards in terms of social integration are greater. No pair of groups can

achieve self-sufficiency and hence social isolation—and this interdependence of social units makes possible a "global integration."

The societies practicing indirect exchange lie mainly in Southeast Asia—Assam, Burma, and a few parts of Indonesia. Ideologically they conceive their systems as "marrying in a circle," and phrase their marriage rule in terms of a kinship category, including mother's brother's daughter and many more distantly related girls, from which a man must select a wife. Both the "circles" and "mother's brother's daughter marriage" have led to endless confusion and controversy among the scholars who, following Lévi-Strauss' lead, have pored over the meager evidence on these groups.

The picture that has emerged is of systems far more complex and dynamic than marrying in a circle would suggest. These societies are usually composed of many small localized patrilineages. It is these lineages that serve as "alliance groups" in the marriage system. These lineages may be ranked, and may be markedly unequal in status, as with the Kachin of Burma (Leach 1954), or they may be unranked, as among the Purum of Assam. In either case, marriage becomes an instrument of political negotiation and status. A few marriages in each generation may serve to maintain the political status of lineages. Other marriages are less important and in some societies need not necessarily conform to the marriage rule.

From the standpoint of any single lineage, some girls may be nonmarriageable because their lineages share common descent at a higher segmentary level. Some lineages may simply be too far away for marriage to be likely. But there remain two other crucial categories of lineages. There are lineages whose girls have married men of one's own lineage (they are "wife-givers") and lineages to which one's own has given women (they are "wife-takers"). The basic marriage rule is that no other lineage can be both wife-giver and wife-taker. While actual patterns of marriage may deviate from the ideal model, most "wrong marriages" (at least those that are politically consequential) are treated *as if* they were right ones, and hence simply readjust the shifting network of alliances. Such an alliance system is usually prominently reflected in the cosmological scheme of a people. The contrast between wife-givers and wife-takers is mirrored in cosmological dualisms (right-left, sun-moon) and in ritual symbolism. This "global" and encompassing structure has led Needham (1962) to make a sharp distinction between such societies, which "prescribe" marriage into a particular category, and others which merely specify "preferred" marriages. This distinction has led to great controversy and to fission between Needham and his students (Korn 1973, Needham 1974) and Lévi-Strauss (1966) himself.

The endless debates about "prescriptive marriage" systems have seemed to outsiders the height of trivial and sterile formalism in kinship studies. But beneath the technical argument has lain a central problem we encountered with Smiths and Joneses, and glimpsed again in discussing kinship and social relations. There is a wide gulf between the ideal conceptual models and ideologies central in a people's thought world and real people competing, choosing, and manipulating. Real people live in a world of ecological pressures, economic and political strivings, individual variability, and the whims of life history. A way of life consists, in a sense, of accommodations and adjustments between a lived-in world and a thought-of world. The debates about "prescriptive marriage" basically reflect the different perspectives we get if we focus on the pragmatic, complex, and muddled patterns of living (in which case the neat formal design of a "marriage system"

dissolves away) or on the crystalline models of thinking (so that the design comes into sharp and clear focus). Anthropologists are still looking for a way to keep both perspectives centrally in view at once.

49.
The Family in Comparative Perspective

The family seems to us the most fundamental social group, the core of a social system. Why, then, not choose this as a starting place for the study of social organization? Why wait until we have dealt with kinship, descent, and marriage? The answer is that the structure of the family, in comparative perspective, is so intricately related to principles of descent and marriage that these principles provide a necessary background for understanding forms of the family.

As usual there are some messy problems of definition. Is "the family" universal? If so, in what sense? Some analysts have emphasized the universality of nuclear family and its crucial functions in all societies of child-rearing and the management of sex. Others argue that this confuses the biological universality of the nuclear family with its social relevance— and point to cases like the Nayar (Case 19) where the "nuclear family" is not a residential unit, an economic corporation, or in fact socially important at all. There are also societies, especially in the Caribbean, where a high percentage of households contain a mother and her children as the stable core. If there is a man around the house, it is as mother's lover, and such arrangements are transitory; the man is not a "father." Such households, which occur with substantial frequency among black working-class Americans, have misleadingly been called matrifocal. (We will return to these phenomena and their interpretation in §72).

Some theorists have tried to solve the problem of variation by distinguishing between the *family*—as a cluster of positions to and through which an individual traces crucial kinship relations—and the *household* or *domestic group*—as a social group, usually corporate, of people who reside together. Even here, the role of "father" is highly variable, and its component elements (mother's husband, mother's lover, begetter of children, guardian of children, and so on) can be differentially divided and assigned to different people. (Thus among the Nayar, mother's husband is in one sense the man who ritually married her before menarche, in another sense her current lover(s); the guardian of the children is mother's brother).

It is probably more useful to say that universally the core of the family is a mother and her dependent children (recall the primate social unit of mother plus young). The usually male roles of providing nurturance (food and labor), being mother's sexual partner, and assuming disciplinary authority and jural responsibility over children can then be assigned to mother's mate, the children's father (forming a nuclear or conjugal family); or all of them but the sexual element can be provided by mother's brothers (forming a consanguine family, as among the Nayar); or the functions may be divided between mate and brothers. Viewing mother and children as forming the family nucleus enables us to fit into the comparative spectrum some of the arrangements that have grown out of women's liberation movements, particularly ones where sexual bonds between women and legal and economic independence have eliminated men from all or most of the roles they have historically played.

Household groups can then be seen as building on the family core—by adding father, by stringing conjugal families together by a rule of descent, by linking several mother-child units to a single husband-father, and so on.

A crucial key to the structure of households and their aggregation into larger communities is a society's system of *residence rules*. Most crucial are rules for postmarital residence. If the wife normally goes to live with her husband's people (virilocal residence), or the husband goes to live with his wife's people (uxorilocal residence), this has a cumulative effect on who lives where and how they are related to one another. But this distinction still does not neatly classify all residence possibilities. Both postmarital residence among the Smiths and Joneses and postmarital residence in the Trobriands are virilocal (Case 27; recall that a young man moves back before marriage to the territory of his matrilineage and hence his mother's brothers). To distinguish them the first has been called viripatrilocal and the second viriavunculocal" ("man's mother's brother's place"). Neolocal residence occurs where the couple establish residence separate from both husband's and wife's families. By further ingenuity in naming, we can come up with a fairly comprehensive scheme.

The problem is to make such classifications meaningful in terms of the culture under study. What does "-local" mean? Is a couple residing across the street from the husband's parents and two doors down from the wife's parents living virilocally, uxorilocally, or neolocally? And how can this be compared with a society where husband's father lives in the same tent and wife's father lives across a hundred miles of desert? What does one do about variation, where some people follow one pattern and others another? As Goodenough (1956) has shown (Case 10), classifying residence can best be done in terms of the categories of the people under study. What do *they* conceive as the alternative forms of residence and how do they decide among them? We run grave risks of classifying as separate "types" two cases they view as equivalent, and classifying as instances of the same "type" choices they regard as different. Talking about "residence rules" cross-culturally can be a useful shorthand, but it disguises many hazards for the unwary. Gone are the days when we talked with confidence of a tribe where "residence is matrilocal"—things are always less simple than that.

We can now survey some of the possible forms of households, while bearing in mind that different forms often occur in the same society. We will see how the forms that seem strange or complicated are a logical expression of the forms of descent, marriage, and residence we have already examined.

Nuclear Family Households

Where nuclear families stand alone, they can best be understood in terms of the *absence* of factors that produce more complex forms. They occur where descent does not link unilineally related men or women together (father and two married sons, married sisters) into larger households and where plural marriage does not produce partial replication (as with three wives and their children, with a common father).

Thus nuclear families, by themselves, tend to occur where descent groups are absent or of lesser importance. In such societies, emphasizing bilateral kinship, nuclear families carry a very heavy "functional load"—as in our own society and among the Eskimo. It is not by chance that our examples come from each end of the continuum of societal scale and complexity. It is in the middle, in tribal societies, that proliferations of more complex households are concentrated.

In bilaterally organized societies such as the Subanun (Case 30), the nuclear family serves as the center of a child's social universe—in it he or she is reared, is cared for, grows up, and learns the culture. Sexual relations and hence reproduction and the continuity of the society are focused in the family. It serves as an economic corporation, owning property and producing (or acquiring) and consuming food. Linkages between nuclear families produce the larger social and political units—bands, villages, and neighborhoods—of a society. However, in other societies nuclear families may be culturally distinguished and socially important, yet be components of larger local groupings that we can also call "households" at a higher level, as we will see shortly.

Complex Households Based on Multiple Marriage

Since polygyny is so common—and is the dominant mode of marriage in tribal Africa and some other areas—polygynous household groupings represent a major form of local grouping. Organizationally the problems in such systems lie in the relationship between co-wives. If we forget about the problems of sharing the same sex partner and use our intuitions about wives sharing the same kitchen, using the same checkbook, and agreeing on whose children get what, we perceive vividly the difficulties of polygynous households.

The most common solution is for each wife to have her own household. The husband plays a secondary role in each; and where, as is common, a wife is sexually taboo for a long period after childbirth, the isolation of households is increased. The households are seldom fully independent economically, since a principal motive for polygyny is to create a joint work force and pool the productive efforts (as well as the reproductive efforts) of several women. But the "subhouseholds" are in many respects separate social units. This does not solve all tensions in polygynous households, and the roles of co-wives are always a delicate matter: there is, for example, a correlation between polygyny and witchcraft accusations.

When co-wives share a single household and hearth, the problems can be multiplied. Some African societies establish separate households for co-wives except when they are sisters (sororal polygyny)—on the assumption that sisters can manage, as they did in childhood, to coexist in the same household.

Case 39: Polygynous Households among the Tallensi

The polygynous family among the Tallensi of Ghana (Cases 12 and 24) well illustrates both this mode of domestic organization and the way it can provide building blocks for larger domestic groupings. (Here recall the Tallensi emphasis on agnatic descent and the ritual focus on the first-born.) Most younger Tallensi men have only a single wife. Their domestic family, centered in a small courtyard and a mud-walled sleeping room, with kitchen and granary, may live in a single homestead, enclosed within mud walls. Sometimes the husband's mother would live with them, and as senior woman would have a separate courtyard and living quarters. More often, in this society where local groups are shallow patrilineages, the man with only one wife will occupy an "apartment" within the homestead of a father or an older brother.

By the time he is middle-aged, a man of substance will have acquired two or more wives. He probably will be living in his own homestead. Each wife will have her own little courtyard, her own sleeping room, her own kitchen. She and her children comprise a *dug* or domestic household group. The senior wife (or the husband's mother) is a kind of leader in the women's realm, but for each wife her apartment is the center of life, a place where she is in charge and where only her children and her husband have free access.

The male head of the homestead group controls the family granary, which supplies the component *dug* groups, and to which they all contribute the produce of their labor. The importance of the *dug* unit in Tallensi social structure is profound. The lines of lineage segmentation normally do not cut across *dug* units, but divide half-brothers with the same father, and their descendants.

Though relations between co-wives are usually fairly amicable due to the separation of their spheres of influence, quarrels over shares of grain, rights of children, and other matters are common. The arrangement of apartments of co-wives reflects their social relationships:

Wives who are clan sisters will usually have adjoining quarters; wives who get on badly will be put in well-separated rooms. . . . If a woman has a quarrelsome disposition . . . her quarters will be separated from those of the next-door wife by a low . . . wall. (Fortes 1949:58)

In the case of polyandry, men and their children cannot build separate households in a mirror image of the polygynous form. A woman cohabiting with several men cannot produce a child by each of them at once. Co-husbands then share a single household. Because they are so often brothers, the problems are minimized in some respects, but structurally these are still unusual forms.

Complex Households Based on Common Descent

Patrilineal or matrilineal descent, and a pattern of residence that aligns a core of lineally related men or women together in a local group, combine to produce many complex family structures. Extended or joint families are produced when, with patrilineal descent, a father and his married sons form a household or two brothers form a household. Often this is a second-order grouping, where the component nuclear families act separately for some purposes and together for others. Extended family households are also possible with matrilineal descent, as among the Zuni and Hopi (Case 26).

The line between households and larger local groupings becomes somewhat arbitrary once we start in this direction. That is, in a segmentary lineage system there will be at each level a group of lineally related kin and their spouses: a man and his wife; a man, his wife, and his sons and their wives; patrilineal first and second cousins and their wives; and so on. For most societies it probably is sensible to use "household" to refer to groups that use a single dwelling and eat meals together (a "hearth group"). But here again, it is impossible to build definitions that make sense of a particular culture under study yet work equally well for all other cultures. Extended family households take many forms, and can be based on parent-child or sibling-sibling links.

Case 40: Patrilineal Extended Families among the Tiv

Among the Tiv of Nigeria, whose segmentary patrilineage system has been glimpsed in Case 25, the domestic unit of production is the compound group. The Tiv compound is an oval or circular arrangement of huts and granaries, with a central open space that is the "center of Tiv family life" (Bohannan and Bohannan 1968:15). The nucleus of the compound group is a senior man, the oldest in the group, who acts as its head. He arbitrates disputes, controls magical forces, and supervises production.

He has several wives, each of whom would normally have a separate hut in the compound. The compound group typically includes the head's minor children and unmarried daughters and his married sons and their wives and children. To this extended family core may be added a younger brother of the head and his wives and children or a nephew of the head. There may also be outsiders—friends or age-mates of the men at the compound—who live there. The membership of the compound group, especially these others attached to the extended family core, may shift considerably over time. The genealogical composition and spatial arrangement of one Tiv compound are diagrammed in Figure 14.2.

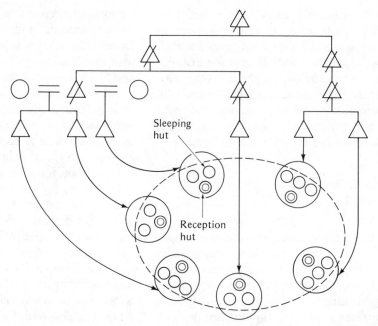

Figure 14.2.   Map and genealogy of a Tiv compound. (After a diagram in P. Bohannan 1954b.)

While in a sense each wife who has a separate hut and her children constitute a separate domestic unit, the larger compound group—a patrilineal extended family augmented by outsiders—is the central domestic unit of everyday Tiv life and of collective economic enterprise. (Bohannan and Bohannan 1968)

A "rule of residence" can produce unilineally related groupings of kin even where no ideology of descent is emphasized. Thus in a *patrilocal band* (§17), where the sons of band members stay put and their wives come in from outside, most male members will come to be related through male links. Moreover, in a tribal society a rule of unlineal descent may be combined with just the opposite rule of residence. Descent groups may be formed by matrilineal descent though a woman goes to live with her husband's paternal kin. In such societies, other factors may keep the men of a matrilineage clustered closely enough that they can still act as an effective corporation. And rarely, as among the Shavante of Central Brazil (Maybury-Lewis 1967), patrilineages occur in conjunction with uxorilocal residence. It should be remembered that even where the rule of descent and the rule of residence correspond, they may not result in neat unilineal groups actually living together. We have seen how, where patrilineal descent is strongly emphasized in ideology, as with the Nuer of Africa, local groups still may include an assortment of bilateral kin and affines as well as patrilineally related men (see Gough 1971).

This leads to the observation that the gulf between an ideal form (nuclear family, extended family household, polygynous household) and the composition of actual households is often very wide. Households are always breaking up due to parental death, divorce, and the like—with widows, orphans, old people, and others attaching to existing households. In some societies, adoption (the jural assignment of a child to new parents, which may or may not entail breaking ties with the old ones) and fosterage are very common. In part of Polynesia, adoption is so frequent as to be almost the normal form. Here, on islands where land is very scarce, it serves among other things as a way of evening out population imbalance between property-owning groups.

If we try to classify the households we actually encounter, we run the risk of defining almost as many types as there are households. A major step in the right direction came from Meyer Fortes (1959), who showed that many different household types represent the same kind of family at different stages in a *developmental cycle*. A household group characteristically passes through a "phase of expansion" during which children are born, a "phase of dispersion" (that may overlap the first) during which children marry, and a "phase of replacement" ending with the death of the original couple. The composition of a household (and hence what type it is according to older theories) depends on what stage of the cycle it happens to be in when we observe it.

We can go even further than this. A single set of cultural principles for making decisions about household membership, descent group membership, and the like, may have extremely variable social outcomes when the principles are applied to the ever-changing circumstances of actual cases. Some families have all daughters, others all sons, and so on. We know a lot about how boys behave toward their mothers' brothers in many societies, but much less about what they do when mother has no brothers.

An emphasis on cultural principles for making decisions in the varying circumstances of social life promises to help to close the gap between the ideal conceptual world of a people and the muddled patterns of actual living.

Thus among the Kwaio of the Solomon Islands (Case 29), where the tiny settlements normally consist of one or several nuclear family households, I encountered one settlement consisting of fourteen people in five households. Yet none of these households included a married couple, nor were there any units of parent and child. The whole settlement consisted of adult bachelors and spinsters and the children of deceased relatives they were fostering. Yet this strange collection of motley households, a classifier's nightmare, was the cumulative result of a series of culturally appropriate decisions made in the face of adversity. If we look more carefully at the cultural principles for deciding among the alternative paths that life opens, rather than simply looking at, classifying, and counting the social groupings that result, we can make sense of the most complex patterns we find.

50.
Kinship and Community

We have already touched on local groups at several points. In discussing cultural ecology, we saw how the emergence of sedentary communities—and their size and permanence—are quite closely tied to subsistence technology and environment. In discussing kinship and descent, we saw how kin groups can be localized; and in taking a comparative look at the family, we glimpsed the forms that these smallest local groups can take. Later we will look at the politics of territorial units, and hence at larger spatial blocks. But it is worth dealing more closely, though briefly, with local groupings in the midrange—*communities*. Communities emerge as important mainly where agriculture makes possible sedentary residence. Given the recency of the agricultural revolution in comparison to man's whole stay on earth, stable and settled communities are a rather late development (see Chapter 5). In tribal societies they characteristically are interlocked with kinship organization. Yet as technological knowledge, market economies, and the like, have increased the scale and density of settlement, localization has become more important and kinship less so. With the rise of cities, or movement to cities in developing countries, kinship recedes into the background. (In Chapter 23, we will examine an emerging anthropological concern with life in urban settings.)

Communities can be roughly classified according to scale. In some agricultural societies, especially those practicing shifting horticulture, homesteads or homestead clusters may be scattered around the landscape and may be moved frequently to follow gardening cycles. On a slightly larger scale, *hamlets* range from a handful of households to a score of them or more. *Villages* contain hundreds or even thousands of people. The development of *towns* has been comparatively late, the culmination of technological and economic changes we looked at in Chapters 5 and 7.

In tribal and peasant societies, it is useful to ask the following questions about the structure of a community.

1. Is it composed of smaller units that are spatially separate and similar to one another in structure?

A village or hamlet may be composed simply of separate households, or it may be some kind of composite. That is, it can be something like an orange in structure, composed of distinguishable segments. Such segments may be clearly visible to an outsider or simply invisible cultural lines between the "pieces." One recurrent pattern is a separation into subhamlets, a cluster of which comprise a village. Another common pattern divides a community into residential areas, or *wards,* with some social and political separation.

2. Are communities or segments associated with descent groups or other kinship units? And if so, is each segment associated with one group or several?

The community may be located in a group's territory and contain its men and their wives. But alternately, the community may be composed of members of several groups. Whether kin groups are spatially segregated into segments, so that each ward or subhamlet corresponds to a descent group, is structurally critical. Even where the segments themselves contain more than one descent group, it is crucial whether at the level of individual households there is separation according to kin group or whether households are "mixed together." If the latter, the arrangement can usually be interpreted as an expression of the precedence of community over kinship. This has been the trend in societies of increased scale and complexity.

3. Are the communities socially independent?

Do most marriages take place *within* the community? In tribal societies one often finds community exogamy, where each settlement (or cluster of settlements) is associated with an exogamous descent group. Here intermarriage provides a linkage between settlements, and no settlement is in the long run socially self-sufficient. Other communities, especially where they are larger and composed of segments, are largely self-contained. That is, most marriages take place within the village, so that in terms of kinship and other social ties the system is a more closed one. Such relatively self-contained communities are particularly characteristic of peasant societies. Economically the closure and self-sufficiency of communities is likely to be much less pronounced. Even in the tribal world, networks of trade and economic specialization are likely to bind communities into wider systems. We will see a vivid example of such a system in Chapter 15 in looking at Trobriand economics. Economic ties beyond the community become even more important in peasant societies. As we will see in Chapter 22, one of the

difficulties in studying peasants is the contrast between the relative closure of the village socially and its openness as part of wider economic and political systems.

The Trobriand Islanders, whom we met in the last two chapters and will encounter again, usefully illustrate the structure of local communities in a tribal society and the way this can articulate with the social and cosmological order of a people.

Case 41: The Trobriand Village

Recall that the Trobrianders are organized in corporate matrilineal subclans, each of which is associated with a territory by traditions of ancestral emergence. In the simplest case, the Trobriand village is the "headquarters" of a single subclan. This means that all or most of its male members, and their wives, live there, while the women of the subclan live elsewhere with their husbands.

As we noted in Case 27, however, a great many Trobriand villages contain segments of two or more subclans. In these villages, where subclan and village do not coincide, we can see that in many ways the whole village—not the subclan—is the most important social unit. "The whole village is the context of family life" (Powell 1969a:188), not simply a person's own subclan segment.

Through processes glimpsed in Case 27, the village may have one "owning" subclan and other subclan segments that are attached to it. (Some Trobriand villages are in fact "compound," in that there are two "owning" subclans, each of which may have subclan segments attached to it—a complexity we can ignore.) The importance of the village, as well as the individual corporate subclans based in it, comes to the fore in gardening: "The village . . . is the effective unit of economic activities. . . . In the making of gardens, whole villages . . . operate as organized corporate bodies under the direction of sub-clan leaders and garden magicians." (Powell 1969b:581)

The spatial arrangement of the Trobriand village reflects both its unity and the partial separation of the subclan segments that make it up. Figure 14.3 shows the plan of a large and internally complex Trobriand village with a very high ranking "chief" (see Case 54). The arrangement is roughly circular, consisting of a central plaza with dancing ground and burial ground, and two concentric rings of buildings with a "street"

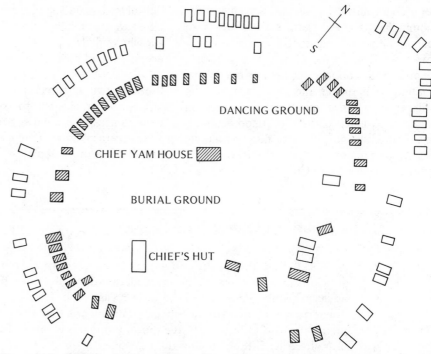

Figure 14.3.   Plan of a Trobriand Village: This village, Omarakana, is the center of the most prosperous district and the seat of the most powerful "chief." (After Malinowski.)

between them. The outer ring of buildings consists of domestic dwelling houses. The inner ring consists of yam storehouses and the bachelor houses in which the amorous adventuring of the young is centered.

In this particular village the presence of the very important "chief" shapes the distribution of residents around the outer circle. As we will see, "chiefs" are entitled to polygynous marriage, and this one had many wives, as well as outsiders resident as his "retainers." In a more typical village, each subclan segment based there would be associated with a sector of the circle. Thus the outer circle of buildings serves to emphasize the partial separation of the segments, while the inner plaza symbolizes the unity of the village.

Such a circular arrangement of the village is not an arbitrary custom. As Lévi-Strauss (1963b) has shown, the circular villages of Indians in central Brazil and other peoples represent a mapping out of basic cosmological principles. For the Trobriands he suggests that the concentric rings reflect a series of symbolic polarities in Trobriand culture.

A circular street runs around the storehouses, with the huts of the married couples built at the outer edge. This Malinowski called the "profane" part of the village. Not only are there oppositions between central and peripheral and between sacred and profane. There are other aspects too. In the storehouses of the inner ring raw food is stored and cooking is not allowed. . . . Food can be cooked and consumed only in or around the family dwellings of the outer ring. The yam-houses are more elaborately constructed and decorated than the dwellings. Only bachelors may live in the inner ring, while married couples must live on the periphery. And finally, the two concentric rings . . . are opposed with respect to sex: "Without overlabouring the point, the central place might be called the male portion of the village and the street that of the women" (Malinowski 1929:10).

In the Trobriands we see, therefore, a complex system of oppositions between sacred and profane, raw and cooked, celibacy and marriage, male and female, central and peripheral. (Lévi-Strauss 1963:137)

One of the most interesting patterns of community organization is that in which the larger communities are modeled on the structure of segmentary lineages. Fustel de Coulanges (1864), in a classic early study of social structure, showed that in ancient Greece and Rome the patrilineal extended family household centering around a sacred hearth fire and shrine provided a model that was replicated not only at higher levels of lineage structure (with lineage shrines and sacred fires) but also in the city-states. Thus an ancient city-state had its sacred fire and shrine symbolizing its unity as though it were a descent group. A strikingly similar pattern has been described by Vogt (1965) among the modern highland Maya of southern Mexico (a pattern we will examine in Chapter 22, Case 90). Vogt suggests that this capacity to replicate a social and ritual pattern at successively higher levels may have enabled the pre-Columbian Maya to create the great temple centers for which they are famous.

51.
Beyond Kinship: Age Sets and Sodalities

Before we turn to economic and political processes in tribal societies, it is worth looking very briefly at forms of social grouping based not on kinship but on age or voluntary association.

In many tribal societies, most notably in East Africa, central Brazil, and parts of New Guinea, social groupings based on age cut across social groupings based on kinship. In *age set* systems, young people—usually only men—are grouped together into a named, corporate unit. As they get older, they stay together in the same group. Thus what was a group of young men is 30 years later a group of middle-aged men; and by that time there may be two new age sets of younger men. These systems often are very complicated, particularly in East Africa where they are most common. A distinction has been made between *cyclical* age set systems, where the same age set appears again every several generations like a duck in a shooting gallery, and *progressive* age set systems, where a named age set appears only once. The distinction is particularly interesting because cyclical and progressive age set systems tend to be mirrored in corresponding contrasts in time reckoning and in the cosmology and world view of a people.

In some African societies, young men of warrior age are separated from normal ties of kinship and community. Most famous anthropologically are the age regiments of the warlike Zulu and warrior age grades of the Masai, where unmarried men form tightly-knit and disciplined segments largely cut off from everyday community life. The Karimojong illustrate a more typical East African system of age sets.

Case 42: Karimojong Age Sets

The Karimojong, tribal pastoralists of Uganda whose cattle-centered economy we glimpsed in Case 6, have an elaborate age-set system.

The general outlines are fairly simple and straightforward. Men are initiated, in young adulthood, into a named age set. Every five or six years, the age set into which men are being initiated is closed, and a new age set is formally opened. At any time, there will be some six age sets active, spanning an age range from young adulthood to old age.

The age sets are grouped into larger divisions or generation sets. A generation set consists of five age sets and bears one of four names. The arrangement of age sets and age grades is cyclical, as shown in Figure 14.4.

There will at any time be two adjacent generation sets represented among the living—A and B, or B and C, or C and D, or D and A. One will be senior, the other junior, and this relationship of seniority and juniority is pervasively related throughout the system.

The generation sets are symbolically paired in alternate fashion, so that B and D and A and C are symbolically linked. Members of one pair wear brass ornaments and are symbolically "yellow"; the other pair wear copper and are symbolically "red." The names of the generation sets remain constant, hence "recycle." The names of age sets are chosen from a stock associated with each pair of generation sets, so they reappear, but not in a fixed sequence.

Note that only two generation sets can be actively represented. This

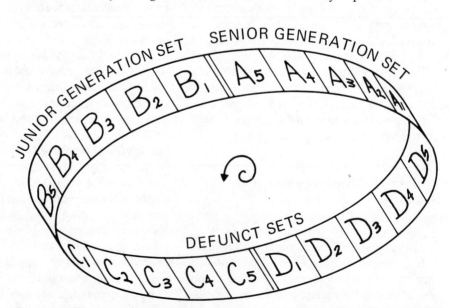

Figure 14.4.   The Karimojong age set system (schematic). (Adapted from Dyson-Hudson (1963).)

occasions no problems halfway through the cycle, when, for example, the last three age sets of the A's constitute the senior generation set (A3, A4, A5—though it will mainly be A5's and some A4's who are still alive and active); and the first two or three age sets of the B's (B1, B2, B3) constitute the junior generation set. But 15 years later, almost all the A's will have died, the B's will be chafing at their juniority, and there will be young men who should appropriately be initiated as C's (hence converting B into the senior generation set). At this stage, the A's ritually bow out and retire from the active scene.

The relationship of seniority and juniority is clearly marked between generation sets and is quite explicitly modeled on the father-son relationship. The senior generation set is in charge of initiating new members into the junior, and in ritual and in secular political contexts the power of elders, deriving from their wisdom, is constantly reinforced.

Each age set is similarly in a junior relationship to the ones above it and in a senior relationship to those below it. How this works apparently depends on where the dividing line is between generation sets. Consider the point where the A's have just retired, the B's have become senior and have opened the first of the C age sets. If all the B's exerted their seniority en masse toward the few C's, there would be too many seniors and not enough juniors; so presumably the B1's and B2's exert authority and seniority vis-à-vis the B4's and B5's, as well as C1's. At the other end of the scale, 25 years later, most of the B's will have died and many of the C1's will be acting as senior (to the point that they can if need be initiate C5's, if there are no survivors among those who have gone B4). Each extant age set has a defined part to play in public life. Senior age sets sit together in litigation; appeals are made to their judgment, and they finally deliver a verdict. The junior age set is engaged much of the time in performing services for their elders—collecting wood, serving meat, performing dances. Each age set is, in addition, in a formally subordinate relationship to the one immediately above, whose members are its "masters"; the ornamental insignia worn by members of an age set are established and limited by the one above it. Complex rules about which brothers, or half-brothers, are initiated in what order help to keep age set relationships parallel to other status relationships.

All this does not imply that Karimojong age sets are tightly organized, tribal-wide corporate groups. Members do not live together, as with the age sets of the Masai and the military age regiments of the Zulu. They continue to play normal familial roles and to live in local groups or "sections" partly based on shallow ties of agnatic descent. Moreover, these sections or clusters of them, scattered widely across barren grazing lands, conduct their age set initiations separately. The public affairs in which age sets function as such are local and regional, not tribal-wide. That means that though all sections of the Karimojong are at the same stage of the age set cycle and all members have common insignia and a common name, the corporate nature of tribe-wide age sets is very tenuous. A Karimojong would not know some fellow-members of his age set from other regions, though he would have a close bond with those of his local area. Yet Dyson-Hudson (1963), their ethnographer, suggests that with such a scattered pattern of settlement and so much individual mobility in pastoral resource use, the age sets perform a crucial function of enabling a man to relate to nonkin, even strangers, in patterned ways and to receive hospitality and protection among members of alien groups.

Age grades differ from age sets in that they constitute a series of levels through which people, usually men, pass in the course of the life cycle. Thus young people are initiated into one age grade; and then, several years later, collectively or one-by-one, into the next higher age grade. Such a sequence of age grades often involves progressive revelation of the sacred mysteries commanded by older men.

The social functions of age sets and age grades vary widely. They may fight together, live together, and so on. In view of the preponderant anthropological attention to kinship, it is interesting that age groups sometimes counterbalance kin groups in providing for collective security in blood feuding and protecting age mates' rights vis-à-vis their own kinsmen. The function of age groups as complementary to, or a substitute for, kinship ties has been emphasized by Eisenstadt (1956) in the major study of age as an organizing principle.

Anthropologists—a few of them—have long been interested in *voluntary associations*— groupings in tribal societies more or less equivalent to fraternities, clubs, and lodges in Western societies. Thus as early reports came in on spectacular or dramatic secret societies such as the Dukduk and

Tamate societies of Melanesia, secret fraternal orders in Africa such as the homicidal Leopards, and Plains Indian military societies, anthropologists tried to sort them out, trace their development, interpret their functions. Webster (1932), Lowie (1920), and Wedgwood (1930) made useful early attempts at synthesis. But though anthropologists have long taken note of such phenomena, not many of them have been very interested. Tiger's (1969) *Men in Groups,* while rightly criticized by feminists for its caricaturing of biological sex roles and its slighting of political action and collective participation by women, has usefully redirected attention to nonkinship groupings in evolutionary perspective. There have also been good studies of voluntary associations in urban situations, such as Little's study of the Poro and Banton's study of the dancing *Compins* of Freetown, Sierra Leone (Case 99, Chapter 23); and studies of the informal networks and nonkinship groupings and coalitions of complex societies (Chapter 23).

At this stage, a glimpse of two classic Melanesian "secret societies" will illustrate the formal and elaborate voluntary associations or *sodalities* found in some parts of the tribal world.

Case 43: Melanesian Secret Societies

The Dukduk secret society of the Bismarck Archipelago in Melanesia takes into its lower grades of membership virtually all male members of the communities in which it is established. Parents wish their sons to belong for the prestige and privileges membership gives. A man who stays outside would almost certainly run afoul sooner or later of one of its secret rules, and so be subject to fines amounting to more that the "fees" which entrance calls for. The higher grades of the society, however, with their closer relation to the "great mystery," are reserved for important men. Entrance and passage through these grades become progressively more difficult and expensive, especially in terms of ceremonial wealth distribution. The innermost circle comprises the most important leaders in the area. The Dukduk conducts elaborate private and public rituals, notable for their masked figures. The Dukduk society serves subtle political functions by linking together with common rules and rites communities that have no ties other than the periodic arrival of the masked Dukduk figures. (Case 46, in Chapter 15, deals with one of these peoples, the Tolai.)

In the Banks and Torres Islands of Melanesia, a number of men's secret societies or *tamate* are found on each island. A few major societies occur throughout the area. The clubhouses of these societies are set apart and forbidden to women and uninitiated boys. To become a member, a candidate must meet initiatory expenses, which vary according to the prestige and dignity of the society; and he must undergo fasting and seclusion. Once a member, he uses the clubhouse as a center of leisure-time activity, though as novice he must help to prepare meals. The ceremonial activities of the *tamate* involve festive dancing, but also periods of plundering and license when members in elaborate masks and costumes (Figure 14.5) impersonate ghosts and chase women and children. Each society has certain mysteries such as devices that produce the noises of "ghosts."

By and large anthropologists have been even more remiss in studying informal relations of friendship and cooperation that cross cut formal groupings based on kinship, or interact with kinship in the formation of everyday action groups. As I have pointed out (Keesing 1972b), anthropologists know a great deal about formally patterned relations of kinship. But they have ignored or underplayed the role of *friendship* in determining who does what with whom in a small-scale society—though in our own society we are vividly, if only intuitively, aware of the importance of friendship. The behavior of higher primates and other mammals often can be interpreted only if we infer that the animals that hang around together *like* one another; and that seems to be true of humans in all societies ("kinship systems" not withstanding), even though social scientists have so far been not much better than chimpanzees at analyzing friendship.

But anthropologists are making some progress. Far too little is known, still, about the way friendship and informal partnerships in gardening, trade, or other enterprises are woven into the fabric of everyday social life. One of the side dividends from an increasing anthropological concern with the organization of complex societies is that in them one *must* pay attention to the ways individual bonds of friendship, economic strategy, and political alliance operate. In tribal societies anthropologists have tended to ignore them as "outside

Figure 14.5. A masked Tamate Masquerader (Banks Island). (After a drawing by Codrington.)

the system" of descent groups and kinship relations. In modern complex societies, one must face the fact that they *are* the system—and that they can give new insights into the forces that shape actual behavior in tribal societies.

Such a quick survey of the complexities of kinship in tribal societies cannot provide a guide for all the forms of kinship grouping, marriage, and family structure the reader might encounter in the non-Western world. Nor will it enable him or her to pick up any technical journal article on kinship and read it with full understanding (though the reader who has worked carefully through these pages might well be pleasantly surprised). But it equips the reader to carry on to understand economics, politics, and other aspects of the organization of small-scale societies; it will serve as a good stepping stone into a somewhat more detailed and technical summary (such as Keesing 1975 or Fox 1967); and it will enable a student to read with considerable technical comprehension anthropological accounts of tribal societies.

At this stage, having glimpsed the major organizational principles and social groupings of tribal societies, we are in a position to examine the economic foundations on which they build.

ECONOMIC SYSTEMS 15

A Kwaio tribesman of the Solomon Islands, Batalamo, examines secretively the fiber bag of strung shell beads he has hidden away. He inspects the five valuables, made of multiple strings, he has been saving for his mortuary feast. He needs only two more to have enough to present at his feast. That would be a respectable feast—but if he could get three or four more instead of only two, his feast would be widely praised. He smiles, thinking of the reaction of his rivals.

But what about troublesome ancestor Kwateta, who has been making Batalamo's gardens grow badly? A small pig consecrated to Kwateta would straighten that out. But he has no extra piglets now, so that would mean getting one from someone else. He could buy one from Geleniu, but to do that he would have to break up one of his carefully saved valuables. Or he might borrow a piglet from his wife's brother Basuka and return one when his sow bore her litter. Brothers-in-law should help one another, and Basuka owes him a few favors. On the other hand Fuikwai might give him a pig in exchange for being taught that curing magic he has been asking about.

But how, Batalamo wonders, will he contribute to his relative Mae's bridewealth payment next week without using one of his largest saved valuables? If he does not contribute generously, Mae's powerful father will not contribute to Batalamo's feast, and that would mean less prestige.

Batalamo is allocating his resources strategically so as to advance his goals. The models of the economist deal with just such patterns of choice and strategy, their statistical outcomes and complex interaction. But the economist deals with these processes in a very different setting. In a vast and impersonal market economy, money as a common thread of value ties decisions and transactions together into complex and systematic webs.

The economist's models have traced these webs of interconnection with great precision and sophistication.

How can we deal with humans as "economic" strategists, with the complexities of economic interconnection, in a setting as different from ours as the Solomon Islands? Here the resources Batalamo commands include his magical knowledge and past favors as well as his shell valuables, his pigs, and his labor; and the knowledge, favors, and labor cannot normally be exchanged for, or valued in, shell beads. The goals he seeks to advance include shell valuables—but note that he wants more of them so that he can give them away in exchange for *prestige,* not material advantage. He must also "maximize" his relations with ancestors, since without their help his family may sicken and die, and his gardens and feasts may fail (see Case 68, Chapter 19).

The economic anthropologist, studying the whole range of human social settings and customs, can begin with few of the assumptions and "givens" that make the economist's success possible. One must take each case as it comes. But in recent years, detailed studies have greatly enriched our knowledge of economic systems in tribal and peasant societies. Moreover, the gap between the subject matter of economics and economic anthropology is narrowing, as the societies anthropologists study become caught up in wider money economies and as economists turn to the study of developing nations.

Meanwhile, anthropologists have hotly debated wider theoretical issues. Are the basic postulates of Western economics culture-bound and applicable only to market economies, perhaps only to capitalist economies? Or do they also apply to the behavior of Batalamo and Mexican peasants? Should economic anthropology study the allocation of scarce resources (like Batalamo's magic) among alternative goals (like keeping ancestors happy)? Or is this just circular double talk? Should economic anthropologists simply study instead the different ways in which societies produce and distribute the material goods they need to satisfy their physical and social wants?

Whether the formal models of economic theory can be stretched to fit tribal and preindustrial societies has seemed to many a sterile and sectarian debate. But it has acquired a new importance as radical economists increasingly challenge the premises of their own science. The assumptions that individuals everywhere maximize values, and that their competitive strivings generate the economic system, have been viewed by radical critics as rationalizations of capitalist individualism (see Rowthorn 1974). Marxist and other radical reinterpretations of economies, including tribal ones, have given the anthropological debates more substance and urgency.

In the pages to follow, we will touch on these issues. Our primary concern will be how the economic systems of tribal and other non-Western peoples are to be understood, and what light they shed on the human condition. The nature of human nature, the motives that move human action, the relation of the individual to the collective, are questions that lie close to the surface when we look at economic systems; and we will pause to ask them, at least indirectly, even though the answers are not fully clear.

52.
What Is "Economic"?

Robbins' (1935:16) classic view of economics as "the science which studies human behavior as a relationship between ends and scarce means which have alternative uses" has been widely quoted in defining the proper scope for economic anthropology. If we take this view of humans as maximizing values, as choosing between desired goals and allocating scarce resources, we face a frustrating conceptual problem. For we cannot then say that any particular spheres of life, or any particular behavior or institutions, are economic. Rather, all purposive behavior has an economic (that is goal-maximizing) aspect. All behavior involves choices, and almost by definition *every* choice maximizes something, however vague.

Economists, studying a society where money and the market bind together the subsystems of "the economy," need not struggle overmuch to delimit their subject matter: saving money to buy a house instead of spending it to go to a baseball game is clearly economic behavior (though not *just* economic behavior!). But the economic anthropologist who believes that the formal models of economics can be applied to the behavior of Batalamo and his friends finds it more difficult to sort economic behavior from religion or politics or kinship. If economics is *economizing*—relating ends and scarce means—then all behavior has an economic facet, and the "economic system" spreads out in all directions.

Some theorists have sought to define the economic realm in a more flexible, but less broadly inclusive way. Monetary transactions are one form of a more general phenomenon: *exchange*. Exchange systems take many forms, yet they all serve to link individual economic acts into wider networks and entail shared standards of valuation.

But a more powerful way to broaden Western economic concepts derives from the insights of Marx. Economics has basically to do with *production;* with how human groups produce and distribute material goods and how social relations are organized in the labor process. Comparative economics would study the technological means and methods of production, the values that motivate production, the distribution of scarce goods, and the social systems whereby a society organizes productive labor and distributes goods. The producers need not be the consumers, so that systems of exchange and redistribution of surpluses are crucial in understanding how

social groups are bound together and how social classes are defined and interrelated. Hence study of exchange systems must be an important facet of comparative economics. But it cannot be the only facet: in tribal and peasant societies, producers are also very often consumers. The food a family eats, the clothes they wear, the house they live in, all may have been produced by the family itself.

If systems of production are examined in tribal as well as complex societies, it can be persuasively argued that the special models of economics only "fit" a particular subclass of human economies: those where the market principle is dominant. Other kinds of models may be needed to interpret the economies of societies where systems of production and exchange are not based, or are only secondarily based, on market principles.

As we have noted, the debate has begun to seem less arcane and exotic now that the theories of the neoclassical "mainstream" economists have been shaken by broadside attacks by radical theorists. But news of those battles has scarcely reached academic anthropology, beset by its own controversies. We will examine these wider questions of theory shortly. For the moment, looking at systems of production and distribution will serve well in leading us into the heart of a society's economics. Looking comparatively at these systems, we can hope to glimpse a broad forest, and see what part of it the economists are skirmishing in—often themselves unable to see beyond local trees to perceive its full breadth.

53.
Systems of Production

We have already viewed in general terms the way subsistence technology can shape and limit a people's culture and social organization (Chapter 12). Shortly we will look more closely at production in the Trobriand Islands of Melanesia, particularly the agricultural system. Once more the Trobrianders will illustrate crucial contrasts with our society in the organization of work and modes of production.

A crucial side of the organization of any society is the *division of labor*. Every society, however primitive its technology, assigns different tasks to men and women. As we saw in our evolutionary sketch of the human past, a division of labor by sex is apparently old. It has roots in primate specialization for defense and the rearing of young (and the attendant sexual dimorphism). At some stage in hominid evolution, the innovation of food-sharing and the emergence of large-scale hunting extended sexual specialization into the food quest. Among modern hunters and gatherers (§17), gleaning wild foods is primarily the task of women, and hunting is primarily the task of men. With the advent of food-producing, sexual divisions of labor have become more complex and diverse—though always there is a tendency, hearkening back to biological dimorphism, for men to do the tasks most

Subsistence cultivation in Zinacantan, Mexico: A peasant farmer clears a maize field. These Mayan-speaking Indians are discussed in detail in Chapter 22. (Courtesy of John Haviland.)

demanding of sheer physical strength, especially strength of shoulder and arm, and those that require the greatest mobility, because nursing mothers must tend their children.

Where subsistence is based on hunting and gathering (§17), the domestic group is likely to perform many of the subsistence tasks independently. However, band members may group together for hunting large game and other subsistence tasks requiring larger numbers. In primarily horticultural or pastoral societies, domestic groups are also likely to be both producers and consumers, though extended or polygynous family groups may enlarge the productive force. Some forms of productive labor (whether fishing, cultivating, hunting, herding, or other work) are often done by larger units working collectively—lineages, village groups, and the like.

Some specialized goods like tools or pots, and some specialized services like magic, may have to be obtained from outside the domestic group. But the division of labor is simple enough that the bulk of subsistence goods can be produced by members of the household group that consumes them. In tribal societies, full-time specialists among able-bodied adults are rare, though many command special skills or knowledge—as priest, artist, potter, canoe carver, or curer—that provide essential services to the community. As we will shortly see, tribal societies are very often not self-sufficient economically, but are tied together in regional networks of trade whereby scarce raw materials or specialized objects of production are circulated within a region. Different language groups then have a complementary role within a regional ecosystem.

The centering of production in the domestic group in small-scale societies leads Sahlins (1972) to class this as the *domestic mode of production.* Sahlins marshals impressive evidence to show that the domestic units in most tribal societies produce far less than their technology would allow—a point worth pondering when viewing these societies in ecological perspective.

Other reexaminations of modes of production in tribal societies have recently come from European Marxist anthropologists, such as Meillasoux, Terray, and Rey. Somewhat misleadingly, these scholars refer to the *lineage mode of production.* Yet lineage organization may emerge at this level of societal scale and complexity not so much to focus productive labor in larger groups as to enable producing units to band together for collective defense and warfare (see, for example, Sahlins 1961 and Vayda 1961). In societies with lineages, larger-scale work groups very often turn out on close inspection to be composed of motley and variable clusters of kin, friends and neighbors, not simply lineage mates.

The Trobriand Islanders will illustrate production and ecology in a society of tribal scale—though one more internally complex and differentiated than most Melanesian societies. The example will also serve to point in the direction of the systems of differentiated social classes to which we will turn in the next chapter.

Case 44: Trobriand Systems of Production

The Trobriand Islands consist of a flat coral island about 30 miles long and several smaller surrounding islands (Figure 15.1). Trobriand villages are scattered along the west coast, with its shallow lagoons, and in the interior. No single village has access to all the material goods its people need; and nowhere in the Trobriands can one obtain some crucial mate-

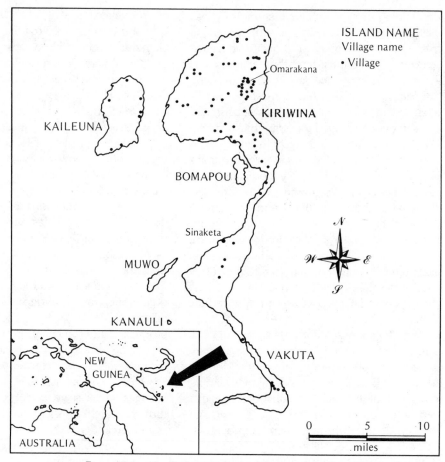

Figure 15.1.   The Trobriand Islands. (After a map by Powell.)

rials. These include the greenstone needed for blades of adzes and axes, which comes from Murua Island to the east; rattan for lashing, and bamboo, which come from Fergusson Island to the south; and clay for pottery, most of which is made in the Amphlett Islands to the south (see Figure 15.2, Case 45).

Furthermore, there are broad regions of specialization on the main island of the Trobriands. Along the western coast, circling the lagoon, are villages that specialize in fishing. The northern section of the island is a rich agricultural area, with villages scattered through the interior. Some villages specialize in a special craft: one in polishing stone tools, another in woodcarving, another in decorating lime pots—all for export. Yet less handsome, everyday articles of almost all kinds can be produced within any Trobriand village—dependent at most on the import of raw materials (Malinowski 1935(1):21–22).

Horticulture is by far the most important source of subsistence in the Trobriands. Our best information comes from the richest and most prosperous (and politically powerful) district in the north. The major crop is the yam, though taro is an important secondary subsistence food.

Because yams can be stored, a regular seasonal cycle of planting and harvest is possible, based on the cycle of winds and rainfall. This annual cycling of the yam season structures many aspects of Trobriand life: trading expeditions, warfare, ceremonies, and even sexual life.

Let us begin the cycle when an area is chosen for the year's cultivation, in this sytem of swidden horticulture. Here we can begin to sort out social units of production. The *gardening team* that will work the large area chosen for gardens usually consists of all residents of a village, even if the men belong to two subclans. In a large village with several subclans, there may be two separate gardening teams.

Even in the simplest case, where the gardening team includes men of only one subclan, it will also include other categories of people—due to the residence pattern where boys grow up in their father's household, then move to their subclan "headquarters." Married women on the gardening team will be in their husbands' places, not their fathers' (where they grew up) or their own (to which their brothers have moved.)

The gardening team does some of its work collectively, under the direction of a garden *magician* who is also its technical expert. The whole garden is divided into smaller squares. Each man has several squares within the large garden, which his *household group* cultivates. Tasks and rituals which call for large-scale cooperation are done by the whole gardening team for the whole garden; daily tasks are done separately by each family.

Trobriand production: Fishermen net mullet using traditional methods on the north coast of Kiriwina Island (1971). (Courtesy of J. W. Leach.)

The Trobrianders distinguish several different modes of collective labor. In some, the villagers or subunits of them join together to do quickly with a concentration of labor jobs that each household group *could* do—with less speed and less camaraderie—by itself. Usually the household whose work of many days is being done in a single day by a large work team provides rations for the workers, who go from plot to plot. In other forms of collective labor, such as erecting large buildings, the work of many men is needed at once to get the job done. Finally, as we will see in detail in Case 54, some Trobrianders command great power and prestige and mobilize and redistribute great surpluses of food and other wealth; their "retainers" contribute labor as well as shares of their crops to maintain the leaders' wealth and prestige. An important leader commands a communal labor force, which erects yam houses, builds canoes, and

Trobriand horticulture: An old man is still planting (in 1972) with a stone-bladed tool. (Courtesy of J. W. Leach.)

undertakes other large-scale projects through which he, and they, derive prestige. Being able to feed a work force, with vegetables that have been contributed by followers, is the prerequisite to such mobilizations of communal labor.

All adults in the Trobriands take a full part in agricultural production. Apart from the special services of the garden magician, who may be the leader of the village or his designated close relative, the division of labor is mainly by sex and age. Men cut the scrub; men and women clear ground and prepare for planting; men plant and women weed; men train yam vines and thin roots; and both sexes take part in the harvest. Tools are simple: sharpened poles for digging and weeding and stone axes and adzes for tree felling.

Each household group produces yams individually on its plots. Two

Urigubu yams are carried to their recipient by the producer and immediate relatives (1974). (Courtesy of J. W. Leach.)

Trobriand agriculture: The empty yamhouses of the wives of the chief of Omarakana village (the successor to Malinowski's "paramount chief") during a drought in 1972. (Courtesy of J. W. Leach.)

factors of this production are crucial here. First, probably the most important sphere of life to a Trobriand couple is their garden production. Vast piles of accumulated yams, far above what they need to feed their household, are their pride and joy—the more the better. They work extremely hard to produce great and "useless" quantities of food in an environment where a livelihood could be won with far more limited efforts.

Second, about half of the yams produced by a household go to the households of the husband's sister and other close female kin, in *urigubu* (Case 36). The yams the household gives away, to other households and to the leader of the sub-clan, are the best and largest it produces. The more and better the yams one presents, the greater is one's prestige. There even are spectacular "giveaway" contests of yams that are duels for prestige between subclans and villages. The symbolic side of Trobriand yam production comes out clearly if we note that many of the yams most highly prized and conspicuously displayed are not used as domestic food at all, and may simply rot. Furthermore, the high-value yams, displayed in storehouses, especially by leaders of high rank, become symbols of prestige and power.

Though the overproduction and lavish exchange and display of yams has commanded anthropological attention for years, it can mislead us if we look at Trobriand ecology. The rich earth that overlies the coral platform of Kiriwina Island supports a large population; in few parts of the tribal world do we find such dense settlement. Yet subsistence of this population depends on sufficient rainfall, which varies from year to year. While in a wet year vast surpluses may accumulate, prolonged drought—which occurred once or twice in a generation—would reduce the horticulturalists to starvation and lead to interdistrict and intervillage wars with survival as the stakes. The lavish extra investment of gardening effort, so laden with symbolic value, provided a buffer for lean years when crop yields fell sharply—and may have provided reserves from the previous year's harvest that might otherwise have been allowed to rot. Famine, and resulting warfare, may have periodically cut back population increases.

Though systems of production in other societies are quite different and are often less dramatic, the Trobriand case usefully illustrates a number of important points.

First, production can be understood only in terms of social organization. Production may, in different contexts or with different scarce goods, take place in a whole range of social groupings of a society. So may the redistribution of surpluses.

As Marxist and ecologically oriented theorists forcefully remind us, it may be putting things backwards to take the social structure as given and show how the social groups involved in production *reflect* this structure. The social organization of production may in an important sense be primary; and formal blueprints of "social structure" may be ideological elaborations and rationalizations of economic relationships. A *mode of production* is best seen from two sides: a technical side whereby humans appropriate or create resources from the natural world; and a social side, where humans are socially organized around the tasks of production.

Second, the relationship between subsistence production, the creation of surpluses, and the emergence of social stratification is critical. As we will see shortly, the Trobriand political system involves a marked stratification—into chiefly and commoner subclans, into headmen or "chiefs" and their followers. This stratification is sustained by the flow of yams "upward" to important men in the form of tribute; these leaders, by redistributing and displaying these surplus yams, reinforce and validate their prestige and power. Trobriand society represents at least an incipient class system. This case suggests how, where productive capacities permit a large and dense

population and the creation of substantial surpluses, a gulf may widen between those who perform productive labor and those who do the conspicuous consuming and redistributing—with the latter acquiring power as well as wealth.

Third, though Trobriand society is in many ways dominated by men politically, women have a highly important and even powerful place symbolically and in social relations, as witness the ideologies of matrilineal descent and, as we will see, the elaborate networks of women's exchange, with prestige as the stakes (see p. 328). Apparently the solidarity of women's communal work groups and their important role in subsistence agriculture are important bases for the symbolic and actual power of Trobriand women. The importance of communal work teams of women, uniting women from different domestic groups, in reinforcing the status of women has been underlined by recent comparative research by Karen Sacks (1974).

Finally, a notion that production in a "primitive" society is concerned largely with meeting subsistence needs is clearly too simple. To understand production—its motives and outcomes—we need to explore the value system of a society. Whether people "work hard" by our standards, or for things we think they should work for, depends on their conceptions of the desirable. In the early colonial period Trobriand Islanders, recruited to dive in their lagoon for pearls by white men, confounded their employers: they would exchange fine pearls only for traditional ceremonial trade goods, not money; they would refuse to dive for pearls when the gardens were in full swing; and they would fish rather than dive for pearls, even when the payment for pearls was 10 or 20 times as great in exchange value as the fish they would barter (Malinowski 1935 I:20). Assertions in popular literature that native peoples are "lazy" and unmotivated should by now be perceived by the reader as implying not a lack of motivation but a pursuit of goals and values different from ours.

Before we examine the modes of exchange whereby scarce goods produced in a society. pass through networks of distribution, it will be useful to look briefly at concepts of *property* in comparative perspective.

54.
Property

Property does not consist of *things*. It is more useful to view property in terms of *relations between people and things,* where the "things" may be as intangible as knowledge of magic. In a non-Western setting, the crucial question is not "Who owns it?" but "Who has what *rights* over it?"

Reflection will show that when an American "owns" a piece of land, he or she is by no means the only one with rights over it. The city, the state, the country have rights over it, as one would discover if one tried to raise chickens in a suburban neighborhood or to deed one's land to the government of China.

When land in a tribe is described as "communally owned," that may mean that a range of people (perhaps members of a lineage) have rights to live or garden there. But rights to sell any particular piece of land, or to claim first fruits, may be vested in individuals or smaller groups. Similarly, when land is described as "owned by the chief," that may only mean that the chief represents a symbolic figurehead. Lineages, households, or individuals may have the major rights over actual tracts of land. Since different rights apply at different levels, generalizations about who owns what are almost always misleading. The European colonial magistrate or administra-

tor's usual first question, "Who owns it?" was often disastrous. The anthropologist must find out who has what rights over what "things" in what contexts—and the answers are seldom simple.

The ways people classify kinds of property—land or livestock, tools, specialized knowledge, and so on—obviously vary according to their mode of subsistence. But the same distinctions appear over and over again: between partible (that is, divisible) and nonpartible property; between movable and immovable property; between personal and collective property (can more than one person use it?); between material and immaterial, and so on.

The ways rights over property are transmitted across generations similarly vary within fairly narrow limits. A recurrent question presented by kinship ties is whether individually held rights over property pass successively down a line of brothers or pass from father to son. *Seniority* is often used to pass rights from oldest son to oldest son (primogeniture), or to assign primary responsibility over property collectively held by a set of siblings. Whether men and women both receive rights over major property is obviously a crucial question, related to ideologies of descent and the symbolic significance of men and women.

The corporate descent group effectively solves important practical problems in managing the relationships between people and scarce goods over long time spans. It keeps property intact while distributing rights—instead of, say, carving land into smaller and smaller pieces; and it maintains the continuity of rights across generations.

55.
Systems of Exchange and Redistribution

We have suggested that market transactions in complex societies are one manifestation of the more general principles of *exchange*.

Study of a society's modes and mechanisms of exchange leads into the redistribution system whereby scarce goods pass through networks to people who did not produce them. Exchanging implies shared standards of value, and links individual acts of valuing and choice into a wider system.

If we are to understand exchange systems in Africa or the Pacific, we will need to broaden our ideas about economic transactions. Many of our usual assumptions about transactions involving goods and services reflect the particular mode of exchange that dominates our economy; they may not fit other systems.

A major set of insights came from the French sociologist Marcel Mauss (1925). Mauss examined evidence on gift-giving in primitive societies and argued that we were likely to misunderstand its essential nature. For "The Gift" in a tribal setting does not simply transfer title to an object from one person to another. Rather, the gift expresses and cements a social relationship: *A gift is a statement about the relationship between giver and receiver.* The thing given is a symbol of that relationship, and hence has value and meaning beyond its material worth. Furthermore, the relationship established or continued by the gift implies *reciprocity*. The relationship between giver and receiver may be symmetrical, as between feast-giving leaders or clans, so that an obligation is created to return in kind. Or the relationship may be asymmetrical: the giver may be dominant, so that he asserts his superior status and the receiver is obligated to reciprocate with tribute or services, or subordinate, as with Trobrianders' yam presentations to their powerful leaders.

Above all, gift-giving expresses and symbolizes human social interdependence. Thus it is enmeshed in systems of kinship and social stratification and reinforces their structure. We have seen how Lévi-Strauss built upon Mauss' insights a model of kinship systems as

modes of exchange, with women as the ultimate scarce good. Important further advances in our understanding of the comparative sociology of exchange, and its symbolic import, have come from recent analyses by Sahlins (1972).

The impersonality of transactions in a market economy, the focus on the goods exchanged rather than the relationship of the exchanging parties, can mislead us in looking at non-Western societies. At times, in fact, we label transactions and relationships "economic" precisely because they *are* impersonal and formal, in contrast to our relations with friends with whom we exchange Christmas cards and presents and wedding gifts. "Business and friendship don't mix" because they rest on different premises about social relations and obligations. In the tribal world, business and kinship and friendship are intertwined.

Karl Polanyi (1957, 1959), an economic historian of heretical bent, has given us further insights about how our Western economic institutions are likely to mislead us. He

Bustling activity of market day animates a clearing in rural Haiti. Tradeswomen are grouped by commodity they sell. (Courtesy of Sidney W. Mintz.)

argues that there are three major modes of exchange in human societies: *reciprocity, redistribution,* and *market exchange.* Market exchange is the exchange of goods at prices based on supply and demand. Redistribution is the movement of goods up to an administrative center and their reallotment downward to consumers. Reciprocity is the exchange of goods that takes place neither through markets nor through administrative hierarchies.

Polanyi sharply contrasts these modes of exchange as reflecting fundamentally different social means to distribute the material goods of a society. Though Polanyi argued at times as though any society could be characterized by the predominance of one of these three modes, his followers in economic anthropology have recognized that all three modes can occur in the same society. Reciprocity and redistribution may well be universal. Still, they argue, one mode is likely to be dominant, while others are peripheral.

Polanyi and Dalton (1961) have proceeded to argue that the basic models of economics, and notions like scarcity, economizing, allocation, and maximizing, properly apply only to systems of market exchange. To talk in such terms about tribal economics is to superimpose notions based on the market onto social institutions that differ in *kind,* not merely in *degree* and the nature of scarce goods. They argue for a comparative economics based on different modes of organization and exchange of the means of material subsistence. This has come to be known as the *substantivist* position.

So-called *formalists* have countered that studying maximization and allocation, and building on the insights and models of economics, can illuminate the workings of tribal and peasant societies. We should, on principle, be able to apply such models to Batalamo's allocation of his scarce resources.

The debate, which has been reverberating in the cloistered halls of anthropology depart-

ments for some years and has scarcely been heard in the outside world, has acquired a new relevance and urgency. The models of the economist have been treated by both formalist and substantivist economic anthropologists with the reverence one accords complicated graphs left on the blackboard by the unseen hand of the previous lecturer, a real Scientist. They are now under sharp attack by radical critics within economics. And these radical economists aim not simply at the details of theory, but at the premises on which they rest. Radical economists point out how economic and political systems are intertwined and how ideologies reinforce and rationalize these structures. What, they ask, is "mainstream" economics a theory of, and why? Neoclassical economics is precisely the theory one would expect a vastly complex system of international corporations, world markets, and interconnected currencies to create to sustain, justify, explain, and predict "itself." And classical economics, correspondingly, was a predictable expression of an earlier era of European capitalism. The foundations of such theories, however sophisticated their superstructures, are premises about human nature (individuals make choices that maximize values—that is, people are basically greedy and selfish) and premises about systems (the behavior of the market is the cumulative product of individual choices). These premises about human nature and the nature of systems constitute a rationale for capitalism (Rowthorn 1974). Marxist critics argue that they do not serve as adequate bases for an economics of socialism, or of precapitalist societies not dominated by the market principle; and beginning from different premises, they point out both general and specific failings of the models of mainstream economic theory.

Marxists and other radical critics of the dogma of mainstream economics point out the sterility of imposing Western standards, defined in purely material terms, for "economic development" ("gross national product," "standard of living"). That "standards of living" are best defined in terms of human relations rather than in terms of wealth and hardware is a hard lesson modern Americans are beginning to learn as they choke on their own prosperity.

The anthropologist who has been trying with formalist zeal to apply mainstream economics to small-scale societies is in a rather precarious position. The sectarian skirmishes between formalists and substantivists have been swept up into much bigger and wider battles. Most important, a comparative economics that seeks the models appropriate to particular modes of production and forms of society becomes a large-scale multidisciplinary quest in which anthropologists command a substantial part of the evidence. If human motives—whether to maximize or share, to compete or cooperate, to consume or exchange—are in substantial part shaped by social relations and value systems, then a comparative economics becomes an exciting exploration of human possibility.

The most successful analysts of tribal and peasant economies have searched for models that seem to work, rather than standing on matters of principle. It may be a virtue that when the most able scholars from both formalist and substantivist camps actually get down to analyzing economic systems, the descriptions they produce seem separated by a less wide gap than their argument would suggest. Exchange systems that differ widely from ours often yield to modes of systematic analysis that draw on many concepts, methods, and models used by economists. In the absence of money, many transactions and values are hard to measure or count, and this poses serious problems. Yet at many points in complex networks it is possible to get data that bring standards of value and equivalence into view; and computer analysis permits us to discern patterns of connection that would otherwise be hidden. Moreover, where tribal peoples are operating according to motives and values that make cultural sense, but not Western "economic" sense, the anthropologist can (or should be able to) interpret the sense and hence broaden theoretical vision.

What matters, then, are not great arguments about principles or what would or would not work. The challenge is to borrow or invent models that *will* work for the data at hand, and to work in a middle range where theories and ethnographic evidence both stay in view.

The fascinating Trobriand exchange system will once more illustrate the sophistication and complexity of systems of redistribution in so-called primitive societies and to give some more general perspectives on economic anthropology and anthropologically illuminated economics.

Case 45: Trobriand Exchange

Here we will summarize the major modes and categories of Trobriand exchange, showing how they fit into a wider comparative perspective. We will begin with the *kula*, one of the most remarkable and fascinating institutions of the tribal world (Malinowski 1922; Uberoi 1962).

KULA

The Trobriand Islands form part of the d'Entrecasteaux Archipelago (Figure 15.2) lying off the southeastern end of New Guinea. Though the

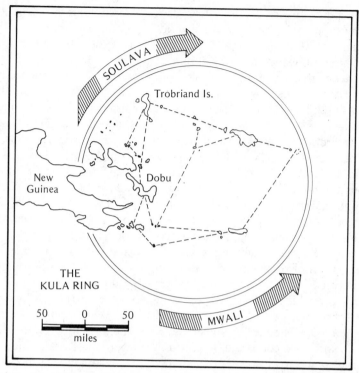

Figure 15.2. The Kula ring: Necklaces *(soulava)* are exchanged clockwise from island group to island group around the ring; armshells *(mwali)* are exchanged from them, in a counterclockwise direction. Paths of exchange are shown in broken lines. (Map by Gilbert Hendren.)

cultures of these islands form a related family, the customs and languages of each group are quite different. Yet they are united into a giant ring of ceremonial exchange several hundred miles across, so that each tribal group is a unit within the whole circle.

What they exchange around the ring are two kinds of intrinsically useless ceremonial objects collectively called *vaygu'a*. Each kind is exchanged around the ring of islands in a different direction. *Soulava*, long necklaces of shell discs, move clockwise around the circle. *Mwali*, white armshells (Figure 15.3), travel counterclockwise. But what does "travel" mean? Who gets the objects? How are they exchanged?

Let us look from the viewpoint of the Trobrianders—only one link in this chain, but the one we know best and are most concerned with here. The essential rule is that I ceremonially and publicly present you, my partner, with a Necklace. You are obligated to give me, some time later, an equally valuable Armshell. Our relationship, as partners, is lifelong, maintained by our periodic exchange of *vaygu'a*. From any point in the Trobriands, a man receives necklaces from partners to the south and west, and armshells from partners to the north and east.

Figure 15.3. Kula valuables: The armshells (left) are made from the spiral trochus shell. The necklaces (right) are made primarily of pink spondylus shell disks strung on fiber.

An average man has a number of *kula* partners, at home and overseas. His partners at home are mainly friends and in-laws; and their exchange of *vaygu'a* is part of a relationship entailing different forms of exchange and assistance. He will also *kula* (that is, exchange *vaygu'a*) with one or two important leaders of high rank.

Kula partnerships within a single district (like the Trobriands) constitute the "inland *kula*." Exchanges in the inland *kula* are smaller-scale, individual, and treated with less ceremonial formality than the overseas *kula*, which involves large-scale voyages and great complexes of magic and ceremony.

The strategies and principles of overseas *kula* transactions, as seen from the perspective of the important coastal Trobriand village of Sinaketa, are well summed up by Malinowski:

Let us suppose that I, a Sinaketa man, am in possession of a pair of big armshells. An overseas expedition from Dobu, in the d'Entrecasteaux Archipelago, arrives at my village. Blowing a conch shell, I take my armshell pair and I offer it to my overseas partner, with some such words, "This is a *vaga* (initial gift)—in due time, thou returnest to me a big *soulava* (necklace) for it!" Next year, when I visit my partner's village, he either is in possession of an equivalent necklace, and this he gives to me as *yotile* (restoration gift), or he has not a necklace good enough to repay my last gift. In this case he will give me a smaller necklace—avowedly not equivalent to my gift—and will give it to me as *basi* (intermediary gift). This means that the main gift has to be repaid on a future occasion and the *basi* is given in token of good faith—but it, in turn, must be repaid by me in the meantime by a gift of small armshells. The final gift, which will be given to me to clinch the whole transaction, would be then called *kudu* (equivalent gift) in contrast to *basi*. . . .

If I . . . happen to be in possession of a pair of armshells more than usually good, the fame of it spreads. It must be noted that each one of the first-class armshells and necklaces has a personal name and history of its own, and as they all circulate around the big ring of the *kula*, they are all well-known, and their appearance in a given district always creates a sensation. Now all my partners— whether from overseas or from within the district—compete for the favour of receiving this particular article of mine, and those who are specially keen try to obtain it by giving me *pokala* (offerings) and *kaributu* (solicitory gifts). (Malinowski 1922:99–100)

A man tries to maintain a reputation as a generous *kula* partner. The more important and numerous the valuables that pass through his hands (for he cannot keep them long or do much with them), the greater his prestige. This requires him both to *give* generously and to *obtain* strategically: he clearly cannot do one without the other. But the Melanesian prestige strategist, like the Western capitalist, sometimes cuts a few corners. Here is how a Dobuan explained his strategies:

Suppose I, Kisian of Tewara, go to the Trobriands and secure an armshell named Monitor Lizard. I then go to Sanaroa and in four different places secure four different shell necklaces, promising each man who gives me a shell necklace, Monitor Lizard in return later. I, Kisian, do not have to be very specific in my promise. It will be conveyed by implication and assumption for the most part. Later, when four men appear in my home at Tewara each expecting Monitor Lizard, only one will get it. The other three are not defrauded permanently, however. They are furious it is true, and their exchange is blocked for the year. Next year, when I, Kisian, go again to the Trobriands I shall represent that I have four necklaces at home waiting for those who will give me four armshells. I obtain more armshells than I obtained previously, and pay my debts a year late. The three men who did not get Monitor Lizard are at a disadvantage in my place, Tewara. Later when they return to their homes they are too far off to be dangerous to me. They are likely to attempt to kill their successful rival, who did get the armshell, Monitor Lizard, by the black art. That is true enough. But that is their own business. I have become a great man by enlarging my exchanges at the expense of blocking theirs for a year. I cannot afford to block their exchange for too long, or my exchanges will never be trusted by anyone again. I am honest in the final issue. (Fortune 1932a:217)

Kula exchange is intimately bound up with the system of social stratification we will look at more closely in the next chapter. A man of chiefly subclan builds, reinforces, and validates his political power not only by accumulating and redistributing yams and other foodstuffs, but also by his participation in the *kula*. The number of *kula* partnerships a high-ranking man possesses, the prestige and power of his partners, and the renown of the valuables that he acquires and passes on constitute symbolic validations of status and power. Note that it is only men who participate in the *kula*.

GIMWALI

Gimwali comprises Trobriand forms of barter—nonmoney transactions according to market principles. Here haggling and publicly acknowledged efforts to get the better of the other man prevail. Within or between Trobriand villages, *gimwali* entails irregular barter of fish for vegetables or of newly manufactured items of various sorts.

Gimwali also takes place, on a large scale, on *kula* expeditions. It is by this means that raw materials and manufactured goods from some segments of the *kula* ring are exchanged through the system to places that lack these objects and resources. Trobrianders thus get pottery, rattan, bamboo, greenstones, and other items through the *gimwali* that accompanies the *kula*.

While *kula* partners are going through their dramatic interchanges, barter is going on around them. The rule is that no *kula* partners can barter—that would mix haggling with ceremonial; but everyone can barter with everyone else's partner.

It has been argued that among other things the *kula* constitutes a kind of regional peace pact under which otherwise hostile peoples can carry out the trade essential in their ecological setting. Such networks and chains of regional trade were common in Melanesia, and apparently are quite old. A crucial element in such trade systems is the production of pottery, widely used in Melanesia, but made in only a few specialized "exporting" centers. In the d'Entrecasteaux, the people of the neighboring Amphlett Islands were the pottery producers; and they, like their counterparts in other Melanesian trading networks, commanded a strategic position (Sahlins 1972; Harding 1967); much of their food was imported from their agriculturally richer neighbors. Large canoes were imported from the islands to the east, as were the greenstones used for axes and adzes. The *gimwali* trade accompanying the *kula* apparently involved a large volume of coconuts, areca nuts for betel chewing, lime, sago, building materials, and manufactured goods such as combs, baskets, and betel-chewing accessories. It is unfortunate that because of the focus of ethnographers on the more spectacular and symbolically central *kula* exchanges, we know too little about the volume and nature of accompanying trade.

Our knowledge of the flow of agricultural produce and the exchange of root vegetables for fish is similarly colored and limited by Malinowski's (and the Trobrianders' own) emphasis on dramatic, formal, and ritualized transactions at the expense of more mundane, impersonal, or informal transactions crucial to ecological adaptation. Thus we know much more about *wasi*, the formal exchange of vegetables for fish between regular partners (see below), than about *vava*, a form of *gimwali* where vegetables are bartered directly for fish. The everyday barter of yams or manufactured items—skirts, lime, spatulas, combs—for other valuables is clearly crucial in Trobriand economics, but the data give only rare glimpses of such exchange.

LAGA

Laga is a transaction type we know little about, but it is conceptually important. This entails the ceremonial transfer of title to a piece of important property; for example, a garden plot or a large pig, in exchange for *vaygu'a*. That is, the ceremonial valuables of the *kula* can be used for commercial transactions, though this is rare and lends a ceremonial character and importance to the exchange.

WASI

A formalized exchange between coastal villages that specialize in fishing and inland villages producing yam surpluses is called *wasi*. Here there are traditional alliances between villages, and within them, there are "partnerships" between a particular fisherman and particular gardeners. After the harvest, the gardeners will take a bunch of taro or yams to their coastal opposite numbers. As soon afterwards as possible, the lagoon dwellers will stage a large fishing expedition. The haul of fish is taken directly to the inland village, where fish bundles are presented in exchange for the earlier yam presentation, according to fixed standards of equivalence.

POKALA

The term *pokala* covers a range of conceptually related transactions. First, it covers the presentation of gifts and services from junior members of a subclan or clan to senior members in exchange for anticipated material benefits and status advantage. Thus *pokala* gifts are a means of securing future political advantage, validating rights to matrilineal inheritance, or rendering tribute to one's ranking leader. It thus implies giving by one of lower status to one of higher status in exchange for obligations—obligations of protection, future status, future material advantage, and so on. In Chapter 17, we will look more closely at the politics of rank and prestige validated by such transactions.

Pokala in a different sense is used to denote tribute to a district chief or some other notable. The term is also used for a gift in the *kula* to solicit favor in a future exchange. The essentials of *pokala* are (1) that it implies status asymmetry, with the giver below the receiver (in the *kula* this is apparently a form of flattery); and (2) that it creates a diffuse or specific obligation, so the giver improves his position vis-à-vis his rivals (even when the "giver" is a village sending tribute).

URIGUBU

We know already that *urigubu* is the presentation of yams by members of a subclan to the husbands of its female members who have married out, particularly by a man's household to his sister's household. This is a major focus of the production of great surpluses of important yams. These *urigubu* presentations are periodically countered by *youlo*, presentations of valuables from a man to his wife's kin.

SAGALI

A *sagali* is a distribution of food in connection with some ceremonial or special occasion—a mortuary feast, a commemorative feast, a competitive enterprise, or the like. Prestige in the system is achieved, expressed, and validated by being able to give away large quantities of food, to sponsor a feast, a war, a work project. Thus an important leader of a village or district gives away in *sagali* much of what he receives through

A *sagali* yam distribution in the Trobriands. (Courtesy of Australian News and Information Bureau.)

Women's exchange in the Trobriands: Women make a presentation of grass skirts at a mortuary feast. (Courtesy of J. W. Leach.)

pokala and *urigubu*. *Sagali* thus functions as a mechanism of redistribution in Polanyi's sense, as well as a means of reciprocity for tribute and services rendered.

The most spectacular distributions of food and other valuables apparently come in the mortuary distributions after a death. Here it is interesting that women play a dramatic and central role, even though neither Malinowski nor H. A. Powell, who did a restudy, have published any detailed information on women's exchange systems.

Only with the work of two women ethnographers in the Trobriands in the early 1970s, the results of which are beginning to be published, have we begun to see that the men's world of high finance and exchange is complemented by and intertwined with a system where women publicly exchange symbolically female valuables and compete for high stakes of prestige.

When a person from a woman's own subclan dies, she and her fellow subclan women give away vast quantities of women's skirts and especially of banana leaf bundles (as many as 15,000 of them) at a special *sagali* mortuary distribution, one of a long series of mortuary distributions. "In

Women's exchange in the Trobriands: This woman, with shaven head and body painted black, is the sister of the dead man. She directs exchanges and here holds center stage. (Courtesy Annette Weiner.)

this ceremony women are the major actresses on-stage in the center of the hamlet playing a role every bit as tough and aggressive and competitive as a big-man'' (Weiner 1974). A woman also plays a central part in the distribution after her father's death, and a lesser part for the death of another person in her father's subclan. These presentations go mainly to the affinally related subclans that have taken a central part in mortuary rites. A woman accumulates her skirts and bundles, aided by her husband, to be publicly given away in return for prestige and center stage, by strategically investing yams she and her husband have received as *urigubu* from her male subclan relatives, as well as by making salable craft goods. She also publicly receives contributions of skirts and bundles from her kin and from her husband's kinswomen to whom the husband has given baskets of yams. "The remembrances of yams once given have as much substance and power as the original gifts of yams themselves" (Weiner 1974).

The Trobrianders have other, less formal, patterns of gift exchange and reciprocal obligation between friends and among kin. This suffices, however, to show the range of intricate transactions whereby scarce goods in the Trobriands are exchanged and distributed.

Here, then, we have a range of modes of exchange. Some are ceremonial and transacted at set standards of equivalence with an obligation of direct return. Others entail much less specific return obligations, such as *pokala*, or entail the supply and demand adjustments of the market, in *gimwali*. For some, the return may simply be prestige, as in some forms of *sagali*.

To understand Trobriand economic systems, we need urgently to know how the exchange subsystems fit together. This would entail knowing more about:

1. How values or valuables are converted from one sphere of exchange to another, and according to what standards of value.
2. How valuables, foodstuffs, raw materials, and manufactured goods flow through the systems and how that flow relates to power, prestige, kinship, and so on.
3. What strategies lead to transactions between, as well as within, the exchange subsystems and to investment in one subsystem rather than another.

Recent data gathered by Annette Weiner provide important clues. She describes a "main road of exchange" traveled by all Trobriand men and women and connecting by side paths to other cycles of exchange. This road connects not only men's wealth and women's wealth but connects agricultural production with the web of social relations and with the mortuary rites that are a major focus of Trobriand culture.

The crucial valued exchange items on the main road are exchange yams. Yams constitute the all-important goods *convertible* into other forms of wealth and ultimately into prestige and power. "If a man has yams he can find everything else that he needs," the Trobrianders told Dr. Weiner. And even in these days when cash has penetrated many areas of the Trobriand economy, "nothing takes the place of distributions of yams at mortuary ceremonies or feasts—nor can cash take the place of giving yams to women—or giving yams in marriage exchanges. . . . Exchanges which involve the creation or maintenance of important relationships have not been replaced [by cash]" (Weiner 1974).

> The circulation of . . . exchange yams . . . produces access to other objects of wealth and other comestibles as well as access to immediate and future obligations. . . . A basket of yams given produces objects received which in turn provide additional roads to other things and people. (Weiner 1974).

Thus a woman can take *urigubu* yams presented to her husband by her brother or matrilineal kin and convert them through exchange into grass skirts or leaf bundles. She can further convert between subsystems by bartering items she manufactures, for example, woven bags, either into women's wealth or into yams that can be further converted. The ultimate goal is enchancement of prestige through the ceremonial presentation of exchange objects (skirts and leaf bundles for women, *kula* valuables and *sagali* for men) and also by the ultimate conversion of exchange yams back to the realm of nature when they rot. The complementary conversion of raw exchange yams into cooked yams is in most contexts disvalued.

Once the yamhouses are filled, the villagers eat very few yams as part of their daily diet. Yams neatly stacked inside a yamhouse are a man's capital—they are a display of his potential. Conversely, the rotting of yams means that a man has fulfilled all his yam exchange obligations, that he has land enough that he has seed yams and subsistence for himself. The natural process of decay is a visual public statement of a man's total control over his social, financial, and ecological environment. (Weiner 1974)

The main road of exchange through which every man and woman converts yams into a measure of prestige leads by side paths into the roads to the *kula* and other subsystems; and through these paths, it opens roads to great power and wealth for men of rank. (We will view the system of rank and politics in Chapter 17.) The web of connection between these exchange subsystems renders any model of gift exchange focusing on direct reciprocity overly simple: "One kind of gift given to A leads to another kind of gift given to B and that in turn leads to another object given to C" (Weiner 1974).

The extraordinary complexity of Trobriand exchange systems defies comprehensive analysis by one ethnographer: it would take a network of data-gathering and analysis comparable to those needed to comprehend the economics of a complex industrial society. But if we had enough data on cycles and strategies of exchange, it seems probable that mathematical models could illuminate the flow of exchange, standards of equivalence, and strategies for achieving Trobriand goals. The latter is a key to the formalist-substantivist debate. The issue is not so much whether non-Western economies could, if we knew enough, be analyzed in terms of formal models; the point is that a range of formal models less culture-bound and ideology-bound than those of Western market systems will be needed. And "achieving Trobriand goals" will require a less simplistic conception of human values and behavior than economists embed in their models.

Sahlins (1972), Godelier (1974), and others have pointed to an emerging answer to the substantivist-formalist debate. The substantivists have been right in spirit, but often wrong in practice—since they have often ended up analyzing institutions with a kind of soggy relativism that makes the motives of people enacting them incomprehensible, and has seemed at times to deny their rationality. The formalists have been right about rationality, but often wrong about the structure of institutions and values and how economic action is expressed in and through them.

The way out is a broadened understanding of how systems of production are organized so as to define the social relations and interests of those within them. All humans act rationally, at least much of the time, in choosing among alternative courses and options. Thus rational calculations are involved in choosing *kula* partners, allowing yams to rot, or deciding to fish rather than dive for pearls. But such rational calculi are not definable in money terms and depend on distinctively Trobriand values.

Moreover, the economic structure within which these rational decisions are pursued is not a cumulative product of maximization strategies by individuals or firms, but a complex outcome of historical forces. The Trobriand wife, managing her household resources, and the low-status man who lives in one of the coastal villages where symbolically defiling stingrays are caught are both acting as rationally as they can, given a system that exploits them and offers limited rewards. But a wealthy man of high rank, who commands deference, controls *kula* valuables, and accumulates prestige, has access to far greater rewards; and the cultural definition of what is rewarding and desirable, and what is polluting or demeaning, is established not by "the culture" but by those who have power to define "the system."

56.
Money and Markets

Traditionally, there was nothing we would want to call "money" in the Trobriands; and the market principle is quite secondary or peripheral in the whole system of production and distribution. In some other Melanesian societies, there are standardized media of exchange that fill many of the functions of money in Western societies.

Case 46: Tolai *Tambu*

The people who have emerged as the Tolai in the colonial period, and have become the most prosperous and powerful cultural force in the emergence of modern Papua New Guinea, originally were a chain of communities of cultural close cousins, tied together by regional trade, intermarriage, feast-giving, and ceremonial (including the Dukduk graded secret society we glimpsed in Case 43).

The networks of trade and marketing, the transactions of marriage that interlinked communities, and the mortuary feasts that were a focus of political power and prestige (as in the Trobriands) depended on *tambu*, strung shell discs that served as currency and ceremonial valuables. The standard length of *tambu* was a fathom, but there were shorter lengths that served as set denominations. There were standard prices for many items purchased with *tambu* (Danks 1887; A. L. Epstein 1963, 1969, n.d.; T. S. Epstein 1964, 1968; Salisbury 1966, 1970).

Tolai *tambu* was closely tied up with the cultural treatment of death: one's worth in life was affirmed by the distribution of *tambu* at one's death. Though strings of *tambu* were used in a wide range of transactions, from the purchase of foodstuffs in markets to payment of bridewealth, it was in these mortuary distributions that their full symbolic significance was expressed. A. L. Epstein (n.d.), assaying an interpretation of *tambu* in

The Rabaul market: Tolai traders deal in Australian currency and traditional *tambu* shell valuables. (Courtesy of Australian News and Information Bureau.)

psychological and symbolic terms, suggests that the emotional centrality of shell valuables in Tolai life expresses a theme of the anal eroticism of early childhood experience. (Recall the psychoanalytic interpretations of cultural phenomena discussed in §34; Epstein's interpretation builds on the insights of psychoanalysts into the preoccupation with money as symbolic feces in industrial capitalist societies.)

Whatever the roots of their preoccupation with *tambu,* Tolai have not behaved as economists of development would anticipate in response to the impact of cash-cropping and substantial Western wealth in recent decades. Although the Tolai are centrally involved in cash-crop production, have amassed considerable wealth, are quite Westernized in education and dress, and have acquired sophistication in Western ways, *tambu* remains centrally important in Tolai life. Even in commercial transactions, such as trade in urban markets, *tambu* is interchangeable with national currency; Tolai can choose between alternative modes of payment. In bridewealth, mortuary distribution, and other traditional transactions, *tambu* retains a central position. As the Tolai Mataungan Association exerts a strong political pressure at national level in Papua New Guinea, traditional *tambu* valuables serve as a symbol of cultural identity and anticolonial sentiment.

Because *tambu* were used in such a wide range of transactions, because anything one could "own" could be bought and sold either in fixed or negotiated prices, and because *tambu* were interchangeable, in standard denominations, these strung shell valuables resemble Western money in many ways. Yet as Dalton (1965) points out, the more peripheral function of markets in a Melanesian society and their central significance as ceremonial valuables call for caution in equating such "currency" with Western money.

Another striking example of moneylike valuables in Melanesia comes from the Kapauku of the highlands of West New Guinea (Irian Jaya).

Case 47: Kapauku "Money"

Pospisil (1963a, b) argues that cowrie shells among the Kapauku of New Guinea constitute true "money." Standard denominations of shells provide a common medium of exchange and a common measure of value. For shells one can buy food, pigs, crops, land, artifacts, labor, and medical and magical services; one can pay fines; one can finance one's marriage, and gain prestige and authority. Though there are common standards of "price" for many goods, these are subject to negotiation; and many prices are directly determined by supply and demand.

A system similar in many ways, though less completely developed, occurs among the Kwaio of the Solomon Islands, who use strung shell beads somewhat similar to Trobriand *soulava*. The largest "denominations" have special ceremonial value; but they can be built from, or dismantled into, shorter lengths or even individual beads (10 of which will purchase an areca nut for betel-chewing). Here recall Batalamo's dilemma with which the chapter began.

Market principles are much more prominent in the societies of West Africa. In this case we must distinguish between the marketplace, which may be colorfully visible, and the abstract principles economists call *the market*. These principles are based on supply and demand and hence reflect statistical patterns of decision by buyer and seller. West African marketplaces fulfill many important functions of communication, security, and sociability; they also are focal points for the trade of specialized goods and surpluses. From the substantivist point of view, as markets they are still "peripheral," since the bulk of production for subsistence does not pass through the market. As tribal peoples have become increasingly urbanized and villagers have become tied more and more into money economies, these African markets have assumed a more central position.

How this shift toward dominance of "the market" in formerly tribal societies is interpreted depends on one's political stance and economic models. The emergence of individualist entrepreneurship and the spread of market principles into traditional economies is viewed by mainstream development economists (and their anthropological counterparts) as a take-off stage necessary to modernization. Marxist critics have provided a counter-interpretation: the spread of capitalist institutions into colonial and postcolonial societies constitutes part of the design for the continuing exploitation of the Third World by the powerful industrial nations (see, for example, Dupré and Rey 1973; Rey 1971.). We will return to these questions in Chapter 25. In looking at the integration and transformation of the economy of the Nigerian Tiv during the colonial period, we will shortly see an example of the early stages of this process (Case 48).

In Chapter 7, we saw how the development of urban centers created a polarization between urban elites and the peasants of the countryside whose surpluses of agricultural produce fed them. As anthropological attention has shifted toward peasants in recent years, the complexity of economics in these social systems has come vividly to light. Peasants, like tribal people, are enmeshed in a mode of production where the household is the main producing unit, and where most of

Kwaio "money": These strings of ground shell discs serve as a general medium of exchange in this Solomon Islands tribal society. A young married woman counts the valuables she has received from her kin at a feast. (Photograph by the author.)

what members consume to subsist is the fruit of their own labor. But peasants produce surpluses of subsistence food, other crops, or small-scale craft goods they feed into the wider economy. Here markets, both in the physical sense of marketplaces and in the abstract economic sense, mold the lives of producers and middlepersons.

In a large and growing literature, the nature of peasant marketing and the way it connects both with local social structure and with religion and subsistence consumption are coming vividly to light.

We will return to these phenomena when we turn to the anthropology of peasant societies in Chapter 22.

57.
The Integration of Economic Systems

We have glimpsed a range of modes of exchange and how within a single society a number of interlinked modes may operate. A major challenge, for non-Western economies, is to see how the various sectors and networks of a society are interlinked. How, for Batalamo, are the demands of subsistence, ancestral support, and feast-giving prestige interconnected? How, for a Trobriand Islander, are the lure of pearl diving or *kula* manipulations balanced against the obligations to reciprocate *wasi* yams with fish or to help an in-law in his garden? How can we map the flow of yams, valuables, prestige, and obligation through the networks of exchange that pervade Trobriand life? How can we relate what a peasant wife does in her kitchen to what she does in the marketplace where she may be seller as well as buyer?

For these analytical tasks we are still inventing and sharpening our tools. Models borrowed from economics enable us to show relationships *within* an economic subsystem better than to show linkages between different subsystems—particularly in these societies where money provides no standard measure of value. The hardest challenges to economic anthropology lie in this middle range, studying interconnections between subsystems.

Here, a few general observations and an example from Africa must suffice. First, a society cannot be characterized by a single dominant mode of exchange without distorting how its economy works. A range of modes and networks of exchange—often entailing reciprocity, redistribution, and market exchange—are interlinked. Furthermore, some of the scarce goods used in subsistence are, in almost all societies, produced by those who consume them. Hence they pass through no networks of distribution outside the producing unit. *An empirical economy consists of interlinked subsystems.*

Second, making decisions about production and exchange involves choices between, as well as within, these subsystems of the economy. Social change often involves no drastic shift in the economic institutions of a society—that is, in its modes of exchange and the social groupings and settings where it takes place. Social change may reflect a shift in statistical patterns of *allocating resources between them.* Time spent in the marketplace rather than the field, or money spent on an outboard engine instead of pigs for the ancestors, cumulatively affect the whole nature of the economy and can produce rapid change or new equilibrium.

Third, in the absence of a pervasive money economy, these allocations involve standards of value and scarce goods that are exceedingly hard to study. To measure prestige, or the satisfaction a Trobriander gets by fishing for *wasi* instead of diving for pearls (and being paid 10 or 20 times what the fish are worth in barter), is a sticky business. Where it is possible at all, it must usually be done by indirection—by studying patterns of choice or by documenting exchanges between things that can be directly evaluated or measured and things that cannot.

We can be partly encouraged by the fact that young Trobrianders manage to learn the values, procedures, and strategies that will enable them to play the games of Trobriand life, to make intelligent and intelligible economic decisions. The anthropologist deeply immersed in such a way of life can hope to make progress in the same direction. That is not to say that Trobrianders or other peoples necessarily understand their economic systems. An observer armed with enough data and a computer might well be able to understand the working of the *kula* as a system better than a Trobriander in Sinaketa village could.

Fourth, as the economic development and the monetization of the non-Western world accelerate, traditional anthropological assumptions that a tribe or community can be studied in isolation, that it is neatly integrated and relatively stable, become less and less realistic and useful. In studies of peasant and developing national economies, anthropologists are looking for ways to analyze how communities fit into wider systems and networks. Here they seek to map that range in between their own rich but narrowly focused knowledge of people, values, customs, and meanings in a particular community and the elegant but abstract global view of the economist. Exploration of the territory between can enrich both disciplines—particularly as economics is pushed toward less culture-bound and ideology-bound assumptions about human behavior.

The integration of subsystems in a non-Western economy and the effects of "modernization" in the form of colonial intrusion and capitalist domination are well illustrated by the Tiv of Nigeria.

Case 48: Integration and Change in the Tiv Economy

Tiv society, as we glimpsed it in Cases 25 and 40, is structured in terms of segmentary patrilineages, with a patrilineal "compound" group as the core unit of production and consumption. Traditionally, Tiv conceived of three categories of exchangeable items. The first category of subsistence items consisted primarily of garden foodstuffs (yams, corn, locust bean, and so on), chickens and goats, and domestic utensils and tools. The second category of valuables consisted of slaves, cattle, a type of large white cloth, and brass rods. The third category consisted solely of rights over persons, especially over women exchanged in marriage.

Within the first (subsistence) category, barter in the spirit of a "market" prevailed: Tiv sought to secure an advantageous exchange. Valuables could likewise be exchanged for other valuables, though one would do so not for pragmatic value but for advantage in the quest for prestige. Exchanges of women were carried out through a highly intricate system of wards and women-exchanging groups.

The three categories of exchangeables are ranked in moral values, with subsistence at the lower end and women at the higher. Exchange within a category is morally neutral, though advantageous exchanges are sought. What the Tiv seeks to achieve is *conversion* from a lower category to a higher category: to parlay food into brass rods or cattle, or to parlay the latter into a wife. Such conversions are the main strategic goals of the Tiv, as means to prestige, influence, and dependents. Downward conversion, as from brass to foodstuffs, constitutes a setback, to be avoided where possible. Accumulation within a category, without upward conversion, shows a failure or inability to play the game properly.

Into this system came British administrators, missionaries, traders, money, and the tentacles of a wider economic system (P. Bohannan 1955, 1959). About 1910, slave dealing was abolished. The administration, regarding the brass rods largely as a form of money, has over the years replaced them with British currency. This largely emptied the "valuables" category. Moreover, in 1927, a well-intending administration prohibited exchange marriages and substituted a system of cash bridewealth as the legal form—thus essentially eliminating the third and highest category, though modern Tiv marriage retains modes of exchange in covert form.

Meanwhile, many new material items that had no place in the old category system were introduced, and cash began to pervade the Tiv economy. This process was speeded by the imposition of a head tax in British money that forced cash-cropping on the Tiv before 1920. Moreover, the agricultural produce of Tivland flows into market channels that bring foodstuffs to urban areas. The Tiv as primary producers are part of a larger system over which they can exert little control. With pacification and transportation, Tiv men have themselves taken to trading subsistence goods over large distances.

How have such far-reaching changes been conceptualized in Tiv culture? Tiv have tried to fit money, and the new hardware one buys with money, into a fourth and lowest category. But money will not stay within these conceptual bounds. Most exchanges in and between categories now take place through the medium of money. Women's subsistence trade for money leads to a draining out of foodstuffs and makes it possible to build up cash through which prestige items can be bought. Their prestige value is eroded correspondingly.

Moreover, the bridewealth payment in cash forces the girl's guardian to trade down—to exchange a woman for money. Since the number of women is limited and monetary wealth rises with the export of food, bridewealth has become inflated. "As Tiv attempt to become more and more wealthy in people, they are merely selling more and more of their foodstuffs and subsistence goods, leaving less and less for their own consumption" (Bohannan 1955; for a critique of Bohannan's interpretation, see Berthoud 1969–1970).

The processes of change that are transforming the Tiv have of course been going on throughout the Third World. Experts on modernization have assured us that the breakdown of tribalism and tradition, the spread of money and market economy, and the emergence of entrepreneurship and individualism are preconditions for "development." If "undeveloped countries" are to raise their standards of living and join the industrial nations, traditional institutions must be destroyed and replaced: drastic social change is both necessary and desirable. Third World peoples are inevitably and rapidly becoming homogenized into a world culture and economy.

The emergence of a sophisticated and articulate radical social science places these assumptions in doubt. Change may be inevitable and necessary in the Third World; but socialist transformations in Cuba, Tanzania, and other countries make it clear that these changes need not be in the direction of capitalist individualism. The "universal" truths about the maximizing propensities of Economic Man and the supply and demand of the market may hold partly true in New York; but they seem vacuous in China—where supply and demand are guided by human plan, inflation is virtually unknown, and humans seem remarkably disposed to cooperate and share, not compete and maximize.

Imposition of alien socialist models imported from the Soviet Union or China

might be as disruptive in Tivland as colonially imposed capitalism has been. But if the radical critique of political economy is substantially correct, that need not be the alternative. Tanzanian socialism, for example, is distinctively African, and builds on the strengths of collective action and group responsibility in traditional kin-based societies—strengths development theorists have condemned as obstacles to "progress."

If alternative paths of economic change and societal organization are potentially open to Third World peoples, but presently hidden, the challenge to economic anthropology is more than academic. In seeking to broaden models of economic systems to incorporate complex, multidimensional calculi of value and the pursuit of symbolic and unmeasurable cultural goals—prestige, harmony, reciprocation, as well as wealth and power—within widely varying social systems, anthropologists are not simply creating better pigeonholes in which to store their knowledge of a vanishing past. Rather, they can help to explore and understand new human alternatives at a time when our present course portends disaster.

Having glimpsed the economics of production and redistribution in small-scale societies, we are in a position to understand those societies where gulfs between producers and those who command and control surpluses have widened into systems of *social classes*.

STRUCTURES OF INEQUALITY
Class and Caste

In talking about the societies of Africa, South and Southeast Asia, the Americas, and the Pacific as "tribal" and "small-scale," we lump together societies that vary enormously in size, internal complexity, and degree of social stratification. Even if we exclude the great civilizations of Mesoamerica and the Andes, of Egypt and China and India, there emerged numerous social systems in the Old and New Worlds that incorporated large populations and reached high orders of complexity. Even stateless societies such as the Tiv and Yakö, whose structurally decentralized and relatively egalitarian descent organization we glimpsed in §42, incorporate sizable populations.

Particularly interesting and theoretically challenging are societies where social stratification separates a population into *kinds* or *classes* of people, whose status and access to valued resources are markedly unequal. We find such complexity emerging in the non-Western world both as historical derivatives of the centers of civilization and as apparently independent developments in various parts of the tribal world.

There is a grave danger—one we will confront again in talking about political systems in the next chapter—of trying to fit "kinds" of systems into typological pigeonholes. First, that would lead us to worry endlessly about trying to define terms like "class," so we can decide which societies have social classes; second, it leads us to worry about what "type" a society belongs to, rather than how it is organized and how it emerged historically; and finally, it obscures the way clusters of historically related societies have developed structurally different patterns due to ecological, demographic, or other factors. A major challenge, as Friedman (1974) has pointed out for the Kachin of Burma and some of their more egalitarian cultural cousins, is to find out how such societies have undergone systematic transformations of a common pattern. It will not do to class them as different "types" and then typologically align, say, the Kachin with a similarly stratified group in North America.

58.

Social Stratification: Strata and Classes

The sexual division of labor universally separates men's and women's roles and defines their spheres of life, whether clearly distinct and polarized, or overlapping. But in tribal societies, as we have seen, production is characteristically centered in domestic groups; men's and women's roles in production are complementary; and most of what people eat they have produced themselves.

As we have seen in nascent form in the Trobriands, the production and redistribution of surpluses can serve to concentrate wealth and power in the hands of a dominant social stratum. (We will examine the Trobriand system of rank in the next chapter.) In more extreme cases, a society may come to be divided into several levels or strata—for example, chiefs, nobles, commoners, slaves—whose role in production, style of life, and status are sharply contrastive.

Are these *social classes*? Are "primitive societies" *classless*? That is the kind of question that is usually best avoided (social scientists are characteristically at their worst when they are trying to define what they mean). But these questions are often asked, and some clarification will be useful.

Social theorists have struggled for three centuries to decide what classes are, and they still do not agree. A useful sorting out is done by the Polish sociologist Stanislaw Ossowski (1963). He takes first of all three aspects of "classness" that are assumed by most writers

on the subject. First, classes constitute a *system* of the most comprehensive groups in the social structure—one can talk about occupations one at a time, but classes must be defined relative to one another, as parts of a system. Second, a class division determines a system of privileges and discriminations not based on biological criteria, such as sex. Third, membership of individuals in a class is relatively permanent (hence, elders cannot constitute a class).

Beyond this, most theorists agree, though with differing emphases, that social classes are vertically ordered, so that class statuses are superior and inferior to one another. Classes thus generate conflicting interests; and at least under some circumstances, such differential status and economic position produce a consciousness of one's class status, one's consequent bond with one's fellows in opposition to other classes, and one's class interests.

This approach is useful, but still rather vague. Marx got at the heart of the matter when he insisted that classes were defined in terms of people's relationship to the means of production, hence to the power to command the labor of others. The proletariat and the bourgeoisie, in classic nineteenth-century capitalism, were polarized in relationship to the means of production. The bourgeoisie commanded the labor of the proletariat, so that those who produced surplus and those who derived the benefit of it were in opposed classes with conflicting interests.

Marx invoked the criterion of class consciousness, a perception of one's common lot, one's class situation, to distinguish true class systems from systems where people in a similar economic situation had no sense of unity or class consciousness—such as the French peasantry or European intelligentsia. Having a common economic lot without a crystallized consciousness, according to one stream of social theory, defines an *estate* (peasant, merchant, noble), not a class. Here perhaps the more neutral term "stratum" sounds less stilted to the modern ear.

How does all that apply to the societies anthropologists study? Do they have classes? Two cases will begin to illustrate anthropological variations on the theme of hierarchy.

Case 49: Rank and Stratification in Tonga

The Tongan Islands of the South Pacific had an aboriginal population of some 25,000. They were grouped into territorial units conceptualized as the lands of large patrilineages. The 13 major territorial groupings *(ha'a)* of modern times trace descent through ancient ancestors. They in turn are segmented into smaller lineages at several levels, though the labels for these lower-level lineages seem not to have been consistently applied.

Tongan society is pervaded by the principle of ranking. The *ha'a* are conceived as ranked according to seniority of descent, reflected in ranked chiefly titles. Within the extended family household, the senior man is classed as *ulumotua* (ancestor). He is succeeded by his younger brother or oldest child, the latter resulting, in some cases, in the *ulumotua* being a woman. Seniority here is determined by a Polynesian principle that rank passes directly down the line of firstborn sons, or sometimes, daughters. Younger brothers and their descendants have a lower rank.

This principle of seniority, through primogeniture—ideally in the male line—was the basis of the elaborate ranking and stratification in the Tongan lineage system. Each descent group, at every segmentary level, had as its nucleus one or more chiefs *('eiki)* and a cluster of "chiefs' attendants" *(matāpule)*. The other lineage members were commoners *(tu'a)*.

The highest-ranking chief in all of Tonga was the Tu'i Tonga, or paramount chief. In recent centuries, his role had become religious; he was the focal point of sacredness, due to his direct descent from ancient ancestors and ultimately the gods. Two other paramount chiefs, the Tu'i Ha'a Takalaua and Tu'i Kanolupolu, represented both great sacredness and broad secular power. They functioned as "national," rather than lineage, leaders.

The chiefs of lineages varied in power and sacredness according to the seniority of their descent. Lesser chiefs headed junior lineages and lower-order segments. Chiefs at all levels commanded deference and exercised a powerful and often arbitrary authority over commoners. Tribute was exacted, taboos were levied. Food surpluses were channeled upward through the status hierarchy, and then downward again to be consumed as reinforcements of the prestige, power, and largesse of the chiefs. So powerful were the great chiefs that they could arbitrarily exact property or life itself from their subjects at will (Gifford 1929). (Sahlins (1958) gives a summary of older sources, and Kaeppler (1971) gives a somewhat revised and newer picture.)

Case 50: Natchez Social Classes

The Natchez Indians of the Lower Mississippi Valley represented the most extreme social stratification in aboriginal North America. About 3500 Natchez lived in nine villages. In the central or Great Village, the divine King, the Great Sun, had his capital. He appointed a Head War Chief, a Master of Temple Ceremonies, two peace chiefs, a maize chief, an administrator of public works, and four festival administrators. The Great Village was the center of divine rule, with a Sun temple.

The class system of the Natchez has been a subject of much anthropological debate. Natchez society was apparently composed of a graded nobility and a large commoner class, called Stinkards by the Nobles. The grades of the nobility included the royal family, or Suns; a class of Nobles; and a lesser class of Honored People. The Great Sun was the oldest son of the highest-ranking Sun woman, White Woman, in this basically matrilineal system. The perquisites of high rank were great: members of higher classes, and especially the Great Sun, had to be treated with deference and honorifics. There was a curious and asymmetrical rule of marriage: a member of the nobility, man or woman, had to marry a Stinkard. The Stinkard husband of a Sun woman did not eat with her, but stood like a servant. She could indulge freely in love affairs, but he could not; and

A Natchez scene: A house in the right foreground, a sun noble being carried on a platform, center, and the Sun Temple in the background. (A reconstruction, courtesy of The American Museum of Natural History.)

when she died he was killed to accompany her. Their children, following the matrilineal principle of affiliation, became Suns. But just what happened to the children of male Suns, Nobles, and Honored People is not quite clear. If, as reported, the children of male members of the nobility dropped one class, rather than all becoming Stinkards (their mothers' class), it would seem that there would soon be an excess of Nobles and Honoreds and not enough Stinkards to provide spouses for the nobility. In addition, some people could apparently rise one class by meritorious deeds.

This puzzle has generated what has come to be called "the Natchez paradox." A searching reexamination of the early reports from which Swanton's early and apparently misleading synthesis was drawn has shed new light on how the Natchez system was organized. First, it seems that collateral matrilineal descendants of the Suns dropped progressively in rank beyond the third degree of collaterality—so the Suns constituted a small royal family rather than a matrilineally constituted highest class. Second, it seems that it was only the sons of Sun and Noble men who dropped only one class; the daughters apparently became Stinkards, acquiring matrilineally their mother's status. Finally, it seems that since only the sons of Nobles dropped one notch, the Honored People consisted only of men, not women. The result of all this is to see basically two social classes—Nobles and Stinkards—with a small royal family of Suns within the nobility and a set of transitionally ranked Honored men. These transitionally ranked Honored men, by great deeds in war, could elevate themselves to Noble status. Stinkard men, by similar brave service, could also elevate themselves to Honored status. One inducement to brave deeds was that Stinkards otherwise were subject to sacrifice in Sun funerals and other state occasions. The Suns thus assured themselves of brave warriors as well as husbands to be disposed of in spiderlike fashion.

The Natchez literature, and the apparent solution to the long-standing "Natchez paradox," are summarized in White, Murdock, and Scaglion (1971).

Applying our conception of "class" to Tonga, Natchez, or other stratified societies in the anthropological world is not simple. Did Stinkards have class consciousness? What was their relation to the means of production?

The best solution seems to be to view the societies of the "primitive" world as running along a continuum. Along most of the range, social classes in the full sense do not occur. But in the middle of the range, systems of social stratification begin to appear. We find ranked social strata with different privileges and differential status and power. At the lower end of this mid-range, these strata are not polarized in relation to the means of production and rights to property. As in the Trobriands, all are subsistence producers, though their access to surpluses and hence prestige and power may be different. But further up the range, people in the top strata may live off the surplus production of lower-ranking groups. And as one moves up the scale toward complex civilizations, the full criteria of "classness" in the Marxist sense are increasingly met, so that the Inca or Aztec can well be viewed as class societies. In fact, class struggle was probably one of the driving forces of social change in a number of early empires.

Though this is not a simplistic notion of social stratification, it still allows some of the variants of inequality in the tribal world to slip through the comparative mesh. In a number of regions individual ranks or titles were used to define status and power. What may look at first glance like a system of social strata, of ranked estates or classes, may turn out to be a system of ranked titles. The Indians of the Northwest Coast provide a classic example.

Case 51: Rank and Title among Northwest Coast Indians

Early accounts described the Indian tribes of the Northwest Coast of North America as organized into ranked social classes, or even "castes." Yet Drucker (1939) argues convincingly that apart from a basic division between freemen and socially inconsequential slaves, there were no social classes at all. Though there were many regional variations among such tribes as Kwakiutl, Nootka, Tlingit, and Haida, common themes emerge. Everywhere it was individuals who had distinctive rank and status, vis-à-vis others in the group. Everywhere, wealth bestowed and validated rank. "Each person's status had its own attributes which were not quite like those of anyone else" (Drucker 1939:216), even though the extent to which they were inherited varied a good deal. In a sense these ranks were like individual titles, a point particularly clear where a person's traditional name served as a kind of summation of his unique status.

So firmly rooted was this association of name and rank that the process of assuming a particular status, social, political, or ritual, consisted in taking (or having bestowed on one) a certain name. The Kwakiutl, among whom the system of naming reached its most profuse elaboration, had separate names for feasts, for potlatches, and for their secret society performances. A personal name was thus a key to its bearer's status and embodied all the rights, economic and ceremonial, to which he was entitled. (Drucker 1939:219)

Though the bulk of societies anthropologists have studied are classless, and only a portion have marked social stratification, the power of class analysis, as developed by Marx and subsequent scholars, can very often still be brought to bear.

First, even in a society without classes in a full sense, there may be an elite that wields the bulk of political and economic power and creates and manipulates ideologies—myths, rituals, property rules, and so on—to serve its own interests. A class analysis leads one to seek out the economic bases of political power, to see the uses to which this power is put by those who have it, to see internal conflict between those in a society who have opposing interests as a driving force of change, and to see "a society" as a temporary stage in the unfolding of social process.

Such perspectives are often more revealing than the closed and ahistorical "functional" interpretations of how the society works and how the culture fits together that have dominated modern anthropology—or at least they are an urgent complementary corrective to them.

Even societies quite far from the class end of the continuum, societies without marked stratification, may be illuminated by such questioning. A society that is egalitarian in class terms but where ritual power and secular authority is in the hands of tribal elders (as in parts of West Africa and Aboriginal Australia) is a far cry from a class system: any man who lives long enough and has the personal attributes of authority may come to wield power as an elder. But it is revealing nonetheless to ask what the basis of the power of weak old men is, and how they use their power to reinforce their interests and bolster that power, even though it is continually passing to younger men as old ones die.

And in the most "egalitarian" society it is usually *adult men* who are equal. Sex cannot in itself be the basis of a true class system. But given the different relations of men and women to the means of production, given the so-frequent male legal control over women, their work, and their bodies, given their differential power and culturally defined value, and given the possibility that both men and women may become conscious as groups of their conflicting interests—given all these parallels to a class relationship—the perspectives of a class analysis very often illuminate the battle of the sexes. This is a theme we glimpsed in Chapter 12 and one on which we will touch at several places in the chapters to come.

All this is to say that from analyses of class relationships, especially in modern European societies, have emerged some valuable insights about the role of conflict and contradictions within social systems and cultures, and about the relationships of ideologies to power—insights that illuminate a much wider range of societies than those from which they were primarily derived.

59.
Caste

Western students of social stratification have viewed the caste system of India with a kind of horrified fascination. For reasons Dumont (1966) has explored, the premises about human relationships that have emerged in the West and the premises of inequality and hierarchy in Indian civilization are so radically different that the way is opened to drastic misunderstanding.

One consequence is some bad comparative sociology. The term "caste" has often been used to designate levels of rigid class systems in various parts of the world, where the lowest strata are exploited and oppressed. Thus "castes" have been identified among the tribal Nupe of Africa, in Guatemala, Japan, modern South Africa, and the American South. All that badly muddles comparative analysis: it often turns out that all such systems have in common—and what links them to caste in India—is the common way they violate our own ideologies of inequality. Such a comparison seems hardly intelligible at all to an Indian social scientist (Sinha 1967).

An excluded or outcaste category, in enforced separation from the dominant society, constitutes a *pariah* class. Members of this class may be excluded from the dominant society because of ritual impurity, as with the Indian untouchables or *eta* of Japan, and may perform essential but polluting economic services. They may be excluded on grounds of race (South African blacks under *apartheid*) or religion (European Jews, for centuries). Pariah classes are excluded from the social structure of the dominant society except as they are exploited, usually economically, by that society. They are accorded a social niche because they do something: European Jews occupied a niche as financiers because they were free to collect interest; Indian untouchables occupied a niche in which they performed unclean services. Both were symbolically polluted.

Caste is a different and special phenomenon, fully developed only on the Indian subcontinent and in Ceylon (Sri Lanka). First, castes are not simply ranked social categories, though their conceptualization in Hindu ideology relates them to the ideal fourfold division of society into *varna*: a priestly class; rulers and warriors; landholders and merchants; and cultivators and menials. Local castes or *jati* are characteristically endogamous corporate groups. Hindu cosmology and rules of purity and pollution prohibit eating and sexual contacts between higher and lower castes. These castes are conceptualized as hierarchically ordered in a fixed rank order, associated with traditional occupations. A person's caste is fixed by birth and is unchanging.

Yet at the level of local caste organization, a quite different and less neat picture has emerged from fine-grained studies (see Marriott 1955b; Singer and Cohn 1968). Castes as local corporate groups are clustered in patterns that vary almost endlessly in local areas. A local caste hierarchy may correspond only very indirectly to the *varna* divisions of Hindu ideology. Thus a dominant group of cultivators may claim the status of warriors, or may dominate Brahmins.

There may simply be no agreed fit to the ideal *varna* categories. Individual castes may jockey for higher ranking, and even their closed endogamous membership may in some areas be permeable. Though ideologies stress the separation of castes, what is most interesting and striking at a local level is their interdependence. (In Case 95, Chapter 22, we will take a closer look at the Indian *jajmani* system of caste interdependence and economic services.)

It is dangerous to lump together social systems in different parts of the world because they are based on inequality and exploitation. Caste is probably best applied only to the Indian scene. But the alternative toward which Dumont (1966) points, taking a relativistic stance in which each culture is to be interpreted in its own terms, is equally limiting and ultimately dangerous. To understand systems of inequality, one must be prepared to

identify oppression and exploitation, whatever cultural symbols and ideologies they are cloaked in. One must see them as products of historic forces; and one must note that it is characteristically ruling classes, and not oppressed ones, that define a cultural ideology which rationalizes these relationships. Caste ideology in India was not created by untouchables, just as the ideologies of nineteenth-century capitalism were not created by factory workers or coal miners (see Mencher 1974 and Meillasoux 1973).

A final type of structured inequality emerges in an unfamiliar light if we examine it in the broadened perspective of anthropology: *slavery.*

60.
Slavery in Anthropological Perspective

We are likely to think of slaves as the lowest class of a society and to view them as economically exploited. Yet neither their low rank nor their exploitation for labor serves to define the position of slaves in all societies where they are found. Nor is slavery confined to large and complex societies. Nearly half the primitive societies in Murdock's (1949) sample, including over two thirds of those in Africa, had some form of slavery (see Miers and Kopytoff 1975).

Slavery is a legal relationship of servitude not governed by a contractual or kinship obligation. The slave hovers in a kind of legal limbo where his master has all the rights—except that, as Malinowski observed, "You can't have your slave and eat him too." He has no kinsmen beyond the nuclear family, if he has one—the master characteristically has no legal duty to keep slave families together.

But the everyday life of slaves is not necessarily lowly or degrading, and they are not necessarily economically exploited chattels. Slaves, not having economic or social interests in conflict or competition with their masters, may acquire great power and responsibility within a family or a court, even though slaves as a category in the wider society are set apart by inequality. Nor was the domestic or court slave usually exploited in the physical and economic ways that a plantation slave was. The "professors" of antiquity were often slaves in the households or courts where they tutored—and presumably exploited young princes with term-paper assignments. But we should not forget, in contrast, the dismal lot of the ancient galley slave, thwarted at every turn. At best his life was a two-sided monotony of either-oar alternatives.

In primitive societies, warfare is the most common source of slaves. How to move slaves outside the boundaries of social group membership, kinship, and legal independence is a problem, and the easiest solution is to capture people who are already outside. Alternatives are enslavement to pay off a debt (so that a child might be sold or "pawned") or to punish a criminal.

When Spaniards plundered the civilizations of the New World and enslaved vast numbers of Indians as miners, and then when plantations created an insatiable demand for slave labor, a tragic new phase in the history of slavery emerged. The consequences of slave labor and plantation systems on family structures and on the emergence of the social systems of the Caribbean, American South, Andes, and other regions will be traced in Chapter 21.

Our first look at structures of inequality in the non-Western world will be extended in the next chapter as we examine the political structures through which power is exercised.

POLITICAL ORGANIZATION 17

In every community anthropologists have studied, they have encountered the processes of "politics"—people leading, organizing, and gaining and using power. Yet paradoxically, if you seek to define what is "political" or to delineate "the political system" in a small-scale society, you face endless frustration.

Looking at tribal societies as stable, isolated systems, we can see certain problems to be solved, by whatever institutional means, that we solve by formal political organization: maintaining territorial rights, maintaining internal order, allocating power to make decisions regarding group action. We can say that the "political organization" of a society comprises whatever rules and roles are used to manage these problems, whether or not there is any formal kind of governmental organization. This refinement of the "take me to your leader" approach has worked fairly well for some purposes. It enables us, for instance, to compare the way these problems are managed across a range of societies from the hunting and gathering band to the centralized state.

But the field anthropologist has increasingly confronted political leaders not in the pristine isolation of a primitive society, but manipulating a colonial administration, fomenting revolution, organizing a faction, uniting ethnic minorities, or running for a position in a government that did not exist five years earlier. Classifying and comparing kinds of "political systems" has increasingly given way to studies of political process at a local level (Swartz et al. 1966; Swartz 1968b). Here we will look at the range of solutions to "political" problems in societies of different scale, and at political processes. But underlying such a sketch will be more important questions about human nature and humans-in-societies. Is the quest for power universal or a product of social and cultural circumstances? Are aggression, conflict, and war basic to the human condition, or do they occur only in some times and places?

61.
Political Institutions: A Comparative View

In modern hunting and gathering societies, political relationships within bands are characteristically devoid of formal, hierarchical structure and are relatively egalitarian. As we saw in §17, those who make decisions that guide group action in hunting, fighting, or maintaining internal harmony are those who have shown ability to make them well. Relations between bands are similarly based more on interpersonal and informal relations than on formal structures.

But the scale of such societies was small, so that the absence of formalized systems of "government" among Australian Aborigines or Andaman Islanders or pygmies posed no major challenge to understanding for the early social anthropologists. As major attention shifted toward African colonies, however, the scale of societies became vast: tens or even hundreds of thousands of tribal Africans maintained ordered and apparently stable territorial relations without any centralized system of government. The challenge to understanding was heightened in British colonies where the governmental policy of "indirect rule" was to use indigenous systems as instruments of administrative control. What *were* the indigenous systems for maintaining political order in stateless, segmentary societies? This question was in the forefront when, in the late 1930s and early 1940s, serious study of political anthropology began.

Recall the segmentary lineage system of Smiths and Joneses illustrated in §42. In the absence of any central political organization, the Elm Street Smiths, normally an independent corporation, may enter into temporary alliances with neighborhood or district Smiths, depending on who the opponents are and what the conflict is about. The classic study of such a system is Evans-Pritchard's (1940) book on the Nuer of the Sudan, which set the framework for 25 years of intensive study of "tribes without rulers" in Africa.

Case 52: Nuer Segmentary Organization

Some 200,000 Nuer live scattered across the swamplands and savanna of the Sudan. Though there is no overarching government, the Nuer maintain a measure of unity and orderly political relations between the territorial divisions Evans-Pritchard calls tribes and between segments of them.

A Nuer tribe is the largest group whose members are duty bound to combine in raiding and defense. Each tribe has a territory, a name, and bonds of common sentiment. Within a tribe, feuds are supposed to be controlled by arbitration.

A tribe is divided into segments. The relationship between segments is conceived in terms of hierarchies of patrilineal descent, as with the Smiths and Joneses, even though the actual correspondence between descent and the composition of territorial groups is quite messy. The basic principle is contextual opposition and alliance: "We fight against the Rengyan, but when either of us is fighting with a third party we combine

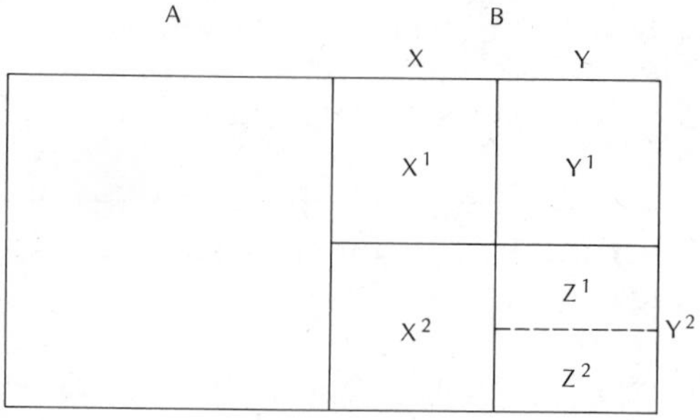

Figure 17.1. Nuer political organization: A and B are the major segments of a Nuer "tribe." X and Y are the major branches of B, and they are in turn divided by segmentation. (From Evans-Pritchard 1940.)

with them" (Evans-Pritchard 1940:143). Evans-Pritchard (1940:143–144) gives the following illustration: "when segment Z^1 fights Z^2, no other section is involved. When Z^1 fights Y^1, Z^1 and Z^2 unite as Y^2. When Y^1 fights X^1, Y^1 and Y^2 unite, and so do X^1 and X^2. When X^1 fights A, X^1, X^2, Y^1, and Y^2 all unite as B. When A raids the Dinka [a neighboring people], A and B may unite."

Disputes begin over many grievances, having to do with cattle, damage to property, adultery, rights over resources, to name a few. The Nuer are prone to fighting, and many disputes lead to bloodshed. Within the same village, Nuer fight with clubs or without weapons. Confrontations between members of different villages can lead to use of spears and to bloody war between men of each village. When a man has been killed, the dead man's close patrilineal kin will try to kill the slayer or one of his close patrilineal kin. The slayer goes to a "Leopard-skin chief" for sanctuary: the latter seeks to mediate and to get the aggrieved lineage to accept "blood cattle" and thus prevent a blood feud. A killing involving members of low-level segments who thus have close social relationships, like Z^1 and Z^2 or even Z^1 and Y^1, is likely to be settled without blood vengeance. The more distantly related are the groups involved, the greater the probability of large-scale fighting between temporary alliances like the X's versus the Y's.

But what about the Leopard-skin chief who arbitrates disputes and provides sanctuary? Does this not indicate some overarching political organization? According to Evans-Pritchard (1940), such a "chief" has ritual powers and a role as mediator and negotiator, but he has no secular authority, no special privileges. His performance in peacemaking is possible because he stands outside the lineage and tribal system, not because he is central in it. He serves an important function which in other segmentary societies must usually be served by persons with conflicting obligations due to cognatic kinship ties that crosscut lineages. His presence enables Nuer to carry the posturing of hostility and threat further than they otherwise could, because he stands in the way of the actual killings most Nuer hope to avoid.

The Nuer political system is interesting in that changing perspectives

A Nuer leopard-skin chief. (Photograph by
E. E. Evans-Pritchard, courtesy of the Clarendon Press, Oxford.)

on how it works and how it can be understood, in the years since Evans-
Pritchard's classic 1940 book *The Nuer*, reveal widening horizons in the
study of social and political organization.

Evans-Pritchard's view of the Nuer was essentially static: his models
show how Nuer society "works" in an ahistorical vacuum where equilibrium prevails. But more recently, studies by Newcomer (1969), Haight
(1972), Gough (1971), and others have reexamined the Nuer more closely
in temporal and ecological context. "Nuer society" emerges as an unstable
stage in a process of invasion and assimilation of their cultural cousins,
the Dinka, that was arrested by colonialism.

For our purposes, it suffices to suggest this change of view by sketching in barest outline a recent exchange between Greuel (1971) and Haight
(1972) regarding the allegedly "powerless" Leopard-skin chief or mediator. Greuel suggested that far from being powerless, the Leopard-skin
chief was a wealthy leader, partly because of the cattle he received for his
services as mediator, who could mobilize the support of a substantial
coalition of followers. If a man murdered a close lineage kinsman, his
relatives would offer blood money; if he murdered a distant outsider, a

blood feud was no threat to community solidarity. But if a man killed a marginally close kinsman or neighbor, where a blood feud would be disruptive of economic and social solidarity, the Leopard-skin chief could often effectively mediate. But he could do so because he could mobilize a dominant coalition with an interest in avoiding internal feuding. Thus, while he had literally no direct power to enforce decisions, he commanded much implicit political power.

Haight (1972), invoking a historical interpretation, questions whether the Leopard-skin chief, who emerged to prominence through personal ability from a particular Leopard-skin lineage, usually was the center of a numerically dominant coalition. In many or most areas, the Leopard-skin lineage was not the dominant lineage; and Haight sees the power of the Leopard-skin chief in these areas as more religious than political. Where in some areas the Leopard-skin lineage exercised political dominance, the Leopard-skin chief might indeed mobilize support of a dominant coalition. But both situations, Haight argues, are best understood in terms of the historical process of conquest whereby the Nuer maintained dominance over the Dinka by absorption, and preserved an egalitarian social order while keeping a firm hold on territories.

Sahlins (1961) has argued that the Nuer and Tiv (Case 25) represent a specialized form of lineage system where each segment corresponds to a territorial bloc, and the arrangement of territories in space corresponds to the genealogical closeness of segments. Such an organization, he suggests, is particularly adaptive when a tribe is expanding into the territory of another people; effective alliances for aggressive "predatory expansion" would emerge at the right time.

Conflicts and feuds within a segmentary system in one sense upset the social order. But as Max Gluckman and his students have argued, they also maintain and renew it. Beyond the local descent group segment (like the Elm Street Smiths in §42), tribesmen seldom unite *for* anything; they unit *against*. Without feuds and conflict, social groupings would be much more atomistic and isolated from one another than they are. Moreover, the process whereby groups and alliances of groups settle feuds reaffirms their unity within a wider social system and moral order. It is Elm Street Smiths whose mothers were Browns who mediate in a feud between Smiths and Browns; and the resolution of feuds thus underlines the webs of kinship that bind groups together rather than the lines of descent that separate them.

In such stateless societies, the possibility often lies latent that from the component lineages or local groups some larger and more effective alliance can be crystallized. Sometimes a charismatic leader drawing on religious symbols or mystical dreams or visions can unite fragmented and opposed groups in a collective war of liberation or conquest or some other dramatic action. Joan of Arc and El Cid illustrate this theme in European history. The Mahdi who united the feuding lineages of the Sudan in a holy war of liberation provides another example. Among such far-flung tribal groups as the Assiniboin Indians of the eastern Plains and the Iban of Borneo (Cases 4 and 31), fragmented local groups have been temporarily united by charismatic leaders whose mission of conquest was revealed in dreams.

In the Mount Hagen region of Papua New

Guinea, the archaeologist Jack Golson has uncovered fascinating though still partial evidence that several times over a span of 6000 years, fragmented local groups may have been united into much larger and more cohesive regional political systems, marked by extensive irrigation and intensification of production.

All this serves as a warning against simplistic typologizing about political systems—a point to which we will shortly return. But to give a better survey of the literature, some "types" will be useful.

Within a descent group like the Elm Street Smiths, political power and authority may be formally defined and assigned or may be flexible and based on personal attainment. A spectrum of possibility in the political organization of Neolithic societies can be illustrated from the Pacific. Here two polar types of leaders are characteristic: "Big Man" and "chief" (Sahlins 1963). The Big Man, characteristic of Melanesia, leans in the direction of the leader in a hunting and gathering society; and the chief, characteristic of Polynesia, leans in the direction of the head of a centralized state. In the middle of this spectrum lie the by-now familiar Trobriand Islanders. The line between a tribal mode of political order and a chiefdom is not always easy to draw, as the Trobriand case will shortly illustrate. Let us look first at a Melanesian Big Man system.

Case 53: The Kwaio "Big Man"

The Kwaio of Melanesia (Cases 29, 32) are fragmented into dozens of local descent groups. Each owns a territory, and there is no central government or political office uniting these small groups politically. Influence, authority, and leadership in secular affairs come from success in mobilizing and manipulating wealth. A Big Man in a descent group is a more successful capitalist than his fellows—the visible capital being strung shell beads and pigs and the invisible capital being prestige. To acquire renown and be respected, a group must give large mortuary feasts honoring its important dead. If a man from group A dies, the dead man's relative from rival group B may be one of several emissaries allowed to bury him. The Big Man of group A will take the lead in a great mobilization of wealth by his group. The pallbearers, including the one from group B, will be rewarded with large quantities of valuables. But all this must be reciprocated. When months or years later an equivalent member of B dies, an A relative has the right to bury him and the B's must give as large a presentation to him as was made in the first feast. What looks like an act of kinship obligation is in fact a duel for prestige between Big Men, on behalf of their groups. A Big Man becomes big by manipulating wealth successfully. To attain great success, he must be an oldest son and he must have a fairly large group of close kin and fellow descent group members to mobilize. His strategy is to make people obligated to him, by contributing to their feasts, financing marriages, and otherwise investing his resources.

A Big Man has no formal authority or powers, no clear-cut position. He is simply a man who leads because people follow, who decides because others defer to him. A Big Man takes the lead in advancing claims or

A Kwaio Big Man in action: A leader gives staging instructions to his kin at a mortuary feast *(left)* and carves pork for distribution *(right).* (Photographs by the author.)

demands against other descent groups and in settling feuds. He maintains internal stability and direction, Kwaio say, like the steersman of a canoe. A Big Man's oldest son may have some slight advantage in the quest for prestige and power. But there is no hereditary succession and no position to succeed to. Bigness is a matter of degree, in a society where every man gives some feasts and plays some part in the game of investment; and many descent groups have no clear-cut Big Man.

In some other Melanesian societies, notably in the New Guinea highlands, the scale and density of population are greater and the production of prestige items—pigs and root crops, and through them, pearl shells and other symbolic valuables—is increased. In such settings, Big Men become bigger and more solidly institutionalized; and the gulf between them and ordinary men widens so that incipient class systems begin to appear. Big Men in the New Guinea highlands may

wield substantial power, as well as command great prestige, through their domination of elaborate exchange cycles. The Te exchange of the Mae Enga (Meggitt 1972) and the Moka exchange of the nearby Melpa (Strathern 1972) are vivid examples. We have noted, in the archaeological evidence from this region (p. 353), the possibility that more complex political systems can emerge from the alliance and political federation of Big Men.

The Melanesian Big Man has become one

of the stereotyped figures in modern political anthropology, and the nature of his power has been contrasted with that of his central African counterpart, the village headman (Gluckman et al. 1949). The Big Man's powers are *personal*. Unlike the village headman, he occupies no office, his powers are achieved, and they are contingent on his continuing leadership as an entrepreneur. Whereas the village headman has authority over people, the Big Man commands resources, manipulating obligations and acquiring prestige (A. L. Epstein 1968).

The Trobriand Islanders combine some elements of the Big Man pattern with a system of chiefly rank, creating a political organization hard to pigeonhole in a classification scheme.

Case 54: Trobriand Political Organization

Recall the central elements in Trobriand social organization: the matrilineal subclans, the rule of residence after marriage that brings married men back to their subclan village, and the *urigubu* presentations of yams from these subclan members to the husbands of their out-married female members.

As we have seen, each matrilineal subclan has a village on its land; and some villages also contain a branch of a second subclan. A number of villages in the same area, related by intermarriage and traditional alliance, form a *cluster* (Powell 1960).

Each village has a leader whose role is in many ways similar to that of the Kwaio Big Man. But there are some crucial differences, for the Trobrianders have a pervasive concept of *rank*. It is not *people* who are ranked, but subclans. Basically there are two ranks, "chiefly" (*guyau*) and commoner. Any village thus is controlled by a subclan that is either of high or low rank. But the high-ranking subclans are themselves in a long-term competitive struggle for prestige and power; and hence there is a publicly known, if not official or clear-cut, ranking of *guyau* subclans.

Now, the leader of a commoner village, attaining his position by manipulating power and wealth and exercising wise leadership, is very much like the Kwaio Big Man, except that he and his group are pieces in a wider design. The leader of a *guyau* village, however, has an important prerogative: he can take more than one wife. If you were a Trobriand man with six wives, imagine what would happen at harvest time. You would get *urigubu* yams from six different subclans. And *urigubu* yams mean prestige. This is precisely how the system works. *Urigubu* presentations become a form of political tribute. The more powerful a subclan, the more subclans in the same cluster and other clusters are placed in a politically subordinate position to it by strategic and manipulated marriage alliances. Sending a wife is, as it were, the first act of a tribute relationship. Commoners must also show formal physical deference to the leaders of the highest-ranking subclans, whose rank is symbolized by the high platforms on which they sit. The leader of a village of high rank symbolizes

Trobriand politics: A chief's yamhouses are filled with prize yams by his followers. (Courtesy of J. W. Leach.)

the status and prestige of his subclan while at the same time steering its decisions and policy and publicly representing it. He may have to mobilize his allies in warfare to maintain or improve its position relative to other important groups. Important leaders take the most prominent roles in *kula* exchanges, so that each flow of armshells and necklaces through the Trobriands validates or adjusts the balance of power and prestige of subclans and clusters.

The leader of the highest-ranking and most powerful subclan in a cluster, by manipulating marriage alliances and effectively distributing wealth, comes to act as leader of that cluster. His role is similar to that of leader with a *guyau* village, but on a larger scale. Once more his authority and powers are far from absolute. They are accorded to him as representative of the will of the subclans in the cluster and because so many people are obligated to support him, or to defer to him, through his manipulations of wealth.

Just as Trobriand men demonstrate and validate their rank by control of prestige exchange systems—notably the *kula* and the food distributions—so women of high-ranking subclans play a dominant role in the prestige exchange of women's valuables. But here as well, individual entrepreneurial success is crucial in asserting and validating status:

As women stand in the center of *sagali* [mortuary distributions], each woman tries to be the number one woman of the day by being able to throw bundles on each transaction. The woman who can meet the challenge of 500 or more payments is the big-woman of the day. . . . In this ceremony [women's mortuary distribution] women are the major actresses—on stage in the center of the hamlet playing a role every bit as tough and aggressive and competitive as a "big-man" (Weiner 1974).

Weiner also points out that since women receive much of that wealth through their husbands and brothers, competitive exchange by women serves to validate the behind-the-scenes status of their male kin and affines.

A leader's rank reflects the rank of his subclan, his authority is that accorded to him by his group, and he contracts his marriages and receives his wealth as an expression of his group's power and prestige. Yet there is no regular hereditary succession to these positions of leadership, the network of strategic marriages must be established afresh by the aspiring leader, and the balance of power is constantly shifting (Powell 1960). We have here a balance between the competitive openness of the Kwaio Big Man system and the formal crystallization of chiefly rank of Polynesian systems.

Trobriand society vividly reveals what is emerging in political and economic anthropology, as well as from Marxist and other radical critiques of complex industrial societies: the complex interconnectedness and interdependence of wealth and power.

In a chiefdom, ranked descent groups are linked into a wider pattern, with a hierarchy of authorities controlling economic, social, and religious activities. The pattern that links groups together creates an interdependence between them. Both the centralized authority and the linkage of groups into wider systems are well illustrated in Polynesia by the Hawaiians.

Case 55: The Hawaiian Political System

The Polynesians of the Hawaiian Islands had an exceedingly complex and, in terms of the Neolithic world, sophisticated political system based on hereditary rank and classes, and theocracy and divine right; yet at the same time it was flexible and constantly shifting in terms of actual political alignments.

Hawaiian society was based on three major hereditary social classes—commoners, nobles, and inferiors. The commoners, by far the most numerous, were agriculturists, fishermen, and artisans—for the most part self-sufficient, but always living and working in the shadow of nobles to whom their very lives could be forfeit at any time, and supplying them with tribute. The nobles, ranked in sacredness, were occupationally specialized as warriors, priests, and political officials. The hereditary ranking of nobles was based on descent from the gods, genealogically traced; rank of individuals and segments was traced in terms of birth order, with highest rank traced through firstborn child (male or female) of the firstborn child, down genealogical trees. The highest-ranking nobles were so sacred that elaborate and extreme deference—for example, prostration—was owed them by lower ranks, under penalty of death.

The islands were divided into chiefdoms, each ruled by a paramount chief whose powers over his subjects were seemingly absolute and were validated by divine right conveyed by his high god. The paramount chief's rule was administered and maintained through a cluster of high-ranking nobles who served as priests, counselors, and military leaders. The districts of his chiefdom were in turn ruled by local chiefs of high rank who exacted tribute and channeled much of it to the paramount chief to support the elaborate religious rites and secular life of the ruling elite. The nobles were supported almost entirely by tribute exacted from commoners in local areas, which in turn were administered by chosen chiefs and overseers of lower rank. The whole system was formally hierarchical, even feudal, in many respects, culminating in the rights of life and death, and dispossession, the paramount chief exercised over his subjects. Being of the highest rank and sacredness himself, this chief approached the status of the god who conveyed on him these divine rights. Secular political powers and ritual relations with the gods were united in his person. Seemingly this almost feudal system was fixed, stable, and immutable.

But in fact it was highly flexible and unstable. The territory of a chiefdom was established and maintained by conquest, and the political fortunes of paramount chiefs waxed and waned with their success or failure in battle and their success in holding their chiefdoms together in the face of insurrection and intrigue. The sacred mandate to rule had continually to be validated by secular success: if a chief lost in battle or a rival successfully challenged him by usurping the paramount chief's sole right to human sacrifice, it showed that he had lost his god's favor or that another's was more powerful. Even if a chief held his chiefdom together or extended its boundaries by conquest, his chosen successor—if there was one—immediately became the focal point of new rivalry and intrigue. Whole islands were added to chiefdoms, or lost; the political map, as well as its ruling cast of characters, was constantly changing. And with each new paramount chief or territorial conquest, the previous ruling elite lost their jobs—and very often their lives, in sacrifice to the new ruler's god. From the highest to the lowest levels of chiefly rule, office and privilege were conferred by a paramount chief and contingent on his political power. Only rarely, when the paramount chiefdom passed through an orderly dynastic succession, was there continuity of power at the lower administrative levels. As in the Trobriand system, the tides of political fortune were always shifting; gaining and preserving power required skilled direction and manipulation of physical and human resources—and a goodly measure of luck (Davenport 1969).

Africa provides not only classic examples of segmentary lineage systems with no overarching political structure, but also a range of societies all the way to enormously sophisticated *states*. The way such central "governments" can build out of localized kin groups is revealed by the political system of the Bunyoro of Uganda.

Case 56: The Bunyoro Lineage System and Kingship

The kingdom of the Nyoro of Uganda, who number about 100,000, is believed to comprise three historically separate ethnic groups: an original agricultural people; a pastoral invading group, the Huma; and a more recently invading Nilotic group, the Bito, from whom the kings of modern times trace descent. Although the Nyoro have been much changed by colonial domination, the general outlines of the traditional system can be reconstructed.

The local groupings of traditional Nyoro society were, at least ideally, segments of patrilineal clans. A cluster of extended family households comprise a dispersed community. Just how these local lineages or clan segments were grouped territorially is difficult to reconstruct, since clans are now intermingled. But rituals, marriage transactions, the legal system, and the kinship terminology suggest that patrilineal descent groups may have been more strongly corporate in the past than in the historic period.

On top of this system, which fits roughly into the Smiths and Joneses pattern, was a system of kingship and political hegemony that resembled in some ways the feudal system of medieval Europe. At its apex was the King, descended from the traditional dynasty of Bito kings. He exercised formal sovereignty over the entire society and land, expressed both in political authority and in sacredness. His health and well-being were critical for the well-being of his people; if he sickened, the entire country suffered.

Authority to administer territories was delegated by the King to chiefs: great chiefs controlled vast territories; lesser chiefs controlled local areas. But chieftainship at all levels was an appointed, not hereditary, power; though it tended to be passed down in families, it could be withdrawn at the King's pleasure. Chieftainships were not strictly ranked, but varied in importance according to the size, population, and wealth of the territory controlled and the closeness of relationship to the King. While the most powerful chiefs were members of the ruling Bito dynasty, most lesser chiefs were Huma cattle herders or peoples of the commoner group, descendants of men who had attracted the favor of a previous King.

The greatest chiefs, mainly Bito relatives of the King, were the "princes" of an aristocracy that commanded deference from commoners and lived from the surplus goods exacted as tribute from these common people. But these great chiefs were potential threats to the King's power, through rebellion and political struggles over succession. Their power was checked by their residence not in the territories they ruled over but in the King's capital; each left the usual affairs of his area in the hands of a deputy. They thus served as links between the King, in whose court they were key figures, and the rural populations that provided foodstuffs, valuables, cattle, and warriors for the King.

Because the King represented, symbolized, and ruled the entire country, it was important that he not be involved primarily with the interests of the Bito. The eldest son of the previous King traditionally held an office as Okwini, the King's "official brother"; and he had primary authority over affairs of the Bito ruling group. A half-sister of the King served as Kalyota, the King's "official sister." She in turn was officially in charge of the aristocratic Bito women, who enjoyed a high rank and prestige and were considered to be "like men," in contrast to commoner women with their domestic duties. Formerly, these women of rank were not allowed to marry or have children. The Kalyota's power was in fact considerable: she held estates like male chiefs, deriving revenue and services from them, and she settled disputes among the Bito women.

Thus, among the Nyoro a patrilineal descent system provided the basic corporate groups and shaped organization at a local level. Yet superimposed on this descent system was a feudal hierarchy, a hereditary aristocracy, and a King with sweeping political power and great sacredness (Beattie 1958, 1960).

Even more striking, in centralization and rigid hierarchical organization, were the great military empires of the Americas and the Middle East whose emergence we sketched in Chapter 7. By this point, however, a comparative typology of political systems has taken us beyond the relatively small-scale societies with which we have been concerned in this segment of the book. We glimpsed very briefly in Chapter 7 the challenges such complex urban states pose for archaeological interpretation, as theorists try to sort out the complex interplay of ecological, economic, demographic, political, ideological, and other variables. In Chapter 23, we will return to the challenges complex societies pose to modern social anthropological analysis and understanding.

Such a comparative study of political institutions is limited and limiting. By placing societies implicitly on a scale of increasing size, centralization, and complexity, such comparison can obscure the dynamics of such systems. Thus the Trobriand political system is in the long run best understood and analyzed not as a way station between New Guinea Big Men and Polynesian chiefs, but as one possible permutation or development of the cultural pattern of the Massim region (other variant forms, involving less marked stratification and wealth, are found in neighboring Murua, the Amphlett Islands, and so on). It is more constructive to probe the ecological and demographic circumstances, and complex processes, whereby Trobriand society assumed its special form through a series of historical transformations (see Friedman 1974; Godelier 1974) than to place it in a typological pigeonhole.

62.
The Processes of Politics

Comparing political institutions inevitably makes assumptions that the societies being compared are relatively independent entities and that the political systems are relatively stable. But these assumptions about discreteness, stability, and integration do not serve us well in understanding the political processes of a rapidly changing and complicated modern world. It is the *processes,* not the institutions, of politics that increasingly command attention.

Political processes, according to a recent attempt at definition, are those "involved in the determination and implementation of public goals and for the differential distribution and use of power . . ." (Swartz 1968b).

The study of political processes is a rapidly moving front in anthropology, partly because on this frontier anthropologists are seeking ways to escape the bonds of the traditional assumptions about closed, stable, integrated societies. First, they are now looking at "fields" of political events that cross the traditional boundaries of societies. We are learning belatedly about the way laws, bureaucracies, and political parties impinge on tribal or village peoples; and about the "political middlemen" who bridge the gulf between the outside world and their own people. Second, they are making no assumptions about stability or equilibrium. Political processes produce new roles, new groups, new conflicts, and new integration. They do not simply keep the system going.

Third, and related, one need not view the

acts of individuals as submerged within "the system." Making no assumption that all participants share the same cultural rules, or that roles and groups are stable, we can *see* individuals as shaping and manipulating patterns of social life, not simply following them.

Studies of conflict and factionalism have dominated the recent literature—partly because conflict is by its nature more dramatic than harmony. Yet the "public goals" of political action may be to avoid conflict or to preserve unity. The leader quietly maintaining his control by building up loyalty and confidence is engaging in political action just as is the fiery orator fomenting revolution. An example of the newer concern with political process, from a village in modern Taiwan, will serve to illustrate.

Case 57: Factionalism and Change in a Taiwanese Village

The Taiwanese village of Hsin Hsing has a population of about 600 Chinese. Their traditional social structure has been built around several patrilineages *(tsu)*, of which two have been most influential. The households of each *tsu* are centered in a small neighborhood or compound in the village. Though there are no marked concentrations of wealth or gulfs of social inequality, important families within the leading *tsu* have steered village politics and controlled alliances with neighboring villages through intermarriage and kinship.

When elections were introduced by the Chinese Nationalist government, elected offices of the village and the district of which it is a part were controlled by these leading families. The outcome of elections was, in effect, arranged so as to follow the traditional power of *tsu* and leading families in them, and to maintain the consensus and outward unanimity of action within *tsu* and village. The "mayor" of the district was chosen by the council of village representatives, again following lines of kinship and traditional influence. The elected officials were members of the gentry—men of education and standing.

But in the latter 1950s, opportunistic men outside the village establishment began to compete with these "respectable" leaders, using vote buying and other manipulations to get elected, and hence gain money and power. The high cost of getting elected, and its unsavory side, led traditional leaders to stay increasingly out of these contests.

Moreover, in 1959 and 1961, the government made election of the district mayor a matter of popular vote and redistricted voting for the district council so that villages no longer each had one representative. At the same time, the country's ruling Kuomintang party intruded increasingly on the local political scene.

The result has been the emergence of political *factions* cross-cutting *tsu* and village lines. Consensus and harmony have been lost in favor of shifting factions, involving the poor and uneducated as well as the gentry, as active forces. Thus in the village of Hsin Hsing, a Farmers' Association and a Public Office faction organized at *district* level have competed for allegiance and control and have divided *tsu* and family alliances. In the competition for votes, one candidate for village mayor chartered a bus to bring back from the city of Taipei 36 eligible voters. The district leadership of a faction enters local politics to provide patronage and avert the defection of supporters—playing on *tsu* unity, or seeking to disrupt it, as suits their cause. The traditional system has not been destroyed, but it has been radically transformed (Gallin 1968).

In Taiwan, with the disruption of traditional equilibrium and political order, the widening of the political arena beyond the local community, the emphasis on change and conflict rather than continuity and control, on process rather than structure, we see in miniature the focal points of the newer political anthropology.

An important conceptual foundation of the emerging anthropology of political processes is a model where social systems are not stable, enduring, "external" frameworks that transcend and constrain individual actors; but rather, where social systems are the statistical outcome of individuals pursuing their strategies and goals.

A crucial pioneering study here was Barth's (1959a) analysis of political processes among the Swat Pathan of northern Pakistan. "The political system" of this segmentary society was not, he argued, maintained in equilibrium because the component social groups were in balanced structural opposition to one another—as in the classic African studies of Nuer, Tiv, and others. Rather, the system was generated and maintained by individual actors seeking to advance their power by strategic choices and coalitions (Barth 1959a, b).

From this analysis of how individual strategies may cumulatively produce systematic integration and equilibrium, Barth has moved toward the study of change. If we see social systems as the outcome of individual decisions, he argues, we are not bound to assumptions of equilibrium: there is no reason why all individuals need pursue the same

strategies, and no reason to assume that—even if they did—the outcomes would preserve "the system" rather than progressively transform it (Barth 1966, 1967).

F. G. Bailey, carrying this model further, has analyzed the political process in India and elsewhere in several important articles and books. In *Stratagems and Spoils* (Bailey 1969), a major synthesis, he elaborates a model of the way individuals seek to maximize power, and of the common themes of strategy, coalition, and conflict that emerge in competitive struggles for power in different times and places. In *Gifts and Poison* (1971), Bailey and his students turn from the public to the private arena and argue that an informal politics of reputation and status in interpersonal relations is crucial in the European communities they studied. They pay special attention to "people competing to remain equal," and to "the tragedy, the bitterness, which we see in conflict between those who are equal and who therefore might have been friends" (Bailey 1971:19).

Viewing individual strategies to maximize and preserve power and reputation as generating "the system" has been highly revealing. We have been led beyond assumptions about stability, led to see how individual motives make sense of collective behavior, led to see informal strategies as well as formal ideologies and rules. But while this reveals one side of politics, it can hide another side.

This distortion is underlined by Talal Asad (1972) in a recent reinterpretation of Barth's (1959a) Swat Pathan evidence. Asad argues that the decision-makers on whom Barth had focused constitute a landed class whose power over their tenants derives from an exploitative economic position with deep historical roots. The system, Asad argues, has been progressively changing. Progressive consolidation of power by landlords, and a polarization between them and the landless peasant class, was accelerated by British colonialism in India and then was stabilized by British military domination of the northern frontier. Asad's critique makes a number of strong points: (1) "A political system" must be seen as part of a wider system, and in a long-range historical perspective: seeming stability may be illusory. (2) Power—who has how much of it and what strategies and options are open for advancing it—is ultimately rooted in economic advantage, and hence in control over resources and means of production. (3) A class analysis reveals how individual consciousness—and hence individual goals, motives, values, and ideologies—are conditioned by the circumstances of one's social class: to make a general model of human motivation from the strategies of an elite is misleading.

Asad also questions the functionalist assumption that political order is maintained within a society through an implicit covenant of consent regarding legitimate authority. The assumption of consent whereby the governed accept political authority as legitimate is implicit in Barth's interpretation, and explicit within the tradition of political anthropology—from Fortes and Evans-Pritchard (1940) through Smith (1956), Easton (1959), and Swartz and others (1966). Asad, in reinterpreting the Swat Pathan material and his own evidence on the Kababish Arabs of the Sudan (1970), argues that a dominant class or group holds political power over a subordinate class or group because historical and economic circumstances have given them the means to do it. The very legitimacy of its authority is an ideology created by the politically powerful and imposed on the powerless: the notion of consent becomes meaningless. Legitimacy is not a social contract, but an instrument of power. (But that is a perspective that comes more vividly to a black convict than to a business executive in suburbia.)

More generally, Asad's critique implies that a political model whereby individuals maximizing power and reputation generate "the system" may be culture-bound and ideology-bound in the same way as maximization models in economics, and for the same reasons. From their vantage point within a social and economic system predicated on competition between individuals, with an ideology emphasizing individualism and competition as virtues, social scientists are prone to project very biased assumptions about human nature and society into their theories.

In their studies of political processes in changing societies, anthropologists are groping for new ways to conceptualize the cultural and the social, the enduring and the changing, the individual and the collective. If they have not reached consensus, they have at least given new life and new excitement to a subject too long rendered dull and lifeless by static models and simplistic typologies.

63.
War, Politics, and Human Nature

Must humans fight? Is conflict inevitable? Are wars generated by our social and biological nature? Or are they generated by imperfect social conditions that could be changed?

If we seek to gain in wisdom and vision from looking at the widest range of human societies, we are led to ask such sweeping questions. The evidence, we will see, is far from clear. As with most major questions about human nature and human life, the evidence can be read in different ways and used to "prove" different theses. One can use ethological, physical anthropological, and ethnographic evidence to "prove" that aggression and fighting over territory are deeply embedded in human biology (Ardrey 1961; Lorenz 1966). Or one can "prove" that humans' basic nature is to cooperate, to share. Any such sweeping interpretation must be suspect. Yet some sifting of the evidence will give us useful perspectives.

In §9, we looked briefly at the biological bases of aggressive reactions—circuits of the evolutionary old limbic system of the brain, and the hormonal and other chemical systems that activate them. But as we saw, a biological mechanism of aggression is not the same thing as a *drive* to aggression. What is peculiarly human is the interconnection between these biologically old mechanisms and cognitive, symbolic systems. Anger, rage, and aggression can be activated by a purely cultural message—a verbal insult, an obscene gesture, a frustrating crossword puzzle, or even the absence of a signal (a telephone that does not ring). So, too, can other emotions— shame, jealousy, fear, and so on. (Thus Firth (1936:473) records that, on the Polynesian island of Tikopia, a man who farted among his companions was so shamed that he jumped from a tree and killed himself.) And when a human is angry, his anger, though physically manifest in quickened pulse and flushed face, may be expressed verbally or in writing, with no physical aggression. Biologically ancient aggression can in humans be transposed by the cognitive powers of memory and symbolism into enduring hate; we are the only animals that can spend years harboring hatred and bent on vengeance.

Biology and "human nature" cannot account for the difference between gentle and peaceful Congo pygmies and fiercely aggressive Yąnomamö or bloodthirsty Mongol hordes building huge pyramids of human skulls. All humans *could* become killers, but only some do. The explanation must lie in particular times and places—in cultural pat-

terning, or sometimes *outside* cultural patterning. (Thus the Semai of Malaya, pictured by Dentan (1968) as "the gentle people," committed terrifying acts of slaughter and cruelty during civil rioting in an urban setting outside their normal cultural framework; and the Balinese, with their cultural emphasis on restraint and harmony, engaged in wholesale slaughter of their fellows in a 1965 political purge.)

Do all societies have war? That, as usual, turns out to be a problem of definition. It is useful to reserve the term "warfare" for collective hostile action by members of a territorial group against another that is regarded by those members as a legitimate policy of the group. If we do, then there are many small-scale societies without wars, though in these societies, homicide and feuding may be endemic. Other specialists, using more inclusive definitions, have found war to be much more widespread.

Quibbling over definitions is usually a waste of time. It is clear from the evidence that interpersonal and intergroup violence takes widely varying forms in different societies. Unless we sort these variations out, we are likely to compare apples with oranges and pears and end with analytical fruit salad. A good deal of sorting out is possible if once more we look at societies in terms of levels of scale, technology, and complexity. Hunters and gatherers do not all fight in the same way for the same reasons; but they have more in common than each would have with Mongol hordes, English Crusaders, or German Panzer divisions.

Among band societies, our data are unfortunately thin. Some bands clearly fought a good deal, for access to special resources, for vengeance, and so on. Thus Warner (1937:155) writes of the Murngin of Australia, "Warfare is one of the most important social activities of the Murngin and surrounding tribes. Without it, Murngin society as it is now constituted could not exist." Yet when peoples of this technological level did fight, combat was usually sporadic, often minimally planned, individualistic, relatively disorganized, and lacking elaborate weaponry and tactics. An unusually formalized mode of combat among Australian Aborigines is worth describing because it counterbalances some recent studies of demographically sparse and politically marginal and subservient hunters and gatherers.

Case 58: Ritualized Combat Among Herbert River Aborigines

The Norwegian naturalist Karl Lumholtz witnessed, in 1882, a remarkable scene of "borboby" ritualized combat among the then-numerous Australian Aborigines of the Herbert River valley in Queensland. He was one of the few observers to see combat among hunters and gatherers in something like their precolonial circumstances and in a nonmarginal ecological zone where populations were substantial. His account is worth quoting at some length:

A borboby is a meeting for contest, where the blacks assemble from many "lands" in order to decide their disputes by combat. . . . As we gradually approached the fighting-ground we met more and more small tribes. . . .

All the natives were armed. They had quantities of spears, whole bundles of nolla-nollas [throwing clubs] and boomerangs, besides their large wooden shields and wooden swords. . . .

[Lumholtz then describes the prepared "battleground" and preliminary threatening posturings and displays by the warriors.]

The warlike ardour increased, and all held their weapons in readiness. Suddenly an old man uttered a terrible war-cry, and swung his bundle of spears over his head. This acted, as it were, like an electric shock on all of them; they all at once gathered together, shouted with all their might, and raised their shields with their left hands, swinging swords, spears, boomerangs, and nolla-nollas in the air. Then they all rushed with a savage war-cry through the grove of gum-trees and marched by a zigzag route against their enemies, who were standing far away on the other side of the plain. At every new turn they stopped and were silent for a moment, then with a terrific howl started afresh, until at the third turn they stood in the middle of the plain directly opposite their opponents, where they remained. . . .

As soon as our men had halted, three men from the hostile ranks came forward in a threatening manner with shields in their left hands and swords held perpendicularly in their right. . . . The three men approached ours very rapidly, running forward with long elastic leaps. Now and then they jumped high in the air like cats, and fell down behind their shields. . . . This manoeuver was repeated until they came within about twenty yards from our men; then they halted in an erect position, the large shields before them and the points of their swords resting on the ground, ready for the fight. . . .

Now the duels were to begin; three men came forward from our side and accepted the challenge, the rest remaining quiet for the present. . . .

While the first three pairs were fighting, others began to exchange blows. There was no regularity in the fight. The duel usually began with spears, then they

Australian Aboriginal men face off with spears in a dispute over the woman in the right foreground. (Photograph taken in Arnhem Land around 1939, courtesy of Rev. H. U. Shepardson.)

came nearer to each other and took to their swords. Sometimes the matter was decided at a distance, boomerangs, nolla-nollas, and spears being thrown against the shields. The natives are exceedingly skillful in parrying, so that they are seldom wounded by the first two kinds of weapons. On the other hand, the spears easily penetrate the shields, and sometimes injure the bearer, who is then regarded as disqualified and must declare himself beaten. There were always some combatants in the field, frequently seven or eight pairs at a time; but the duellists were constantly changing.

The women gather up the weapons, and when a warrior has to engage in several duels, his wives continually supply him with weapons. The other women stand and look on, watching the conflict with the greatest attention, for they have much at stake. Many a one changes husbands on that night. As the natives frequently rob one another of their wives, the conflicts arising from this cause are settled by borboby, the victor retaining the woman.

The old women also take part in the fray. They stand behind the combatants with the same kind of sticks as those used for digging up roots. They hold the stick with both hands, beat the ground hard with it, and jump up and down in a state of wild excitement [here it does not take much Freudian imagination to notice a symbolic linkage of sex and war.] They cry to the men, egging and urging them on, four or five frequently surrounding one man and acting as if perfectly mad. . . .

If one of the men is conquered, the old women gather around him and protect him with their sticks, parrying the sword blows of his opponent, constantly shouting, "Do not kill him, do not kill him."

The duels . . . lasted only about three-quarters of an hour. . . . As soon as the sun had set the conflict ceased. . . . As a result of the borboby several family revolutions had already taken place, men had lost their wives and women had acquired new husbands. In the cool morning of the next day the duels were continued for an hour; then the crowds scattered, each tribe returning to its own "land." (Lumholtz 1889:119–127)

Though killings seem to have been rare in such combat, among some other Aboriginal groups it seems to have been quite common. As we noted in §17, recent studies suggest that stereotypes of peaceful and gentle hunter-gatherers have been quite misleading.

In food-producing societies, warfare was very often a vicious and deadly business, where neighboring kin groups or tribes were in constant danger. The frequency and scale of fighting, for many societies, is hard to assess. Very often our evidence comes from a period, just before Europeans imposed a peace, when traditional balances had been upset by new weapons and other outside influences.

Tribal warfare very often had two facets, and writers have had difficulty keeping both in view. The first side involves elaborate posturing and even pageantry, "productions" in the male realm that involved a great deal of action with very few casualties. Ritualized forms of combat and carefully followed "rules of play" often command attention: a tribal war often looked more like a football game than a ruthless struggle for territory or principle. Robert Gardner's classic anthropological firm *Dead Birds* shows vividly this side of tribal warfare in New Guinea, though the other emerges as well.

This appearance of formal posturing in tribal warfare has often obscured its more serious and vicious side (Fried and others 1968). Warfare to gain territory and hence adjust ecological balances has emerged as far

more important among shifting horticulturists than early writers had thought (Vayda 1961). Recent studies, especially in New Guinea, give a picture not of stability and equilibrium but of a constantly shifting scene where peoples are driven out and scattered and territories expand and contract. The impression Europeans got of a primitive world with groups and tribes that had been there "since time immemorial" was an illusion; the stability they found they often had created by their own intrusion.

In the New Guinea highlands, where group sizes reach a scale more comparable with Africa than in most of Melanesia, yet where a colonially-imposed peace is recent and fragile, anthropologists have encountered intergroup warfare that kills many, scatters survivors, and appropriates territories. Thus the Maring (Case 14) fight to capture one another's territories; the demographically dwindling Fore (Case 16) are threatened by proliferating neighbors. Among the densely settled and tightly organized Mae Enga, hostile neighboring clans covet one another's garden lands in the face of rising land shortage. When wars break out they often involve hundreds of warriors, sometimes in alliances of clans. Battle formations and military manoeuvers are reminiscent of Napoleonic Europe, casualties are heavy, settlements are burned, and territories are captured and held. Meggitt (personal communication) estimates that as many as one third of Mae Enga men died in such fighting.

Ritualized combat on the traditional "battlefield" gives a vivid picture of one side of tribal warfare. But more often, aggression against the neighbors took the form of ambushes, of surprise attacks on undefended hamlets or people working in the gardens, and often killing of women and children. Ethnographers working in societies where warfare is or was endemic have vividly reported the traumatic costs, social and psychological, of living in a state of war with neighboring communities such that sudden death is a daily threat. A romanticization of tribal life that minimizes the prevalence and staggering cost of endemic warfare is sorely misleading.

One who set out to demonstrate through tribal warfare that aggression and cruelty run biologically deep in humans could make a persuasive case: torture of captives and other bloody doings seem to bring out deep satisfactions (Freeman 1964). There is also an organizational side to this. In the tribal world of "we" versus "they," the people over the next hill are likely to be enemies, and the people beyond that to be scarcely human. In such a world, "our" ancestors can easily develop an insatiable demand for "their" heads; or becoming a man may require homicidal raiding of the neighbors. Without governments to prevent or halt hostilities, tribal groups may live in constant danger.

In more complex societies with centralized political systems, the fragmented group-versus-group pattern of tribal warfare gave way to new forms. War as an instrument of the state, with conquest, slaves, or tribute as its aims, was on a very different scale than tribal warfare. If there are deep biological roots to human aggression, their expression is probably more immediate and dramatic for the hunter or warrior than for the mercenary or merchant; the latter enjoyed his violence at the colosseum or the public execution or sacrifice.

And that provides a partial answer to those who surmise from the evidence of ethology and early man that killing and aggression are the nature of the beast. Given our new understanding of continuities with the animal past and our knowledge of protohumans and early humans subsisting as hunters for hundreds of thousands of years, it would be surprising if *Homo sapiens* was by biological nature a docile animal. But with the development of culture, humans created a world of symbolic goals, meanings, and satisfactions, an imagined as well as a sensed world. Aggression can be displaced, channeled, aimed symbolically rather than physically. Culturally created organization can limit and direct its expression, channeling "human nature" into a wide range of social forms (Montagu 1972).

To despair that human life on global scale could be stable and peaceful—on grounds that "human nature" inevitably produces conflict and war—is too simple and pessimistic. To anticipate a golden age when reason and goodness will prevail and people will stop killing one another because it is madness is too simple and optimistic.

In a world where pushing a red button could kill millions and turn the planet into a burned-out wasteland, humans cannot depend on suppressing individual hostile feelings, hoping that all people will love all other people all the time. They will not, and many of them at any moment will be wanting to kill one another. The solutions, if there are any, must lie in our capacities to build new symbolic systems and to create new and more encompassing organizational forms. The progression from band and tribe to vast state partly has been a matter of expanding the scale of the "we." The "they" against whom humans focus their hostility and aggression has shifted from the village across the mountain to the country across the sea. The *con-*

ceptual model has not changed radically; it is the social systems that have been transformed. We have reached a critical point where higher levels of social and political organization that would unite peoples in common human enterprise cannot be achieved without a radical reorganization of our conceptual model. We have run out of human "theys" we can afford to hate and kill. Can we do without them? Science gives no answer, but we have no choice but to try.

SOCIAL CONTROL

18

A culture consists of more or less shared rules for playing the game of ordered social life. Yet these accepted standards of social life are continually at odds with the drives and goals of individuals; and because of this gap between collective standards and private interests, rules are violated, or individuals play by their own rules. So the social scientist sees two sides of the same problem. One must explain and understand *why people follow rules* that thwart their private goals, and one must understand how social order is maintained when the rules of the game are ignored or broken.

Here, first, we will look more closely at those forces that promote conformity to cultural codes. Then we will examine the mechanisms and process of "primitive law," the way peoples in non-Western cultural settings control conflict and respond to breaches of social rules.

64.
The Forces of Social Conformity

Conformity and deviance are like a layer cake, and most social scientists have concentrated on the icing and the top layers. Writings on "deviance and conformity," especially in sociology, usually begin with a narrow conception of a "norm," as something people say should or should not be done. You violate a norm if you steal, cheat, marry two men at once, go nude in church, drive through a stoplight, or (if you are a man) wear lipstick— whether or not you break a formal law. You conform when you follow such norms; you deviate if you violate them.

Some norms are indeed public and are consciously followed or broken. The anthropologist's knowledge about language codes reveals more subtle "rules," akin to those of syntax or phonology. These "rules" are implicit in our behavior, deeply ingrained in habit and unconscious mental processes. Yet our following them lies at the heart of ordered social life. The man who robs a bank is, in sociological terms, criminally deviant. But the anthropologist can perceive him as a routine-bound conformist as well. He comes to the bank appropriately clothed, walking rather than crawling, on the sidewalk rather than the roof or the gutter. He utters or writes his demands in hopelessly conventional English, and he makes his getaway on the right side of the street. One must conform unconsciously to a myriad of cultural rules and conventions to commit a "grammatical" bank robbery—which is, in fact, a complex act of communication. A Trobriand Islander would be hard-pressed to rob an American bank.

The rules we break, or would like to break, lie toward the surface of that complex and intricate system of shared knowledge we call culture. To communicate, we are and must be rule followers. We will, for ease of explication, call those standards of behavior we talk and consciously think about as public norms. Our unconscious rule-following on lower, hidden, levels does not explain why we follow public norms as often as we do, but it gives a different perspective on them. Another source of new perspectives on conformity and deviance is our growing understanding of our biological heritage. Since the writings of Freud, a conflict between human biological drives and the rules of ordered social life has usually been taken for granted. We are, biologically, animals—and to behave as humans exacts a cost of frustration and repression.

Our views of human biosocial life have changed dramatically with modern animal behavior studies. As we noted in §34, Freud was imagining the individual animal, driven by its aggressive nature and sexuality and free to express these natural drives. But we have seen animals in *groups*. That primates are "programmed" with drives for dominance, aggression, and sexuality does not imply their free expression: the young baboon may be as thwarted as a Viennese psychiatric patient. Social organization—whether animal or human—requires that individual organisms pursuing their goals mesh together into ordered patterns of communication, acknowledged rights and powers, and collective action.

Moreover, the very notion of our biological drives being "blocked" seems unrealistic at this stage. In looking at human social organization and political and economic behavior in the preceding chapters, we have not been seeing a thwarting of the biological nature we glimpsed in the early chapters. Rather, we have seen *channeling* and, at times, *deflection* of these primate biological patterns. Culture reshapes, and redefines, and directs biological goal-seeking. It defines for people in a particular time and place what *dominating* is, what a *territory* is, which mates are desirable (and even what to do if you find one). That is, a cultural code defines the goal states toward which people should strive, building on but reshaping the templates laid down biologically. If we think of these goal states in terms of a game, culture does not prevent people from playing a biologically satisfying game. It lays out the strategies for play and lays down the rules.

Anthropological questions about conformity and deviance mainly ask why, in these games of life, people cheat as seldom as they do. Or they ask why people play them at all. We will look quickly at some of the pressures that guide humans into these cultural games and keep their play within accepted bounds.

First, childhood learning gives a person his or her conception of what kind of world this is and what one should be trying to do in and about it. It further underlines—by precept, example, folktale, game, myth, and so on— the moral virtues of one's people and the costs of wrongdoing. Anthropologists have observed that ways of life differ in the degree to which they depend on the "internalization" of moral standards to guide behavior. Some peoples rely more heavily on *external* forces of social approval and disapproval. The contrast has been drawn, perhaps too sharply, in terms of "guilt sanctions" and "shame sanctions" (Mead 1940; Hsu 1953). Later a dramatic instruction in the moral order of one's people may come in an initiation ceremonial. We have seen that the initiates, before their symbolic rebirth, are frequently placed in seclusion. In such periods, intensive indoctrination in the moral virtues of one's people is common.

The pressures for conformity to the ways of one's group are familiar to all of us. The peer-group subcultures of American young people provide vivid examples. Even "nonconformity" is likely to be highly conformist and stereotyped: beards and bare feet can be a "uniform" just as much as Brooks Brothers suits and basic black with pearls.

Nor does the seeming conformity to custom in "primitive" societies necessarily imply great conservatism and lack of change, as earlier writers had often thought. American teenage subcultures or dress fashions should immediately show us the flaws in the supposed equation, conformity = lack of change. As we saw in Chapter 12, change and innovation are constant even in small-scale tribal societies.

Probably the most compelling pressures to conform come from enlightened self-interest. The cynic who sees humans as motivated only by self-interest and the idealist who sees human destiny in selfless giving and sharing are seeing the grays of social life in black or white. Humans have constructed the mazes

of social life—because they have had to—so that the paths through them to individual goals are opened only by cooperation, by sharing, and by rule-following.

Sometimes the rewards of playing the game together and of helping one's fellows are immediate and direct. Sometimes they are long range, as when a young person willingly serves titled leaders and elders in the expectation that later he will attain such status. Our society is rapidly losing a cycling kind of giving and return that is shaped by the life cycle and often axiomatic in the moral system of a tribal people: parents who care for their children when they are young and helpless will be cared for by them when they are old and helpless. Sometimes the rewards are diffuse, as with family cooperation or the satisfaction of friendship, security, or popularity.

We have seen (§40) the peculiar moral force of *kinship*. Fulfilling obligations to one's relatives would seem to run counter to self-interest. But if kinsmen do not always live up to ideal standards, they meet obligations well enough that kinship seems to have an extraordinary moral force. Why? On closer inspection, following kinship obligations turns out to advance, not conflict with, self interest; and very often, group interests *are* self-interests.

This can well remind us that a self-interest model of society is in part an expression of a Western economic and political ideology. It is clear that human tendencies to be individualistic and motivated by self-interest are reinforced by childhood experience that emphasizes competitive individualism. That childhood experience in sharing and cooperation can lead to a substantial submergence of individual interests within group interests—as emphasized in socialist ideologies—is equally clear from modern reorganizations of society in China, Cuba, Tanzania, Israel, with its kibbutzim, and elsewhere.

Even in tribal societies that stress entrepreneurial individualism, as with many Melanesian peoples, self-interest and kinship obligation are so interwoven that group interests and kinship norms are reinforced by personal strategies.

Case 59: Kwaio Kinship and Self-Interest

The Kwaio of the Solomon Islands (Cases 29, 30, and 53) can get married, or advance their position in the game of prestige, only by amassing large quantities of shell valuables and ceremonially presenting them to other people. Yet as a Kwaio man tries to accumulate his capital for such a presentation, he constantly has to give away the valuables he is saving—to help finance a feast, marriage, or fine on behalf of a relative. Having spent months acquiring two or three large strings of shell, he may give them away to help someone else acquire prestige or get married. Why? Because of moral obligations of kinship? Closer examination brings two crucial facts to light. First, to get married or give a feast large enough to bring prestige, a man has to mobilize more valuables at a single time than he would be able to accumulate in a decade. Great numbers of his kinsmen must contribute to his mobilization of wealth, just as he has contributed to those of his relatives. Some do so because they are obligated to reciprocate his help to them. Others are making him obligated to help them at some future time. Second, by helping kinsmen one is in fact investing. A man who saved his capital rather than investing it would not only lose prestige by being stingy but he would be unable to amass enough valuables to acquire prestige through feasting. The trick, as in playing the stock market, is to come out ahead. Only a genius at financial manipulation can acquire great prestige as a feast-giving Big Man (Case 53).

Though following or manipulating the rules is very often the best way to advance self-interests, people encounter over and over again situations where a shortcut across the boundaries of permissibility would get them to the goal faster. Rule-following does generate a measure of tension, frustration, and temptation.

One way to relieve these stresses is to suspend the rules at some special occasion or in some special context. A good orgy every now and then can be useful as well as enjoyable (in many societies the neighbors join in instead of calling the police). Sexual license in a limited situation, or overt hostility against the rules of the Establishment, can be an effective way of "blowing off steam." Privileged sexual access outside of marriage, as between a man and his wife's sister, can relieve potential conflict and tension. *Joking relationships* involving joking and often sexual license between certain classes of relatives have been a classic focus of attention in social anthropology. So, too, have been the opposite side of the same coin, *avoidance relationships,* where strict rules of decorum or even of complete avoidance restrict interaction between a man and his mother-in-law, his sister-in-law, his sister, or some such relative or class of relatives. Avoidance relationships, like joking relationships, occur in the strain points of a kinship system; but they control pressures and tensions by ritualized distantness rather than blowing off steam.

Case 60: Familiarity and Avoidance in the Trobriands

Trobrianders illustrate both privileged familiarity and avoidance, though neither is in as extreme a form as found in some tribal areas. These customs will prove important in Chapter 20. Though Trobriand brother and sister have common concerns in the subclan, and her sons are his heirs, the gulf of her sexuality separates them. From childhood onward, their relations are marked by distance and avoidance of any close contacts. As the sister begins her amorous adventuring, her brother must refrain from any knowledge of it. Even when she marries, matters surrounding her reproductive life are forbidden territory to him. The tabooed relationship between brother and sister is the most emotionally charged and morally fundamental rule in Trobriand culture.

But a man's father's sister has a very different relationship with him. "Her presence always carries with it the suggestion of license, of indecent jokes and improper stories" (Malinowski 1929:535). She is a kind of prototypical sexual object for him—usually considerably older and hence seldom an actual sexual partner—though that is quite permissible—but treated with sexual familiarity and openness. A man cannot mingle with both paternal aunt and sister at the same time: the rules for each contrast too sharply.

Supernaturals often, though not always, keep a close watch on the moral conduct of the living. Moreover, customary rules and procedures are very often given a stamp of divine origin that validates them and gives them an aura of being ultimate, absolute, and sacred. To break the rules of social life is very often to break the laws that govern the universe.

A powerful force of social control in many societies is *witchcraft*—malevolent power that operates through individuals as an involuntary force. Even in the outwardly peaceful and restrained social setting of Pueblo Indians in Zuni or Hopi, violence may erupt with the driving of a witch into the desert. In many societies in Africa, North America, and elsewhere, the deviant who failed to meet the norms of kinship or play by the rules—or simply was more successful than everyone else—would be likely to be singled out as a witch and killed or exiled. Witchcraft accusations, which may in some societies assign responsibility for every death that occurs, give a splendid means to get rid of those who cheat, deviate, or succeed too much—and a splendid incentive to be an upstanding citizen. Fear that witchcraft will be directed against one makes conformity to the norms of social life strategically wise.

Case 61: Kaguru Witchcraft and Social Control

The Kaguru of Tanzania believe that many of their fellows, male and female, possess *uhai,* supernatural powers of witchcraft. Beliefs in witchcraft are conceptually quite separate from Kaguru religious beliefs, which center around propitiation of ancestors.

Kaguru believe that most misfortunes, from death and illness to crop failure, loss of articles, and bad luck in hunting, result from witchcraft. Witches represent an inversion of the moral and symbolic values of the Kaguru, with their evil and antisocial intents and, in the most feared forms of witchcraft, their clan incest, cannibalism, and nakedness.

A Kaguru who suspects he is a victim of witchcraft will often suspect who the witch is; but he may go to a diviner to find or confirm the witch's identity. In the past, an accused suspect would be tried by the local community, usually with an ordeal. If found guilty, he or she would be clubbed to death. If innocent, the accuser would pay a large fine. Now public witchcraft accusations are illegal, but the suspected witch may learn of the charge in gossip or through some sign; or his garden may be damaged or his house burned. A man against whom such accusations are directed several times would probably move somewhere else.

Who is accused? Members of your own matrilineal clan are not supposed to be apt to direct witchcraft at you, but many accusations occur even within the closer bounds of a matrilineage. Although anyone might be a witch, the following are particularly suspect: (1) economically successful persons; (2) powerful chiefs and headmen; (3) nonconformists; (4) a wife her husband cannot easily control; (5) a woman envious of her co-wives; (6) people who refuse to meet important obligations to their kin (Beidelman 1963:74).

How does witchcraft serve as a force of social control? Beidelman (1963) notes that the powerful man may in fact encourage beliefs in his powers of witchcraft so as to increase his influence and control. A powerful man might be feared as a witch, but it would take corresponding power to accuse him. It is not clear how successfully, and by what means, witchcraft accusations could be used in olden times to eliminate the strong man who went too far in wealth or power. Certainly political rivalries and disputed succession bring witchcraft accusations and suspicions to the fore. For the man of more limited means and powers, the threat of witchcraft accusations was a strong force for conformity and approved social behavior.

For most Kaguru, accusations or threats of witchcraft enforce conformity. This is done through fear of accusation against nonconformists and through fear of nonconformity being punished by the witchcraft of others. (Beidelman 1963:96–97)

Witchcraft is distinguished from sorcery, or black magic performed by a magician to achieve his ends. Comparative study of witchcraft has been an important theme in modern social anthropology. The premise that witchcraft accusations will follow the "stress lines" of a social structure underlies most of this research. Are accusations usually directed against kin? against affines? against unrelated neighbors? against co-wives? Systematic correlations between forms of social structure and the nature of witchcraft have supported and reinforced this premise.

Control of deviant behavior may also be maintained by blood feuding. Thus among the Kwaio of the Solomon Islands, a man would put up a bounty to avenge the killing of his close relative. Any member of the killer's descent group, or one of his close bilateral relatives, would be a suitable blood victim, and whoever killed one could claim the bounty. Often the killer's group would themselves provide a victim or even do the deed themselves to claim the bounty. The offered victim would be a girl thought wanton or quarrelsome or lazy, a boy or man who had made a dangerous swear, or some other "undesirable." Bad boys and girls had considerably shorter life expectancy than good ones. (Modern Kwaio pagans, discouraged by the British administration from this mode of getting rid of undesirables, send them to become Christians.)

Conformity to the rules that govern social life is not a harsh burden of culture, a thwarting of drives. First, human goals are socially shaped and conventional. Second, to pursue them requires conformity to many implicit codes for communication, whether or not one plays according to the "rules." Third, the apparent conflicts between self-interest and socially acceptable behavior are misleading. Individuals striving for personal goals are players in a game that requires shared conventions, coalitions, and cooperation in a common enterprise. Staying within the boundaries—which are never that narrow—becomes a means of advancing one's position. In the long run, self-interest is social interest. With the wrath of supernaturals or the scorn or jealousy of one's fellow players, one seldom can win the games of social life. One often cannot play at all.

But that is only one side of the picture . . .

65.
Law: A Comparative View

Rules are broken, expectations are flouted, order is disrupted. However small-scale and closely integrated a society is, some people try to beat the system or operate outside the bounds of custom and the restraint of rules. Moreover, even though people may agree in principle about matters of custom, conflicts arise about who has what rights over particular people or pieces of property.

Societies respond in widely varying ways to breaches of social standards or conflicts over rights. A killing or theft may set into motion a formal procedure of courts and punishments; or the offended party and his kin may simply retaliate in kind if they can. Between these extremes lies a great range of procedures and institutions that in some ways resemble Western legal process and in other ways are quite different.

So the anthropologist is left in a familiar conceptual dilemma. Should one turn the concept of "law" into a very flexible but shapeless piece of elastic and put it around anything that does in some society what law does in ours? Or shall we extend the Western concept of law but retain its shape, and then try it on tribal societies to see where it fits and where it does not? Add to this conceptual dilemma the compulsive nit-picking to which the legally minded are prone and you can understand the endless debates about what is or is not "law" in non-Western societies.

Not being jurists or headhunters, we will avoid splitting hairs. What matters is that we glimpse the range of ways in which societies manage breaches of the rules; and that by seeing "law" in comparative perspective, we avoid ethnocentric views of other peoples and attain a clearer view of ourselves.

A few first principles will serve us well in making sense of the range of cultural variation we will sample. First, if we start out to find *the* legal system in a society, our quest may be misguided from the outset. There may be several "legal systems" in the same society. Different people may make decisions in different kinds of groups, or cases, or settings, with reference to different sets of standards. The different legal subsystems in a society may involve different spheres of life. They may involve different kinds of violations. Thus our distinction between civil and criminal offenses may be mirrored in a non-Western society with a contrast between "private delicts" and "public delicts." Or they may involve different groups. Thus cases involving members of a lineage may activate one set of legal mechanisms, cases involving members of a larger community another, and cases involving members of different communities a third.

But how do we know a legal system, or a legal process, when we find one? Is it because there is a clear and codified (if not written) set of "laws"? No, says Pospisil (1968), a leading specialist. He argues that such abstract rules are rare and specialized in human societies, mainly limited to Western societies since the codification of Roman law. Legal principles are more often implicit, flexible, and constantly changing. Increasingly, the legal processes and legal principles of a society have come to light by looking at *cases,* at specific instances where conflicts of rights or breaches of rules are socially resolved. The legal principles of a

society emerge from the study of *decisions* in these cases.

Who makes these decisions? In what settings and by what processes? And if there is no formal code of laws, what guidelines, principles, or precedents are used to make them? How are they enforced? Each of these questions, if followed out, would show a wide range of variation. Here we can afford only a quick glimpse at each.

Who makes legal decisions? Where the social organization is simple, as in band societies, they are likely to be made by the leader of the band. What legal powers he exercises may be contingent on his success in leading the hunt, dealing with supernaturals, or maintaining internal or external peace. So, too, the Big Man of Melanesia has power to make legal decisions only to the extent people defer to his skill and wisdom and his success and power as an entrepreneur.

In a tribal society, even where the leader of a descent group or community has formal rights based on his *position,* not simply his personal power, these are likely to be binding only to members of his own group. In a segmentary lineage system, who has the right to make decisions may depend on who the contending sides are and what the case is about. Offenses involving members of different corporations may lead to blood feuding or warfare, or they may be settled according to "legal" principles to avoid or end armed confrontation.

This usefully shows that—except to some degree in more complex societies where formal courts and legal specialists have developed—legal action is intertwined with politics. The power to make binding decisions in cases of conflict is, in less complex societies, political power. But for us to try to draw, or erase, a line between legal and political would be a waste of time. It is better to think of the political and legal as two ways of looking at events, sometimes the same events: each point of view illuminates a different facet.

In what settings do legal processes take place? In a society without formal legal institutions, the setting for litigation may be a feast, a spontaneous or arranged gathering, or some more organized council of those who make and influence decisions in a community. In some parts of the tribal world, particularly Africa, formal legal systems involving courts, trials, judges, appeals, and so on, are highly elaborated. Those who make legal decisions in them may be legal specialists; or they may be those who exercise political or religious leadership in other settings. The Tswana will illustrate elaborated legal systems in Africa.

Case 62: The Tswana Court System

The Tswana tribes of south-central Africa have a complex and hierarchical court system, paralleling the political hierarchy. Each local patrilineage or "ward" has its own court, with the headman as judge; and each village had its court and judge. These lower courts had jurisdiction in civil cases (that is, cases dealing with status, property, and contracts); but difficult cases could be referred to a higher court. A "criminal" case, involving an offense such as homicide or sorcery, could be reviewed at local levels; but decisions were made by the trival chief's court, complete with legal specialists and elaborate formal proceedings.

In a Tswana court case, the judge and his advisers faced the litigants. Formal statements by the litigants were followed by testimony by witnesses and examination by the court advisers, deeply steeped in the subtle and detailed principles of Tswana law. The advisers debated the merits of the case, after which the judge summarized the evidence and delivered the verdict.

The complexities and detail of Tswana law, as known by legal specialists who act in the courts, are impressive. Schapera (1955), their ethnographer, had years of experience in Tswana legal matters; yet when invited to act as an adviser to the court, he felt insufficiently versed in the intricacies of Tswana law to do so with the skill of a Tswana specialist.

Even in a society with elaborated courts, informal litigation may often be used to settle cases out of court. This underlines the need to look for more subtle and undramatic legal processes side by side with formal legal systems.

Case 63: The Kpelle Moot

Among the West African Kpelle of Liberia, a political structure of town, district, and regional chiefs is paralleled by a hierarchy of formal courts. However, this formal system of courts and official legal decision-making has major disadvantages for settling disputes among kin, affines, and neighbors whose social relations must be maintained after the particular legal issue at hand has been resolved. The formal courts, coercive in imposing decisions in black and white terms, tend to leave the litigants polarized and bitter.

A more effective means of settling disputes among people who need to preserve the fabric of social relations is the "house palaver," or moot. Moots, in an anthropological borrowing from legal terminology, are informally constituted and unofficial gatherings—usually of kin or neighbors or other interested parties—who hear the case and attempt to work out a solution.

Among the Kpelle, it is usually domestic problems—a marital conflict, an unpaid debt between kin, a quarrel over inheritance—that are settled through airing of the dispute before a moot. The group is an *ad hoc* cluster of interested and concerned parties, mainly kin and neighbors. The gathering is held at the home of the complainant, who calls the moot, under the auspices of a kinsman who acts as mediator. The mediator is a respected elder skilled in dispute settlement.

As the circumstances are laid out by the parties to the case, the group attempts to determine where truth and blame lie and to reach some consensual settlement. The testimony, conducted in an orderly fashion,

Dispute settlement in a tribal society: A Kwaio man proffers shell valuables in compensation for seducing his neighbor's daughter (Solomon Islands). (Photograph by the author.)

may move far from the specific details at issue: frequently the precipitating issue is the culmination of years of friction and historical enmity, which can be aired.

When a settlement is reached, it usually is payment of a light fine and an apology. The proceedings close, as they began, with religious blessings; but the tension has usually been dissipated, and the group drinks beer or rum together. Gibbs, the ethnographer (1963), argues that the Kpelle moot is a means of social and psychological therapy as well as a mechanism of dispute settlement.

Where there is no formal political structure uniting members of different kin groups, mechanisms for managing disputes are likely to be based on negotiation or confrontation between the individuals or kin groups involved. In stateless societies, disputes can easily erupt into feuding. Thus an offense may be managed either through legal negotiation or outside the framework of law. We have already illustrated some of the mechanisms—such as the Nuer Leopard-skin chief and the intervention of kinsmen with divided allegiances—that militate against open hostility. Some other examples of legal mechanisms for dispute settlement among hunters and gatherers and tribesmen will further illustrate the range of possibilities. The first, the ordeal, is widespread in the tribal world.

Case 64: Ordeals among the Ifugao

Among the Ifugao of the Philippines, criminal cases and such civil cases as property disputes are often settled by ordeals. A person accused of an offense who persistently denies guilt may submit to an ordeal as a challenge; or the accuser may challenge the individual to prove his or her innocence. An accused person or a party to a dispute who refuses to submit to an ordeal is considered to be in the wrong.

There are several forms of ordeals. In the hot water ordeal, a person must reach into a pot of boiling water, pull out a pebble, and then replace it. In other Ifugao regions, a red hot knife is lowered onto a person's hand. In either case, if the party is guilty his hand will be badly burned; if innocent (or in the right, in the case of a property dispute), it will not be badly burned, and the accuser or rival must pay compensation. Two parties to a dispute must both have the knife lowered onto both of their hands; the one who is in the right will be less badly burned.

Finally, there are several forms of duels and wrestling matches where the parties to a dispute put their case to the test. Here, as in the individual ordeals, supernatural support swings to the party who is in the right.

The ordeals and contests are supervised by a *monkalun*, or arbiter, a neutral party who in these cases acts as an umpire. In other forms of litigation a *monkalun* acts as go-between and attempts to reach a compromise or bring the facts to light by negotiating with and probing the parties to the dispute (Barton 1919).

An Ifugao ordeal: An accused man picks a pebble from boiling water. (From an old photograph by R. F. Barton, courtesy of the Lowie Museum of Anthropology, University of California, Berkeley.)

Case 65: Eskimo Song Duels

Among Eskimo groups, with no formal mechanisms of government or courts, disputes are resolved with a "court" of public opinion, the small-scale Eskimo community. With no formal or codified set of rules, the Eskimo are free to treat each dispute over wife stealing, homicide, or the like, as a unique constellation of people and circumstances (Hoebel 1954).

For disputes less serious than homicide, most Eskimo groups have an unusual and effective way of blowing off the steam of hostility while resolving the legal issue: the song duel. Here each party to the dispute composes songs that ridicule his adversary and set out in exaggerated fashion his grievance or his version of the disputed events. Ribald satire, taunts, innuendo, distortion, and buffoonery bring mirth from the onlookers as the songs go back and forth. By the time the "case" has been made by each party, the litigants have blown off steam and public opinion has swung toward a decision that will redress valid grievances or dismiss weak ones. A perhaps more important function than legal decision-making is that by their song duel the disputing pair have had their say in public and can resume their normal relationship—stung only temporarily by the "little, sharp words, like . . . wooden splinters" (Rasmussen 1922:236).

Case 66: Dispute Settlement among Herbert River Australian Aborigines

In Case 58, borboby, ritualized combat between aggrieved parties of Australian Aborigines, was described by Lumholtz. Among these Aboriginal groups, such formal duelling was a major means for settling disputes over women or stolen property. Lumholtz' summary is again useful.

Here all disputes and legal conflicts were settled, not only between tribes but also between individuals. . . . With the exception of the murder of a member of the same tribe, the aboriginal Australian knows only one crime, and that is theft, and the punishment for violating the right of possession is not inflicted by the community, but by the individual wronged. The thief is challenged by his victim to a duel with wooden swords and shields; and the matter is settled sometimes privately, the relatives of both parties serving as witnesses, sometimes publicly at the borboby, where two hundred to three hundred meet from various tribes to decide all their disputes. . . .

In these duels the issue does not depend wholly on physical strength, as the relatives play a conspicuous part in the matter. The possession of many strong men on his side is a great moral support to the combatant. He knows that his opponent, through fear for his relatives, will not carry the conflict to the extreme; he is also certain that, if necessary, they will interfere and prevent his getting wounded. . . . Mortal wounds are extremely rare. (Lumholtz 1889:125–127)

What standards are used to make legal decisions, if there is no formal legal code? The conception of culture adopted here enables us to see this clearly. To operate in the world—to garden or build houses or conduct religious rituals—humans need an implicit set of "rules" for acting, doing, and deciding. These need not be completely shared or consistent or neat; they are constantly being changed and adapted. Learning them and using them is easy for human beings. Verbalizing them, or writing them down in ways that accurately correspond to implicit codes, is difficult and—generations of jurists and ethnographers notwithstanding—perhaps impossible. One of the central elements in the mystery of human behavior is how conceptual codes are linked to the ever shifting and complicated situations, the unique crystallizations of circumstance, we encounter in the world. Writing down a legal code takes one side of this miraculous and flexible linkage and hardens it into rigid laws. We then need enormous human wisdom and skill to reintroduce this flexibility into a system of courts—to follow the "spirit" of the law rather than the "letter," to recognize and cope with the uniqueness of each case. That, in a sense, is what the art of jurisprudence is all about. Tribal "jurists," unburdened by the letter of the law and able to treat each pattern of circumstances afresh, are doing what humans do very well. Those who argue cases, or decide them, can cite general principles and precedents to support their contentions: it is the essence of law, primitive or modern, that it be "legitimate." But the implicit codes whereby ideal principles and rules of thumb are translated into actual decisions and plans may remain largely hidden to those who use them.

How are legal decisions enforced? If they are without any effective sanctions and can be violated with impunity, we would hardly want to call them legal. The "teeth" in the law may include physical punishment, forfeiture or destruction of property, banishment, and so on. The pressures to settle matters according to legal procedures and to accept legal decisions may be more subtle than the threat of direct punishment. The alternatives to legal settlement may be warfare or bloody vengeance outside legal channels.

We tend to think of law in terms of social control—and indeed a useful way to make a first exploration of legal processes in a non-Western society is to see what rules a people consider binding and what happens when they are broken. Yet the mechanisms and processes that are set into action when such rules are broken may not serve only as means of social control. Taking a person to court or claiming compensation for a grievance may be a matter of economic strategy, political rivalry, descent group segmentation, or reli-gious principle. The affairs of life in the tribal world—or even of ours—refuse to stay in the tidy pigeonholes of the social scientist. Legal action is social action, in all its manifold complexity. Frake's vivid picture of litigation among a Subanun (Case 30) group in the Philippines will help to leave us with a view of law as a facet of social life, not a separate compartment.

Litigation in Lipay . . . cannot be fully under-stood if we regard it only as a means of maintaining social control. A large share, if not the majority, of legal cases deal with offenses so minor that only the fertile imagination of a Subanun legal authority can magnify them into a serious threat to some person or to society in general. . . . A festivity with-out litigation is almost as unthinkable as one with-out drink.

In some respects a Lipay trial is more compara-ble to an American poker game than to our legal proceedings. It is a contest of skill, in this case of verbal skill, accompanied by social merry-making, in which the loser pays a forfeit. He pays for much the same reason we pay a poker debt: so he can play the game again. . . .

Litigation nevertheless has far greater signifi-cance in Lipay than this poker game analogy implies. For it is more than recreation. Litigation, together with the rights and duties it generates, so pervades Lipay life that one could not consistently refuse to pay fines and remain a functioning mem-ber of society. Along with drinking, feasting, and ceremonializing, litigation provides patterned means of interaction linking the independent nuclear families of Lipay into a social unit, even though there are no formal group ties of compara-ble extent. The importance of litigation as a social activity makes understandable its prevalence among the peaceful and, by our standards, "law-abiding" residents of Lipay. (Frake 1963:221)

RELIGION
Ritual, Myth, and Cosmos

19

Humans not only weave intricate webs of custom that regulate and order their social lives. They also spin out wider designs of the universe, the forces that govern it, and their place in it. Religious beliefs and rituals are basic in these designs. So, too, are fundamental premises about the way things and events are interrelated, the nature of time and space, the way the world is and should be.

The religion and world view of a people are less immediately apparent, less readily studied, than their agriculture or their kinship system. Anthropologists have tended to look at them obliquely, as reflections or projections of social life, rather than as intellectual systems in their own right. But in recent years, major new insights have emerged as the thought worlds of non-Western peoples have been more systematically explored and mapped. In this chapter, we will examine the religious systems of tribal peoples, emphasizing the new perspectives and models and

necessarily sampling only briefly the rich variety of ritual and belief in non-Western societies.

66.
Religion in Comparative Perspective

What is religion? What is the difference between religion and magic? What is myth? Ritual? Such questions catch the anthropologist in the usual dilemma—trying on the one hand to render faithfully the shape and distinctiveness of a particular culture, and on the other to compare similar institutions in a range of societies. As particularist and ethnographer, one can show that any set of comparative classifications distorts the culture one studies; as generalist, a scholar keeps trying to devise better analytical categories.

Numerous scholars have sought to find a common denominator for all forms of religion. Recently, many have moved back toward Tylor's classic definition of religion as a "belief in spiritual beings." Thus, Goody (1961), Horton (1960), and Spiro (1966) have seen the extension of "social" relations to superhuman beings or forces as the feature common to all religions. Others, following Durkheim, have sought to find some special quality of "sacredness" that demarcates the religious from the secular.

Religions vary enormously in the powers and agencies they posit in the universe and the ways people relate to them. There may be a range of deities, a single deity, or none— simply spirits or even impersonal and diffuse powers. These agencies may intervene constantly in human affairs or be uninvolved and distant; they may be punitive or benevolent. In dealing with them, humans may feel awe and reverence, or fear; but they may also bargain with supernaturals or seek to outwit them. Religions may govern people's moral conduct or be unconcerned with morality. Such variety makes a search for common denominators frustrating and not very productive.

Students of comparative religion have been given to typologies. Some religions were animistic: they viewed the natural world as inhabited by in-dwelling spirits. Others were totemic (§17), positing a mystical relationship between clans and birds or animals. Ancestor worship was another common pattern; animatism, where a mystical spiritual force such as Polynesian *mana* or Eastern Woodlands *orenda* gave power to human effort, was yet another. In the religions of hunting and gathering peoples, Catholic missionary scholars sought evidence of an early monotheism, a primitive "high god."

Such early typological schemes have proven to be misleadingly simplistic. On closer examination, religions characteristically turn out to be too subtly complicated to fit into such a set of pigeonholes. A single religion characteristically turns out to be a "mixture" of different "types." Some elements of a people's belief system often seem on the surface to be incompatible with others. Thus, the Tallensi (Cases 24 and 39) and some other West African peoples believe that each person's life follows a foreordained destiny. But at the same time they believe that individuals have the power to choose paths of good or evil and that lineage ancestors control and may intervene in the unfolding of a person's life (themes that Fortes (1959c) compares with the ancient themes of Oedipus and Job). We will shortly see how (Case 67), for one West African religion, such seemingly contradictory themes are woven into a subtle and complex system of belief.

That does not mean that comparative religion must be bereft of comparison or that any kind of religion will be found in association with any kind of social system in any kind of ecosystem. We will return in §63 to modern and more sophisticated attempts to show systematic relationships between thought-of worlds and lived-in worlds.

For the moment, it is most revealing to ask why humans in all or almost all times and places have created a world of unseen entities and forces that parallels, lies behind, or explains the world perceived directly by human senses. We ask not what religions *are*, but what they *do*, and hence, *why* they are.

Religions, first of all, *explain*. They answer existential questions: how the world came to be, how humans are related to natural species and forces, why humans die, and why their efforts succeed and fail. Undoubtedly, not all individuals in a society worry about such questions. But every society has its philosophers who seek answers to existential questions; while others carry on assured that there *are* answers, and are more concerned with coping, solving, and striving than with explaining.

Second, religions *validate*. Religions posit controlling forces in the universe that sustain the moral and social order of a people. Ancestors, spirits, or gods reinforce rules and give validity and meaning to human acts. In a complex and hierarchical social system, religion sustains the power of rulers or priests or elites and reinforces a status quo. We will consider in §72 another theme: religion can be a revolutionary force as well as a conservative one.

Third, religions reinforce human ability to cope with the fragility of human life—with death and illness, famine, flood, failure. By reinforcing humans psychologically at times of tragedy, anxiety, and crisis, religion gives security and meaning in a world which, "seen in naturalistic terms, appears to be full of the unpredictable, the capricious, the accidentally tragic" (Kluckhohn 1942). And religion also heightens the intensity of shared experience, of social communion.

Clifford Geertz, in an important essay, formulates a definition of religions in terms of what they do, and amplifies his definition brilliantly.

A religion is a system of symbols which acts to establish powerful, pervasive, and long-lasting moods and motivations in men by formulating conceptions of a general order of existence and clothing these conceptions with such an aura of factuality that the moods and motivations seem uniquely realistic. (1966a:4)

Religion, in other words, defines the way the world *is* in such a way that it establishes an appropriate stance to take toward it—a way of feeling, acting, and living in it. Both the nature of the world and human emotions and motives are mutually confirmed and reinforced. It is this double-sidedness, this creation through religions of both "models of" and "models for," that makes them so central in human experience.

The way a religion codifies a view of the world, and hence sustains a stance toward life, is vividly illustrated by the view of the cosmos held by the Kalabari of Nigeria.

Case 67: The World View of the Kalabari

The Kalabari, a fishing people who live in the swampy delta of the Niger River in Nigeria, have a highly complicated system of cosmological beliefs—a system that would seem to exemplify the "mystical" or "magical" mode of thinking many writers have attributed to primitive peoples. The contrast with a modern scientific view of the universe would seem profound.

Three orders of existence are postulated by the Kalabari as lying behind "the place of people"—the observable world of human beings and things. The first level is the world of "spirits." It is with the beings of this level that the living are most concerned, and with which their relations are mediated by ritual. The spirit world is populated by beings of various sorts. All of them are normally invisible and are manifest, like the wind, in different places.

First, every object or living thing has a spirit that guides or animates its behavior. When a person dies, or a pot breaks, spirit and physical form have become separated. But more important to people's daily lives are three categories of "free" spirits. First, there are ancestral spirits, dead members of the Kalabari lineages which watch over every member, rewarding them when kinship norms are observed and punishing them when they are violated. Second, there are "village heroes." These formerly lived with the Kalabari, but came from other places bringing new customs. Whereas ancestors are concerned with lineages, village heroes are concerned with the whole village—composed of several lineages—and its unity and community enterprises. The effectiveness of the village head relies heavily on support by village heroes.

A final category of spirits is the "water people," who are manifest as humans and also as pythons, or rainbows. They are identified not with human groups but with the creeks and swamps that are central to Kalabari subsistence. Water people control weather and fishing and are responsible for deviant human behavior, whether positive (innovation or acquisition of unusual wealth) or negative (violation of norms or mental abnormality).

This triangle of spirit forces, interacting with one another as well as with the living, shapes and guides human life. Ritual cycles alternately reinforce relations with ancestors, village heroes, and water people.

But beyond the spirit world, and more abstract and remote from human life, are other orders of existence. A personal creator, shaping each individual's destiny from before birth, lays the design of his or her life. A pattern of power or of failure is preordained for any individual, and the events of life are simply its unfolding. Even the time and manner of a person's death are laid down before birth. Even the destiny of a lineage, or a village, is viewed as laid down, though it has no creator as such.

Finally, on a still more remote and abstract level, Kalabari conceive the entire world and all of its beings as created by a "Great Creator," and all the events of the world as the immutable unfolding of an ultimate pattern of destiny. Although offerings are made to one's personal creator, the mood is one of resignation rather than manipulation: "The Creator never loses a case," say Kalabari. The Great Creator is in most respects remote from human life.

Does this elaborate and, in scientific terms, fanciful scheme reflect a mystical mode of thought remote from modern science? In one sense, like all religious systems, it does, says the anthropological interpreter Robin Horton (1962). That is, rather than keeping systematic control of the relationship between "the theory" and the evidence of observation, Kalabari allow a complex pattern of secondary and contingent explanation. When sacrifice attains the desired result, this reinforces belief; when it does not, some other explanation—a competing spirit, a ritual mistake, or the like—is invoked. The belief is not called into question. The same, of course, is true of Christian prayer.

But is the contrast between Kalabari religious explanation and Western science really that profound? Horton argues that this reflects illusions about science overemphasizing its objectivity and precision and misconstruing the relationship between data and theoretical model (see §2).

The world of the spirits is, in one sense, modeled on the everyday world of Kalabari life. But to make the events of that life intelligible, the spirit world represents a transformation that sorts out the component forces and spheres of human life. Thus, for example, village heroes appropriately represent the ties of community that transcend the separate loyalties of kinship and lineage. They came from outside places, not Kalabari lineages; they contributed innovations that distinguish the customs of each particular village; they simply disappeared, they did not die; and they left no descendants. They were creatures of community, without any of the ties of human kinship. Similarly, Horton argues, a model in science very often represents a transformation of the phenomena in the world of observables that gave rise to it. Thus the physicist's models of atomic structure are "hybridized" transformations of the revolutions of planets that served as a prototype for them.

Moreover, there is for the scientist no single level of reality, and no single model to represent it. Rather, the same "matter" can be described in terms of subatomic particles or macromolecules. The nature of the explanatory or predictive task determines the appropriate model. Thus the models of time and space that suffice for a highway engineering project must be modified in sending a rocket to the moon, and must be modified again to deal with theoretical problems of astrophysics. A chemical manufacturer making caustic soda out of salt can use a simple chemical model, while a much more complex second-order model is required for dealing with a related theoretical problem in physics.

Similarly, the orders of existence postulated by the Kalabari are invoked in different contexts to explain different orders of phenomena, to answer different orders of questions. A temporary success or failure is intelligible in terms of the vicissitudes of relations with spirits; a series of catastrophes or failures is seen as the unfolding of destiny.

Furthermore, seeming contradictions between levels of explanatory models are as basic to the conceptualizations of science as the cosmology of the Kalabari, yet the levels complement and augment one another. Just as the successively higher levels of Kalabari existence are more and more abstract, less and less related to immediate experience and mundane existence, so too are the increasingly abstract models of physics. By eliminating features relevant at lower levels, each more abstract level unifies a greater range of phenomena with less and less specification of content. "As tools of understanding, successive levels of Kalabari reality are committed to explaining more and more in terms of less and less" (Horton 1962). Horton argues that this is as true of the models of modern atomic physics, with its hypothetical particles and statistical models, as of the Kalabari conception of Great Creator and cosmic destiny.

The sophistication and complexity of cosmologies among many "primitive" peoples give lie to the early assertions that "the natives" had childlike, credulous minds and religions dominated by fear, obsessive ritualism, superstition, or meaningless mumbo-jumbo. Thus materially unencumbered Australian Aborigines have incredibly subtle, philosophically challenging mystical cosmologies that posit a spiritual plane of existence that was prior to the world of sensory experience (in the "dreamtime") but now lies behind or parallel to it. Mervyn Meggitt (personal communication) describes how the old Walbiri man who was his spiritual guide eventually told him gently that he, Meggitt, had reached his philosophical depth and could follow no further into the mysteries of the cosmos. Probably no Westerner has ever fully penetrated these Aboriginal philosophical realms (see Stanner 1956, 1963, 1965; Meggitt 1972). Similarly, the old African hunter and philosopher Ogotemmeli spread out for his ethnographer pupils a vast and incredibly sophisticated vista of the cosmology of his people, the Dogon (Griaule and Dieterlen 1960).

The impression of credulity and mumbo-jumbo comes in part from tribal world views where a logic of magic prevails. "Magical thinking" reflects a model of the universe that is far more deterministic than ours, a universe where things do not just happen by chance or accident. If a snake bites a man, it is the venom that directly causes his death. But what caused the snake and that particular man to intersect at a particular moment on a particular path? Why does one snake-bite victim recover and another die? Most of us do not ask these questions. Most tribal peoples demand answers to them.

In such a universe, death, illness, and crop failure call for explanation. And such a far-reaching determinism invites people to try to manipulate the course of events in socially approved or socially disapproved ways. A sorcerer who uses fingernail parings of his intended victim, or a magician who draws animals to ensure the abundance of game, is building on a logic quite different from ours— a logic where influences are spread by "contagion" and where like produces like. Such an all-embracing determinism and "magical" pattern of thinking dominate the tribal world.

"Magic," then, represents human attempts to manipulate chains of cause and effect between events that to us are unrelated, in ways that to us are irrational. Magic, like prayer, works in the eye of the believer because the system of belief contains an explanation for both success and failure: the magician's beliefs are confirmed whether the garden grows well or dies. Paradoxically, the advance of Western science comes not from explaining more things, but from explaining fewer things more systematically.

Is magic part of religion, or is it a distinct cultural realm? Where the magician works pragmatically at his routine, recites his spell, and hence "compels" the desired effects to come about, magic contrasts with the religious mood of supplication and spiritual communion: the magician seems more like a mechanic than a priest. But a hard line between "magic" and "religion" is often difficult to draw and culturally meaningless in terms of a particular people under study. Anthropologists have learned the hard way that to understand belief systems they must discard as many rigid definitions and preconceptions as possible and find out how another people conceptualize their universe, see the place of humans in it, and relate to and communicate with unseen beings and powers. Striving to understand the religious philosophy of a non-Western people, whether it be from a Zen master, an Indian guru, or a tribal priest, demands every ounce of one's analytical and intuitive powers, and often more.

But that is not to say that all peoples are

equally concerned with elaborating models of the cosmos and philosophies of the human condition. Some peoples are relatively pragmatic, down to earth, uninterested in ultimate answers and cosmological complexities. Moreover, Walbiri or Dogon or other tribal philosophers cannot be lightly assumed to represent "their culture." In some cases, their syntheses may be purely personal; and at least, the man or woman on the path may be quite unconcerned with such matters. The anthropologist straining to conceptualize and codify a belief system may exaggerate systematization and consistency in the process of piecing together individual views of "shared" beliefs (see §69).

67.
Religion and Social Structure

Anthropologists have long perceived that a people's religious beliefs and their social organization are closely interrelated. It is clear that the supernatural order is to some extent modeled on human social relationships. Conversely, religious beliefs validate and regulate social relations.

One way to interpret the close relationship between religious and social is to view religion as a sort of distortion and projection of the human world. Thus, one can find relationships between the kinds of supernaturals posited by a people and the scale of their political organization. People with fragmented clans often have a cult of ancestral spirits for each clan, and people with a centralized state are more likely to have a high god or centralized pantheon. Sacrifice, which has fascinated Western scholars (partly because of biblical and other early Semitic sacrifice), takes on a new light if we look at it this way. If we view relations with supernaturals as modeled on relations between the living, we see "sacrifice" as a category that lumps together a wide range of quite different transactions between

subordinate humans and subordinate supernaturals. The transactions among the living on which various forms of "sacrifice" are modeled range from tribute to bribery, manipulation to receive special advantage, obeisance, or expiation. Because the supernatural world is immaterial, what is given is converted to ethereal "substance" (while the sacrificers usually eat the material remains). What the supernaturals give in return is similarly intangible.

Similarly, ancestral spirits who punish the living for their violations of taboos or ritual procedures can be seen as a projection of the authority system of the living—the lineage elders elevated to a supernatural plane. Studies have correlated the nature of authority and the way it is transferred across generations with the nature of religious belief and ritual.

But in asking such questions, as in studying sacrifice comparatively, we may distort understanding by separating the realms of "religion" and "social structure." To people who live in a lineage system, ancestral lineage members ("spirits") may be ever-present, and in communication with them every day: they are unseen co-resident members of the lineage. A sacrifice may be a ritual gathering of living and dead members at which the living ones solicit the greater powers of the dead ones. Kopytoff (1971) argues that in many West African religions ancestors are defined, treated, and accorded powers as the eldest elders in the lineage system.

The classic study in this genre is Durkheim's (1912) analysis of Australian Aboriginal religion. In worshipping the "totem" animals that symbolized each group, the Aborigines were in fact worshipping the units of society itself. Particularly in the seasonal *intichiuma* rite, the temporary social and emotional bonds that pulled together diverse groups were projected upon the cosmos: religion was society writ large.

Another classic is Hertz's study (1907) of double funerals in Borneo. At a first funeral, the dead man was buried and surviving relatives went into a ritual seclusion from social contact. Then the purified skull was exhumed, and a second funeral was staged which sent the spirit to the afterlife and freed the mourners to rejoin normal social life. Hertz interprets this as a treatment of death as a rite of passage to a new status (as with initiation ceremonies). The afterlife is invented so as to avoid treating death as final, and the second funeral reincorporates the living into their world and sends the spirit into its new one.

Here it will be useful to examine in closer detail the religious system of another tribal people, one we have encountered in previous chapters, to see systematic relations between religion and social structure.

Case 68: Kwaio Social Structure and Religion

Recall from Case 29 how the Melanesian Kwaio of the Solomon Islands are organized into small descent groups, composed of agnatic and cognatic descendants of the ancestors who founded the territory on which they live. We will see shortly, in Case 69, how Kwaio cosmology partitions the world into a sacred realm where ancestors hold sway and from which women are mainly excluded; we will also see the mirror image of the sacred, a polluted realm that is dangerous to men.

Here we will look more closely at the realm of the sacred, the relation of the living with their ancestors, and the linkages between descent groupings and systems of ancestors, shrines, and ritual.

What supernaturals inhabit the Kwaio universe, and what is their relation to the living? Kwaio believe their world to be inhabited, and in many ways controlled, by ancestral ghosts or *adalo*. *Adalo* are unseen and diffuse, "like the wind." But they interact and communicate with the living indirectly, through *events*, and directly, through priests. The places where this direct communication is centered—notably priests' men's houses and shrines, which are in groves mainly on high hills or above settlements—are especially sacred.

Every adult man and woman, after death, is transmuted into ancestorhood as a ghost. *Adalo*, ancestral ghosts, are distinguished as "minor" and "important." Minor *adalo* are the ghosts of those one has known in life—close relatives in the parental and grandparental generations, whose activities as ghosts are relevant only to their living close kin. Important ancestors are ghosts that have risen to prominence through the generations; most of them appear on genealogies six or more generations above their oldest living descendants. Minor *adalo* sometimes serve as intermediaries on behalf of their living kin, in dealing with important *adalo*. *Adalo*, like living Kwaio men (Case 53), vary in "bigness." There is in practice a large category of *adalo* from previous generations who are not attributed special and dangerous powers and singled out for special sacrifice, but who are in a kind of limbo.

A Kwaio feast giver talks to his ancestors while making an offering of taro and coconuts to ensure dry weather. (Photograph by the author.)

A most interesting parallel is thus suggested between ancestors and the kin groups of the living. Each descent group has a cluster of powerful ancestors, usually two or three, to whom its priest sacrifices pigs. Usually one of these ancestors is primary in power (hence, corresponding to a Kwaio Big Man, in the "big ghost's" role vis-à-vis other descent-group ghosts). At the time of sacrifice, the priest calls the names of a line of previous priests and of remembered descent-group men, mainly but not exclusively agnatic ex-members. The ghost of a man who established primary rights and interests in his mother's descent group, not his father's (Cases 29 and 32), is likely to have somewhat marginal status in the ancestral cult of the group where he was a nonagnate. But if he maintained a ritual involvement with his agnatic group, he is likely to be accorded ancestral status in it—a reflection on the ancestral plane of divisible and multiple descent-group membership (Keesing 1968b).

A pig sacrificed to the "big" ancestor or ancestors is conceived as going to all of the descent group's ancestral ghosts, through the "big ghost" (as ancestral Big Man). While one can conceive of the "ancestral descent group" as a supernatural projection of the social structure, it makes more cultural sense to see the descent group as a single perpetual corporation comprising both the living and their ancestors.

Just as the living are fragmented into locally based descent corporations, so the ancestral cults are limited and locally based. Ancestral ghosts are concerned only with their own descendants. The living are concerned only with their own ancestors. The "concern" of ancestors in the affairs of the living is two-sided. Ancestors infuse the efforts of the living with supernatural power (*mana*) when they are pleased with the way the living are raising pigs consecrated to them, are following correct ritual proce-

Kwaio sacrifice: A priest speaks to his ancestors in a shrine as the smoke of a sacrificial pig rises to them. (Photograph by the author.)

dures, and in particular, are following rigid pollution taboos concerned with the symbolic uncleanness of women. (We will return to Kwaio pollution beliefs in Case 69.) When the ancestors are displeased with the living, most often due to pollution violations, they visit sickness and death on their descendants—and can be assuaged only by sacrifice of expiatory pigs.

Ancestors are concerned with the conduct of all their *cognatic* descendants. This has a number of implications.

1. The "big" ancestor(s) of a descent group are propitiated not only by descent-group members (most of whom are agnates), but also by the descendants of out-marrying female members. Male cognatic descendants have a right to participate in descent-group sacrifices, so that the religious "congregations" are broadly cognatic and unite members of different local groups.

Kwaio magic: A priest bespells a twig being used in a rite. (Photograph by the author.)

2. From the standpoint of a particular individual, the circle of ancestors to which sacred pigs are consecrated (usually 8 to 12 for a man, and somewhat less for a woman) is broadly bilateral. Thus an individual may propitiate ancestors (to whom he is related through both father and mother) that are "from" six or eight or more different descent groups, groups to which he traces cognatic descent and in whose territories he has secondary rights of residence and land use.

The cluster of powerful ancestors, patrilateral and matrilateral, for whom an individual raises propitiatory pigs [is] a direct reflection of the bundles of rights and kinship relationships he receives through each parent. The sacred pigs in his pen are, as it were, the embodiment of these networks of kinship ties, and as they mix with the sacred pigs his wife raises for her own ancestors, they symbolize the bundles the two parents combine to pass to their children. (Keesing 1970:758)

3. Ritual relationships with distant and powerful ancestors, more remote than the founding ancestors of descent groups, serve to express and reflect hierarchical and lateral relationships between descent groups.

a. Normally, a cluster of members of a particular descent group (call it group A) who share common descent from a powerful ancestor in group B (through marriage of a B woman to an A man several generations previously) send sacrificial pigs to the B priest. However, the latter may authorize one of the A descendants to act as an officiant in his stead and to found a shrine for the B ancestor. Through this process, "branch offices" are created. Through the passage of generations, the cumulative result of laterally proliferating shrines may be propitiation of the same distant ancestor by a half-dozen priests and descent groups at separate shrines. In time, rather separate cults of ritual and magic may attach to each of these separate shrines, so that the same ancestor has a number of different local manifestations and cults. (One might think here of different Virgin Mary's around the Catholic world.) And each of these may produce "branch offices." The ritual relationships between priests of different shrines symbolically express their coordinate or subordinate status.

b. Descent groups are conceived as related agnatically, through segmentation, as well as cognatically due to out-marriage and the lateral spread of shrines. Again, the ritual relations between priests expresses the seniority or juniority of agnatically related groups. Through such processes, Kwaio conceive local descent groups as hierarchically related and interconnected in time and space—even though their local political autonomy is unchallenged. The Kwaio landscape, dotted with shrines, is thus conceptualized in terms of genealogical hierarchies and temporal unfoldings, not contemporary political relationships.

4. Relations to a few most powerful and ancient ancestors unite many Kwaio within a broad region. As many as 50–75 percent of Kwaio in a region share common descent from one of several ancient ancestors; and this—expressed in ritual eating of propitiatory pigs by men at mortuary feasts and by restrictions regarding blood feuding—provides a bond of distant kinship between marginally related individuals and groups.

A final important connection between the social and supernatural planes concerns the status of women. Though women are placed in a subordinate and polluted position according to the cosmological scheme, and are excluded from the sacred realm most of the time, their position is less marginal than it might seem at first. Women can and often do take a prominent place in the realm of feasting and high finance; some emulate men by giving speeches and making large presentations. They exercise extensive domestic power and can achieve substantial financial independence—and they support their enterprises supernaturally by raising propitiatory pigs to their own ancestors. The women of a descent group undergo a sacrament at times of shared sacredness and can eat pork at some feasts: there is a minimally developed "women's auxiliary" to a descent group's ancestral cult, concerned with attracting money and mediated by a male priest. Some women acquire considerable sacredness themselves, especially after menopause; an old woman who is the last survivor of her generation has considerable sacredness as well as power. Finally, the emphasis on descent through women as well as through men is a symbolic underlining of the relatively coordinate status of women in many contexts.

All this is expressed in the ancestral cults. A number of the most powerful *adalo*—including 3 of the 10 most commonly propitiated—were women, not men, in life. These powerful female ancestors excelled either in female pursuits, notably taro gardening (for which they confer power); or in normally male pursuits, notably blood feuding (in which they confer power or from which they confer protection), or feasting (for which they confer powers of attracting money).

Thus the Kwaio, though relatively unconcerned with details of theology, have created a universe whose supernaturals mirror in many ways the organization of the living. And relations between the living and ancestral ghosts, expressed in hierarchies of shrines and cults of sacrifice, both reflect and reinforce relationships between the living.

Such interpretations, beginning with the social structure of a people and seeing religious systems as reflections or extensions of the social world, as projections of society on the cosmos, have been highly revealing. But they introduce a characteristic distortion. Our social world is our only vantage point on life. It is inevitable and obvious that our models of the cosmos should be drawn from that world. But one cannot legitimately argue from the resulting parallels and resemblances that religion is "nothing more" than a projection of social life. Why project at all? And as Geertz (1966a) cogently suggests, one could profitably focus on the way the world of the living is *transformed* in creating a model of the cosmos. Increasingly, we are perceiving that religions must be viewed as ideational systems, and their overall structure mapped. A focus on the parallels between religious and social has predisposed us to look at those segments of religious experience where the closest parallels occur, at the expense of the rest.

Both the powers and the limitations of a sociological and symbolic approach to religious systems come out clearly in recent concern with cultures in which male and female realms sharply contrast and in which women are believed to be dangerous and polluting. We glimpsed such systems in Chapter 12, in considering the relationship of religious beliefs in ecological adaptation: recall the New Guinea Fore, with their brain cannibalism transmitting deadly *kuru* (Case 16), and the elaborated sexual polarization and homosexual cults among the Marind Anim of the southern coast of New Guinea (Case 15).

A number of writers have suggested that beliefs in pollution or genital mutilation, such as circumcision or subincision, are best explained as projections on the cosmos of the psychic anxieties and conflicts of individuals. Here recall Freeman's (1968) interpretation (Case 13) of the thunder god of the Malayan Semang as a punishing father figure. Using similar premises about the relationship of individual psychology to collective belief, a number of writers of psychoanalytic bent have seen a fear of menstrual blood and other pollution by women as due to male castration anxiety.

Mary Douglas, a leading figure in symbolic

and sociological approaches to religious ritual and belief, argues that such a symbolic preoccupation with bodily orifices and substances need not simply express individual psychic concerns. The concerns and conflicts may be social and collective and public, not psychological and private.

We cannot possibly interpret rituals concerning excreta, breast milk, saliva and the rest unless we are prepared to see in the body a symbol of society. . . . It is easy to see that the body of a sacrificial ox is being used as a diagram of a social situation. But when we try to interpret rituals of the human body in the same way, the psychological tradition turns its face away from society, back toward the individual. Public rituals may express public concerns when they use . . . door posts or animal sacrifices: but public rituals enacted on the human body are taken to express personal and private concerns. (Douglas 1966:138)

In *Purity and Danger* (1966), Douglas examines the ritual use of the human body, particularly in pollution taboos. She notes that the human body is used to symbolize the body politic, the social structure. Powers and dangers focus on the margins of the society—in the anomalous, the marginal and threatening. And mirroring social threats and dangers, it is the bodily orifices and substances—menstrual blood, spittle, urine, feces—that threaten and pollute.

The polarization of men and women, and a separation of the social realm into sacred and polluted spheres of life, define categories that must be rigidly kept separate. The Kwaio will again serve us well in illustrating how a symbolic division of the cosmos expresses lines of cleavage in the social structure and is reflected in spatial organization and ritual.

Case 69: Sacredness and Pollution Among the Kwaio

Kwaio *adalo,* or ancestors, move in a realm where sacredness prevails. Communicating with *adalo* is sacred and dangerous, and it is done by men. Men, as we saw in Case 68, act as priests. All the male cognatic descendants of descent-group ancestors take part in purificatory rites of sacrifice; ritually adult men eat sacred propitiatory pigs as well.

From all these events women are excluded, because women's bodies are polluted. Urination and defecation by women are polluting. Menstruation is more polluting; and most polluting of all is childbirth. The most common culturally defined cause of illness, death, or misfortune is violation by women of the rigid pollution taboos.

The major preoccupations of Kwaio ritual are with keeping sacred and polluted realms properly demarcated from the everyday "mundane" realm of gardening, eating, talking, and sleeping. As Douglas' analyses would lead us to expect, separation of these categories is ritually central: and it is symbolically expressed in a series of dualistic oppositions:

Female	:	Male
Polluted	:	Sacred
Down	:	Up

Thus, men and women have to eat out of separate cooking vessels, drink from separate bamboos, and so on. Male and female, sacred and polluted, are vividly defined as symbolic mirror images of one another.

This symbolic cosmological model is mapped onto the spatial layout of a tiny Kwaio settlement (Figure 19.1). At the upper margin of the clearing is the men's house where men sleep and eat, and which is sacred and off-limits to women. At the lower margin is the menstrual hut, polluted and off-limits to men. In the central clearing, which is "mundane," are one or more domestic dwelling houses. But even in each house, the uphill side (from the fireplace upward) is restricted to men; the downhill side is open to both men and women. Thus an invisible line runs across mid-clearing, with the uphill side preeminently the province of men. (With characteristic flexibility, male dogma allows Kwaio women to cross this line and go as far as the margins of the men's house to scrape the clearing, pick up pigs' droppings, and carry firewood.) A man may move freely between dwelling house and men's house, and a woman between dwelling house and menstrual hut. But transitions, especially downward, are carefully observed. A woman must leave pipe and bag behind. If she takes firewood from the house, she must first light an intermediate stick before lighting a fire in the menstrual hut. If a man is sacred through sacrifice or a woman is polluted by menstruation, more drastic rites of desacralization or purification must be performed before the mundane realm can be entered. This cosmological and social mirror-imaging of sacredness and pollution is even more dramatically apparent in the most sacred of men's activities and the most polluting of women's: a high sacrifice by cremating a pig, and childbirth. The woman giving birth retires into a hut in the

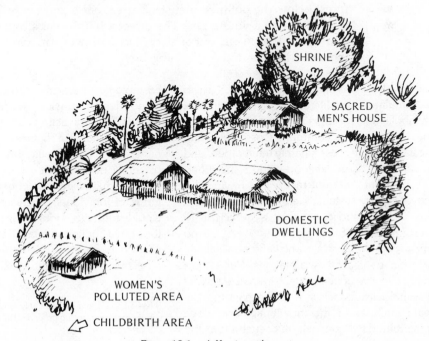

Figure 19.1.   A Kwaio settlement.

Kwaio pollution: A Kwaio girl battens down the thatch on a menstrual hut as gusty winds increase; pieces of the thatch blown into the clearing above would cause pollution. (Photograph by the author.)

forest below the polluted menstrual area, out of all contact with men, and is attended by a young girl. The priest who sacrifices retires to the men's house near the shrine, out of all contact with women, and takes to his bed, where he is attended by a young boy.[1]

There seems little doubt, as such cases accumulate in the literature, that the kinds of symbolic and sociological structuring Douglas has analyzed are common. Cosmology and social structure are intimately intertwined, and neither can be understood without the other.

But that does not mean that having discovered such systematic structure, a sociological and symbolic analysis is sufficient to account for it. Such patterning need by no means rule out the relevance and applicability of psychoanalytic interpretations. Public rites and collective concerns can dramatize private psychological conflicts. If in the past the private fantasies of the individuals who have contributed to the evolution of such ritual and

cosmological systems had not struck a responsive chord with their fellows—perhaps articulating and acting out psychic conflicts shared by many of their fellows—they would never have been institutionalized in the first place. If rituals were simply public performances that were no longer meaningful in terms of individual psychic experience, they would not have endured (in the Kwaio case, they have continued intact despite 70 years of missionary effort). But conversely, once such a belief system is institutionalized, it perpetu-

[1]Here I have drawn on an analysis of a parallel symbolic system in a neighboring group by Elli and Pierre Maranda (1970).

ates the anxieties that may have given initial rise to it, and creates new ones. Kwaio men, having given their womenfolk powers of life and death over them, worry continually about being polluted. The point is that psychological and sociological "explanations" have often been viewed as mutually exclusive; but they should, instead, be viewed as mutually reinforcing.

But what about the kinds of ecologically adaptive functions of religious behavior we sketched in Chapter 12? What about Maring religious ritual and its apparent function as an environmental homeostat, as argued by Rappaport (Case 14)? What about Lindenbaum's argument (p. 213) that pollution taboos operate as "supernatural birth control" and occur in Melanesian societies with high population density as a ritual way of maintaining demographic balance?

And what about the sexual politics whereby men, in gaining control over things sacred and defining women as polluted, achieve impregnable dominance? And could this dominance—involving as it so often does elaborate ritual mummery, sexual anxiety, initiatory brutalizing, and collective display behavior—disguise and maintain deep-seated male anxiety and feelings of inadequacy? Is male supremacy a hollow and precarious victory when it is achieved at such cost?

The latter questions express my conviction, a conviction shared by Shirley Lindenbaum (1972, 1973), Michelle Rosaldo (1974), and some other recent authors, that sexual politics, social structure, cosmology and ritual, and psychology form a tightly knit complex. Though in the past specialists in one or another mode of explanation have tended to dismiss other modes as if they were contradictory, we urgently need less simplistic models that map their interconnectedness.

And if Lindenbaum (1972) and Rappaport (1971) are right, ecological factors are crucial as well. Lindenbaum's argument

regarding sexual polarity takes Mary Douglas' ideas an important further step. If the human body serves as a symbol of the body politic, then what it symbolizes may include a people's perception of their society's demographic state, their relationship to their environment, their relationship to neighboring peoples. Similarly, as Rappaport suggests for the Maring, supernaturals may be personifications of natural forces or diseases (recall the Tsembaga Maring red spirits that cause malarial fever and live in the river valleys where anopheline mosquitoes happen also to be; see p. 208).

A point we made in Chapter 12 remains urgent, however. Symbolic systems are elaborated to cope with psychological stress as well as environmental-ecological-demographic problems. Moreover, since a people's perceptions of such problems are often oblique and distorted, their symbolic responses may often worsen the problems they seek to deal with (recall that Fore endocannibalism, which spreads the fatal *kuru* disease, may be a symbolic response to perceived demographic decline).

Thus ritual behavior that has ecologically adaptive consequences may evolve. But so may ritual behavior that is ecologically maladaptive, anxiety provoking, or oppressive. A system of pollution beliefs may indeed be in part a means of supernatural birth control; but if so, it is a bitter pill.

68.
Myth and Ritual

Myth and ritual, being exotic and easily recorded in far corners of the tribal world, have long fascinated anthropologists. Moreover, the esoterica of the tribal world early stirred a sense of connection between the dark rites and bizarre beliefs of the primitive and the ancient heritage of early Europe—as witness the continued popularity of Frazer's *The Golden Bough*.

Myths are accounts about how the world came to be the way it is, about a super-ordinary realm of events before (or behind) the experienced natural world; they are accounts believed to be true and in some sense sacred. Religious rituals are tightly structured performances of prescribed actions accorded sacred or religious meaning.

Since rituals very often dramatize and act out the stories told in myth, and since the myths correspondingly explain and rationalize ritual performances, anthropologists were led into a long and fruitless debate about which was a reflection of which. Since there are many bodies of myth without corresponding rites, and since there are many bodies of ritual without corresponding myths, scholars should have known better. (There are peoples, such as the Kwaio of Melanesia, who have highly complex systems of ritual but have no myths at all.)

More constructively, modern social anthropologists have sought to trace the relations among ritual, myth, and social structure. Radcliffe-Brown's (1922) classic interpretation of the rites of the Andaman Islanders set the way for social-anthropological study of ritual. In the realm of myth, the way was opened by Malinowski's (1925) sociological interpretation of Trobriand myths. He insisted that Trobriand myths made sense not as disembodied texts for the psychoanalyst or Frazerian antiquarian. Rather, they were living social events, intelligible only in the context of real humans in real places involved in continuing political relations.

Case 70: Trobriand Origin Myths

In any Trobriand village, an essential element of life is the recounting of what we would call myths. Members of a Trobriand subclan know, mark, and recount the history of the "hole" from which its ancestress and her brother emerged from the underworld. In that underworld, in the days before life on the earth, people lived as they do now. The ancestral brother and sister brought up with them sacred objects and knowledge, skills and crafts, and the magic that distinguish this group from others. Is this myth an attempt at primitive "explanation"? Is it an expression of the deep surgings of the unconscious—of incestuous desire or whatever? Or is it some disguised encapsulation of actual history? No, says Malinowski. It can only be understood in the rich context of Trobriand life and cultural meaning. Brother and sister emerged because they represent the two essential elements of the subclan; a husband did not emerge because he is, in terms of the subclan, an irrelevant outsider. The ancestral pair lived in separate houses because the relationship of brother and sister is marked by sharp taboos. But why recite the myth at all? Because it validates the rights of the subclan to the territory and encapsulates the magic and skills that make them sociologically and ritually unique. The myth of local emergence is the *property* of the local subclan; it does not float in limbo to be examined by a psychoanalyst, and it can be understood only in terms of how, when, and with whom it is *used*.

Other origin myths known by all Trobrianders relate the emergence of the four clans, legitimizing their food taboos, but, more particularly, matters of rank and precedence. Finally, other local myths deal with the relative rank, position, and dispersion of high-ranking subclans beyond their point of original emergence. Such myths, Malinowski says, *validate* the political structure and provide a *mythological charter* to justify and reinforce present social relations. Pulling Trobriand myths out of this social context, we would not understand them (Malinowski 1925).

The French anthropologist Claude Lévi-Strauss disagrees. As we will see, Lévi-Strauss is seeking to explicate the universal workings of the human mind by looking at varied cultural forms as its artifacts. The realm of myth is crucial in this enterprise because here human thought has its widest freedom. Not every imaginable form of marriage, house style, or residence pattern is actually found; there are too many constraints, too many possibilities that are unworkable for ecological, technological, or purely physical reasons. But humans can *think* all of these possibilities, and in myth their thoughts have freest reign.

What do humans use this realm of myth for? Lévi-Strauss (1969, 1971, 1974) argues that peoples everywhere are plagued intellectually by the contradictions of existence—by death; by man's dual character, as part of nature yet transformed by culture; by dichotomies of spirit and body; by the contradictions of descent from a first man (where did a nonincestuous first mate come from?); and so on. The realm of myth is used above all to tinker endlessly with these contradictions, by transposing them symbolically. Thus the gulf between life and death can be symbolically mediated by rephrasing the contrast mythically as between an antelope (herbivore) and a lion (carnivore). By introducing a hyena, which eats animals it does not kill, one then in effect denies the contradiction.

Lévi-Strauss' original insistence that a myth, such as the story of Oedipus or of Asdiwal in Northwest Coast mythology (Lévi-Strauss 1967) could be understood by itself

has been modified considerably in his monumental four-volume *Mythologiques*. In *The Raw and the Cooked* (1969), the first volume, he examines a whole complex of myths among Indian tribes of central Brazil and draws heavily on cultural evidence in his interpretation. His exceedingly complicated and involuted decipherment of their "myth-o-logic" is an analytical tour de force. Subsequent volumes (1971—1974) trace out ever-widening webs of myth through the Americas—for myths and mythic themes and symbols, unlike kinship systems, refuse to stay inside societal boundaries. Lévi-Strauss ends with a sweeping vision of cultures, the mind, and the human condition.

But is he right? Lévi-Strauss is solving puzzles, and often doing it with few clues along the way and little "evidence" at the end that the puzzle has been pieced together correctly. Lévi-Strauss' often daring assumptions about the cognitive worlds of other people, as understood from the ethnographic page in a Paris study, have raised many an anthropological doubt. One of the grave problems in this whole mode of analysis is to introduce more controls on a method that can discover, or create, structure in any cultural material. Whether Lévi-Strauss' interpretations endure, there is little doubt that myths have a logic, structure, and richness we had not suspected and that most of the work of deciphering them still lies ahead. Here a rapprochement of structuralist interpretations—which emphasize an intellectualist cognitive view of myth—and psychoanalytic interpretations—

which view myths as projective systems—is badly needed.

Anthropological study of *ritual* has also undergone major transformations in recent years. Rites had been viewed by Durkheim (1912) and Radcliffe-Brown (1922) as reinforcing collective sentiment and social integration. The *content* of rites—whether the priest zigged or zagged, held a stick in his left hand or a leaf in his right—was a secondary and seldom manageable problem.

As the content of cultural systems has been shown to be increasingly systematic, with the bits and pieces seeming less and less arbitrary in relation to one another, such questions now seem crucial. Anthropologists are now beginning to ask them effectively. The nature of ritual symbols has been revealed dramatically in the work of Victor Turner. Exploring the rituals of the East African Ndembu, Turner (1967) has mapped an extraordinarily rich structure of symbolism.

Case 71: Ndembu Ritual Symbols

The key to ritual symbolism among the Ndembu of Zambia is a set of major symbolic objects and qualities that recur in many ritual settings: colors, especially red, white, and black; certain trees and plants; and other "things" accorded central importance in the Ndembu environment. Let us take, for instance, a certain tree, *mudyi*, which exudes a milky sap when cut. The tree is used in several rituals, and we can ask what it "stands for." The answer is that it stands for a wide range of things: a broad fan of conceptually related meanings, from the basic and physiological (breast milk, nursing) to the social (mother-child relations, matrilineal descent) and abstract (dependency, purity). An actual ritual procedure involves not one symbolic object but a series of them in sequence. What, then, does the ritual "mean," if each object could have such a wide spectrum of possible meanings? A sequence of acts involving these objects, like a musical score or a sequence of words, has a *syntax;* and the possible meaning of each is limited and shaped by their combination and arrangement to form a message. But here again the message is not simple and unambiguous, because it is stated on many levels. A rite may at the same time be a statement about mothers and children, men and their matrilineages, and dependency of the living on their ancestors. Moreover, these multiple levels of meaning relate what is abstract and social with the "gut feelings" and emotions of individuals related to their primary experience.

Here, then, are the beginnings of a theory of symbolism that transcends the Freudian and the crudely sociological: the royal sceptor is neither simply a phallic symbol nor a symbol of the unity of the state—it is both, and that is why it "works."

Individual concerns are systematically related to public concerns; collectively enacted dramas have private and unconscious meanings.

In ritual, as in myth, humans reveal a fascination with the gulf that divides them, as creatures of culture, from animals and other phenomena of the world of nature. As we will see in §77, two recent and important studies have examined the symbolic position of women in terms of the culture-nature polarity and have independently reached similar conclusions. Ardener (1972) argues that in most if not all times and places, elaborations of cultural ideologies have been creations of men, not of women. That, he says, is why so often women's views of the social world, as well as the lives of women, have been slighted anthropologically. But why? Ardener goes on to argue the pervasiveness of a symbolic association between women and the world of nature.

The same theme has been explored by Sherry Ortner (1974). Ortner argues that the generative powers of women's sexuality are never controlled by men, always marginal and peripheral to the tight world of cultural control where power rests in men's hands. Women are both cultural and natural beings; and that position of liminality—"betwixt and between"—is reflected cosmologically (in symbolic associations between women, nature, darkness, blood, the moon, the left hand, and so on) and in the characteristic exclusion of women from the center of a society's public stage. We will return to these questions in §77.

The sexual politics of women's roles can serve to remind us that myths, rituals, and religious belief systems do not arise in a political vacuum, and cannot be taken lightly (as Lévi-Strauss and some others have taken them) as collective creations of human consciousness. Religious ideologies reflect, reinforce, and perpetuate political power. It is always well to ask what class interests are served by ideologies (even if the "classes" are simply those defined by sex and age, in a classless society); and to ask who creates them to what ends. Creating and using ideologies reveals the exercise of power as well as the logic of the mind.

This brief look at a field of greatly expanding anthropological interest must suffice for the moment. We will reinforce it in the next chapter. There, shifting our focus slightly, we will return to a question we posed in Chapters 8, 9, and 10, but were insufficiently equipped to deal with systematically: How are cultures as ideational systems organized and integrated?

Armed now with extensive ethnographic evidence, especially on many facets of society and culture among the Trobriand Islanders, we can return to problems of structure and integration with hope of deepened understanding. Since many aspects of cultural integration concern general premises of philosophy and world view, this quest will at the same time extend and deepen our understanding of religion in non-Western societies.

WORLD VIEW AND CULTURAL INTEGRATION

How does a culture fit together? How well integrated is a culture? These questions seem straightforward and sensible enough. But they set traps for the unwary.

Consider an imaginary New Guinea tribe of 500 people. They have customs and a language different from those of neighboring tribes. The "culture" of this tribe "exists" only in a peculiar sense. If all 500 died in an epidemic, the culture would disappear. If, as has been known to happen in New Guinea, all 500 appended themselves to the neighboring tribe, and if they adopted its language and customs and stopped using those they had learned as children, the culture would essentially disappear (except as it survived in memory for a generation or more). A culture is thus manifest in, sustained by, and transmitted between the minds and brains of individual human beings.

Cultural artifacts, things a people make, can remain, of course. And for some recent humans, writing has enabled elements of culture to survive, as the fossilised imprint of minds. But this is not the case with the hypothetical New Guineans.

Each of the 500 members of the tribe has built up a mental guidebook about the world (an "internal model of reality"; Gregory 1969, 1970). Each has some conception of what his or her fellows mean, expect, and do. And each of the 500 mental guidebooks is to some extent unique and different from those of the 499 other people in the tribe. This is inevitable in a world where no two people have the same genetic makeup and life experiences, and where minds have no direct access to other minds. Each guidebook is not only unique, it is partial. Each person has a special perspective on social life and his or her place in it—as male or female, as 10 years old or 60, as priest or farmer, as first-born or last-born, as rich or poor. One does not have to know all the "rules" or perceive the total system in order to play one's own part.

What, then, is the culture of the tribe? It is a 501st version or model constructed by an observer. The culture serves as a heuristic (that is, strategically useful) simplification; it is a useful way of summarizing and codifying what the 500 tribespersons know and believe in order to interpret what they do and say. It is a way to understand how they understand one another. But this 501st version the observer constructs, and finds it useful to attribute to 500 other human beings, *cannot* correspond to the actual mental guidebook of any one of them. The 501st version is a composite: it seeks to show the total system from all vantage points, as no single participant sees it. This composite is generalized and abstract, whereas individual thought worlds are rich in particularities as well as general "rules"; and the composite version is systematic, fitting together into a wider, consistent design what for many or most individuals are partly disconnected segments. Finally, in constructing the culture of the 500 people, the anthropologist seeks not merely to understand what they are doing and meaning but also to communicate about it to colleagues who have never heard their language or been to New Guinea.

Reminded of what a culture is, we are in a position to see the peculiarities and pitfalls of the questions with which the chapter began. How does a culture fit together? An anthropologist too easily forgets that he or she is the one who did much of the fitting together. In asking about cultural integration, about how cultures fit together as total systems, we must thus remember that there is a danger of the observer exaggerating connectedness and consistencies and logical integration in the process of piecing together an idealized composite model of the culture. We will

shortly see Geetz' warnings to this effect.

But the consistencies, the structures, the logics are more than creations of the observer. Even though these structures and connections may remain partly hidden from people's conscious knowledge, and even though they may be but imperfectly and partially realized in the minds and behaviors of individuals, they nevertheless seem to have a systematic continuity and integration over time. In some sense, and in some way, the logical designs seem to transcend their imperfect and partial realizations in individual minds, as continuing collective ideational systems. In what sense, and in what way, are issues that deeply divide anthropological theorists.

How integrated cultures are and how the structures and logics of a culture can be uncovered and described have been central questions in anthropology for many years. In this chapter we will probe these structures, drawing heavily on the background knowledge of Trobriand culture we have built up as a source of illustration and illumination.

69.
The Nature of Cultural Integration

The American anthropologist Robert Lowie (1920), in a passage in which he sought to emphasize how modern ways of life represent accumulations of borrowed elements, once referred to civilization as a "thing of shreds and patches." Critics were quick to point out the defects in the analogy. For the "shreds and patches" are not simply a random collection, randomly arranged. A culture, as its patterning is brought to light, is fantastically intricate, a web of interlinked symbols and meanings on many levels. An element— whether it is a design for house entrances, a ritual procedure, or a dress style—is limited not only by physical possibilities but also by the "rules" of symbolic ordering in the culture. If it is "arbitrary" in the sense that it is not biologically laid down, it is far from arbitrary in the sense that any element could equally well be fitted into a cultural design. When a people conceive the cosmos dualistically in terms of male and female, right and left, and up and down, then what men's costumes can be like, and how the right sides of houses can be designed, must fit this symbolic pattern. Elements are borrowed not as shreds and patches, randomly combined; they are borrowed only if they fit a culture's symbolic designs or can be recut or recolored to fit. Furthermore, there are webs of "functional" interconnection between customs. Elements of a culture fit together in a social and organizational logic, as well as in symbolic patterns: economic relationships, kinship customs, and political institutions must form a coherent system that "works" in a particular environment.

A people's taboo on talking to mothers-in-law, their mode of inheriting property, the sleeping arrangements in the house, their kinship categories, and their theory of procreation may be elements of an integrated system. They may express a set of basic premises about the cosmos and human social relations. But these underlying designs distinctive of a culture are abstract and subtle. The people cannot usually talk about them. They lie hidden beneath the details of custom and do not yield to any mode of direct exploration. For many years, anthropologists have groped for ways of uncovering and describing these underlying patterns of order and integration that constitute each culture's unique view of the world.

Our evidence on the Trobrianders has many gaps, but it will serve to illustrate some forms of cultural integration and some approaches to the underlying premises and symbolic order of a culture.

Case 72: The Integration of Trobriand Culture

We can glimpse an important level of cultural integration by pulling together some elements of Trobriand social organization, custom, and belief. We can then see how elements that seem peculiar by themselves become intelligible in terms of a wider design. Many of these items have been introduced in preceding chapters. Here we will set out schematically a series of "strange" customs and belief.

1. The doctrine of subclan perpetuity
   a. A brother and sister emerged together from the underworld and founded the subclan.
   b. The spirits of the dead descendants of this ancestral pair continue to be "members" of the subclan, along with the living. Though as *baloma,* or spirits, they have moved to a new plane of existence centered in Tuma, the island of the dead, their association with their subclan continues. (We will soon examine the *milamala* festival at which they annually return to visit living members of the subclan.)
   c. New children born into the subclan are reincarnations of subclan spirits whose period as *baloma* has come to an end. The subclan existed of old when men lived underground; and it has always been and will always be the same.

2. The Trobriand theory of conception

    a. Copulation by the father does not "cause" the birth of a child—which is the reincarnation of a spirit of the mother's subclan. (There is an enormous literature and controversy about what Trobrianders "really mean" here.)

    b. The child's "blood" comes from the mother and her siblings.

    c. The child physically resembles the father, not the mother, because his repeated intercourse with the mother "molds" the child.

3. The avoidance relationship between brother and sister

    a. Brother and sister must avoid close social contact or any intimacy.

    b. The brother must avoid all knowledge of his sister's sexual affairs.

    c. When she marries, he must avoid any direct involvement in her reproductive life.

4. The rule of residence

    a. A Trobriand girl and her brother grow up in their father's household, usually in a different village from her subclan's.

    b. Whereas the brother returns to his subclan village in adolescence, the daughter remains with her father until she marries.

    c. She then goes to live with her husband; thus at no stage in her life cycle does she normally live with her male subclan relatives in their territory.

5. Rules of exogamy

    a. A Trobriander is forbidden to marry, or have intercourse with, a girl in his subclan.

    b. Though marriage with them is regarded as wrong, sexual affairs with girls in different subclans of one's own clan are regarded as naughty and dangerous (and hence add spice to life).

6. The relationship of a father to his children

    a. The father is said to be a "relative by marriage" to his children.

    b. Half-siblings with the same mother and different father are treated as similar to full siblings. Yet half-siblings with the same father and different mothers are treated as nonrelatives. If they are boy and girl, it is regarded as all right for them to have sexual relations. Trobrianders say that the reason they cannot marry is that this would snarl up the *urigubu* yam presentations.

    c. A daughter belongs to her mother's corporate subclan, which is dependent on her and its other girls for members in the next generation. Yet when she marries, it is her *father* and *his* subclan—not her own—with whom her husband's people exchange valuables.

    d. When the married daughter wants to become pregnant, her father asks his subclan ancestors to ask the ancestors of his wife's and daughter's subclan to send a spirit child.

7. The relationship of children to their paternal aunt

    a. For a boy, the aunt is the prototype of a sexually eligible woman, with whom he can joke freely or have sexual intercourse.

    b. Her daughter is said by Trobrianders to be the ideal wife for him.

    c. It is a girl's paternal aunt who takes the lead in events surrounding her pregnancy and childbirth; her aunt, not her mother, makes her a pregnancy cloak, for example.

8. *Urigubu* and relations between affines

   a. *Urigubu* yam presentations, in the ideal form, go from a man to his sister's husband.

   b. A second form of *urigubu* yam presentation is from a married son to his father.

   c. *Urigubu* is more widely a relationship between a corporate subclan and its female members' husbands and their subclans.

   d. When a spouse dies, his or her own subclan members cannot have any contact with the body, or outwardly mourn; these things are done by the kin of the surviving spouse, who then receive valuables from the dead spouse's subclan at the mortuary feast.

We could keep widening the circle of customs and show how they fit together; but at this stage enough elements have been brought out to indicate that they are not simply "shreds and patches." Simply in setting out these customs and beliefs this way, their connectedness begins to emerge. We can see it more clearly if we penetrate deeper to find a symbolic structure underlying them.

We view our connectedness to our father and mother in terms of "blood relationship," which extends through them to uncles, grandmothers, cousins, and so forth. The Trobrianders view the connection between subclan members, and most vividly between brother, sister, and the sister's child, in terms of "blood." Blood implies perpetuity and continuity, as in (1) and (2b) in the outline.

Yet if the blood and the immaterial continuity with the spirits give perpetuity and unity to the subclan—as the dogma of conception insists—these cannot make the subclan independent and self-perpetuating. In the brother and sister taboo and rule against subclan incest, blood and sexual relations are inimical and sharply separate. We can think in symbolic terms of the rule BLOOD ⊃ NO SEX ("if blood, then no sex"). In the denial of physiological paternity, we can see its mirror image, SEX ⊃ NO BLOOD.

The dogma of subclan perpetuity and conception symbolically asserts that the subclan is self-contained and self-sustaining. But Trobriand ideologists come to terms with ecological, physical, and political necessity and recognize the dependence of the subclan for a complex of services they themselves cannot provide. In the separation of blood and sex, this need for bonds outside the subclan is symbolically expressed.

But Trobriand ideology can define those bonds outside the subclan as radically different from those of blood. They are bonds of influence, but not of substance—as expressed most directly in the father's "molding" of the child (Leach 1961). The bonds outside the subclan are created by marriage, and most of them terminate when the marriage ends. We can view these ties as "affinal," and understand the Trobrianders now when they tell the ethnographer that the father is a "relative by marriage" (6a in the outline)—that is, connected by bonds of influence but not substance.

We can see why they say paternal half-siblings share no common blood (6b).

Because the child's subclan is linked by an "affinal" and hence sexual bond to the father's subclan, father's sister is the prototypical sexual object, with whom a son can joke or have sexual relations (7a). Because the mother and her brother are separated by the gulf of taboo (3c), he and other men of her own subclan must avoid involvement in matters connected with her sexuality and reproductive life. Hence it is their "affines," the father's subclan, who receive marriage presentations (6c), who assist in her becoming pregnant (6d), and who provide magical and ritual services connected with her pregnancy and childbirth (7c) (Robinson 1962). When a Trobriander is mourned and buried by his or her spouse's relatives, not fellow members of his or her own subclan (8d), it is because the evil "mist" emanating from the dead could spread to those of common blood; but it cannot pass across the bonds of affinity, where no common substance provides a connection. When the affines have been rewarded for this final service at the mortuary rites, the affinal relation between the two subclans comes to an end (though the children continue to trace relationships of bilateral kinship, based on influence but not blood, through a dead father; Sider 1967).

Thus the men of a subclan must send their sisters out for the sexuality, "molding," and childbearing they themselves can take no part in; and then must get back the sisters' sons who will be their successors. This sending away in a symbolic sense is reflected in the physical pattern of residence (4). A subclan's dependence on its affines for the services and influences its own members cannot provide is first of all expressed in the relationship of a man to his sister's husband, and in the next generation, in the relation of these two brothers-in-law toward children of the marriage (where the father and his sisters provide services the mother's brother cannot). Because a son is a member of his maternal uncle's subclan, his relation to his father structurally resembles and continues his uncle's "brother-in-law" relation to his father.

This comes out in *urigubu* transactions (8). *Urigubu* transfers of yams can be viewed in part as a contractual obligation whereby a corporate subclan rewards its affines for the services they have provided. That a father can receive *urigubu* from his married son as well as or in succession from his brother-in-law (8b) makes sense if we see the young man as stepping into his maternal uncle's shoes. Here it is worth remembering back also to the Crow equivalence rule posited to account for Trobriand kinship terms: a woman's brother is equivalent to her son in the reckoning of kinship.

Such webs of logic and interconnection can be traced throughout a culture. They show well the flaws in the shreds and patches analogy and the way seemingly strange customs fall into place when we see them as elements of a wider design. We will see shortly how even more elements fall into place if we penetrate to a deeper level in the symbolic structure of a culture.

But as Geertz (1966b:65—67) points out, the "integration" of a culture is partly the creation of the analyst, a composite version pieced together by the anthropologist. (Recall the 501st version of the hypothetical New Guinea society with which the chapter began.) The extent to which a culture fits together into a total system, a neatly integrated whole—even in the most stable and isolated tribal society—is now a problem to be investigated. The Trobriand illustrations show how cultures do make sense, and fit together, in a way a newcomer to anthropology might well not suspect. But as Geertz suggests, if we assumed that Trobriand culture should be totally integrated and self-consistent, it would be easy to create just as striking a picture of discontinuities and logical contradictions, showing how badly integrated Trobriand culture is. One of the remarkable things about humans is our ability to tolerate and operate with inconsistent and contradictory beliefs and customs: the world is filled with soldiers fighting for peace, adulterous Christians, rich Communists, and quarreling kinsfolk.

By piecing together an internally consistent and integrated composite view of Trobriand culture, the anthropologist not only may obscure inconsistencies and contradictions. The observer also obscures deep lines of cleavage in the social system, and thus hides the dynamics of the society. Though Trobriand men and women, chiefs and commoners, may have shared codes of expectation that make ordered social life possible, the notion of a culture badly oversimplifies matters. A commoner shuffles along on his knees with head bowed before a leader of high rank and presents as tribute the valuables and yams which the leader uses in ceremonial exchanges and feasting. Both of them share a common culture in the sense that the high-ranking leader knows how to demand and receive obeisance and the commoner knows when and how he has to give it. But to say that those kinds of knowledge, pieced together into a composite, constitute Trobriand culture obscures our understanding of how Trobriand society works and how it changes, and our understanding of how individual Trobrianders see their world. As Talal Asad has recently argued forcefully, "The notion of holistic integration in functional anthropology assumes that ideologies are necessarily socially homogeneous and temporarily closed"; yet the people an anthropologist studies are characteristically made up of "classes or other groups in dialectical opposition to each other for whom social meanings are continually being reconstructed on the basis of evolving material circumstances; the process of reconstitution always involves tensions and fluctuations . . ." (Asad 1974:215). The interests of Trobriand chiefs and commoners, men and women, may be deeply in conflict; and Trobriand culture as pieced together by Malinowski represents a temporary state of the battle lines.

That there is no recorded history of the development of social stratification, the *kula* ring, or matrilineal descent in the Trobriands should not mislead us into seeing a spurious unity, integration, or equilibrium of Trobriand society and culture.

These challenges to anthropological assumptions and dogma are beginning to have an impact in many realms. We will return to them.

For the moment, we will return to another approach to cultural structure, one that builds on models from linguistics. But as this and other approaches to cultural integration are explored, the force of Asad's critique should stimulate critical reservations and questioning.

"Ethnoscience" or "ethnographic semantics" (§26) builds on the assumption that the things and events in a people's conceptual world will be mirrored in the semantic categories of their language (Tyler 1969). By finding out what "things" there are in a people's world, and what features of that world they treat as distinctive in assigning meanings, one could avoid superimposing our preconceptions and cultural biases on their conceptual system. Moreover, by using systematic eliciting methods modeled on those in linguistics, one could hopefully achieve greater rigor than the usual style of fieldwork permits.

Thus Frake (1961) has explored and mapped with great rigor the way the Subanun of the Philippines diagnose skin diseases. He has since sought to extend this method to Subanun social interaction ("how to ask for a drink in Subanun" (1964b)); to social organization and ecology (the principles governing their shifting of settlements and gardens (1962a)); and to relations with supernaturals (1964a).

Frake and other students of "ethnoscience" are attempting not only to map the structure of small subsystems of folk classification with increased sophistication and rigor; they also hope to transcend the artificiality of a "chapter title" approach to a people's culture. "Economics," "political structure," and so on, are misleading but convenient organizing devices in a comparative survey like ours. But if we hope to describe the structure of a people's own conceptual world, they are worse than misleading. We want to find out what realms people divide their world into, not force it into our predevised compartments. Their systems might turn out to correspond in some respects to "chapter title" comparative frameworks. But that is something we would have to discover about another people's world; we cannot use a method that assumes it.

Case 73: Subanun "Religious Behavior"

In Subanun culture (see Case 30), regular "meals" are on some occasions replaced by a "festive meal," where several families eat together and normal food is augmented by meat and rice wine. The events in the course of such a festive meal constitute a festivity.

One type of festivity differs from others in that some of the participants are not mortals but are invisible supernaturals. The latter receive food from the mortals. Such presentations of food are called *kanu*, or offerings. These offerings distinguish one type of festivity, a ceremony, from other types such as "labor-recruiting feasts" and "hospitality feasts." Note that there is no Subanun word for "ceremony"; yet it can be identified as a relevant segment of the Subanun world of experience by the way culturally distinctive acts and things are used.

Planning and staging these offerings, and the ceremonies built around them, is a central theme of Subanun life. Offerings involve elaborate plans and organization and are deemed crucial to successful living. This sphere of Subanun life can be conveniently labeled as religious behavior. But, insists Frake, that is not because it fits some general definition of "religion": from a standpoint of the Subanun thought world, that is irrelevant.

What matters is that this and other domains of Subanun culture, as they are described by the ethnographer, follow distinctions and categories relevant to the Subanun themselves (Frake 1964a).

Using such an approach to explore the structure of Trobriand culture on the basis of published information would be dangerous and difficult. Though Malinowski gives extensive linguistic materials, the full sets and contextual materials we would need to reconstruct semantic structure are rare (but compare Tambiah 1969). Yet Trobriand folk classification can usefully illustrate one point often missed in the ethnoscience procedure of looking at domains one at a time in isolation—at the classification of plants, or kinsmen, or birds, or firewood, or supernaturals. The logic of one subsystem may be intelligible only in terms of another, and the same symbolic principles may be used to order different domains.

Case 74: Trobriand "Animal" Categories

The fauna of the Trobriands are sparse—reptiles, birds, bats, crabs, and insects. We do not know from Malinowski's writings how the Trobrianders classify different kinds of birds or snakes or what not (though it is a good guess that like many Pacific islanders they class birds and bats in the same category). But what concern us here are two higher-level categories that embrace all of these land creatures: "things of the below" and "things of the above." The former include snakes, crabs, iguanas, and lizards. The latter include birds, bats, and insects.

Analyzing these categories in ethnoscience fashion, we might see the distinction between them in terms of terrestrial versus flying creatures—the "below and above" suggest that apparently insects that do not fly are still in the "above" category, which is puzzling. Digging deeper, one might discover that "things of the below" are classed together because they come out of holes in the ground, and particularly because they all change their skins. But what kind of categorization is that? Looking only at this domain, we would probably remain mystified.

Students of symbolism like Leach and Douglas would insist that the anthropologist's job is to go further than just describing the semantics of folk classification in the manner of ethnoscience. These are cultural creations, and we want to understand the logic of their creation—to know why as well as what. Leach (1965) would have us look very closely at those strange animals that are neither fish nor fowl, that fall in the middle in a scheme of classification. He would have us look carefully at "odd" distinctions like shedding of skin, and would have us note that on the rare occasions when evil spirits take visible form, it is as reptiles. And he might have us note that when women who are witches change their form and become invisible flying *mulukuausi* that prey on men at night and at sea, their presence can be recognized by the smell of decaying flesh—what may be a symbolic transition between life and death. But why are these changes of form and state important? Snakeskins, witches, night, sea—is it all a giant puzzle? And why "creatures of the below"? If there is a structure in all this, it is deeper and more subtle.

Case 75: The Structure of Trobriand Culture

To try to lay bare the whole structure of Trobriand culture would be far beyond our scope—if indeed it is possible using spotty library evidence, or possible for anthropology at all. But some of the possibilities can at least be glimpsed.

We can begin with some basics of Trobriand cosmology. Recall that the ancestors long ago lived underground and then emerged through the subclan holes into the world. The *baloma*, spirits of the dead, live underground as well, though the details are vague (Malinowski 1916:170–171). We can draw these dualistic contrasts:

BELOW	:	ABOVE
SPIRITS	:	MEN
IMMATERIAL	:	MATERIAL
INVISIBLE	:	VISIBLE

To these further analysis would add such contrasts as

DARKNESS	:	LIGHT
IMMORTAL	:	MORTAL
DEATH	:	LIFE

In such a scheme of symbolic dualisms it is worth looking always at mediating states and beings. Thus in dreams and visions the living can communicate with the spirits. The subclan holes (and holes in general) are avenues between above and below. So, symbolically, is the sea, on which spirit children come from Tuma, the land of the dead. Invisible witches, at night and at sea, may begin to make sense. But why are evil spirits manifest as reptiles; why changing skins, why "creatures of the below"?

In their earlier existence men were immortal, and underground. When they aged, they sloughed their skins and grew new ones, as the *baloma* still do. Shortly after emerging from the subclan holes to the world above, men lost their immortality in a seemingly trivial incident. But the snakes, crabs, and lizards that emerge from holes and still change their skins are mediators to the underworld and retain the vestiges of immortality; in contrast to men and to birds, bats, and insects, they are creatures of the BELOW. It is as a creature of the BELOW, a snake or iguana, that an evil spirit becomes visible to men. Crabs, which brought sorcery to men from the spirit world, are slow to die, for they too are medial creatures of the BELOW.

Elsewhere in Trobriand culture we could discern further symbolic contrasts that partly mesh with the preceding dualisms:

MOON	:	SUN
FEMALE	:	MALE
LOW	:	HIGH
COMMONER	:	"CHIEF"
AFFINITY	:	BLOOD

Moreover, there are the symbolic polarities to which Lévi-Strauss called our attention in his glimpse of the Trobriand village (Case 41):

PERIPHERAL	:	CENTRAL
COOKED	:	RAW
MARRIAGE	:	NONMARRIAGE
PROFANE	:	SACRED

A careful look at these arrays of dualisms shows that they do not simply line up in two columns such that everything in the right column or left column goes together in all contexts. Items in opposite columns may be contextually united—so that SPIRITS and SACRED clearly are not contrasted, and continuity of BLOOD passes through the FEMALE line.

Symbolic oppositions and mediations between them may be important elements in the structure of a culture. But they do not simply hang on pegs in a fixed array—they are *used;* and there is a "grammar" for using them in different contexts. How the symbolic system of a culture is used can be illustrated if we speculate about the highpoint of the Trobriand year, the *milamala.*

The *milamala* is, in outward appearance, a harvest festival—a period of dancing, feasting, ceremonial visiting, exchanges of food and valuables, and heightened sexual activity. The *milamala* activities begin after the yams have been harvested, displayed, distributed in *urigubu,* and ceremoniously stored in yam houses. At this point, marking the annual break in the gardening and work cycle, a food distribution (*sagali*) and pageantry lead up to the first playing of slit drums and commencement of dancing. The *milamala* takes place through the first half of a lunar month and ends at the full moon. As the moon waxes, activities become more intense, with dancing going on through the night, organized visits by girls or boys of a village to a neighboring village to enjoy its sexual hospitality, and even organized visits by the whole population of a village to a neighboring village, with accompanying political maneuvering, mock threat, and exchange of ceremonial valuables.

But there are a number of curious features that suggest a more subtle symbolic theme. They suggest that this is a context (or "frame"; see p. 169) where symbolic polarities are joined or reversed. Female and male, the spirits and the living, the periphery and the center, the below and the above are united or reversed.

One element in this union of polarities, or reversal, is expressed in the realm of sexuality. Recall that it is the bachelor houses in the center of the village, the male domain, that are the focal settings for premarital sex. The symbolic polarity of inner and outer circles of the village may in fact express not a symbolic contrast between MARRIAGE and NONMAR-RIAGE, as Lévi-Strauss has argued (see Case 41), but one between REGU-LATED SEX and UNREGULATED SEX (Boon 1972:127). Premarital sex reaches its height during *milamala* and acquires a kind of overt recognition, cultural embellishment, and collective character in intervillage sexual visiting. The shift of emphasis from individual, regulated, domestic sex to collective, unrestricted premarital sex and from periphery to center of the village hints that *milamala* is not only a time of liminality (Turner 1967) but

Trobriand men don women's grass skirts for a dance. Reversal of polarities in the *milamala*. (Courtesy of Australian News and Information Bureau.)

a time when polarities are mediated or reversed. Given the polarities between MOON:SUN and DARK:LIGHT, the way the *milamala* reaches its climax at full moon probably reflects their symbolic union in this liminal period of heightened cultural intensity. Apparently the dancing in the village center, which attracts men and women around the slit drums— one symbolically male, another symbolically female—serves as a medium for the union of dualities. Men wear their festive ornaments emphasizing maleness in the day, during *milamala,* then take them off at night; and in some of the dances the male dancers put on women's grass skirts. Cooked food, symbolic of the women's and domestic realm, is normally taboo within the central plaza. But in the opening feast of *milamala* cooked food is set out and distributed there.

But the most dramatic union of symbolic oppositions in *milamala* is the return of the *baloma* spirits to their village. Through the *milamala* period the spirits are present and are given food offerings and ceremonial valuables (the "spirit" of which they take). The element of symbolic reversal comes out vividly in the high platforms made for *baloma* of high rank— placing them ABOVE rather than BELOW. Moreover the *baloma* enforce the suspension of the normal rules of life. If they are not satisfied with people's conduct, as well as with presentations of food and valuables, they can spoil weather or even the next gardening cycle. "Everybody had to be bound on pleasure, dancing, and sexual license, in order to please the *baloma*" Malinowski (1916:185). The *milamala* ends at full moon when the *baloma* are ritually sent back to their spirit home. Viewing *milamala* as a liminal period during which polarities are mediated, reversed, or shifted illuminates some aspects of ritual and behavior. So, too, does viewing it as a rite of cosmic regeneration (compare Eliade 1970, Lanternari 1955); and there are still other symbolic themes that await analysis.

The Trobriand material, though incomplete, is rich and provocative: small wonder that it has stimulated so many attempts at analysis and reinterpretation since Malinowski's day. Tambiah's (1969) analysis of the language of Trobriand magic, for example, hints at the rich symbolic structure in the use of colors, folk botany, direction, and other realms. But we have gone far enough to show how such symbolic analysis can bring the structure of a culture to light.

Can such analysis tell us something about Trobriand life, about the behavior of individual Trobrianders? Can such abstract symbolic interpretations tell us anything about the motives, perceptions, and behavior of real people? Peter Wilson (1969) argues that they can, and illustrates with a Trobriand example.

Case 76: Trobriand Water Bottles

Malinowski (1929:98–99) recounted an event that puzzled him. The son of an important chief discovered his wife in the arms of his half-brother. He reacted with visible anger; but instead of smashing his wife or her lover, he smashed all of his wife's water bottles. And then, seemingly satisfied, he appeared publicly "sitting beside his wife in perfect harmony." Malinowski notes elsewhere that when a husband is angry with his wife he may express this by breaking her water bottles or destroying her grass skirt (1929:21). But this seemed to Malinowski an inadequate and hence idiosyncratic response to his wife and half-brother caught in the act of adultery.

We know enough about displaced aggression to understand that by redirecting anger at the water bottles the husband diverted his aggression from direct assault on the adulterous couple. Redirecting aggression—kicking a wall in frustration—is an old part of our mammalian heritage. But why the water bottles? And is it coincidental that the wife had taken her water bottles as a pretext to meet her lover? Wilson (1969:286) notes a myth in which women who are raped while getting water are more upset about the breaking of their water bottles than their physical violation. He notes that the waterhole is "the women's club and centre of gossip" (Malinowski 1929:17) and that filling water bottles is an exclusively female duty. Moreover, water is the medium through which conception occurs. Not only does a spirit child usually enter a woman's body through water (so that if she wants to avoid conception she stays away from the water); but her brother or mother's brother may facilitate conception by collecting water in a wooden baler (*not* a water bottle) and leaving it in her hut overnight. Wilson argues that there is a symbolic association of water with the reproductive powers of women. (As we will see in Chapter 24, these powers are universally beyond the control of men and are a frequent point of elaboration of sex role symbolism and conflict.) He further notes that the symbolic line drawn in Trobriand culture between men's and women's realms centers around the head. Wilson (1969:287) argues that symbolically "A woman's head . . . is that part of her which is the junction and starting point for passion, conception and creation, for the psychological or emotional and physiological process of birth."

That the power of creation symbolically brings together head and water emerges in the Trobriand myth of incest. A woman's brother brings water into her house—but he does so, inappropriately, in water bottles, not a baler. The girl's mother will not bring it to her, so she goes to get it herself; and in doing so, she inadvertently knocks over the coconut shell containing coconut oil brewed by her brother into love potions. Some of it spills on her head; she is seized with desire for her brother and they rush to the sea shore and have intercourse.

Wilson believes that water bottles, also made of coconut shells, symbolically represent the sexual relationship between husband and wife, being carried on women's heads, containers of water as the medium of life, and symbols *par excellence* of women's domestic role. He argues that they serve, correspondingly, as symbols of the incest taboo that separates a woman from her brother and matrilineal kin.

To a husband, his wife's water bottles indicate her sexuality and his right to that sexuality. The water within them, and the fact that she carries them on her head, signifies her life-giving powers and her relation to her brother. To a brother water bottles signify the incest taboo and the water within them his rights to her children. To a woman a water bottle is the symbolic nexus of her total social position: her relationship with her husband and thence her sexuality, her relationship with her brother and thence her procreative duties. (Wilson 1969:288)

For the adulterous wife to have taken her water bottles as pretext to meet her lover, for the cuckolded husband to have displaced his aggression by smashing them and not her, and for their fellow Trobrianders to have accepted this as a quite appropriate response is not strange or idiosyncratic, Wilson argues. Rather, these constitute appropriate messages in a symbolic code Trobrianders share and (however unconsciously) "understand."

As we move to these deeper levels of structure, more elements of a culture fall into place. But the solid foundations of ethnoscience, have dissolved into something less tangible. How do we know Trobrianders think in terms of these symbolic patterns or use them in ordering their culture? These uncertainties mount as we go deeper; and many anthropologists would be unwilling to follow this far.

Can one penetrate more deeply still? Are there even more basic premises and principles that give a culture its unique shape? One avenue of approach is through the structure of the language. As we noted in Chapter 9, Whorf saw language not simply as expressing thought but as channeling and shaping it. A people's language lays down and expresses their models of time, space, and causality. Could we find more basic designs of the Trobrianders' world in the structure of their language? Dorothy Lee's own fieldwork with the Wintu Indians of California, and Whorf's explorations of Hopi language and world view, had convinced Lee that this was possible. Though she never met a Trobriander or heard one speak, she "lived" her way into their language by immersing herself in Malinowski's rich linguistic texts. A first attempt to draw the Trobriand world view (Lee 1940) contrasted it with that of an English speaker. But she had misgivings whether one could faithfully render the Trobriand world view in terms of what it was not, in terms of contrasts. In a second paper, Lee (1949:401—415) tried to draw the Trobriand world in its own terms—an immensely difficult challenge when one must write in English about another language.

Case 77: The Trobriand World View as Structured in Language

Among the Trobriand Islanders, as with other peoples, "language . . . incorporates the premises of the culture, and codifies reality in such a way that it presents it as absolute" to its speakers. The speakers of Trobriand (or Kiriwinan) "are concerned with being, and being alone. Change and becoming are foreign to their thinking. An object or event is grasped and evaluated in terms of itself alone." It is not defined, which implies contrast with other things, but is conceived in terms of what it is. "Each event is grasped timelessly," seen in relation to other things only in that it is part of an "ordained pattern."

> If I were to go with a Trobriander to a garden where the taytu, a species of yam, had just been harvested, I would come back and tell you: "There are good taytu there; just the right degree of ripeness, large and perfectly shaped; not a blight to be seen, not one rotten spot. . . ." The Trobriander would come back and say "Taytu"; and he would have said all that I did and more. . . . (Lee 1949:402)

> History and mythical reality are not "the past" to the Trobriander. They are forever present, participating in all current being, giving meaning to all his activities and all existence. . . . (403)

> To be good [an object] must be the same always. . . . Trobriand being never came into existence; it has always been, exactly as now. . . . (405)

> To the Trobriander, events do not fall of themselves into a pattern of causal relationships . . . the magician does not cause certain things to be; he does them. (400–407)

> The Trobriander performs acts because of the activity itself, not for its effects; . . . he values objects because they are good, not good for. . . . (408)

> [Yet] being has no independent existence. It is itself only as part of an established pattern. . . . Being is seen . . . as a fixed point in a single, changeless whole. (409)

> For members of our culture, value lies ideally in change, in moving away from the established pattern. . . . The Trobriander, on the contrary, expects and wants next year to be the same as this year and as the year before his culture emerged from underground. (413)

Finally, Lee speculates on the level and the relevance of such linguistically structured contrast in world view:

> Do we who base our behavior on relationships, read these relationships into reality, or are they given? Which codification is true to reality. . . . Our peculiar codification makes us blind to other aspects of reality. . . . Or makes these meaningless when presented. But one codification does not exhaust reality. . . . The Trobrianders, according to our view of life, should be bored automatons. Actually they act as they want to act, poised and sure, in activities which hold meaning and satisfaction. (415)

Lee's intuitions, like Whorf's analyses of the Hopi world view, capture the imagination with their vividness. And they become doubly plausible to those caught up in a counterculture that challenges the pervasive and destructive rationality of Western thought and seeks a more mystical and holistic vision of the world in the wisdom of other peoples.

But at this stage, Lee's interpretations seem mainly wrong. It may be that Trobrianders see their world in a very different way than we see ours. But this is not shaped profoundly by their grammatical system. Rather, in terms of modern linguistic theory (§25 and §26), the contrasts between English and Kiriwinan Lee describes reflect relatively superficial grammatical differences. The underlying logical or propositional structure of both languages (that is, the basic level at which thoughts are encoded) is quite similar. These underlying propositions are then converted by the special derivational (transformational) rules of each language into surface-structure representations. It is contrasts in the "output" rules of the two languages that Lee is characterizing in an intuitive fashion—hence, not contrasts in the logic of thinking.

Whether Trobrianders perceive "cause" in a way different from English speakers cannot be inferred from linguistic surface structures. But whatever philosophical elaborations on causality they may make (as in their theory of conception), it seems likely that it is part of their mammalian equipment, on which their ability to learn and survive depends, that they understand causal relations: that a canoe paddle stuck in the water and pushed in one direction will lead the canoe to go in the other direction; that pulling a roasted taro out of the fire leads a hand to be burned; and that a puncture of the skin with a sharp weapon leads blood to come out. And Trobrianders, like other humans, can communicate with one another about such relationships, using the special conventions of their language. Similarly, linguistic conventions for expressing verb tenses may be largely irrelevant for understanding a people's perception of time.

Other scholars have taken the whole range of customs and behavior as sources of clues about the deepest levels of "world view" or cultural integration. Many American anthropologists have considered a culture to be something like a geometry in its internal order. That is, there are a great many specific theorems, corollaries, principles, and relationships; but they are elaborations and implications of a smaller set of more general principles. Finally, underlying the whole system are a few general axioms, the "givens" of the system, cultural equivalents of "a straight line is the shortest distance between two points." House styles, kinship taboos, and ritual routines are viewed as like the specific theorems and rules of geometry. The anthropologist must search beneath them to find the underlying givens of the system.

A major attempt of this sort was Clyde Kluckhohn's exploration of the basic givens of Navaho Indian culture, based on years of intimate experience with Navaho life and analysis of Navaho custom and belief. From evidence as diverse as sandpainting designs, curing ceremonies, kinship arrangements, political action, and fears of witchcraft, Kluckhohn (1949) inferred a set of basic premises about the universe in terms of which these details make sense. The following premises are illustrative:

The universe is orderly: all events are caused and interrelated.
   a. Knowledge is power.
   b. The basic quest is for harmony.
   c. Harmony can be restored by orderly procedures.
   d. One price of disorder, in human terms, is illness.
The universe tends to be personalized.
The universe is full of dangers.
Evil and good are complementary, and both are ever present.
Morality is conceived in traditionalistic and situational terms rather than in terms of abstract absolutes.
Human relations are premised upon familistic individualism.

Similarly deep involvement in the thought world of another Indian people, the Ojibwa, led A. I. Hallowell to explore the categories, assumptions, and logic in terms of which Ojibwa order experience. These studies bring out particularly clearly how some of the distinctions we take most for granted—animate versus inanimate, natural versus supernatural—are by no means universal in human experience. Hallowell's most important writings are collected in *Culture and Experience* (1955). His insights regarding the cognitive structuring of reality and the psychology of self had a sophistication that prefigured subsequent anthropological exploration of culture and cognition.

These approaches reflected the tradition, following Franz Boas, that cultures are highly diverse and that the human infant is highly plastic, open to the shaping of a unique culture. More recently, Lévi-Strauss has approached the underlying structure and integration of cultures from a more universalistic point of view.

Lévi-Strauss was strongly influenced by his contact with the linguist Roman Jakobson, a pioneer in the structural analysis of sound systems. Jakobson elaborated and refined the theory of distinctive features in phonology. At the time he and Lévi-Strauss were in closest contact, he was refining a method of analyzing sound systems in terms of the way, in each language, a set of binary features (voiced versus unvoiced, tense versus lax) was drawn from a wider universal set to define the relevant contrasts in sound. Such a structural system lay beneath the continuous world of sound, creating a pattern by defining contrasts. The human mind was creating structure, unconsciously imposing order on flux.

For Lévi-Strauss, this was an exciting paradigm for the understanding of perception, of mind, and of culture. In his earlier work he sought to analyze the stuff of a culture—its kinship system, its art, its economic system— to find structural patterns distinctive of that culture. Each culture had its distinctive structural patterns, manifest in these different realms (and perhaps even correlated with the phonological structures of the language; Lévi-Strauss 1945). He has retained through the years his fascination with the unique content of a culture, its conceptualization of plants and animals, its forms of art and marriage. But increasingly Lévi-Strauss has emphasized not cultural uniqueness but universals. The human mind, the instrument through which cultures are created and passed and through

which the world is perceived, imposes the same formal order, the same structures, in all times and places.

In the realms of culture, as in phonology, the logic of thinking is binary—based on sets of two-way contrasts (A or not-A, B or not-B). The tribesman directs this relatively simple mode of relational thought at the world of sensory experience: the animals, plants, constellations, individuals, and groups that are his direct evidence about the world. Like the French handyman who solves infinitely variable repair problems by rearranging the pieces and materials at hand, tribal peoples endlessly rearrange and classify their universe of experience. The precise arrangements are almost infinitely variable, but the mode of arrangement, the structure of the designs, is repeated over and over. It is as though the human mind were a snowflake machine which never precisely replicated the same pattern, but which always produced the same *kind* of pattern.

Lévi-Strauss does not argue that there is a "primitive mind," a qualitatively different way of thinking, as had Lévy-Bruhl (1923). Modern humans live in a conceptual world whose building materials have been enormously expanded by microscope, telescope, the stuff of science, and the language of mathematics; we have also become specialists, more like electronics expert than handyman. The mode of thought is the same; the products of thought have been transformed.

The same symbolic polarities—culture versus nature, sacred versus profane, male versus female, right versus left, sun versus moon—run through the domains of a culture. The same formal arrangements of contrast recur again and again within one culture, or from one culture to another. The differences are in the realm of content, so that it is possible to show how one design is a replica or a transformation of another.

Because the same modes of thinking are

applied by tribal peoples to a world of direct sensory experience that is very much the same in jungle or desert, the same elements, themes, and contrasts occur over and over again on different continents: fire, moon, and sun; the contrast between the sexes, between our group and outsiders, between nature and culture; the use of animals and plants to symbolize relations between human groups. Human intellect grapples with the existential contradictions and problems humans face—death, human origin, the contrast between people and animals (and hence culture and nature)—using a logic of polarity and mediation. As we saw in §64, the realm of myth has increasingly preoccupied Lévi-Strauss as a meeting ground where human intellect confronts the paradoxes and contradictions of existence.

In exploring the structures of myth in his monumental four-volume *Mythologiques* (1969–1973), Lévi-Straus has moved between and above cultures and even continents. And he has been pushed to and beyond the limitations of the phonological model of cultural structure. He searches, in the subtle designs of music, for ways of capturing the more holistically patterned structures of cultures; but they mainly elude his grasp. And at the end of the last volume, *l'Homme Nu* (1971), he points to a mode of thinking and perceiving which is complementary to the logical structures of language—a mode characterized by pattern, integration, and harmony that cannot be dissected by the analytical instruments at hand. The structures of language and the designs of art and music seem poles apart.

Lévi-Strauss' challenge to the premise that each culture is unique expresses the urgency of an anthropological search for underlying universals of mind, experience, and culture. There is unquestionably a wide range in the ways people conceive the universe to be ordered, in people's views of themselves, of time, of change. Yet these increasingly seem to be variations within a common design, a design imposed by the structure of the human brain and perceptual equipment and the common elements of our biological endowment and social life. But the difficulties Lévi-Strauss has encountered in probing the deeper structures of mind can well warn researchers that we have only begun to understand the vast systemic complexities and subtleties of mind and brain.

Whether these deeper levels are accessible to our probing, and describable in language if we could uncover them, has recently been questioned from another direction. This is a bold theoretical exploration of art, culture, and the human mind by Gregory Bateson (1972b). The areas of life where humans spin out rational plans, formulate rules, and organize and classify may represent only the uppermost layers of mental process. Like an iceberg, the human mind reveals only its surface conformations to consciousness and outward inspection. In the deep realms of unconscious thought, the mind deals not with things but with relationships and patterns ("primary process"). Bateson argues that our consciousness inevitably deals with bits and pieces, with segments carved out of wholes: the very process of conscious thought distorts and disrupts. So, too, does the attempt to describe these deep patterns in the channels of language.

In art, humans attempt to reconstitute whole patterns, to recapture lost integration. The painter or musician or sculptor is saying something in that medium about total patterns, about the way elements fit together into wholes, about the relationship between levels. The esthetic gestalt or perceptual vision of total pattern reconstitutes in the mind the fragmented pieces of experience. So, perhaps, does ritual. Recall the *mudyi* tree used in Ndembu ritual, the milk-exuding wood that symbolizes breast milk, motherhood, and matrilineal descent. These multiple levels of meaning, the restatement of the same pattern of relationship in terms of different "things," may similarly recapture a perceptual integration, a vision of how things fit together, that humans lose in their everyday life.

There is a congruence between the contrast Bateson draws between the "secondary process" of logic and language and the "primary process" of art and music and the contrast Lévi-Strauss draws in his latest work. That the gulf may be deep and biologically based is suggested by recent research on hemispheral lateralization (left and right brain hemispheres) in *Homo sapiens*. Research by Sperry, Bogen, and others on split-brain patients has underlined a contrast between logical, lineal modes of thinking normally centered in the left (and dominant) cerebral hemisphere, where language faculties are concentrated; and integrative, intuitive, total-pattern modes centered in the right hemisphere (see Ornstein 1973). These findings are still controversial and difficult to interpret. But they suggest that there are neural correlates to the frustrations of anthropologists trying to write "cultural grammars" (Keesing 1972a), to discover the geometry of cultural integration, or to interpret myths structurally.

Anthropologists have never gotten very far in systematically mapping any culture as an ideational system. Bateson's warnings, and emerging evidence on the vast complexity and multiple levels of mind and brain, hardly give cause for optimism.

Through burgeoning research in formal theories of intelligence (including the mathematical design of robots and the decipherment of genetically coded information), scientific explorers may reach major breakthroughs in understanding and describing complex natural systems. Neurophysiology may, through probings of the brain, increasingly open windows on the structures and processes of the mind. But all is not optimistic. Along many frontiers of science researchers are facing awesome and intractable complexity. We can do well to remember, soberly, that the observing instrument, the human brain, is a product of evolution; and it is by no means unlimited in power. Put baldly, the left hemisphere may be unable to analyze what the right hemisphere is seeing and doing.

ANTHROPOLOGY AND THE PRESENT

Part

Studying the diverse ways of life in small-scale societies has given anthropology special and crucial understanding of human diversity and human possibility. But the very social and economic systems of the West that took adventurers and, later, scholars to the frontiers of "civilization" were subjugating and destroying the peoples along these frontiers. In the 100 years in which anthropology has been a serious academic enterprise, the ascendance and dominance of the West has been complete: hundreds of societies have been obliterated or swallowed up. Only in the last 30 years have the tentacles of colonialism been thrown off by independence movements—in many cases, only to take a new hold again in more subtle fashion.

Anthropology, if it is to be useful and if it is to survive, cannot simply be a study of ways of life now vanishing or vanished. Anthropologists must study what is happening now, what is happening in African towns as well as rural villages, what is happening in Chicago as well as on Polynesian islands.

But many now argue that anthropology must do more. They see the historical role of anthropologists on the frontiers of colonialism as yet another manifestation of European expansionism—in short, of imperialism. They see the Westernization of the Third World not simply as "culture change" or "acculturation," but as subjugation of hundreds of peoples into a worldwide capitalist system of exploitation—as sources of cheap labor, raw materials, and markets. The transformation of tribal societies caught up in this system has not simply been a matter of peoples acquiring new hardware and new ideas and beginning to participate in a world economy. Western domination, old and new, has hammered Third World peoples into a common mold as sources of cheap labor and has drained their lands of raw materials. Pride and identity have been broken. Anthropologists who take this critical stance toward their own history, their own society, and their own discipline now argue forcefully that anthropology must be, as much as anything else, a study of imperialism and its impact. And they argue that if anthropology is to free itself from colonialism, it must become genuinely a study by and for Third World peoples, not simply a study *of* them.

Part 4 will examine the relevance of anthropology to the crises of the latter twentieth century. We will pay special attention to the radical reappraisal of anthropology, of colonialism old and new, and of the emergence of power in the Third World out of the ruins of colonialism.

RESPONSE TO CATACLYSM 21
The Tribal World and
the Expansion of the West

Here we will glimpse the cataclysmic impact of European expansion on tribal societies. First, we will briefly introduce a perspective on colonialism—and of anthropology in colonialism—that will provide a background for the sections and chapters to follow. Then we will consider the processes of change along the frontiers of colonialism, building on but extending the theories of social change sketched in Chapter 12. Finally, in a series of subsections, we will examine different facets of the impact of the West on non-Western societies.

70.
Colonialism and the Anthropological Perspective

To understand colonialism and its historical impact requires a drastic rethinking of many assumptions and myths. It is a rethinking many young people in Western industrialized societies have already gone through in the last decade, catalyzed by the anguish of Vietnam and the rising power of Third World peoples. For others, cherished myths of the West are still accepted; and familiar assumptions remain unchallenged. The pages that follow may be provocative to many, but they will challenge the reader to further thought.

Americans brought up on the myths that are a national heritage—kindly old mission fathers, George Washington chopping down cherry trees, Abe Lincoln freeing slaves, and Teddy Roosevelt charging up San Juan Hill—are not likely to have a critical perspective on their own history and the history of Western civilization to which they are joint heirs unless they have worked hard to reeducate themselves. (Britons brought up on tales of empire, on myths about Nelson, Kitchener, Livingstone, Gordon, the Black Hole of Calcutta, and the rest, are likely to have a similar difficulty.)

A global understanding of Western expansion and its impact requires a reanalysis of the most sacrosanct institutions of the West. A notable example is Christianity. What began as a religion of the oppressed had, by the Crusades and particularly the age of Spanish and Portuguese "discovery," become the religion of the conqueror. Historically, Christianity has been both an imperialist, expansionist force in its own right and a servant of empire in subjugating conquered peoples and organizing them into communities where their labor could be exploited. Thus missionary priests rode beside the *conquistadores* in the Americas and the Phillippines, baptizing souls and sending gold to the coffers of Spain and the Vatican—just as three centuries later, missionaries in Darkest Africa brought light to the savages, supported by corporate wealth, and clothed them in raiment from the mills of industrial England. [1]

A reinterpretation of European history and the systemics of colonialism would take dozens of volumes—volumes that are beginning to be written by Western historians who have broken loose from the smug assumptions of empire and their own moral supremacy, and by growing ranks of Third World historians. It would be presumptuous even to try to sketch the vast intricacies and global systemics of imperialism as it unfolded over 500 years of European expansion.

But what is urgent is that the reader acquire some sense of the way economic strategies dictated ideologies; of the way events in one cluster of far-away islands were tied in with the world economy and events in other corners of the world; of the way peoples were moved around like pawns as sources of slave labor or a cheap equivalent; and of the way fellow humans—whatever their skin color—were accorded or denied humanity depending on the demands of profit.

The latter point will serve as a beginning. Pervasive racism whereby dark-skinned peoples have been despised and treated like animals is a continuing theme of the colonial period. But to see racism primarily in terms of European prejudice against people of different skin colors is far too shallow. A deeper analysis reveals that most often people have been treated as subhuman when it was economically profitable to deny their humanity. Eric Williams, an Oxford-trained black historian who later became Prime Minister of Trinidad Tobago, has argued compellingly that the slave trade whereby Africans were shipped to the Caribbean and the Americas was strongly supported and rationalized by the power of British society as long as the Caribbean sugar plantations were sources of great profit (Williams 1944).

From the royal family down through the highest levels of British society and throughout the merchant class, slavery was rationalized and supported. Humanitarian protests were drowned out by the voices of those pursuing burgeoning profits. The high rungs of British Christianity not only defended the slave trade, but participated actively in it (as did Christians in the British colonies of eastern North America, including many Quakers). Slavery was not hidden from genteel British society: it was displayed on every side as the foundation of prosperity. But when the tide of profit and economic power swung away from the Caribbean sugar plantations to the mills of industrial England, humanitarian voices somehow began to be heard: abolitionism, the ideology of free trade, and shifts in the balance of economic power were closely intertwined. And in 1807 England banned the slave trade to the Caribbean (Williams 1944). But as Williams notes, before African slaves were economically advantageous in the Caribbean, poor whites had been sent from

---

[1]Some of the early missionaries were great scholars and humanists, as we will see; but that did not substantially affect impact of Christianity as an historic force in conquest and subjugation.

England in virtual bondage and their labor exploited under conditions almost as bad as those endured by the black slaves later. Their humanity as fellow white men was recognized only when black slaves became more useful with the advent of sugar plantations. In the Americas, an expanding cotton industry made slavery economically advantageous for another half-century. Calls for abolition began to be heard clearly in New England only when the balance of economic power shifted from the agricultural South, which needed slaves, to the industrial North, which needed cheap factory labor.

That the roots of racism are primarily economic is underlined by what happened when the Caribbean sugar industry collapsed. Instead of shipping slaves from Africa, England shipped Indian laborers, under conditions of virtual slavery, to the sugar fields of Fiji and other parts of the tropical world (Tinker 1974); Melanesians were shipped to the sugar fields of Queensland in the infamous "blackbirding" labor trade (Corris 1973).

That racism has been a pervasive and devastating element in colonialism is undeniable. But whether the boundaries of humanity were drawn so as to include or exclude Irishmen or Italians, and whether the inhumanity was focused on black Africans or Chinese, was more often based on where profit or economic threat lay than on notions of racial superiority. The latter have been rationalizations for profitable inhumanity. This begins to show—through inevitably, in overly broad generalizations—the economic roots of the ideologies of colonialism, in its various phases. Another illustration may be useful. When Spanish power in the New World went through its final disintegration in the Spanish-American War, the United States faced the question of whether to acquire Cuba as a colony or make that island nominally independent as a sugar-producing satellite. The same question arose with the Philippines, where a Filipino independence movement had achieved virtual control by the time Admiral Dewey destroyed the ancient and scarcely operative Spanish fleet based in Manila. Pomeroy (1970, 1973) vividly shows how the interests that supported U.S. colonization of the Philippines (mostly northern industrialists anxious for a strong base from which to compete for the vast markets of China and stand against rising Japanese naval power) and the interests opposed to colonial incorporation (mostly southern agriculturalists afraid of cheap competition from a tropical colony) fought a bitter battle through their political spokesmen in Congress. The issue was fought out with noble rhetoric about the rights of brown peoples to freedom versus the responsibilities of the white race to civilize the childlike Filipinos: but the issues and motives were basically economic. Later, when the balance of economic power shifted, the Philippines became a nominally independent economic satellite, with an alliance between a small Filipino land-owning elite and American big business (a neocolonial arrangement which set the pattern that was to follow in South Vietnam, South Korea, and Taiwan; see Pomeroy 1970, 1973). Here, once more, the economic roots of ideologies—in this case, about paternalistic responsibility or independence, colonialism or neocolonialism—are laid bare.

Another urgently needed perspective on colonialism is to see the vast and subtle skein of interconnections which have tied together events and policies in different parts of the colonial world. We will see some elements of this network in the sections to follow.

The flow of raw materials to the burgeoning factories of England, Germany, and New England, the cheap labor of the natives in faraway plantations (and the worldwide relocation of African slaves and of Indians, Chinese, Filipinos, and others to supply cheap labor where needed), the creation of markets in

South Asia, Africa, South America, and elsewhere for the cloth and hardware of industry, all tied tribal societies and non-Western states into a worldwide system of exploitation and oppression—in the name of progress and Christianity, and in pursuit of wealth and power.

Again, where moral duty and humanitarian sentiment usefully served to rationalize profitable exploitation, they burst forth with great passion and zeal. Where it was more profitable to leave moral considerations aside, this was managed. Thus when the British conquest of India gave control of the poppy-growing areas of Bengal, the East India Company was given a government monopoly to export opium to China. The British did all they could to spread opium addiction in southern China, where little opium had previously been used; and this trade was joined by American ships taking opium to China from the poppy fields of Turkey. (Ironically, a number of old New England families made their fortunes in this opium trade, creating in Turkey the poppy industry the U.S. government has recently been trying to stamp out.)

Similar webs of interconnection tied together colonial policy in the Moluccas and Peru, in Tahiti and Barbados, in Tanganyika and German New Guinea, in New Caledonia and Indochina—each part of a worldwide network of imperialism extending outward from London, Lisbon, Cadiz, Hamburg, Amsterdam, Paris, Boston, and other centers of commerce. And they continue to do so, even as Third World peoples exercise nominal independence: huge investment by giant U.S. corporations, or by their Japanese, British, or increasingly multinational equivalents, shapes economic events and political decisions in several dozen "independent" countries.

This brief introductory sketch of colonialism will have to serve for the moment: to go further would require chapters and books. These are beginning to be written, and the searching reader can go on to find them. The challenge to rethink and relearn a less mythical history of the West is urgent.

Anthropologists have mainly worked around the distant fringes of this vast worldwide system. They have had a special kind of perspective on colonialism and its consequences—a perspective that has given them some advantages, but has exacted serious costs as well. It will be well to glimpse this perspective and its limitations before we go on.

Along the fringes of colonialism, and later in colonial territories, representatives of the West mainly saw strange peoples through some lens of purpose: the missionary, to convert them; the administrator, to pacify and govern them; the trader, to exploit them; the planter, to lure them into hard labor with the temptations of hardware.

When in the twentieth century professional anthropologists began to do fieldwork in the colonies, they saw tribesmen from a distinctive point of view. First, in the close encounter of fieldwork they saw the humanity, dignity, and value of the ways of life they observed. They found the stereotypes of treacherous, lazy native and of noble savage to be equally far from the mark. Bonds of common humanity compellingly united fieldworker with subjects. But the anthropologist's field of view, being local, was also myopic. One could not clearly see—for the view of the forest was obscured by the particularities of local trees—how the stability of one's tribe, a society seemingly in equilibrium, had been largely created by colonialism. One could not clearly see, from the vantage point of a single village in a single tribe, how the populations of a region were bound together in networks of "international relations"—of trade, exchange, the flow of ideas—and how they often filled complementary niches in a wider ecosystem. And one could not see how the small local manifestations of colonialism—the trader, the plantation owner, the administrator, the missionary—were part of a vast worldwide design of imperialism. In a society without written records, the anthropologist could easily fail to see how "the system" reflected a century or two of Western influence, often indirect and subtle and often having begun long before direct contact with Europeans.

This narrowness of view, in space and in time, has exacted an enormous cost in anthropological understanding. It is the special (though not exclusively) anthropological myopia to see the microscopic and miss the macroscopic, to explain general phenomena in local terms, to see fragments and build them into wholes, to explain the present—a precipitate of history—in terms of itself.

The special strategy of anthropological research has been to try to understand a community—its social structure, its culture and world view, its economy—more or less in its own terms: to see a people as a microcosm of humanity. Yet when the common shaping force in communities around the world has been capitalism in its successive manifestations, and when events on one continent have been reflexes of events or another, this narrow view has often been inadequate.

We will return to this theme at several points. First, before we look at the cataclysmic impact of European civilization on small-scale societies, it is worth extending and refining our understanding of the processes of cultural change so as to enable us to grasp more clearly how different peoples have responded to their subordination by Western power.

71.
Colonialism, Westernization, and Processes of Change

Before glimpsing the impact of the West on small-scale societies, it is well to underline a point that might otherwise be forgotten. Exploitation, conquest, genocide, and ethnocide—the planned destruction of ways of

life—are very old. Europeans did not invent them.

Early military empires spread death and devastation and enslaved neighboring peoples in the ancient Middle East, Mesoamerica, South America, and Asia. Conquering peoples speaking Bantu and Hamitic languages swept across sub-Saharan Africa, imposing conquest states and exterminating, enslaving, or absorbing those who stood in their path. Grisly relics of Neanderthals and *Homo erectus* suggest that eating or bashing one's neighbor, or at least evicting him, is an early human—probably hominid—foreign policy. The experience of being enslaved, exploited, subjugated, and forced to change customs to satisfy the designs or customs of the conquerors goes back at least some 5000 years to the early empires of Mesopotamia. They were, as we saw in §21 and §22, a concomitant of the rise of urbanization and social classes that came with the widening gulf between producers and those who controlled surpluses.

Presumably, though we seldom have adequate records, the reactions, adaptations, and transformations of peoples subjugated by early empires parallel those recorded along the frontiers of colonialism. (We do get glimpses of early responses, as in biblical records of Israelite adaptations to subjugation.)

While the human costs of subjugation and exploitation have always been staggering, European imperialism, imposing these costs on a vast scale and in new ways, represents a new phase in human history.

One new element in Western history has been the awesome acceleration of technology since the Industrial Revolution, bringing vast power and affluence to the industrial nations. These nations have had not only an increasingly overwhelming advantage in power, but also an increasing appetite for raw materials and markets and increasingly direct access to remote parts of the world. In the latter twentieth century, technology has pushed humans toward a common world culture of airplanes, television, and computers. While polarizing the world into "developed" and "underdeveloped," it has made Western-style "development" an almost universal aspiration.

The destruction or forced transformation of tribal peoples reached a new scale with the worldwide imperialism of the Industrial Revolution. But ironically both oppression of minority enclaves and the emptiness and alienation of industrial societies have reemerged in the socialist states forged in revolution against capitalist class systems. Thus in the Stalinist wake of the Russian revolution, many thousands of Kazakhs and other minority peoples were exterminated; a socialist police state founded on terror replaced a Czarist one; and Soviet society reconstituted

in new form the alienation and bureaucratic emptiness of industrial capitalist society. Chinese incorporation of Tibet liberated a huge population of serfs and slaves from a feudal theocratic system, but at an enormous cost. Socialist imperialism has at its worst been as destructive of lives, freedoms, and cultural integrity as capitalist imperialism ever was. And in Third World countries that have emerged from colonialism, the record of genocide and oppression against tribal and other minorities is appalling. Capitalist countries built the Industiral Revolution on the blood and sweat of Third World peoples; but in this century Western technology has become a worldwide instrument of power whose use to oppress the weak has known no geographical or ideological bounds.

Joining the community of nations: Representatives of the U.N. Trustee-Council talk with New Guinea Highlanders about the path toward independence, then a decade away. (Courtesy of Australian News and Information Bureau.)

Finally, as we saw in the last section, worldwide networks in the flow of labor, raw materials, and manufactured goods generated and sustained colonialism. These interconnections have had different consequences for subjugated peoples from older systems of empire where tribute, plunder, and slaves flowed back to Ur or Tenochtitlan or Rome. Moreover, worldwide imperialism has produced parallel phenomena in different parts of the world and thus has been global rather than regional in impact.

The pace of change quickens: New Guinea Highlanders listen to campaign rhetoric in the 1964 House of Assembly election. (Courtesy of Australian News and Information Bureau.)

Benabena tribesmen from Highland New Guinea examine the latest transformation in their once-isolated valley. In a decade of rapid change, the Benabena have been swept up in an economy of cattle, trucks, and transistor radios (Courtesy of Department of Information and Extension Services, Papua, New Guinea.)

In the next section, we will examine the confrontation between European power and tribal peoples. First, we will relate these phenomena of domination and Westernization to the theoretical foundations built up in Chapter 8 and the model of sociocultural change sketched in Chapter 12.

We will see that many small-scale societies simply vanished under the juggernaut of European expansion, their populations decimated by disease and slaughter, their lands appropriated, their communities gone and customs destroyed. Where peoples were more isolated, or sufficiently numerous to withstand the impact of colonial domination, they became tied into the periphery of a global economy and had to accommodate to a new world in which they were inferior and subordinate.

With peoples that have had to adjust to the power of colonial domination, the kind of model of ecological adaptation and cultural development we sketched in Chapter 12 becomes inadequate. For a culture provides guides for living in a world that no longer exists; and people must cope psychologically with a radically changed universe. Consider a New Guinea tribesman who in a decade has gone from his tribe's traditional model of the cosmos—a world with his people at its center, populated by ghosts and spirits and controlled by magic—through a series of radical shifts. A fundamentalist missionary may have persuaded him that in the Book of Genesis and what follows lies the source of the white man's power. Within five more years he is voting for a representative in the Assembly, is co-owner of a truck, and has heard about men landing on a moon that ten years earlier he had regarded as a totemic spirit. Moreover, the tribesman has had to reconcile himself not only to the power and wealth of whites in the colonial world but to a racism that relegates him to the scorned status of a "native." How humans can cope with such chaotic cognitive and emotional stresses without blowing their minds remains a mystery. (Sometimes they do not; we will see in §72 the millenial movements, anticipating an earthly paradise, that represent a kind of organized and collective mind-blowing under such stress.)

In a classic case study, Clifford Geertz suggested that one crucial step toward understanding such drastic change is to distinguish carefully (as we learned to do in §24) between *cultural* structure and *social* structure. Cultural structure is an organized system of knowledge, more or less shared by individuals, that enables them to communicate, share meanings, and do things together toward common ends. Social structure is the network of social relations among the actors on the social stage, in contrast to the scripts they follow and understandings they share. In his case study of a Javanese funeral, Geertz (1957) shows what can go wrong when cultural guides to appropriate action no longer fit changed social circumstances due to the impact of Westernization and the new tides of national politics.

Case 78: A Javanese Funeral

The Javanese town of Modjokuto in many respects still represents the peasant cultural traditions of rural Java, including a religious system that combines elements of Islam, Hinduism, and the older animistic beliefs. Essential here are communal feasts, *slametan,* where at important stages in the life cycle members of neighborhood groups gather to make offerings to

A Javanese funeral *slametan:* Three Islamic priests perform the mortuary rites (Solo, Central Java). (Courtesy of Masri Singarimbun.)

the spirits and to partake together of the ritual meal. Moslem prayers are part of the proceedings; and Moslem ritual has a particularly central place in the subdued procedure of a funeral, where the living bid leave of the social bonds broken by death.

But in recent decades, political parties, religious fission, and other discordant elements of modern Indonesian life have torn the harmony of Modjokuto social life. Particularly important has been a split between Masjumi and Permai factions. The Masjumi comprise a national party, militantly Moslem, which presses for a purified form of Islam as the state religion. The Permai party, strong in Modjokuto, would emphasize the "traditional" Hindu and animistic rites and, being vocally anti-Moslem, would eliminate Islamic prayer and ritual in such affairs as marriage and funerals.

This split precipitated a crisis in Modjokuto when a 10-year-old boy, nephew of a Permai man, died. The *Modin*, or religious officiant, remained absent. The ritual washing of the corpse, the quiet and orderly procedure culminating in a *slametan* reaffirming the unity of the commu- nity in the face of death, were still not performed. Finally a Masjumi man friendly with the Permai involved tried to conduct the essential rites. In the midst of all this, the grief the normal funeral rites keep under control burst forth.

Finally the dead boy's parents arrived from the city. Being less committed religiously, the father authorized the *Modin* to carry on in the Moslem fashion—though not before the mother had expressed a grief that would normally have remained beneath the surface. By the time the funeral *slametan* had been performed the unity it was intended to affirm had been badly and publicly torn (Geertz 1957).

Distinguishing between a cultural system and changed social realities to which the old system is no longer appropriate, as Geertz would have us do, is a step in the right direction. But it is only a partial step, and it poses dangers.

For Javanese culture exists, if it can be said to exist, not out in some ethereal realm between or beyond the minds of individual Javanese, but as a composite of what individual Javanese know and believe.

Recall our hypothetical tribe of 500 New Guineans at the beginning of the last chapter and the anthropologist's 501st composite version of their culture. Even in a traditional society such as the Trobriands before European intrusion, there would have been considerable diversity in cultural knowledge and belief.

Not every individual has the same mental mapping of "the rules" of social life. Many of these rules are not verbalized, as we have seen, but are implicit. Individuals must learn them by watching and devising theories: Trobriand culture is not magically implanted in the heads of Trobriand children (the way the children are implanted by subclan ancestors). Each individual learns a partly unique version of his or her culture. Any society thus contains a *reservoir of diversity* in cultural codes. The culture includes sets of alternative and even contradictory principles and rules.

Moreover, the complex hierarchical structure of cultural knowledge and the flexibility with which cultural principles are applied to the ever-changing and unique circumstances of the real world mean that enacting, or changing, cultural routines is not a simple matter. A general ideal principle—such as, in

the Trobriands, that things given should be reciprocated or that matrilineal kinsmen should help one another—applies to a great range of concrete situations. Yet how the principle is applied to a particular type of transaction or relationship in a particular situation may be subject to different interpretations. How soon the return should be, whether it is to be in kind or in some other form of equivalence, whether the obligation remains despite the death of one party, whether kinship obligation overrides direct reciprocity in some case—all these considerations may be redefined or reinterpreted without any major change of the general principles of reciprocity and kinship. And since actual situations are endlessly variable, what may shift are not even the specific details of "rules," but simply which ones apply in what combinations in what instances.

Under the impact of European conquest and domination, tribal peoples' struggles to survive, adapt, and find new meaning have heightened the complexity of the interplay between cultural knowledge and the changing world to which it is applied.

Think back on the effects of money on the Tiv economy (Case 48). The Tiv are being caught up in a vast system of interconnected events and things, including money, that is changing what they do, what they have, and what they can choose. These new circumstances of life are very difficult for the Tiv to fit into their conceptual scheme. When a Tiv man bemoans the fact that he now has to "sell" his daughter in marriage, hence to trade down from the most valued exchange category to the least valued, we cannot simply talk about "culture change." The change in

Tiv culture is of a different order than the changes in Tiv social life and economic circumstances; and that is part of the problem.

Diversity in cultural codes makes change in an ongoing society doubly hard to understand—especially if we cancel out diversity to produce an idealized description of "the culture." In a society undergoing rapid change, diversity increases so much that no composite is even possible. Among the modern Tiv one could find government officials with radios and trucks, conservative elders, young men employed as entrepreneurs, Christian evangelists, and leftist politicians. A single idealized picture of changing Tiv culture clearly will not do—it is changing in all directions for different people.

The drastic and dramatic impact of Westernization on small-scale societies, and the world-wide processes of social and economic transformation that are going on in latter twentieth century, push anthropological understanding to—and beyond—its limit. Will our theories prove adequate? Perhaps. It is a question to which we will return in Chapter 23. We have suggested the weakness of an idealized composite conception of culture in the face of rapid change and diversity. In any case, the reason for distinguishing culture, as an ideational system, from social and ecological systems is not to examine ideational worlds by themselves. Though for some purposes that may be enough, it does not suffice for understanding real people facing real problems and alternatives. The challenge is to see how ideational world, ecosystem, and social process interact in wider systems. Consider the market economy in a Nigerian city. Within the physical setting of a marketplace, transactions interlink Tiv traders with Hausa, Ibo, Yoruba, and members of many other tribal groups, plus Europeans, Arabs, Indians, and others. Each has a highly variable version of different cultural traditions. These cultural patterns shape decision-mak-

ing and value commitments, and they affect the flow of goods into the market system from rural areas (so that large-scale Tiv refusal to sell foodstuffs or grow beniseed might make a slight ripple in the market). But the patterns of decision and the flow of goods and money depend on a wider worldwide market *system* that very few Nigerian participants begin to understand—a system within which Nigeria is peripheral. Events that transform the lives of Nigerians emanate from London or New York boardrooms or stock exchanges or oil producers' private airplanes.

Perhaps it is illusory to imagine that the Tiv ever controlled their own destiny: they have been part of wider systems, social, economic, and ecological, throughout their history. But in the colonial and postcolonial periods, their lives have been progressively pulled further from their own grasp.

As the Tiv example underlines, colonial subjugation—the suppression of warfare or polygyny or bridewealth—may have far-

Urban Africa: A street scene in Lagos, Nigeria. Traditional anthropological concepts of "culture" and "social structure" are clumsy tools for interpreting such complexity, diversity, and change. (Courtesy of United Nations.)

reaching and pervasive ramifications through a culture that may erode its very foundations. Even a seemingly minor transformation in technology due to European influence in an isolated society marginal to direct colonial impact may have far-reaching and unforeseen consequences, as Lauriston Sharp's classic case from Australia illustrates strikingly.

Case 79: Steel Axes for Stone Age Australians

The Yir-Yoront of remote northern Australia, though they had some early and bloody encounters with Europeans, preserved their aboriginal culture largely intact until the 1930s. In 1915 a mission station was established three days away from the heart of their territory, and the first important influences of European civilization began to be felt.

The most important tool for the Yir-Yoront was a polished stone axe. Technologically, it was used for a great many operations crucial in their physical adaptation. But it had an equally central role in the social and symbolic organization. First, stone axes were scarce and owned only by senior men. Women and children had to borrow axes from their immediate male kin to perform their assigned labors. The axe constituted a crucial symbol of masculinity and the male realm, as the only exclusively male item women had to use. All dyadic (two-person) relations among the Yir-Yoront defined one person as senior and the other as junior or subordinate: and the axe helped to express this asymmetry. Second, the axe heads had to be obtained from quarries 400 miles to the south, from which they were traded by networks of trade partners in exchange for stingray barb spears. This trade was conducted at annual ceremonial gatherings, providing what was a high point of Yir-Yoront interest. Third, the axes had an important place in the totemic cosmology of the Yir-Yoront. Every element in the traditional way of life had a defined and mythologically validated place in the scheme of things, an association with a patrilineal clan and its ancestors. The axe was, symbolically, the sacred possession of one clan.

The missionaries had set up their station in part to protect the Aborigines from destructive outside influences. They carefully made available only those things they deemed would materially improve the Yir-Yoront standard of living and open the way for a spiritually enriched life. Most importantly these included short-handled steel axes, which the missionaries gave away in quantities and made widely available. The intent was to improve Yir-Yoront technology in a major way, hence freeing time for more important things.

But the result of the steel axes, and other new items, was far more drastic than the missionaries anticipated. The changes were not mainly in the technological realm, where the steel axe did not have the profound advantages that the suppliers expected. Lauriston Sharp, who studied the

Yir-Yoront, wryly notes that it may have increased their time spent sleeping.

But in other realms, the steel axe had profound and disruptive consequences. Women and young boys acquired axes of their own, as they became plentiful. This led to a "revolutionary confusion" of the rules of sex, age, and subordination. The axe as a symbol of the male realm was destroyed. Trading partnerships and the annual tribal gatherings dwindled in interest and importance as the need for stone axe heads disappeared. Moreover, the steel axes and other European items—with no defined place in the cosmological scheme that viewed the present as a precipitate of the ancestral past—became central points in the breakdown of traditional beliefs and values.

> The steel axe . . . has no distinctive origin myth, nor are mythical ancestors associated with it. Can anyone, sitting in the shade of a *ti* tree one afternoon, create a myth to resolve this confusion? No one has, and the horrid suspicion arises as to the authenticity of the origin myths, which failed to take into account this vast new universe of the white man. The steel axe . . . is not only replacing the stone axe physically, but is hacking at the supports of the entire cultural system. (Sharp 1952)

The processes of social and cultural change along the frontiers of colonialism not only reveal great devastation; they also show the enormous resiliency and adaptive capacity of human beings—a dramatic ability to survive in the face of oppression and devastation, as long as life itself remains.

A decade or two ago, many anthropologists saw Aboriginal Australians as a vanishing people so devastated by European conquest and so overwhelmed by the vast gulf between their ancient ways and those of European civilization that they were quite unable to adapt. The stereotypic Aborigine was living in despair and tragic squalor on the fringe of a mission station, drinking his life away. The squalor, tragedy, and oppression are real enough (Rowley 1970—1971), but the vanishing Aborigines are not vanishing. Their population is markedly on the rise, and so is their political consciousness and power. Urban leaders press their demands on white Australian society; and on tribal reserves, new political power, and revitalization of tradition-

al culture, are gathering force. The remarkable human capacity to endure exploitation and oppression, to adapt, to regroup, to change, and to survive has been dramatically revealed amid the devastation of colonialism. And the capacity of the once-devastated to rise again is a major theme of the modern Third World.

A little understood facet of adaptation to rapid cultural change and Westernization is why some peoples have at least outwardly adjusted quickly and flexibly to new circumstances, new life-styles, and new opportunities, while others have been conservative or unsuccessful in changing their ways.

Some kind of congruence—or lack of it—between the old and the new is partly involved. Thus some peoples have even in precolonial times been receptive to new ideas and new things, while others have hearkened back with solid conservatism to old ways.

Receptiveness to change seems particularly characteristic of some New Guinea cultures. Many years ago Margaret Mead (1938)

Anticolonialism in the Trobriands: Leaders of the Kabisawali movement have melded their knowledge of revolutionary struggle in the Third World with traditional cultural strengths and symbols. (Courtesy of J. W. Leach.)

described the Mountain Arapesh as an "importing culture" that had been borrowing customs from the neighbors long before Europeans arrived. The Chimbu of the highlands, and a number of other New Guinea highlands people, seem neither to codify models of the past systematically nor place strong value on old ways. Faced with a bewildering set of changes—from stone tools to transistors, Toyotas, and tourists—the Chimbu have been remarkably flexible in their adaptations to a new world of the twentieth century (Brown 1972).

A fusion of the old and new, a capacity not only to adapt to Western cultural elements but to exploit them, has also been characteristic of the Melanesian Tolai of coastal New Britain (Case 46). The Tolai have become highly successful entrepreneurs in

the colonial economy and have acquired great political power through a political movement, the Mataungan Association, that combines traditional cultural symbols and principles with Western-style wealth, power, and political organization; and they have become a major force in the emergence of a new nation in Papua New Guinea. The traditional culture, more than in the Chimbu case, is a focal point of identity. A similarly striking blend of cultural conservatism and radical political and economic reorganization is underway in the modern Trobriands. Though there is an airfield near Omarakana Village in the yam-growing heart of Kiriwina Island, *kula* exchange continues unabated and mortuary distributions and yam exchanges flourish. Yet the leader of what amounts to a Trobriand cultural renaissance is a young political activist leader, John Kasaipwalova, ex-student of the University of Papua New Guinea, who has organized the Kabisawali Association. This cooperative society, strongly communalist in orientation and highly sophisticated economically, is running an art shop in Port Moresby, operating charter tourist flights, and organizing a strong political movement.

Other striking examples of successful adaptation to introduced economy and culture are found in Southeast Asia (for example, the Minangkabau of Sumatra, highly successful as entrepreneurs and effective participants in an international economy) and in Africa.

In contrast, conservatism can be a strategy for survival as well as a cultural orientation. One element here is apparently old: some ways of life conceptualize time and the past in ways that make change difficult, and have a kind of tight systemic integration that reduces flexibility, pragmatism, and innovation. A second element derives from the impact of the West. As we have seen, when a people are pressed by the forces of change, a hearkening back to the past may be a crucial—sometimes a desperate—way of trying to survive as a people: of preserving identity and integrity in the face of powerlessness, decimation, and degradation.

Congruence between the old and the new, and adaptation to radically changed conditions of life, can also be approached in psychological terms, using (with appropriate

Trobriand political transformation: John Kasaipwalova, leader of the Kabisawali movement, addresses his followers after a 1973 confrontation with Papua New Guinea riot police. (Courtesy of J. W. Leach.)

cross-cultural cautions) instruments of psychological research. Two recent studies by G. D. and L. S. Spindler will serve to illustrate.

Case 80: The Menomini and Blood Indians

The Spindlers used Rorschach tests and their own culture-specific testing methods to probe the personality of Menomini Indians in Wisconsin. They divided the Menomini into five categories, ranging from the very conservative native-oriented to those who had fully adopted white middle-class culture. They found that Menomini in each category had a distinctive personality pattern. The native-oriented groups show a psychological pattern congruent with the restraint and control and dependence on supernatural power appropriate to the old Menomini ways of life: inward orientation, fatalism, lack of overt emotional responsiveness. Those Indians who have adopted white ways have achieved a reorganization of personality congruent with the success orientation, competitiveness, and punctuality their jobs demand of them—though not without costs of anxiety. The transitional group in the middle of the continuum of change show cognitive disorganization and its social expression (G. D. Spindler 1955; L. S. Spindler 1962).

> Some are striving for an orderly way of life, toward goals recognizable in the surrounding non-Indian community; others are withdrawn and mostly just vegetate; others go on destructive rampages. . . . (G. D. Spindler 1968:329)

The Blood Indians of Canada show marked and significant contrasts. Like the Menomini, they represent a continuum in their adoption of the dominant culture and in their standard of living. Yet the bulk have adopted many white ways without abandoning their identity as Indians. Most still speak their own language and retain many Indian customs and beliefs. Beneath the spectrum of differences between modern Blood in socioeconomic status, the Spindlers found a continuum in underlying culture. Much less psychological reorganization seems to have occurred than among the Menomini in adaptation to changed ways of life. Apparently traditional Blood culture and the cognitive and emotional organization it fostered were congruent with the alien culture and new alternatives in a way Menomini patterns were not. The aggressive, competitive, acquisitive way of life of the Blood as hunters of the plains apparently fit sufficiently neatly the modes of life and livelihood whites introduced to the Alberta plains—especially cattle ranching—that the Blood could adopt new ways without fully abandoning old ones, and without a radical shift of psychological integration.

In their more recent work (Spindler and Spindler 1971; G. D. Spindler 1973) the Spindlers view these differential responses to change more in cognitive terms than in the terms of depth psychology and cultural congruence. In situations of colonial subjugation, people use the best survival strategies they perceive (in terms of the opportunities their subordinate status affords and the cultural materials available for conceptualizing and dealing with them). "Instrumental linkages"—ways of getting to valued goals by cognitively (and economically and physically) available paths—are explored and used to adapt as best possible. That for some peoples this means retaining the traditional language and seeking wages and excitement as cowboys, that for others it means withdrawing into traditional isolation or individual alcoholic escape, and for others that it means adopting the life-style of Wisconsin suburbia is not a matter of culture, of personality, of "acculturation," of conservatism, or even of adaptation. It is a matter of survival by the means at hand.

The patterns of change and adaptation we will glimpse in the pages to follow present a double challenge to interpretation and understanding. On the one hand, by subjecting a wide range of distinctive human ways of life to extreme pressure, subjugation, and drastic change, European imperialism provides crucial evidence on how humans adapt, change, learn, and survive. Theories of traditional societies that cannot cope with such transformation are only academic exercises. On the other hand, the Western imperialism that has swept around the world and has connected subjugated peoples into a worldwide network constitutes a vast historical phenomenon whose roots and consequences demand special understanding. And the struggles of Third World peoples to forge from these common experiences a new vision and new freedom have thrown a new light on past anthropology (Hymes 1973; Asad 1973), and have given anthropologists a challenge to rethinking and new involvement. This challenge will centrally concern us in Chapter 25.

72.

The Impact of the West on Small-Scale Societies

The impact of the West on small-scale societies produced pheonomena of physical and cultural destruction that had parallels in earlier empires, as we have noted; but they were in many respects new in human history.

What happened to tribal peoples in the path of European expansion depended on a number of factors:

1. The size, political organization, and technology of the society subjugated.
2. The time period of initial subjugation (and, consequently, the goals Europeans were pursuing and the technology they commanded).
3. The location of the society, in terms of remoteness or ease of access and of the desirability to Europeans of the territory they occupied.
4. The cultural orientation of the subjugated peoples relative to European culture and what Europeans wanted from and demanded of them.

5. The colonial policy of the colonizers (which has varied in different times and places from ruthless extermination to benevolent paternalism).

We will sketch here a number of the processes that have taken place along the frontiers of colonialism. These are by no means a series of "types" of contact; many peoples subjugated by colonialism were subjected to several of these processes at once or in different stages. They serve to illustrate not types but recurrent themes and processes in different parts of the colonized world.

Physical Decimation by Extermination, Disease, and Enslavement

In many parts of the colonized world, populations of tribal people were decimated early in the contact period. There are many cases where massacres—of Australian Aborigines, North and South American Indians, and many others—destroyed substantial proportions of aboriginal populations. Systematic extermination ("A good Indian is a dead Indian" or its equivalent on other colonial frontiers) was often a keystone of European policy or the practice of early colonial settlers.

Though adequate statistics are seldom available, European disease was a more devastating blade cutting through tribal populations, often in advance of colonial settlement. Most vicious of the killing diseases was smallpox, accidentally or intentionally spread by Europeans to populations with no immunity. The populations of aboriginal Australia were decimated by smallpox and other diseases in the early contact period. When European settlement of Australia began in 1788, some 250,000 to 300,000 Aborigines inhabited the continent. By 1798, smallpox epidemics were raging across Australia, reaching far into the interior long before direct contact was made. Tuberculosis, whooping cough, measles, leprosy, influenza, and venereal disease were also spread. Though large numbers of Aborigines were slaughtered by the colonists, most were killed not by guns but by epidemics.

For some North American Indian groups, we have better statistics. Those from the once-rich and powerful Mandan of the upper Missouri are extreme but illuminating. In 1750, at the beginning of the fur trade, some 9000 Mandan lived in large, permanent villages. Smallpox epidemics, beginning as early as 1764, had by 1782 so reduced and weakened the Mandan that they were vulnerable to raids by the nomadic Teton Sioux on one side and the Assiniboin on the other. By about 1800, the population had been reduced to about 1500. In 1837, when another devastating smallpox epidemic swept through the two villages into which the surviving Mandan had regrouped, the population was almost completely wiped out. The num-

The prosperous and powerful Mandan Indians: Here the Bull Dance of the *okipa* ceremony is performed before the earth lodges of a Mandan village. The inhabitants numbered in the thousands. (From a painting by George Catlin, courtesy of the National Collection of Fine Arts, Smithsonian Institution.)

ber of survivors was, at most, 63 adults, perhaps substantially less (Bowers 1950; Bruner 1961). Devistation by disease may well have been equally drastic in a number of other parts of North America.

When massive extermination by systematic hunting or massacre and the toll of disease were coupled with enslavement for forced labor in mines or fields, the demographic catastrophes of colonialism were even more staggering. Wilbert (1972) assesses the appalling cost in human life of the Spanish conquest of South America. He estimates that only 4 percent of the pre-Columbian Indian population of some 50 million survived the first few decades after the Spanish conquest. Tens of thousands were directly hunted out and massacred. Hundreds of thousands died, broken, enslaved as miners to feed Spanish lust for gold and silver; and millions died of introduced diseases and starvation.

The most tragic and appalling consequence of colonial conquest of tribal societies was thus complete physical destruction or near-extermination. Scattered survivors clustered together as refugees, fleeing beyond colonial frontiers or in despair clinging to bare survival on the periphery of fort, town, or mission. Though cultures and languages may have survived such catastrophic destruction, the patterns of social life they infused with meaning and the lands on which subsistence had depended had been swept away.

Armed Resistance

Where the gulf in numbers and technology between Europeans and tribesmen was vast, large-scale resistance was impossible. Yet in some parts of the world, tribal peoples engaged in long and effective armed struggle against invading colonialists. The Hollywood tradition of whooping redskins trying to massacre wagon trains and African savages threatening intrepid explorers has hardly done justice to these struggles or prepared us to understand them.

The most effective resistance to European conquest did not always come from highly centralized militaristic societies with large armies that could be put into the field. As the fairly rapid collapse of the Aztec and Inca states in the face of Spanish invasion illustrate, highly organized armies were often more vulnerable to dramatic defeat than small, mobile forces. And empires that had held surrounding peoples in subjugation were vulnerable to the uprising of their subjects in support of the invaders.

But even with 300 years of further technological advance at their command, the European forces in the Zulu wars and the Ashanti wars were temporarily held in check by tightly organized, mobile resistance by warrior peoples. Here a charismatic leader often played a major role, as with Tshaka, the great Zulu chief. Even more successful in withstanding imperialist conquest was the brilliant Samory of Guinea (Person 1971). Samory's epic resistance to French invasion is celebrated by the patriots of African independence movements. He achieved among his people a degree of political order that could well be an inspiration:

In all, he . . . fought 13 major engagements with the French and . . . moved his empire a distance of some 600 km. in the process. He displayed . . . [a] combination of military and administrative genius. . . .

In him we can see the sort of leader who might well have achieved modernization of his own state, independent of European control. That he had the ability and the instinct is clear from his military tactics, his organization of trade and his spectacular administration of his constantly moving empire. . . . If Samory had not had to face the French there is every indication that he had the organizing genius and sufficient control of his people to have created a state responsive to the needs of the approaching twentieth century. (Crowder 1968:87—89).

Brave resistance against conquest came not only from militarily formidable forces such as those of Tshaka or Samory, but also from technologically and numerically weak peoples such as the South African Bushmen—who fought desperately and with surprising success for their hunting territories until their eventual near-extermination. Bellicosity has continued to be a viable foreign policy for a few isolated hunter-gatherers: some Andaman Islanders in the Indian Ocean continue to greet outsiders with a shower of arrows and retain their independence, despite a Soviet naval base not far away.

In the Americas, wise and inspirational leadership was a key factor in the long resistance of such people as the Seminole, led by Osceola, and the Nez Percé, led by Chief Joseph. Resistance to invasion in some areas catalyzed a people into united struggle even though there were no overarching political

"Billy Bowlegs": A Seminole leader in the fight against colonial conquest. (From a painting by C. F. Wimar, courtesy of the St. Louis Art Museum.)

institutions to provide a framework of command. One of the most striking cases was the resistance of the Yaqui of northwestern Mexico. The Yaqui population was about 30,000, living in autonomous communities without centralized political leadership. Yet confronted by the threat of subjugation by Spanish armies and the incursion of a slave trader, the Yaqui put a military force of 7000 men in the field. In campaigns between 1608 and 1610, Captain Hurtaide and his army of Spaniards and Indian allies were routed three times by well-organized and fierce Yaqui warriors; in the last and largest battle, Hurtaide's forces were crushed and the Spanish captain narrowly avoided capture (Spicer 1961).

In the Pacific, the most dramatic large-scale resistance came from the Maori. In the Maori wars, Polynesian warriors in their palisaded hill forts held British infantry at bay with remarkable success in the face of superior firepower. The Chamorro of Guam fought long and bitterly against Spanish conquest and were virtually wiped out. Even in Melanesia, with smaller populations and greater political fragmentation, there were cases of effective resistance—notably in New Caledonia, where in the so-called Kanaka Revolt of 1878, Melanesians killed many settlers and recaptured most of their large island before being crushed.

But however bravely tribal peoples resisted, they were eventually conquered and subjugated by the increasingly powerful forces of European technology. By the early twentieth century, only marginal peoples maintained political autonomy; and all of them were in remote jungles, deserts, or snowfields around which colonial or national boundaries had been drawn.

Colonialism and Disruptions of the Social Order

Even in advance of actual colonial subjugation, the penetration of European power and technology profoundly changed political relationships and balances of power and ecology. In a few cases this resulted in a kind of cultural efflorescence. Most dramatic perhaps was the emergence of nomadic horse cultures on the American plains. In an amazingly rapid burst of cultural adaptation, such peoples as the Cheyenne were transformed from sedentary maize-cultivating villagers into buffalo-hunting nomadic warriors on horseback; and from the other direction, Great Basin Shoshonean hunters and gatherers such as the Comanche underwent a similar transformation. Further to the northeast, at the margins of the plains and woodlands, such people as the Mandan and Assiniboin capitalized on their established position as wealthy traders astride the main trade routes to become purveyors of buffalo hides to European traders

further east and purveyors of guns and other European goods to the Plains nomads (see Jablow 1951; Bruner 1961).

Disruptions of the balance of power were often unintentional consequences of colonialism. Thus an enterprising Tongan chief captured a British warship in 1806, killed all the crew other than those he needed to man its cannons, and then—using them—invaded and conquered the Tongan capital. And in the western Solomon Islands, steel tools and firearms reinforced the power of chiefs whose ancestors had a lust for human heads. What had been a small-scale sporadic raiding of the neighbors became waves of attack by armadas of canoes. Warriors armed with firearms wiped out entire populations on neighboring islands, returning with canoes full of head

A rich Mandan leader's earth lodge. The Mandan amassed great wealth and power as middle persons with the flowering of Plains cultures. (From a painting by Carl Bodmer, courtesy of The American Museum of Natural History.)

trophies. The main bases of escalated head-hunting were firearms, which rendered useless traditional means of escape and defense, and the steel tools that made possible large-scale production of canoes and freed large fighting forces from subsistence labor. Similarly, the bloody wars and vast-scale cannibalism recorded in early nineteenth-century Fiji were drastic escalations of traditional patterns due to introduced firearms and European-fueled conflict. (The presence of Europeans in the armed camps of warring chiefs also contributed. "In the early days many Fijian chiefs had . . . tame white men, regarding them as mannerless but useful; to have one was part of a chief's prestige" (Furnas 1947:215).)

The effects of the slave trade on West African peoples, even in advance of colonial penetration of the interior, were disastrous. By setting tribe against tribe, exploiting the gulfs between social classes, draining populations, destroying communities, and creating wealthy African leaders as middlemen, the slave trade nourished inhumanity and human tragedy on a staggering scale. The apologists of imperialism were correct in noting that slavery had existed in Africa long before Europeans arrived. But traditional African slavery did not force slaves into plantation labor, did not take them to distant and alien lands, and usually did not prevent their establishing and preserving families. And they were technically correct that it was Africans who were selling one another into bondage. But this argument hardly holds up to close examination and reflection. If an economic system can induce people to sell their grandmothers, or in this case their neighbors, is this more an indictment of grandmother-salesmen or of the system that turns humans into units of profit?

When colonial control was sealed, the effects on the colonized communities depended on their position in the scheme of things—on where they were and what the colonizers wanted from them. There was, of course, a tremendous gulf between the life of laborers in silver mines or sugar fields and that of people living in a relatively isolated jungle village in British colonial Africa, administered by indirect rule through a local headman. But given the worldwide design of colonialism, it is not surprising that parallel transformations of social life took place in widely separated regions of the colonial world.

One transformation that seems to have been a recurrent adaptation to exploitation of cheap (or slave) labor on plantations or in other colonial production was a relative exclusion of males from the core of the family. Where male labor was a cheap exploited commodity, and women kept the household together and produced subsistence food as best possible, women came to provide continuity and strength in the domestic group and in women-centered networks, particularly known anthropologically from the Caribbean. Men characteristically became attached to the domestic group of mother and children tenuously or temporarily, as lovers or husbands in brittle and transient relationships. The erosion of male pride and identity in such circumstances emerges in the literature; and, partly as response to it, so do patterns of *machismo* or the equivalent. Male-female relationships have become hostile and fragile; men compete for honor, prestige, and reputation in a world where they are denied power and economic rewards. This theme has been an important focus of debate in peasant and urban studies, notably through Oscar Lewis' theories of the "culture of poverty" and its critics. We will return in more detail to this theme in Chapter 22.

Peter Wilson gives a vivid picture of the scrambling for reputation in his recent book *Crab Antics* (1972), a study of the English-speaking islands of the Caribbean. He also shows another recurrent theme of the colonial situation: social stratification defined in colonialist terms.

Case 81: "Crab Antics" in the British Caribbean

Wilson argues that in the formerly British Caribbean, as a historical product of plantation exploitation and the imposition of alien standards, rigid and vicious systems of social stratification have emerged. Those who have historically acquired land or other sources of wealth, characteristically by serving colonialist interests, constitute an elite—defined in terms of light skin color, Christian virtue, and emulation of British aristocratic ways. "Good" families try subtly to outmaneuver one another in "respectability" as defined in European terms; and this elite, by intermarriage, outside education, and the manipulation of wealth, preserves its hold over the far more numerous poor people who work as laborers, sharecroppers, fishermen, and so on.

Wilson's primary focus is on the small English-speaking island of Providencia, now part of Colombia. He shows vividly the operations of the small "respectable" elite who dominate the economic and social life of the island.

But what of "crab antics"? In Providencia, the term derives from the way crabs in a barrel, in trying to crawl out, pull one another back down the sides: gains are at someone else's expense. Crab antics are the subtle battles for *reputation* among the lower-class Providencian men. Unlike the status games enhancing respectability, the quest for reputation is open to the poor. A good man is one who works hard; but most particularly, he exemplifies a set of male virtues: bravado, hard drinking, sexual conquests. As in the *machismo* of Mexico and other parts of the Spanish-speaking Americas, material poverty and powerlessness are countered by an ostentatious display of bravado, courage, toughness, and predatory sexual aggression; and relations between the sexes are polarized accordingly. This, in the Caribbean, is the opposite face of the domestic group where women provide strength, continuity, and the means of economic survival, and where men's economic contributions are meager and sporadic.

Wilson argues that the two themes of respectability and reputation are pervasive principles of Caribbean social organization. He views the quest for respectability as a product of British colonialism, with its racism and its emphases on class differences, aristocratic manner, Christian virtue, and "breeding." But the quest for reputation, he argues, is an indigenous and egalitarian value system, a creation of the people and an adaptation to adversity. In this, Wilson probably underestimates the degree to which the quest for reputation—a kind of vicious egalitarianism at best—is a product of colonial exploitation and the poverty it has produced. It is a status game among those left bereft of power and material reward, a game that exploits women and oppresses the weak. It is worth recalling F. C. Bailey's observations in *Gifts and Poison* (1971), based on his and his students' studies of social relations in European villages, about the desperate in-fighting for status where the goal is not to get ahead but to stay even (§62). We will return to the debate about the roots of status conflict among the poor and powerless when we look more closely at peasant societies in Chapter 22.

The transformation of traditional societies in the face of colonialism and its aftermath is an urgent theme of modern anthropology. We will return to it in Chapters 22 and 23, where we examine anthropological studies of peasant communities and urban settings and in Chapter 24 when we look at the experience of women in anthropological perspective. And we will face it again squarely in Chapter 25 when we view "development" and "modernization" in relation to anthropology and the Third World.

Syncretism and Cultural Synthesis

Wherever European ways of life have burst upon small-scale societies, cultural borrowing has taken place—by choice and under duress. Peoples have adopted steel tools and handshaking, and have been forced into Mother Hubbard dresses and monogamy.

The synthesis of old and borrowed elements—*syncretism*—has been most striking in the realm of religion, where Christianity has been spread to every continent. Many of the most striking examples come from the New World, particularly from Mesoamerica.

Recall that processes of conquest, incorporation, and cultural borrowing, from Olmecs through Aztecs, had created complex syntheses of cultural elements before the Spanish invaded. Syntheses of Catholicism with traditional belief systems carried these old processes to much more dramatic degree: there was a vast gulf between the religion of the *conquistadores* and the Mesoamerican priestly cults of war, fertility, sun and rain, worship of feathered serpent, jaguar, and other gods, and human sacrifice. But striking syntheses were to emerge, sometimes very quickly.

Early sixteenth-century Catholic missionaries had some advantages that fundamentalist Protestants two or three centuries later lacked. Catholicism embodied a rich pageantry and complex ceremonial cycle. It offered roles to men and women, young and old. Its priests, believing in the devil, spirits, and magic, could deal with the older religion in ways Mesoamerican peoples could squarely comprehend. And Catholicism provided, in its multiple manifestations of the Virgin and the Trinity, both an approximation of multiple deities and physical objects for veneration.

Perhaps the most striking example of religious syncretism is the cult of the Virgin of Guadalupe, the patron saint of Mexico.

Case 82: The Virgin of Guadalupe

In 1531, 10 years after the Spanish conquest of Mexico, the Virgin Mary appeared to Juan Diego, a Christianized Indian, and addressed him in Nahuatl, the Aztec language. She commanded him, in this and subsequent visions, to have a church built in her honor on the site of their encounter, the Hill of Tepeyac.

This was the site where the Aztecs had worshipped their earth and fertility goddess Tonantzin, Our Lady Mother. The veneration of the Virgin of Guadalupe in the early centuries of the cult was in reality a worship of Tonantzin by a subjugated people, as Spanish Churchmen well realized:

> Now that the Church of Our Lady of Guadalupe has been built there . . . they call her Tonantzin. . . . It seems to be a satanic device to mask idolatry . . . and they come from far away to visit that Tonantzin, . . . as of old (Sahagun).

> On the hill where Our Lady of Guadalupe is they adored the idol of a goddess they called Tonantzin, which means Our Mother, and this is also the name they give Our Lady. . . . They always say they are going to Tonantzin or they are celebrating Tonantzin and many of them understand this in the old way and not in the modern ways. (Martin de Léon)

Such syncretism persisted in the seventeenth century: "It is the purpose of the wicked to [worship] the goddess and not the most Holy Virgin, or both together" (Jacinto la Serna).

In the seventeenth century, the Guadalupe cult provided a focus for the emergence of Mexican colonial society, and the first emergence of a national culture that offered a place for the oppressed Indian.

> To Mexicans [the Virgin] . . . not only . . . is a supernatural mother . . . she embodies their major political and religious aspirations. To the Indian groups the [Virgin] . . . is . . . an embodiment of life and hope; it restores to them the hope of salvation. . . . The Spanish Conquest signified not only military defeat, but the defeat also of the old gods and the decline of the old ritual. . . . [The Virgin] . . . represents on one level the return of Tonantzin. . . . On another level, the myth of the apparition served as a . . . testimony that the Indian . . . was capable of being saved. (Wolf 1958:37)

The Indian was not only exploited and oppressed: his very humanity was denied by many of the conquerors and Churchmen, who could absolve themselves of moral responsibility for murder and slavery. Wolf goes on to show that the Virgin also served the needs of an emerging group of Mexicans with Spanish fathers and Indian mothers—who, like "half-castes" in so many colonial situations, were denied a place in both worlds.

What had begun as the worship of an Aztec goddess in transformed guise under the swords of the *conquistadores* and the merciless watch of the Inquisition-minded friars thus was transformed into a symbol of the new Mexico rising from colonialism—so that in the War of Independence against Spain, and later when the agrarian revolutionary Emiliano Zapata and his men fought against the domination of corrupt landowners and Church, the Virgin of Guadalupe led them into battle (Wolf 1958).

In rural Indian communities in Mesoamerica, cultural syntheses of old and new are visible in many realms of life. One is *compadrazgo*, or ritual co-parenthood (Case 91), where a Hispanic Catholic pattern has been melded with kinship-based social systems of Mesoamerica (Davila 1971). In religion, new beliefs and traditional ones are blended or coexist, as in highland Mayan communities such as Zinacantan in southern Mexico.

Case 83: Religion in Zinacantan

The casual visitor to the center of the Chiapas *municipio* of Zinacantan is likely, despite the striking dress of its peasant inhabitants, to infer that Catholicism is a dominant force in the community. A church crowned with crosses dominates the central plaza, with lesser churches scattered through the town center and chapels in each of the outlying hamlets. On the steep, surrounding hills are clusters of large crosses. Within the Church of San Lorenzo, candles, altars, and painted figures of Catholic saints further reinforce the impression of a pious Catholic flock.

Through years of anthropological study, the external trappings of Christianity have seemed a progressively thinner veneer beneath which lies a complex Mayan religious system (Vogt 1969; 1970).

The people of Zinacantan, Zinacantecos, continue to conceive the world as shaped in a large cube. The upper surface of the cube comprises the high mountains and deep valleys of highland Chiapas—with a low earth mound in the ceremonial center of Zinacantan as the "navel" of the world.

The cubical world rests on the shoulders of gods. Beneath it is the "lower world," the shape of an ancient Maya pyramid. Sun and moon, seen as sacred cosmic forces, symbolically male and female, move across the sky above the cube, and humans orient their lives to these movements. The sun is symbolically associated with the Catholic God, the moon with the Virgin Mary; but the Zinacanteco world remains pervasively Mayan.

The universe is inhabited by numerous classes of spiritual beings which play a crucial part in human life. The most important beings are the ancestral gods, who dwell in the mountains around Zinacantan. They are remote ancestors of the Zinacantecos, and were ordered to dwell in the mountains by the gods that support the earth. In their mountain houses, the ancestors survey and confer about the social affairs of their descendants and await offerings of chickens, candles, incense, and liquor. The ancestors not only maintain the rules of proper Zinacanteco social and ritual life and guide the correct behavior of their descendants; they also keep a zealous watch over deviations from the straight lines of propriety, as we will see.

Another deity, the Earth Owner, controls the things and products of the earth on which life depends—the maize crops, rain, the earth, trees, waterholes, and the other sources of subsistence and necessary material props of life. The attitudes toward the Earth Owner, who must be propitiated with offerings when these products of the earth are used, are ambivalent, marked by both danger and dependence.

Since the Spanish conquest, the Zinacantecos have acquired 55 "saints," carved or plaster images of Catholic saints and other sacred objects. Each saint has a personality and a mythic history. The most important, notably San Sebastian, are the centers of elaborate cults and annual ceremonial activities. The Zinacantecos view them as gods with extraordinary powers, with their "homes" in Catholic churches. Like the ancestral gods, they expect offerings of candles, incense, and flowers. The Zinacantecos view a Catholic mass as a prayer to the saint to whom a fiesta is dedicated. A *Ladino* (Spanish-speaking Mexican) priest is asked to perform the mass. But the position of orthodox Catholicism in Zinacantan is suggested by the reaction if the priest cannot come: the saint is expected to be enraged, but to visit punishment upon the derelict priest, not the community—which has done its part by soliciting the priest.

Zinacantecos have two kinds of "souls." Each person has an "inner soul," located in the heart. This inner soul has 13 components—one or more of which can leave the body in sleep, in fright, in sexual excitement, or when the ancestors cause soul loss due to bad behavior. Shamans play a continuing part in Zinacantan by curing illnesses due to the loss of soul components, restoring the balance with the ancestors and thus reincorporating and reintegrating the patient's inner soul. It is not only humans that have inner souls:

Virtually everything that is important and valuable to Zinacantecos also possesses an "inner soul": domesticated animals and plants . . .; salt, which possesses a very strong "inner soul"; houses and the household fires; the wooden crosses

A Zinacanteco curing ceremony combines traditional Mayan ritual with Christian derived symbols. (Courtesy of John Haviland.)

erected on sacred mountains, inside caves and beside waterholes; the saints . . .; musical instruments . . .; and all the various deities in the Zinacanteco pantheon. . . . The most important interaction going on in the universe is not between persons, nor between persons and objects, . . . but . . . between "inner souls" inside these persons and material objects. (Vogt 1970:10–11)

Every Zinacanteco individual has a second kind of "soul," an "animal spirit companion." The spirit companions of the living, one for each person, live in a mountain that towers above central Zinacantan, in separate supernatural corrals: one of jaguars, another of coyotes, another of ocelots, another of small animals such as opossums. A person's animal spirit companion shares his or her same inner soul, so that one's well-being depends on one's animal spirit companion being properly protected and cared for by the ancestral gods. A person's animal companion may be turned out of its corral by the ancestral gods if that person has transgressed cultural rules; and a shaman must intercede to have the ancestors restore the companion to its corral.

Ostensibly Christian rites, including those that involve cross shrines, turn out on closer inspection to be vehicles for the traditional Mayan religious system. The hundreds of *krus* (from Spanish "cross') shrines, called *kalvario* (from "Calvary"), are in actuality places where the ancestral gods meet, deliberate about the conduct of their descendants, and await ritual offerings. As we will see in Case 90, these shrines are hierarchically ordered in terms of an underlying patrilineage system. The Zinacantecos see the cross altars as doorways to the gods. A set of religious symbols—flowers, incense, and rum—serve to define sacred contexts in which communication with the gods can take place.

What outwardly appears to be a Catholic ceremony thus has a meaning to the Zinacantecos that hearkens back to the religion of their ancestors, and established communication with them.

With flowers on the crosses, incense burning . . ., liquor being consumed . . ., and music being played . . ., the stage is set for efficient communication with the supernaturals through prayers and offerings, typically candles, which are regarded as tortillas and meat for the gods, and black chickens whose "inner souls" are eagerly consumed by the gods. . . .

The supernaturals . . . will . . . reciprocate by restoring the "inner soul" of a patient, by sending rain for a thirsty maize crop or by eliminating . . . evils and setting things right for the Zinacantecos. (Vogt 1970:16)

Syncretism is also striking in the black cultures of the Caribbean. Perhaps best known and most intriguing to outsiders have been the "voodoo" cults of Haiti. But similar syntheses of West African spiritualism with European and New World beliefs and rites occur in many areas around the Caribbean. These elaborations of West African elements in the Caribbean have been documented vividly by Melville Herskovits (1937) and subsequent scholars.

In Southeast Asia and India, syncretism is

an ancient phenomenon, long predating European influence. Sri Lanka (Ceylon), with its syntheses of Buddhist, South Indian, and indigenous cultural elements, provides many examples; there Westernization is yet another layer. And Indonesia, with its complex syntheses of Malayo-Polynesian, Hindu, Islamic, and other elements, further illustrates the theme of cultural synthesis (recall the Javanese funeral in Case 78).

The borrowing and synthesis of cultural elements as a response to Western imperialism is strikingly illustrated by the emergence of pidgin languages, and the "cultures of intercultural communication" they express, in different parts of the world. A pidgin is a language developed in a contact situation that is composed of grammatical structures and lexicon drawn from two or more languages. It serves as a lingua franca for people on both sides of a cross-cultural encounter. It also serves as a means for tribal or other non-Western peoples speaking different languages but thrown together by imperialism to communicate and survive.

A Chinese-English pidgin developed in the trade on the China coast. More striking examples come from the Pacific, notably in Melanesia, when the earlier China coast pidgin gave rise to a pidgin called biche-la-mar. Through plantation labor in alien settings, this early Pacific pidgin evolved into New Guinea pidgin, synthesizing Melanesian, English, German, and other elements. In the Solomons and New Hebrides, a somewhat different pidgin evolved during the labor trade through which Melanesians from many language groups were taken to the sugar fields of Queensland and Fiji.

In West Africa, a pidgin derived from

Cultural syncretism: A Trobriand Islands cricket team dances in traditional dress (in 1973) as it enters the playing field for a game; this team is called "the Airplanes," and their dance imitates a plane banking. (Courtesy of J. W. Leach.)

English, Portuguese, and a cluster of West African languages apparently served as a vehicle for the slave trade and as a means of survival for slaves. There are a number of shared elements in Black English (Case 8), in the dialects of the Carolina coast (of which Gullah is the best known), and in the Creole dialects of the Caribbean. Now that linguists have gone beyond earlier racist and ethnocentric dismissals of these as debased forms of speech, these common patterns are emerging.

Creole languages illustrate a further development. Pidgins are always second languages used in intercultural settings (and are characteristically simplified and condensed); but in some places, they have developed into the primary language of a people. When a pidgin is transformed into a first or "native" language, it is classed as a creole language; and in "creolization" the language becomes correspondingly more richly developed.

Swahili, in East Africa, illustrates another theme. Swahili began as a language of exploitation—as a pidgin composed of East African, Arabic, Portuguese, and other elements. It emerged through the development of trading and slavery, especially the trade of slaves to the Islamic empires. In the period of European colonialism, it became the vehicle of white supremacy, settlement, and exploitation. Yet since the independence of the West African states, Swahili has become a symbol of struggle and freedom, especially in Tanzania. What had been a vehicle of exploitation and oppression had at the same time been a means of survival and a way to unity. *Uhuru* became a rallying cry of independence in Kenya; and Swahili has become a keystone of socialism in Tanzania.

Cultural synthesis in the face of colonial subjugation is anthropologically challenging not only in revealing the human capacity to adapt to oppression and adversity but in underlining the complexity of cultural integration. When cultural *content* changes markedly, do underlying structures and deeper premises remain unchanged? Do elements of a culture lie latent though overt behavior may conform to the demands of the conqueror? The survival of traditional religion in Zinacantan suggests that overt compliance to the demands of conquest may sometimes mask extreme conservatism. When control is relaxed, latent knowledge may become covert practice; and eventually old patterns may spring forth. Striking illustrations come from the margins of the Caribbean where escaped slaves, such as the so-called Bush Negros of Guyana and Surinam (Price 1973), have established communities where traditional social and religious patterns flowered anew. In the Pacific, the way cultural patterns can persist despite marked outward changes in a people's mode of life is vividly revealed by events of the last century on Tanna Island in the New Hebrides. The Melanesian inhabitants had been decimated in mid-nineteenth century by the brutal "blackbirding" labor trade to Australia, by European attacks, and by introduced diseases. By the early twentieth century, observers reported that the traditional culture had disappeared and that the remnant population was fully Christianized and rapidly adopting European ways. Yet in 1940, the "John Frum" movement, an anti-European cult led by a human manifestation of the ancient spirit of Karaperamun, sprang forth. Old patterns suppressed by the theocratic Presbyterian Church for half a century—polygyny, dancing, kava drinking—suddenly reappeared full-blown. It appears that the cultural structure on which these customs rested had been there all along.

Even where new customs and beliefs fully replace the old in the course of change, the deeper premises and values of the traditional culture may continue to shape a people's world view and orientation to life. However, this is an elusive question: the very subtlety and depth of these underlying cultural patterns makes them hard to get at and hard to interpret, for reasons we glimpsed in the last chapter.

The Impact of Christianity

Anthropologists and missionaries have, at least in stereotype, been at odds with one another for many decades. The caricatured missionary is a strait-laced, repressed, and narrow-minded Bible thumper trying to get the native women to cover their bosoms decently; the anthropologist is a bearded degenerate given to taking his clothes off and sampling wild rites.

Things are more complicated than that. There is an old and enduring tradition of great missionary scholarship. Though many of the friars that accompanied the *conquistadores* in the Americas and in the Phillippines engaged in brutal repression and played an active and often sordid part in the subjugation of conquered populations, there were also many champions of humanism and justice; and there were some great scholars and statesmen like Sahagun and Las Casas and Lafitau who compiled rich records of indigenous cultures and championed the humanity of the conquered. In the nineteenth and early twentieth centuries, such figures as Junod, Codrington, Leenhardt, and Schebesta have enormously enriched anthropological knowledge. And in recent years, missionary ethnographers and linguists have continued to provide valuable evidence on tribal societies.

But there are deep gulfs between the premises, as well as the styles, of missionary work and anthropology that have led to considerable friction and controversy. Here, a critique of missionary work will be set out that takes a rather different direction than the traditional anthropological challenge. Many readers, who accept the missionary's premise that he bears the Divine Word and thus has

an urgent duty to spread the faith, will not agree with this critique: but the questions are worth raising even though the answers individuals reach will inevitably differ.

Anthropologists who have battled missionaries through the years have often bolstered their position with a cultural relativism and romanticism about the "primitive" that seem increasingly anachronistic. The anthropologist who finds himself in defense of infanticide, head-hunting, or the segregation and subordination of women, and in opposition to missionization, can well be uncomfortable about the premises from which he argues. But if one suspends both the premises of Christian duty and the equally shaky premises of cultural relativism, one can look penetratingly at Christianity and its spread under imperialism as historical phenomena—and one can find stronger grounds for questioning the missionary enterprise.

First, historically Christianity was brought to Latin America, the Philippines, and elsewhere as an instrument of conquest and subjugation. In the sixteenth and seventeenth centuries, Catholicism was literally spread by the sword; and subjugation of conquered peoples and the exacting of tribute and forced labor in mines and fields was as much the work of missionaries as of soldiers. In later centuries, Protestant and Catholic missionaries have been less directly used as instruments of government policy. But they have come under the aegis of colonialism and have been in its vanguard; and in many ways, direct and indirect, they have played a part in the subjugation of non-Western peoples.

Second, a major basis for Christian success, where Christianity has been successful, has been the inference by subjugated peoples that Europeans were rich and powerful because of the supernatural support they enjoyed. The White Man's deity must be the source of the White Man's power. Missionaries have seldom tried to dispel this assumption, and in most places have consciously exploited it. (So today the "miracles" of airplanes and penicillin help fundamentalist Protestants in New Guinea spread an ancient Middle Eastern theology that denies the major foundations of twentieth-century scientific knowledge.) From the perspective of the tribal peoples the inference is not surprising. If earth were invaded by an extraterrestrial civilization vastly more powerful and technologically advanced than ours, with a religion of ancestor worship, most Europeans would probably abandon Christianity and become ancestor worshippers. The premise on which any such ideological export rests is fundamentally exploitative.

By imposing European standards and European theology on societies to which they are alien, missionization has been pervasively racist and has eroded the self-conception of subjugated peoples. Colonized peoples have been proffered images of a white-skinned Jesus and a white-skinned God. They have usually, at least implicitly, been promised second-class citizenship in the White Man's heaven. They have been treated as children to be uplifted, not as men and women.

The most blatant racism and exploitation have been disappearing. Africans, Asians, and Pacific islanders serve as priests, deacons, or bishops. But paternalism, patronage, and racism remain; Christianity continues in many regions to serve alien interests; and the wounds to peoples' self-conception and to the integrity of their cultures remain deep and unhealed. It is worth quoting from the recent Declaration of Barbados, which emanated from a 1971 conference co-sponsored by the World Council of Churches and the Department of Anthropology, University of Basel, on the plight of South American Indians.

Evangelisation, the work of the religious missions in Latin America also reflects and complements the reigning colonial situation with the values of which it is imbued. The missionary presence has always implied the imposition of criteria and patterns of thought and behavior alien to the colonised Indian societies. A religious pretext has too often justified the economic and human exploitation of the aboriginal population.

The inherent ethnocentric aspect of the evangelisation process is also a component of the colonialist ideology and is based on the following characteristics:

1. its essentially discriminatory nature implicit in the hostile relationship to Indian culture conceived as pagan and heretical;

2. its vicarial aspect, implying the re-identification of the Indian and his consequent submission in exchange for future supernatural compensations;

3. its spurious quality given the common situation of missionaries seeking only some form of personal salvation, material or spiritual;

4. the fact that the missions have become a great land and labour enterprise, in conjunction with the dominant imperial interests. (Bartolome et al. 1971:5)

It is worth emphasizing as well that despite the enormous power of Europeans, missionization has been less than dramatically successful in many parts of the Third World. In many parts of Africa where strong missionary effort has been directed for as much as a century, only a small percentage of converts have been won. Islam is now expanding in Africa much more rapidly than Christianity; and decades of missionary effort in China and India have had few lasting results.

One reason for resistance to missionization in tribal areas has been the gulf between traditional belief systems, focusing on ancestor worship or belief in multiple supernatural powers, and the beliefs missionaries sought to introduce. At least in the early decades of Christian influence in tribal communities, belief in ancestors or spirits was characteristically retained; and God and the devil were added as a new force in the cosmos. Thus in Papua New Guinea a new Catholic cathedral was opened with appropriate participation by the most powerful sorcerers. In the British

Solomons an Anglican bishop whose father was a pagan priest drove porpoises ashore in a porpoise drive to obtain the teeth as ceremonial valuables, clutching a crucifix (in lieu of a traditional sacred baton); and he blessed the first kill in traditional fashion—but in Latin.

We saw from Mesoamerica that the rich pageantry of Catholicism offered rewarding replacement for much that had been swept away. One of the many impediments to the success of fundamentalist Protestant missionaries has been the austerity and emptiness of the new life proffered in place of the old. A pall of Protestant gloom hangs over many a community in the Pacific and tropical South America that once throbbed with life, laughter, and song. The concept of sin must rank with smallpox among our most damaging exports.

Christianity as a worldwide force is also illuminated by examining its ideological and economic roots. Christianity, from its beginnings as a religion of the oppressed, has from the Crusades onward been a religion of expansion and conquest. The treasuries of the Vatican attest to the immense wealth that has flowed directly to the Church from Christianization of the New World and parts of Asia; and the Church in the Third World continues to be an extraordinarily wealthy and powerful force controlling land and resources. Protestantism, as Weber (1956) and Tawney (1926) have compellingly argued, has historically been closely associated with the rise of capitalism, supported indirectly by the corporate wealth of Europe and the United States. Spreading Christianity has on the one hand been part of the moral justification (the white man's burden) Europeans have used to rationalize their subjugation of the world. And on the other hand, it has been a direct instrument of imperialism to spread religion while gaining raw materials, markets, and cheap labor. From the critical

standpoint of the student of political economy, who views ideologies as expressing underlying economic and political interests, it is not surprising that European religion has taken these forms. The civilization that produced an insatiable lust for profit has produced a religion with an insatiable lust for souls. And a religion that preaches the nobility of poverty, the virtue of passivity, and the joys of the next world has served rather nicely the interests of colonial powers and modern neo-colonialists' pursuit of raw materials, docile cheap labor, and profit.

The conclusions drawn in the Declaration of Barbados are strongly worded, but they bear reflection:

We conclude that the suspension of all missionary activity is the most appropriate policy on behalf of both Indian society as well as the moral integrity of the churches involved. Until this objective can be realized the missions must support and contribute to Indian liberation in the following manner:

1. overcome the intrinsic Herodianism of the evangelical process, itself a mechanism of colonialisation, Europeanisation and alienation of Indian society;

2. assume a position of true respect for Indian culture, ending the long and shameful history of despotism and intolerance characteristic of missionary work, which rarely manifests sensitivity to aboriginal religious sentiments and values;

3. halt both the theft of Indian property by religious missionaries who appropriate labour, lands and natural resources as their own, and the indifference in the face of Indian expropriation by third parties;

4. extinguish the sumptuous and lavish spirit of the missions themselves, expressed in various forms but all too often based on exploitation of Indian labour.

5. stop the competition among religious groups and confessions for Indian souls—a common occurrence leading to the buying and selling of believers and internal strife provoked by conflicting religious loyalties;

6. suppress the secular practice of removing Indian children from their families for long periods in boarding schools where they are imbued with values not their own, converting them in this way into marginal individuals, incapable of living either in the larger national society or their native communities;

7. break with the pseudo-moralist isolation which imposes a false puritanical ethic, incapacitating the Indian for coping with the national society—an ethic which the churches have been unable to impose on that same national society;

8. abandon those blackmail procedures implicit in the offering of goods and services to Indian society in return for total submission;

9. suspend immediately all practices of population displacement or concentration in order to evangelise and assimilate more effectively, a process that often provokes an increase in morbidity, mortality and family disorganization among Indian communities;

10. end the criminal practice of serving as intermediaries for the exploitation of Indian labour. (Bartolome et al. 1971:5—6)

But there is another side. Many Christian missionaries have devoted their lives in ways that have greatly enriched the communities where they worked. Many, in immersing themselves in other languages and cultures, have produced important records of ways now vanishing. But more important, in valuing these old ways and seeing Christianization as a challenge to creative synthesis of old and new, the best missionaries have helped to enrich human lives and provide effective bridges to participation in a world community. In a great many colonial regions, missions provided educational systems while colonial governments did not; and consequently, when the stage was set for the emergence of Third World leaders in decolonization, many who took the stage were able to do so because of their mission education. Missionaries, living in local communities where colonial exploitation had tragically disruptive consequences, have often been vocal critics of government policy or practice. No treatment of Christianity in the Third World could wisely overlook this humanitarian side.

Moreover, as we will see in Chapter 25, anthropologists' critiques of the involvement of missionaries as a part of imperialist design can no longer overlook their own historic involvement as well. It is no accident that after its critique of missionary exploitation, the

Declaration of Barbados goes on to lay bare the exploitative aspects of anthropology.

Anthropological critiques of missionaries have too often been based on a romantic idealism about tribal ways of life, sustained by a philosophy of cultural relativism. Such a relativism denies the very real oppression in tribal societies and the costs of endemic warfare, fear, and disease. Christian missionaries, in helping to bring medical care, education, and peace to tribal communities, have very often dramatically improved the material conditions of life (even if too often, by condemning customs they have not understood, they have caused needless erosion of social life and its satisfactions). Europeans, as conquerors, have had the power to force change on the conquered; and Christianity has been a more benign and humanitarian force, most of the time, than many other instruments the conquerors have used to impose their will and their standards.

It is urgent not simply to condemn missionary effort retrospectively but to understand its roots and its impact. But it is urgent above all to insist that, while change and the transformation of traditional societies and cultures are inevitable and necessary, the formerly colonized must create their *own* new worlds, their own syntheses of the old and new. If Third World peoples are to emerge from the ruins of colonialism and escape the tentacles of neocolonialism, they must find their own solutions, their own ways to transcend the oppression of the past while drawing on its wisdom and values. In this challenge, Christianity is increasingly seen by many Third World peoples as an alien system serving alien interests. But that must be for others to choose.

Millenarianism, Revitalization, and Anticolonial Struggle

Whether he was in ancestral village, plantation, or mining town, the tribesman was no longer the center of his world. He was rejected and despised, an inferior being: he was a "native." "Natives" are a creation of colonialism, of a racist denial of humanity. The "native" became a semihuman, scorned creature in his own country. Proud men were turned into "boys," led to despise the color of their skin and the ways of their forefathers.

The consequences for the social and psychological integration of colonized peoples have been deep and tragic. The psychology of being a "native" has been most searchingly explored by the psychiatrist Franz Fanon (1965), who has revealed a cost of colonialism—and a source of anticolonialist rage and frustration—that had remained largely hidden from the colonizers. It was more reassuring to deny the humanity of the natives and decry the barbarism of their customs, and then to seek to uplift them. One could ratio-

nalize exploitation with a sense of moral responsibility.

Faced with massive external threat, some peoples made conservatism a stance for survival, a way of preserving cultural and individual identity. With traditional social systems breaking down, they have sought to preserve central rites and symbols. As we have seen, the once-numerous and powerful Mandan Indians of the upper Missouri were devastated by smallpox and enemy raids. They were also controlled by a series of fur companies, in the end being controlled and dominated by the American Fur Company. Yet through this period, they struggled to maintain their cultural integrity and identity, with numbers decimated and autonomy gone, by carrying on their elaborate religious ceremonial. Most notable was the great *okipa* ceremony, requiring

The Mandan Indian *okipa* ceremony: Continued performance of this rite became a symbol of cultural integrity in the face of subordination and decimation. (From a painting by Carl Bodmer, courtesy of The American Museum of Natural History.)

scores of participants (Catlin 1867; Bowers 1950). With numbers so far reduced, this required more men than they could muster; so the neighboring Hidatsa, with whom they had coalesced for sheer survival, were incorporated into the rite. And in this period, the Mandan attempted to preserve their culture by adopting into the tribe Indians from surrounding groups, and even French trappers and their half-Indian children; the only condition for being a Mandan was raising one's children as culturally Mandan. Yet even this desperate means for survival was to fail: Mandan language and culture have now vanished, driven into final extinction by a conscious U.S. government policy of assimilation that forced dispersal of the remnant Mandan communities (Bruner 1961).

Subjected to extreme pressures by the onslaught of European power, and forced to reject their centrality in the scheme of things

and to become subjugated "natives," tribal peoples often came to view their culture as a "thing." The customs, values, and rites that, as in the Mandan case, had been taken for granted as part of human life came to be seen from an external point of view: a peoples' *culture* could become a *symbol*. Once this external view was taken, the old ways could symbolize a golden age of past glories and freedoms; or they could be rejected as delusions, as having kept from one's forefathers the power of the White Man.

Millennial (or millenarian) movements that promised a future paradise on earth have arisen on many colonial frontiers. Some hearkened back to the glory of the past. Most dramatic were the two Ghost Dance cults that spread across Plains Indian tribes when their power and independence had been broken and the buffalo on which life depended had vanished.

Case 84: The Ghost Dance Religions

In 1869, a Paiute prophet named Wodziwob had religious visions which foretold the end of the existing world, the ousting of the whites, the return of dead relatives, and the restoration of Indian lands and integrity. These doctrines spread rapidly among Plains tribes whose ways of life had disintegrated under white pressure and the extermination of the buffalo.

Figure 21.1. "Bulletproof" ghost shirt: This Arapaho (Plains American Indian) shirt was part of the magical equipment of the Ghost Dance adherents, supposedly protecting them against the white man's guns. It is of leather, with both traditional Indian symbols and what appear to be Christian symbols (the cross). (After Mooney 1896.)

The Ghost Dance: An Arapaho brave in rigid dance position. (Photograph 1893 by James Mooney, courtesy of National Anthropological Archives, Smithsonian Institution.)

Though attempts at military resistance generated by cult doctrines were smashed, the cult spread widely and diversified into local versions. Then in 1890, a second Ghost Dance cult inspired by another Paiute prophet, Wovoka, spread eastward across the Plains tribes and even to some Eastern Woodlands tribes. Again the cult stressed return to traditional ways of life that had broken down. If the patterns of traditional culture were purified and restored, the vanishing buffalo would return, the dead ancestors would come back, and the Indians could drive out the whites with magical protection against the power of bullets (Mooney 1896).

Millenarian movements that reject a traditional culture and formulate some new social order as a means to a millennium have drawn much attention from anthropologists and other scholars. Most dramatic and intensively studied are the "cargo cults" of New Guinea and neighboring areas of Melanesia (Worsley 1957; Thrupp 1962; Lanternari 1963; Jarvie 1963). In these movements, the material power and prosperity of the White Man are seen as valued goals; and the traditional culture is viewed as an obstacle to achieving them. By following the doctrine of the cult, and (usually) following the leadership of its visionary leader in reorganizing social life, a people expect to achieve the millennium. The classic "Vailala madness" of New Guinea is a dramatic illustration of such a movement, clearly oriented toward a mystical and "irrational" millennium and the acquisition of European material goods and rejecting the religious symbols of the past.

Case 85: The Vailala Madness

As of 1919, the Elema of coastal New Guinea had experienced the waves of European influence: missionary teachings, early experience as plantation laborers, introduction of the few items of European hardware the Elema could afford, and pacification.

In that year, a movement broke out among the Elema that for a time set whole villages into collective "head he go round," a psychophysical state reminiscent of the dancing mania of plague-ridden medieval Europe. People lost control of their limbs, reeled drunkenly, and eventually lost consciousness. Who formulated the ideology is not clear. Central in it was a belief that the dead would return, bringing with them a fabulous cargo of European material goods—knives, cloth, canned goods, axes, and so on. Sacred bull-roarers and other ritual objects were destroyed in a wave of iconoclasm, in communities where dramatic rituals and spectacular men's houses had been focal points of life. The Elema abandoned normal gardening projects and devoted their efforts to elaborate preparations for the return of the dead (Williams 1923).

Within a year most overt forms of the movement had subsided. When Williams, the government anthropologist, returned in 1933, a few traces of it remained, though there were vague traditions that some of the prophecies had come true.

Interpretations of "cargo cults" and other millennial movements have come not only from anthropologists but from psychologists, historians, sociologists, and students of comparative religion. Many writers have stressed exploitation and economic inequality. Aberle (1962) has emphasized relative deprivation, a perceived gap between the desired and possible, between new aspirations and abilities to satisfy them. Anthropologists have been sensitive to cultural factors as well—congruences between new doctrines and old patterns of belief and magical explanation, relations between the role of cult prophet and traditional leader. But too few analysts of millenarianism in the Pacific have taken a sufficiently global view of imperialism, with its racism and exploitation, as the force to which modern millennial movements have been a response (and hence, the experiences of plantation labor, of being "natives," of being caught up in an economy of trade stores, calico, and tobacco).

And a wariness about psychological explanation in social science has misled many students of millenarian and other social movements into missing a vital perspective (one basic to Marxist interpretations of social change): that it is a transformation of consciousness, a new vision of one's position in the scheme of things, that opens the possibility of radical change—whether by mystical or political means. It has been the crystallization of a *collective self-identity* that has opened the way for dramatic movements of change. What is needed is for people to perceive their own way of life in a new perspective (relative to the dominant group's), usually with one or more leaders providing the ideology and charismatic force. However carefully we probe economic and sociological factors, dramatic transformations of social life cannot be anticipated or understood if we overlook the psychological and symbolic elements in the chemistry of radical change and the catalysis of new consciousness.

This then leads to another limitation of recent fascination with millenarian movements. Preoccupation with the esoteric, with collective fantasy, has often obscured a continuum between millennial cults and more political responses to colonial subjugation—a continuum with modern revolutionary struggles at the other end.

In Melanesia itself, there have been more directly political responses to colonial domination, though it is characteristic that they have been cloaked in religious symbols. Such Melanesian movements have painted a much more realistic vision of the new social order, where the goal is a transformation of the social order by human effort and planning, not supernatural intervention, and where this path has been pursued more by political than mystical means. Sometimes, as in the Paliau movement on Manus Island northeast of New Guinea (Schwartz 1962) and the rise of the Mataungan Association on New Britain (Case 46), the plans and methods have been so clearly political that they have become part of the ongoing political process of an emerging nation. In others, such as Maasina Rule (Case 86) in the Solomon Islands, political action and doctrines for social reorganization have been melded with messianic beliefs and have been expressed in religious guise; and too often European observers have exaggerated the millennial content in order to sustain their stereotypes and rationalize their colonialist aims or economic and religious interests.

Case 86: Maasina Rule in the Solomon Islands

The Solomon Islands were the scene of major World War II sea and land battles. A volunteer Melanesian Labor Corps, mainly from Malaita Island, worked with American troops. From their encounter with staggering quantities of military hardware and American egalitarian ideologies, a Malaitan named Nori and a group of compatriots formulated a new doctrine. The different tribal peoples were to join together, united by a council of nine head chiefs, to negotiate their demands with the returning British administration (which they hoped might be replaced by Americans). Each tribal group was to organize into communal villages, structured on the model of military units—with roll calls, chiefs to supervise communal labor, and drills with wooden rifles. Fragmented local kin groups joined together, building large communal gardens for subsistence and anticipated trade.

Maasina Rule, "The Rule of Brotherhood," was to unite the Solomon Islanders in a new social, economic, and political order in which they would be free and wealthy like the Americans—for which their new way of life was to prepare them. Malaitans refused to work on plantations and staged large demonstrations in confrontation of the administration. The British jailed the nine head chiefs, but their places were filled again. Supernatural doctrines of the millennium and the imminent return of

Prologue to Maasina rule: A Malaita labor corpsman uses farm machinery on a large-scale agricultural project to feed U.S. troops. (A World War II photograph in the author's collection.)

Americans swept the island; and as prophecies failed to materialize, as old conflicts and ecological pressures welled up, and as the British government imposed a heavy-handed repression, the active movement subsided after about seven years of overt social ferment.

European observers consistently exaggerated the millenarian content and wild credulity of the movement, and thus escaped dealing with a political content that prefigured the modern movement toward independence, and with a political organization that violated colonialist stereotypes about the "natives."

The continuum from religious millenarianism to political struggle is important and revealing. The deep destruction of identity in colonialism creates an explosive situation. Catalyzed by millenarian vision, it can lead to religious cultism, where people are powerless and the gulf between ways of life is vast. But where people have greater power and a clearer and more global perception of the colonial situation, destruction of identity has led to rebellion, political struggle, or wars of liberation. In retrospect, the Mau Mau movement of Kenya was not a fanatic cult of religious murder as it was painted by the white colonists, but a highly effective war of liberation against an entrenched enemy.

Anthropologists, because of their predilection for studying the exotic and for working among powerless and peripheral small-scale societies, have characteristically focused on millennial cults and religious rather than political quests for liberation from colonial oppression. As we will see in Chapter 25, they have found themselves standing apart from—and often rejected by—peoples who have wrested themselves free from colonial or neocolonial domination.

Colonial Policy and the Adaptation of the Colonized

As we noted at the beginning of this section, the adaptation of tribal peoples to colonial subjugation depended in substantial part on where they were, and hence what Europeans wanted from them—whether cheap labor, land, or simply peaceful submission in the wilderness. It also has depended on the colonial policy of a particular country and era, so that it is a gross oversimplification to paint colonialists of all times and places with the same broad brush strokes or to condemn each for the collective sins of all. Europeans were more or less exploitative, more or less ruthless, more or less benevolent, in search of lands and profits; and in different times and places they have pursued different goals for the "natives," running the gamut from extermination to assimilation.

When colonial settlement was the aim—especially in temperate zones of the world, such as North America, Australia, South Africa, and New Zealand—the "natives" had to be removed from the new land that had been "discovered." By extermination and herding of the survivors into barren and unwanted reserves, European settlers could take possession of fertile land and resources in the name of some crown or another.

However, some tribal peoples, instead of succumbing conveniently or disappearing into the wastelands, adopted European ways with apparent ease and enthusiasm and began beating the White Man at his own game. The best-known case was that of the Cherokee. Before and after their desperate forced move to Oklahoma, the Cherokee were dramatically successful in adopting white economic patterns, technology, literacy, and customs and reshaping them to their own ends and their own design. Yet the Cherokee Nation was twice destroyed by white greed, land hunger, and fear of Cherokee power and success.

Equally striking, and less well known, was a somewhat similar adaptation by the most populous and politically integrated Australian Aborigines, the "five tribes" of central Victoria.

Case 87: The Five Tribes and the "Coranderrk Rebellion"

Five Australian language groups or "tribes," the Woiwurrung, Bunurong, Wodthaurung, Jajourong, and Tangerong, had a complex regional system of trade, intermarriage, and ceremonial within a kind of political confederacy (Howitt 1904).

Decimated by disease in the early contact period, the five tribes were deprived of their lands by the sort of deception and broken promises familiar from the American frontier. In 1863, the survivors of the five tribes were given a reservation at Coranderrk, under protection of Queen Victoria.

Many of the Aborigines by then spoke good English; many read newspapers, and some wrote letters to the editors.

Coranderrk: Dick and Ellen Richards (right) in front of their houses with their neighbors about 1876. (Photograph by Friedrich Kruger, copyright the National Museum of Victoria.)

In 1874 more than half the population in school was considered "equal to European children of their age." . . . Some were good farmers. . . . They cleared heavy timber, built houses, strung fences, grew saleable crops and ran some cattle. Many had jobs at European wages; they raised their living standard by craft work for sale, and by wages earned outside the reserve. (Stanner 1973:107)

The Aborigines had European furniture, dishes, bedding, sewing machines, and kerosene lamps. Their reserve had a library for which Aborigines bought novels, magazines, and portraits of Queen Victoria (Stanner 1973; Barwick n.d.).

In the first decade, the reserve at Coranderrk was managed by an intelligent and capable man who encouraged the community to work out its own laws and transform their society. The people changed their old prescriptive marriage system, giving young women freedom to choose their own husbands, subject only to the rule of clan exogamy.

Yet by 1875, the Victorian Board for the Protection of the Aborigines was increasingly pressured by whites fearful of the economic success of the Coranderrk Aborigines: they not only held land the settlers wanted and were becoming prosperous, organized, and vocal in their protests against injustice; they also threatened the stereotype of Aborigines as childlike savages incapable of civilized life—a stereotype white settlers used to rationalize their strategies of extermination and usurpation of land. The Board, itself dominated by self-serving and hypocritical "protectors" of Aboriginal rights, fired the benevolent head of the Coranderrk Reserve and imposed a series of repressive measures designed to wreck

The vanishing black fellow as racist myth: The stereotype of Australian Aborigines as unable to cope with an advanced civilization has been used to justify decades of oppression. These Aboriginal cricketers, photographed in 1867, astounded Victorian England with their superb play. (Courtesy of the Mitchell Library, Sydney.)

the economic and political organization of the Aborigines. In the face of this, the Aborigines did the only thing they could do: they protested, in the form of strikes, demonstrations, and complaints to authority—though not violence. Under pressure, factionalism began to split the Aboriginal camp into a "progressive" faction (including a number of half-Aboriginals) bent on assimilation and a "conservative" faction bent on preserving cultural identity.[2]

In governmental enquiries into the Coranderrk situation a myth was fostered that the reserve had been a den of gambling and prostitution and had been an economic failure. And over succeeding decades the lands of the reserve were broken up and ceded to whites. By the 1920s, only the cemetery and a 500-acre reserve to which the Coranderrk remnants were moved remained from the 27,000 acres given to the Aborigines: the rest was in the hands of whites. Yet Australian histories of Victoria still perpetuate the myth that the Aboriginal reserves, notably Coranderrk, were "failures" and use that to justify their expropriation by land-hungry Europeans (Barwick n.d.; Stanner 1973).

[2]A similar split among the Cherokee after their tragic forced march along the "Trail of Tears" to Oklahoma, between the conservative Ross Party and the assimilationist Treaty Party, has been a major theme of Cherokee adaptation. White mythologists have attributed the successful adaptation and cultural achievements of the Cherokee—such as the creation of a syllabary by Sequoyah—to the infusion of "white blood"; and have used the division to bolster racism against traditional Indians and their culture and the political and economic ascendancy of Americanized Cherokee. (see Wahrhaftig and Thomas 1969.)

Where the aim of Europeans was not settlement but pacification, subjugation, and colonial control, the range of options was wider. The first order of the day was to force political capitulation. How that was to be accomplished—whether by conquest, political intrigue, or simply imposition of the *Pax Britannica* or its equivalent—was both a matter of location and a matter of the political organization of the people to be subjugated.

Where a non-Western people had a strong and centralized government, it had to be forced to capitulate to ultimate colonial control within a web of empire. The process of subjugation, but also of cultural misunderstanding by the colonizing power, is vividly illustrated by a famous issue of sovereignty in West Africa.

Case 88: The Golden Stool of Ashanti

The most sacred symbol of the great Ashanti Kingdom of West Africa was the Golden Stool. It had been introduced to the Ashanti by a celebrated magician, who had proclaimed that it contained the *sunsum*, or "soul," of the Ashanti people. He warned that "with it was bound up their power, their honour, their welfare, and that if ever it were captured or destroyed the nation would perish" (B. W. Smith 1926). The Stool was never sat upon, never allowed to touch the ground; only on great occasions was its sacred power invoked by the Ashanti king.

In 1910, the British governor made a series of demands to the leaders of the Ashanti he had summoned to the fort of Kumasi, to which they had come "outwardly submissive, but inwardly boiling over with indignation" (E. W. Smith 1926:5). His speech stands out as a gem of colonialist history:

Now Kings and Chiefs . . . what must I do to the man, whoever he is, who has failed to give to the Queen [of England], who is the paramount power in this country, the Stool to which she is entitled? Where is the Golden Stool? Why am I not sitting on the Golden Stool at this moment? (Rattray 1923)

The governor, of course, thought the Golden Stool was an "appurtenance of the kingly office," and expected that this symbol of his authority should be given, like the Stone of Scone, to the English monarch.

Within a week the Ashanti nation was at war with England. Perhaps Governor Hodgson suspected his mistake when he and his forces were subsequently besieged at Kumasi by tens of thousands of Ashanti warriors.

A characteristic strategy Europeans used was to support a particular leader fighting with his rivals for power, make him "king," give him the means to conquer other leaders, and then use him to achieve European domination. A classic case was Cakobau of Fiji, chief of the tiny island of Bau, who was armed and supported by the British, was turned into a

A first colonial strategy: Find the "chiefs" and manipulate them. New Guinea chiefs deal with Commodore Erskine on H.M.S. Nelson (1884), holding the "emblems of authority" presented to them. (Courtesy of Australian News and Information Bureau.)

"king," and then ceded his kingdom to Queen Victoria—who guaranteed hegemony of Fiji to his successors.

The people Europeans sought to bring under their control often perceived the political symbols of sovereignty invoked by the whites as quite meaningless, or they manipulated them to their own ends. The Mandan Indians of the upper Missouri once more provide a striking case.

Case 89: Mandan Acceptance of European "Sovereignty"

Precontact Mandan trade with the Plains tribes involved partnerships. The important Mandan men were strikingly rich, powerful, and aristocratic. In their trading partnerships with influential men from other groups, the Mandan ritually defined their partners as "father," fictively incorporating them into the kinship system. They in turn were adopted as the fictive fathers of Plains leaders. This was a means of both strategic alliance and manipulation. "Plains Indian trade was accomplished by barter between fictitious relatives. . . . A vast network of ritual kinship relationships extended throughout the entire Plains" (Bruner 1961:201). When Europeans arrived and demanded sovereignty, what the Mandan wanted from them was trading partnerships and power. La Verendrye, the first European to arrive, was received with ceremonial display and deference. "One of the chiefs begged La Verendrye, whom he addressed as father, to adopt the principal Mandan men as his children. This he did, by placing his hands on the head of each chief. The Mandan replied with "shouts of joy and thankfulness" (Bruner 1961:198), and were incorporated (from La Verendrye's point of view) under sovereignty of the king of France.

In 1762, Mandan territory was formally ceded by the king of France to Spain. In 1794, the British built a trading post among the Mandan; but two years later, a Spanish expedition visited the Mandan—who promptly adopted their leader. "He distributed flags, medals, and presents to the chiefs, who promised to follow the counsels of "their Great Father the Spaniard" (Bruner 1961:207). Then, in 1803, the area was ceded to the United States under the terms of the Louisiana Purchase; and shortly afterwards, Lewis and Clark visited them. "The American explorers distributed flags, medals, presents, and officers' uniforms to the Indian Chiefs, who now promised to follow the consel of their Great Father the President" (Bruner 1961:207). However, the Mandan privately observed to

The Hidatsa, neighbors of the Mandan Indians, bargain with a royal tourist, Prince Maximilian of Wied, in 1832. (From an engraving by Carl Bodmer, courtesy of the National Anthropological Archives, Smithsonian Institution.)

a British trader that in the Lewis and Clark expedition there were "only two sensible men . . ., the worker of iron and the mender of guns" (Masson 1889:330, quoted by Bruner 1961).

In this early contact situation, another cultural misunderstanding loomed large. A pervasive principle of Mandan culture was that the power of important men could be transferred to younger and less powerful men through the medium of female sexuality. Thus young men would gain power by sending their wives to sleep with powerful older men. When Europeans arrived, with their obvious wealth and power, the Mandan strategically sent their womenfolk to sleep with the explorers. So in the early literature of the contact period, Mandan women are described as wanton and promiscuous (Bruner 1961).

Elsewhere, subjugation to colonialism had to be achieved by conquest and naked force (as with the Navaho or Sioux, who were militarily crushed, then herded onto barren reservations) or by less direct imposition of control. In the Pacific and Africa, control was often imposed indirectly through local headmen—sometimes leaders in the traditional political system, but often superimposed for colonialist convenience. Imposition of a head tax was a favorite strategy of the colonialists: it forced overt recognition of subjugation, since from the standpoint of the conquered it amounted to the exaction of tribute; but more important, it forced the "natives" to go to work on plantations or mines, or wherever cheap labor was needed. And it brought the colonized regions into a capitalist cash economy, creating markets for cloth, steel tools, sugar, tea, and tobacco. (The spread of tobacco would be a tale in itself; the Germans in New Guinea, for example, conducted schools to teach the "natives" how to smoke.)

Even where colonial administration was relatively benevolent, colonial administrators often rivaled or surpassed missionaries in their misunderstandings of local culture. The reader who has traced in the preceding pages the labyrinths of custom and belief in the Trobriand Islands can appreciate the confusions a well-meaning government administrator there

could fall into. *Urigubu* payments, matrilineal descent, plural marriage, the *kula,* the dogma of procreation—all these could lead an Englishman applying his "common sense" into disastrous misunderstandings. Thus Malinowski (1935,I:103) writes of the Resident Magistrate who, in land disputes, "adopted a method natural to the European but fatal in a matrilineal community. He would inquire whose father had cut the disputed plot in olden days, a question which, under maternal

Apartheid in South Africa: Bus sign—non-Europeans only. (Courtesy of United Nations.)

Aborigines in an affluent society: These Arnhem Land Australians live in shattering poverty, with appalling infant mortality, at the margins of a giant mining complex. (Courtesy of Sreten Bozic.)

descent, was beside the point and usually admitted of no answer, since the fathers of both litigants probably belonged to other communities."

A heavy-handed approach to cultural change has marked many colonial situations, but most strikingly in cases where massive settlement by colonists has made surviving indigenous peoples an obstacle and an embarassment. Where the indigenous peoples outnumber settlers, as in South Africa and Zimbabwe (Rhodesia), ruthless separation and *apartheid* have been keynotes of policy. But where the surviving indigenous peoples have been numerically few and consigned to reservations, paternalism has often given way to pressures for assimilation. Often this has meant systematic destruction of aboriginal cultures. As we have noted, the Mandan Indians, whose desperate efforts for cultural survival we encountered in the preceding pages, were finally destroyed by a deliberate policy that broke up the large village that was the keystone of cultural integration (the remnant of the nine big villages of the early contact period) and forced Mandan to scatter into dispersed homesteads. The language and culture of the once-proud Mandan have been completely destroyed for 25 years—a tragic case of forced cultural extinction or ethnocide (Bruner 1961).

Colonial administrations have varied in their treatment of tribal peoples from ruthless suppression to paternalistic protectionism and sympathy to local custom. Protection against excesses of exploitation has been a theme of the modern colonial period. Thus a British administration in the Trobriand Island prohibited diving for pearl shell by any outsiders; isolated peoples have sometimes been quarantined as best possible from the spread of Western diseases; and an effort has often been made to respect local custom where feasible. Such benevolent (if often condescending) colonial government replaced older and more ruthless styles in many areas in later decades, as ideologies changed and social conscience became focused on the morality of colonialism. The white man's burden became heavier as the costs of leading a colonial people toward and through self-government came to outweigh the profits flowing back to the colonizing nation. Yet the cynic

The old and the new in Australia: This huge mining complex, carved out of an aboriginal reserve in Arnhem Land, brings great wealth to European investors and helps to support an affluent society at the expense of the original inhabitants (Courtesy of Sreten Bozic.)

can find much evidence that even now, when the stakes are sufficiently high, native peoples who stand in the way of dam, uranium or copper mine, or airfield will be brushed aside as efficiently as ever. We will return to the phenomena of the postcolonial colonialisms of our time in Chapter 25. First, a closer look at the anthropological study of peasant communities, urban settings, and complex societies will enlarge our view and expand our theoretical perspectives on the problems and challenges of the present.

PEASANTS

22

Anthropology acquired its special stamp, and its special skills, from studies of exotic "primitive" peoples. Yet modern anthropology has increasingly focused on peasant villagers, on townspeople, and now on city dwellers. In part, this attention has been generated by anthropology's aspirations to universality: having set about to make scientific generalizations about the human condition and the widest ranges of cultural and social variation, anthropologists could hardly look only at "primitive" peoples. And this has been all the more urgent since those "primitives" have been so rapidly vanishing. An anthropology that confined itself to the tribal world would soon be only an arcane pursuit in libraries.

But anthropological study of peasant communities and particularly of urbanites poses special and serious problems. As we saw in the last chapter, concepts of culture, social structure, and the like—which anthropologists found meaningful in small-scale, homogeneous, and stable communities—are less useful in a peasant marketplace or a city neighborhood. Moreover, the special virtue of anthropological research, its close view of the life of a community, exacts a serious cost when the anthropologist is looking at a small part of a wider system. By seeking what is closest, one may be myopic in seeing the wider forces shaping the local situation.

In this chapter, we will examine anthropological study of peasants—looking first at a kind of standard anthropological view of the peasant condition, and then subjecting it to a critical reassessment. In Chapter 23, we will look at the special challenge to anthropology of the study of complex civilizations and the study of urban settings.

73.

Peasants: A Conventional Anthropological View

As we noted in §21 and §22, there have been peasants as long as there have been stratified urban societies; but anthropologists have been slow in turning their attention to peasant communities.

What is a peasant? Most writers agree that an agricultural mode of life, with an emphasis on subsistence farming but a dependence on the products and markets of the wider society, is a dominant feature of peasant life everywhere. The peasant lives at once in a world of his own and a wider one. The center of that wider world on whose margins the peasant lives is the city.

But are these really the essential elements in defining the peasant condition? E. R. Wolf (1966a:3—4) argues that the peasant is a cultivator with a special kind of relationship to the world outside: "peasants are rural cultivators whose surpluses are transferred to a dominant group of rulers that uses the surpluses both to underwrite its own standard of living and to distribute the remainder to groups ... that ... must be fed for their specific goods and services." What makes peasants peasants is their existence with a *state,* where they are subject to "the demands and interests of power holders" outside their social stratum, usually but not always centered in cities.

Peasants have been part of the human scene since the emergence of civilization in the Middle East and Mesoamerica. Our detailed knowledge of their economic life, social organization, and world view has been built up mainly through field studies of modern communities. The picture that is emerging reveals peasants struggling to maintain life, continuity, and a measure of dignity while trapped on a kind of treadmill, exploited by elites and entrapped in poverty and powerlessness. Compared to the lot of tribal people, in the center of their own conceptual universe, it is a difficult and often desperate existence.

Anthropologists working in peasant communities in the last 30 years have built up detailed records of the texture of social relations in many parts of the peasant world and have explored economy, religion, and political processes. In seeing peasant communities basically as they had seen tribal communities—as more or less closed and self-contained, and often as devoid of known history—anthropologists have drawn a picture of the peasant condition which is both vivid and revealing and in many cases inadequate. In the paragraphs to follow, we will present an orthodox picture of the peasant condition. Then we will step back to look at a wider picture of the forces that have created and shaped life in peasant communities, in the centuries before anthropologists arrived as well as in the two or three decades when they have been watching. Like a number of other recent critics, I will argue that the "standard" view of the peasant condition has been inadequate and misleading—that the view most anthropologists have gotten and the interpretations many have drawn have been partial and limited.

Peasant Social Organization

Many peasant communities in both the New and Old Worlds have patterns of social organization that reflect elements of the tribal social systems from which they grew. Unilineal descent groupings may remain important. Thus patrilineages play significant roles in peasant social life in corners of the world as widely separated as Mexico, the Balkans, and China (Case 57).

The Mayan Indians of Zinacantan, whose religious system we examined in the last chapter, provide a vivid example of unilineal descent groupings in peasant communities.

Case 90: Descent Groups and Zinacantan Social Organization

Zinacantan, whose complex synthesis of Mayan and Catholic religious beliefs we glimpsed in Case 83, is organized in a way that subtly reflects an underlying patrilineal descent system.

Zinacantan has a population of some 8000, living in a classically Mayan settlement pattern of a ceremonial center and 15 outlying hamlets. The most important social units are domestic groups, composed of kinsmen who live in a single house compound and share a single supply of maize (corn). Normally, a compound contains at least two houses, around a central patio. Each domestic group is symbolically centered around a "house cross" that reflects its ritual unity.

Most Zinacanteco domestic groups are patrilocal extended families, the minimal local segments of patrilineages. The essential requirement is that it contain both men and women, so as to be economically viable. The most common pattern—a senior man, his wife, his married sons and their wives, and any unmarried children—reflects the practice of virilocal residence and patrilineal inheritance. (See photograph, p. 310.)

These domestic groups (for which there is no label in their language, Tzotzil) are in turn clustered into larger localized groupings along patrilineal lines. Several patrilineally related domestic groups, living on adjacent lands inherited from their ancestors, comprise an unnamed shallow patrilineage some four generations in depth.

One or several patrilineages (or, rarely, as many as 13 of them) are in turn clustered into ritually defined groupings which Vogt (1969, 1970) calls *sna*. These clusters, ranging from some 15 to 150 people, collectively perform ceremonies for the ancestral gods and Earth Owner (Case 83) twice a year. The senior members and shamans of the component lineages take part in these ceremonies in defined hierarchies of ritual rank. The ceremonies focus around cross shrines that are a formal analogue of the house crosses, on a more inclusive scale (Vogt 1969).

Zinacantan has a complex system of personal naming. One of the three names each individual bears is an Indian surname, of which there are some 70. These names are patrilineally transmitted within lineages; and since there is a rule against marriage between people with the same surname, this produces exogamous groupings Vogt calls "patriclans."

The *sna* patrilineage clusters are in turn aligned around particular waterholes, with from 2 to 13 patrilineage clusters using a single water supply for their livestock and household use. There is some seasonal dispersal and regrouping during rainy season and dry season. Each water-

A Zinacanteco woman and her baby in front of her house. (Courtesy of Frank Cancian.)

hole is highly sacred; its ritual importance is marked by a series of cross shrines, both beside the hole and on a hill above, where the ancestors of the component *sna* are believed to assemble. The same twice-annual ceremonial conducted by each *sna* is also performed a few days earlier by the whole waterhole group. At these ceremonies, the social and ritual unity of the patrilineages that share a common waterhole, and their collective bonds with their ancestors, are symbolically expressed.

Vogt (1965) has argued that the symbolic complex whereby a patrilineal group is symbolically related to its ancestors through crosses, which constitute an entryway to the sacred, is replicated at successively more inclusive levels of social structure: the domestic group, the *sna*, the waterhole grouping. The ritual unity is expressed ceremonially by sacred meals within which the ranking of the human participants is carefully observed—a pattern again repeated on a larger scale at each hierarchical level of the social structure. Vogt suggests that this replication of the same formal pattern at more and more inclusive levels may have provided a mechanism for the symbolic unity of the great temple centers of Classic Maya society.

In other peasant societies, as in the southern European agrarian communities that have received increasing anthropological attention, the underlying social systems are the old feudal ones of medieval centuries progressively transformed by emerging modern nations.

Unilineal kin groups are seldom important in such settings, though networks of kinship and intermarriage weave together the households that are the primary constituent groupings. Coalitions of friends and neighbors, formed to pursue collective economic strategies and characteristically temporary, have turned up over and over again in rural European settings—though as P. Schneider et al.

(1972) rightly insist, *all* societies are organized in both more formal and enduring groups and *ad hoc* coalitions; it is their relative importance and spheres of relevance that vary.

"Fictive kinship" ties, relations modeled on parental, fraternal, or grandparental roles, are often important in extending or complementing bonds of kinship and affinity.

Best known is *compadrazgo,* or co-parenthood, of Mesoamerica, primarily derived through Catholicism from southern European customs but with roots in Mexican Indian cultures as well. Comparable but historically unrelated systems of fictive kinship have turned up as far away as Japan and Nepal.

Case 91: *Compadrazgo* in Mexico

Compadrazgo in Mesoamerica overtly derives from the Catholic institution of baptism: a "godfather" and "godmother" sponsor a child ritually in the baptism; they provide spiritual responsibility for the child complementary to the responsibility of father and mother for the child's physical development. While a child's relationship to *padrino* (godfather) and *madrina* (godmother) is important—marked by respect and obedience from the child and guidance and assistance from the sponsors—it is the relationship between sponsors and *parents* that has received special elaboration in Mesoamerica.

The sponsors and parents establish bonds of ritual co-parenthood which (especially between godfather and father) are important additions to kinship bonds. The reciprocal term *compadre* is used for this relationship, which characteristically has strong associations of sacredness and entails ritual respect and formalized reciprocity.

Mexican and other Latin American elaborations of *compadrazgo* have extended the range and importance of these ties far beyond the original

Catholic derivation in the sponsorship of baptism. The relationship may unite the sponsor to the grandparents, as well as parents, of the child or otherwise extend the dyadic relationship into a multiple one. And sponsorship in other ritual events, not simply baptism, may lead an individual to have multiple ritual parents.

The variation in regional forms of *compadrazgo* presumably reflects differences in the pre-Columbian Indian cultures onto which the Spanish model has been superimposed (Davila 1971). These regional variations in the range of *compadre* relationships, their social entailments and relationships to family structure, and their function in the social life of communities have been extensively studied.

Characteristically, sponsors are nonkin or distant kin. A major function of *compadrazgo* is thus to extend the range of close personal relations beyond the circle of kin. In most communities, fairly free choice of a sponsor is possible. Where the social system is relatively egalitarian, the *compadre* relationship is characteristically symmetrical in terms of status. But where differences in wealth and power are marked, sponsorship by a wealthy or powerful man becomes a political strategy—a way of maintaining status (for the sponsor) and seeking upward mobility (for the son) and patronage (for the father).

The symbolic modeling of *compadrazgo* on kinship is evident not only in terminology and role relationships; it is also apparent in the inalienable, enduring sacred nature of the bonds of sponsorship and co-parenthood, the axioms of moral obligation they entail, and the extension of incest taboos to relations of *compadrazgo* (Davila 1971).

Despite wider ties of actual and fictive kinship, the peasant community characteristically differs from its tribal counterpart in the independence of household groups. These may be extended families of various sorts or nuclear family households.

Economically, these family households characteristically act as separate corporations, as units of production and as competitors for scarce resources and income. In many peasant communities these households stand relatively isolated and are not organized into lineages or other kin groups. The fragmentation into nuclear families, and their economic competition, are very often reflected in the texture of social relations. The competition and hostile distrust that often prevail between families have been described in such terms as "atomism" (Rubel and Kupferer 1968). Here it is worth recalling once more Bailey's (1971) observations from rural European villages, in *Gifts and Poisons*, of subtle struggles for status, the often vicious business of staying even with one's fellows. Similar observations have come from many peasant communities.

Foster (1961) has underlined the emphasis on *dyadic* relations in peasant life—that is, the way pairs of individuals are, in many different spheres of life, bound into relationships almost similar to contracts, though they are not enforced in law. Ties outside the family are, at least in the Mexican village of Tzintzuntzan, primarily between individuals rather than groups. They persist partly because they are never precisely balanced, and hence call for continuing reciprocity. Some dyadic ties are between persons of equal status; others are with *patrons* of superior status (including deities as well as people), who exploit and are "exploited" by the lower-status clients for mutual benefit. Ties to powerful patrons outside the community help to link its residents into wider social networks.

Considerable variation in the wider structure of communities has been documented (as would hardly be surprising when one is talking about regions as diverse as Europe, India, China, and Mexico). But in social organization, as in many aspects of peasant life, strikingly similar patterns turn up in different parts of the world. One of the important variants is what Wolf (1957) calls the "closed corporate community"—where the community communally controls land, restricts its own membership, has its own religious system, and imposes barriers between its members and the outside world.

Peasant Economics

The peasant household head and his wife lead a two-sided existence economically. First, they are primarily subsistence cultivators. They and their family subsist primarily on the fruits of their own labor. Their limited technology and resources characteristically force them to scrape by from year to year, vulnerable to crop failure and demands from outside elites. Second, they contribute to an outside economy in the form of agricultural surpluses, or specialized products. Through markets and other networks of transactions, household products go to maintain external elites and the specialists that provide services for elites. But peasants' participation within the outside economy is limited and channeled by the social organization and pressures of the community, which guide economic decisions, as well as by limited means of production.

Case 92: Pottery Production in Amatenango

In the Guatemalan peasant community of Amatenango (Nash 1961), households engage in agricultural pursuits both for subsistence and for trade with neighboring communities. There is a lively trade for foodstuffs between communities, with each one partly specialized in its agricultural output. But Amatenango is more notable within the region for another specialized form of production: pottery making. Within an area nearly 40 miles long by 30 across, it is the only center for pottery production. People in every surrounding village must acquire and use Amatenango pottery. Thus pottery production is economically crucial to the households of Amatenango.

Practically every one of the 280 households in Amatenango makes pottery, through a combination of effort by men and women. The raw materials are freely available, the tools are minimal, and the needed skills are learned in childhood. Yet there is wide variation in the pottery output of the various households. Moreover, although pots are sold for money in markets, no household appears to produce nearly as many pots as it could. Why?

Manning Nash kept detailed records of pottery production in several households. He found that there is a seasonal rhythm in pottery making. Production reaches a peak just before a fiesta in Amatenango or a neigh-

Peasant subsistence: These Highland Mayan Indians from Zinacantan, Mexico, depend on the maize and other crops they grow themselves for daily subsistence; craft goods and other produce are sold in markets. (Courtesy of Frank Cancian.)

boring community. First, this is because that is when the household most needs cash; second, though the prices are not highest at these times, there is a convenient influx of potential buyers, so marketing is easy. Nash found also that there is a negative association between pottery production and wealth in land. The family with wealth in land can provide more of its own food, hence needs cash less; and more of its productive effort is likely to be devoted to agriculture.

But doesn't a household, like a firm, seek to maximize its gain— whether by pottery or agricultural production? And if so, why is production limited and its peaks seasonal? Because as a unit in a complex system of kinship, local grouping, and religious organization, the Amatenango household is severely constrained by leveling mechanisms. "Getting ahead" of other households is in general neither feasible nor desirable. Household economic gains would in any case be short-lived: movable wealth is quickly consumed, and wealth in land is fractionated by inheritance in each generation. The leveling devices are rather subtle. First, what wealth a family has is drained by the costs of one of the many civil and religious offices in which a man must serve during his adult life. A wealthy household is particularly subject to the financial drain of ritual office. One office, the *alferez* (for which four men are selected each year), is particularly expensive and costs a tremendous amount; a family may take years to recoup. In addition, the household that outdid its neighbors in a quest for wealth would become highly vulnerable to witchcraft or accusations of witchcraft. Thus, the performance of a pottery-producing Amatenango household in the outside market economy is controlled by a series of social forces and mechanisms within the community. Despite the economic advantages on paper, it is not to a family's long-term social advantage to maximize its income by producing as much pottery as it could.

The operation of such leveling mechanisms has been vividly documented in other highland Mayan communities. The *cargo* system of Zinacantan is the best known.

Case 93: Cargos in Zinacantan

The cargo system in Zinacantan is a hierarchy of religious offices organized around Catholic churches and saints. The system in Zinacantan consists of 61 positions in 4 levels of a ceremonial ladder.

A major life goal for a Zinacanteco man is to serve for a year at each of the four cargo levels, and hence pass through the whole ladder and become a *pasado,* or honored ritually senior man. When a man holds a cargo, he must move into the ceremonial center and engage in an expensive annual round of ceremonies. The costs of liquor, food, and ritual items such as fireworks, incense, candles, and costumes are enormous, especially for the higher levels of the ceremonial ladder.

At the lower level are 28 *mayordomos,* who serve as caretakers of particular saints or hamlet chapels; and 12 *mayores,* who are ranked, and serve as policemen, errand boys, and ceremonial functionaries. At the second level, there are 14 *alfereces,* named for particular saints and organized into two ranked orders, senior and junior. They spend much of the year giving ceremonial meals and dancing for the saints.

The third and fourth level cargoholders are collectively classed as Elders. The third level comprises four *regidores;* the fourth and highest level comprises two *alcaldes viejos.* The Elders manage the cargo system. An old man who has not been able to get through all levels of the cargo hierarchy can be appointed to a post of terminal cargo seniority. Finally, there are ritual advisers who assist cargoholders at various levels; and there are auxiliary personnel—musicians, scribes, and sacristans—who serve for periods longer than a year. These advisers and auxiliary personnel help to maintain the intricacies of ceremonial in the cargo system despite the annually shifting incumbents.

Whereas in some related Mesoamerican systems a civil hierarchy and religious hierarchy are interconnected into a single complex, with civil and religious services undertaken on an alternating basis, the Zinacantan

The cargo system in Zinacantan: The *Alcaldes Viejos* examine the lists of those waiting to assume cargos. (Courtesy of Frank Cancian.)

cargo system is not directly tied to the complicated civil officialdom (Cancian 1965).

The cost of holding one of the cargos, especially at higher levels, is so great that an individual must save for years, as well as borrow heavily and call on outstanding obligations to kin, to assemble the needed resources. After a year in a cargo, an individual characteristically retires from the limelight with savings spent, heavily in debt, and with outstanding "credit" (in the form of obligations) largely repaid. To build up once more to a position where one can ascend to a higher rung of the cargo ladder is likely to take years of hard work and support of others.

Other leveling mechanisms in Mayan and many other peasant communities are witchcraft accusations or fear of being bewitched, and malevolent gossip, dwelling endlessly upon status and its correlates as part of the deadly game of staying even (Bailey 1971).

How the surpluses or craft specialties produced by peasants enter the wider society and flow to urban elites has varied widely in different times and places. Many ruling elites have exacted grain or other products from peasants, imposing demands for quotas or shares of crops. When wealthy landlords or feudal seigneurs own the land, they have been able to exact tribute in the form of agricultural labor; the peasant is given an amount of produce sufficient for survival, while the bulk of production supports the feudal elite or landed aristocracy. More commonly in the recent period studied by anthropologists, peasant produce enters the wider society through markets.

We now have a number of good studies of peasant marketing in Central America and Mexico. In most Mesoamerican markets the producer himself seeks out the most advantageous selling conditions, rather than working through a trader as middleman. Thus the Amatenango potter and the Zinacanteco farmer or weaver (or their spouses) bring their wares to the market—a market most often controlled by Spanish-speaking *ladinos* who manipulate transactions to their advantage and the disadvantage of Indians. In many parts of the peasant world, the producers live far from the marketplace, and their wares are transported and sold by middlepersons. Thus the Tiv of Nigeria (Case 48) are likely to send their produce to urban markets via trucks operated by Tiv entrepreneurs; and the same patterns have emerged among the Chimbu and other New Guinea peoples. An interesting pattern, where women act as entrepreneurs, occurs in Haiti, in the Caribbean.

Case 94: Markets in Haiti

There are some 65,000 market traders in Haiti—about 1 person out of 50 in the total population. Fifty thousand are women; in addition, most of the peasants who buy and sell in markets are women. A woman brings her crop to the marketplace, selling some export items like coffee to licensed buyers and selling the rest to *revendeuses*, market traders (Mintz 1959).

There are large market centers in the towns, connected by bus routes to numerous, less permanent rural marketplaces. Within a rural area, alternate marketplaces operate on different days, forming a "market ring" similar to those found in West Africa and Mexico.

Revendeuses can move and manipulate goods between marketplaces so as to buy and sell according to advantageous shifts in supply and demand. Many operate within a narrow geographical range on modest capital.

But larger-scale "operators" may move goods from one region to another or from urban center to countryside. Even larger-scale "operators" may buy manufactured or other goods in the main port and wholesale them to local market traders. Such "operators" obviously need more capital and maneuver financially on a larger scale than local market traders.

Such market operations have not eliminated the interpersonal relations of alliance and obligation as encountered in the Trobriands. For Haitians try to establish a favored trade relationship they call *pratik,* whereby particular partners transact recurrent business according to price or credit concessions (Mintz 1961). Thus there is a personal, not impersonal, relationship, and a sense of mutual obligation. A *revendeuse* tries to establish *pratik* connections, as many as possible, on both ends of her trading, to render supply and sale more secure.

Transactions are based on cash currency according to fluctuating supply and demand. The Haitian system works efficiently because small quantities are traded, crops are diversified (so risks are minimized), capital is minimal, and goods are mobile. The *revendeuse* needs to make little profit, and by having stocks of commodities she can move from market to market, is able to come out ahead. (See photograph, p. 319.)

Studies of peasant marketing have been a major theme of recent economic anthropology. The papers in Yamey and Firth (1964) and Dalton (1972a) can lead interested readers into this literature.

Where peasant social organization is more complex, as with the caste systems of India and Sri Lanka (Ceylon), the flow of surpluses and of goods and services through social hierarchies is more intricate.

Case 95: The Jajmani System in Rampur

The *jajmani* system, a mode of reciprocal service and caste interdependence widespread in traditional village India, is well illustrated by its workings in the village of Rampur, near Delhi (Lewis and Barnouw 1956). In Rampur, the Jat caste dominates the scene, with its control of land and agriculture; even the local Brahmans are its subservient tenants. The remaining 10 castes include such occupational specialists as leatherworkers, sweepers, potters, washermen, and barbers.

The *jajman* is a kind of patron who provides grain, or reciprocal services, to his *kamin,* or worker, in exchange for the traditional services of his caste. The Jats, controlling the land and its output of grain, are the dominant *jajman* in Rampur; the other castes provide them services and receive grain, money, and sometimes supplies, clothing, or other benefits.

The *jajmani* relationship between a particular Jat family or group of families and a particular *kamin* is hereditary, so that such linkages were quite stable through time. The duties of a potter to his *jajman* are to supply earthenware vessels and to render certain services at weddings; in return he receives grain commensurate in value with the vessels, and additional grain when his children marry. A carpenter, in exchange for repairing agricultural tools, receives a fixed ration of grain each year; a barber, in exchange for shaving and cutting hair, can take as much grain at harvest time as he can carry. Some *jajmani* linkages between caste specialists may occur, so that a barber may give shaves and haircuts to a potter and his family and receive earthenware vessels in return. However, in Rampur, as in many other parts of India, the *jajmani* system is undergoing change and breakdown as new jobs become available in urban centers, technological changes affect the traditional division of labor, and cash becomes more centrally important (Lewis and Barnouw 1956).

Plantation labor, in colonial or postcolonial situations, may also enable impoverished peasants to augment their subsistence economy—though always to support some outside elite by hard labor for scant reward. Highland Mayan communites such as Zinacantan (Cases 83 and 90) and Chamula augment their impoverished economies by working on coffee plantations owned by wealthy *ladinos.*

In many areas of Latin America and South Asia (as in Rampur), land-owning elites still control the means of agricultural production; and peasants have nothing to contribute but their labor, in return for meager subsistence.

Development projects that have attempted to improve the economic lot of peasants, in India, Indonesia, Latin America, and many other regions, have been frustrated by the apparent conservatism, inflexibility, and suspicion of peasant communities. Foster (1967) and many others have seen the peasant stance toward life—the world view we will shortly sketch and the economic and social fragmentation—as thwarting effective social change. Foster cites the case of a UNESCO-sponsored community development program which sought to improve the economic lot of the Tarascan-speaking Indians of Tzintzuntzan in Mexico.

Case 96: CREFAL in Tzintzuntzan

The regional Center for the Development of Fundamental Education in Latin America (CREFAL) attempted to reorganize the economy of Tzintzuntzan by organizing the production of pottery, textiles, furniture, and embroidery for tourists, and introducing chicken ranching. Technicians were brought in. They persuaded potters to experiment with new kilns, created a weaving industry, established a furniture cooperative, and loaned money to begin six chicken ranching businesses. Yet within a fairly short time, these innovations had collapsed. Foster (1967) blames peasant conservatism, suspicion, and lack of motivation for the failure of the development project.

The theme of desperate frustration but inability to transform or break out of the system in which they are enmeshed runs through the anthropological literature on peasants. It is summed up vividly by May Diaz:

Peasants live in a social world in which they are economically and politically disadvantaged. They have neither sufficient capital nor power to make an impression on the urban society. But they have no illusions about their position. Indeed, often they have no notion at all of that imaginary world which offers social mobility, entrepreneurs . . . , and the possibility of economic growth, rather than a stability fluctuating on the edge of disaster. (1967:56)

The Peasant World View

The morality and value system of peasants, and their view of the world and their place in it, show vividly the pathological side of peasant life. Peasants are locked into a world that has passed them by. It has condemned them to poverty in comparison to urban elites. Their status is demeaned on all sides, and their self-conception is eroded. Pride and achievement, as well as money and the material things it buys, can easily become scarce "goods."

Foster, drawing on his work in Tzintzuntzan, sees the peasant world view as characterized by the "image of limited good." That is, the peasant sees his social, economic, and natural universe "as one in which all the desired things in life such as land, wealth, health, friendship and love, manliness and honor, respect and status, power and influence, security and safety, exist in finite quantity and are always in short supply" (Foster

1965). From this would seem to follow the emphases many have noted in peasant societies: families competing independently against one another, with each seeking to conceal its advances and to guard against loss of relative position to others; competition for friendship and love, within families and outside them; preoccupation with health and illness; and an emphasis on manliness and honor (as with Mexican *machismo*). The peasant, in this view, can become almost paranoid about the possibility that others may be getting ahead or that, by his success, others will suspect he is getting ahead—leaving him open to gossip or to more dangerous sanctions of witchcraft or violence.

The religious ceremonials and ritual offices of Latin American peasants can be seen in part as leveling devices, as in Amatenango and Zinacantan. Ritual office requires the outlay of money in exchange for a prestige that is soon dissipated. By going to the top of the religious ladder, a man slides back down the economic ladder to join his fellows. In peasant societies, the moral order is predicated on everyone trying to do everyone else in—at least beyond the close bonds of the family.

74.
Peasant Studies: Broadened Perspectives

This picture of peasants, recent critics have argued, is precisely the one an observer gets if for the purposes of study one immerses oneself in a single community and takes the wider society for granted. It sees symptoms, not causes; it sees fragments, not systems; and it sees timelessness, not long-term process. The system to which peasants are adapting, and the strategies they have devised to cope with it, are usually products of centuries of exploitation, in successive modes or phases.

A critique of peasant studies can thus well begin with a broad perspective of the forces that have created the situation of modern peasantries. André Gunder Frank, in his studies of Latin American colonialism and its consequences, provides such a sweeping view, though inevitably with some oversimplification.

Frank sees colonialism as creating constellations of economic interest, each with what he calls a "metropolis" at its center and with "satellite" economic regions or sectors; and each of these satellites may on smaller scale consist of a minor metropolis and its satellites. Thus, in Latin America, a major Spanish center such as La Paz or Santiago was a metropolis in relation to its satellite mining regions and latifundia (quasi-feudal agricultural estates). But a mining center would itself be a "micrometropolis" in relation to the agricultural developments that grew up in the surrounding countryside. What is a metropolis at one level is thus a satellite of some larger metropolis. Far-off European centers in Spain and Portugal were the central metropolises in the early history of South America, but the rise of British power shifted Spain and Portugal into satellite positions (see Frank 1969:15—17).

Frank's thesis is that underdevelopment, and hence the plight of peasants, is not basically a consequence of traditional societies in which some sectors have become urbanized and partly modernized and rural sectors have been left behind. Rather, he argues that underdevelopment in Latin America—and by extension, parts of Africa and Asia—has been systematically *created* by colonialist exploitation.

The regions of Latin America which are today the most backward—parts of Central America and the Caribbean, the Northeast of Brazil, the areas in the Andes and in Mexico where the indigenous population predominates, and the mining zones of Brazil, Bolivia, and Central Mexico—have in common the fact that in the early period (and, in many cases, in the present as well), they were the areas where the exploitation of natural, and to an even greater extent human, resources was most extreme. . . . The degree and type of dependence on the metropolis of the world capitalist system is the key factor in the economic and class structure of Latin America. (Frank 1973:21—22)

Frank has documented "the development of underdevelopment" in Chile, Brazil, Mexico, and Cuba in telling detail (1969, 1973). His studies show how the constant drain of wealth from the areas of Latin America most productive in the colonial and postcolonial periods has produced incredible poverty and has not only hampered but systematically destroyed indigenous economic development. He also shows how the emergence of a Latin American landowning bourgeoisie was shaped by European interests. What was demanded of Mesoamerican or Andean Indians, how landowning interests operated, and whether exploitation took the form of mining or the production of sugar, coffee, bananas, or other commodities depended on the fluctuations of world capitalism.

Because of commerce and foreign capital, the economic and political interests of the mining, agricultural, and commercial bourgeoisie were never directed toward internal economic development. The relations of production and the class structure of the latifundia and of mining and its economic and social "hinterlands" developed in response to the predatory needs of the overseas and the Latin American metropolis. They were not the result of the transfer, in the sixteenth century, of Iberian feudal institutions to the New World, as is so often and so erroneously alleged. (Frank 1973:23)

What happened in the colony was determined by its ties with the metropolis and by the intrinsic nature of the capitalist system. It was not isolation but integration which created the reality of Brazilian underdevelopment. The life of the interior was determined through a whole chain of metropolises and satellites which extended from England via Portugal and Salvador de Bahia or Rio de Janeiro to the farthest outpost of this interior. (Frank 1969:166)

Frank quotes old sources that show clearly how shifts in trade or European politics and economics, and events around the colonial world, affected the systems of exploitation and domination in various parts of Latin America. Thus is 1794, the viceroy of New Spain wrote warning the king about the growth of local manufacture in Mexico that had arisen initially during an economic depression in Spain:

With no help of any kind . . . they have progressed enormously; to such a degree that one is amazed by certain types of manufactures, principally cottons and cloth for rebozos. . . . In these domains it is very difficult to prohibit the manufacture of those things which are made here. . . . The only way to destroy such local manufactures would be to send the same or similar products from Europe, to be sold at lower prices. This is what has happened to the great factory and guild which existed for all sorts of silk textiles, now barely remembered. (Frank 1973:24)

From Mexico, Frank quotes contemporary assessments of the Mexican peasantry under General Diaz, a period which saw "the systematic organization of a capitalist regime."

In a short time, a large number of latifundia were established, and the popular *caudillos* [military leaders] of the Diaz revolution, along with a large number of foreigners, formed a landed aristocracy. At the same time, the Church quickly recovered its former power by purchasing haciendas through intermediaries or inheriting them from the dying, who were terrified by visions of hell's fires. . . . Daily, the consequences of this policy became more evident. Larger harvests were gathered every year, land values rose and labor costs fell steadily, and the wretchedness of the poor deepened as the wealth of the landowners increased. Thus, capitalist organization proved to be the most effective method of increasing the enslavement and poverty of the people and aggravating the inequalities between the poor and the rich. (Gonzalez Roa and Jose Covarrubias, quoted in Frank 1973:39)

Neocolonialism and underdevelopment in Brazil: Urban affluence in São Paulo, exploited workers, and hinterland poor peasants are part of a vast system sustained by massive foreign investment. (Courtesy of Brazilian Government Trade Bureau.)

Frank argues compellingly that "independence" in Latin America accompanied the decline of Spanish and Portuguese power and the increasing power and wealth of the New World creole bourgeoisie who controlled mines and lands but not politics. The liberal philosophy of the eighteenth century, which in Europe had advanced the interests of the industrial bourgeoise, was adopted in Latin America to advance the interests of the landholders and mine owners. The political ascendancy of a landed aristocracy in Latin America, drawing its wealth from export, systematically generated the underdevelopment of rural peasantry and established the structure of class exploitation and internal colonialism that continues into the 1970s. The Western industrial powers, in the twentieth-century system of neocolonialism that has brought large mining companies to Chile, fruit companies to Mesoamerica, multinational oil companies to Venezuela and staggering foreign investment to Brazil, have reinforced these old structures of inequality and exploitation and have further polarized the class interests of rich and poor.

Frank shows that it has mainly been those regions of the Americas which did not provide the incentive for plantations, mines, or other modes of economic exploitation (because of poor climate, sparse resources, low population, or marginality) that have become most prosperous and developed in the twentieth century. He shows how historically areas such as Cuba, Barbados, and parts of Colombia were prosperous and rapidly developing economically until shifts in capitalist investment and trade brought plantation economies and the destruction of local prosperity.

The same colonialist development of underdevelopment has produced similar class polarization and desperate poverty among exploited peasants in Southeast Asia. Thus we find in Indonesia, Sri Lanka (Ceylon), Malaysia, the Philippines, and other areas the same polarization, the same poverty. The continuous stream of modernization and development in Japan, and its present wealth and prosperity in contrast to its neighbors to the southwest, further supports Frank's interpretation: whereas in most of South and Southeast Asia wealth was drained off for several centuries, Japan remained free of colonial domination and developed on an impressive upward course. The contrast with colonially exploited Indonesia, especially Java—where Dutch investment was greatest—is stark. The disastrous course of what Geertz (1963) calls "agricultural involution" in Indonesia, where more and more people have squeezed out a decreasingly adequate subsistence with decreasing efficiency, was the product of a colonialism that poured profits back to the metropolis.

The mechanisms of nineteenth-century population increase in Java remain little understood despite Geertz's exploration.

Similar explosions of peasant population occurred in other parts of the world in roughly the same period. Wolf's comparative study of twentieth-century peasant wars suggests that population pressures contributed to the deterioration of peasant life and hence to the inflammability of the social systems.

Mexico had a population of 5.8 million at the beginning of the nineteenth century; in 1910—at the outbreak of the revolution—it had 16.5 million. European Russia had a population of 20 million in 1725; at the turn of the twentieth century it had 87 million. China numbered 275 million in 1775, 430 million in 1850 and close to 600 million at the time of the revolution. Vietnam is estimated to have sustained a population of between 6 and 14 million in 1820; it had 30.5 million inhabitants in 1962. Algeria had an indigenous population of 10.5 million in 1963, representing a fourfold increase since the beginnings of French occupation in the first part of the nineteenth century. Cuba had 550,000 inhabitants in 1800; by 1953 it had 5.8 million. (Wolf 1969b:367—368)

Drastic rises in population, and in many areas continuing expropriation of peasant lands by landowning classes, have aggravated conditions of peasant life in many parts of the world—and have contributed to the capitalist conversion of subsistence farmers into cheap laborers.

What has all this to do with peasant studies in anthropology?

First, the peasant community is part of a regional system—usually, in Frank's terms, as a kind of microsatellite within a constellation of such satellites, economically and politically tied to a micrometropolis; and it is at the end of a chain of colonial relationships (if, following Frank and others, we see colonialism as an internal as well as external relationship). In many regions of the Andes and parts of Mesoamerica, peasants continue to live within a modern version of the old quasi-feudal latifundia, exchanging their labor on hacienda or plantation for meager means of subsistence.

Agricultural involution in Java: The development of underdevelopment through colonial exploitation. The population explosion in colonial Java and the draining off of wealth by the Dutch has left Javanese peasants on a treadmill where more and more people must be fed with less and less efficiency and possibility for economic growth. (Courtesy of Masri Singarimbun.)

In other areas such as Mexico, land reform programs have outwardly given peasants their own land, but in many regions, this process has resulted in most of the best land passing into the hands of *mestizo* landowning classes. The self-sufficiency of the peasant is always an illusion; the seeming closure of the peasant community is a defense but not a reality.

Frank's perspective would lead us not simply to look at a peasant community— Zinacantan, Chamula, Mitla, Tepotzlán, Tzintzuntzan, Amatenango, Panajachel—as an isolate; we would be led to look at the region-al structure of ethnic and economic relations that shapes peasants' lives. The Mexican sociologist Rodolfo Stavenhagen has taken such a view of the highland Mayan Indians of southern Mexico and Guatemala, a view that contrasts sharply with studies by American anthropologists of the cultures of Zinacantan, Chamula, Tenejapa, and other Mayan communities. Stavenhagen views the internal colonialism of *ladinos* vis-à-vis Mayan Indians as constituting a regional system of racism and exploitation, with (in highland Mexico) San Cristobal las Casas as its micrometropolis. (San Cristobal is itself a mountain satellite, maintained substantially for exploitation of the surrounding Indian communities, in relation to the prosperous valley city of Tuxtla Gutierrez, a center of coffee production and regional industry and commerce.)

Stavenhagen shows vividly how the structure of *ladino* domination and exploitation embraces the social and economic life of the Indian communities in the mountains around San Cristobal so much studied by anthropologists.

The well known bargaining of Indian markets is an instrument used by Ladinos in order to depress price levels of Indian products. In San Cristobal . . . the Ladino women who place themselves at the city entrance on market days . . . almost violently force the submissive, incoming Indians to sell their wares at prices that they impose and which are lower than those which prevail at the market.

These various forms of exploitation which victimize the Indian trader, both as seller and buyer, are due to economic and political dominance of the urban Ladinos. This power is reinforced by the cultural superiority as expressed by their knowledge of price-building mechanisms, of the laws of the country; above all, of the Spanish language, which . . . represents one more factor of inferiority and social oppression. . . . Under these conditions, the Indian has no access to national legal institutions which protect his individual rights. (Stavenhagen 1975:254)

Although at first sight compadrazgo [see Case 91] may appear to be an institution in which Indians and Ladinos face each other on a level of equality, in fact it contributes to accentuate the Indians' condition of inferiority and dependence. Compadrazgo is one among many institutions in a complex system which keeps the Indian subordinated to the Ladino in all aspects of social and economic life. (Stavenhagen 1975:255)

Mayan-speaking Indians in the San Cristobal market. (Photographs by the author.)

[The cargo system in such communities as Zinacantan prevents] economic pre-eminence of those individuals who for some reason have been able to accumulate a greater amount of goods than their peers. This wealth is not reabsorbed by the community, it is consumed in liquor, ceremonial clothing, firecrackers and fireworks, and in hundreds of articles employed in . . . "institutionalized waste." These expenses required by the ceremonial economy associated with the functioning of the political and religious organizations are transformed into income for those who provide these articles for the community. These purveyors are urbanized Ladinos. . . . We may thus conclude that the structure which maintains equality within the Indian community, preventing the emergence of social classes, also contributes to the whole Indian community's dependence on the city, that is, to the differentiation of social classes between Indians and Ladinos. (Stavenhagen 1975:259)

Stavenhagen argues that the very old relationship of internal colonialism between *ladinos* and Indians, whereby Indians maintained relatively closed communities and cultural integrity at a cost of subordination, exploitation, and racism, is being transformed by the emergence of a class system due to the capitalist development of the region. Having lost much of their best land to *ladinos* in the process of "land reform," and being threatened by overpopulation and ecological destruction, with erosion of their subsistence base, Indians are increasingly locked into exploitative wage labor on coffee plantations and in other *ladino* enterprises. And as they increasingly become plantation laborers, the older system of ethnic domination is being transformed to a class relationship between capitalist and worker (Stavenhagen 1975).

While we have undoubtedly learned a great deal from studies of the Mayan Indian communities as if they were cultural isolates, these studies have also given a one-sided and often distorted picture of the peasant condition.

Recent insights into the highland Maya cargo systems further underline the limitations of the usual anthropological perspective. First, it is becoming clear that though the cargo systems do force the prosperous peasant to redistribute much of his wealth, they do not always cycle him back to the lower levels of the economic ladder. In highland Maya communities, as in peasant communities more generally, there very often is considerable economic inequality between families; and a ceremonial system that is costly but prestigious can be an instrument through which prosperity buys longer-range power, not simply a year's prominence. Anthropologists have often underestimated the economic inequalities in peasant communities (partly because family budgets are so often well hidden). A second insight into the cargo system has come with the discovery of historical documents that reveal how the cults of saints were specifically created by the Spanish conquerors according to a detailed plan, as one instrument for the subjugation and Christianization of the Indians. It remains true that the Indians turned the cults into their own distinctive cultural design. Yet the tendency to see the cargo systems, and Mayan religious syncretism generally, in cultural rather than historical terms further suggests the cost of bringing to peasant communities the theoretical orientations derived from studying tribal communities.

Frank's sweeping perspective highlights most anthropologists' relative innocence of historical vision. Close immersion in the life of a tribal or peasant community for a year or two has often given a limited view in time as well as in space. Anthropological sterotypes of the conservatism, docility, and fatalism of the peasant bear closer inspection from this point of view.

First, peasant hostility and suspicion to outsiders—whether indigenous urban landowner or anthropologist or Peace Corps volunteer or CREFAL technician—is historically well founded and realistic. Centuries of lies, oppression, and forced servitude hardly make either trust of outsiders or the optimism of Protestant ethic entrepreneurship a realistic stance. (See Harris 1971:475—487; Huizer:1970). Also, the progressive transformation of the modes and structures of exploitation over many decades and centuries has seldom improved the peasant's lot: for him to be optimistic that well-intentioned programs for education or economic development will markedly improve his condition would hardly be realistic—or wise. Peasants know, in most cases better than anthropologists, that only deep social revolution which transforms the class relationship between exploiter and exploited and breaks the system of internal colonialism will substantially change their lives.

And this leads to a second major inadequacy of the "peasant fatalism" view, emphasizing as it does passive resignation, destructive internal conflict, and ignorance of the wider world. Peasants have risen, time and time again, to try to break the bonds of oppression and the chains that tie them in colonial servitude and poverty.

Case 97: Peasant Resistance in Michoacan

In the Mexican state of Michoacan, Tarascan peasants—whose forefathers had resisted Toltec and Aztec domination—rose in the 1920s against oppression by wealthy landowners and their allies in the church. The Michoacan Socialist Party, some of whose members came from Tzintzuntzan and surrounding communities, demanded land redistribution—and the leaders were liquidated by government forces in 1921. Tarascan peasant villagers, led by Primo Tapia of Naranja (Huizer 1970; Friedrich 1965; Mugica, 1946), continued to press their claims for land reform.

In 1923 many peasants from the Liga of Michoacan participated in the I Congreso Nacional Agrarista in Mexico City. Primo Tapia brought with him a proposal for a new agrarian law . . . to give . . . workers living on haciendas full rights to petition for land. Another issue was that large units for the cultivation of sisal, cotton, sugar, henequen, or rice would not be left untouched but given as a whole to the peasants. . . . One of the major manifestations of the Liga was a demonstration of 8000 peasants at the railway station of Patzcuaro [only a few miles from Tzintzuntzan] when the presidential train passed. (Huizer 1970:453)

Primo Tapia succeeded in forcing some land redistribution. But in 1926 he was shot by the army.

Foster has commented on the wide gulf between the conservative and passive people of Tzintzuntzan (they of the "limited good") and the historically activist peasants of some Tarascan communities, notably Naranja, near Primo Tapia's home village where land redistribution was successfully pressed. But Huizer (1970), citing evidence from Van Zantwijk (1967), suggests that the passivity and conservatism of the Tzintzuntzenos had not prevented their struggling against oppression in the 1920s; rather, he suggests that peasant resistance has been broken under pressure by the Church and wealthy landowners: "The communities where the image of the limited good prevails suffered severe physical and spiritual repression from a combination of the landed elite and the religious authorities" (Huizer 1970:304). Conservatism in the face of oppression becomes a survival strategy: "Traditionalism is . . . related to the over-all social structure of the country as a form of protection against the dangers of pauperization."

Similar peasant struggles against oppression have occurred in many parts of the world (see, for example, Wolf 1969a). In Mesoamerica, the Mayan Indians of the highlands rose against their oppressors, in the nineteenth century in messianic form, but earlier with guerilla resistance. The lowland Mayans of Yucatan were in revolt and virtual secession through much of the nineteenth century before they were subdued into a system of exploitation in the production of henequen fiber for rope (Reed 1965).

In Indonesia, some 200,000 Javanese died in an unsuccessful struggle for liberation from Dutch rule between 1825 and 1830. The Philippine revolution of 1896 to 1898 was in part, as earlier in South America, a struggle by a local landed aristocracy created by colonialism for independence from a weakened colonial power, Spain. But it was also, in rural areas, a peasant revolt. The Philippine revolution succeeded in wresting power from Spain, only to fall victim to a burst of imperialist pressure from the United States (Pomeroy 1970). In a bloody war with many parallels to the war in Vietnam, Philippine independence was crushed by the U.S. Army at a cost of some 500,000 lives (Pomeroy 1970:96); and the Philippines became an American colony. Peasant revolutionary movements have, of course, been a major theme of the twentieth century (Wolf 1969a). In the hinterlands of Guatemala, Nicaragua, Colombia, Uruguay, Argentina, Boliva, Brazil, and across the world in Malaysia, the Phil-

ippines, and other regions, peasants press for social revolutions that will give them land, power, and freedom from oppression by the wealthy landowning classes created by colonialism and supported by the Western powers and foreign corporations.

The relatively circumscribed and partial view peasants have of their society exacts a cost when they rise to change their lot. Peasant rebellions, despite images of masses armed with pitchforks, seldom have turned into successful revolutions without a vanguard of leadership from urban centers. As Wolf observes:

Where the peasantry has successfully rebelled against the established order—under its own banner and with its own leaders—it was sometimes able to reshape the social structures of the countryside . . .; but it did not lay hold of the State, of the cities which house the centers of control, of the strategic non-agricultural resources of the society. . . . Thus a peasant rebellion which takes place in a complex society already caught up in commercialization and industrialization tends to be self-limiting, and hence anachronistic. [See Debray 1967 for an argument of the vulnerability of peasant rebellions to outside repression.] The peasant Utopia is the free village, untrammeled by tax collectors, labour recruiters, large landowners, officials. Ruled over, but never ruling, peasants also lack any acquaintance with the operation of the State as a complex machinery. . . . Peasants in rebellion are natural anarchists. (Wolf 1969b: 371—372).

Wolf argues, on the basis of comparative study of the revolutions in Mexico, Russia, China, Vietnam, Algeria, and Cuba where peasants played a central part, that those peasants likely to rise successfully are not the poorest and landless; rather, they are the middle peasants who have sufficient control or leverage over their own resources to rise in challenge to their overlords. Wolf's study also points to another peasant condition likely to breed or catalyze rebellion: relative marginality, and hence relative freedom from outside control, and relative mobility. Wolf points to the participation of a "tactically mobile peasantry" (particularly a peasantry ethnically distinct from more centrally located groups, and with mountain fastnesses to retreat to) in twentieth century wars of revolution (Wolf 1969a, b).

The "conservatism" of peasants in being unreceptive to development projects proffered by Peace Corps volunteers or other well-intentioned representatives of the West is scarcely surprising. First, peasants have no reason to trust outsiders who command wealth and power. Even if the aid projects are well conceived and sensitive to · cultural nuances (as they most often have not been), they promise piecemeal and gradual improvement. Such piecemeal aid promised by economic development specialists to improve peasant standards of living aims at alleviating symptoms rather than curing causes. Its usual goals, implicit or explicit, have been to decrease peasant unrest by alleviating peasant poverty—and thereby, to reinforce the oppressive structure of landowning elites and foreign investment that keeps peasants in bondage. Small wonder that peasants do not embrace such projects as paths to salvation. Of the abortive CREFAL project in Tzintzuntzan, Huizer (1970:305) points to this contradiction: "We can . . . ask how the peasants living under these circumstances would have reacted if the visitors from the development agencies had come to help them fight against the repressive system instead of to offer minor improvement schemes which would actually emphasize rather than relieve the state of frustration in which the peasants live."

The kind of broadened perspective toward which Frank's view pushes us illuminates peasant communities in Europe as well as in the Third World. Anthropologists have in recent years begun to pay increasing attention

to peasants in Greece, Spain, Italy, France, Austria, and other European countries, and around the southern and eastern rim of the Mediterranean. From some of these studies, especially in the last few years, have come perspectives that begin to transcend the limitations of older peasant studies.

We will illustrate from some recent studies of peasants in Spain. The older view of peasant societies focused on a particular community, and, taking it as the center of the analytical universe, traced out networks of connection to the wider society. Yet as Frank's interpretation should lead us to expect, regional *clusters* of peasant communities, tied politically and economically to a particular micrometropolis, turn out to have a complex organization, cultural commonality, and economic interrelationship older studies had mainly missed. Thus, in the Andalusian province of Huelva, Aguilera (1972) found a "multicommunity" of 17 peasant communities, linked together by a common cultural pattern, economic interrelationship, and ritual.

Studies of peasant communities within the wider context of a modernizing nation point toward a broadened view of peasant economies and a broadened view of development. The modernization and increased affluence of a country like Spain does not necessarily push peasants along toward greater prosperity. Industrialization, agribusiness, tourism, and inflation can place a marginal peasant community in a desperate situation where their traditional sources of income, in the form of agricultural or craft produce, yield a sharply decreasing return in buying power.

Modernization under such circumstances characteristically pulls peasant communities toward increasing openness and secularization. A common pattern is out-migration of large segments of the population to the cities as wage laborers in industry. (Enormous numbers of southern Europeans and other

Mediterranean peoples are working in the factories of West Germany, so this migration may extend beyond the metropolis of one's own country.) Such opening outward and proletarianization of a peasantry has been described, for Spain, by Aceves (1971), Barrett (1974), Brandes (1972), and Schneider et al. (1972). But at the same time, these authors make it abundantly clear that modernization need not lead to the abandonment or destruction of "traditional" institutions. Peasants in Spain and elsewhere adapt traditional values and cultural patterns to new agricultural opportunities and economic strategies. As Tipps (1973:214) has pointed out,

"modernization can no longer be equated simply with the destruction of tradition, for the latter is not a prerequisite of modernization— since in many instances 'traditional' institutions and values may facilitate rather than impede the social changes usually associated with modernization."

In Almonaster la Real, the Spanish community studied by Aguilera (1972), a poor ecological setting afforded no attractive opportunities to marked modernization. With grains, the traditional cash crop, at a marked disadvantage in the Spanish national economy due to agribusiness, the people of Almonaster had two main choices: either to concen-

In Almonaster La Real, Spain, girls, dressed in traditional costumes, marching in a ritual parade, *romeria,* during the important folk/Catholic rituals of the 3d day of May (Day of the Cross). (Courtesy of Francisco E. Aguilera.)

trate on several alternative sources of cash (pulpwood, pigs, and tourism) so as to raise their economic standard in line with modernization elsewhere in Spain—but at a sacrifice of drastic out-migration and reduced community life; or on the other hand, to accept a markedly limited standard of living by concentrating on subsistence production and lesser cash production—and be able to keep the community and its traditional integration and ritual life relatively intact. For the moment, the people of Almonaster have opted mainly for community integrity rather than marked modernization (Aguilera 1972).

Such views of European peasant communities, seeing them within a wider economic, demographic, and political system rather than as closed cultural entities, are leading us well beyond the limited and static view of the peasant condition that dominated the earlier literature on peasants. The classic picture of peasants as beset by suspicion and an obstructionist conservatism is, in the process, being balanced by the realization that the poor and powerless, in adapting to their often dismal alternatives, are very often following strategies and making realistic and skillful choices (see Johnson 1971).

CIVILIZATIONS AND CITIES

23

Can anthropologists illuminate civilizations as well as communities? Can they shed light on the human condition in a city as well as in a village? These challenges confront anthropologists as they work in emerging Third World nations, in countries such as India, Indonesia, or Japan with ancient and complex cultural traditions, and in urban neighborhoods in Chicago or Rio de Janeiro.

In §75, we will look briefly at the challenge to anthropologists represented by the interplay of local cultural traditions with the traditions of a civilization. In §76, we will turn to the burgeoning anthropological concern with people in cities.

75.
Great and Little Traditions

Can anthropology illuminate complex national cultures and the cultural and religious traditions of the great civilizations? Has the anthro-

pologist some special insights beyond—or between—those of historians, sociologists, or political scientists? Can the anthropologist see both the forest and the local trees?

Anthropology, if it is to be genuinely comparative and not culture-bound in reverse, cannot simply stop when social systems get too complicated. Moreover, the anthropologist's sensitivity toward cultural patterns and the close and human perspective he or she gets from living in and studying local communities often make generalizations about complex states by colleagues in other disciplines seem inadequate.

But can anthropologists do better? The attempts are interesting, but so far have been fraught with difficulty. A leading pioneer here was Robert Redfield, who went from a simple contrast between "folk" and "urban" to more sophisticated conceptions of the variety and workings of complex states. This development can be traced in a posthumous collection of Redfield's papers (M. P. Redfield 1962). Thus Redfield came to distinguish, for example, between "primary civilizations" and "secondary civilizations." The former have developed from an indigenous folk tradition, as in India, China, Mesopotamia, and Egypt; the latter result from the superimposition of an outside civilized tradition on indigenous ones.

But apart from such vast-scale classifica-tions and developmental sequences, anthro-pologists are far from being able to concep-tualize the complex ongoing process and cultural richness of modern states.

Religious beliefs and rites in village India illustrate the interplay between "great" and "little" traditions that makes studies of total societies particularly difficult. Here, religion in an Indian village in Uttar Pradesh will usefully illustrate.

Case 98: Religion in Kishan Garhi

The village of Kishan Garhi is ancient and centrally located in the area of primary and early Aryan influence. Hence the influence of Sanskritic religion and the Hindu Great Tradition could be expected to be old and deep. It is. But that does not mean that religion in Kishan Garhi is simply an enactment of the rites, and a building on the beliefs, of the Great Tradition.

Fifteen of 19 religious festivals in Kishan Garhi are sanctioned in universal Sanskrit texts; 8 of them were probably universally observed in traditional India, and many others have wide regional distribution. But 4 festivals in Kishan Garhi have no Sanskritic rationales. Many of the festivals widespread in India are not represented. Moreover, there are considerable diversity and disagreement about the connections to the Great Tradition of many of the rites in Kishan Garhi, and there are many elements of ritual procedure within Sanskrit-based festivals that have no apparent connection to the ancient epics that provide their rationale. If the combination of old and "new" (that is, ancient Sanskritic) elements gives an index of how far the rise of a Great Tradition has transformed religion in this village setting, then "we must conclude that spread and Sanskriti-zation in Kishan Garhi have scarcely begun, despite their having contin-ued there for some 3000 years" (Marriott 1955a:196).

By what processes does a great tradition develop from and diffuse into little traditions? Marriott sees both an upward and a downward spread of cultural patterns. Through universalization, local customs and patterns are incorporated into a developing religious literature and hence are spread through the Great Tradition to much wider areas, where they may com-pete with and restructure existing patterns. Through parochialization, the religious patterns that are elaborated by a sophisticated and educated priestly elite are filtered down to local levels. In both directions, upward and downward, these religious elements are transformed.

> Seen through its festivals and deities, the religion of the village of Kishan Garhi
> may be conceived as resulting from continuous processes of communication
> between a little, local tradition and greater traditions which have their places
> partly inside and partly outside the village. . . . A focus upon the small half-world
> of the village and a perspective upon the universe of Indian Civilization thus
> remain mutually indispensable for whole understanding, whether of Hinduism or
> of the traditional forms of India's social structure (Marriott 1955a).

As we noted in §59, the student of Indian society also faces on a village level a tremendous range of variation in caste organization and its relationship to the caste ideology of the Great Tradition. As Marriott (1955a) puts it, "The intricacies of the Hindu system of caste ranking cannot be imagined as existing in any but small packages"; but from such small, diverse, yet mutually relevant packages, how can one depict that vast and complicated bundle that is India?

This split vision of the whole and its parts is what gives the anthropologist a great advantage in understanding a complex civilization; but it gives headaches as well, as one finds oneself increasingly unable to describe the wider view without distorting the smaller.

As the anthropologist begins to develop models to relate traditional local communities to great traditions, he or she faces the further conceptual problems of dealing with rapid and vast-scale social change. A picture of modern India must deal with the intricacies of national and regional politics, with the workings of caste in urban settings as well as villages, with nuclear power plants as well as ancient modes of agriculture.

Anthropologists in India and other complex societies have increasingly found participant observation and fieldwork in depth only partially adequate research methods. The broader sweep of sociological survey techniques, as modified to fit non-Western settings, has proved necessary as well. Moreover, in extending vision above a village level or directing it into urban settings, the anthropologist finds that it is not enough to look at what people do within organized groups. Any given individual—say, a market trader—lives in a world on which many different individuals impinge: his family and kin, of course, but now more often as individuals than as members of his group; also his trading associates, sources of financial assistance, suppliers, buyers, and so on. He moves in a wider range of settings than did a tribesman, and he deals individually with different kinds of people in each of them. As we will shortly see, to describe such patterns of social life, anthropologists have increasingly explored models of networks linking individuals, or clusters of people who temporarily join in collective action. Such studies reveal pattern and process in small parts of large systems. If they give no clear total view of these wider systems, they help to balance and correct older ways of looking at societies as stable arrangements of groups.

Hence the frustrations and rewards of studying complex civilizations anthropologically. The description of India, China, or Japan by a political scientist or historian often seems starkly oversimplified to the anthropologist who knows life there from the ground up—from living with real people in local communities, rural or urban. It is clear that the anthropologist, in trying to do better, can breathe life into generalizations and can show how relations between kinsmen, friends, or patron and client go on in between the "cracks" of the formal social and political structure (Wolf 1966b). It is also clear that, in the attempt, he or she can help to create better ways of viewing social process that colleagues will be wise to try out in jungle or desert as well. But whether one can reconstitute from this knowledge of the parts, of people and processes, a clearer picture of the whole—of how a society works and how its culture is distinctive—remains in doubt.

Such studies of complex societies have increasingly led anthropologists not only to look outward from a village or small town at the national economy, political system, and religion that impinge on it but to go into the cities—where the power is, where the action is, and to which villagers are increasingly drawn.

76.
Anthropological Study of Cities

Anthropologists, with their inclination to study small and isolated societies, were rather slow to tackle complex civilizations in the center—in cities—as well as on the margins, in peasant villages. But in recent years anthropologists have gone to town, making the most of necessity. In Africa, Asia, Latin America and, on small scales, in the Pacific, peasant and tribal villagers have flocked to urban centers and surrounding slums. Cities are where the action is, in the Third World and in industrial states. An anthropology that aspires to study universals, to see the human condition in the widest possible perspective, cannot study only hamlets and villages. An urban anthropology has emerged, taking anthropological researchers not only to Third World cities, but also to the neighborhoods next to universities.

But to see urban anthropology as a single subfield or specialization is misleading. Some urban anthropologists are predominantly interested in cities—in how and why urban centers have developed in different times and places, in how variable cities are, in how cities create new modes of human experience. In

short, for many, cities are *subjects for study*. But to many other urban anthropologists, cities represent not subjects but *settings*: one studies a neighborhood, a housing project, a street corner, as before one had studied a village or a band—as a microcosm, a social world in miniature.

Comparative studies of cities have raised important questions. How much like the cities of the United States or Europe are the cities of Latin America or Africa? Do urban bureaucracies or urban poverty lead to similar patterns in different countries? To what extent do the cities of Japan or India remain distinctively Asian? Do colonial and postcolonial Third World cities contrast with cities that have grown up free of colonial domination? Are rural-urban ties still close?

Comparison of urban experience in Third World settings also throws in question the generalizations sociologists have long made on the basis of studies in Western cities—for example, do kinship ties shrink in range and importance? Do nuclear families become predominant? Cast in the crucible of cross-cultural doubt are other widespread assumptions about the stresses of urban life—such as the supposed effects of crowding on aggression and frustration. Thus Anderson (1972) argues, of urban Chinese in Hong Kong, that due to cultural ways of dealing with crowding, the supposed pathological effects are minimized. An anthropology that studies urban life in comparative perspective can perhaps fulfill in this new realm the historic role of anthropology in the social sciences: sorting the culture-bound from the universal, and hence pushing toward a genuinely comparative understanding of human ways.

How similar have cities been in different times and places? How similar are Bangkok and Bombay? And how similar to Baltimore? How similar to Babylon?

Gideon Sjoberg has made a noteworthy attempt to pull together the evidence on "preindustrial cities," particularly the cities of antiquity. He arrives at an idealized model of the pre-industrial city to which actual cities were an approximation—a kind of composite standard. The ancient city was characteristically the center of government and religion; it housed elites; and it was only secondarily the center of commerce. Ethnic groups tended to form separate enclaves, within which extended family households were strong. Commerce tended to be in the hands of low and outcaste classes; and men, especially elders, of an hereditary elite held political and religious power. Religious ideology and education tended to perpetuate the elite, hence to be conservative forces (Sjoberg 1960).

But as Southall (1973a) and others have pointed out, such an idealized composite hides many of the most interesting variations. Southall cites a number of cases, such as Early Dynastic Sumeria, Aztec Mexico, Damascus, Carthage, and medieval and Renaissance Europe, where merchants were rich and powerful, not polluted or peripheral. For most of the characteristics of Sjoberg's ideal composite, one can find exceptions. And where this is not the case (for example, where such characteristics as male dominance or the conservatism and elite-reinforcing functions of education seem to have held true in all preindustrial cities), they hold equally true in tribal societies or rural communities; hence they in no way define the uniqueness of city life.

Technology and industrialization have progressively transformed cities everywhere, creating the possibility of larger populations, more extensive political control, new modes of production, and new class relationships. But is the industrialized city as much of an idealized composite as the preindustrial city as sketched by Sjoberg?

Looking at the great cities of Latin America, Asia, or Africa, one sees sharp contrasts with Western industrial cities in the shattering poverty and squalor, and in squatter settlements, as well as similarities in scale and the complexity and fragmentation of social relations. Most of the great Third World cities have in varying degrees been created by colonialism, old and new—São Paulo, La Paz, Santiago, Singapore, Bombay, Hong Kong, Manila. It is thus not surprising that the class systems, economic patterns, and relations to the hinterlands of these Third World cities are in some ways similar: tied as satellites to Europe and serving as colonial metropolises in relation to satellites in the hinterlands (to use Frank's terms), they have undergone parallel development. Nor is it surprising that these colonial metropolises differ from London, New York, or Paris in having squatter settlements, in drawing poor wage labor from rural areas, and so on; they evolved to serve the interests of the metropolitan states, under their economic domination.

Striking evidence on the variation in urban patterns comes from those few cases where non-Western countries had precolonial cities and particularly where the path to industrialization was followed substantially free of European domination.

Case 99: Urbanization in Japan

In Japan, the first capital city of Heijoku (Nara) was built on a Chinese model at the beginning of the eighth century; and the subsequent feudal and then industrial cities have evolved in ways distinctively Japanese. After the Meiji Restoration of 1868, Japan industrialized with amazing rapidity—so that by the Russo-Japanese War (1904) Japan had a powerful

Western-style war machine and the industrial might to support it. The rise of giant industrial firms and banks, which dominated politics as well as economics, helped to shape the great expansion of such cities as Tokyo and Osaka. By 1920, Tokyo had a population of almost two million. The distinctiveness of Japan's cities and urban life has been reconstructed by Yazaki (1963, 1968, 1973), Smith (1973), and others—drawing for recent centuries on detailed census records. Smith notes that preindustrial eighteenth-century Japanese cities had small individual families, not larger extended families, as crucial constituent units; and these household groups were highly mobile. He argues that rather than nuclear families becoming separate and mobile due to urban industrialization, as urbanization theorists would have it, in the Japanese sequence household independence and mobility apparently preceded industrialization. He suggests that this pattern may have contributed to the remarkably rapid and effective adaptation of Japanese society to industrialization. Smith also suggests that the pattern whereby single heirs inherited control over household property contributed to the emergence of family business firms, some of which grew into the great *zaibatsu* family corporations of industrial Japan. (Bellah (1957) and others have suggested that other aspects of Tokugawa-period Japanese culture provided "preadaptations" to industrialization.)

That Japanese urban society is still distinctively Japanese culturally is reinforced by Thomas Rohlen's study of a Tokyo banking firm. Rohlen found the bank, in its quasi-familial bureaucratic structure and many other respects, to be a kind of microcosm of Japanese culture. Bank trainees, for example, underwent a kind of *zen* job orientation whereby the appropriate humility, respect, and loyalty were instilled (Rohlen 1974; see also Nakane 1970).

Other perspectives on what is distinctive about non-colonial Third World cities—and hence, on what is unique to Western urban experience—have come from such settings as Addis Ababa in Ethiopia (see Shack 1973), the Yoruba cities of West Africa (Lloyd 1973), and the old precolonial cities of India (Rowe 1973). These old Indian cities, like ancient Greek or Mayan ones, represent a model of the cosmos. "All the Indian royal cities . . . are built after the mythical model of the celestial city where, in the age of gold, the universal Sovereign dwelt" (Eliade 1959:5). "The symbolism of the house, the temple, and the city are realities in the Hindu scheme of life" (Rowe 1973:211).

The old Yoruba towns had populations of up to 50,000. They contrasted with urban centers in the West in many ways—most notably in the high percentage of subsistence cultivators within the towns. In this century, modernization has swelled Nigerian populations and increased migration to urban areas, so that Ibadan, with 97 percent Yoruba population, has grown to well over a million. Here the old and the new are melded in revealing ways: "The . . . physical structure and morphology of Ibadan . . . represents a convergence of two traditions of urbanism—a non-mechanistic, pre-industrial African tradition more akin to the mediaeval urbanism in Europe, and a technologically oriented European tradition" (Mabogunje 1967:35).

The emergence and growth of cities mean movement from the countryside. Individuals or families flock from villages to the city, in quest of wage labor or following the lure of bright lights. (In fact, despite efforts in some Third World countries and socialist states to stem the tide of urban migration and to focus development in rural areas, the lure of the city is so world-wide and pervasive that special economic or sociological "explanations" may be too narrow. We are in danger of building special explanations of general phenomena.)

So a major challenge to the urban anthropologist is to understand the relationship between rural communities and urbanites, and to interpret the transformation of rural cultural patterns in urban settings. Do old values, old fabrics of kinship and community, bind people together in urban settings? Pocock (1960) and others have argued that where urban centers have grown up outside a framework of exploitation and colonial domination, rural and urban remain a single system, sustained by the same cultural patterns. When urbanization breaks those bonds of continuity, it is because the fragmentation of wage labor in colonial and postcolonial urbanization has disrupted them—when ties of shared culture are transformed into class relationships; when urban wealth creates rural poverty and draws the poor to the urban margins; and when urban workers, often leaving families behind, are drawn from different ethnic groups and regions.

The colonial cities of the nineteenth century were described as parasitic, funneling wanted products out to the West without inducing economic transformation. Now that most of them have become the capital cities of independent countries, local elites have been co-opted alongside the white elites who remain in greater numbers than before, though they have retreated from open political dominance to more subtle diplomatic, commercial, military, and general aid-to-development domi-

nance. Considering that the gap between urban luxury and both urban and rural poverty is also greater than before, and that they serve as channels through which the United States alone consumes 60 per cent of the world's natural resources . . . these Asian [and other Third World] cities can hardly be considered less parasitic than before. The spatial segregation and social solidarity of the immigrant ethnic communities remain marked and, in the conditions of extreme overcrowding and underemployment, doubtless necessary to survival. (Southall 1973a:10)

Within such cities—what might be called neocolonial cities, in contrast to those of the modern West or of Japan and China—traditional bonds of kinship and community may remain strong. In ethnic enclaves, as Southall notes, such cultural patterns may serve as crucial survival strategies whereby identity is preserved and collective action and "belonging" are maintained. (The same is true, of course, of the ethnic enclaves of Western cities where internal colonialism has produced the often surprising cohesion of the black ghetto or Chinatown.) Kinship ties, both within and between families, may remain more important than the theories of urban sociologists had suggested. Thus Bruner (1973) and others have shown how important and strong are ties of kinship in urban settings of the Third World, a theme that emerges as well in the autobiographical materials collected from Mexico and Puerto Rico by Oscar Lewis (1961, 1966). And studies of ghetto blacks in the United States, notably the recent work of Carol Stack (1974), have emphasized the centrality and enduring resilience of bonds of kinship, despite the fragmentation, impersonality, and mass scale of urban life.

But in many areas of the Third World, especially neocolonial cities where individuals and families are pulled from rural communities for wage labor, bonds of kinship and community are at least temporarily sundered in urban migration. Here voluntary associations and other institutions, in some ways modeled on the close ties of kin and neighbors, may emerge as sources of strength, identity, and survival—and as ways of incorporating new arrivals in a hostile environment.

Case 100: The Dancing Compins of Freetown

In the city of Freetown, Sierra Leone, Temne peoples have formed voluntary associations of a sort common in West Africa (Banton 1957; Little 1967). These are known as "dancing compins." Their ostensible function is is perform "plays" of traditional music and dancing. Performances are given for the weddings of members (both men and women), for special occasions such as visits by important people, and to raise funds.

Each compin is tightly organized, with officials, committees, and treasuries to which members contribute weekly and at the death of a fellow member. They maintain close discipline over members and compete for a good reputation for conduct as well as for performances. Fines are levied on members for breaches of rules, and great stress is laid on mutual aid in times of need.

Most members of a dancing compin are migrants from rural towns and villages, and there is a strong local and regional bias in their membership. In many respects they function as an urban counterpart to the kinship-based corporations of traditional Temne society. They also serve to socialize new arrivals to the city in the ways of the world, and provide a closely knit group that contributes to their security in this new and otherwise often hostile setting.

The origin of the dancing compins reveals another side of their importance and appeal. The Temne were long regarded as the "hillbillies" of Sierra Leone by other peoples from less conservative groups. For young Temne establishment of the first compin by a somewhat revolutionary Temne schoolmaster provided a rallying point around which they could build a new urban identity. As compins became established and acquired prestige, their combination of what was sophisticated and new with what was received from valued traditional elements of Temne culture gave them added influence. Some younger men used them as springboards to political leadership in tribal matters.

Thus, by founding voluntary associations individual Temne raised their prestige and rose in the social scale. These organizations provided new leadership roles. . . . By resuscitating certain aspects of the traditional culture and adapting it to urban needs these young men were able to further their modernist ambitions. (Little 1967:160)

It is therefore not quite true to say that the close ties to relatives, friends, and neighbors that are the framework of social life in the small communities characteristic of the first 99.9 percent of human (and late hominid) existence on earth have been transformed and replaced in the lives of city dwellers, whose social relationships are now shallow, transient, and mainly with strangers. But it is certainly true that fragmentation of social relationships in urban life has drastically changed the texture of social interaction. To the encounters with known peoples and places, the textures of intimacy and familiarity, that prevail in small communities have been added ranges of encounters that are impersonal, transitory, and shallow—structured by the vast economic differentiation and bureaucratic complexity of the city as well as by sheer masses of people. Such theorists of urbanization as Banton (1973) and Southall (1973a) have sought to characterize what is distinctively new about urban ways of life in terms of these changed fabrics of social relations. Thus Southall (1973a:6) defines "urban" in terms of "high spatial density of social interactions," rather than on the sheer aggregation of people and buildings.

A large part of these multitudinous social interactions may be very shallow and fleeting. . . . Such . . . fleeting interactions are an essential aspect of urban life; but . . . another, equally important, aspect of the same high density . . . is that it also permits and facilitates the emergence and maintenance of profoundly personal relationships, . . . effective solidary relationships with a few neighbors, kinsfolk, and friends. (Southall 1973a:6—7)

The life of the U.S. urban ghetto black and Latin American or Asian slum dweller has been a major focus of recent urban study. In part, this has been motivated by liberal humanistic concern, or sometimes revolutionary zeal; it has also been a response to the availability of research funding to "treat" the social unrest that has exploded into violence. Anthropological studies of the urban poor, whether in black ghettos or Third World cities, raise a broad range of questions and doubts. We will return to them in Chapter 25.

In studying the poor and powerless in urban settings, anthropologists often make too blithely a common liberal assumption: there is a problem "out there," so let us go and cure it. But the roots of "the problem" are not simply "out there." Radical critics have argued that they are in the corporate power structure that has created the economy of exploitation, the ideology of racism, and the social system of discrimination. From this perspective, curing the symptoms by urban renewal projects, "headstart" programs, job training, or other piecemeal remedies so as to lift the poor into the mainstream of society can be only partly successful; especially in global perspective, such an approach can only succeed in creating small new elites and widening and polarizing oppressive class relationships. Such remedies may succeed in giv-

Apartheid and international investment: The gate of a South African factory, a subsidiary of a giant U.S. corporation. (Courtesy of United Nations.)

ing a few black executives token power in multinational corporations, but these very corporations shape and sustain exploitation and oppression in South Africa or Latin America. On a massive scale, remedies of this kind may succeed in incorporating many blacks into the industrial labor force; but the relative affluence of American workers is sustained at the expense of the poor in Latin America, Asia, and Africa.

The desperate poverty in which so many urbanites in the Third World or black America are trapped can easily be seen as pathological. Thus Oscar Lewis has painted a dramatic picture of an international culture of poverty, with many broad similarities that transcend regional and national variations. This picture has been highly controversial. Lewis suggests, and seeks to document with his selected life-history materials, that the poor (at least in Western societies) pattern their lives partly on, but are largely excluded from, the major institutions of the dominant society. Their social and economic lives and psychological adaptions are shaped by exclusion and deprivation. Socially, the result is a lack of stable marriages and solid family life, with lovers drifting in and out, children leaving home early in search of an adventure that masks their economic frustration, and so on. Psychologically, "a strong feeling of marginality, of helplessness, of dependence and of inferiority" prevails (Lewis 1966:xlvii).

Lewis' writings have provoked a storm of criticism. He has been rightly criticized for underplaying the creative, positive value systems and social relationships that preserve solidarity amid adversity and for a too-narrow conception of the roots of poverty. It has been a characteristic strategy of the dominant society, whether in external or internal colonialism, to caricature blacks or Indians or "natives" as lazy, shiftless, promiscuous, or otherwise lacking in the virtues that would enable them to prosper and get ahead. The

problems of the poor are laid at the feet of the poor. Lewis is by no means simplistic, moralistic, and racist in the way many observers of black America have been; but his picture of urban poverty is too narrow and has been vulnerable to the same critical onslaught (Valentine 1968; Leacock 1971).

Recall the discussion in §68 of *machismo* and of the quest for honor and reputation in Latin America and the Mediterranean; and the discussion of woman-centered networks in §68. Anthropological interpretations of social relations, whether in rural communities or urban enclaves, are always in danger of myopia—of seeing phenomena within too narrow a frame, of being naive about the wider shaping forces of economic systems and of historic processes. Explanations for what goes on in the narrow frame are sought within the frame, not outside it; and that often leads to misleading and partial interpretations. It is the special and perhaps deepest dilemma of anthropological method that in viewing human life from close-up, anthropologists see a richness of everyday experience other social scientists characteristically miss; but they are in constant danger of local, partial understandings of events shaped by outside forces.

And that raises a special concern of urban anthropology: method. Are the methods that sufficed in studying a tribal hamlet, and were at least partly successful in a peasant village, adequate to the scale, fragmentation, and diversity of urban social life? Can (or should) the urban anthropologist study in ways urban sociologists do not? An anthropologist arrives in the city with a bag of methodological tricks that is not, when unpacked in the view of colleagues in other disciplines, very impressive. They emphasize deep and long immersion, not breadth or systematic sampling; they focus on "culture," hence on what is shared, on a consensus of values and common premises about the social life. Do these methods work in cities?

One strategy has been to take small slices of a vast urban setting and look at them with the closeup lens of anthropological observation over extended time periods. This may involve close participation in small groups, such as gangs, as in Keiser's study of the Vice Lords in Chicago.

Case 101: The Vice Lords

The Vice Lord Nation comprises a union of local black youth gangs in Chicago, studied by anthropologist Lincoln Keiser (1969). The Vice Lords originated in a reformatory in 1958; and by the mid-1960s their original nucleus had expanded to a wide range of neighborhoods—originally filling a temporary vacuum in the power struggles of local youth gangs (the Clovers, the Imperial Chaplains, the Cave Men), and eventually attracting established fighters from other gangs and recruiting local strength.

What had begun as a small social club, giving parties and providing neighborhood solidarity, had under the pressures of surrounding youth gangs become a formidable fighting gang. It was organized in a series of noncontiguous territories, streets within which the Vice Lords had primary power. The Vice Lord Nation was divided first of all into "branches" (the Albany Lords, the Madison Lords, the Maniac Lords, the War Lords . . .), with the City Lords as the original and most powerful subgroup. Each branch had a particular set of officers and a territory. The formal offices provided a structure of leadership when a particular leader was arrested. The City Lords are in turn segmented into local "sections." These sections are subordinate to the City Lord officers; but the junior branches likewise acknowledge the seniority of the City Lord leaders. It is only they who call the infrequent meetings of the entire Vice Lord Nation. Finally, each branch or section is divided into small "cliques" with strong internal solidarity; these, too, are usually named (Gallant Men, Rat Pack, Magnificent Seven).

If all this sounds disconcertingly reminiscent of a segmentary lineage system, it is. When the gang fights or "gangbangs" that are a focus of group prestige and solidarity break out, they operate in a way not unlike our hypothetical Smiths and Joneses in Chapter 13, or the Nuer of the Sudan (Case 52, Chapter 17).

If the Vice Lords involved in the gangbang are members of the same section, then it is section membership that will be significant; if the Vice Lords are members of different sections, but the same branch, then it is branch membership that is significant; and if the Vice Lords are members of different branches, it is club membership that will be significant. (Keiser 1969:31)

Within a branch or section, there is also a kind of age-grading (Seniors, Juniors, Midgets). Each local grouping also has a kind of women's auxiliary, girls who are known as Vice Ladies. This does not imply necessarily that Vice Ladies are the mates of particular Vice Lords, and does not imply that they are more or less passive and subservient toward the men: one of Keiser's informants recounted vividly how a group of Vice Ladies bashed up a group of Lords with bricks, knives, and clubs when a youth and his Vice Lady girlfriend came to blows.

Fights occurred in planned and unplanned encounters and confrontations (for example, at a dance, a party, a game) or as operations of invasion and defense of club territory. Fights often trigger cycles of feuding. All this is a fairly rough business, when the weapons might include guns and knives as well as fists: killings were not infrequent.

Vice Lord groups also engaged in other operations—"hustling" (begging, stealing, or gambling), "wolf packing" (beating up passersby), "pulling jive" (drinking wine), shooting craps, or simply informally cruising together. Keiser vividly analyzes the ideologies central in the culture of such black youth gangs that give meaning to their actions: a valuation of "soul" (see also Keil's (1966) study of the Urban Blues), of "brotherhood," of "heart" (bravery and daring), and of playing the "game" successfully (that is, conning people, getting the best of interpersonal encounters, beating the system).

Personal status within the Vice Lords and similar gangs depends on displaying virtues of loyalty, bravery, and sheer audacity—but particularly of success and courage in fighting. Note here a partial convergence to the values of *machismo* and "crab antics" (Case 81).

This usefully reminds us that the Vice Lords and their rivals do not exist in a social vacuum, and that—unlike the pre-colonial Nuer—they are not ultimately in control of their own territories and their own social system. They have been economically in an often desperate plight, surviving in a world of armed robbery and drug use the wider society wages war against through police repression. The bravery and violence of black youth gangs have been nurtured by desperate anger and frustration fomented by poverty, alienation, and brutalization in reform schools and prisons.

It is noteworthy that in latter 1960s the Vice Lords were undergoing a dramatic transformation under the impact of black nationalism and an influx of community-development funds. As economic opportunities opened and a sense of black identity was strengthened, gang fighting was giving way to political unity, militancy, and economic gain.

Other studies, such as Elliot Liebow's *Tally's Corner* (1967), have taken small slices of life and traced their connections outward. Liebow studied a small and shifting collection of black men in Washington, D.C., whose lives carried them to and clustered them around a particular street corner. He traced their lives outward from it into short-lived jobs, sexual and marital relationships, and webs of friendship. Such studies of small groups or local settings are by no means distinctively new and anthropological: studies of the bank-wiring group in a New England factory and of a street corner gang (Whyte 1955) have been sociological classics for decades. And in recent years, sociologists as well as anthropologists have flocked to ghetto housing projects, hippie communes, Divine Light *ashrams,* and other small-scale settings.

Perhaps it is idle to worry about whether participant-observers of small groups carry anthropological, sociological, or some other credentials. But the more urgent question is whether participant observation in small groups, as microcosms of some wider system, is adequate to the complexity of urban life. For characteristically, an urban gang or commune or tenement is the focus for only part of the social life of its participants. For each, daily social life reaches beyond these warm and close settings to the vast impersonal world of jobs and stores and buses and streets. The challenge to systematic exploration of individual social relations in urban settings across this whole range has been faced squarely by British social anthropologists in urbanizing Africa. Particularly anthropologists trained in or influenced by the "Manchester School" of social anthropology—Max Gluckman and his students—have sought to generalize anthropological methodology to deal with the fragmentation of urban life.

Thus Theo Van Velsen, Clyde Mitchell, and others, have developed "situational analysis," where some collective happening—a dance, a public meeting, a marriage—is analyzed under a close microscope to reveal who participates and why. Such analysis can show how the strategies and conflicts manifest in the particular incident reflect the structures and processes of the wider society. Situational analyses that move from the concrete and immediate to show general processes and networks have developed from strategies first worked out for studying conflict and social relations in African tribal settings—the "structural dramas" examined by Victor Turner

(1957) among the Ndembu, the "extended case method" explored by Van Velsen (1967) and others. But in urban settings, particularly where change is rapid, participants are mobile, and ethnic backgrounds are varied, such situational analysis must reveal processes and conflicts against a background of fluidity and diversity, not of shared institutions and values.

A related development has been "network analysis" (Barnes 1972). Here, scholars such as Mitchell, Epstein, Barnes, Kapferer, and Boissevain have sought to trace the activities of individuals as they move through the full range of social relationships. By showing how and why urbanites enter into economic, political, and kinship relationships, and how they strategically use their networks of connection, urban anthropologists can move beyond both a static framework of institutional analysis and the distortion that comes from looking only at that portion of each person's life that is spent in the small group—a gang or residence or bar—the anthropologist happens to be observing. Network analysis has been partly successful in mapping patterns of social relations so that the properties of networks can be examined mathematically. But here the formalisms have often been superficial and analogical. There is a danger of becoming carried away with the formal elegance of it all and forgetting what the numbers or diagrams mean—of the usually tenuous relationship between the formalism and the world. But this is a common temptation in social science, one anthropologists have usually avoided only by their imprecision.

One consequence of this tracing of interpersonal relationships across a range of contexts has been a searching reexamination of tribal societies. Scholars such as Boissevain (1968, 1973), and Barth (1966b, 1967) have argued with considerable force that the "corporate groups" of the older models of social structure have badly oversimplified the flux of social relations in small-scale societies, where individuals move from context to context enacting different roles, dealing with different people, and pursuing strategies akin to those found in urban settings. A converging critique has come from scholars who have explored social relations from a standpoint of the conceptual codes of the actors and found the older models simplistic and inadequate (recall Case 32, where we looked at Kwaio social relations). Newer models stressing roles, contexts, networks, or "quasi groups" may help to illuminate social life in small-scale tribal societies as well as cities. Too often, anthropologists have talked about clans and lineages and not about the mixed and temporary clusters of friends and neighbors who get jobs done together.

The challenge of interpreting the range of human experience in urban settings, and understanding the forces that shape adaptations to urbanism, is urgent and immediate. Anthropology cannot survive as a study of remote, powerless, and exotic peoples. There are few of them left, and access to them has been made difficult not only by scarcity of research funds and a growing population of aspiring fieldworkers, but also by a rising hostility in the Third World to "being studied" by a discipline historically associated with colonialism.

Cities are where the action is, where the future apparently lies if there is to be one. Anthropology must be there, though it will continue to be in the hinterlands as well.

But studying Third World cities or black ghettos poses massive ethical and political, as well as methodological, problems. Should anthropologists be studying in white suburbia and executive offices, as well as among the oppressed and powerless in slums and shanty towns? Should the anthropologists studying there be white, or should they be Africans or Pacific islanders? Such questions loom large in present anthropology. We will return to them shortly, after we look at another facet of the relation between anthropology and the oppressed: the worlds of women.

WOMEN AND ANTHROPOLOGY

24

The women's movement has sent waves of changed consciousness through academic fields and institutions. Studies of women and by women have begun to come to the fore—belatedly—in many disciplines; and anthropology is no exception.

The communities anthropologists have studied have been populated by females and males in roughly equal number. Yet the experience of women, the texture of their lives and their perspectives on social events, have rarely been adequately reported. Even though twentieth-century anthropologists have included many distinguished women (Benedict, Mead, Parsons, Blackwood, Seligmann, Wedgwood, Richards, Kaberry, Bunzel, Du Bois, and others, did outstanding work before World War II), with few exceptions they were pulled into the worlds of men in the societies they studied, and worked mainly in them.

Now women are beginning to receive their due, as women anthropologists expand in numbers and guide their interpretations with their own expanded consciousness. But sexism is still pervasive in anthropological theory and practice, and the task of rethinking and reworking has only begun.

In the section to follow, we will briefly examine the role of women in an emerging comparative perspective, outlining the problems of interpretation that loom large and suggesting some lines of needed rethinking in an anthropology of women.

77.
Women's Worlds

In some of the literature of the women's movement, ancient societies where women were dominant—primitive matriarchies—have been a prominent theme. As 16 women social anthropologists compellingly argue in *Woman, Culture, and Society* (Rosaldo and Lamphere 1974), there is no evidence that matriarchal societies have ever existed. The apparent universality of male dominance—at least in public and political realms—must be a starting point for an anthropology of women. The point is urgent. If women are to achieve full liberation, it will be through means that have never before been open: hearkening back to myths of an imagined past power will not help.

Women's Subordination, Biological Differences, and Cultures

The apparently universal fact of female subordination—though subordination in different degree and different forms—challenges understanding and interpretation. Is male dominance strongly rooted in human biology, hence immutable? Are male and female sex roles and personality patterns shaped mainly by genes and by body chemistry? Or are they in substantial degree learned and hence culturally shaped? These questions were glimpsed in Chapter 4. We return to them now better equipped to seek partial answers.

The most useful place to begin to assess the interface between biology and culture in shaping sex roles and male dominance is with the universality of childbearing and child caring by women. Though men cannot bear children and cannot (without modern technology) nurse them, they can care for them once weaned. But the mother-child bond, culturally patterned on biological foundations, is such that nurturing and care remain mainly in the hands of women in all societies through the crucial formative years.

Rosaldo (1974) argues that the assignment to women of the tasks of childrearing has led in every known society to a separation between the domestic realm and the "public" realm. Women have their major roots and major commitment in the domestic realm:

women's roles center around hearth and home. The public realm is preeminently the world of men, though in various times and places women have come to play a central part on the public stage, as well as behind the scenes.

Put quite simply, men have no single commitment as enduring, time-consuming, and emotionally compelling—as close to seeming necessary and natural—as the relation of a woman to her infant child; and so men are free to form those broader associations that we call "society," universalistic systems of order, meaning, and commitment that link particular mother-child groups. (Rosaldo 1974:24)

The question remains why, apparently universally and for both men and women, it is the roles associated with men, and with the public realm, that are most highly valued—roles of warrior, elder, priest, or chief. Women's domestic virtues are virtues of subordination and second-class citizenship.

Before the question of subordination is squarely faced, a word about the shaping forces of biology is needed. One-sided distortion of a very complex interplay between human biological potentials and their cultural shaping and expression has come both from ethologists and feminists. The argument of some ethologists that female subordination and sex roles are biologically laid down in humans, and the argument of some feminists that sex role differences are entirely created by cultural experience, are both wrong.

Rosaldo examines the cultural expressions of female subordination even in societies where women have relatively high status and power and sex role polarization is not extreme—societies such as the Arapesh (Mead 1935), where women were excluded from sacred rites and were required to act like ignorant children; the Merina of Malagasy (Keenan 1974), where men speak publicly with formal allusion while women are "cultural idiots, who are expected to blurt out what they mean; and the Yoruba, where women control trading and economics yet must kneel to serve their husbands and feign ignorance and obedience" (Rosaldo 1974:20). Can such subordination be accounted for on the basis of "different hormonal cycles, infant activity levels, sexual capacities, or emotional orientations" (Rosaldo 1974:20)?

Will they explain the constant factor in the secret flute cults of the Arapesh, the Merina woman's lack of subtlety, or the bowing and scraping of the Yoruba wife? Although there is no doubt that biology is important, and that human society is constrained and directed in its development by facts of a physical kind, I find it difficult to see how these could possibly lead to moral evaluations. Biological research may illuminate the range in human inclinations and possibilities, but it cannot account for the interpretation of these facts in a cultural order. It can tell us about the average endowments of groups or of particular individuals, but it cannot explain the fact that cultures everywhere have given Man, as a category opposed to Woman, social value and moral worth. . . . Biology . . . becomes significant only as it is interpreted by human actors and associated with characteristic modes of action.(Rosaldo 1974:22—23)

How wide is the range of variation in cultural interpretations of biology? Cultural variations in sex roles—and the plasticity of human infants to the shaping of culture— were undoubtedly overstressed in the American anthropology of the first half of the century, dominated as it was by Franz Boas and his students (see Freeman 1969). Margaret Mead's classic studies of adolescent girls in Samoa and of sex roles in New Guinea can be seen in retrospect to have greatly overemphasized human plasticity and cultural variability (see, for example, Freeman 1974; Fortune 1939)—a particular irony, since her book *Sex and Temperament in Three Primitive Societies* (1935) has loomed large in feminist literature.

It is too simple to say, as Rosaldo (1974:22) does, that "facts of a physical kind . . . could [not]lead to moral evaluations." Rites, rules, and religions are not simply collective creations of a people; they are created by those classes or strata within a society that have the power to define them for, or to impose them on, the group. If there are physical-biological bases for male *power* over women, then the multitude of ideational systems created by men to reinforce and rationalize their dominance would be fully comprehensible. The fantastic creative powers of the human mind to elaborate symbolic systems are *biologically* open to men and women, rich and poor, old and young: but they may not be *politically* open. Biology does not explain the content of male ideologies, but it may account to substantial degree for male power to create ideologies.

But this is still too simple. First, we have not drawn a convincing connection between biological differences of males and females and men's political dominance—and there may well not be any direct one. Second, to the extent that male dominance is universal, it is political dominance in the public realm; in the domestic realm, and behind the scenes, women often wield great power even if it is not publicly recognized and ideologically reinforced. Third, male power is characteristically tinged with insecurity and envy: the pride and power are vulnerable.

An adequate account of the interplay between biology, sexual politics, and the asymmetry of sex roles, toward which anthropologists are moving, will have to be complex and subtle, not simplistic. It will have to be "interactionist," seeing not chains of cause and effect but webs of interconnectedness.

An important set of insights has come from related observations by Edwin Ardener (1972) and Sherry Ortner (1974) (see §65). If men have political control in the public realms of a society, there is always one power—the greatest power of all—that remains mysterious and beyond their control: the power of life itself, of giving birth. Men may arrange or exchange legal rights over women's offspring, but the power of creating life (and of sustaining it with breast milk) remains beyond their grasp. Pregnancy and birth are processes that seem dark, mysterious, and threatening—yet are envied.

Two explorations of this complex of envy, threat, and ambivalence toward the uncontrollable reproductive powers of women foreshadow this interpretation vividly, hence bear note before we pass on to the conclusions Ardener and Ortner draw. The first is the psychoanalyst Bruno Bettelheim's classic interpretation of male genital mutilation—circumcision, subincision, and related initiatory mutilation—as the symbolic expression of male envy of women's reproductive powers. Men, in incising the penis, symbolically are creating analogues of menstrual blood and female genitals. (The men of Wogeo Island off northern New Guinea actually let blood from their penises periodically, quite explicitly in imitation of menstruation (Hogbin 1970). A second interesting line of related interpretation comes from the anthropologist Alan Dundes. Dundes argues that male envy of the power of women to give birth is reflected in fantasies of anal birth that are widely recurrent in mythology; and he argues that men who write books (or otherwise display their "creations") are symbolically compensating for that inability to create life (Dundes 1962).

Back to Ardener and Ortner. Noting this envy of uncontrollable power by the men who create cultural ideologies, Ardener suggests that women are often symbolically linked with the wild world of nature, in contrast to the ordered, controlled world of culture. The double meaning of "man" in English and many other languages—man versus woman and man versus animal—may be a reflection of such a symbolic relegation of woman to the periphery. Woman, as "not-man," is symbolically marginal or liminal, neither fully in the world of nature or the world of culture.

Ortner, drawing inspiration from Simone de Beauvoir (1953) as well as Lévi-Strauss, explores a similar theme. "Woman's body seems to doom her to mere reproduction of life; the male, in contrast, lacking natural creative functions, must (or has the opportunity to) assert his creativity externally, artificially through the medium of technology and symbols" (Ortner 1974:75). In one sense, the male creations are sterile and superficial in contrast to the creation of life. But paradoxically, "he creates relatively lasting, eternal, transcendant objects, while the woman creates only perishables—human beings" (Ortner 1974:75). De Beauvoir suggested that cultural valuation of the taking of life by men (in hunting and warfare) above the creation of life by women reflects a celebration not of destruction but of risking life; and Ortner builds on this to argue that warfare and hunting are social and cultural, while giving birth is natural. (Here she may be carrying the zeal of symbolic analysis a bit far: hunting could equally be the height of human *animality,* while childbirth is almost universally a social event surrounded with cultural procedures.)

Ortner argues that at an unconscious level the association between women and the realm of nature may be universal, though cultural elaborations of this symbolic pattern apparently are not. This would dovetail well with a kind of composite comparative view of sex roles that seems needed—pointing as it does to the precariousness and ambivalence that underlie male dominance in the public realm.

We gain other elements needed for such a composite view by looking at the possible interplay between genetic predispositions and socialization experience during the life cycle. It seems increasingly certain (§11 and §35) that individual humans differ considerably in genetically coded foundations of personality which are translated in the maturation process into different metabolic rates, different hormonal levels, and probably to different propensities to excitability, to passivity, to aggressiveness, to such loosely defined patterns as "introversion" or "extroversion," and perhaps to various cognitive styles. Given a particular biological predisposition to high excitability and aggressiveness, a particular male infant would probably grow up to become somewhat more bellicose than most of his male companions whether he was raised among the violent Yąnomamö (Chapter 1) or the peaceful Balinese. Yet the most peace-loving Yąnomamö would be regarded as a violent madman in Bali; so cultural fostering, patterning, and channeling of such propensities is obviously crucial. (Moreover, it seems probable that dietary deficiencies and other factors may biochemically alter genetically programmed propensities. Recall Bolton's argument (Case 11) that the aggressive behavior of the Qolla Indians of the Andes may be partly due to deficiencies and imbalances in blood sugar levels.)

We do not yet know how detailed these genetic templates of personality are, how wide the statistical range of variation in these genetic patterns might be, and how flexible various genetic predispositions are to the shaping of cultural experience. It is thus impossible to say with any certainty whether the statistical ranges in the various genetic propensities to personality are the same for men and for women, and if not, to what extent they overlap. There are many evolutionary reasons to expect that they are not the same, and a fair amount of experimental evidence to support this expectation (see Freedman 1974). However, here the danger of typological thinking is as great as with "race." First, in many biological respects sexuality is a continuum with female and male at opposite

poles, not a simple dichotomy. Second, if there are sex differences in the distribution of the genetic foundations of personality, there are undoubtedly hundreds of complexes of interacting genetic information involved; and each complex must have its own range of distribution. For most, the ranges for men and for women probably largely overlap; for many, they are probably the same. It is poor evolutionary biology and genetics to insist or assume that the genetic templates of personality are identical for men and women despite the physical differences between the sexes; but it is equally poor biology to assert that men are more active or aggressive and women more passive and submissive (or "emotional," "intuitive," and so on), since it grossly ignores ranges of individual differences.

A good deal of the writing on sex roles inspired by the women's movement has probably overstated the cultural factors and understated their biological foundations. But from this literature has come a long overdue awakening of concern with women's life cycles, hence a challenging of the sexist biases of much social science theory. Nancy Chodorow (1971, 1974) and others have argued strongly that the sex roles into which men and women are channeled contrast more because of asymmetries in the life cycle and life situation of men and women than because of differences in their genes and hormones.

The contrast begins with the universal role of women in bearing and raising children, within domestic settings. This, Chodorow argues, creates a bond of continuity and identification between daughter and mother. A girl grows up in a world that she will herself recreate as mother—a domestic role of familiar people and things and recurrent familiar tasks. But a son, beginning in a domestic world of women in strong physical and emotional dependence upon his mother, must be removed from that world. The world of men—whether the boy is introduced to it traumatically through initiation or gradually—is a world of public drama, competition, strife, and danger, a world of roles and rules. A boy must become a Man, in that special and even more limited sense (Kipling: "Be a man, my son . . ."). A girl does not have to become a woman—she matures gradually into one, however traumatic the shift may be from a home in which she is a daughter to her home as wife and mother. Chodorow convincingly argues that these asymmetries in socialization experience would account—*even if* there were no differences in genetic potentialities—for culturally standardized contrasts between women's and men's roles and personalities. Chodorow's psychoanalytic interpretation of the contrasts in "ego boundaries" and "gender identity" is vividly argued. She suggests that despite their subordination, the identity of women may be stronger and less fragile than the identity of men. But she notes that the psychological security of women is threatened by life experiences as well:

Women's biosexual experiences . . . all involve some challenges to the boundaries of her body ego (me-'not-me' in relation to her blood or milk, to a man who penetrates her, to a child once part of her body). These are important and fundamental human experiences that are probably intrinsically meaningful and at the same time complicated for women everywhere. (Chodorow 1974:59—60)

Chodorow's explorations underline the cost to social science theory of years of male bias and inattention to the lives of women. Where a few years ago there were only a few important anthropological studies of women, there is now a trickle of information from around the world, growing steadily into a stream. And with further information and awakening consciousness have come challenges to the sexism of theory. If the activities of women are accorded secondary interest and importance by the people anthropolo-

gists have studied, these cultural valuations have been unquestioningly accepted by observers coming themselves from a sexist society; and these biases have been perpetuated in theory as well as observational bias. "Man the hunter" has been on center stage, while woman the gatherer remained behind the scenes. The public settings where men strut, debate, fight, feast, and sacrifice have commanded attention in theory as well as ethnography. Even the basics of cultural theory can well bear reexamination. As we noted in Chapter 20, the notion of "a culture" shared by a people is too simple to deal with the gulfs of consciousness between social classes, between men and women, between young and old. Ardener raises the point that in many societies women do not have a comprehensive picture of "the culture" in the way that men, or some men, do. Rosaldo and Ortner suggest that the relative isolation and fragmentation of the domestic settings where women so often spend most of their lives may militate against their having a kind of universalist and abstract model of "the system." This further reinforces the point made in Chapter 20 that how different versions or differential models of a way of life are distributed in societies—and how this relates to its political structure—badly needs further study.

Paths to Liberation

The challenge of liberating anthropological theory and the challenge of liberating anthropology departments has been a major struggle in recent years. The issues go far beyond academia and anthropology. The major underlying question faced by the authors in *Woman, Culture, and Society* is not "How do we need to change anthropological theory and practice so as to reflect adequately the roles and experiences of women?" but rather, "How must the world be restructured to end and transcend subordination and oppression of women?'' The quest to uncover the foundations of subordination is motivated partly by intellectual urgency; but more strongly, by the challenge to overturn these foundations and build a new and liberated social order.

Some critics in the women's movement (Leacock 1974; Caulfield, personal communication; Schlegel 1974) would argue that the emphasis of authors such as Rosaldo, Ortner, and Chodorow on universals in the experience of women and their biosocial and psychological roots is misleading. Perhaps women have been subordinate in some sense in all traditional societies. But there have been enormous differences in the status of women, their economic position in relation to the means of production, and their power in domestic and public realms. If one is to understand the oppression of women, these critics would argue, one should look at these variations and should have a keen sense of history and process—a sense that is dulled if one emphasizes universals. By studying the power of women, and its limits, in such societies as the Iroquois or Cherokee or Hopi or Minangkabau or Dahomey one can see more clearly the sources of power and the domains where it can be exercised. One can see the relationship of women's status and power not only to the economics of production but to a social organization of production where women work together in groups larger than domestic units—hence where collective consciousness and collective power can be reinforced. Extreme sex polarization, as in many societies in Melanesia where the sexes are rigidly separated by pollution taboos (§63) or in Arab societies, may reinforce male power. But there is not only a strong cost of male insecurity; the isolation of women in a realm forbidden and dangerous to men may give women a collective strength and a life of their own beyond what is possible in isolated domestic families where women's status is ostensibly higher (see, for example, Fernea 1965).

An emphasis on the variation of women's roles, and on the economic and historic roots of these differences, is particularly needed to understand the transformations in the lives of women brought about by the industrial revolution and capitalist economy. As Leacock (1974:363) observes, "so many cultures that formerly allowed great individual autonomy within the imperatives of *reciprocity,* have shifted towards social-economic structures based on the Western-type nuclear family and the economic *dependency* of women and children on individual wage-earning men."

The separation between domestic realm and public realm may in some sense be universal (though see Schlegel 1974); and events and roles in the public realm may universally be male dominated and more highly valued than domestic ones. But that obscures a drastic transformation engendered by the industrial revolution and the rise of wage labor. In tribal and peasant societies, *production,* the socially valued creation of the material means of life, takes place mainly within the domestic group. Women and men play complementary roles in this production though the roles and recognition of each vary considerably.

With the advent of industrial wage labor, socially valued production takes place not in domestic settings but in factories. Women's domestic labor is cut off from production and from the corresponding social valuation; it is the money the wage-earning husband brings home that becomes the family's attachment to the wider world, and its means of survival (see Zaretzky 1973).

Both the universal themes of women's subordination and the variations in women's

Vaccination of cattle by a female veterinarian in Mongolia. (WHO photo by E. Schwab.)

power and status point to the same primary avenue of liberation. Men have not had full control over women's sexuality and reproductive powers; but women have had even less control over their own bodies. Women have been prisoners of their own biology; bearing and raising children through the prime years of life has not only tied women to hearth and home but has often left them physically drained and broken.

But the technology of birth control potentially gives women control over their own sexuality and reproductive powers. And this makes possible revolutionary changes in the social relations of reproduction, and the social systems in which they are embedded. Birth control provides only the *possibility* of freedom from subordination. It does not by itself constitute that freedom as long as women are isolated in separate households, dependent on male wage-earners, and playing a subordi-

nate role as sex objects and homemakers. In modern industrial societies men too are entrapped as wage-earners in the same system that has created the modern forms of women's subordination. Liberation for women partly entails women getting equal rights and access to the highly valued, traditional, male roles in public realms. (It also entails transforming and revaluing traditionally female roles.) But in industrial societies liberation will not come from women freeing themselves from domestic tasks of child-rearing and homemaking and joining the wage-labor force. Freedom from subordination and alienation in modern industrial societies—for both men and women—seems possible only through major changes in the social and economic relations of production (see Zaretzky 1973). Americans may be appalled by the frustration of individual enterprise in the modern socialist societies of China or Cuba. But it is noteworthy that it is only in such societies where social organization has been drastically rebuilt from the ground up that the relationships of men and women have been radically transformed and women have achieved full and independent participation in economic and political life. These particular modes of reorganization may not be commensurate with the values of Western industrial societies or their great stress on individualism and personal freedom. But it must surely be instructive that where the social relations of production have remained substantially unchanged, the liberation of women to join the world of male wage-earners has been partial and piecemeal. Replacing the alienation of the kitchen with the alienation of industrial wage-labor or secretarial jobs may be a hollow victory.

Here it is doubly ironic that Western societies have felt they have had so much to teach the "underdeveloped" societies of the Third World and so little to learn from them. When humans desperately need to find ways of relating to one another and to their ecosystem that are less exploitative and pathological, the many and varied traditional ways of life are crucial sources of wisdom.

As we will reflect in the final chapter, Third World peoples exploring syntheses of traditional values and social organization and Western models of modernization may in the long run have more to teach the West than to learn. Through syntheses of old and new the fateful uniformity of a single world culture can perhaps be avoided. In the process, possible designs for rebuilding the roles of women and men may be more effectively explored in Burma or South Yemen than in Boston.

That raises a final point. The cultural relativism that has guided so much anthropological thinking (§30) has led anthropologists to look at other ways of life in their own terms. Whatever customs, values, and beliefs a people accepted as valid and meaningful for them were treated by the anthropologist as alternative human possibilities, legitimate and valuable in their own right. In counterpoint to this relativism, it is worth considering that every tribal way of life is oppressive to some members of the society—if we adopt some standard of what constitutes "oppression" that is maximally culture-free and universalistic (a standard that need assume only a few basic rights to survival, physical and psychological well-being and dignity, and a measure of freedom of self-expression and self-realization). In every society some individuals or classes—whether children, women, the poor, the landless, the elderly, the mentally subnormal—are oppressed.

Is it the anthropologist's right or responsibility to seek to transform other people's societies? Can or should one try to make the people whose way of life one is sharing and studying aware of the wider forces of outside economics and politics that impinge on their community? And if the anthropologist can legitimately help to catalyze people's consciousness about their place in a wider world, can (or should) he or she try to avoid awakening or heightening their consciousness about where power lies in their own society and how the roots of oppression might be cut away?

Such questions loom increasingly large as a younger generation of anthropologists challenge the notion of a value-free, neutral, objective, and uninvolved social science; as the historical association of anthropology with colonialism becomes more clear; and as Third World peoples increasingly resist "being studied."

We now turn directly to these urgent questions.

ANTHROPOLOGY AND THE THIRD WORLD

25

In World War II, many anthropologists served their country in ways that brought their specialized knowledge to bear, as experts on the peoples of battle zones or as analysts of Nazi Germany or Imperial Japan. And after the war, as the United States acquired Pacific territories, as U.S. aid money was massively spent in the underdeveloped world, and as former colonies moved to independence, anthropologists sought in many regions to apply their knowledge to improve the lot of rural communities around the world. Through the fifties and early sixties, "applied anthropology" explored the possibilities and frustrations of trying to transform technology, health practices, or political structure in small-scale communities. The anthropologist, sensitive to cultural nuances and to potential misunderstandings that could frustrate a doctor giving injections or an agricultural expert introducing tractors, sometimes was able to avert confusion or disaster.

British anthropology had had a period of similar concern with practical problems and ameliorating the stresses of culture change through the thirties, in colonial Africa and the Pacific.

Through the postwar period few anthropologists questioned the national aims and policies that created these local situations. Anthropology had served the United States and England well in wartime; and in the postwar world of independence movements, foreign aid, and Cold War it continued to serve.

For U.S. anthropology all this was to change in an Indochina war that divided the nation, alienated a good many million people from the policies of their government (including major sections of academic communities), and led to widespread questioning of historic Western policies and institutions. (For many British scholars the same realizations had come earlier in the agonies of Africa, and for French scholars, in the blood of Algeria and Indochina.)

Though the Indochina war crystallized a

new political consciousness among hundreds of thousands of intellectuals and shook many disciplines and academic institutions to their foundations, it perhaps had a special impact in anthropology. One reason why the impact of political protest and awareness on anthropology was so traumatic was that academic anthropologists had formed a small and rather clubbish community until the 1960s; and political polarization shattered many of the bonds of community. Another reason is that the decade of major political protest saw a population explosion among academic anthropologists and anthropology departments in the United States, the United Kingdom, and through Commonwealth countries; the younger generation of anthropologists were in graduate schools when they were centers of political action and awareness, and their subsequent diaspora to new campuses and new departments has profoundly affected the spirit of involvement, of ethical and political concern. Finally, anthropologists had for decades regarded themselves as champions of powerless and marginal peoples, humanistically involved in ways of life others scorned as "primitive." For their humanism to be challenged by the angry voices of Native Americans, U.S. blacks, Africans, or Asians, and by their own radical colleagues, was particularly traumatic.

The tide of protest against "anthropological colonialism" coming from Third World peoples was not merely a moral and intellectual challenge. These peoples increasingly were independent—and in India, Africa, and other regions, Western social science research became a political issue. The people anthropology had historically studied finally had the power to step out from under the lens of observation and close the "laboratory" doors.

In the sections to follow we will examine the historic role of anthropology in colonial settings, and we will consider ethical and political issues of field research. Finally, we will end this exploration of anthropology with some reflections about variations in human ways, and the perspectives Third World peoples can bring to the desperate human struggle to avert ecological, demographic, or nuclear disaster.

78. Anthropology and Colonialism

The successive waves of European expansion that engulfed the non-Western world brought to the frontiers a number of astute, sympathetic observers of exotic peoples and customs. Gifted missionaries, soldiers, explorers, and other pioneer scholars of the colonial frontiers created the foundations on which later theorists such as Morgan, Tylor, Frazer, and Durkheim built. One could trace connections between colonial expansionism and ethnographic observation as far back as the Spanish conquest of Mexico, or perhaps as Tacitus among the Germanic tribes, or even Herodotus.

But since it is the relationship between anthropology as a professional discipline and colonialism that has been searchingly reexamined, it is most useful to begin at about the turn of the twentieth century, when amateur ethnologists began to give way to professionals.

Whether and in what ways anthropologists have been instruments of colonial domination could be asked of South Asia or the Pacific, but it has been raised mainly in connection with North America, and with Africa.

Vine de Loria's (1969) hilarious but biting attacks on the anthropology of North American Indians, intentionally overstated, have boldly forced a rethinking. Anthropologists seeking to reconstruct and preserve vanishing ways of life had seen themselves as champions of the Indian. They cared when no one else did, valued what no one else did. That the still-viable Pueblo societies had closed ranks to exclude anthropologists and preserve their sacred secrets had seemed a local anomaly; elsewhere toothless elders unfolded the ways of a remembered past, grateful that someone would listen, care, and perhaps pay a little.

But now the anger and pride of the Pueblos has spread on all sides as once-broken and powerless peoples have begun to rise. The friendly anthropologist had too often looked away when confronted with years of broken treaties, oppression, and shattering poverty, and had gone on piecing together remembered fragments of the old days. The summer visitors from universities and museums often left cumulations of bitterness building up behind them. And some anthropologists, working with the Bureau of Indian Affairs, had actively implemented policies of assimilationism whose cost is now being realized and which have become a target for the rhetoric of Red Power. Anthropologists have become political symbols and foils for rhetoric, and have been caricatured into a kind of composite villain. The criticisms are only partial truths. But they hit close enough to home to force a rethinking, a new awareness, and a soul-searching that have long been needed.

Other radical critics of anthropology and colonialism have charged that the social anthropologists, mainly British and South African, who studied British colonial Africa in the 1930s were instruments of colonial policy who developed their models of lineage structure and politics to establish and maintain colonial control. Thus it has been pointed out that functionalist studies of tribal politics served the interests of colonial administration through "indirect rule." Many studies of political and kinship institutions were funded by a government whose administrators needed to know how these institutions could be used to maintain colonial control within a framework of local custom. It has been pointed out that

in coming to live with a tribal people and record their social life, an anthropologist used "his people's" subordinate position to intrude upon them and gain their cooperation; and it has been pointed out that anthropologists were assuming their own niche in the hierarchy of colonial control that included district administrators, missionaries, planters, and traders. Finally, the roles of particular anthropologists vis-à-vis colonial regimes and their relationship with their subjects have been harshly judged.

It is important to remember that anthropologists were genuinely concerned with what they perceived to be the well-being of the human beings in the tribal communities they knew—and it seemed much better for well-intentioned administrators to understand local social structures than to act in ignorance. What was seldom if ever questioned in the Africa of the 1930s or 1940s was the inevitability of colonial rule. Independence seemed, to most, to be many decades away, if it was ever to come. Colonialism was an established fact and even a moral responsibility. The challenge was to rule well, not badly; and anthropologists did what they could to make colonialism benevolent. Moreover, their appreciation of their subjects as human beings, and their sympathy for different values and ways of life, set them off from most other whites in colonial settings.

Recent extreme condemnations of functionalist anthropology as a handmaiden of colonialism or of such leading figures as Evans-Pritchard or Nadel as instruments of colonial domination are too simplistic. The question of individual commitment should be treated with particular caution. The comments of Saudi Arabian-born Marxist anthropologist Talal Asad are worth quoting:

I believe it to be both mistaken and unjust to attribute invidious political motives to anthropologists studying primitive societies. . . . Most social anthropologists held and still hold radical or liberal political views. Nevertheless, it remains true that classic functionalism prevented them from effecting a fruitful conjunction between their political commitments and their sociological analysis. (Asad 1970:10)

Rather, the critique must be more global. Asad's more recent observations are incisive:

The basic reality which made prewar social anthropology . . . feasible and effective . . . was the power relationship between dominating . . . and dominated . . . cultures. We then need to ask . . . how this relationship has affected . . . the uses to which . . . knowledge was put; the theoretical treatment of particular topics; the mode of perceiving and objectifying alien societies; and the anthropologist's claim of political neutrality.

. . . the general drift of anthropological understanding did not constitute a basic challenge to the unequal world represented by the colonial system. Nor was the colonial system as such . . . analyzed. . . .

. . . the scientistic definition of anthropology as a disinterested (objective, value free) study of "other cultures" helped to mark off the anthropologist's enterprise from that of the trader, the missionary, the administrator . . .; but did it not also render him unable to envisage and argue for a radically different political future for the subordinate people he studied and thus serve to merge that enterprise *in effect* with that of dominant status-quo Europeans? If the anthropologist sometimes endorsed or condemned particular social changes affecting "his people," did he, in this ad hoc commitment do any more than many colonial Europeans who accepted colonialism as a system? If he was sometimes accusingly called "a Red," "a socialist" or "an anarchist" by administrators and settlers, did this not merely reveal one facet of the hysterically intolerant character of colonialism as a system, with which he chose nevertheless to live *professionally* at peace? (Asad 1973:17–18)

As Jacques Maquet (1964:260) has put it, "What matters is that anthropology was oriented as though it wanted to preserve the existing situation." Though neither a con-

demnation of individual anthropologists nor a blanket dismissal of "functionalism" is justified or illuminating, it is important that the relationship between theory and its wider historical and ideological context be understood (here, Maquet's critique is highly illuminating). The balanced discussion by Richard Brown (1973) of the work of a brilliant humanistic scholar, Godfrey Wilson, in the setting of a government-sponsored institute in colonial northern Rhodesia well illuminates the complex interplay of theory and application, and of personal commitment and colonial policy.

Euro-American anthropology has developed within a vastly powerful expansionist civilization that has swept across and subjugated the entire world. Its historic role has been to study small-scale exotic societies as the juggernaut rolled over them or pushed them into submission at the margins of the world white men wanted.

It is too simple to attack past anthropologists for not condemning the evils of colonialism more globally and more insistently. Had they done so, they would not have run the gauntlet of colonial administrations whose permission and support they needed to get where they were going. In the 1930s, a vocally anticolonial anthropologist would have been an armchair scholar. Nor was it likely that many anthropologists would have been able to step outside the framework of their institutions—despite all the insistence about cross-cultural perspectives—to take a systemic, critical stance toward world-wide imperialism.

Finally, it is worth pointing out that the contradictions in the stance of many a humanistic anthropologist in the 1930s who accommodated himself to the realities of a colonialist system were no more stark than those of a 1970s radical academic in a U.S. or British university who accommodates himself to a bourgeois life-style in an affluent society.

But by the same token, anthropologists should not be surprised that newly independent Third World peoples have often turned on their benevolent anthropological "friends" and condemned them as another bunch of colonialists—as wolves in cheap clothing. Above all, the anthropological challenge is not to condemn errors of the past but to learn from them: to redefine the premises of fieldwork.

Now that the systemics of world-wide domination are opened to view, the nature of this domination has changed. No longer are colonialists clothing and civilizing the savages; now neocolonialists are developing the underdeveloped. The anthropologist who wants to do fieldwork in a remote tribal pocket must run the gauntlet of an independent postcolonial government likely to be hostile to what is seen as a holdover from colonialism (the missionary may well have the same problem). But often, the anthropologist (or other

Rule Britannia: The flag of colonialism is raised over Port Moresby, New Guinea, in 1884. Almost a century later, the descendants of these Papuan spectators are struggling to achieve more-than-nominal independence. (Courtesy of Australian News and Information Bureau.)

social scientist) is there sponsored by the United Nations or Ford Foundation to study or guide "modernization" or "development," and the postcolonial African or Asian elites the researcher deals with are enmeshed in a neocolonial system through which metropolitan countries continue to control and exploit their countries. Rhetoric about anthropology and the old colonialism will only dimly illuminate the ties between anthropology and the new colonialism. It is to these that we now turn.

79.
Applied Anthropology, Development Studies, and Neocolonialism

British anthropologists became seriously and closely involved in colonial administration, and hence the practical application of anthropological knowledge, in the 1920s and especially the 1930s. There had been earlier links with government anthropologists in New Guinea and Africa, and a long tradition of colonial administrator-ethnologists. In U.S. anthropology there had been a long involvement in Indian affairs, including a tradition of government anthropology through the Bureau of American Ethnology that produced distinguished scholars such as Powell and Mooney. But the United States had no colonial empire other than the Philippines and a few scattered islands, and the practical problems of administration there received only scattered anthropological attention.

World War II changed the face of American anthropology as dozens of anthropologists sought to assess the character of the enemy or played a part in the liberation and administration of Pacific and Asian regions. After the war, with Americans administering the Micronesian islands of the northern Pacific, anthropologists became centrally involved in the practical problems of administration and policy. Through the late forties, the fifties, and the early sixties, U.S. investment in rebuilding the war-torn world and aiding developing countries in modernization brought many scholars into "applied anthropology."

Applied Anthropology

Scholars seeking to apply anthropological knowledge to community development or directed social change have often had mixed feelings about transforming old and valued ways: somewhat romantic appreciation of traditional cultures runs very deep in anthropology. But in general, "applied anthropologists" have accepted the inevitability of change and the desirability of improved education, community health, and participation in government. And in general, they have accepted the colonial or postcolonial social and political system that impinged on the community they were working in (in India, Peru, Mexico, or Micronesia) as inevitable, if not necessarily as benevolent. They sought to make the impact of a wider system on local communities less disruptive and painful than it would have been without their intermediation, or to shape local reform and revitalization.

A classic case of anthropological involvement in cultural change is the Cornell Peru Project in the Vicos Valley.

Case 102: The Cornell Peru Project

A Peruvian anthropologist trained at Cornell had done field research from 1950 to 1952 in the Vicos Valley of Peru. Vicos was a manor or large estate with a population of about 1700 monolingual Quechua-speaking

Indians. Since early colonial times they had been bound as serfs or peons to the land.

Vicos was a public manor, owned by the Public Benefit Society (like many such manors) and providing revenue (at least in theory) to state charities. An individual or company rents such a manor, at auction, for 5 or 10 years. The renter, inevitably a Spanish-speaking *mestizo*, acquired the rights of a feudal lord over the serfs: he could not only demand farm labor to work the best lands commercially, but could demand household and other services as well. In "return" the serfs were given enough of the poorer agricultural land to eke out a marginal subsistence.

The Vicos serfs, like the villagers of Zinacantan (Chapter 22), had a religious hierarchy wherein respected elders who had given a life service to the scattered "community" took center stage in religious ritual for a year. But the *mestizo patron* and his agents had complete power over the peons. All efforts to break out of this desperate exploitative system had been ruthlessly crushed by a coalition of landlords, clergy, and police.

When the industrial firm renting Vicos went bankrupt in 1952 with five years of its lease remaining, Cornell University—through the leadership of anthropologist Alan Holmberg—stepped in and subleased the property. Their goal was to try to implement a bold and ambitious program of social change, in the role of *patron* into which they had stepped.

The Cornell Peru Project lasted five years. In this period, new farm technology and improved crops were able to lift agricultural production sharply, hence improve diet and bring an inflow of money for further capital improvement. With the aid of Peruvian authoritiies, education was improved. The work of peons in commercial production was channeled toward collective goals, and their manor services were paid. (Cornell enlisted the existing overseer into the operation, but in pursuit of the project's goals.) Political decision-making was increasingly passed to a committee of the former straw-bosses, progressively refilled with younger men committed to development goals.

When the five years were completed, Cornell sought to enable the peons to purchase the manor from the Public Benefit Society. For five years, power elites in the region and powerful government figures who themselves were absentee landlords sought to block the freeing of the serfs and their control over their own destiny. Through political pressure from the United States and sympathetic Peruvian intellectuals, the Vicos community finally became independent in 1962—though Cornell continued to play a supervisory role.

The transformation of Vicos, through a program that was unabashedly paternalistic, was viewed by Holmberg (1965:7) in retrospect as a bold demonstration that Peru's "serf and suppressed peasant populations, once freed and given encouragement, technical assistance and learning, can pull themselves up by their own bootstraps and become productive citizens of the nation." He was optimistic that the Peruvian government's programs of land reform "may go a long way towards a more peaceful and rapid development of the country as a whole" (Holmberg 1965:7).

At times anthropologists have had great surges of optimism about what they could tell governments and colonial administrators, or do themselves, to bridge cultural boundaries and make change more smooth or less costly in human terms. At other times the enormity and complexity of the problems and the inadequacies of their knowledge and theories have raised grave doubts and discouragement. The truth of what can and might be accomplished through "applied anthropology" lies somewhere between these poles of optimism and pessimism.

The optimism is generated by the fact that an anthropologist who has lived in a local community, who knows its leaders, its language, its details of custom, can very often see what is going wrong and how it might be set right. Many changes, procedures, laws or policies that seem sensible enough to the administrator, the missionary, or the doctor may lead to problems the anthropologist can foresee immediately. What would happen in the Trobriand Islands if a missionary converted the "chiefs" and prohibited plural marriages? What might happen in a society where bridewealth signified a contract between corporate descent groups and defined rights over the children, if an administrator or missionary outlawed bridewealth payments as "degrading to women"? What might happen among a people who believe in the magical power of substances introduced into the body, if a well-meaning doctor gives injections or takes blood samples? I vividly remember watching nervously (and wondering how to avert a massacre or at least be on the winning side) while a member of a visiting medical team took fingernail and hair clippings from Kwaio pagans in the Solomon Islands and put them in cellophane bags; six months earlier a medical missionary had been speared nearby.

Administering, converting, educating, or ministering to the health of a tribal or peasant people involves communication across cultural boundaries, in both directions. Misunderstandings run rampant on both sides, as messages in one cultural code are interpreted in terms of another. The anthropologist, specialist in the nature of cultural codes and conversant with each one, has often been able to serve as "cultural interpreter" or anticipate what messages would be misread and why.

Anthropologists have sometimes been able to suggest creative syntheses between the cultural traditions of a people and the changed situations and demands of modern life. A constitution may be possible that recognizes and builds on the authority of traditional leaders rather than bypassing them. A business cooperative might be formed in which the pattern of rights and responsibilities is modeled on traditional corporate or work groups (such as the Trobriand subclan or gardening team). Schools might teach the traditions, arts, and skills of a people instead of European history, helping to foster the pride and cultural identity so crucial to a people as they undergo sweeping changes.

Why, then, the pessimism? Basically, because anthropologists are no better than other social scientists in predicting and anticipating human behavior, in all its manifold complexity. When communication takes place between peoples, we are prone to view this as *two cultures interacting*. But cultures do not interact; warm-blooded individual human beings do, with all their idiosyncrasies and unpredictability. An anthropologist might, for example, persuade the government to build a well in the village he or she studied—and seemingly have anticipated and guarded against cultural misunderstanding. Yet the project might be rejected · because political rivalry between two local leaders leads one to condemn the well, or because someone put a curse on it during a quarrel with his wife. Such turns of events are no more predictable in a village setting than they are in a modern nation.

There is another and related problem. When an anthropologist penetrates into another way of life, he or she does so in layers or stages. After several months of fieldwork, a researcher learns the formal rules and groupings that lie on the surface of a society and its culture. At this stage one may feel a confidence and understanding that later evaporates into a feeling of ignorance as one penetrates to a deeper level. Such alternating stages of insight and impotence continue as one probes further. Those who have penetrated most deeply into another way of life are more often left with a feeling of how complex it is and how profound and unpredictable are the ramifications of any decision or event than they are with a feeling that all is known, that prediction is possible.

Yet too often attempts at applied anthropology have been made in the flush of superficial understanding. Particularly when administrators need answers, they are not likely to want to wait years. Too often the role of consultant has taken the anthropologist into an area just long enough for the formal outlines to come into focus, and not long enough for them to dissolve into a blur again. This premature feeling of confidence has also been fostered by the involvement of partially trained or inexperienced anthropologists. Saving the world by anthropology, as by any other means, looks easier to the idealistic neophyte than to the experienced and battle-scarred campaigner. The partial cultural understanding of Peace Corps volunteers may produce the same overoptimism about the scale of the problems and the effectiveness of the tools we command to solve them. Both sources of premature confidence have contributed to a disillusionment on the part of some governments and anthropologists as to what anthropology can contribute in guiding policy. In the U.S. administration of Micronesian islands, for instance, the possibilities of applied anthropology were "oversold" in the early stages, and a more sober reassessment has been necessary.

A final problem in applying anthropological knowledge to practical policy is that very often the choice is between a set of dismal alternatives. It is often not a question of which course of action will work best; but rather, which will work less badly than the others. A people whose old order is breaking down, yet who if they opt for Western ways will be condemned by geography and resources to a life of poverty and isolation, have no desirable alternatives. They are the victims of a world that oppressed, exploited, impoverished, and isolated them; they can neither fully join nor ignore it. In such situations, the satisfaction of applied anthropology are few and the successes are still failures.

Beyond Applied Anthropology

"Applied anthropology" has been questioned in latter years by a number of anthropologists of varying persuasions. Glynn Cochrane (1971), for example, has called for a more broadly conceived "development anthropology"; and he has argued that the anthropologically sophisticated administrator, with more practical approaches and more decisive commitment to development goals, can often do better as an agent of change than the professional anthropologist. (There is something to be said for this criticism: academics are notoriously wishy-washy and slow in making decisions; but on the other side, administrators in cross-cultural situations have a strong record for making bad decisions quickly.) Other criticisms have come from such scholars as Sol Tax, calling for a more bold, decisive, and politically conscious "action anthropology" that would seek to challenge the wider system that is oppressing local communities and to tackle urgent human problems directly rather than, as has usually been the case, as a by-product of fieldwork directed to other goals.

As events in the late sixties were to make dramatically clear, we need to go further still. With Project Camelot, an abortive attempt to use social science to enable the U.S. government to manipulate the course of politics in Latin American countries, the uses and abuses of applied anthropology began to emerge (see Horowitz 1965). Subsequent revelations about CIA and Defense Department funding behind seemingly innocuous research on the northern frontier of India brought a storm of protest from the Indian government and bitter division among the anthropologists involved (Berreman 1969). Participation of anthropologists in the forced resettlement of Vietnamese villagers and the manipulation of Montagnard tribesmen—often under a cloak of deception—cast a further pall on "applied anthropology" at a time when opposition to the Vietnam war had polarized the country, alienated millions of Americans from the policies of their government, and shattered the credibility of the myths of the Cold War. The bitterest and most disruptive division in American anthropology focused on clandestine participation of scholars in secret U.S. government programs to reinforce a pro-American regime in Thailand and prevent the tide of revolution from spilling over from Indochina.

Meanwhile, in Latin America, U.S.-financed programs of economic development and "land reform"—Kennedy's Alliance for Progress and subsequent programs—sought to create stability, reduce peasant unrest, and

erode support for revolutionary movements in Bolivia, Ecuador, Colombia, Brazil, Peru, Chile, Paraguay, Guatemala, Nicaragua, and other areas. And anthropologists found themselves studying ways to alleviate the symptoms of suffering in oppressed rural communities while reinforcing the ruling classes and systems of economic domination that were causing the suffering.

Anthropologists doing applied research in black American or Chicano or Native American communities similarly found themselves being paid to find out what was wrong with black families or why Native Americans drank all the time instead of working—to find cures for local symptoms that would settle community unrest. The social and economic system that generated oppression in minority enclaves was the very system government and foundations sought to preserve and strengthen.

Realization by many individuals within anthropology that the system they were serving was oppressing the people whose lives they sought to improve has placed the tradition of "applied anthropology" in a harsh new light. It has been one element in a transformed consciousness about the role of the United States, England, France, Japan, Germany, and other industrial nations in the postcolonial Third World. Many anthropologists have become aware of the systemics of what Third World writers have called "neocolonialism" (Alavi 1964; Nkrumah 1965).

The new colonialism, as viewed by these critics, is a system whereby the metropolitan countries maintain a quasi-colonial relationship with nominally independent states. Heavy overseas investment, characteristically by multinational corporations (or, in the case of Japan, by government-linked corporations), extracts minerals and other raw materials from African, Asian, Pacific, and Latin American countries (for example, oil from Venezuela; copper from Chile, Zambia, and

Papua New Guinea; bauxite from Jamaica; timber from Indonesia and the Philippines). For such investment, the prime requirement is political stability, and a malleable local elite that can be tempted with money and development schemes.

There are many variations on the theme of neocolonialism. In formerly French West Africa, in such countries as Senegal and Cameroun, French government advisers and businessmen drive around in elegant Citroens and dominate government policy and public life. Only the fiery patriot Sekou Toure of Guinea resisted French domination and turned down federation with France; and when the French left they ripped out all the telephones and destroyed everything they could.

The United States has created a string of client states, has armed them to the teeth, and has supported military dictatorships in a score of Latin American, Asian, and other countries. In Chile, a popularly elected socialist government was overturned in 1973 with active U.S. support; at the time of writing, martial law sustains a landowning elite in the Philippines, where U.S. and Japanese investment has been enormous. In Brazil, staggering overseas investment in the development of the interior has gone hand in hand with sordid political repression and the massive arming by the United States of a military dictatorship—guaranteeing political and hence economic stability at the expense of freedom, and rewarding a small millionaire aristocracy amid vast poverty, squalor, and suffering. The same theme is repeated on a lesser scale over and over in Latin America.

The threat to this system is that poverty and repression will lead to revolution—as in Cuba. So aid projects to "develop" rural areas, and token land reform that does little or nothing to redistribute wealth or power, are undertaken to create hope among the hope-

What price progress? Brazil's Trans-Amazon Highway network is being carved out of rain forest at a cost of ecological devastation, the destruction of Indian populations and their cultures, and the forced resettlement of thousands of poor farmers along the highway margins. (Courtesy of Brazilian Government Trade Bureau.)

less and powerless. Token development is replacing religion as the opiate of the masses.

And there in the village has been the anthropologist or the Peace Corps volunteer trying to teach people to use tractors instead of water buffaloes, to raise slightly the productivity of miserable and overworked land holdings, to read and write, or to improve village sanitation. The elites that control the most productive land and rake the benefits from foreign aid are far from view, in the cities, behind high walls, in glittering villas, in penthouses. (And their children are likely to be at Harvard or Oxford.)

One irony, as Kathleen Gough (1968) points out, is that the anthropologist—if allowed to do research in Third World countries at all—is likely to be welcome only in those countries that are client states of the West. Where independence and sovereignty have been genuine, not nominal, Western anthropologists have usually been excluded as imperialists in yet another guise. And given the historic role of anthropologists, however naive and innocent they may have been about its implications, such a stance is sensible enough.

Gough's conclusion, one that a number of her colleagues have come to share, is that the anthropologist's role as a champion of freedom and dignity for common people should be to support social revolution in neocolonialist countries. If anthropologists do not stand with the oppressed, she argues—if they accept the status quo in the countries where they work, despite political repression and gross inequalities in power and wealth—then they themselves are oppressors.

Such rhetoric, urging as it does support of socialist revolution, resistance to world capitalism, and active political involvement, goes too far for many—most—students or anthropologists to accept. To people who have been brought up to think that fighting back the forces of communism is the historic destiny of the United States and that capitalism and democracy go hand in hand, such talk is downright heretical if not treasonous. But the challenge to question assumptions and dogma is squarely laid down, for those bold enough to undertake it—whatever the outcome.

At least, the bitter political debate in anthropology has given the lie to the widespread assumption that social science can be objective and neutral—that it can be free of ideological and political commitments and can seek truth without involvement. It is being realized that not taking a political position, not making a moral commitment, is not neutral: it *is* making a commitment—to the support and continuation of the system of which one is a part and within which one is working anthropologically. If one does not "notice" oppression or injustice or exploitation because one is only a scientist and science does not concern itself with political issues, then one is being myopic and self-deluding about objectivity. Ultimately amorality is immorality.

The myth of scientific objectivity has also begun to fall apart through an awareness of the ideological bias implicit in social science theory. Theories that seem to build on common sense in fact build on the premises of the economic and political system of the theorizer. Thus the assumptions that the individual is the appropriate locus of explanation, that social systems are created and maintained by cumulative individual acts of maximization and self-interest, and that the roots of such self-interest lie deep in human nature are premises of Western capitalist ideology that have been promulgated since Adam Smith's time to rationalize and explain the political economy of Western nations. The anthropologist or sociologist or economist who uses such models may take these premises to be obvious, objective, and beyond question. The rise of radical counterinterpretations within Western social sciences (including a belated discovery of the extensive body of Marxist scholarship) has given new insight into the ideological biases of "establishment" social science.

All this points to a need to broaden and generalize the intellectual base of anthropology and other social sciences—the need for a "critical and self-reflexive" study of human assumptions and the distortions in our special view of the world (Scholte 1972). It also points to a need to redefine the relationship of anthropology to the Third World, a need for decolonization of anthropology both at the level of theory and at the level of practice. It is to these problems that we now turn.

80.
Decolonizing Anthropology

Anthropology has aspired to be a general study of the human condition, ranging widely in time and space to see contrasts and similarities. But the kind of perspective we have taken underlines the fact that a Chinese anthropology or an ancient Indian anthropology or a Trobriand anthropology might have begun with very different premises and achieved very different perspectives. (Seeing anthropology as a product of colonial expansion, and of the romantic quest for the "primitive" as a recurrent Western fantasy, helps us to understand why Chinese, Indians, and Trobrianders did *not* elaborate anthropological theories—for the very enterprise is peculiarly Western.)

The *contents* of anthropological theory, as well as its underlying assumptions, reflect the special cultural heritage of Western Europe. Consider how many of the analytic categories anthropology has sought to refine and generalize to classify events in other peoples' worlds derive initially from the folk categories of modern European languages or from Greek and Latin—such terms as "family," "kinship," "supernatural," "religion," "economic," "laws," "property," and "magic," or concepts like "cause," "institutions," and "function." Anthropologists rather rarely find equivalents of most of these terms in non-European languages. How different might a comparative study of man be that had begun with a different set of folk categories and sought to make them precise?

Perceptions of other peoples' behavior are similarly deflected by the cultural assumptions of the observer, as a classic study of an American Indian society by a Chinese scholar reveals vividly.

Case 103: A Chinese View of the Zuni

In 1935, a Chinese anthropologist, Li An-Che, spent three months living in a Zuni Indian household. The Zuni were anthropologically well documented by such observers as Stevenson and Bunzel. Yet after his brief immersion in Zuni life, Li was puzzled by the almost stereotyped view of their culture given by American anthropologists.

Where the Americans had seen in Zuni religion an extreme preoccupation with formal detail but a lack of emotional commitment, Li was impressed with the reverence and depth of feeling beneath outward formalism. Where Americans had been struck by the lack of competitiveness, and inferred that Zuni were reluctant to assume leadership, Li saw a misplaced application of our own cultural logic: "In the competitive Western world . . . where, if one does not push ahead, one is surely pushed behind" the absence of ambition implies the absence of leadership. "But in another society where mutual give and take is harmoniously assumed among all beings of the world, one might be . . . humble" and still be a leader among men. "Thus leadership is naturally assumed . . . [and] followed by others who do not see in the act of following any degree of humiliation" (Li An-Che 1937:68).

Where Americans had been struck by the lack of parental discipline, Li saw a child's behavior as shaped by a united adult front. He indirectly expresses wonder at the way Americans deal with their children: "To get bodily enjoyment by caressing the baby as a plaything and calling this love is not the pattern in Zuni" (70). Finally, Li was struck, in a way American observers had not been, by the mirror image relationship between the position of a wife in a patrilineally oriented society like China and the position of a husband among the matrilineal Zuni. He agrees that "It is not correct to say that woman rules man in Zuni, but what is . . . important . . . is that woman is not ruled by man at all" (75).

What Li infers from the very different view of Zuni culture his perspective as a Chinese presented is that observers see some but not all elements in an unfamiliar cultural pattern and "are easily led astray by their own background in supplying the missing logic with their own" (70).

The psychoanalyst-anthropologist George Devereux (1967) has recently reminded anthropologists vividly of what they were beginning to discover in the 1940s—that the depths of the observer's psyche affect the process of perception, through "countertransference." Many of the psychological orientations involved are at least in part shared and cultural—attitudes toward sex or dirt or intimacy; and these may lead anthropological observers to perceive selectively or react inappropriately to other people's signals.

All this underlines an urgent need for one kind of decolonization of anthropology, at an intellectual level. Third World scholars studying human behavior in comparative settings—perhaps most urgently, in Western industrialized countries—could contribute crucially to the emergence of a genuinely universal and generalized study of human ways. As recent debates and discussion (see, for example, Lewis 1974 and Caulfield 1973) have underlined, there needs to be a decolonization of anthropology that brings to bear the power of both "inside" and "outside" views. The central theme of Lewis' argument, building on other critiques by Third World scholars, is that in a decolonized anthropology white anthropologists would not study black or Native American communities; rather black anthropologists should study black communities, Native Americans should study Native American communities, and so on (Lewis 1974).

But as Caulfield and others have countered, there are some flaws in this argument. One is that a black anthropologist who has grown up in a middle-class suburban setting and has gotten an anthropology PhD may be separated by wide gulfs of social class from ghetto blacks—and may be as much "outside" in terms of culture and class as a white anthropologist would be (though politically he *might* be defined as an "insider"). Second, the anthropological cost of an inside view is at least as great as the benefit. A corollary of Lewis' view would seem to be that only white middle-class ethnographers should study American suburbia. Yet they may be precisely the wrong ones to do it, because they take too much for granted, accepting strange behavior (like saving trading stamps or taking pet dogs to doctors) as commonplace and undeserving of comment. The heightened perception of a Trobriand anthropologist or a Kachin anthropologist would be likely to cast more vivid comparative light on American upper-middle-class behavior than an anthropologist who grew up in these settings. Unfortunately, when academic opportunities have opened to formerly colonized peoples, or when Third World scholars from India, Indonesia, or the Philippines or Nigeria have been trained anthropologically, they have usually been indoctrinated with the technical jargon and theoretical prejudices of Anglo-American or continental anthropology. In the process of acquiring a PhD from Oxford, Chicago, the Sorbonne, or Leiden, a Third World anthropologist is likely to be so indoctrinated in the traditional assumptions of the discipline that he emerges perceiving the world in the manner of Radcliffe-Brown or Lévi-Strauss. Part of the challenge in decolonizing anthropology is for Third World students to be encouraged to question and challenge the premises and categories of Anglo-American or French anthropology, not simply apply them in emulation of their teachers.

There is some power in an inside view as well: intuitions can be brought to bear, and native actors can often see the oversimplifications in anthropological descriptions. Conventional anthropological descriptions may be possible only because of the ethnographer's limited evidence and relative ignorance of how subtle and complicated another people's social world really is. As I have observed, "the anthropologist who can confidently write about 'the lineage' in an African tribe would be hard-pressed to write in a similar vein about 'the department' in his university—because he knows too much" (Keesing 1972c:38.) The inadequacies, oversimplifications, and distortions of anthropology fieldwork—the costs of an "outside" view—are becoming painfully clear as students in formerly colonial areas learn what anthropologists have written about their people. In Papua New Guinea, for example, there is a growing body of critical commentary from Trobrianders, Dobuans, Enga, Arapesh, and other students from anthropologically classic societies on the flaws of ethnography and the frailties of ethnographers. These obvious benefits of an inside perspective highlight the need for and value of a dialectic between inside and outside views, so that benefits of each can be achieved and the limits of each

can be transcended. It seems more appropriate to recast Lewis' critique.

What is needed is a genuine decolonization of anthropology; and having anthropologists study only people of their own culture or skin color gives only a partial and illusory decolonization. The colonialism in anthropology has not simply come from white anthropologists studying nonwhite Third World people. Rather, it has come from the rich, powerful, and dominant studying the poor, powerless, and subordinate; and racism has been more symptom and by-product than cause of this exploitation. (As we noted in §70, the boundaries between oppressed and oppressor, between the victims and perpetrators of racism or its equivalent, have shifted historically with tides of economic exploitation: poor whites and southern Europeans and Irish have been victims, as well as Africans and Asians, when it was economically advantageous to deny them full human status.) A decolonized anthropology will have to balance this asymmetry of power and seek to create a dialectical and symmetrical relationship between the studier and the studied.

As we will shortly see, this means a new ethic of fieldwork where subjects are accorded full rights, where they participate as collaborators in the process of ethnography and its rewards. But it also means that anthropology can no longer concern itself only with powerless, poor, marginal communities far from where wealth and power are manipulated. An anthropology not only of suburbia but of bureaucracies, corporations, governments, and legal systems is urgently needed. As we have seen in previous sections, the anthropologist's view from a small marginal community often leaves hidden the wider systemic forces of economy and politics that shape local events. Anthropologists—Third World anthropologists and Anglo-American anthropologists who can look critically at their own institutions—need to be where decisions are made, as well as in distant communities where their impact is felt.

Some anthropologists will of course continue to work in remote and powerless communities, though the list of places where this is still possible in the Third World shrinks each year as consciousness of sovereignty and strength of identity rise among the formerly colonized. How can the relationship of ethnographer to tribal or peasant villager be decolonized? What ethical questions have arisen with new urgency?

One of many realizations that came from the Indochina war was the realization that the isolated community whose culture an ethnographer describes may not stay isolated; and that what an anthropologist writes may be used to defraud or destroy the people who shared their lives and ways with him. Cora Dubois has noted that the Japanese executed some of her close friends and informants on the remote Indonesian Island of Alor in World War II because they innocently spoke of an America they had heard about from her (Dubois 1960). Such tragedies were magnified in Vietnam. The French anthropologist Georges Condominas, himself related through a grandparent to the Vietnamese mountain people he studied, the Mnong Gar, has voiced his outrage and bitterness at the barbarous misuse of his writings. In 1957, he wrote a poetic book in French about the Mnong Gar that drew heavily on the wisdom of a Mnong Gar philosopher friend and sage. The U.S. government, without his permission, translated the book and other works on the Mnong Gar into English and distributed them to U.S. Special Forces (Green Beret) units trying to force Vietnamese mountain villagers into joining their military operations. U.S. soldiers tortured Condominas' philosopher-friend-informant to death trying to force him to divulge the information they knew he knew. And the Mnong Gar that survived the carnage of war were scattered as virtual prisoners in refugee camps, their villages destroyed by army units equipped with an anthropological guide book.

Such catastrophic invasions of the trust and good faith that makes fieldwork possible have given many anthropologists a heightened sense of the awesome responsibility they take over other people's lives.

Should the ethnographer disguise names and places to try to guard against abuse of this trust? Probably so, in most cases. But the protection is probably usually illusory—anyone sufficiently interested who gets to the general area can find out in a few minutes or hours the real names of communities, clans, or individuals despite efforts to protect anonymity.

There are other ethical issues in fieldwork beyond placing one's subjects in jeopardy. Do the people have any real choice in being studied or not being studied, or is it forced on them by the ethnographer or the local administration? Do they have a right to their privacy? Do they have the right (and the power) to close off sacred areas of their culture from outside view and exposure? Do they have rights over their pictures, or confidentially disclosed information? Are individuals protected from slanderous gossip or embarrassing disclosure?

Should an anthropologist try to reciprocate the hospitality and trust that have been offered with a return of book royalties? With sharing of his or her knowledge of the outside world? With continuing human concern and involvement after fieldwork ends?

What is the ethnographer's responsibility if he or she encounters events—infanticide, head-hunting, incest, polygyny, murder, theft—that violate the laws of the region? Can he or she protect the confidence of the people who opened these events to observation?

What is the responsibility of an ethnographer who encounters injustice or oppression against the community studied, especially if it is perpetrated by the government whose permission is needed to continue the study? An anthropologist working in a Brazilian Indian village found out that the Indians were being systematically swindled by the local representative of the Indian Protection Service. When he denounced the swindler to his superiors in the central government he discovered that these superiors were organizing and profiting from the fraud—and quickly found himself in trouble with the immigration authorities.

What is the ethnographer's responsibility when he or she encounters oppression *within* the community studied—where infants are killed, mental defectives are abused, women, young people, or commoners are exploited or oppressed? Can the ethnographer only observe? The anthropologist has a more global view of the world, a more adequate theory of disease, perhaps a more sophisticated view of how life could be improved. But does he or she, given greater power in a colonial relationship, have a moral or political right to introduce changes? An ethnographer who perceives that women are oppressed in a society where they are blamed and punished for sorcery, secluded because they are polluted, or abused because they are weak may believe that these women could and should liberate themselves. But is it yet another expression of an anthropologist's colonialist power to try to initiate social change or foment "class" struggle?

To all these questions there are no simple all-purpose answers. But they constitute critical challenges to anthropological responsibility and further shatter the myth that doing anthropology is or could be objective and morally neutral. When one enters human situations one assumes human responsibilities; and when one enters a powerless, marginal community as intermediary of an outside world, one's responsibilities are awesome. Often no satisfactory answers to these ques-

tions are possible, other than not doing anthropology—or not doing it in Third World communities one enters as representative of the dominant world powers. The anthropologist who applies in vain for permission to do fieldwork in a Third World country may feel thwarted by fumbling bureaucracy; but such refusal often reflects not clumsy obstructionism but an awareness heightened beyond that of the anthropologist of how exploitative and dangerous seemingly innocent fieldwork can be, and how fraught with colonial premises the ethnographic situation can be.

Decolonizing the anthropology of Third World communities from within the discipline is easy to talk about but enormously difficult to achieve—as long as there are such disparities of wealth and power in the world. Anthropologists should not wonder that the issue is so often being taken out of their hands. Third World countries are increasingly discovering that the simplest and most thorough way to decolonize anthropology is to keep anthropologists at home. The issues do not go away, however; they are merely shifted to the urban poor the anthropologist decides to study instead when a visa or grant for fieldwork in Africa or New Guinea is turned down.

The dilemmas are deep, difficult, and urgent. On their outcome depends what anthropology will become, and whether it will endure, in the next 20 years.

81.

Anthropology and Survival in an Age of Crisis

Whether anthropology survives is a trivial question compared to the larger problems that loom. Many demographers and ecologists warn that the human population is outstripping the possible limits of food production, and that the world ecosystem is at the brink of irreparable damage and probable destruction. Human efforts at control and solution seem piecemeal, partial, and too late. The very systems and strategies that have created vast technological power, and the very structures of mind and society that have made possible spectacular evolutionary success, have set off a spiral they cannot control. The quest for power and control over nature seems now to have led into the trap of nature's intricate and infinite web.

There is hope, but it does not lie in doing the same things harder, better, and faster. It must lie in wisdom and control (in the sense of systemic integration, restraint, and balance, not in the sense of more power). And it is precisely in these realms that the culture of technology and technocracy the West has been spreading around the globe is most lacking.

It is too simple to say, as Gregory Bateson (1972a) does, that it is pathological Western (or human?) ways of thinking that have gotten us into this desperate situation. It is also ways of organizing, systems of economic and political organization. To say that these systems are products of pathological ways of thinking, as Bateson would seem to, is at least half wrong: ways of thinking are also reflections or realizations of modes of organization. In the realm of ecological balance, we can well compare Japan and China. In both, philosophical emphasis on harmony and wisdom, not power and technology, have been central themes. Yet modern China leads the world in ecological control, recycling of wastes, and restraint in resource consumption, while Japan sinks increasingly into a mire of chemical slime amid a brown cloud of pollution. The Chinese, we might well conclude, have created a social system where traditional values and modern wisdom can be expressed and applied; the Japanese have created (partly in emulation of the West) an economic and social system that systematically violates the wisdom of Zen while paying surface homage to it. (It remains to be seen whether China can

preserve this restraint and wisdom as industrialization increases.)

A world dramatically made small by air travel and world-wide communication poses problems of cultural conflict and social integration on a scale unmatched in human history. Since the early empires of Mesopotamia, countless ethnic minorities have been swallowed up in larger states. Their languages and customs were different; and hence the laws and customs of the dominant group could not easily be adopted by, or forced upon, them. How, then, could one reconcile social and political integration with cultural distinctiveness?

The problem is as old as written history. The "solutions"—suppression, assimilation, genocide, indirect rule, separatism—have seldom worked and have seldom been reconcilable with moral codes. In the latter twentieth century, this problem confronts humans on a scale, and with a global danger, never faced before.

Throughout the world, peoples emerging from tribalism to "underdeveloped nationhood," and from "underdeveloped" to "developed," are seeking and demanding the material fruits of Western technology. For better or worse, Western "standards of living" are rapidly becoming universal aspirations. But what can this mean in cultural terms? To join into the world economy, and the community of nations, must people abandon their traditional world view, values, and conventions? In many segments of their lives, the question has become academic for formerly tribal peoples. The impact of the West has broken down economic self-sufficiency, sent the young away from village settings and flocking to cities. Kinship groupings larger than the family have disintegrated or lost their functions. Old religions have been abandoned. Traditional leaders have been bypassed by Western-educated politicians. The old order—were there some compelling reason to preserve it—is gone beyond preservation. New levels of unity are being carved out that bind together formerly diverse tribal peoples.

Are non-Western peoples to lose their cultural distinctiveness? Does a standardization of legal treatment, education, and opportunity in a nation of diverse peoples necessarily mean a cultural uniformity? Must members of a minority group reject what is distinctive of their way of life to achieve equal opportunity? Humans are stumbling toward answers, and meanwhile, killing and hating one another.

No modern nation has solved or managed without great costs and grave problems the paradox of reconciling cultural pluralism with political unity and internal order. Some have done better than others. The United States has incorporated large immigrant groups from East and West—with their adaptations ranging from rapid and enthusiastic assimilation to the cultural separatism of Chinatown. Yet the dilemma of American blacks and Chicanos—to create a new cultural identity and achieve pride and dignity without isolating themselves from the economic and political mainstream—affords no easy answer. That is not a singular dilemma. It must be dealt with on a massive scale in the Soviet Union, China, and India. It faces peoples in Africa, Asia, Latin America, and the Pacific. Do the Kachins of Burma, who through centuries of invasion and political turmoil have preserved their cultural identity, lose it now as part of a modern nation? In the Philippines, with scores of local languages and distinct cultural traditions, can representative government and administrative flexibility preserve the integrity of these traditions? And at the same time, can the boundaries of each group be kept open enough that from them can emerge into the national society those who aspire to be doctors, politicians, or physicists?

In one sense, cultural distinctiveness is an artifact of tribalism—and tribalism and its extension, nationalism, pose grave dangers of mass devastation in a nuclear age. Yet in another sense, the richness of cultural diversity is a crucial human resource. The cancelling out of cultural differences and the emergence of a standardized world culture might—while solving some problems of political integration—deprive humanity of sources of wisdom and vision, and a reservoir of diversity and alternatives, we cannot afford to lose. One of the crucial secrets of evolutionary adaptation is diversity, between individuals but also between local populations. The canceling out of human diversity may in the long run exact staggering costs. Yet solutions to the problems of reconciling cultural pluralism with world order still lie beyond the horizon of our vision.

Here Bateson's views can be brought to bear. He points out that it is the exaggerated emphasis on rationality and control over nature that has brought great technological power to the West. And it is precisely this philosophy as well as this technology that is being exported to the Third World through "modernization." Ironically, it may well be that the West has as much to learn from Third World peoples as to teach them.

Does anthropology provide grounds for hope that humans can work out regional and planetary strategies for survival?

As modern thinkers apparently must, the anthropologist has moments of crushing pessimism when humanity seems in a downward spiral—poisoning and polluting the environment, madly overpopulating the planet, crushing the highest aspirations of the human spirit, and visiting death and destruction in the name of petty principles. But philosophizing on the human condition, one is also led by visions of what we could be, if we would. One's views of human nature, of social life, of cultural order and possibility, fluctuate accordingly.

Given the political and economic climate

of the Western world at the time of writing, it takes rather more mental effort to imagine an idyllic 1984 than an Orwellian one. But anthropology is documenting more and more compellingly the remarkable capacity of humans to change their ideas and behavior drastically.

These paragraphs are being written in Papua New Guinea as people who grew up in the Stone Age drive past in their cars, fly in (or behind the controls of) airplanes, and debate their country's political future. And I have just been reading the words of B. M. Narokobi, who has emerged from a Mountain Arapesh[1] village to become a brilliantly able lawyer:

[We can] build a new society based on communal sharing, inter-dependence, mutual trust, self-reliance and love. We cannot hope to build a new society by being half committed to the imperialistic and capitalistic life styles. We have arrived at the point where the only honest road to choose is a total commitment to the ideology of human development. Let those who believe take the first step and build our nation based on interdependent communities. . . . I am convinced we can build a new society . . . free . . . of many constraints of . . . past societies. . . . Modern civilization is yet to answer many basic needs of humans everywhere. There is no harm in trying an alternative which might answer our true needs.(Narokobi 1974:2)

Perhaps this is an unrealistic optimism. But at this point, the success of new modes of

[1]Anthropologically famous from the work of Margaret Mead (1935, 1938).

political and economic organization is urgent not only for new nations like Papua New Guinea but for humans everywhere. And the ability of formerly tribal peoples to emerge into a new world and imagine a better one gives hope that the rich and powerful nations might change their courses before it is too late.

The challenge, somehow, is to achieve for the industrial nations what their massive invasion has forced on less powerful peoples—a radical restructuring of world view and experience, and a new integration. Whether that is possible can well be doubted. Collective exploration of new visions, and the transformation or dismantling of established systems and vested powers, will be extraordinarily difficult, perhaps impossible.

An understanding of human diversity is urgent if such visions and transformations are to be possible. Whatever wisdom cultural anthropology has gleaned in its sweeping study of human ways is wisdom about diversity—its extent, its nature, its roots. That wisdom, used wisely, can be a crucial human resource: for in understanding human differences we can glimpse new human possibilities. Visions of society must be broadened, but they must be wisely constrained. If they are not illuminated by sound understanding of human nature—biological, social, and cultural—and of the limits of human possibility, they could speed disaster, not avert it. Here we have no better source of wisdom than the diverse ways of life, the multifold human possibilities, we have glimpsed in these pages.

GLOSSARY

Abbevilian: A technique of biface (two-edged) core-tool making widespread in the European Lower Paleolithic.

Aboriginal: If capitalized adjective: Pertaining to Australian Aborigines. If uncapitalized adjective: Pertaining to an indigenous population.

Aborigine, Australian: A member of the indigenous population of Australia.

Acculturation: Culture change due to contact between societies; most often used to refer to adaptation of subordinate tribal societies to domination by Western societies.

Acheulian: A complex of stone tools rather more sophisticated than Oldowan, and marked by core tools such as hand-axes; characteristic of many *Homo erectus* and some early *Homo sapiens* populations (covering a time span of several hundred thousand years).

Achieved Status: A social position a person assumes, not according to the circumstances of birth and inheritance, but according to his or her acts, accomplishments, qualifications, and such. (As opposed to *Ascribed Status.*)

Action Group: A group of people joined temporarily to accomplish some task or take part in some collective action.

Adaptive Radiation: Proliferation and differentation of an evolving group of organisms, marked by the diversification of species in adaptation to different environments.

Adaptation, Biological: Evolutionary modification of organisms or biological structures to fit into a particular environment.

Adze: A cutting tool differing from an axe in that the blade is hafted at right angles to the handle (like a hoe) rather than parallel to it.

Affine: A relative by marriage. (Normally, however, the spouse of a parent's sibling and, reciprocally, the child of one's spouse's sibling are classed with *consanguineal* relatives, not affines).

Affinity: Relationship by marriage. May include the relationship between corporate groups linked by marriage between their members.

Age Grade: A social category based on age, within a series of such categories, through which individuals pass in the course of the life cycle. (Also known as *age class.*)

Age Set: A category (or corporate group) based on age, within a hierarchy of such categories. Differs from age grades in that one remains in the same age set as it becomes progressively more senior rather than moving up a ladder of categories.

Agnate: A person related by patrilineal descent.

Agnatic Descent: See *Patrilineal Descent.*

Algorithm: A set of computational or logical operations; that is, a programmed routine.

Agriculture: In general sense, cultivation of crops; in narrow and more technical sense, cultivation using plows (as contrasted with *horticulture* (q.v.), in which only digging sticks, hoes, and such are used).

Alliance: A system whereby descent groups or other kin groups are linked by a rule of prescriptive or recurrent marriage so that the groups remain in an affinal relationship to one another across generations.

Analog: Of a communications system, using the magnitude of continuous variables (loudness, size, temperature) to communicate messages or represent relationships. (Cf. *Digital.*)

Anasazi: The Pueblo Indian cultural pattern, in the Southwest (U.S.), which emerges archaeologically with Basketmaker cultures and continues to the modern Hopi.

Ancestor Worship: The worship or propitiation of ancestors, particularly characteristic of societies organized in terms of corporate descent groups.

Animatism: A belief that the natural world is pervaded or animated by impersonal spiritual force(s), such as Melanesian *mana* or North American Indian *orenda.*

Animism: A belief in in-dwelling spirits in natural objects and phenomena.

Ape: Primate suborder, including the great apes (gorilla, chimpanzee, orangutan) and the gibbons.

Apical Ancestor (Ancestress):   The ancestor or ancestress from which descent is traced. (The "apex" of the triangle of descendants.)

Applied Anthropology: The use of anthropological knowledge and expertise to deal with problems in the "real world"; for example, the introduction of technological innovations, public health, or economic development schemes (or, in physical anthropology, the design of airplane seats or cockpits).

Arboreal: Characterizing the way of life of an animal that lives entirely or mainly in trees.

Archaic: In prehistory, used to designate a stage in a particular regional sequence of development (hence it has different precise meanings in different regions).

Artificial Intelligence: A generic term for mathematical representations of the programs of biological organisms, especially the programs of the brain, that simulate the processes of intelligence (for example, problem-solving, pattern recognition). This includes, but is not limited to, the use of such mathematical representations in programming computers or building robots to simulate human performance.

Ascribed Status: A social position or category to which one belongs, or which one assumes, by virtue of who one is, rather than what one does; that is, due to the circumstances of birth, inheritance, kinship relationship, and such. (As opposed to *Achieved Status.*)

Association: A social group based on shared interest or voluntary participation.

Asymmetrical Alliance: In alliance theory, a marriage system involving indirect exchange. (Patrilateral alliance is considered by some theorists to be nonexistent or impossible, so matrilateral alliance—marriage with MBD or a girl classed with her—is the form commonly referred to as asymmetrical.)

Atlatl: A spearthrower, an artificial extension of the human arm that increases throwing velocity.

Aurignacian: An Upper Paleolithic cultural tradition in Western Europe marked by refined stone tools and cave paintings.

Australopithecine: Hominid forms, spanning the late Pliocene and early Pleistocene epochs, some of which were apprently human ancestors.

Austronesian: A family of languages spoken in the Indonesian Zone (including Malay, Indonesian, and Philippine languages), in most of Melanesia (other than New Guinea), in Polynesia, in Micronesia, in parts of Taiwan, and in Madagascar (Malagasy). (Also known as *Malayo-Polynesian.*)

Avoidance Relationship: A patterned social relationship whereby individuals in a particular kinship relationship (for example, mother-in-law/son-in-law, brother/sister) must avoid social contact or behave in formal and constrained ways.

Avunculocal: (Postmarital) residence of a person with mother's brother. Since characteristically this entails residence of a couple with the *husband's* maternal uncle, the terms *viri-avunculocal* or *avuncu-virilocal* are more precise.

B.P.: Before the present (indicating dates of prehistoric events).

Baboons: Large ground-living Old World monkeys, powerful and with large canine teeth.

Band: In primate studies, a social group occupying a home range; in hunting and gathering societies, a social group occupying a territory.

Bantu: A widespread language family in sub-Saharan Africa, originally derived from the Cameroon highlands.

Barrio: A neighborhood grouping within an urban setting, marked by a sense of community (in Latin America, historically derived from such neighborhood kinship groupings as the Aztec *calpulli*).

Big Man System: A mode of leadership characteristic of Melanesia (including New Guinea), whereby the leader ("Big Man") commands a following by manipulation of wealth. The leader's powers depend on personal skill and on continuing entrepreneurial and political success, and hence are not hereditary.

Bilateral Kinship: Kinship traced to relatives through both father and mother. (Also known as *consanguineal kinship.*)

Binary Opposition: A two-sided contrast (nature vs. culture, voiced vs. unvoiced), used to establish a semantic, symbolic, or other distinction.

Binocular Vision: The capacity to see objects with both eyes, hence three-dimensionally, with overlapping fields of vision.

Bipedal: Walking upright on the hind legs. (As a noun, *biped.*)

Blood-Feuding: A state of continuing warfare and hostility between groups marked by homicide and retaliatory murder.

Blood Group: A classification of red blood cells, based on reaction of the cells with particular sets of antibodies. There are several blood group systems (ABO, MN, and so on).

Boasian: Characterizing the anthropology of Franz Boas, his students, and those they trained, marked by a concern for ethnographic detail, a careful search for historical and other connections, an emphasis on the diversity of cultures, and an insistence that human behavior is primarily a product of diverse cultural experience.

Bonding: Formation of biologically channeled psychological attachment to the mother (or mother-figure), other close attachment figures, or a mate. (See *Pair Bond.*)

Brachiation: A mode of locomotion by swinging arm over arm along a horizontal branch or other support, characteristic particularly of gibbons.

Breeding Isolate: A population whose members seldom if ever mate with members of other populations.

Bride Price: See *Bridewealth.*

Bridewealth: Marriage payments from the husband and his kin to the bride's kin. Characteristically these payments balance a transfer of rights over the wife's sexuality, work services, residence, fertility, and such.

Bronze Age: A stage or level of technological development marked by the use of bronze tools and characteristically accompanied (where it emerged in Europe, China, and elsewhere) by marked social stratification and a specialization of labor.

Bushman: Member of the Khoisan (Hottentot) speaking populations of southern Africa, physically distinct from surrounding peoples; historically, hunter-gatherers.

Canine Teeth: Pointed or cone-shaped teeth in front corners of mammalian mouths, often specialized for biting and aggressive display.

Carbon 14 Dating: Dating of organic archaeological materials by calculating the percentage of radioactive carbon, which decays at a constant rate.

Cargo Cult: A millennial movement characteristic of Melanesia in the Southwest Pacific, marked by the expectation that Western material goods will be received by supernatural means.

Cargo System: In Mesoamerica, a Spanish-derived hierarchy of religious offices, or religious and political offices, through which individuals pass as temporary holders of these offices *(Cargos)*.

Carnivore: Meat-eating animal.

Caste: In the Indian subcontinent, an endogamous social group incorporated within the stratified hierarchy of Hindu ideology. Some sociologists would apply the term more generally to endogamous, ranked social classes.

Category: A collectivity of things (people, items, events, and so on) classed together because of some culturally relevant feature(s) they share. In kinship theory, *category* refers to the position (advanced notably by Leach and Needham) that kin terms ("relationship terms") relate broad categories of "kinds" of people.

Caudillo: In Latin America a leader whose power has come from exploits as a war leader.

Cerebral Cortex: Outer layer of the brain, highly developed in higher primates and particularly in humans; this convoluted gray tissue is the physical center of most higher brain functions.

Chatelperronian: An early Upper Paleolithic tool industry in Western Europe. (Also known as *Lower Perigordian.*)

Chiefdom: A political system in which kin groups are linked together through a hierarchy of political and/or religious leadership.

Chopper: Early stone tool technology marked by the use of edged pebbles held in the palm.

Choukoutien: Cave site near Peking where rich *Homo erectus* fossil finds were made in the 1930s.

Chinampas: Mode of intensive cultivation by the Aztecs, in lagoons and drained swamps of the valley of Mexico, where gardens were built up from rich mud and vegetable materials.

Chronology, Absolute: The dating of time levels (especially those of ancient geologic periods or fossils) in terms of absolute age (that is, reckoned in years).

Chronology, Relative: The dating of ancient time periods or fossil remains not in terms of their absolute age (in years) but in terms of their serial order (older or younger) relative to one another. The sorting out of time sequences where the dates of each period cannot be established.

Circuits: In cybernetic analysis, any path along which information ("news of a difference") can travel within a system (as with the electronic circuits of a thermostat or the connections that link the stick of a blind man with his brain).

Clan: A unilineal descent group or category whose members trace patrilineal descent (patri-clan) or matrilineal descent (matri-clan) from an apical ancestor/ancestress, but do not know the genealogical links that connect them to this apical ancestor.

Class: *See Social Class.*

Class Analysis: A mode of social analysis, pioneered by Marx and Engels, in which the underlying dynamics of a society are sought, beneath superficialities and the camouflage of ideologies, in the historically rooted interests and conflicts of social classes in relation to means of production, labor and its fruits, and the distribution of power.

Classificatory System: A mode of kinship classification in which collateral kin are terminologically equated with lineal kin (FB=F, MZ=M, and so on).

Cline: In population genetics, a pattern of distribution where frequencies of alternative genes vary along a continuous gradient.

Clovis: A distinctive projectile blade type used by big-game hunters in North America some 11,000 years ago, and the associated cultural tradition.

Coding: The organization of information in a particular physical or logical representation. For example, a TV picture is organized as a set of electronic signals and then re-coded by a transducer—the TV set—into visual images. A page of a book could be coded as a written visual image, as magnetic signals in a computer, as sound patterns (if read aloud), as dots and dashes in Morse code, or neurologically in someone's brain.

Cognate: A bilateral (consanguineal) kinsman or kinswoman.

Cognatic: *Sense 1:* A mode of descent reckoning where all descendants of an apical ancestor (ancestress) through any combination of male or female links are included (preferred sense). *Sense 2:* Synonymous with *bilateral* or *consanguineal* (q.v.), as in "cognatic kinship" (the same as "bilateral kinship").

Cognition: The processes of thinking and memory.

Cognitive: Related to the processes of cognition, the processes of *thinking* and *knowing* (in contrast to emotions and motivation).

Collateral: In kinship terminologies, the siblings of lineal relatives (parents, grandparents) and their descendants.

Compadrazgo: In Latin America and other Spanish-influenced areas (for example, Guam), ritual coparenthood, where godparents play roles complementary to parents in relation to children.

Comparative Method: In anthropology, a method for investigating cross-cultural recurrences in (and hence for testing theories about) the relationship between different customs, practices, and institutions (for example, the relationship between child-rearing practices and religious beliefs). In linguistics, the comparative method is a way of assessing historical relationships between languages on the basis of regularities in sound shifts and their correspondences.

Competence, Linguistic: A speaker's knowledge of his language (mainly unconscious), which is drawn on in speaking and understanding speech (*transformational* linguistics).

Competitive Exclusion: The principle that no two species in the same area can occupy precisely the same ecological niche: one will inevitably out-compete the other.

Complementary Filiation: In the work of Fortes, Goody, and others, the relationship between a person and his/her maternal uncle and his lineage (in a patrilineal descent system), or between a person and his/her paternal aunt/uncle and their lineage (in a matrilineal descent system).

Componential Analysis: A mode of analysis, originally used for phonological systems but later used for defining the meanings of sets of contrasting words (notably kinship terms), whereby several dimensions of contrast (high vs. low, male vs. female, and so on) intersect to define the uniqueness of each phoneme or each word in the set, in terms of their contrast with the rest.

Consanguineal: A relative by birth (that is, a "blood" relative), as distinguished from in-laws *(affines)* and step-relatives.

Contagious Magic: Magic that depends on an assumed (magical, mystical, spiritual) contact between the object on which magic is performed and the person or object it is supposed to affect.

Core Tools: Stone tools made by chipping flakes or chips off a core which is cut into the desired shape.

Corporate Group: A social group whose members act as a legal individual in terms of collective rights to property, a common group name, collective responsibility, or other common interests.

Cosmology: A people's beliefs and assumptions regarding the world—what entities and forces control it, how the universe is organized, and what humans' role and place within the world are.

Creole: In linguistics, a language derived historically from a contact *lingua franca* (that is, a *pidgin*) which has become the native language of a population (and correspondingly has usually become more lexically rich and syntactically complex than the pidgin from which it was derived).

Cro-Magnon: A modern human population *(Homo sapiens)* associated with European Upper Paleolithic cultures.

Cross-Cousin: A cousin related to ego through ego's mother's brother or ego's father's sister (that is, cross-cousins are the children of a brother and sister).

Cross-Cousin Marriage: In alliance theory (especially in its early versions), a rule or practice of marriage between father's sister's child and mother's brother's child (a man's marriage with MBD is *matilateral,* while FZD is *patrilateral*).

Cross-Cultural: Pertaining to comparison between different ways of life.

Cultural Ecology: The study of human populations, and their culturally patterned behavior, as components within ecosystems.

Cultural Materialism: The position, argued most forcefully by Marvin Harris, that cultures represent primarily adaptive solutions to the material circumstances of life, and hence that people with similar technologies in similar environments will tend to evolve similar modes of social grouping, similar belief systems, and so on.

Cultural Relativism: An ethical position insisting that since cultures are diverse and unique, and embody different conceptions of the desirable, they can be understood and evaluated only in terms of their own standards and values.

Culture: The system of knowledge more or less shared by members of a society.

Culture and Personality: The attempt, most characteristic of American anthropology in the 1940s and 1950s to find regularities in the relationship between a people's child-rearing practices (and the personality configurations they tend to produce through childhood experience) and their cultural beliefs and institutions.

Culture-Bound: Applicable only to a particular society and its way of life, of a generalization that is purported to be true of man in general.

Culture of Poverty: The theory, initially advanced by Oscar Lewis, that a generally similar way of life (marked by exploitative and fragile sexual relations, psychological stress and fragile family structures) occurs among the urban poor in many parts of the world.

Cybernetics: A cluster of related subdisciplines that deal with information processing, control, feedback systems, and such. More generally, the sciences of communication, systems, and information, dealing with biological systems and artificial intelligence.

Cynocephalus Baboons: Several closely related species of baboons (*papio* spp.), savanna or forest-dwelling, marked by single-level, multi-male troop structures.

DNA: Deoxyribenucleic acid; the large organic molecules that convey genetic information.

Deductive: In scientific or logical inference, a chain of reasoning that proceeds from known general principles or theories or theorems and traces out what their consequences and implications would be. (Cf. *Inductive.*)

Deep Structure: In transformational linguistics, the underlying syntactic pattern of a sentence that conveys meaning.

Demography: The study of populations and of the statistics and dynamics of reproduction.

Dentition: Tooth pattern (number, shape, and arrangement) of an organism.

Derivation: In grammatical theory, the chain of rule-governed steps connecting an underlying syntactic *deep structure* with its surface structure representation.

Desacralization: The process of becoming secular, of moving from a state of sacredness (of sacralization).

Descent: A relationship defined by connection to an ancestor (or ancestress) through a culturally recognized sequence of parent-child links (from father to son to son's son=patrilineal descent; from mother to daughter to daughter's daughter=matrilineal descent).

Descent Group: A kin group whose membership is based on a rule of descent. Appropriate descent status (patrilineal, matrilineal, or cognatic, depending on the society) entitles a person to be a member of the group.

Developmental Cycle: In the anthropology of social organization, the process whereby a domestic family established by a marriage proliferates with the birth of children, disperses with their marriages, and eventually is extinguished.

Dialect: A variety of a language characteristic of a particular geographic region or social class.

Dialectical: Pertaining to a mode of analysis in terms of oppositions and their resolution; more generally, a relationship of the sort now called *feedback* (in cybernetics) whereby forces or messages or propositions interact cyclically.

Dialectical Materialism: The term used by Marx and Engels to describe their conception of the historical process of socioeconomic and ideological change.

Diffusion: The spread of elements of custom or technology from one society to another, especially across the "primitive" world in pre-European times. It was a focus of anthropological study from 1910 to 1930.

Digital: Of a communications system, using binary contrasts (yes-no, on-off, black-white) to transmit information. (Cf. *Analog.*)

Dimorphism (Sexual):   A physical contrast between male and female of the same species, as in size, coloration, and body form.

Direct Exchange: A system of alliance (prescriptive marriage) whereby two kin groups exchange wives directly (so that wife-givers are the same people as wife-takers). (Also known as *échange restreint.*)

Discovery Procedures: In linguistics (and other sciences), a set of methods and strategies for working from observations to hypotheses and theories.

Distinctive Features: In phonology, semantics, or symbolic analysis, two-way contrasts (high vs. low, front vs. back, right vs. left, nature vs. culture); a set of contrasting items (phonemes, words, and so on) are defined by combinations of these distinctive features. (For example, a phoneme is defined as vowel-front-high-tense, in contrast to the other phonemes in the set.)

Divination: In the tribal and ancient world, obtaining information or securing decisions from supernaturals.

Division of Labor: The performance of different tasks by different kinds of classes of people—most basically, between men and women, young and adult and old); but in complex societies, increasingly specialized.

Domestic Group: A social group occupying or centered in a dwelling house, living (and usually eating) together, and characteristically exercising corporate control over family property.

Domestic Mode of Production: Term used by Sahlins for economic systems where the bulk of production takes place within the domestic family.

Dominance: In animal behavior, a relationship whereby one animal maintains physical domination over another, often forming hierarchical "pecking orders."

Double Descent: A system whereby two systems of social groups or categories exist (for different purposes) in the same society, one based on patrilineal descent and the other on matrilineal descent (so a person belongs to his/her father's patrilineal group and his/her mother's matrilineal group).

Dowry: The valuables or estate transferred by a bride's relatives to her, her husband, or her children in connection with her marriage.

Dreamtime: In Australian Aboriginal cosmology, a mode of existence believed to have preceded the visible mundane one (a time of sacred beings and events celebrated in ritual and myth) and to lie behind that realm of perceptible events in the present.

Drift (Genetic):   Change in the frequencies of genes within a population due to random genetic sampling in the reproductive process.

Dryopithecine: A subfamily of Old World of Miocene-age primates from which the great apes and hominids are probably descended.

Dualism: A mode of conceptual organization in terms of opposites: yin vs. yang, nature vs. culture, or male vs. female, and so on.

Dyadic Contract: Enduring obligations entailing exchanges of goods and services between two individuals; especially important, according to Foster, in some peasant communities.

Ecological Niche: The place of a species within an ecosystem: its habitat, food supply, relationship to predators or prey, and so on.

Electra Complex: In psychoanalytic theory, ambivalence and hostility between mother and daughter in relation to the father's sexuality.

Elementary System (of Kinship):   In Lévi-Strauss' theory, systems of kinship and marital alliance where all members of one's society are potentially incorporated in kinship categories and where these categories serve to define a system of marital alliance (exchange of women between groups).

Elite: The dominant class or classes in a complex stratified society, with political power and a prestigious life style sustained by strategic control, direct or indirect, over resources and the means of production.

Emic: Term coined by Kenneth Pike (from "phonemic") for description of a structural system in terms of the units and distinctions relevant in the system, and for description of a stream of events (speech, behavior) in terms of the units and contrasts perceived as relevant by the actors participating in those events. (Cf. *Etic.*)

Enculturation: A child's learning of his or her culture.

Endogamy: A requirement for marriage within a defined category or range or group or community ("in-marriage"). All societies are minimally endogamous in that they limit marriage to members of the same species; most limit marriage to members of the opposite sex.

Entrepreneur: A business person who makes investments of resources, entailing risk, in pursuit of profitable return.

Eocene: A geological epoch that began about 58 million years ago and lasted until about 34 million years ago.

Epicanthic Fold: A fatty fold of tissue at the outer margins of the eye characteristic of east and north Asian populations (for example, Chinese).

Estate: Property, property in land; in the theory of social stratification, a stratum, a category of persons within a stratified society lacking the full cohesiveness of a social class but marked by a cluster of occupational statuses, and attendant prestige, power, and privilege (or, for one of low estate, their absence).

Estrus: Period of sexual receptivity (heat) in female mammals.

Ethnocentrism: Viewing other peoples and ways of life in terms of one's own cultural assumptions, customs, and values.

Ethnographic Present: The hypothetical time baseline where (in various parts of the world, at different times) Europeans first intruded on the tribal world.

Ethnographic Semantics: See *Ethnoscience.*

Ethnography: The documenting and analyzing of a particular culture through field research.

Ethnography of Communication: Term proposed by Dell Hymes for analysis of the way speech and other communicative modes are culturally conceptualized and used in social situations—the cultural uses of speech and nonlinguistic communication.

Ethnology: The study of human cultures in historical and comparative perspective.

Ethnoscience: An anthropological approach seeking to analyze how a people perceive and operate in their cultural world by systematic analysis of their cultural labels for "things" and ways of classifying and talking about them.

Ethology: The scientific study of the behavior of animals in natural settings.

Etic: Term coined by Kenneth Pike (from "phonetic") for description of a structural system, or a stream of events, in objective physical terms independent of those defined within the system or perceived as relevant by participants in the events. An "external" observer's-eye-view (which can contrast with, or be a step in working toward, an "emic" analysis). (Cf. *Emic.*)

Evolution: Descent with modification; the process of progressive change in organisms.

Exchange: Reciprocal transfer of valuables, rights, commodities, and so on between individuals or groups.

Exogamy: A requirement for marriage outside a particular social group or range of kinship.

Extended Case Method: Mode of social anthropological analysis that focuses on an event (a ceremony, a political meeting, and such) and explores the network of social relations, the cultural patterns, and the individual interests that led participants to act as they did.

Extended Family: A domestic group or composite of domestic groups consisting of two or more nuclear families linked together through parent and child (patrilineal extended family, matrilineal extended family) or through siblings (fraternal or sororal extended family).

Factor Analysis: Statistical procedures whereby, from a large set of coefficients of correlation between different variables, clusters of related variables are identified.

Fallow: The period or process whereby the fertility of soil is regenerated after a crop has been harvested.

Feedback: In a cybernetic system, a communication circuit such that an increase in A leads to an increase in B, leads to a further increase in A, and so on (*positive feedback,* as in an armaments race), or such that an increase in A leads to a change in B that triggers a corrective decrease in A (*negative feedback,* as in a thermostat).

Feudal: A system of social and economic organization where estates in land are held by conferred right (in fief) by members of a privileged class, who can then command the labor of serfs.

Feuding: Continuing hostility, enmity, and recurrent aggression between social groups.

Fictive Kinship: Relations, such as *compadrazgo,* between nonrelatives whose nature, affective content, and social obligations are modelled on those appropriate to blood relatives.

Fieldwork: A broad term for research in which social/cultural anthropologists (and other social scientists) engage, involving close study of, and partial participation in, the life of a community or group (characteristically in a setting that contrasts culturally with that in which the observer normally lives).

Filiation: Relationship to or through one's father and one's mother; the relationship between parents and children, or the basing of rights on this relationship.

Flake Tool: A tool struck as a flake from a stone core.

Folsom: Fluted stone projectile points of big-game hunters of prehistoric North America (about 11000 B.P.), and the associated cultural tradition.

Foramen Magnum: Hole in base of skull through which the spinal cord passes.

Formal: Having to do with form; in scientific method, explicitly stated in logical or mathematical terms.

Formalist: In economic anthropology, the premise that if they are rendered sufficiently broad and abstract, the models of (neoclassical) economic theory can be applied to all human societies. (Cf. *Substantivist.*)

Formative Period: In prehistory, a term used for a stage in a regional sequence (hence with different referents in different parts of the world).

Fossil: Parts of an organism that have become mineralized or have left casts in surrounding materials.

Founder Principle: Establishment of a new population by a few members of a parent population, which then represent a partial sample of the original gene pool.

Fraternal Polyandry: Marriage of a woman to two or more brothers.

Functionalism: Modes of theoretical interpretation in social science that search for the interconnections between social institutions—how they fit together and what they *do*—rather than seek causal explanations.

Galton's Problem: In comparative (cross-cultural) anthropological research, the difficulty of drawing a sample of societies/cultures that are not historically related in such a way that the same traits occur due to common origin or contact.

Gene: The unit of hereditary material.

Gene Pool: All the genes in a breeding population.

Genealogy: A pedigree: a web of relationship traced through parents and children. In kinship theory, the position (advanced notably by Lounsbury and Scheffler) that kinship terms serve primarily to define genealogical relations between individuals.

Generative Grammar: Generic term for the school of linguistic theory, pioneered by Noam Chomsky, that seeks to describe in logicomathematical terms the implicit linguistic knowledge of native speakers. A linguist's grammar of a language constructed within this theoretical tradition. (Also known as *transformational* or *transformational-generative (TG) grammar.*)

Generative Semantics: A recent development in *transformational* linguistics where the deepest levels of syntax are conceived as highly abstract semantic relationships (that is, logical relationships expressing meanings of sentences).

Genotype: The genetic composition of an organism. (Cf. *Phenotype.*)

Genus: In biological classification (biosystematics), a set of closely related species.

Ghetto: In medieval Europe, ethnic enclaves within towns. In modern urban setting, slum areas where subordinate ethnic groups are concentrated.

Gleaning: Collecting of foods, especially gathering of wild foods.

Gracile: Light, slender in bodily build (characteristic of some early hominid populations).

Grammar: The formal structure of knowledge of a language a native speaker draws on in speaking and understanding speech; a linguistic description that attempts to represent this implicit knowledge.

Great Apes: The large apes (gorillas, chimpanzees, orangutan), in contrast to the gibbon group (gibbon, siamang).

Great Tradition: The cultural pattern of a major civilization, as represented in its religion, literature, art, and so on. In contrast with the *little traditions* (q.v.) distinctive of local communities.

Günz: First of the major Pleistocene glaciations (named for the Alpine sequence).

Hamadryas Baboons: Desert-dwelling baboons *(Papio hamadryas)* important for their distinctive multilevel social organization.

Hamitic: A family of East African languages, of which Amharic (Ethiopia) is an important member.

Headman: The legitimately empowered head political authority of a village (Central Africa), or a colonially created equivalent.

Hemispheral Lateralization: The development in humans of complementarity of the two cerebral hemispheres of the brain (so that the left hemisphere is normally—in right-handed individuals—the center of linguistic and logical operations; the right, the center of associative, integrative, holistic thought processes).

Hemoglobin: Red protein in blood cells; it transports oxygen to and from bodily tissues in vertebrates. Abnormal forms (such as the sickle cell) are used in population genetics to trace population connections.

Heterarchical: Organized in terms of separate subsystems at the same level; acephalous, or lacking a central hierarchy of command or control.

Heterozygous: In genetics, having two different forms of a gene (technically called "alleles") at the same location on matching chromosomes (one form inherited from each parent). (Cf. *Homozygous.*)

Hierarchical: Organized in terms of vertical levels, with lower elements of the system (whether it be a political organization or a classification system or a computer program) subsumed under or controlled by those at higher levels.

Holocene: The current division of the Quaternary geological period (12,000 B.P.).

Home Range: An area within which a primate social group forages (distinct from a *territory* in that a home range is not defended against encroachment by other groups of the same species.)

Hominid: Member of the family of the order Primates to which man and his closest fossil ancestors are assigned.

Homo habilis: Term used by L. Leakey, and accepted by many specialists, for hominid fossils at the dawn of the Pleistocene transitional to the genus *Homo* and associated with tool industries.

Homo sapiens: The human species.

Homo sapiens sapiens: The subspecies of biologically modern human populations that have diversified within the last 40,000 years.

Homozygous: In genetics, having a pair of the same form of a gene (allele), one from each parent. (Cf. *Heterozygous.*)

Horticulture: Cultivation of crops using digging stick or hoe, but not plow. (Cf. *Agriculture.*)

Human Relations Area Files (HRAF):   An extensive set of files, maintained at many universities, in which ethnographic evidence from a large sample of societies is stored according to a detailed indexing system—so that a range of cross-cultural evidence on a particular subject can be readily compiled.

Hunter-Gatherers: Human populations that rely in subsistence exclusively or almost exclusively on wild foods, hunted and collected. Some modern hunter-gatherers receive subsistence food from governments or missions or do minimal cultivating, but their relationship to their environment continues to be predatory and opportunistic.

Hunting and Gathering: A mode of subsistence based on hunting and collecting of wild foods.

Hysteria: A class of mental disturbances marked by fantasy and an extreme physical response to psychic stress (for example, rigidity, going berserk); subject to a high degree of cultural patterning (for example, Arctic Hysteria, Witiko Psychosis, Amok, and other possession states).

Iconic: Of communications systems, the modeling of signs on their referents. (For example, a snarl is patterned on a bite, a beckoning gesture indicates the desired direction of movement.) (Cf. *Noniconic.*)

Ideational: Pertaining to the mental realm of ideas, rather than the physical world of things and events. (Cf. *Phenomena.*)

Idiolect: The special version of a language known and used by each individual speaker.

Ideology: A cultural belief system, particularly one that entails systematic distortion or masking of the true nature of social, political, and economic relations.

Image of Limited Good: A world view, supposed to be characteristic of many Mesoamerican (and other) peasants, whereby the good things of the world (money, honor, reputation, success) are in limited, finite supply—hence where you can attain your goals only at other people's expense (George Foster).

Immunochemistry: Studies of the biochemistry of bodily defenses against infection and intrusive agents through the formation of antibodies.

Incest Taboo: A rule prohibiting sexual relations between immediate kin (father and daughter, mother and son, brother and sister) and others culturally defined as in an equivalent relationship. Differs from *exogamy,* which prohibits marriage but not necessarily sexual relations.

Indirect Exchange: A system of alliance (prescriptive marriage) whereby kin groups exchange wives indirectly, so that a man must marry his actual or classificatory MBD (matrilateral alliance) or FZD (patrilateral alliance; said not to exist) but so that wife-givers cannot be wife-takers. (Also known as *échange géneralisé.*)

Inductive: In scientific inference, a chain of discovery that leads from observed data toward theoretical principles that could account for them. (Cf. *Deductive.*)

Indigenous: Native (adj.), pertaining to the original inhabitants and their way of life.

Infanticide: Killing of infants, required or sanctioned by custom in many small-scale societies.

Interaction: Social behavior in which two or more individuals communicate and respond to one another's behavior.

Internal Models of Reality: Term coined by Kenneth Craik and used by R. L. Gregory, the specialist on visual perception, to denote the knowledge of a person's world he or she has stored in the brain in terms of which incoming sensory information is interpreted.

Intersexuality: Hermaphroditism; physical conditions where the sexual characteristics and genitalia of male and female are ambiguous or mixed.

Jajmani System: A system of interdependence between Indian landowners and those who provide specialized services in exchange for subsistence food.

Joint Family: See *Extended Family.*

Joking Relationship: A relationship of privileged familiarity or license between kinsmen in a particular relationship.

Jural: Relating to law, legal principles, or contractual obligation.

Kindred: A category comprising a person's relatives, or relatives within a certain range of distance, from which groups are formed, where ego is born, marries, gives a feast, and so on.

Kin Group: A social group whose members define their relationship (or their eligibility for membership) on kinship or common descent.

Kinship: Relationship based on or modeled on the culturally recognized connection between parents and children (and extended to siblings and through parents to more distant relatives).

Kinship Terminology: A system of linguistic categories for denoting kinds of relatives.

Knuckle Walking: A mode of locomotion, characteristic of some great apes (most notably, gorillas), where weight rests on the feet and on the knuckles, in a stooped position; thought by Washburn to have been a possible mode of locomotion of early hominids.

Kuru: A virally transmitted neurological disease occurring among the Fore of the Eastern Highlands of Papua New Guinea, and apparently transmitted by ritual consumption of the brains of the dead.

Ladino: In Southern Mexico and Guatemala, a Spanish-speaking participant in the national culture (in contrast to a person who is culturally and linguistically Indian).

Language: 1. A code for symbolic communication consisting of a set of symbols and a set of rules (a *grammar*) for constructing messages. (Thus a computer uses a man-made artificial language of digital signals.) 2. A naturally evolved human code for vocal communication (a *natural language*) or a system (for example, of hand signs) based on a natural language.

Language Acquisition: The learning by a child of his or her native language, and the processes whereby this is accomplished.

Langue, La: The grammatical code of a language, as contrasted with actual speaking; a speaker's (unconscious) knowledge of his language, which he uses in speaking (F. de Saussure). (As opposed to *la Parole.*)

Lateralization: See *Hemispheral Lateralization.*

Latifundia: Great estates (in ancient Rome, postcolonial Latin America, and elsewhere) run by absentee landlords.

Levirate: A system where a dead man's brother (or equivalent close male relative) succeeds to his status as husband by marrying his widow.

Levalloisian: A sophisticated stone tool industry of the European Upper Paleolithic, marked by flake blades.

Lexicon: A dictionary. In linguistic theories of grammatical competence, the mental "dictionary" in which words (and wordlike elements), their meanings, and their grammatical possibilities are assumed to be organized.

Liminal: In symbolic analysis, a state or category that is in-between or outside normal states or categories. This may be a state of transition between social categories (as when initiates are taken off into seclusion, or when on a honeymoon bride and groom go off together), or a category that is outside a normal framework (hermaphrodites, in relation to men and women).

Lineage: A unilineal descent group based on patrilineal descent (patrilineage) or matrilineal descent (matrilineage) whose members trace descent from an apical ancestor/ancestress by known genealogical links.

Lineage Mode of Production: In Marxist anthropology, a subsistence-oriented system of production (characteristically horticulturalist or pastoralist) where domestic groups that are the primary producing units are grouped into corporate lineages or clans with substantial collective rights and interests.

Litigation: Legal dispute.

Little Traditions: The patterns of culture distinctive of local communities or regions within a complex society. (Cf. *Great Tradition.*)

Lungshan: A Chinese cultural tradition, derived from the Yangshao one that preceded it, beginning around 3000 B.C.

Machismo: A quest for manly honor and reputation, marked by bravado, sexual predation, and such, characteristic of men in many Latin American societies.

Magdalenian: The last Upper Paleolithic cultural tradition in Western Europe, marked by extensive use of bone as well as stone tools.

Maize: Corn.

Malars: Cheekbones.

Malaysian: Pertaining to the peoples and cultures of the Southeast Asian zone comprising the Malay Peninsula, Sumatra, Java, Borneo, Eastern Indonesian islands, and the Philippines (within which languages of the Indonesian branch of Austronesian are spoken).

Manioc: A tropical root crop (cassava, tapioca) yielding a starchy tuber.

Market: The abstract relationship of supply and demand in the buying and selling processes of a money economy. (Cf. *Marketplace.*)

Marketplace: A physical setting within which buying and selling (and barter) take place. (Cf. *Market.*)

Marxist: Pertaining to the theories of Karl Marx regarding socioeconomic systems, social change, and class struggle, and the body of scholarship derived from these theories.

Matrilateral: Based on relationship on the mother's side.

Matrilineage: See *Lineage.*

Matrilineal: A principle of descent from an ancestress through her daughter, her daughter's daughter, and so on (in the female line).

Matrilocal: See *Uxorilocal.*

Maximization: A theoretical assumption that individuals (or groups or firms) will make decisions rationally in such a way as to achieve maximum reward—an assumption underlying classical and neoclassical economics and formalist economic anthropology.

Means of Production: In Marxist analysis, the technical, material, and social skills—technology, broadly conceived—that is, tools, and human resources whereby scarce goods are created. (In Marxist theory, the means of production and the social relations of production, as a system, define a *mode of production.*)

Mediator: In dispute settlement, a go-between; in symbolic anthropology, a middle-term that mediates a symbolic opposition (for example, a tamed wild animal might symbolically serve to mediate an opposition between nature and culture).

Melanesian: Geographically, pertaining to the area of the Southwest Pacific from New Guinea through New Caledonia and the New Hebrides (and by some definitions, Fiji), occupied by dark-skinned, frizzly-haired peoples. More narrowly, it pertains to speakers of diverse Austronesian languages within this region, or to these languages.

Mesoamerica: The area of Central America from the north-central part of Mexico to Honduras.

Mesolithic: Traditional archaeological term for the mixed food-collecting economies of the post-Pleistocene period, particularly in Europe.

Messianic Movement: A social movement with a doctrine of a new world, to be accessible to members of the group by the leadership of a spiritual intermediary (a messiah).

Mestizo: In Latin America, a Spanish-speaking participant in the national culture (often conceived to be of mixed Indian-European descent).

Metacommunication: Term coined by Gregory Bateson for "messages about messages"; that is, for messages (between animals, humans, machines) that define the premises according to which messages are to be interpreted (seriousness, play, threat, and so on) and/or define the relationship between the communicators.

Metropolis—Satellite: The relationship between a major or minor economic and political center and its hinterlands, or those secondary centers for which it served as the hub of trade, exploitation, and control (particularly developed in the theories of André Gunder Frank).

Microevolutionary: Pertaining to the diversification and local adaptation of regional populations.

Microlith: Small stone points used in rows to edge blades and projectiles (characteristic of parts of Mesolithic Europe and the Near East).

Micronesian: Pertaining to the peoples and cultures of the central and north Pacific islands (including the Gilbert and Ellice group, the Marshall Islands, the Caroline Islands, and the Marianas) where Micronesian languages of the Austronesian family are spoken.

Middleperson ("Middleman"): A go-between, particularly someone who mediates in economic transactions (for example, one who buys from A and sells to B, C, D).

Millennial Movement: A social movement with a doctrine of a new world (a millennium) to be attained at least in part by spiritual means. (Also known as *millenarian movement.*)

Millet: A grain extensively cultivated in Africa and the Middle East.

Mindel: The second major glaciation of the Pleistocene (named for the Alpine sequence).

Miocene: Geological epoch from about 25 million years ago to about 12 million years ago.

Mode of Production: In Marxist theory, a social system that represents technological means of production and a system of social relations through which the material bases of life are produced and exchanged (and by which the society is sustained through time in the reproduction of its members and their social groupings).

Moiety: A division of a society into two social categories or groups characteristically by a rule of patrilineal descent (patrimoiety) or matrilineal descent (matrimoiety).

Molars: Square, broad cheek teeth.

Molecular Genetics: Study of the bases of genetic coding at a molecular level, in terms of biochemistry (DNA, RNA, protein synthesis, and so on).

Moot: An informal hearing of a legal dispute by peers and neighbors.

Morphological: Having to do with form, particularly physical form and structure.

Mortuary (Feast, Rite): Having to do with funerals or more generally with the disposal of the dead or the relationship of the living to the recently deceased.

Mousterian: A generic term for the diverse and specialized tool industries characteristic of Neanderthal populations.

Mutation: Change in genetic material.

Natal: Pertaining to the group or kinship connections of one's birth (as opposed to those acquired in marriage).

National Character: In *culture and personality* research (important in American anthropology in the 1940s and 1950s), a mode of personality (or "character") more or less standardized among members of a society (here, a nation) as a result of their shared culture and relatively similar childhood experience.

Natural Selection: Process of differential reproduction whereby some genes within a gene pool are selected as adaptive to the environment, and others are discarded.

Nature: In symbolic analysis, especially as pioneered in the work of Claude Lévi-Strauss, a polarity between the realm of plants and animals and the world of humans. (As opposed to *Culture.*)

Neanderthals: Fossil hominids, the earliest member of *Homo sapiens,* living from about 150,000 years ago to about 50,000 years ago.

Negrito: Member of dark-skinned, short-statured populations living in Southeast Asian rain forest pockets (in Malaysia, Philippines, and elsewhere), formerly more widespread.

Neoclassical Economics: The mainstream theoretical approach in Western economics, admitting the need for Keynesian economic planning and manipulation, but arguing that under conditions of international free trade, maximum efficiency in production and marketing will be achieved.

Neocolonialism: The process whereby industrial nations control the political and economic life of nominally independent countries through investment and support of local elites.

Neolithic: "New Stone Age": the level of technology, marked by food producing and the use of ground and polished stone tools, characteristic of much of the "tribal" world before the advent of colonialism.

Neolocal: Residence of a couple after marriage in a new household not linked spatially to that of the groom or the bride. (Cf. *Virilocal, Uxorilocal.*)

Network: In sociological analysis, a mode of tracing and analyzing the relations between individuals as though they formed a pattern of connected points whose nature and arrangement can then be studied. More loosely in folk sociology, the friends and associates who provide contacts and support for a person.

Neurophysiology: Study of the physical structure and operation of the central nervous system, and particularly the brain.

New Archaeology: An approach in prehistory that stresses not the reconstruction of past historic sequences but the formulation and testing of theories about cultural and ecological processes.

New World: North, Central, and South America.

Nocturnal: Of animals active at night.

Nomadism: A mode of life based on the shifting of population in order to move with livestock (in accordance with needs for pasturage), to collect wild foods, or to hunt.

Noniconic: Of communications systems, a relationship between a sign and its referent whereby the sign is not modeled on the thing, event, or relationship it represents; that is, the sign is a *symbol*. (Cf. *Iconic*.)

Nonunilineal Descent: An alternative term to *cognatic descent*. Since cognatic descendents *include* patrilineal descendants and matrilineal descendants, this usage is unfortunate. I have suggested that the term be used in societies that recognize a unilineal core within a cognatic descent category to denote descent status through at least one alternate-sex link (that is, non-agnatic where descent includes at least one female link; non-uterine where it includes at least one male link).

Nonverbal Communication: Communication by gesture, expression, body movement, eye contact, and such. Often used (instead of *nonlinguistic* communication) to refer to modes of communication other than speech or writing.

Norm: An explicit or implicit standard or principle for appropriate behavior.

Nuclear Family: A family unit consisting of parents and their dependent children.

Oedipus Complex: In psychoanalytic theory, the relationship of conflict and ambivalence between father and son in relation to the sexuality of mother.

Old World: Asia, Europe, Africa, and the Pacific.

Oldowan: A complex of crude stone tools, of which a pebble chopper is most distinctive, characteristic of late australopithicines and some *Homo erectus* populations.

Olduvai Gorge: A region of rich fossil deposits in Tanzania.

Oligocene: The geological epoch that began about 34 million years ago and lasted until about 25 million years ago.

Olmec: An early Mesoamerican cultural tradition, centered around Vera Cruz, and marked by religious architecture and deities (such as the jaguar god) reflected in subsequent Mesoamerican civilizations.

Ordeal: A physical test used to establish guilt or innocence or to establish which litigant is in the right.

Pair Bond: A close and continuing psychological and physical attachment between sexual mates.

Paleolithic: "Old Stone Age": the vast period marked by chipped and flaked stone tool industries.

Paleontology: Study of the fossil remains of extinct life forms.

Parallel Cousin: Ego's father's brother's child or mother's sister's child, or more distant cousin classed terminologically with these first cousins.

Pariah: In India, an outcaste, an untouchable; more generally, a member of a social group or category excluded from normal participation and rights in a society.

Parole, La: Speech, as contrasted with the grammatical structure of which speech is an expression (F. de Saussure). (As opposed to *la Langue*.)

Pastoralism: A mode of life where herding (of cattle, sheep, camels, goats, horses, and such) provides the major subsistence.

Parricide (= Patricide): Killing of the father, a central theme in Freud's *Totem and Taboo* theory of hominid evolution and the emergence of culture.

Patrilateral: Based on relationship through the father's side.

Patrilineage: See *lineage.*

Patrilineal Descent: Descent traced through a line of ancestors in the male line. (Also known as *agnatic descent.*)

Patrilocal: See *Virilocal.*

Patrilocal Band: A mode of social organization, believed by some scholars to have been characteristic of most hunting and gathering societies, where men remain in their territories and wives marry in—hence where men tend to be related in the male line.

Patron: A person in a position of power who maintains subordinates through wealth and largesse in return for labor and support.

Peasant: A member of a social class or estate, characteristically agrarian, whose productive labor supports an elite, characteristically urban, as well as providing subsistence.

Performance: Actual speech behavior and speech production, expressing or drawing on a speaker's linguistic competence but subject to errors and false start, and various psychological limitations (transformational linguistics).

Perigordian: An early Upper Paleolithic tool industry in Western Europe, showing continuities with Mousterian industries.

Personal Culture: The version of a culture (as a system of knowledge) of a particular individual, distinctive in some respects from the version of any other person.

Personal Kindred: See *Kindred.*

Phenomenal: Pertaining to the realm of observable phenomena: things and events. (Cf. *Ideational.*)

Phenotype: The observed physical expression (as manifest through growth and development) of the genetic specification *(genotype)* of an organism.

Phoneme: In linguistics, a distinctive unit of sound contrasting with other such units. Whether phonemes exist as psychologically real or linguistically salient elements, or simply represent stages in the application of phonological rules, is presently being debated by specialists.

Phonetics: In linguistics, the sound patterns of speech and the notations used for describing these acoustical patterns. Since phonetic description includes many contrasts that are irrelevant to speakers and hearers of a language, the linguist moves toward a *phonemic* notation that includes only the contrasts the linguistic code defines as relevant.

Phonology: In linguistics, (the study of) sound systems of languages.

Phratry: A grouping of clans related by traditions of common descent or historical alliance based on kinship.

Pidgin: A contact language or *lingua franca,* characteristically somewhat simplified and condensed, and not used as a native language. (Cf. *Creole.*)

Pigmentation: Skin color, a result of melanin in the skin (apparently highly concentrated as an adaptation to tropical solar radiation).

Pleistocene: The geological epoch that began about 3 million years ago and lasted until about 10,000 years ago.

Pliocene: Geological epoch beginning about 12 million years ago and lasting until about 3 million years ago.

Polarity: A division into polar opposites. In symbolic analysis, a two-way contrast (right-left, sun-moon, nature-culture); sociologically, marked opposition between social categories or classes (men-women, workers-bourgeoisie).

Political Economy: Study of the relationship between economic systems, political power, and ideologies.

Pollution (Symbolic):   A belief that some state, substance, or class of persons is dirty, defiled, or ritually contaminating.

Polyandry: Marriage of a woman to two or more men.

Polygyny: Marriage of a man to two or more women.

Polymorphism: In genetics, the occurrence of alternative forms of a gene (alleles) at the same chromosome location. In a *balanced polymorphism,* such alternative forms are held in statistical balance or equilibrium by adaptive pressures.

Polynesian: Pertaining to the peoples, cultures, and Austronesian languages of a triangular zone in the Pacific from Hawaii to New Zealand to Easter Island.

Polytypic: Of a population, marked by alternative genetic patterns or polymorphisms.

Population Genetics: Statistical study of the genetics of populations; concerned with gene frequencies and the environmental factors that shape adaptations within gene pools.

Potassium-Argon Dating: Absolute age of a geological specimen determined by measuring percentages of radioactive potassium and argon.

Potlatch: A feast marked by distribution and destruction of valuables, as a demonstration of wealth and status, characteristic of the Kwakiutl and some other Northwest Coast (U.S.) Indians.

Preferential: Of a marriage pattern (for example, marriage with a cross-cousin or a brother's widow), socially valued and desirable, but not enjoined.

Prehensile: Grasping (of a hand or tail).

Prehistory: Study of the ways of life and sequences and processes of cultural development prior to the advent of written records. (Also known as *prehistoric archaeology.*)

Prescriptive Marriage.   In alliance theory, a requirement that marriage be with a partner in a particular kinship category. Even where "incorrect" marriages occur, they are likely to be classed as if they were correct, and kinship relations readjusted accordingly.

Prestation: A transfer of scarce goods laden with symbolic significance.

Primary Group: A small group marked by personal interaction between its members.

Primate: Member of the order of mammals to which humans, apes, monkeys, and prosimians belong.

Primogeniture: A rule or principle whereby the oldest son has the right of inheritance of the family estate.

Productivity: Of a communicative code (especially human languages), the possibility of constructing complex messages from the elements of the code, according to a grammer; it permits the creation of new messages.

Program: A coded set of instructions (an *algorithm,* q.v.) for performing a series of computations, logical operations, or physical acts. The genetically coded information in cells, the routines in a computer, and the procedures for translating mental messages ("pick up the cup"; "tie the shoelace") into muscular movements can be viewed as programs.

Projection (Psychological):   A process whereby the mind imputes its own creations (in the form of fantasy) on the external world.

Projective Test: A psychological test, such as the Rorschach or Thematic Appperception Test, in which a subject responds to an ambiguous or relatively undefined stimulus; and, by filling in content, provides psychodiagnostic evidence.

Prosimian: Member of one of the two suborders of primates (vs. *Anthropoidea*), including lemurs, tarsiers, and others.

Proto-:   Prefix indicating first, earliest, earliest stages or forms of. (As in *protocultural.*)

Psychological Reality: The view that a cognitive theory or model (in psychology, anthropology, or linguistics) corresponds in some fairly direct way to what is actually happening in the minds (and brains) of the people being studied.

Pueblo: A village composed of compound dwellings (characteristically of adobe brick), particularly among Indians of the U.S. Southwest.

Pygmy: Small in stature; member of a short-statured population, especially of a population in Zaire and other West-Central African rain forests.

Quadruped: Having four feet; walking on four legs.

RNA (Ribonucleic Acid):   A substance basic in the biochemistry of genetic reproduction and protein synthesis which carries coded instructions from cell nuclei to surrounding cytoplasm.

Race: A population, geographically separated to some degree, hence distinguished from other populations of the same species in genetic frequencies.

Ramapithecus: A genus of Old World fossil primates, probably ancestral hominids, living about 15 to 12 million years B.P.

Reciprocity: A mode of exchange marked by continuing obligation to reciprocate, particularly in kind.

Redistribution: A mode of distribution of surplus commodities whereby they flow upward through a political hierarchy (as taxes, tribute, and such) and are then redistributed downward.

Reproductive Isolation: The evolutionary separation of two or more populations in the process of speciation so that mating between their members produces a sharply lower (or nil) frequency of viable (or fertile) offspring.

Residence Rules: Cultural principles for deciding residential affiliation. Most commonly, *postmarital* residence rules, defining where and with whom a couple should reside after they marry.

Revitalization: The transformation of a community by some conscious new commitment to ideals or a way of life—either one that is new or one that embodies the ways and virtues of the past.

Riss: The third major Pleistocene glaciation (named for the Alpine sequence).

Rite of Passage: A ritual dramatizing the transition from one social state to another (for example, a wedding, a Bar Mitzvah, an initiation).

Ritual: A stylized, repetitive pattern of behavior (in humans, in most cases culturally patterned, collective behavior). Often used only of religious ritual, that is, stylized behavior deemed to be sacred.

Role: The behavior patterns appropriate to an individual acting in a particular social capacity. (See *Social Identity.*)

Root Crops: Cultigens that produce edible tubers, usually starchy—taro, yams, potatoes, sweet potatoes, manioc.

Rorschach: A projective test in which a subject reports what he or she "sees" in a standard set of ink-blot cards; used in psychiatric diagnosis and cross-cultural research.

Sacralization: The process of becoming sacred; the transition from the realm of the secular or ordinary to the realm of the sacred. (Cf. *Desacralization.*)

Sacred: Having to do with ultimate or superhuman powers in the universe; having a special religious significance or aura.

Sago: The starchy pith of a Southeast Asian and Pacific palm (*Metroxylon* spp.) from which edible flour can be extracted.

Savanna: Open grasslands, characteristic of much of East Africa in prehistoric and modern times.

Schizophrenia (Schizophrenic):   A class of acute mental illnesses, with genetic, chemical, and experiential etiological roots, marked by withdrawal and inability to distinguish reality from fantasy.

Secondary Group: A group whose members interact indirectly through an organizational structure (for example, a business corporation, operating through a board of directors), but do not all interact face to face.

Secondary Growth: The vegetation that grows back when primary forest is cut down (as in *swidden* horticulture).

Secret Society: A group such as a fraternity, masonic order, or its equivalent in the tribal world (for example, Dukduk, Tamate, Leopards).

Section System: In alliance theory and Australian kinship studies, division of a society into 2, 4, or 8 social categories through rules or descent and alliance. Symmetrical rules of marital alliance, enjoining marriage with a member of one of the sections, are a normal accompaniment of such systems.

Sedentary: Living in settled communities.

Segmentary: Of descent systems, defining descent categories with reference to more and more remote apical ancestors so that the descent categories form a tree-like structure (including successively wider ranges of descendants.)

Self Concept: A person's view (conscious and unconscious) of his or her worth, nature, and standing in the eyes of others.

Semantics: The study of linguistic meaning: how "words" represent meanings and how their arrangement in sentences conveys propositions.

Semiotics: Study of signs and signaling; the comparative study of communications systems. First envisioned by the linguist Fernand de Saussure, semiotics has expanded (especially in Continental Europe) and is now a burgeoning field.

Settlement Pattern: The spatial dispersion and arrangement of a population, as patterned by cultural principles for forming groups, choosing residential attachments, and using resources.

Sexual Dimorphism: Occurrence of one form of a trait in males of a species and a different form in females.

Sexual Selection: Change in the frequency of genes within a population as a statistical result of choices in the process of mating (for example, on the basis of sexual displays or courtship ritual).

Shaman: A person in a tribal society believed to have special powers of communicating with supernatural beings or forces, who does so on behalf of others.

Shang: Bronze Age dynasty in China beginning 1500 B.C.

Shifting Cultivation: See *Swidden (Cultivation)*.

Sickle Cell: A form of abnormal hemoglobin, common in some African populations (and among black Americans), that, when inherited in homozygous form, can produce an often fatal anemia.

Sister-Exchange: Exchange of sisters in marriage by a pair of men.

Situational Analysis: In modern social anthropology, analysis of social relations in a complex society by taking a particular social event as the focus and tracing out the wider ties of the participants, and how and why they play the parts they do.

Slash-and-Burn: See *Swidden (Cultivation)*.

Slavery: A system of relationship between masters and slaves whereby the slaves stand outside the normal social system and are without rights of citizenship, kinship, and legal personhood.

Social Class: A division of society, defined in terms of its relationship to the means of production, within a system of such classes, hierarchically ordered, and marked by a consciousness of their collective identity and interests.

Social Identity: A social position or capacity (for example, salesperson, customer, physician) in which a person assumes in a particular setting. (See *Role.*)

Social System: A system of ordered social relations maintained over time.

Socialization: A child's incorporation into his or her society through learning of the culture.

Society: A population marked by relative separation from surrounding populations and a distinctive culture. (Complex societies may include two or more distinctive cultural groups incorporated within a single social system.)

Sociocultural System: The patterns of behavior characteristic of a population sharing a distinctive culture within an ecosystem.

Sociolinguistics: The study of the social variations and uses of language, the use of language in social contexts, the relationship of variant speech usages to social stratification or subgroups, and so forth.

Sodality: A social group based on interest or voluntary participation.

Solutrean: An Upper Paleolithic culture of western Europe marked by beautifully formed blades.

Sorcery: Malevolent magic, consciously directed by humans against one another. (Cf. *Witchcraft.*)

Sororal Polygyny: Marriage of a man to two or more sisters.

Sororate: A form of secondary marriage whereby, upon the death of a wife, her sister or some other close relative marries the surviving husband. This perpetuates the marital contract between groups.

Speciation: The evolutionary process whereby geographically separated populations evolve differences that eventually result in reproductive isolation, or genetic incompatibility that precludes their producing fully viable or fertile offspring through interbreeding.

Species: In biological classification (biosystematics), a form of organism whose populations are separated from those of related organisms by reproductive isolation.

Speech Levels: Dialects within a society differentiated according to social class, education, and other criteria—so that command of (and a right to use) the higher level(s) bring prestige and serve as a marker of status.

Status: The rights and duties in a reciprocal role relationship (social identity relationship); the rights, privileges, and duties, and social worth accorded to members of a social class or category.

Subculture: The culture distinctive of a particular subgroup, region, or social class.

Subsistence Economy: The technical processes and social relationships whereby the foodstuffs and other physical means of life are produced and consumed.

Subspecies: A population within a species marked by distinctive genetic patterns due to geographic isolation, but still capable of interbreeding successfully with other subspecies. (See *Species; Reproductive Isolation.*)

Stratification: Hierarchical separation of a society into social classes or estates ranked in power, privilege, and prestige and in the relation of their members to the means of production.

Stratigraphy: In geology or archaeology, layers built up over time (within which the relative age of associated objects, or minerals, can be determined).

Subincision: A form of male genital mutilation, characteristic of some Australian Aborigines, in which the underside of the penis is slit open as a mode of ritual initiation.

Substantivist: In economic anthropology, the position that the models of (neoclassical) economics properly apply only to capitalist economies where the market principle is pervasive (hence that tribal societies where other modes of production and redistribution predominate must be analyzed in terms of different models). In substantivist theory, economics is properly concerned not with maximizing-behavior but with the ways in which humans produce and distribute the material goods that sustain their existence.

Succession: Assumption of an office that has been vacated; the pattern whereby successors are chosen.

Surface Structure: In transformational linguistics, the syntactic string that is converted into sound by phonological rules, in the derivation of a sentence.

Surplus: In economics, production that exceeds the subsistence needs of the producers.

Swahili: A language widely spoken in East Africa; originally, derives from a pidgin with extensive Portuguese and Arabic lexicon.

Swidden (Cultivation): Garden(ing) in which forest is cleared and burned, crops are planted and harvested, and the land is then allowed to lie fallow and develop secondary growth before it is cultivated again. (Also known as *shifting cultivation*.)

Symbiosis: Mutual interdependence and complementarity within a system, as where two organisms or populations complement one another within an ecosystem or a parasite is beneficial to its host.

Symbol: A sign that is related to the thing it refers to (its referent) in a conventional (rather than natural) manner (that is, is arbitrary). A *cultural* (or *ritual*) symbol is an object or other sign that has a range of culturally salient meanings.

Symmetrical Alliance: In alliance theory, a marriage system involving *direct exchange*, q.v.

Sympathetic Magic: Magic that depends on a resemblance or perceived similarity between the object, substance, or action used in performing the magic and the desired effect.

Sympatry: A relationship where two or more organisms are reproductively isolated and exploit different ecological niches within the same environment.

Syncretism: Synthesis of the elements of two or more cultures, particularly religious beliefs and ritual practices.

Syntax: (Study of) the formal system whereby linguistic elements (words and word-like elements) are constructed in sentences.

Systems Theory: A body of theoretical models for dealing with the organization of complex natural (or artificial) systems, in terms of cybernetic regulation, information, and bioenergetics. The formal study of biological (and quasi-biological) systems.

Taboo: Sacred; forbidden, especially by supernatural sanctions (from Polynesian *tapu*).

TAT (Thematic Apperception Test): A projective test in which subjects compose stories in response to drawings of ambiguous social situations. Used in psychological testing and (often with culturally adapted drawings) in cross-cultural research, to tap the subject's world of fantasy and hence psychodynamics.

Taro: A class of tropical plants of the lily family (for example, genera *Colocasia* and *Alocasia*) with heart-shaped "elephant ear" leaves, widely cultivated for their starchy corms (tubers).

Territoriality: In animals, use of and defensive reactions toward a particular area.

Territory: The part of a home range exclusively occupied by members of a primate social group and defended against encroachment.

Totemism: Symbolic association between a social group (for example, a lineage or clan) and a kind of bird, plant, or natural phenomenon. In "classic" forms a member of the social group has some special religious relationship (for example, a food taboo) toward members of the natural species.

Transformational Grammar: A school of linguistic theory, pioneered by Noam Chomsky, that seeks to describe formally, in logicomathematical terms the linguistic knowledge native speakers of a language draw on in speaking and understanding speech. (See also *Generative.*)

Transformational Rule: In transformational linguistics, a syntactic rule that applies in the derivation of sentences by modifying and rearranging tree structures (hence serving as a step in the connection between a deep structure and its surface structure representation).

Transhumance: Seasonal movement of nomadic peoples according to the availability of pasturage.

Tribal: Pertaining to small-scale food-producing societies without centralized political organization; more generally, stateless, technologically "primitive" societies.

Tribe: A small-scale society characterized by a distinctive language and culture (though it need have no political unity).

Troop: Among primates, a relatively structured and enduring social group.

Ubaid: Early Mesopotamian period (4750-3500 B.C.) marked by waterworks for irrigation and flood control and the emergence of temple centers.

Ultimogeniture: A rare pattern of inheritance in which the appropriate family heir is the youngest son or youngest sibling.

Universal: Of humans, characteristic of the species in all times and places, rather than a (variable) product of particular culturally patterned experience.

Unilineal: *Patrilineal* (agnatic) or *matrilineal* (uterine) descent, q.v.

Unvoiced: In language, a sound produced without vibration of the vocal cords. (In whispering, all sounds are unvoiced; in normal speech "t" is unvoiced, "d" is voiced.)

Urban: Pertaining to cities or life in cities.

Urbanization: The movement of rural or small-town populations into cities; the growth of cities.

Uruk: Mesopotamian (Near East) period of early urbanization marked by the emergence of cities and temples (3500-3200 B.C.)

Uterine: See *Matrilineal.*

Uxorilocal: Residence of a married couple with the wife's kin (formerly called "matrilocal").

Values: Conceptions of the desirable principles that guide human choice.

Varna: The four major castes, or paths of life, in Hindu ideology.

Viri-avunculocal: Residence of a married couple with the husband's matrilineal kin.

Virilocal: Residence of a married couple with the husband's kin (formerly called "patrilocal"). Residence rules can be further distinguished as viri-patrilocal (or patri-virilocal): residence with the husband's father; and viri-avunculocal (or avunculo-virilocal): residence with the husband's maternal uncle.

Viri-patrilocal: Postmarital residence with the groom's father (or with his people).

Vocalization: Production of sounds (by animals).

Voiced: Of a sound in speaking, produced in accompaniment to the vibration of the vocal cords. (Cf. *Unvoiced.*)

Vowel: In language, a sound produced by the unobstructed passage of air through the vocal chamber, concentrated in a particular sound frequency by varying the shape of that chamber by moving tongue or lips.

Ward: A partially separated neighborhood division of a village, town, or city whose members have some sense of community solidarity (may be based on descent or kinship).

Whorfian Hypothesis: The hypothesis, most strongly stated by the American linguist B. L. Whorf, that a language embodies or encodes a model *of* the world, in its grammatical structure, as well as a way of talking about it; and hence that habitual thought patterns tend to run along the channels cut by linguistic structures.

Witchcraft: Malevolent power that operates through humans as an involuntary force. (Cf. *Sorcery.*)

World View: A people's basic assumption about what kind of world they live in, what forces or entities control it, and what the place of humans is.

Würm: The last major Pleistocene glaciation (named for the Alpine sequence).

Yam: A class of tropical plants, mainly twining creepers, widely cultivated for their starchy tubers (though many species grow wild). Mainly genus *Diascorea*. Not related to the sweet potato *(Ipomoea batatas)*.

Yangshao: An early Chinese cultural tradition, prior to 3000 B.C., with farmers living in villages and cultivating millet and other grains.

SUGGESTIONS FOR FURTHER READING

For each of the numbered sections of the text, I have suggested a brief list of further readings. These will provide a student access to additional technical materials in the field. The suggested readings include key articles, general books (or chapters of general books), and edited compilations of readings in the subfield. The latter give a sampling of the technical literature, often containing useful introductions as well as technical bibliographies.

Depending on the library resources available to the student, additional means of finding technical literature may be available. One of the best sources is the catalog to the Peabody Museum Library (Harvard University), which is indexed by subject and author and includes detailed cataloging of journal articles as well as books.

Major anthropology journals of possible interest to the student include *American Anthropologist, Ethnology, Man, Journal of Anthropological Research* (formerly *Southwestern Journal of Anthropology*), *Current Anthropology, Africa, Journal of the Royal Anthropological Institute* (until 1965), *Oceania, L'Homme, Journal of American Folklore, Journal of the Polynesian Society, Bijdragen Tot de Land,—Taal,—en Volkenkunde, Anthropos, Ethnohistory* and *Comparative Studies in Society and History*.

Some of the numbered sections of the text have been grouped together in the recommended readings below, since the same readings are useful for several sections.

Section 1

Clifton, J. 1968. Cultural Anthropology: Aspirations and Approaches. In J. Clifton, ed., *Introduction to Cultural Anthropology*. Boston: Houghton Mifflin Company.

Frantz, C. 1972. *The Student Anthropologist's Handbook*. Cambridge, Mass.: Schenkman Publishing Co.

Fried, M. 1972. *The Study of Anthropology*. New York: Thomas Y. Crowell Company.

Hatch, E. 1973. *Theories of Man and Culture*. New York: Columbia University Press.

Sturtevant, W. 1968. The Fields of Anthropology. In M. H. Fried, *Readings in Anthropology*. 2d. ed., Vol. 1. New York: Thomas Y. Crowell Company.

Tax, S., ed. 1964. *Horizons of Anthropology*. Chicago: Aldine Publishing Company.

Section 2

Brown, R. 1963. *Explanation in Social Science*. Chicago: Aldine Publishing Company.

Hempel, C. G. 1965. *Aspects of Scientific Explanation, and Other Essays in the Philosophy of Science*. New York: Free Press.

Kuhn, T. S. 1970. *The Structure of Scientific Revolutions.* 2d. ed. Chicago: University of Chicago Press.

Naroll, R., and R. Cohen, eds. 1970. *A Handbook of Method in Cultural Anthropology.* Garden City, N.Y.: Natural History Press.

Pelto, P. J. 1970. *Anthropological Research: The Structure of Inquiry.* New York: Harper & Row, Publishers.

Popper, K. R. 1959. *The Logic of Scientific Discovery.* Rev. ed. New York: Harper & Row, Publishers.

————. 1972. *Objective Knowledge: An Evolutionary Approach.* New York: Oxford University Press.

Section 3

Berreman, G. D. 1968. Ethnography: Method and Product. In J. Clifton, ed., *Introduction to Cultural Anthropology.* Boston: Houghton Mifflin Company.

————. 1962. *Behind Many Masks: Ethnography and Impression Management in a Himalayan Village.* Ithaca, N.Y.: Society for Applied Anthropology, Monograph No. 4.

Bowen, E. S. 1954. *Return to Laughter.* New York: Harcourt Brace Jovanovich, Inc.

Casagrande, J. B., ed. 1960. *In the Company of Man.* New York: Harper & Row, Publishers.

Edgerton, R. B., and L. L. Langness. 1974. *Methods and Styles in the Study of Culture.* San Francisco: Chandler and Sharp.

Epstein, A. L., ed. 1967. *The Craft of Social Anthropology.* London: Tavistock.

Freilich, M., ed. 1970. *Marginal Natives: Anthropologists at Work.* New York: Harper & Row, Publishers.

Golde, P., ed. 1970. *Women in the Field.* Chicago: Aldine Publishing Company.

Henry, F., and S. Saberwal, eds. 1969. *Stress and Response in Fieldwork.* New York: Holt, Rinehart and Winston.

Jongmans, D. G., and P. C. Gutkind, ed. 1967. *Anthropologists in the Field.* Assen: Van Gorcum.

Paul, B. 1963. Interview Techniques and Field Relationships. In A. L. Kroeber, ed., *Anthropology Today.* Chicago: University of Chicago Press.

Spindler, G. D., ed. 1970. *Being an Anthropologist: Fieldwork in Eleven Cultures.* New York: Holt, Rinehart and Winston.

Williams, T. R. 1967. *Field Methods in the Study of Culture.* New York: Holt, Rinehart and Winston.

Sections 4 to 5

Alland, A., Jr. 1973. *Evolution and Human Behavior: An Introduction to Darwinian Anthropology.* New York: Doubleday & Company, Inc.

Birdsell, J. 1975. *Human Evolution: An Introduction to the New Physical Anthropology.* Chicago: Rand McNally & Company.

Buettner-Janusch, J. 1973. *Physical Anthropology: A Perspective.* New York: John Wiley & Sons, Inc.

Campbell, B. 1974. *Human Evolution: An Introduction to Man's Adaptations.* Chicago: Aldine Publishing Company.

Howell, F. C. 1971. *Early Man.* 2d. ed. New York: Time-Life Books.

Kelso, A. J. 1974. *Physical Anthropology: An Introduction.* New York: J. B. Lippincott Company.

Pfeiffer, J. E. 1972. *The Emergence of Man,* 2d. ed., New York: Harper & Row, Publishers.

Pilbeam, D. 1972. *The Ascent of Man: An Introduction to Human Evolution.* New York: The Macmillan Company.

Simons, E. L. 1972. *Primate Evolution: An Introduction to Man's Place in Nature.* New York: The Macmillan Company.

Sections 6 to 9

Chance, M. R. A., and C. Jolly. 1970. *Social Groups of Monkeys, Apes and Men.* London: Jonathan Cape, Ltd.

DeVore, I. 1965. *Primate Behavior.* New York: Holt, Rinehart and Winston.

Dolhinow, P., ed. 1972. *Primate Patterns.* New York: Holt, Rinehart and Winston.

Jay, P. (P. J. Dolhinow), ed. 1968. *Primates: Studies in Adaptation and Variability.* New York: Holt, Rinehart and Winston.

Jolly, A. 1972. *The Evolution of Primate Behavior.* New York: The Macmillan Company.

Kummer, H. 1971. *Primate Societies. Group Techniques of Ecological Adaptation.* Chicago: Aldine Publishing Company.

Lancaster, J. B. 1975. *Primate Behavior and the Emergence of Human Culture.* New York: Holt, Rinehart and Winston.

Section 10

Hewes, G. W. 1973. Primate Communication and the Gestural Origin of Language, *Current Anthropology* 14(1-2):5-24.

Hockett, C. F., and R. Ascher. 1964. The Human Revolution. *Current Anthropology* 5:135-168.

Holloway, R. J., Jr. 1969. Culture: A Human Domain. *Current Anthropology* 10:395-407.

Wescott, R., ed. 1974. *Language Origins.* Silver Spring, Md.: Linstok Press.

Section 11

Freedman, D. G. 1974. *Human Infancy: An Evolutionary Perspective.* New York: John Wiley & Sons, Inc.

Freeman, J. D. 1970. Human Nature and Culture. In R.

O. Slatyer et al., eds., *Man and the New Biology*. Canberra: Australian National University Press.

Hainline, L. J. 1965. Culture and Biological Adaptation. *American Anthropologist* 67:1174-1197.

Section 12

Dobzhansky, T. 1971. *Genetics of the Evolutionary Process*. New York: Columbia University Press.

Mayr, E. 1970. *Populations, Species, and Evolution*. Cambridge, Mass.: Harvard University Press.

Section 13

Alland, A., Jr. 1973. *Human Diversity*. Garden City, N.Y.: Anchor Press/Doubleday.

Baker, P. T., and J. S. Weiner, eds. 1966. *The Biology of Human Adaptability*. Oxford: Clarendon Press.

Brace, C. L. 1964. A Nonracial Approach towards the Understanding of Human Diversity. In A. Montagu, ed., *The Concept of Race*. New York: The Free Press.

Brace, C. L., G. R. Gamble, and J. T. Bond, eds. 1972. *Race and Intelligence*. Washington, D.C.: American Anthropological Association.

Brace, C. L. and J. Metress, eds. 1973. *Man on Evolutionary Perspective*. New York: John Wiley & Sons, Inc.

Buettner-Janusch, J. 1973. *Physical Anthropology: A Perspective*. New York: John Wiley & Sons, Inc.

Mead, M., et al., eds. 1968. *Science and the Concept of Race*. New York: Columbia University Press.

Section 14

D'Andrade, R. G. 1966. Sex Differences and Cultural Institutions. In E. E. Maccoby, ed., *The Development of Sex Differences*. Stanford, Calif.: Stanford University Press.

Freedman, D. G. 1974. *Human Infancy: An Evolutionary Perspective*. New York: John Wiley & Sons, Inc.

————. 1968. Personality Development in Infancy: A Biological Approach. In S. L. Washburn and P. Jay, eds. *Perspectives on Human Evolution*, Vol. I. New York: Holt, Rinehart and Winston.

Section 15

Binford, L. R., and S. Binford, eds. 1968. *New Perspectives in Archaeology*. Chicago: Aldine Publishing Co.

Deetz, J. 1967. *Invitation to Archaeology*. Garden City, N.Y.: Natural History Press.

Fagan, B. 1972. *In the Beginning: An Introduction to Archaeology*. Boston: Little, Brown and Company.

Hole, F., and R. F. Heizer. 1973. *Introduction to Prehistoric Archaeology*. 3d. ed. New York: Holt, Rinehart and Winston.

Meighan, C. 1966. *Archaeology: An Introduction*. San Francisco: Chandler Publishing Company.

Section 16

Bordes, F. 1968. *The Old Stone Age*. New York: McGraw-Hill, Inc.

Bushnell, G. H. S. 1968. *The First Americans*. New York: McGraw-Hill, Inc.

Butzer, K. W. 1969. *Environment and Archaeology: An Introduction to Pleistocene Geography*. Chicago: Aldine Publishing Company.

Chard, C. S. 1975. *Man in Prehistory*. 2d. ed. New York: McGraw-Hill, Inc.

Clark, J. D. 1970. *The Prehistory of Africa*. New York: Praeger Publishers, Inc.

Fagan, B. M. 1974. *Men of the Earth: An Introduction to World Prehistory*. Boston: Little, Brown and Company.

Jennings, J. D. 1968. *Prehistory of North America*. New York: McGraw-Hill, Inc.

Meggers, B. J. 1972. *Prehistoric America*. Chicago: Aldine Publishing Company.

Mulvaney, D. J. 1969. *The Prehistory of Australia*. New York: Praeger Publishers, Inc.

Patterson, T. C. 1973. *America's Past: A New World Archaeology*. Glenview, Ill.: Scott, Foresman and Company.

Section 17

Bicchieri, M. G., ed. 1972. *Hunters and Gatherers Today: A Socioeconomic Study of Eleven Such Cultures in the Twentieth Century*. New York: Holt, Rinehart and Winston.

Coon, C. S. 1971. *The Hunting Peoples*. Boston: Little, Brown and Company.

Graburn, N. H. H., and B. S. Strong. 1973. *Circumpolar Peoples: An Anthropological Perspective*. Pacific Palisades, Calif.: Goodyear Publishing Company.

Lee, R. B., and I. DeVore, eds. 1968. *Man the Hunter*. Chicago: Aldine Publishing Company.

————. 1974. *Kalahari Hunter Gatherers*. Cambridge, Mass.: Harvard University Press.

Oswalt, W. H. 1973. *Habitat and Technology: The Evolution of Hunting*. New York: Holt, Rinehart and Winston.

Service, E. R. 1966. *The Hunters*. Englewood Cliffs, N.J.: Prentice-Hall, Inc.

Section 18

Hodges, H. 1970. *Technology in the Ancient World*. New York: Alfred A. Knopf, Inc.

Marshack, A. 1972. *The Roots of Civilization*. New York: McGraw-Hill, Inc.

Struever, S. 1971. *Prehistoric Agriculture.* American Museum of Natural History Sourcebook in Anthropology. New York: Doubleday & Company, Inc.

Ucko, P. J., and G. W. Dimbleby, eds. 1969. *The Domestication and Exploitation of Plants and Animals.* Chicago: Aldine Publishing Company.

Section 19

Chard, C. S. 1975. *Man in Prehistory.* 2d. ed. New York: McGraw-Hill, Inc.

Fagan, B. M. 1974. *Men of the Earth: An Introduction to World Prehistory.* Boston: Little, Brown and Company.

Section 20

Conklin, H. C. 1954. An Ethnoecological Approach to Shifting Agriculture. *Transcripts of New York Academy of Sciences* 17(2):133-142.

De Schlippe, P. 1956. *Shifting Cultivation in Africa.* London: Routledge & Kegan Paul Ltd.

Irons, W., and N. Dyson-Hudson, eds. 1972. *Perspectives on Nomadism.* Leiden: W. J. Brill (International Studies in Sociology and Social Anthropology, Vol. 13).

Phillips, E. D. 1965. *The Royal Hordes: Nomad Peoples of the Steppes.* New York: McGraw-Hill, Inc.

Vayda, A. P., ed. 1969. *Environment and Cultural Behavior: Ecological Studies in Cultural Anthropology.* Garden City, N.Y.: Natural History Press.

———, and R. A. Rappaport. 1968. *Ecology, Cultural and Noncultural.* In J. Clifton, ed., *Introduction to Cultural Anthropology.* Boston: Houghton Mifflin Company.

Sections 21 to 22

Adams, R. N. 1966. *The Evolution of Urban Society.* Chicago: Aldine Publishing Company.

Krader, L. 1968. *The Formation of the State.* Englewood Cliffs, N.J.: Prentice-Hall, Inc.

Sanders, W. T., and B. J. Price. 1968. *Mesoamerica: The Evolution of a Civilization.* New York: Random House, Inc.

Sections 23 to 24

Geertz, C. 1973. *The Interpretation of Cultures.* New York: Basic Books (especially "Thick Description" and "The Impact of the Concept of Culture on the Concept of Man").

Goodenough, W. H. 1961. Comment on Cultural Evolution. *Daedalus* 90:521-528.

———. 1971. *Culture, Language, and Society.* McCaleb Module in Anthropology. Reading, Mass.: Addison-Wesley Publishing Company.

Kay, P. 1965. Ethnography and the Theory of Culture. *Bucknell Review* 19:106-113 (reprinted as Bobbs-Merrill reprint).

Kluckhohn, C., and W. Kelly. 1945. *The Concept of Culture.* In R. Linton, ed., *The Science of Man in the World Crisis.* New York: Columbia University Press.

Kroeber, A. L., and C. Kluckhohn. 1952. *Culture: A Critical Review of Concepts and Definitions.* Papers of the Peabody Museum of American Archaeology and Ethnology, Harvard University, Vol. 47.

Spradley, J. P. *Foundations of Cultural Knowledge.* In J. P. Spradley, ed., *Culture and Cognition: Rules, Maps, and Plans.* San Francisco: Chandler Publishing Company.

Section 25

Bolinger, D. 1968. *Aspects of Language.* New York: Harcourt Brace Jovanovich, Inc.

Chomsky, N. 1973. *Language and Mind.* 2d. ed. New York: Harcourt Brace Jovanovich, Inc.

Grinder, J., and S. Elgin. 1973. *Transformational Grammar: History, Theory, Practice.* New York: Holt, Rinehart and Winston.

Langacker, R. W. 1968. *Language and its Structure.* New York: Harcourt Brace Jovanovich, Inc.

Section 26

Brown, R. 1973. *A First Language.* Cambridge, Mass.: Harvard University Press.

Burling, R. 1969. Linguistics and Ethnographic Description. *American Anthropologist* 71:817-827.

Goodenough, W. H. 1971. *Culture, Language, and Society.* McCaleb Module in Anthropology. Reading, Mass.: Addison-Wesley Publishing Company.

Keesing, R. M. 1972. Paradigms Lost: The New Ethnography and the New Linguistics. *Southwestern Journal of Anthropology* 28:299-332.

Lenneberg, E. 1969. On Explaining Language. *Science* 164:635-643.

McNeill, D. 1970. *The Acquisition of Language.* New York: Harper & Row, Publishers.

Spradley, J. P. 1972. *Culture and Cognition: Rules, Maps and Plans.* New York: Chandler Publishing Company.

Tyler, S., ed. 1969. *Cognitive Anthropology.* New York: Holt, Rinehart and Winston.

Whorf, B. L. 1956. *Language, Thought and Reality.* Cambridge, Mass.: MIT Press.

Section 27

Bauman, R., and J. Sherzer, eds. 1974. *Explorations in the Ethnography of Speaking.* New York: Cambridge University Press.

Burling, R. 1970. *Man's Many Voices: Language in its Cultural Context.* New York: Holt, Rinehart and Winston.

Fishman, J. A., ed. 1968. *Readings in the Sociology of Language.* The Hague: Mouton.

Gumperz, J. J., and D. Hymes, eds. 1972. *Directions in Sociolinguistics.* New York: Holt, Rinehart and Winston.

Hymes, D. 1974. *Foundations in Sociolinguistics: An Ethnographic Approach.* Philadelphia: University of Pennsylvania Press.

Labov, W. 1972. *Sociolinguistics Patterns.* Philadelphia: University of Pennsylvania Press.

Section 28

Bateson, G. 1972. *Steps to an Ecology of Mind.* Philadelphia: Intext Publishing Group.

Birdwhistell, R. 1970. *Kinesics and Context.* Philadelphia: University of Pennsylvania Press.

Eibl-Eibesfeldt, I. 1975. *Ethology: The Biology of Behavior.* 2d. ed. New York: Holt, Rinehart and Winston.

Hall, E. T. 1959. *The Silent Language.* Garden City, N.Y.: Doubleday & Company, Inc.

———. 1966. *The Hidden Dimension.* Garden City, N.Y.: Doubleday & Company, Inc.

Sections 29 to 30

Geertz, C. 1965. The Impact of the Concept of Culture on the Concept of Man. In J. R. Platt, ed., *New Views on the Nature of Man.* Chicago: University of Chicago Press.

Herskovits, M. H. 1972. *Cultural Relativism: Perspectives in Cultural Pluralism.* New York: Random House, Inc.

Keesing, R. M. 1972. Paradigms Lost: The New Ethnography and the New Linguistics. *Southwestern Journal of Anthropology* 28:299-332.

Section 31

Eggan, F. 1954. Social Anthropology and the Method of Controlled Comparison. *American Anthropologist* 56:743-763.

Evans-Pritchard, E. E. 1965. *The Comparative Method in Social Anthropology.* In E. E. Evans-Pritchard, ed., *The Position of Women and Other Essays.* London: Faber & Faber, Ltd.

Ford, C. S., ed. 1967. *Cross-Cultural Approaches.* New Haven, Conn.: HRAF Press.

Kobben, A. F. J. 1967. Why Exceptions? The Logic of Cross-Cultural Analysis. *Current Anthropology* 8:3-34.

Moore, F. W., ed. 1961. *Readings in Cross-Cultural Methodology.* New Haven, Conn.: HRAF Press.

Nadel, S. F. 1952. Witchcraft in Four African Societies: An Essay in Comparison. *American Anthropologist* 54:18-29.

Naroll, R. 1968. Some Thoughts on Comparative Method in Cultural Anthropology. In H. M. Blalock, ed., *Methodology in Social Research.* New York: McGraw-Hill, Inc.

———. 1970. What Have We Learned from Cross-Cultural Studies? *American Anthropologist* 72:1227-1288.

Naroll, R., and R. Cohen, eds. 1970. *A Handbook of Method in Cultural Anthropology* (esp. Parts V, VI, and VII). Garden City, N.Y.: Natural History Press.

Whiting, J. W. M. 1968. Methods and Problems in Cross-Cultural Research. In G. Lindzey and A. Aronson, eds., *The Handbook of Social Psychology.* 2d. ed., Vol. 2. Reading, Mass.: Addison-Wesley Publishing Company, Inc.

Sections 32 to 34

Barnouw, V. 1973. *Culture and Personality.* Rev. ed. Homewood, Ill.: Dorsey Press.

Child, I. L. 1968. Personality in Culture. In E. F. Borgatta and W. V. Lambert, eds., *Handbook of Personality Theory and Research.* Chicago: Rand McNally, Inc.

Cole, M., and S. Scribner. 1974. *Culture and Thought: A Psychological Introduction.* New York: John Wiley & Sons, Inc.

De Vos, G., and A. Hippler. 1969. Cultural Psychology: Comparative Studies of Human Behavior. In G. Lindzey and A. Aronson, eds., *Handbook of Social Psychology,* Vol. 4. Cambridge, Mass.: Addison-Wesley Publishing Company, Inc.

Edgerton, R. B. 1971. *The Individual in Cultural Adaptation: A Study of Four East African Peoples.* Berkeley: University of California Press.

Hsu, F. L. K., ed. 1972. *Psychological Anthropology.* 2d. ed. Cambridge: Schenkman Publishing Company.

Hunt, R., ed. 1967. *Personalities and Cultures.* Garden City, N.Y.: Natural History Press.

Le Vine, R. A. 1973. *Culture, Behavior, and Personality.* Chicago: Aldine Publishing Company.

———, ed. 1974. *Culture and Personality: Contemporary Readings.* Chicago: Aldine Publishing Company.

Spiro, M. E. 1968. Culture and Personality. In D. L. Sills, ed., *International Encyclopedia of the Social Sciences,* Vol. 3:558-563. New York: Crowell Collier and Macmillan, Inc.

Wallace, A. F. C. 1961. Mental Illness, Biology and Culture. In F. L. K. Hsu, ed., *Psychological Anthropology.* Homewood, Ill.: Dorsey Press.

Wallace, A. F. C. 1970. *Culture and Personality.* 2d. ed. New York: Random House, Inc.

Section 35

Ainsworth, M. D. S. 1967. *Infancy in Uganda.* Baltimore: Johns Hopkins University Press.

Brown, R. 1973. *A First Language.* Cambridge, Mass.: Harvard University Press.

Ferguson, C. A., and D. Slobin, eds. 1973. *Readings in Child Language Acquisition.* New York: Holt, Rinehart and Winston.

Freeman, J. D. 1974. Kinship, Attachment Behaviour and the Primary Bond. In J. R. Goody, ed., *The Character of Kinship.* Cambridge: Cambridge University Press.

Hutt, S. J., and C. Hutt, eds. 1973. *Early Human Development.* London: Oxford University Press.

Kagan, J. 1972. Do Infants Think? *Scientific American,* March.

McNeill, D. 1970. *The Acquisition of Language.* New York: Harper & Row, Publishers.

Piaget, J. 1970. Piaget's Theory. In P. H. Mussen, ed., *Carmichael's Manual of Child Psychology,* 3d. ed., Vol. 1, pp. 703-732. New York: John Wiley & Sons, Inc.

Shimahara, N. 1970. Enculturation: A Reconsideration. *Current Anthropology* 11:143-234.

Whiting, B. B., ed. 1963. *Six Cultures: Studies of Child Rearing.* New York: John Wiley & Sons, Inc.

Williams, T. R. 1972. *Introduction to Socialization: Human Culture Transmitted.* St. Louis: The C. V. Mosby Company.

Yarrow, M., J. Campbell, and R. Burton. 1968. *Child Rearing: An Inquiry into Research and Methods.* San Francisco: Jossey-Bass.

Section 36

Cohen, Y. A., ed. 1961. *Social Structure and Personality.* New York: Holt, Rinehart and Winston.

Smelser, N. J., and W. T. Smelser, eds. 1963. *Personality and Social Systems.* New York: John Wiley & Sons, Inc.

Section 37

Damas, D., ed. 1969. *Contributions to Anthropology: Ecological Essays.* National Museum of Canada Anthropological Bulletin No. 86. Ottawa.

Friedman, J. 1974. Marxism, Structuralism and Vulgar Materialism. *Man* 9:444-469.

Godelier, M. 1974. Anthropology and Biology: Towards a New Form of Co-operation. *International Social Science Journal* 26(4):611-635.

Harris, M. 1975. *Culture, People, Nature: An Introduction to General Anthropology.* New York: Thomas Y. Crowell Company.

Heider, K. G. 1972. Environment, Subsistence, and Society. *Annual Review of Anthropology* 1:207-226. Palo Alto, Calif.: Annual Reviews, Inc.

Kottak, C. P. 1974. *Anthropology: The Exploration of Human Diversity.* New York: Random House, Inc.

Meggers, B. J. 1971. *Amazonia: Man and Nature in a Counterfeit Paradise.* Chicago: Aldine Publishing Company.

Netting, R. M. 1971. *The Ecological Approach in Cultural Study.* Reading, Pa.: Addison-Wesley Publishing Company, Inc.

Rappaport, R. 1971. Nature, Culture, and Ecological Anthropology. In H. Shapiro, ed., *Man, Culture and Society,* pp. 237-267. London: Oxford University Press.

Vayda, A. P. 1968. Primitive Warfare. *International Encyclopedia of Social Science* 16:468-472. New York: The Macmillan Company.

————. 1969. "An Ecological Approach in Cultural Anthropology". *Bucknell Review,* 17:112-119.

————, and R. Rappaport. 1968. Ecology, Cultural and Noncultural. In J. A. Clifton, ed., *Introduction to Cultural Anthropology.* Boston: Houghton Mifflin Company.

Watson, R. A., and P. J. Watson. 1969. *Man and Nature.* New York: Harcourt Brace Jovanovich, Inc.

Section 38

Goodenough, W. H. 1970. *Description and Comparison in Social Anthropology.* Chicago: Aldine Publishing Company.

————. 1971. *Culture, Language, and Society.* McCaleb Module in Anthropology. Reading, Mass.: Addison-Wesley Publishing Company, Inc.

Section 39

See references to Section 35 for childhood; Section 51 for age groupings; and Section 77 for sex roles.

For the aged, see:

Cowgill, D. O., and L. D. Holmes, eds. 1972. *Aging and Modernization.* New York: Appleton-Century-Crofts.

Simmons, L. W. 1945. *The Role of the Aged in Primitive Society.* New Haven, Conn.: Yale University Press.

Sections 40 to 44

Bohannan, P. J., and J. Middleton, eds. 1968. *Kinship and Social Organization.* Garden City, N.Y.: Natural History Press.

Eggan, F. 1968. Kinship: An Introduction. *International Encyclopedia of the Social Sciences* 8:390-401. New York: The Macmillan Company.

Fox, R. 1967. *Kinship and Marriage*. Baltimore: Penguin Books, Inc.

Goody, J. R. 1968. Kinship: Descent Groups. *International Encyclopedia of the Social Sciences* 8:401-408.

————, ed. 1971. *Kinship: Selected Readings*. Baltimore: Penguin Books, Inc.

Graburn, N. H. H. 1971. *Readings in Kinship and Social Structure*. New York: Harper & Row, Publishers.

Keesing, R. M. 1975. *Kin Groups and Social Structure*. New York: Holt, Rinehart and Winston.

Sahlins, M. 1968. *Tribesmen*. Englewood Cliffs, N.J.: Prentice-Hall, Inc.

Scheffler, H. W. 1974. Kinship, Descent and Alliance. In J. J. Honigmann, ed., *Handbook of Social and Cultural Anthropology*. Skokie, Ill.: Rand McNally & Company.

Schneider, D. 1968. *American Kinship: A Cultural Account*. Englewood Cliffs, N.J.: Prentice-Hall, Inc.

————, and K. Gough, eds. 1961. *Matrilineal Kinship*. Berkeley: University of California Press.

Section 45

Boissevain, J. 1968. The Place of Non-Groups in the Social Sciences. *Man* (n.s.) 3:542-556.

Keesing, R. M. 1975. *Kin Groups and Social Structure* (Chap. 8). New York: Holt, Rinehart and Winston.

Sections 46 to 50

Bohannan, P. J., and J. Middleton, eds. 1968. *Marriage, Family and Residence*. Garden City, N.Y.: Natural History Press.

Fox, R. 1967. *Kinship and Marriage*. Baltimore: Penguin Books, Inc.

Goody, J. R. 1972. *Domestic Groups*. Addison-Wesley Modules in Social Anthropology. Reading, Mass.: Addison-Wesley Publishing Company, Inc.

————, and S. N. Tambiah, eds. 1973. *Bridewealth and Dowry*. Cambridge: Cambridge University Press.

Keesing, R. M. 1975. *Kin Groups and Social Structure*. New York: Holt, Rinehart and Winston.

Leach, E. R. 1971. Marriage, Primitive. In *Encyclopedia Britannica* 938-947.

Section 51

Eisenstadt, S. N. 1956. *From Generation to Generation: Age Groups and Social Structure*. New York: The Free Press.

Hammond, D. 1972. *Associations*. McCaleb Module in Anthropology No. 14. Reading, Mass.: Addison-Wesley Publishing Company, Inc.

Lowie, R. H. 1947. *Primitive Society* (Chaps. 10 and 11). New York: Liveright Publishing Corp.

Van Gennep, A. 1960. *The Rites of Passage*. London: Routledge & Kegan Paul Ltd.

Wedgewood, C. H. 1930. The Nature and Functions of Secret Societies. *Oceania* 1:129-145.

Sections 52 to 57

Belshaw, C. 1965. *Traditional Exchange and Modern Markets*. Englewood Cliffs, N.J.: Prentice-Hall, Inc.

Bohannan, P., and G. Dalton, eds. 1962. *Markets in Africa*. Evanston, Ill.: Northwestern University Press.

Dalton, G., ed. 1967. *Tribal and Peasant Economics*. Garden City, N.Y.: Natural History Press.

Firth, R., ed. 1967. *Themes in Economic Anthropology*. ASA Monographs, 6. London: Tavistock.

Godelier, M. 1972. *Rationality and Irrationality in Economics*. Trans. by B. Pearce. New York: Monthly Review Press.

LeClair, E. E., and H. Schneider. 1968. *Economic Anthropology*. New York: Holt, Rinehart and Winston.

Nash, M. 1966. *Primitive and Peasant Economic Systems*. San Francisco: Chandler Publishing Company.

Sahlins, M. 1971. Economic Anthropology and Anthropological Economics. *Social Science Information* 8(5):13-33.

————. 1972. *Stone Age Economics*. Chicago: Aldine Publishing Company.

Schneider, H. K. 1974. *Economic Man: The Economics of Anthropology*. New York: The Free Press.

Section 58

Bendix, R., and S. M. Lipset, eds. 1966. *Class, Status, and Power: Social Stratification in Comparative Perspective*. 2d. ed. New York: Free Press.

Bohannan, P. 1963. *Social Anthropology*. New York: Holt, Rinehart and Winston.

Cox, O. C. 1970. *Caste, Class, and Race*. New York: Monthly Review Press.

Eisenstadt, S. N. 1971. *Social Differentiation and Social Stratification*. Glenview, Ill.: Scott, Foresman and Company.

Fried, M. 1967. *The Evolution of Political Society*. New York: Random House, Inc.

Kwan, K. M., and T. Shibutani. 1965. *Ethnic Stratification*. New York: Macmillan, Inc.

Ossowski, S. 1963. *Class Structure in the Social Consciousness*. New York: Free Press.

Plotnicov, L., and A. Tuden. 1969. *Essays in Comparative Social Stratification*. Pittsburgh: University of Pittsburgh Press.

————. 1970. *Social Stratification in Africa*. New York: Macmillan, Inc.

Section 59

Berreman, G. 1973. *Caste in the Modern World.* Morristown, N.J.: General Learning Press.

Beteille, A. 1970. *Social Inequality.* London: Penguin Books.

De Reuck, A., and J. Knight, eds. 1967. *Caste and Race: Comparative Approaches.* London: J. and A. Churchill, Ltd.

Dumont, L. 1970. *Homo Hierarchicus.* Chicago: University of Chicago Press.

Leach, E. R., ed. 1960. *Aspects of Caste in South India, Ceylon, and Northwest Pakistan.* Cambridge Papers in Social Anthropology, 2. Cambridge: Cambridge University Press.

Marriott, M., ed. 1955. *Village India: Studies in the Little Community.* Chicago: University of Chicago Press.

Mencher, J. P., 1974. The Caste System Upside Down, or The-Not-So-Mysterious East. *Current Anthropology* 15:469-?.

Singer, M., and B. S. Cohn, eds. 1968. *Structure and Change in Indian Society.* Viking Fund Publications in Anthropology, 47. Chicago: Aldine Publishing Company.

Section 60

Bohannan, P. 1963. *Social Anthropology.* New York: Holt, Rinehart and Winston.

Miers, S., and I. Kopytoff, eds. 1975. *Slavery in Pre-Colonial Africa.* Madison: University of Wisconsin Press.

Richardson, P. 1971. *Empire and Slavery.* New York: Harper & Row, Publishers.

Winks, R., ed. 1972. *Slavery: A Comparative Perspective.* New York: New York University Press.

Sections 61 to 62

Asad, T. 1972. Market Model. Class Structure and Consent: A Reconsideration of Swat Political Organization. *Man* 7:74-94.

Bailey, F. G. 1969. *Stratagems and Spoils: A Social Anthropology of Politics.* Oxford: Basil Blackwell & Mott, Ltd.

Balandier, G. 1970. *Political Anthropology.* New York: Random House, Inc.

Barth, F., ed. 1969. *Ethnic Groups and Boundaries.* Boston: Little, Brown and Company.

Cohen, A. 1969. Political Anthropology: The Analysis of the Symbolism of Power Relations. *Man* (n.s.) 4: 215-235.

Cohen, R., and J. Middleton, eds. 1967. *Comparative Political Systems.* Garden City, N.Y.: Natural History Press.

Eisenstadt, S. N. 1963. *Political Systems of Empires.* New York: Free Press.

Fortes, M., and E. Evans-Pritchard, eds. 1940. *African Political Systems.* London: Oxford University Press.

Fried, M., 1967. *The Evolution of Political Society.* New York: Random House, Inc.

Sahlins, M. 1963. Poor Man, Rich Man, Big Man, Chief: Political Types in Melanesia and Polynesia. *Comparative Studies in Society and History* 5:285-300.

Swartz, M., ed. 1968. *Local Level Politics.* Chicago: Aldine Publishing Company.

Swartz, M., V. Turner, and A. Tuden, eds. 1966. *Political Anthropology.* Chicago: Aldine Publishing Company.

Section 63

Bohannan, P. J., ed. 1967. *Law and Warfare.* Garden City, N.Y.: Natural History Press.

Fried, M., M. Harris, and R. Murphy, eds. 1968. *War: The Anthropology of Armed Conflict and Aggression.* Garden City, N.Y.: Natural History Press.

Montagu, M. F. A., ed. 1972. *Man and Aggression.* 2d. ed. London: Oxford University Press.

Otten, C. M., ed. 1973. *Aggression and Evolution.* Lexington, Mass.: Xerox Corporation.

Otterbein, K. F. 1970. *The Evolution of War: A Cross-Cultural Study.* New Haven, Conn.: HRAF Press.

Sections 64 to 65

Bohannan, P. J., ed. 1967. *Law and Warfare.* Garden City, N.Y.: Natural History Press.

Diamond, A. L. 1971. *Primitive Law, Past and Present.* London: Methuen & Co., Ltd.

Hoebel, E. A. 1954. *The Law of Primitive Man.* Cambridge, Mass.: Harvard University Press.

Marwick, M. 1970. *Witchcraft and Sorcery.* London: Penguin Books.

Middleton, J., ed. 1967. *Magic, Witchcraft, and Curing.* Garden City, N.Y.: Natural History Press.

Nader, L., ed. 1965. *The Ethnography of Law.* American Anthropologist Special Publication, Vol. 67, 6, Part 2.

———. 1968. *Law in Culture and Society.* Chicago: Aldine Publishing Company.

Pospisil, L. 1958. *Kapauku Papuans and Their Law.* New Haven, Conn.: Yale University Publications in Anthropology, 54.

———. 1968. "Law and Order." In J. Clifton, ed., *Introduction to Cultural Anthropology.* Boston: Houghton Mifflin Company.

———. 1974. *Anthropology of Law: A Comparative Theory.* New Haven, Conn.: HRAF Press.

Section 66

Banton, M., ed. 1966. *Anthropological Approaches to the Study of Religion*. ASA Monographs, 3. London: Tavistock. (See especially articles by Geertz and Spiro).

Evans-Pritchard, E. E. 1965. *Theories of Primitive Religion*. London: Oxford University Press.

Geertz, C. 1966a. Religion as a Cultural System. In M. Banton, ed., *Anthropological Approaches to the Study of Religion*. ASA Monographs, 3. London: Tavistock.

Horton, R. The Kalabari World View: An Outline and Interpretation. *Africa* 32:197-220.

La Barre, W. 1972. *The Ghost Dance*. New York: Dell Publishing Co., Inc.

Leslie, C., ed. 1960. *Anthropology of Folk Religion*. New York: Random House, Inc.

Lessa, W. A., and E. Z. Vogt. 1972. *Reader in Comparative Religion: An Anthropological Approach*. 3d. ed. New York: Harper & Row.

Middleton, J., ed. 1967. *Myth and Cosmos*. Garden City, N.Y.: Natural History Press.

————, ed. 1967. *Gods and Rituals: Readings in Religious Beliefs and Practices*. Garden City, N.Y.: Natural History Press.

Wallace, A. F. C. 1967. *Religion: An Anthropological View*. New York: Random House, Inc.

Section 67

Douglas, M. 1966. *Purity and Danger*. Baltimore: Penguin Books.

————. 1970. *Natural Symbols: Explorations in Cosmology*. London: Cresset.

Evans-Pritchard, E. 1953. The Nuer Conception of Spirit in Relation to the Social Order. *American Anthropologist* 55:201-214.

Goody, J. 1962. *Death, Property and the Ancestors*. London: Tavistock.

Hertz, R. 1960. *Death and the Right Hand*. New York: Free Press.

Lévi-Strauss, C. 1963. *Totemism*. Boston: Beacon Press.

Lewis, I. M. 1972 *Ecstatic Religion: An Anthropological Study of Spirit Possession and Shamanism*. London: Penguin Books.

Section 68

Cohen, P. S. 1969. Theories of Myth. *Man*, (n.s.), 4:337-353.

Firth, R. 1973. *Symbols, Public and Private*. Ithaca, N.Y.: Cornell University Press.

Georges, R. A., ed. 1968. *Studies on Mythology*. Homewood, Ill.: Dorsey Press.

La Fontaine, J., ed. 1972. *The Interpretation of Ritual*. Cambridge: Cambridge University Press.

Leach, E. R., ed. 1967. *The Structural Study of Myth and Totemism*. London: Tavistock.

————. 1970. *Natural Symbols: Explorations in Cosmology*. New York: Pantheon Books, Inc.

Maranda, P., ed. 1972. *Mythology*. London: Penguin Books.

Middleton, J., ed. 1967. *Gods and Rituals: Readings in Religious Beliefs and Practices*. Garden City, N.Y.: Natural History Press.

Turner, V. 1967. *The Forest of Symbols*. Ithaca, N.Y.: Cornell University Press.

————. 1969. *The Ritual Process*. Chicago: Aldine-Atherton.

Section 69

Bateson, G. 1972. *Steps to an Ecology of Mind*. Philadelphia: Intext Publishing Group.

Geertz, C. 1957. Ethos, World-View and the Analysis of Sacred Symbols. *Antioch Review* 17:421-437.

————. 1962. The Growth of Culture and the Evolution of Mind. In J. Scher, ed., *Theories of the Mind*, pp. 713-740. New York: Free Press.

Hallowell, A. I. 1955. *Culture and Experience*. Philadelphia: University of Pennsylvania Press.

Kluckhohn, C. 1949. The Philosophy of the Navaho Indians. In F. S. C. Northrop, ed., *Ideological Differences and World Order*. New Haven, Conn.: Yale University Press.

Leach, E. R. 1974. *Claude Lévi-Strauss*. Rev. ed. New York: Viking Press.

Lévi-Strauss, C. 1963. *Structural Anthropology*. New York: Basic Books, Inc.

————. 1966. *The Savage Mind*. Chicago: University of Chicago Press.

Ornstein, R. 1973. *The Psychology of Consciousness*. San Francisco: W. H. Freeman and Co.

Paz, O. 1970. *Claude Lévi-Strauss: An Introduction*. Ithaca, N.Y.: Cornell University Press.

Section 70

Austen, R. A. 1969. *Modern Imperialism: Western Overseas Expansion and its Aftermath*. Lexington, Mass.: D. C. Heath & Company.

Horowitz, D. 1969. *Empire and Revolution: A Radical Interpretation of Contemporary History*. New York: Random House, Inc.

Jalee, P. 1970. *Pillage of the Third World*. New York: Monthly Review Press.

Owen, R., and R. Sutcliffe, eds. 1973. *Studies in the*

Theory of Imperialism. London: Longman Group Ltd.

Rhodes, R. I., ed. 1970. *Imperialism and Underdevelopment: A Reader.* New York: Monthly Review Press.

Sections 71 to 72

Aceves, J. B., ed. 1972. *Aspects of Cultural Change.* Southern Anthropological Society Proceedings, 6. Athens, Ga.: University of Georgia Press.

Asad, T., ed. 1973. *Anthropology and the Colonial Encounter.* London: Ithaca Press.

Bohannan, P., and F. Plog, eds. 1967. *Beyond the Frontier: Social Process and Cultural Change.* Garden City, N.Y.: Natural History Press.

Eisenstadt, S. N. 1973. *Tradition, Change, and Modernity.* New York: John Wiley & Sons, Inc.

Fanon, F. 1965. *The Wretched of the Earth.* London: Macgibbon & Kee.

Hymes, D., ed. 1973. *Reinventing Anthropology.* New York: Random House, Inc.

Mair, L. 1969. *Anthropology and Social Change.* LSE Monograph 38. London: Athlone.

Price, R. 1973. *Maroon Societies.* New York: Doubleday & Company, Inc.

Spicer, E. H., ed. 1961. *Perspectives in American Indian Culture Change.* Chicago: University of Chicago Press.

Steward, J. H., ed. 1967. *Contemporary Change in Traditional Societies* (3 vols.). Urbana: University of Illinois Press.

Tarupp, S. L. 1970. *Millennial Dreams in Action: Studies in Revolutionary Religious Movements.* New York: Schocken Books, Inc.

Turnbull, C. 1962. *The Lonely African.* New York: Simon & Schuster, Inc.

Wallace, A. F. C. 1956. Revitalization Movements. *American Anthropologist* 58: 264-281.

Worsley, P. 1968. *The Trumpet Shall Sound.* 2d. ed. New York: Schocken Books, Inc.

Sections 73 to 74

Bock, P. K., ed. 1968. *Peasants in the Modern World.* Albuquerque: University of New Mexico Press.

Critchfield, R. 1973. *The Golden Bowl be Broken: Peasant Life in Four Cultures.* Bloomington, Ind.: Indiana University Press.

Frank, A. G. 1969. *Latin America: Underdevelopment or Revolution.* New York: Monthly Review Press.

———. 1973. *Lumpenbourgeoisie, Lumpendevelopment: Dependence, Class and Politics in Latin America.* New York: Monthly Review Press.

Hobsbawm, E. J. 1959. *Primitive Rebels.* New York: Free Press.

Hunter, G. 1969. *Modernizing Peasant Societies: A Comparative Study in Asia and Africa.* London: Oxford University Press.

Potter, J. M., M. N. Diaz, and G. M. Foster, eds. 1967. *Peasant Society: A Reader.* Boston: Little, Brown & Company.

Redfield, R. 1956. *Peasant Society and Culture.* Chicago: University of Chicago Press.

Rogers, E. M., and L. Svenning. 1969. *Modernization among Peasants: The Impact of Communication.* New York: Holt, Rinehart and Winston.

Stavenhagen, R. 1975. *Social Classes in Agrarian Societies.* Garden City, N.Y.: Doubleday & Company, Inc.

Wolf, E. R., 1966. *Peasants.* Englewood Cliffs, N.J.: Prentice-Hall, Inc.

———. 1969. On Peasant Rebellions. *International Social Science Journal,* 21 2:286-294.

———. 1969. *Peasants Wars of the Twentieth Century.* New York: Harper & Row.

Worsley, P. 1970. *The Third World.* Chicago: University of Chicago Press.

Section 75

Banton, M., ed. 1966. *The Social Anthropology of Complex Societies.* ASA Monographs, 4. London: Tavistock.

Eisenstadt, S. N. 1961. Anthropological Studies of Complex Societies. *Current Anthropology* 2:201-210.

Marriott, M., ed. 1955. *Village India: Studies in the Little Community.* Chicago: University of Chicago Press.

Redfield, R. 1956. *Peasant Society and Culture: An Anthropological Approach to Civilization.* Chicago: University of Chicago Press.

Section 76

Barnes, J. A. (cont.). 1972. *Networks in Social Anthropology.* Reading, Mass.: Addison-Wesley Modules in Anthropology.

Boissevain, J., and J. C. Mitchell, eds. 1973. *Network Analysis: Studies in Human Interaction.* The Hague: Mouton.

Eddy, E. M., ed. 1968. *Urban Anthropology: Research Perspectives and Strategies.* Southern Anthropological Society Proceedings, 2. Athens, Ga.: Southern Anthropological Society.

Foster, G. M., and R. V. Kemper, eds. 1973. *Anthropologists in Cities.* Boston: Little, Brown & Company.

Fox, R. G. 1972. Rationale and Romance in Urban Anthropology. *Urban Anthropology* 1:205-233.

Friedl, J., and N. J. Chrisman, eds. 1975. *City Ways: A Selective Reader in Urban Anthropology.*

Keish, R. L., and D. Jacobson, eds. 1974. *Urban Socio-*

Cultural Systems. New York: Holt, Rinehart and Winston.

Mangin, W. P., ed. 1970. *Peasants in Cities: Readings in the Anthropology of Urbanization.* Boston: Houghton Mifflin Company.

Mitchell, J. C., ed. 1970. *Social Networks in Urban Situations.* New York: Humanities Press.

Southall, A., ed. 1973. *Urban Anthropology: Cross-Cultural Studies of Urbanization.* New York: Oxford University Press.

Weaver, T., and D. White, eds. 1972. *The Anthropology of Urban Environments.* Boulder, Colo.: Society for Applied Anthropology.

Section 77

Ardener, E. 1972. Belief and the Problem of Women. In J. La Fontaine, ed., *The Interpretation of Ritual.* Cambridge: Cambridge University Press.

Friedl, E. 1975. *Women and Men: An Anthropologist's View.* New York: Holt, Rinehart and Winston.

Mitchell, J. 1971. *Women's Estate.* New York: Random House, Inc.

———. 1974. *Psychoanalysis and Feminism.* London: Allen Wayne.

Paulme, D. 1971. *Women of Tropical Africa.* Berkeley: University of California Press.

Reiter, R., ed. In Press. *Toward an Anthropology of Women.*

Rosaldo, M. Z., and L. Lamphere. 1974. *Woman, Culture, and Society.* Stanford: Stanford University Press.

Schlegel, A. 1972. *Male Dominance + Female Autonomy: Domestic Authority in Matrilineal Societies.* New Haven, Conn.: HRAF Press.

Section 78

Asad, T., ed. 1973. *Anthropology and the Colonial Encounter.* London: Ithaca Press.

Hymes, D., ed. 1973. *Reinventing Anthropology.* New York: Random House, Inc.

Sections 79 to 80

Barnes, J. 1967 Some Ethical Problems in Modern Field Work. In D. Jongmans and P. Gutkind, eds., *Anthropologists in the Field.* New York: Humanities Press.

Clifton, J. A., ed. 1970. *Applied Anthropology: Readings in the Uses of the Science of Man.* Boston: Houghton Mifflin Company.

Foster, G. M. 1973. *Traditional Societies and Technological Change.* New York: Holt, Rinehart and Winston.

Goodenough, W. H. 1963. *Cooperation in Change.* New York: Russell Sage Foundation.

Hymes, D., ed. 1973. *Reinventing Anthropology.* New York: Random House, Inc.

Leacock, E. B., ed. 1971. *The Culture of Poverty: A Critique.* New York: Simon & Schuster, Inc.

Spicer, E. H., ed. 1952. *Human Problems in Technological Change: A Casebook.* New York: Russell Sage Foundation.

Valentine, C. A. 1968. *Culture and Poverty: Critique and Counter-Proposals.* Chicago: University of Chicago Press.

Valentine, C. A., and B. Valentine. 1971. *Anthropological Interpretations of Black Culture.* Reading, Mass.: Addison-Wesley Modules in Anthropology.

Weaver, T., ed. 1973. *To See Ourselves.* Glenview, Ill.: Scott, Foresman and Company

BIBLIOGRAPHY

Aberle, D. F. 1961. Matrilineal Descent in Cross-Cultural Perspective. In D. Schneider and K. Gough, eds., *Matrilineal Kinship.* Berkeley: University of California Press.

———. 1962. A Note on Relative Deprivation Theory as Applied to Millenarian and Other Cult Movements. In S. L. Thrupp, ed., *Millennial Dreams in Action. Comparative Studies in Society and History,* Supplement 2. The Hague.

———, A. K. Cohen, A. Davis, M. Levy, and F. X. Sutton. 1950. The Functional Prerequisites of a Society. *Ethics* 60:100-111.

———, U. Bronfenbrenner, E. Hess, D. Miller, D. M. Schneider, and J. Spuhler. 1963. The Incest Taboo and the Mating Patterns of Animals. *American Anthropologist* 65:253-265.

Aceves, J. 1971. *Social Change in a Spanish Village.* Cambridge, Mass.: Schenkman Publishing Co.

Acheson, J. E. 1972. Limited Good or Limited Goods? Response to Economic Opportunity in a Tarascan Pueblo. *American Anthropologist* 74:1152-1169.

Adams, R. M. 1966. *The Evolution of Urban Society.* Chicago: Aldine Publishing Company.

Aguilera, F. E. 1972. *Santa Eulalia's People: The Anatomy of an Andalucian Multicommunity.* Unpublished Ph.D. dissertation, University of Pennsylvania.

Aiyappan, A. 1945. Iravas and Culture Change. *Bulletin of the Madras Government Museum* (n.s.) General Section, Vol. 5, No. 1.

Alavi, Hamza. 1964. Imperialism: New and Old. *Socialist Register.*

Alland, A. A. 1972a. *Human Diversity.* New York: Columbia University Press.

———. 1972b. *The Human Imperative.* New York: Columbia University Press.

———. 1973. *Evolution and Human Behavior.* 2d ed. Garden City, N.Y.: Doubleday & Company, Inc.

Altmann, S. A. 1967. The Structure of Primate Social Communication. In S. A. Altmann, ed., *Social Communication among Primates.* Chicago: University of Chicago Press.

Anderson, E. N., Jr. 1972. Some Chinese Methods of Dealing with Crowding. *Urban Anthropology* 1:141-150.

Anderson, R. S. 1975. *The Organization of Phonology.* New York: Academic Press, Inc.

Ardener, E. 1972. Belief and the Problem of Women. In J. LaFontaine, ed., *The Interpretation of Ritual.* Cambridge: Cambridge University Press.

Ardrey, R. 1961. *African Genesis.* New York: Dell Publishing Co., Inc.

———. 1966. *The Territorial Imperative.* New York: Dell Publishing Co., Inc.

Asad, T. 1970. *The Kababish Arabs: Power, Authority and Consent in a Nomadic Tribe.* London: Conrad Hurst and Co.

———. 1972. Market Model, Class Structure and Consent: A Reconsideration of Swat Political Organization. *Man* (n.s.) 7:74-94.

Asad, T., ed. 1973. *Anthropology and the Colonial Encounter.* London: Ithaca Press.

———. 1974. The Concept of Rationality in Anthropology. *Economy and Society* 3(2):211-218.

Aschmann, H. 1959. The Central Desert of Baja California: Demography and Ecology. Ibero-Americana 42:316.

Bailey, F. G. 1969. *Stratagems and Spoils: A Social Anthropology of Politics.* New York: Schocken Books, Inc.

———. 1971. *Gifts and Poison.* Oxford: Basil Blackwell & Mott, Ltd.

Baker, D. T. 1969. Human Adaptation to High Altitude. *Science* 163:1149-1156.

Baker, P. T., and J. S. Weiner, eds. 1966. *The Biology of Human Adaptability.* Oxford: Clarendon Press.

Banton, M. 1957. *West African City: A Study of Tribal Life in Freetown.* London: Oxford University Press.

———. 1973. Urbanization and Role Analysis. In A. Southall, ed., *Urban Anthropology.* London: Oxford University Press.

Barnes, J. A. 1962. African Models in the New Guinea Highlands. *Man* 62:5-9.

———. 1967. *Inquest on the Murngin.* Royal Anthropological Institute of Great Britain and Ireland. Occasional Paper No. 26.

———. 1971. *Three Styles in the Study of Kinship.* London: Tavistock Publications.

———. 1972. *Networks in Social Anthropology.* Reading, Mass.: Addison-Wesley Modules in Anthropology.

Barnett, H. G. 1956. *Anthropology in Administration.* New York: Harper & Row, Publishers.

Barrett, R. A. 1974. *Benabarre.* New York: Holt, Rinehart and Winston.

Barth, F. 1956. Ecological Relationships of Ethnic Groups in Swat, North Pakistan. *American Anthropologist* 58:1079-1089.

———. 1959a. *Political Leadership Among Swat Pathans.* London: Athlone Press.

———. 1959b. Segmentary Opposition and the Theory of Games: A Study of Pathan Organization. *Journal of the Royal Anthropological Institute,* 89:5-21.

———. 1966a. *Models of Social Organization.* Royal Anthropological Institute Occasional Papers, No. 23. London: Royal Anthropological Institute.

———. 1966b. Anthropological models and social reality. *Proceedings of the Royal Society* 165:20-25.

———. 1967. On the Study of Social Change. *American Anthropologist* 69:661-669.

Bartolome, M. A., et al. 1971. *Declaration of Barbados: For the Liberation of the Indians.* Copenhagen: International Work Group for Indigenous Affairs. (From proceedings of the Barbados symposium, January, 1971, sponsored by World Council of Churches Programme to Combat Racism and University of Berne.)

Barton, R. F. 1919. Ifugao Law. In *American Archaeology and Ethnography,* 15. Berkeley: University of California Press.

Barwick, D. 1972. Coranderrk and Cumaroogunga: Pioneers and Policy. In T. S. Epstein and D. H. Penny, eds., *Opportunity and Response.* London: C. Hurst & Company.

———, n.d. Rebellion at Coranderrk. Unpublished MS.

Bateson, G. 1955. A Theory of Play and Fantasy. *Psychiatric Research Reports* 2:39-51. American Psychiatric Association. (Reprinted in Bateson 1972a)

———. 1958. *Naven.* 2d ed. Stanford, Calif.: Stanford University Press.

———. 1968. Redundancy and Coding. In T. A. Sebeok, ed., *Animal Communication.* Bloomington: Indiana University Press, (Reprinted in Bateson 1972a)

———. 1972a. *Steps to an Ecology of Mind.* San Francisco: Chandler Publishing Company.

————. 1972b. Style, Grace and Information in Primitive Art. In *Steps to an Ecology of Mind.* Philadelphia: Intext.

Bauer, K. 1970. An Immunological Timescale for Primate Evolution Consistent with Fossil Evidence. *Humangenetik* 10:344-350.

Beattie, J. 1958. *Nyoro Kinship, Marriage, and Affinity.* London: Oxford University Press.

————. 1960. *The Bunyoro: An African Kingdom.* New York: Holt, Rinehart and Winston.

Beauvoir, Simone de. 1953. *The Second Sex.* Trans. and ed. by H. M. Parshley. New York: Alfred A. Knopf, Inc.

Beidelman, T. O. 1963. Witchcraft in Ukaguru. In J. Middleton and E. Winter, eds., *Witchcraft and Sorcery in East Africa,* London: Routledge & Kegan Paul Ltd.

Bellah, R. N. 1957. *Tokugawa Religion: The Values of Pre-Industrial Japan.* New York: The Free Press.

Bereiter, C., S. Engelmann, J. Osborn, and P. A. Reidford. 1966. An Academically Oriented Preschool for Culturally Deprived Children. In F. Hechinger, ed., *Preschool Education Today.* New York: Doubleday & Company, Inc.

Berlin, B., and P. Kay. 1969. *Basic Color Terms: Their Universality and Evolution.* Berkeley: University of California Press.

Berreman, G. D. 1969. Academic Colonialism: Not So Innocent Abroad. In *The Nation,* Nov. 10, 1969. (Reprinted in T. Weaver, ed. 1973. *To See Ourselves.* Glenview, Ill.: Scott, Foresman and Company.)

Berthoud, G. 1969-1970. La Validité des Concepts de 'Multicentricité' et de 'Sphères d'Echange' en Anthropologie Economique. *Archives Suisses d'Anthropologie Generale* 34:35-64.

Bicchieri, M. G., ed. 1972. *Hunters and Gatherers Today: A Socioeconomic Study of Eleven Such Cultures in the Twentieth Century.* New York: Holt, Rinehart and Winston.

Binford, L. R. 1968. Post Pleistocene Adaptations. In L. R. and S. Binford, eds., *New Perspectives in Archaeology.* Chicago: Aldine Publishing Co.

————. 1972. *An Archeological Perspective.* New York: Seminar Press.

————, and S. Binford, eds. 1968. *New Perspectives in Archaeology.* Chicago: Aldine Publishing Co.

Birdwhistell, R. 1970. *Kinesics and Context.* Philadelphia: University of Pennsylvania Press.

Black, M. 1959. Linguistic Relativity: The Views of Benjamin Lee Whorf. *Philosophical Review* 68:228-238.

Blurton-Jones, N. 1972a. *Ethological Studies of Child Behaviour.* Cambridge: Cambridge University Press.

————. 1972b. Nonverbal Communication in Children. In R. Hinde, ed., *Nonverbal Communication.* Cambridge: Cambridge University Press.

Bogen, J. 1969. The Other Side of the Brain, II: An Appositional Mind. *Bulletin of the Los Angeles Neurological Society* 34:135-162.

Bohannan, L. 1958. Political Aspects of Tiv Social Organization. In J. Middleton and D. Tait, eds., *Tribes without Rulers.* London: Routledge & Kegan Paul Ltd.

————, and P. Bohannan. 1968. *Tiv Economy.* Evanston, Ill.: Northwestern University Press.

Bohannan, P. 1954. *Tiv Farm and Settlement.* London: H. M. Stationery Office.

————. 1955. Some Principles of Exchange and Investment among the Tiv. *American Anthropologist* 57:60-70.

Bohannan, P. 1959. The Impact of Money on an African Subsistence Economy. *Journal of Economic History* 19:491-503.

———. 1963. *Social Anthropology.* New York: Holt, Rinehart and Winston, Inc.

Boissevain, J. 1968. The Place of Non-Groups in the Social Sciences. *Man* (N.S.) 3:542-556.

Bolton, R. 1973. Aggression and Hypoglycemia among the Qolla: A Study in Psychobiological Anthropology. *Ethology* 12:227-257.

Boole, G. 1854. *An Investigation of the Laws of Thought, on Which Are Founded the Mathematical Theories of Logic and Probabilities.* (Republished 1951, New York: Dover Books.)

Boon, J. 1972. *From Symbolism to Structuralism: Levi-Strauss in a Literary Tradition.* New York: Harper & Row, Publishers.

Bordes, F. 1968. *The Old Stone Age.* New York: McGraw-Hill Inc.

Bott, E. 1971. *Family and Social Networks.* 2d ed. London: Tavistock Publications.

Bowers, A. W. 1950. *Mandan Social and Ceremonial Organization.* Chicago: University of Chicago Press.

Bowlby, J. 1969. Attachment and Loss. Vol. I: *Attachment.* London: Hogarth Press.

Brace, C. L. 1964. A Nonracial Approach Towards the Understanding of Human Diversity. In A. Montagu, ed., *The Concept of Race.* New York: The Free Press.

———. 1968. Ridiculed, Rejected, But Still Our Ancestor, Neanderthal. *Natural History,* May.

———, and F. B. Livingstone. 1971. On Creeping Jensenism. In C. L. Brace, G. R. Gamble and J. T. Bond, eds., *Race and Intelligence.* Anthropological Studies, 8. Washington, D.C.: American Anthropological Association.

Brame, M. K., ed. 1972. *Contributions to Generative Phonology.* Austin: University of Texas Press.

Brandes, S. H. 1972. El Impacto de la Emigración en un Pueblo de la Sierra de Bèjar. *Ethnica* 4:9-28.

Brookfield, H. C., and P. Brown. 1963. *Struggle for Land: Agriculture and Group Territories among the Chimbu of the New Guinea Highlands.* London: Oxford University Press.

Brose, D. S., and M. H. Wolpoff. 1971. Early Upper Paleolithic Man and Late Middle Paleolithic Tools. *American Anthropologist* 75:1156-1194.

Brown, P. 1972. *The Chimbu: A Study of Change in the New Guinea Highlands.* Cambridge, Mass.: Schenkman Publishing Co.

Brown, R. 1973. Anthropology and Colonial Rule: Godfrey Wilson and the Rhodes-Livingston Institute, Northern Rhodesia. In T. Asad, ed., *Anthropology and the Colonial Encounter.* London: Ithaca Press.

Bruner, E. M. 1961. Mandan. In E. H. Spicer, ed., *Perspectives in American Indian Culture Change.* Chicago: University of Chicago Press.

———. 1973. Kin and Non-Kin. In A. Southall, ed., *Urban Anthropology.* London: Oxford University Press.

Buchbinder, G. 1973. *Maring Microadaptation: A Study of Demographic, Nutritional, Genetic and Phenotypic Variation in a Highland New Guinea Population.* Unpublished Ph.D. dissertation, Columbia University.

Butzer, K. W. 1971. *Environment and Archaeology: An Ecological Approach to Prehistory.* 2d edition. Chicago: Aldine Publishing Company.

Campbell, B. G. 1963. Quantitative Taxonomy. In B. Campbell, ed., *Classification and Human Evolution.* Chicago: Aldine Publishing Company.

————. 1970. The Roots of Language. In J. Morton, ed., *Biological and Social Factors in Psycholinguistics.* Urbana: University of Illinois Press.

————, ed. 1972. *Sexual Selection and the Descent of Man.* Chicago: Aldine Press.

Cancian, F. 1965. *Economics and Prestige in a Maya Community: The Religious Cargo System in Zincantan.* Stanford, Calif.: Stanford University Press.

————. 1972. *Change and Uncertainty in a Peasant Economy.* Stanford, Calif.: Stanford University Press.

Catlin, G. 1867. *O-Kee-Pa.* Philadelphia. (Republished as *George Catlin's O-Kee-Pa.* J. Ewens, ed. 1954. New Haven, Conn.: Yale University Press.)

Caulfield, M. D. 1972. Culture and Imperialism: Proposing a New Dialectic. In D. Hymes, ed., *Reinventing Anthropology.* New York: Random House, Inc.

————. 1973. Participant Observation or Partisan Participation? Paper presented to International Anthropological Congress, Chicago.

————. 1975. Imperialism, the Family and Cultures of Resistance, *Socialist Revolution.*

Chagnon, N. A. 1968a. *Yąnomamö: The Fierce People.* New York: Holt, Rinehart and Winston.

————. 1968b. Yąnomamö Social Organization and Warfare. In M. Fried, M. Harns, and R. Murphy, eds. *The Anthropology of Armed Conflict and Aggression.* Garden City, N.Y.: Natural History Press. (Page reference is to reprinting in M. Fried, ed. 1973. *Explorations in Anthropology.* New York: Thomas Y. Crowell Company.)

Chance, M. R. A., and C. Jolly. 1970. *Social Groups of Monkeys, Apes and Men.* London: Jonathan Cape, Ltd.

Chang, K.-C. 1968. Archeology of Ancient China. *Science* 162:519-526.

————. 1970. The Beginning of Agriculture in the Far East. *Antiquity* 44:175-185.

Chodorow, N. 1974. Family Structure and Feminine Personality. In M. Z. Rosaldo and L. Lamphere, eds. *Woman, Culture, and Society.* Stanford, Calif.: Stanford University Press.

Chomsky, N. 1957. *Syntactic Structures.* The Hague: Mouton and Company.

————. 1959. Review of *Verbal Behavior* by B. F. Skinner. *Language* 35:26-58.

————. 1964. *Current Issues in Linguistic Theory.* The Hague: Mouton and Company.

————. 1965. *Aspects of the Theory of Syntax.* Cambridge, Mass.: MIT Press.

————. 1966. Topics in the Theory of Generative Grammar. In T. Sebeok, ed., *Current Trends in Linguistics,* III. The Hague: Mouton and Company.

————. 1973. *Language and Mind.* 2d ed. New York: Harcourt Brace Jovanovich, Inc.

————, and M. Halle. 1968. *The Sound Patterns of English.* New York: Harper & Row, Publishers.

Clark, J. D. 1967. The Problem of Neolithic Culture in Subsaharan Africa. In W. W. Bishop and J. D. Clark, eds., *Background to Evolution in Africa.* Chicago: University of Chicago Press.

Clarke, W. C. 1971. *Place and People.* Berkeley: University of California Press.

Cline, W. 1936. *Notes on the People of Siwah and el-Garah in the Libyan Desert.* Menasha, Wis.: George Banta, Inc.

Cochrane, G. 1971. *Development Anthropology.* New York: Oxford University Press.

Codrington, R. H. 1891. *The Melanesians: Studies in Their Anthropology and Folklore.* Oxford: Clarendon Press. (Reprinted 1957 by HRAF Press, New Haven, Conn.)

Colby, B. N. 1973. A Partial Grammar of Eskimo Folktales. *American Anthropologist* 75(3):645-662.

Cole, M., and S. Scribner. 1974. *Culture and Thought: A Psychological Introduction.* New York: John Wiley & Sons, Inc.

Condominas, G. 1957. *Nous avons mangé la forêt: chronique de Sar Luk, village Mnong Ga.* Paris: Mercure de France.

Conklin, H. C. 1955. Hanunóo Color Categories. *Southwestern Journal of Anthropology* 11:339-344.

————. 1957. *Hanunóo Agriculture in the Philippines.* Rome: FAO.

————. 1962. Lexicographic Treatment of Folk Taxonomies. In F. W. Householder and S. Saporta, eds., *Problems in Lexicography.* Bloomington: Indiana University Research Center in Anthropology, Folklore and Linguistics, Pub. 21.

————. 1973. Review of *Basic Color Terms: Their Universality and Evolution,* by B. Berlin and P. Kay (Berkeley: University of California Press) in *American Anthropologist* 75(4):931-942.

Coon, C. S. 1962. *The Origin of Races.* New York: Alfred A. Knopf, Inc.

————. 1965. *The Living Races of Man.* New York: Alfred A. Knopf, Inc.

————. 1971. *The Hunting Peoples.* Boston: Little, Brown and Company.

Corris, P. 1973. *Passage, Port and Plantation: A History of Solomon Islands Labour Migration 1870-1914.* Melbourne: Melbourne University Press.

Coult, A. D., and R. W. Habenstein. 1965. *Cross Tabulations of Murdock's World Ethnographic Sample: A Reference Handbook.* Columbia: University of Missouri Press.

Crowder, M. 1968. *West Africa under Colonial Rule.* London: Hutchinson Publishing Group, Ltd.

————, ed. 1971. *West African Resistance: The Military Response to Colonial Occupation.* London: Hutchinson Publishing Group, Ltd.

Dalton, G. 1961. Economic Theory and Primitive Society. *American Anthropologist* 63:1-25.

————. 1965. Primitive Money. *American Anthropologist* 67:44-65.

————, ed. 1972a. *Studies in Economic Anthropology.* Washington, D.C.: American Anthropological Association.

————. 1972b. Peasantries in Anthropology and History. *Current Anthropology* 13:385-415.

Damas, D., ed. 1969. Band Societies: Proceedings of the Conference on Band Organization. Ottawa *National Museum of Canada Bulletin,* No. 86.

D'Andrade, R. G. 1966. Sex Differences and Cultural Institutions. In E. E. Maccaby, ed., *The Development of Sex Differences.* Stanford, Calif.: Stanford University Press.

Danks, B. 1887. On the Shell-Money of New Britain. *Journal of the Royal Anthropological Institute* 17:305-317.

Darwin, C. 1871. *The Descent of Man and Selection in Relation to Sex.* New York: Random House, Inc. (Modern Library edition.)

Davenport, W. 1969. The Hawaiian Cultural Revolution: Some Political and Economic Considerations. *American Anthropologist* 71:1-20.

Davila, M. 1971. Compadrazgo: Fictive Kinship in Latin America. In N. Graburn, ed., *Readings in Kinship and Social Structure.* New York: Harper & Row, Publishers.

Debray, R. 1967. *Revolution in the Revolution? Armed Struggle and Political Struggle in Latin America.* Trans. by B. Ortiz. New York: Grove Press, Inc.

De Loria, V. 1969. *Custer Died for Your Sins: An Indian Manifesto.* New York: The Macmillan Company.

Dentan, R. K. 1968. *The Semai: A Nonviolent People of Malaya.* New York: Holt, Rinehart and Winston.

De Sonneville-Bordes, D. 1963. Upper Paleolithic Cultures in Western Europe. *Science* 142(3590):347-355.

Devereux, G. 1953. Why Oedipus Killed Laius. *International Journal of Psychoanalysis* 35:132-141.

———. 1967. *From Anxiety to Method in the Behavioral Sciences.* Preface by W. LaBarre. The Hague: Mouton and Company.

———. 1975. *Fantasy as a Reflection of Reality.* Paper presented at 46th ANZAAS Congress, Canberra, Australia. January.

DeVore, I., ed. 1965. *Primate Behavior: Field Studies of Monkeys and Apes.* New York: Holt, Rinehart and Winston.

———. 1968. Comment. In L. R. and S. Binford, eds., *New Perspectives in Archaeology.* Chicago: Aldine Publishing Company.

De Szwart, H. S. 1969. Developmental Psycholinguistics. In D. Elkind and J. Flavell, eds., *Studies in Cognitive Development.* London: Oxford University Press.

Diamond, M. 1965. A Critical Evaluation of the Ontogeny of Human Sexual Behavior. *Quarterly Review of Biology* 40:2.

Diaz, M. N. 1967. Introduction: Economic Relations in Peasant Society. In M. J. Potter, M. N. Diaz and G. M. Foster, eds., *Peasant Society: A Reader.* Boston: Little, Brown and Company.

Dimond, S. J. 1972. *The Double Brain.* Edinburgh: Churchill Livingstone.

———, and J. G. Beaumont, eds. 1974. *Hemispheral Functions in the Human Brain.* New York: John Wiley & Sons, Inc.

Dobzhansky, T. 1967. On Types, Genotypes and the Genetic Diversity in Populations. In J. N. Spubler, ed., *Genetic Diversity and Human Behavior.* New York: Wenner-Gren Foundation for Anthropological Research.

———. 1967. *Genetic Diversity of Environments.* Proceedings of the 5th Berkeley Symposium on Mathematical Statistics and Probability, Vol. 4:295-304.

Dolhinow, P., ed. 1972. *Primate Patterns.* New York: Holt, Rinehart and Winston.

———, and N. Bishop. 1970. The Development of Motor Skills and the Social Relationships among Primates Through Play. *Minnesota Symposia on Child Psychology* 4:141-198.

Douglas, M. 1966. *Purity and Danger.* Baltimore: Penguin Books, Inc.

———. 1970. *Natural Symbols: Explorations in Cosmology.* London: Cresset.

Driver, H. E. 1961. *Indians of North America.* Chicago: University of Chicago Press.

———, and K. F. Schuessler. 1967. Correlational Analysis of Murdock's Ethnographic Sample. *American Anthropologist* 69:332-352.

Drucker, P. 1939. Rank, Wealth, and Kinship in Northwest Coast Society. *American Anthropologist* 41:55-65. (Reprinted in Hoebel, Jennings, Smith, eds. 1955. *Readings in Anthropology.* New York: McGraw-Hill, Inc.)

Du Bois, C. 1960. *People of Alor: A Social-Psychological Study of an East Indian Island.* 2d ed. Cambridge, Mass.: Harvard University Press.

Dumont, L. 1966. *Homo-Hierarchicus: Essai Sur le Système des Castes.* Bibliothèque des Sciences Humaines. Paris: Gallimard.

Dundes, A. 1962. Earth Diver: Creation of the Mythopoeic Male. *American Anthropologist* 64:1032-1051.

Dupré, G., and P.-P. Rey. 1973. Reflections on the Pertinence of a Theory of the History of Exchange. *Economy and Society* 2:131-163.

Durkheim, E. 1912. *Les Formes Elémentaires de la Vie Réligieuse: Le Système Totemique en Australia.* Paris: Presses Universitaires.

———, and M. Mauss. 1901-1902. *De Quelques Formes Primitive de Classification.* Contribution a l'Etude des Représentations Collectives. *L'Année Sociologique* 6:1-

72. (Translated as *Primitive Classification*. 1963. Chicago: University of Chicago Press.)

Dyson-Hudson, N. 1963. The Karimojong Age System. *Ethnology* 2(3):353-401.

———. 1966. *Karimojong Politics*. Oxford: Oxford University Press.

———, and R. Dyson-Hudson. 1970. The Food Production of a Semi-Nomadic Society: The Karimojong, Uganda. In P. F. M. McLoughlin, ed., *African Food Production Systems*. Baltimore: The Johns Hopkins Press.

Dyson-Hudson, R., and N. Dyson-Hudson. 1969. Subsistence Herding in Uganda. *Scientific American,* February, 76-89.

Easton, D. 1959. Political Anthropology. In B. Siegel, ed. *Biennial Review of Anthropology, 2.*

Edgerton, R. B. 1964. Pokot Intersexuality: An East African Example of the Resolution of Sexual Incongruity. *American Anthropologist* 66:1288-1299.

Eibl-Eibesfeldt, I. 1968. Ethological Perspectives on Primate Studies. In P. Jay, ed., *Primates: Studies in Adaptation and Variability*. New York: Holt, Rinehart and Winston.

———. 1975. *Ethology: The Biology or Behavior*. 2d ed. New York: Holt, Rinehart and Winston.

Eisenstadt, S. N. 1956. *From Generation to Generation*. New York: The Free Press.

Ekman, P. 1972. *Expressions of Emotions in Man and Animals: A Centenary Volume*. New York: Academic Press, Inc.

———, ed. 1973. *Darwin and Facial Expression: A Century of Research in Review*. New York: Academic Press, Inc.

———, and W. Friesen. 1969. The Repertoire of Nonverbal Behavior: Categories, Origins, Usage and Coding. *Semiotica* 1:49-98.

———, R. Sorenson, and E. W. Friesen, 1969. Pan-Cultural Elements in Facial Displays of Emotion. *Science* 164:86-88.

Eliade, M. 1959. *Cosmos and History: The Myth of the External Return*. New York: Harper & Row, Publishers.

———. 1970. Cargo Cults and Cosmic Regeneration. In S. L. Thrupp, ed., *Millennial Dreams in Action: Studies in Revolutionary Religious Movements*. New York: Schocken Books, Inc.

Elwin, V. 1968. *The Kingdom of the Young*. London: Oxford University Press.

Epstein, A. L. 1963. Tambu: A Primitive Shell Money. *Discovery* 24:28-32.

———. 1968. Power, Politics and Leadership; Some Central African and Melanesian Contrasts. In M. J. Swartz, ed., *Local Level Politics*. Chicago: Aldine Publishing Co.

———. 1969. *Matupit: Land, Politics and Change Among the Tolai of New Britain*. Berkeley: University of California Press.

———. n.d. *Tambu: The Shell-Money of the Tolai*. Unpublished MS.

Epstein, T. S. 1964. Personal Capital Formation among the Tolai of New Britain. In R. Firth and B. Yamey, eds., *Capital, Saving and Credit in Peasant Societies*. Chicago: Aldine Publishing Co.

———. 1968. *Capitalism, Primitive and Modern*. Manchester: Manchester University Press.

Evans-Pritchard, E. E. 1940. *The Nuer*. Oxford: Clarendon Press.

———. 1951. *Kinship and Marriage among the Nuer*. Oxford: Clarendon Press.

———, ed. 1954. *The Institutions of Primitive Society*. New York: The Free Press.

———. 1956. *Nuer Religion*. Oxford: Clarendon Press.

Fanon, F. 1965. *The Wretched of the Earth*. Preface by J. P. Sartre. Trans. from French by C. Farrington. London: Macgibbon & Kee.

Fernea, E. W. 1965. *Guests of the Sheik: An Ethnography of an Iraqui Village.* New York: Doubleday & Company, Inc.

Firth, R. 1936. *We The Tikopia.* London: George Allen and Unwin, Ltd.

——, ed. 1956. *Two Studies of Kinship in London.* London: Athlone Press.

——, ed. 1957. *Man and Culture: An Evaluation of the Work of Bronislaw Malinowski.* London: Routledge & Kegan Paul Ltd.

——. 1956. A Note on Descent Groups in Polynesia. *Man* 57:4-8.

——, ed. 1967. *Themes in Economic Anthropology.* ASA Monographs, 6. London: Tavistock Publications.

——. 1973. *Symbols, Public and Private.* Ithaca, N.Y.: Cornell University Press.

Fischer, J. L. 1964. Solutions for the Natchez Paradox. *Ethnology* 3:53-65.

Fishman, J. A. 1960. A Systematization of the Whorfian Hypothesis. *Behavioral Science,* 5:232-239.

——, ed. 1968. *Readings in the Sociology of Language.* The Hague: Mouton and Company.

Flannery, K. V. 1968. Archeological Systems Theory and Early Mesoamerica. In B. J. Meggers, ed., *Anthropological Archeology in the Americas.* Washington, D.C.: Anthropological Society of Washington.

——. 1969. Origins and Ecological Effects of Early Domestication in Iran and the Near East. In P. J. Ucko and G. W. Dimbleby, eds., *The Domestication and Exploitation of Plants and Animals.* Chicago: Aldine Publishing Company.

Ford, C. S. 1945. *A Comparative Study of Reproduction.* Yale Publications in Anthropology, 32. New Haven, Conn.: Yale University Press.

Forde, C. D. 1934. *Habitat, Economy and Society.* New York: E. P. Dutton & Co., Inc. (Rev. ed. 1950.)

——. 1950. Double Descent among the Yakö. In A. R. Radcliffe-Brown and C. D. Forde, eds., *African Systems of Kinship and Marriage.* London: Oxford University Press.

——. 1963. On Some Further Unconsidered Aspects of Descent. *Man* 63:12-13.

——. 1971. Ecology and Social Structure. *Proceedings of the Royal Anthropological Institute,* 15-30.

Fortes, M. 1945. *The Dynamics of Clanship among the Tallensi.* London: Oxford University Press (for International African Institute).

——. 1949. *The Web of Kinship among the Tallensi.* London: Oxford University Press (for International African Institute).

——. 1959*a*. Primitive Kinship. *Scientific American* 200(6):146-157.

——. 1959*b*. Introduction. In J. Goody, ed., *The Developmental Cycle in Domestic Groups.* Cambridge Papers in Social Anthropology, 1. London: Cambridge University Press.

——. 1959*c. Oedipus and Job in West African Religion.* Cambridge: Cambridge University Press.

——. 1960. Ancestor Worship in Africa. In M. Fortes and G. Dieterlen, eds., *African Systems of Thought.* London: Oxford University Press (for International African Institute).

——. 1974. The First Born. *Journal of Child Psychology and Psychiatry* 15:81-104.

Fortune, R. 1932*a. Sorcerers of Dobu.* London: Routledge & Kegan Paul Ltd.

——. 1932*b*. Incest. *Encyclopedia of the Social Sciences* 6:620. New York: The Macmillan Company.

——. 1939. Arapesh Warfare. *American Anthropologist* 41:22-41.

Fossey, D. 1971. More Years with Mountain Gorillas. *National Geographic,* 140, October.

Foster, G. M. 1961. The Dyadic Contract: A Model for the Social Structure of a Mexican Peasant Village. *American Anthropologist* 63:1173-1192.

———. 1962. *Traditional Cultures and the Impact of Technological Change.* New York: Harper & Row, Publishers.

———. 1965. Peasant Society and the Image of Limited Good. *American Anthropologist* 67:293-315.

———. 1967. *Tzintzuntzan: Mexican Peasants in a Changing Community.* Boston: Little, Brown and Company.

———. 1972. A Second Look at Limited Good. *Anthropological Quarterly* 45:57-64.

———. 1973. *Traditional Societies and Technological Change.* New York: Holt, Rinehart and Winston.

Foulks, E. K. 1972. The Arctic Hysterias of the North Alaskan Eskimo. *Anthropological Studies,* No. 10. Washington, D.C.: American Anthropological Association.

Fox, R. 1967. *Kinship and Marriage: An Anthropological Perspective.* Harmondsworth; Penguin.

Frake, C. O. 1960. The Eastern Subanun of Mindanao. In G. P. Murdock, ed., *Social Structure in Southeast Asia.* Viking Fund Publications in Anthropology, 29. New York: Wenner-Gren Foundation for Anthropological Research.

———. 1961. The Diagnosis of Disease among the Subanun of Mindanao. *American Anthropologist* 63:113-132.

———. 1962a. Cultural Ecology and Ethnography. *American Anthropologist* 64:53-59.

———. 1962b. The Ethnographic Study of Cognitive Systems. In T. Gladwin and W. Sturtevant, eds., *Anthropology and Human Behavior.* Washington, D.C.: Anthropological Society of Washington.

———. 1963. Litigation in Lipay: A Study in Subanun Law. In *Proceedings of the Ninth Pacific Science Congress of the Pacific Science Association* 3:217-222. Bangkok (1957).

———. 1964a. A Structural Description of Subanun "Religious Behavior." In W. Goodenough, ed., *Explorations in Cultural Anthropology.* New York: McGraw-Hill, Inc.

———. 1964b. How to Ask for a Drink in Subanun. In J. Gumperz and D. Hymes, eds., *The Ethnography of Communication.* American Anthropologist Special Publication 66(6), part 2.

Frank, A. G. 1969. *Latin America: Underdevelopment or Revolution.* New York: Monthly Review Press.

———. 1973. *Lumpenbourgeoisie, Lumpendevelopment: Dependence, Class and Politics in Latin America.* New York: Monthly Review Press.

Frazer, J. G. 1890. *The Golden Bough: A Study in Magic and Religion.* 12 vols. London: Macmillan and Company.

Freedman, D. G. 1968. Personality Development in Infancy: A Biological Approach. In S. L. Washburn and P. Jay, eds., *Perspectives on Human Evolution,* Vol. I. New York: Holt, Rinehart and Winston.

———. 1974. *Human Infancy: An Evolutionary Perspective.* New York: John Wiley & Sons, Inc.

Freeman, J. D. 1955. Iban Agriculture. *Colonial Research Studies,* No. 18. London: Colonial Office.

———. 1958. The Family Structure of the Iban of Borneo. In J. Goody, ed., *The*

Developmental Cycle in Domestic Groups. Cambridge Papers in Social Anthropology. Cambridge: Cambridge University Press.

———. 1960. The Iban of Borneo. In G. P. Murdock, ed., *Social Structures in Southeast Asia.* Chicago: Quadrangle Press.

———. 1964. Human Aggression in Anthropological Perspective. In J. D. Carthy and F. J. Ebling, eds., *The Natural History of Aggression.* New York: Academic Press, Inc. (Reprinted in revised form in Otten, ed., 1973.)

———. 1967. Totem and Taboo: A Reappraisal. In W. Muensterberger and S. Axelrod, eds., *The Psychoanalytic Study of Society,* Vol. IV.

———. 1968. Thunder, Blood, and the Nicknaming of God's Creatures. *Psychoanalytic Quarterly* 37:353-399.

———. 1969. On the Concept of the Kindred. *Journal of the Royal Anthropological Institute* 91:192-220.

———. 1970. Human Nature and Culture. In D. Slatyer, ed., *Man and the New Biology.* Canberra: A.N.U. Press.

———. 1974. Kinship, Attachment Behaviour and the Primary Bond. In J. R. Goody, ed., *The Character of Kinship.* Cambridge: Cambridge University Press.

Freud, S. 1950. *Totem and Taboo.* London: Routledge & Kegan Paul Ltd.

Fried, M., M. Harris, and R. Murphy, eds. 1968. *War: The Anthropology of Armed Conflict and Aggression.* Garden City, N.Y.: Natural History Press.

Friedman, J. 1974. Marxism, Structuralism and Vulgar Materialism. *Man* 9(3):444-469.

Friedrich, P. 1965. A Mexican Cacigazgo. *Ethology* 4:190-209.

Fromm, E., and M. Maccoby. 1970. *Social Character in a Mexican Village.* Englewood Cliffs, N.J.: Prentice-Hall, Inc.

Furnas, J. C. 1947. *Anatomy of Paradise.* New York: William Sloane Associates.

Fustel de Coulanges, N. D. 1864. *Le Cité Antique.* (Trans. as *The Ancient City.* 1956.) Garden City, N.Y.: Doubleday & Company, Inc.)

Gallin, B. 1968. Political Factionalism and Its Impact on Chinese Village Social Organization in Taiwan. In M. Swartz, ed., *Local Level Politics.* pp. 377-400. Chicago: Aldine Publishing Company.

Gardner, B., and R. A. Gardner. 1971. Two-Way Communication with an Infant Chimpanzee. In A. Schrier and F. Stollnite, eds., *Behavior of Nonhuman Primates,* Vol. 4. New York: Academic Press, Inc.

Gardner, R. A., and B. T. Gardner. 1969. Teaching Sign-Language to a Chimpanzee. *Science* 165:664-672.

Gazzaniga, M. 1970. *The Bisected Brain.* New York: Appleton-Century-Crofts.

Geertz, C. 1957. Ritual and Social Change: A Javanese Example. *American Anthropologist* 59:32-54.

———. 1960. *The Religion of Java.* New York: The Free Press.

———. 1962a. Studies in Peasant Life: Community and Society. In B. J. Siegel, ed., *Biennial Review of Anthropology, 1961.* Stanford, California: Stanford University Press.

———. 1962b. The Growth of Culture and the Evolution of Mind. In J. Scher, ed., *Theories of the Mind.* New York: The Free Press.

———. 1963. *Agricultural Involution.* Berkeley: University of California Press.

———. 1966a. Religion as a Cultural System. In M. Banton, ed., *Anthropological Approaches to the Study of Religion.* ASA Monographs, 3. London: Tavistock Publications.

———. 1966b. *Person, Time, and Conduct in Bali: An Essay in Cultural Analysis.*

Cultural Report Studies, 14. New Haven, Conn.: Southeast Asia Studies.

Geertz, C. 1966c. The Impact of the Concept of Culture on the Concept of Man. In J. R. Platt, ed., *New Views on the Nature of Man.* Chicago: University of Chicago Press. (Page refs. are to reprinting in Geertz 1973b.)

――――. 1967. The Cerebral Savage: On the Work of Claude Lévi-Strauss. *Encounter* 28:25-32.

――――. 1972. Deep Play: Notes on the Balinese Cockfight. *Daedalus* 101:1-37.

――――. 1973a. Thick Description. In C. Geertz, ed., *The Interpretation of Cultures.* New York: Basic Books, Inc., Publishers.

――――, ed. 1973b. *The Interpretation of Cultures.* New York: Basic Books, Inc., Publishers.

――――. n.d. *Common Sense as a Cultural System.* Forthcoming MS.

Geschwind, N. 1967. The Neural Basis of Language. In K. Salzinger and S. Salzinger, eds., *Research in Verbal Behavior and Some Neurophysiological Implications.* New York: Academic Press, Inc.

――――. 1970. The Organization of Language and the Brain. *Science* 170:940-944.

――――. 1974. *Selected Papers on Language and the Brain.* Dordrecht, Holland: D. Reidel.

Gibbs, J. L. 1963. The Kpelle Moot: A Therapeutic Model for the Informal Settlement of Disputes. *Africa* 33:1-11.

Gifford, E. W. 1929. Tongan Society. *Bernice P. Bishop Museum Bulletin,* No. 61. Honolulu: Bishop Museum.

Glickman, M. 1972. The Nuer and the Dinka: A Further Note. *Man* (n.s.) 7:586-594.

Gluckman, M. 1940. The Kingdom of the Zulu of Southeast Africa. In M. Fortes and E. E. Evans-Pritchard, eds., *African Political Systems.* London: Oxford University Press.

――――. 1955. *Custom and Conflict in Africa.* Oxford: Basil Blackwell & Mott, Ltd.

――――, ed. 1962. *Essays in the Ritual of Social Relations.* Manchester: Manchester University Press.

――――. 1963. *Order and Rebellion in Tribal Africa.* London: Cohen and West.

――――, J. C. Mitchell, and J. A. Barnes. 1949. The Village Headman in British Central Africa. *Africa* 19:89-106.

Godelier, M. 1972. *Rationality and Irrationality in Economics.* Trans. by B. Pearce. New York: Monthly Review Press.

――――. 1974. Anthropology and Biology: Towards a New Form of Co-operation. *International Social Science Journal* 26(4):611-635.

Goldenweiser, A. A. 1910. Totemism: An Analytical Study. *Journal of American Folklore* 23:1-115.

Gonzales, N. S. de. 1970. Toward a Definition of Matrifocality. In N. E. Whitten and J. F. Szwed, eds., *Afro-American Anthropology: Contemporary Perspectives.* New York: The Free Press.

Goodale, J. C. 1962. Marriage Contracts among the Tiwi. *Ethnology* 1:452-466.

――――. 1971. *Tiwi Wives: A Study of the Women of Melville Island, North Australia.* American Ethnological Society Monograph, No. 51. Seattle: University of Washington Press.

Goodenough, W. H. 1955. A Problem in Malayo-Polynesian Social Organization. *American Anthropologist* 57:71-83.

――――. 1956. Residence Rules. *Southwestern Journal of Anthropology* 12:22-37.

――――. 1957. Cultural Anthropology and Linguistics. In P. Garvin, ed., *Report of the Seventh Annual Round Table Meeting on Linguistics and Language Study.* Monograph Series on Language and Linguistics, 9. Washington D.C.: Georgetown University.

———. 1961. Comment on Cultural Evolution. *Daedalus* 90:521-528.

———. 1963. *Cooperation in Change.* New York: Russell Sage Foundation.

———. 1970. *Description and Comparison in Cultural Anthropology.* Lewis Henry Morgan Lectures, 1968. Chicago: Aldine Publishing Co.

Goodman, M. 1963. Man's Place in the Phylogeny of the Primates as Reflected in Serum Proteins. In S. L. Washburn, ed., *Classification and Human Evolution.* Chicago: Aldine Publishing Co.

———. Phylogeny and Taxonomy of the Catarrhine Primates from Immuno-diffusion Data In B. Chiarelli, ed., *Taxonomy and Phylogeny of Old World Primates with Reference to the Origin of Man.* Turin, Italy: Rosenberg and Sellier.

———. 1974. Biochemical Evidence on Human Phylogeny. *Annual Reviews of Anthropology,* Vol. 3.

Goody, J. R. 1961. Religion and Ritual: The Definitional Problem. *British Journal of Sociology* 12:142-164.

———. 1969. Adoption in Cross-Cultural Perspective. *Comparative Studies in Society and History* II:55-78.

Gorman, C. F. 1969. Hoabinhian: A Pebble Tool Complex with early Plant Associations in Southeast Asia. *Science,* February 14.

———. 1971. The Hoabinhian and After: Subsistence Patterns in Southeast Asia during the Late Pleistocene and Early Recent Periods. *World Archaeology* 2:300-320.

Gough, E. K. 1959. The Nayars and the Definition of Marriage. *Journal of the Royal Anthropological Institute* 23-34.

———. 1961. Variation in Matrilineal Systems. In D. Schneider and K. Gough, eds., *Matrilineal Kinship,* Part 2. Berkeley: University of California Press.

———. 1968. World Revolution and the Science of Man. In T. Roszak, ed., *The Dissenting Academy.* New York: Random House, Inc. (Reprinted in M. T. Weaver, ed. 1973. *To See Ourselves.* Glenview, Ill.: Scott, Foresman and Co.)

———. 1971. Nuer Kinship and Marriage: A Reexamination. In T. Beidelman, ed., *The Translation of Culture.*

Gould, R. A. 1969. *Yiwara: Foragers of the Australian Desert.* New York: Charles Scribner's Sons.

———. 1971. The Archaeologist as Ethnographer: A Case From the Western Desert of Australia. *World Archaeology,* 3(1):143-177.

Greenberg, J. H. 1963. Introduction. In J. H. Greenberg, ed., *Universals of Language.* Cambridge, Mass.: MIT Press.

Gregory, R. L. 1969. On How Little Information Controls So Much Behaviour. In C. H. Waddington, ed., *Towards a Theoretical Biology,* Vol. I. Chicago: Aldine Publishing Company.

———. 1970. Information processing in biological and artificial brains. In H. E. Von Gierke, W. D. Keidel, H. L. Oestreicher, eds., *Principles and Practice of Bionics,* 73-80. Slough, England: Techvision.

Greuel, P. J. 1971. The Leopard-Skin Chief: An Examination of Political Power among the Nuer. *American Anthropologist* 73:1115-1120.

Griaule, M., and G. Dieterlen. 1960. The Dogon of the French Sudan. In C. D. Forde, ed., *African Worlds.* London: Oxford University Press.

Grinder, J. T., and S. H. Elgin. 1973. *Guide to Transformational Grammar: History, Theory, Practice.* New York: Holt, Rinehart and Winston.

Gulliver, P. H. 1965. *The Family Herds.* London: Routledge & Kegan Paul Ltd.

Haffer, J. 1969. Speciation in Amazonian Forest Birds. *Science* 165:131-137.

Haight, B. 1972. A Note on the Leopard-Skin Chief. *American Anthropologist* 74:1313-1318.

Hall, E. T. 1959. *The Silent Language.* Garden City, N.Y.: Doubleday & Company, Inc.

———. 1966. *The Hidden Dimension.* Garden City, N.Y.: Doubleday & Company, Inc.

———. 1972. Art, Space, and the Human Experience. In G. Kepes, ed., *Arts of the Environment.* New York: George Braziller, Inc.

Hall, K. R. L. 1963. Tool-Using Performances as Indicators of Behavioral Adaptability. *Current Anthropology* 4:479-494. (Reprinted in P. C. Jay, ed. 1968. *Primates: Studies in Adaptation and Variability.* New York: Holt, Rinehart and Winston.)

Hallowell, A. I. 1955. *Culture and Experience.* Philadelphia: University of Pennsylvania Press.

———. 1963. American Indians, White and Black: The Phenomenon of Transculturation. *Current Anthropology* 4:519-531.

Hallpike, C. R. 1973. Functionalist Interpretations of Primitive Warfare. *Man* 8(3):451-470.

Hardin, G. 1959. *Nature and Man's Fate.* New York: Holt, Rinehart and Winston.

Harding, T. G. 1967. *Voyagers of the Vitiaz Strait.* American Ethnological Society Monograph 44. Seattle: University of Washington Press.

Harris, M. 1968. *The Rise of Cultural Theory.* New York: Thomas Y. Crowell Company.

———. 1971. *Culture, Man and Nature: An Introduction to General Anthropology.* New York: Thomas Y. Crowell Company.

Hart, C. W. M. 1955. Contrasts Between Prepubertal and Postpubertal Education. In G. D. Spindler, ed., *Education and Anthropology.* Stanford: Stanford University Press.

Hawkins, G. S. 1964. Stonehenge: A Neolithic Computer. *Nature* 202:1258-1261.

Heinzelin, J. de. 1962. Ishango. *Scientific American,* June, 105-116.

Herdt, G. H. 1973. *The Milamala and Falling Stars: Aspects of Religious Organization in the Trobriands.* Unpublished MS.

Herman, G. T., and A. D. Walker. 1972. The Syntactic Inference Problem Applied to Biological Systems. In B. Meltzer and D. Michie, eds., *Machine Intelligence,* 7. New York: John Wiley & Son, Inc.

Herskovits, M. J. 1938. *Dahomey: An Ancient West African Kingdom.* 2 vols. Locust Valley, N.Y.: J. J. Augustin, Inc.

———. 1937. African Gods and Catholic Saints in New World Religious Beliefs. *American Anthropologist* 39:635-643.

———. 1951. Tender and Tough-Minded Anthropology and the Study of Values in Culture. *Southwestern Journal of Anthropology* 7:22-31.

———. 1955. *Cultural Anthropology.* New York: Alfred A. Knopf, Inc.

———. 1972. *Cultural Relativism: Perspectives in Cultural Pluralism.* New York: Random House, Inc.

Hertz, R. 1907. Contribution à une Etude sur la Représentation Collective de la Mort. *Année Sociologique* 10:48-137. (Trans. in *Death and the Right Hand.* 1960. New York: The Free Press.)

———. 1909. Le Préeminence de la Main Droite: Etude sur la Polarité Religieuse. *Revue Philosophique* 58:553-580. (Trans. in *Death and the Right Hand,* 1960. New York: The Free Press.)

Hewes, G. W. 1973. Primate Communication and the Gestural Origin of Language. *Current Anthropology* 14:5-24.

Hiernaux, J. 1964. The Concept of Race and the Taxonomy of Mankind. In A. Montagu, ed., *The Concept of Race*. New York: The Free Press.

———. 1968. *La Diversité Humaine en Afrique Subsaharienne*. Brussels, Belgium: Editions de l'Institut de Sociologie Université Libre de Bruxelles.

Hockett, C. F. 1960. The Origin of Speech. *Scientific American* 203(September):88-111.

Hoebel, E. A. 1954. *The Law of Primitive Man: A Study in Comparative Legal Dynamics*. Cambridge, Mass.: Harvard University Press.

Hogbin, H. I. 1970. *The Island of Menstruating Men: Religion in Wogeo, N.G.* San Francisco: Chandler Publishing Company.

Holloway, R. J., Jr., 1969. Culture: A Human Domain. *Current Anthropology* 10:395-407.

Holmberg, A. R. 1965. The Changing Values and Institutions of Vicos in the Context of National Development. *American Behavioral Scientist* 8:3-8.

Horowitz, I. L. 1965. The Life and Death of Project Camelot. *Trans-Action,* December. (Reprinted in M. T. Weaver, ed. 1973. *To See Ourselves*. Glenview, Ill.: Scott, Foresman and Co.)

Horton, R. 1960. A Definition of Religion and Its Uses. *Journal of Royal Anthropological Institute* 90:201-226.

———. 1962. The Kalabari World View: An Outline and Interpretation. *Africa* 32:197-220.

Howell, F. C. 1969. Foreward to R. H. Klein. *Man and Culture in the Late Pleistocene*. San Francisco: Chandler Publishing Company.

Howells, W. W. 1966. Population Distances: Biological, Linguistic, Geographical and Environmental. *Current Anthropology* 7:531-540.

Howitt, A. W. 1904. *The Native Tribes of South-East Australia*. London: Macmillan and Company.

Hsu, F. L. K. 1953. *Americans and Chinese: Two Ways of Life*. New York: Abelard-Schuman, Inc.

Huizer, G. 1970. "Resistance to Change" and Radical Peasant Mobilization: Foster and Erasmus Reconsidered. *Human Organization* 29(4):303-313.

Huxley, T. H. 1863. *Man's Place in Nature*. Ann Arbor: University of Michigan Press. (Ann Arbor Paperbacks ed., 1959).

Hymes, D., ed. 1964. *Language in Culture and Society: A Reader in Linguistics and Anthropology*. New York: Harper & Row, Publishers.

———, ed. 1973. *Reinventing Anthropology*. New York: Random House, Inc.

Itani, J. 1965. Savanna Chimpanzees. *Kagahu Asahi,* 25.

———, and A. Suzuki. 1967. The Social Unit of Chimpanzees. *Primates* 8:355-381.

Izawa, K. 1970. Unit Groups of Chimpanzees and Their Nomadism in the Savanna Woodland. *Primates* 11.

Jablow, J. 1951. *The Cheyenne in Plains Indian Trade Relations 1795-1840*. Monographs of the American Ethnological Society, 19. Locust Valley, N.Y.: J. J. Augustin, Inc.

Jarvie, I. C. 1963. Theories of Cargo Cults: A Critical Analysis. *Oceania* 34(1):1-31 and 34(2):108-136.

Jay, P. 1968a. Primate Field Studies and Human Evolution. In P. Jay ed., *Primates: Studies in Adaptation and Variability*. New York: Holt, Rinehart and Winston.

———, ed. 1968b. *Primates: Studies in Adaptation and Variability*. New York: Holt, Rinehart and Winston.

Johnson, A. W. 1971. Security and Risk-Taking among Poor Peasants: A Brazilian Case. In G. Dalton, ed., *Studies in Economic Anthropology*. Washington, D.C.: American Anthropological Association.

Jolly, A. 1972. *The Evolution of Primate Behavior.* New York: Crowell-Collier and Macmillan, Inc.

Jolly, C. 1970. The Seed Eaters. *Man* 5(1):5-26.

Jones, D. J. 1970. Towards a Native Anthropology. *Human Organization* 29(4):251-
259.

Jorgenson, J. G. 1972. *The Sun Dance Religion: Power for the Powerless.* Chicago:
University of Chicago Press.

Junod, H. A. 1927. *The Life of a South African Tribe.* 2d ed. London: Macmillan and
Co.

Kaeppler, A. L. 1971. Rank in Tonga. *Ethnology* 10(2):174-193.

Keenan, E. 1974. Norm-Makers, Norm-Breakers: Uses of Speech by Men and Women in
a Malagasy Community. In R. Bauman and J. Sherzer, eds., *Explorations in the
Ethnography of Speaking.* Cambridge, England: Cambridge University Press.

Keesing, R. M. 1966. Kwaio Kindreds, *Southwestern Journal of Anthropology* 22
(4):346-353.

———. 1968a. On Descent and Descent Groups. *Current Anthropology* 9:453-454.

———. 1968b. Nonunilineal Descent and the Contextual Definition of Status. *American
Anthropologist* 70:82-84.

———. 1970. Shrines, Ancestors, and Cognatic Descent: The Kwaio and Tallensi.
American Anthropologist 72:755-775.

———. 1971. Descent, Residence, and Cultural Codes. In L. Hiatt and C. Jayarwardena, eds., *Anthropology in Oceania.* Sydney: Angus and Robertson.

———. 1972a. Paradigms Lost: The New Ethnography and the New Linguistics. *Southwestern Journal of Anthropology* 23:299-332.

———. 1972b. Simple Models of Complexity: The Lure of Kinship. In P. Reining, ed.,
Kinship Studies in the Morgan Centennial Year. Washington, D.C.: Anthropological
Society of Washington.

———. 1972c. The Anthropologist's Dilemma: Empathy and Analysis Among the
Solomon Islanders. *Expedition* 3:32-39.

———. 1974. Transformational Linguistics and Structural Anthropology. *Cultural Her-
maneutics* 2:243-266.

———. 1975. *Kin Groups and Social Structure.* New York: Holt, Rinehart and Winston.

Keil, C. 1966. *Urban Blues.* Chicago: University of Chicago Press.

Keiser, R. L. 1969. *The Vice Lords: Warriors of the Streets.* New York: Holt, Rinehart and
Winston.

Kemp, W. B. 1971. The Flow of Energy in a Hunting Society. *Scientific American,*
September.

King, J. L., and T. H. Jukes. 1969. Non-Darwinian Evolution. *Science* 164:788-798.

Klein, M. 1950. *Contributions to Psychoanalysis 1921-1945.* London: Hogarth Press.

———, and J. Riviere. 1937. *Love, Hate and Reparation.* New York: W. W. Norton &
Company, Inc.

Kluchkhohn, C. 1942. Myths and Rituals: A General Theory. *Harvard Theological
Review* 35:45-79.

———. 1949. The Philosophy of the Navaho Indians. In F. S. C. Northrop, ed.,
Ideological Differences and World Order. New Haven, Conn.: Yale University Press.

———. 1953. Universal Categories of Culture. In A. L. Kroeber, ed., *Anthropology
Today.* Chicago: University of Chicago Press.

———, and W. H. Kelly. 1945. The Concept of Culture. In R. Linton, ed., *The Science
of Man in the World Crisis.* New York: Columbia University Press.

Köbben, A. J. F. 1967. Why Exceptions? The Logic of Cross-Cultural Analysis. *Current Anthropology* 3:19.

Kohne, D. E. 1970. Evolution of Higher-Organism DNA. *Quarterly Review* 3:327-375.

Konner, M. 1972. Aspects of the Developmental Ethology of a Foraging People. In N. Blurton-Jones, ed., *Ethological Studies of Child Behaviour*. London: Cambridge University Press.

Kopytoff, I. 1964. Family and Lineage among the Suku of the Congo. In R. F. Gray and P. H. Gulliver, eds., *The Family Estate in Africa*. London: Routledge & Kegan Paul Ltd.

———. 1965. The Suku of Southwestern Congo. In J. Gibbs, Jr., ed, *Peoples of Africa*. New York: Holt, Rinehart and Winston.

———. 1971. Ancestors as Elders in Africa. *Africa* 41(11):129-142.

Korn, F. 1973. *Elementary Structures Reconsidered: Lévi-Strauss on Kinship*. Berkeley: University of California Press.

Kortlandt, A. 1973. Comment on G. Hewes "Primate Communication and the Gestural Origin of Language." *Current Anthropology* 14(1-2):13-14.

Krader, L. 1968. *The Formation of the State*. Englewood Cliffs, N.J.: Prentice-Hall, Inc.

Kroeber, A. L. 1948. *Anthropology*. New York: Harcourt Brace and Jovanovich.

———, and C. Kluckhohn. 1952. *Culture: A Critical Review of Concepts and Definitions*. Peabody Museum Papers 47, 1. Cambridge, Mass.: Harvard University Press.

Kuhn, T. S. 1970. *The Structure of Scientific Revolutions*. 2d ed. Chicago: University of Chicago Press.

Kummer, H. 1968. *Social Organization of Hamadryas Baboons: A Field Study*. Basle: S. Karger.

———. 1971. *Primate Societies: Group Techniques of Ecological Adaptation*. Chicago: Aldine & Atherton, Inc.

Labarre, W. 1967. Preface to G. Devereux, *From Anxiety to Method in the Behavioral Sciences*. The Hague: Mouton and Co.

———. 1970. *The Ghost Dance: The Origins of Religion*. Garden City, N.Y.: Doubleday & Company, Inc.

Labov, W. 1970a. The Study of Language in its Social Context. *Studium Generale* 23:30-87.

———. 1970b. The Logic of Nonstandard English. In *Language and Poverty: Perspectives on a Theme*. Chicago: Markham Publishing Co.

———. 1972. *Sociolinguistic Patterns*. Philadelphia: University of Pennsylvania Press.

Lafitau, J. F. 1924. *Les Moeurs des Sauvages Amériquains Comparées aux Moeurs des Premiers Temps*. Paris: Saugrain l'Âiné.

Lakoff, G. 1971. Presupposition and Relative Well-Formedness. In D. D. Steinberg and L. A. Jakobovits, eds., *Semantics: An Interdisciplinary Reader in Philosophy, Linguistics, and Psychology*. London: Cambridge University Press.

Lancaster, J. B. 1968. Primate Communication Systems and the Emergence of Human Language. In P. Jay, ed., *Primates: Studies in Adaptation and Variability*. New York: Holt, Rinehart and Winston.

Lanternari, V. 1955. L'Annua Festa 'Milamala' Dei Trobriandesi: Interpetazione Psichologica e Functionale. *Revirta di Antropologia*. 42:3-24.

———. 1963. *Religions of the Oppressed: a Study of Modern Messiaric Cults*. New York: Alfred A. Knopf, Inc.

Leach, E. R. 1954. *Political Systems of Highland Burma*. Cambridge, Mass.: Harvard University Press.

Leach, E. R. 1955. Polyandry, Inheritance, and the Definition of Marriage, with Particular Reference to Sinhalese Customary Law. *Man* 55:182-186.

———. 1957. Aspects of Bridewealth and Marriage Stability among the Kachin and Lakher. *Man* 57:59.

———. 1958. Magical Hair. *Journal of the Royal Anthropological Institute* 88:147-164.

———. 1959. Concerning Trobriand Clans and the Kinship Category Tabu. In J. Goody, ed., *The Developmental Cycle of Domestic Groups.* Cambridge Papers in Social Anthropology 1. London: Cambridge University Press.

———, ed. 1960. *Aspects of Caste in South India, Ceylon and Northwest Pakistan.* Cambridge Papers in Social Anthropology 2. London: Cambridge University Press.

———. 1961. *Pul Eliya, a Village in Ceylon: A Study of Land Tenure and Kinship.* London: Cambridge University Press.

———. 1962. *Rethinking Anthropology.* London: Athlone Press.

———. 1965. Anthropological Aspects of Language: Animal Categories and Verbal Abuse. In E. Lenneberg, ed., *New Directions in the Study of Language.* Cambridge, Mass.: MIT Press.

———. 1969. *Genesis as Myth, and Other Essays.* London: Gossman Publishers.

———. 1971. Marriage, Primitive. *Encyclopedia Britannica:* 938-947.

Leacock, E. B., ed. 1971. *The Culture of Poverty: A Critique.* New York: Simon & Schuster, Inc.

———. 1972. Introduction to F. Engels. *Origin of the Family, Private Property and the State.* New York: International Publishers Co., Inc.

———. 1974. Review of S. Goldberg, *The Inevitability of Patriarchy,* (New York: Morrow and Co., 1973). *American Anthropologist* 76(2):363-365.

LeCam, L., J. Neyman, and E. Scott, eds. 1972. *Proceedings of the Sixth Berkeley Symposium on Mathematical Probability.* Vol. 5: Darwinian, Neo-Darwinian and Non-Darwinian Evolution. Berkeley: University of California Press.

Lee, D. D. 1940. A Primitive System of Values. *Philosophy of Science* 7:355-378.

———. 1949. Being and Value in a Primitive Culture. *Journal of Philosophy* 46(13): 401—415.

Lee, R. B. 1968a. What Hunters Do for a Living. In R. B. Lee and I. DeVore, eds., *Man the Hunter.* Chicago: Aldine Publishing Company.

———. 1968b. Comment. In L. R. and S. Binford, eds., *New Perspectives in Archaeology.* Chicago: Aldine Publishing Company.

———. 1969. !Kung Bushman Subsistence: An Input-Output Analysis. In A. P. Vayda, ed. *Environment and Cultural Behavior.* Garden City, N.Y.: Natural History Press. (Revision of a paper originally published in D. Damas, ed. 1969. *Ecological Essays.* Ottawa: Queens Printer.)

———, and I. DeVore, eds. 1968a. *Man the Hunter.* Chicago: Aldine Publishing Company.

———. 1968b. Problems in the Study of Hunters and Gatherers. In R. B. Lee and I. DeVore, eds., *Man the Hunter.* Chicago: Aldine Publishing Company.

———, eds. 1974. *Kalahari Hunter Gatherers.* Cambridge: Harvard University Press.

Lenneberg, E. H. 1967. *The Biological Foundations of Language.* New York: John Wiley & Sons, Inc.

———. 1969. On Explaining Language. *Science* 164:635-643.

Leroi-Gourhan, A. 1968. The Evolution of Paleolithic Art. *Scientific American,* February.

Levine, R. A. 1966. *Dreams and Deeds: Achievement Motivation in Nigeria.* Chicago: University of Chicago Press.

———. 1973. *Culture, Behavior, and Personality: An Introduction to the Comparative Study of Psychosocial Adaptation.* Chicago: Adline-Atherton, Inc.

Lévi-Strauss, C. 1945. L'Analyse structurale en linguistique et an anthropologie. *Word* (Journal of Linguistic Circle of New York) 1(2).

———. 1949. *Les Structures Elementaires de la Parente.* Paris: Plon. (Trans. as *The Elementary Structures of Kinship.* 1969. Boston: Beacon Press.)

———. 1962. *La Pensée Sauvage.* Paris: Plon. (Trans. as *The Savage Mind.* 1966. Chicago: University of Chicago Press.)

———. 1963a. *Structural Anthropology.* New York: Basic Books, Inc., Publishers.

———. 1963b. Do Dual Organizations Exist? In C. Lévi-Strauss, ed., *Structural Anthropology.* Paris: Plon.

———. 1967. The story of Asdiwal. In E. R. Leach, ed., *The Structural Study of Myth and Totemism.* A.S.A. Monographs. London: Tavistock Publications.

———. 1968. The Concept of Primitiveness. In R. B. Lee and I. De Vore, eds., *Man the Hunter.* Chicago: Aldine Publishing Company.

———. 1969. *The Raw and the Cooked.* New York: Harper & Row, Publishers. (Translation of *Le Cru et le Cuit.* 1964. Paris: Plon.)

———. 1969. *Mythologiques, III: L'Origine de Manières de Table.* Paris: Plon.

———. 1971. *Mythologiques IV: L'Homme Nu.* Paris: Plon.

———. 1973. *An Introduction to the Science of Mythology, Vol. II: From Honey to Ashes.* New York: Harper & Row, Publishers. (Translation of *Mythologiques: Du Miel aux Cendres.*)

Levy-Bruhl, L. 1912. *Les Fonctions Mentales dans les Societiés Inférieures.* Paris: F. Alcan. (Trans. as *How Natives Think.* 1966. New York: Washington Square Press.)

———. 1923. *Primitive Mentality.* London: George Allen & Unwin Ltd. (Trans. by L. A. Clare.)

Lewis, D. K. 1973. Anthropology and Colonialism. *Current Anthropology* 14:581-602.

Lewis, O. 1961. *The Children of Sanchez.* New York: Random House, Inc.

———. 1966. *La Vida.* New York: Random House, Inc.

———, and V. Barnouw. 1956. Caste and Jajmani System in a North Indian Village. *Scientific American* 83(2):66-81.

Li An-Che 1937. Zuni: Some Observations and Queries. *American Anthropologist* 39:62-76.

Lieberman, P., and E. S. Crelin. 1971. On the Speech of Neanderthal Man. *Linguistic Inquiry* 2:203-222.

———, ———, and D. H. Klatt. 1972. Phonetic Ability and Related Anatomy of the Newborn and Adult Human, Neanderthal Man, and the Chimpanzee. *American Anthropologist* 74(3).

Liebow, E. 1967. *Tally's Corner.* Boston: Little, Brown and Company.

Lienhardt, G. 1961. *Divinity and Experience: The Religion of the Dinka.* Oxford: Clarendon Press.

Lindenbaum, S. 1972. Sorcerers, Ghosts and Polluting Women: An Analysis of Religious Belief and Population Control. *Ethnology* 11(3):241-253.

———. 1973. *A Wife Is the Hand of Man.* A paper presented at American Anthropological Association annual meeting, New Orleans.

Linton, R. 1940. Acculturation. In R. Linton, ed., *Acculturation in Seven American Indian Tribes.* Gloucester, Mass.: Peter Smith.

Little, K. 1965. *West African Urbanization: A Study of Voluntary Associations in Social Change.* London: Cambridge University Press.

———. 1967. Voluntary Associations in Urban Life: A Case Study of Differential

Adaptations. In M. Freedman, ed., *Social Organization: Essays Presented to Raymond Firth.* Chicago: Aldine Publishing Company.

Livingstone, F. B. 1958. Anthropological Implications of Sickle-Cell Gene Distribution in West Africa. *American Anthropologist* 60:533-562.

——. 1964. On the Nonexistence of Human Races. In A. Montagu, ed., *The Concept of Race.* New York: The Free Press.

——. 1969. Genetics, Ecology, and the Origins of Incest and Exogamy. *Current Anthropology* 10(1):45-49.

Lloyd, P. C. 1965. The Political Structure of African Kingdoms: An Exploratory Model. In M. Banton, ed., *Political Systems and the Distribution of Power.* ASA Monographs, 2. London: Tavistock Publications.

——. 1973. The Yoruba: An Urban People? In A. Southall, ed., *Urban Anthropology.* London: Oxford University Press.

——, A. Mabogunje and B. Awe, eds. 1967. *The City of Ibadan.* London: Cambridge University Press.

Löffler, R. 1971. The Representative Mediator and the New Peasant. *American Anthropologist* 73:1077-1091.

Lorenz, K. 1966. *On Aggression.* New York: Harcourt Brace Jovanovich, Inc.

Lounsbury, F. G. 1964. A Formal Account of the Crow- and Omaha-type Kinship Terminologies. In W. Goodenough, ed., *Explorations in Cultural Anthropology.* New York: McGraw-Hill, Inc.

——. 1965. Another View of the Trobriand Kinship Categories. In E. A. Hammel, ed., *Formal Semantic Analysis.* American Anthropologist Special Publication 4(67), part 2. Menasha, Wis.: American Anthropological Association.

Lowie, R. H. 1920. *Primitive Society.* New York: Liveright.

Lumholtz, C. 1889. *Among Cannibals.* New York: Charles Scribner and Sons.

McLean, P. D. 1964. Man and His Animal Brain. *Modern Medicine,* February: 95-106.

McGrew, W. C. 1972. *An Ethological Study of Children's Behaviour.* London: Academic Press.

McLean, P. D. 1964. Man and his Animal Brain. *Modern Medicine,* February: 95-106.

——. 1968. Alternative Neural Pathways to Violence. In M. L. Nag., ed., *Alternatives to Violence.* New York: Time-Life Books.

——. 1969. The Paranoid Streak in Man. In A. Koestler and J. R. Smythies, eds., *Beyond Reductionism: New Perspectives in the Life Sciences.* London: Hutchinson and Co.

——. 1970. The Triune Brain, Emotion and Scientific Bias. In *The Neurosciences: Second Study Program.* F. O. Schmitt et. al. New York: Rockefeller University Press.

——. 1973. A Triune Concept of the Brain. In T. J. Boag, et al., eds., *A Triune Concept of the Brain and Behaviour.* Toronto: University of Toronto Press.

McNeill, D. 1966. Developmental Psycholinguistics. In F. Smith and G. A. Miller, eds., *The Genesis of Language.* Cambridge, Mass.: MIT Press.

——. 1970a. The Development of Language. In P. A. Mussen, ed., *Carmichael's Manual of Child Psychology.* New York: John Wiley & Sons, Inc.

——. 1970b. *The Acquisition of Language.* New York: Harper & Row, Publishers.

MacNeish, R. S. 1964. The Origins of New World Civilization. *Scientific American,* November. (Page citations in J. Jorgenson, ed., 1972. *Biology and Culture in Modern Perspective.* San Francisco: W. H. Freeman and Co.)

——. 1971. Early Man in the Andes. *Scientific American* 224:36-46.

Mabogunje, A. L. 1967. The Morphology of Ibadan. In P. C. Lloyd, A. L. Mabogunje, and B. Awe, eds., *The City of Ibadan.* London: Cambridge University Press.

———. 1968. *Urbanization in Nigeria.* London: University of London Press.

Malinowski, B. 1916. Baloma: The Spirits of the Dead in the Trobriand Islands. *Journal of the Royal Anthropological Institute* 46:353-430. (Reprinted in *Magic, Science and Religion.* 1954. Boston: Beacon Press.)

———. 1919. Kula: The Circulating Exchange of Valuables in the Archipelagoes of Eastern New Guinea. *Man* 20:97-105.

———. 1922. *Argonauts of the Western Pacific.* London: Routledge & Kegan Paul Ltd.

———. 1925. Magic, Science and Religion. In J. Needham, ed., *Science, Religion and Reality.* London. (Reprinted in *Magic, Science and Religion,* 1954.)

———. 1926. *Myth in Primitive Psychology.* London. (Reprinted in *Magic, Science and Religion,* 1954)

———. 1927. *Sex and Repression in Savage Society.* London: Routledge & Kegan Paul Ltd.

———. 1929. *The Sexual Life of Savages in Northwestern Melanesia.* London: Routledge & Kegan Paul Ltd.

———. 1931. Culture. In *Encyclopedia of the Social Sciences.* New York: The Macmillan Company.

———. 1935. *Coral Gardens and Their Magic.* 2 vols. London: George Allen & Unwin Ltd.

———. 1944. *A Scientific Theory of Culture and Other Essays.* Chapel Hill: University of North Carolina Press. (Reprinted by Oxford University Press, 1960.)

Maquet, J. 1964. Objectivity in Anthropology. *Current Anthropology* 5:47-55.

Maranda, P., and E. Maranda. 1970. Le Crâne et l'Uterus: Deux Théoremes Nord-Malaitains. In J. Pouillon and P. Maranda, eds., *Echanges et Communications: Mélanges offerts à Claude Lévi-Strauss.* The Hague: Mouton and Company.

Marler, P. 1965. Communication in Monkeys and Apes. In I. DeVore, ed., *Primate Behavior: Field Studies of Monkeys and Apes.* New York: Holt, Rinehart and Winston, Inc.

Marriott, M. 1955a. Little Communities in Indigenous Civilization. In M. Marriott, ed., *Village India.* Chicago: University of Chicago Press.

———, ed. 1955b. *Village India: Studies in the Little Community.* Chicago: University of Chicago Press.

Marshack, A. 1964. Lunar Notation on Upper Paleolithic Remains. *Science,* November 6.

———. 1972. *The Roots of Civilization.* New York: McGraw-Hill, Inc.

Marshall, L. 1959. Marriage among the !Kung Bushmen. *Africa* 29:335-364.

———. 1960. !Kung Bushmen Bands. *Africa* 30:325-355.

———. 1965. The !Kung Bushmen of the Kalahari Desert. In J. Gibbs, Jr., ed., *Peoples of Africa.* New York: Holt, Rinehart and Winston.

Martin, P. S., and H. E. Wright, eds. 1967. *Pleistocene Extinctions: The Search for a Cause.* New Haven, Conn.: Yale University Press.

Masson, L. R., ed. 1889. *Les Bourgeois de la Compagnie du Nord-Ouest,* Vol. 1. Quebec.

Mauss, M. 1925. *Essai sur le Don. L'Année Sociologique* (n.s.t.)I:30-186. (Trans. as *The Gift: Forms and Functions of Exchange in Archaic Society.* 1954. New York: The Free Press.)

Maybury-Lewis, D. H. P. 1967. *Akwe-Shavante Society.* Oxford: Clarendon Press.

Mead, M. 1928. *Coming of Age in Samoa.* New York: William Morrow and Company, Inc.

———. 1938. The Mountain Arapesh. Part 1: An Importing Culture. *American Museum of Natural History Anthropological Papers,* 36:139-349.

Mead, M. 1935. *Sex and Temperament in Three Primitive Societies.* New York: William Morrow and Company, Inc.

———. 1940. Social Change and Cultural Surrogates. *Journal of Educational Sociology* 14(2):92-109.

———. 1957. Toward More Vivid Utopias. *Science* 126:957-961.

———. 1949. *Male and Female.* New York: William Morrow and Company, Inc.

Meggers, B. J. 1971. *Amazonia: Man and Culture in a Counterfeit Paradise.* Chicago: Aldine-Atherton, Inc.

Meggitt, J. J. 1964. Male-Female Relationships in the Highlands of Australian New Guinea. In J. B. Watson, ed., *New Guinea: The Central Highlands.* American Anthropologist Special Publication 66, part 2.

———. 1965. *The Lineage System of the Mae Enga of the New Guinea Highlands.* Edinburgh: Oliver & Boyd.

Meggitt, M. 1972a. Understanding Australian Aboriginal Society: Kinship Systems or Cultural Categories. In P. Reining, ed., *Kinship in the Morgan Centennial Year.* Washington, D.C.: Anthropological Society of Washington.

———. 1972b. System and Subsystem: The Te Exchange Cycle among the Mae Enga. *Human Ecology* 1:111-123.

Meillasoux, C. 1960. Essai d'Interprétation de Phénomène Economique dans les Societes Traditionnelles d'Auto-Subsistance. *Cahiers d'Etudes Africaines* 4.

———, ed. 1971. *The Development of Indigenous Trade and Markets in West Africa.* Oxford: Oxford University Press.

———. 1972. From Reproduction to Production. *Economy and Society* 1:93-105.

———. 1973. Are there Castes in India? *Economy and Society* 2:89-111.

Mencher, J. P. 1974. The Caste System Upside Down, or The-Not-So-Mysterious East. *Current Anthropology* 15:469-493.

Meyers, J. T. 1971. The Origins of Agriculture: An Evaluation of Three Hypotheses. In S. Struever, ed., *Prehistoric Agriculture.* Garden City, N.Y.: Natural History Press.

Michels, J. W. 1972a. *Dating Methods in Archaeology.* New York: Seminar Press.

———. 1972b. Dating Methods. In *Annual Reviews of Anthropology,* 1. Palo Alto, Calif.: Annual Reviews Press.

Middleton, J., and P. Bohannan, eds. 1968. *Kinship and Social Organization.* Garden City, N.Y.: Natural History Press.

Miers, S., and I. Kopytoff, eds. 1975. *Slavery in Pre-Colonial Africa.* Madison: University of Wisconsin Press.

Miller, G. A. 1972. Linguistic Communication as a Biological Process. In J. W. Pringle, ed., *Biology and the Human Sciences.* London: Oxford University Press.

Mintz, S. W. 1959. Internal Market Systems as Mechanisms of Social Articulation. In V. F. Ray, ed., *Proceedings of the American Ethnological Society.* Seattle: University of Washington Press.

———. 1961. Pratik: Haitian Personal Economic Relationships. In *Proceedings of the 1961 Annual Spring Meeting of the American Ethnological Society.* Seattle: University of Washington Press.

Mitchell, J. 1974. *Psychoanalysis and Feminism.* London: Allen Wayne.

Mitchell, J. C. 1969. The Concept and Use of Social Networks. In J. C. Mitchell, ed., *Social Networks in Urban Situations.* 2d ed. Manchester, England: Manchester University Press.

Molitz, H. 1965. Contemporary Instinct Theory and the Fixed Action Pattern. *Psychology Review* 72:27-47.

Montagu, M. F. A. 1968. *The Natural Superiority of Women*. Rev. ed. New York: the Macmillan Company.

———. ed. 1972. *Man and Agression*. 2nd ed. New York: Oxford University Press.

Montague, S. 1971. Trobriand Kinship and the Virgin Birth Controversy. *Man* 6:353-368.

Mooney, J. 1896. *The Ghost Dance Religion*. Bureau of American Ethnology, Annual Report 14. Washington, D.C.: U.S. Government Printing Office.

Moore, O. K. 1957. Divination—a New Perspective. *American Anthropologist* 59:69-74.

Morgan, L. H. 1870. *Systems of Consanguinity and Affinity in the Human Family*. Washington, D.C.: Smithsonian Institution.

———. 1877. *Ancient Society*. New York: Henry Holt and Company.

Morris, D. 1967. *The Naked Ape*. New York: McGraw-Hill, Inc.

———, ed. 1967. *Private Ethology*. Chicago: Aldine Publishing Company.

Mugica, A. M. 1946. *Primo Tapia: Semblanza de un Revolucionano Michaocano*. 2d ed. Mexico.

Murdock, G. P. 1945. The Common Denominators of Cultures. In R. Linton, ed., *The Science of Man in the World Crisis*. New York: Columbia University Press.

———. 1949. *Social Structure*. New York: The Macmillan Company.

———. 1957. World Ethnographic Sample. *American Anthropologist* 59:664-687.

———. 1967. Ethnographic Atlas: A Summary. *Ethnology* 6:109-236.

Nakane, C. 1970. *Japanese Society*. Berkeley: University of California Press.

Narokobi, B. M. 1974. To Build a New Society We Must Build From the Base. *Papua New Guinea Post Courier,* October 22.

Naroll, R. 1970. What Have We Learned from Cross-Cultural Studies? *American Anthropologist* 72:1227-1288.

———, and R. Cohen, eds. 1970. *A Handbook of Method in Cultural Anthropology*. Garden City, N.Y.: Natural History Press.

Nash, M. 1961. The Social Context of Economic Choice in a Small Society. *Man* 61(219).

Needham, R. 1962. *Structure and Sentiment: A Test Case in Social Anthropology*. Chicago: University of Chicago Press.

———. 1964. Blood, Thunder and the Mockery of Animals. *Sociologus* 14:136-149.

———. 1971. Remarks on the Analysis of Kinship and Marriage. In R. Needham, ed., *Kinship and Marriage*. ASA Monographs, 11. London: Tavistock.

———, ed. 1973. *Right and Left: Essays on Dual Symbolic Classification*. Chicago: University of Chicago Press.

———. 1974. Remarks and Inventions. Skeptical Essays about Kinship. New York: Barnes & Noble, Inc.

Neel, J. V. 1970. Lessons from a 'Primitive' People. *Science* 170:805-822.

Newcomer, P. J. 1972. The Nuer are Dinka: An Essay on Origins and Environmental Determinism. *Man* (n.s.) 7:5-11.

Nkrumah, K. 1965. *Neo-colonialism: The Last Stage of Imperialism*. New York: International Publishing Company.

Ornstein, R. E. 1973. *The Psychology of Consciousness*. San Francisco: W. H. Freeman and Co., Publishers.

Ortner, S. B. 1974. Is Female to Male as Nature is to Culture? In M. Z. Rosaldo and L. Lamphere, eds. *Woman, Culture, and Society*. Stanford: Stanford University Press.

Osgood, C. 1971. Where Do Sentences Come From? In D. D. Steinberg and L. A. Jakobovits, eds., *Semantics: An Interdisciplinary Reader in Philosophy, Linguistics, and Psychology*. Cambridge: Cambridge University Press.

Ossowski, S. 1963. *Class Structure in the Social Consciousness.* Trans. by S. Patterson. London: Routledge and Kegan Paul Ltd.

Otterbein, K. F. 1963. Marquesan Polyandry. *Marriage and Family Living* 25(2).

Oxnard, C. E. 1969. Evolution of the Human Shoulder: Some Possible Pathways. *American Journal of Physical Anthropology* 30:319.

Pastner, S. 1971. Camels, Sheep and Nomad Social Organization: A Comment on Rubel's Model. *Man* (n.s.) 6:285-288.

Peacock, J. L. 1968. *Rites of Modernization: Symbolic and Social Aspects of Indonesian Proletarian Drama.* Chicago: University of Chicago Press.

Person, Y. 1971. Guinea-Samori. In M. Crowder, ed., *West African Resistance: The Military Response to Colonial Occupation.* London: Hutchinson Publishing Group, Ltd.

Peters, 1972. A New Start for an Old Problem: Evolution of the Capacity for Language. *Man* 7:13-19.

Pfeiffer, J. E. 1972. *The Emergence of Man.* 2d ed. New York: Harper & Row, Publishers.

Piaget, J. 1970. Piaget's Theory. In P. H. Mussen, ed., *Carmichael's Manual of Child Psychology,* Vol. 1. 3d ed. 703-732. New York: John Wiley & Sons, Inc.

Pike, K. L. 1967. *Language in Relation to a Unified Theory of the Structure of Human Behavior.* The Hague: Mouton and Company.

Pilbeam, D. 1972. *The Ascent of Man: An Introduction to Human Evolution.* New York: The Macmillan Company.

Ploog, D. 1970. Social Communication among Animals. In F. O. Schmitt, ed., *The Neurosciences: Second Study Program.* New York: Rockefeller University Press.

———, and T. Melnechuk. 1969. Primate Communications. *Neuroscience Research Program Bulletin* 7:419-510.

Plotnicov, L. 1967. *Strangers to the City: Urban Man in Jos, Nigeria.* Pittsburgh: University of Pittsburgh Press.

Pocock, D. F. 1960. Sociologies: Rural and Urban. *Contributions to Indian Sociology* 4:63-81.

Polanyi, K. 1957. The Economy as Instituted Process. In K. Polanyi et al., eds., *Trade and Market in the Early Empires.* New York: The Free Press.

———. 1959. Anthropology and Economic Theory. In M. H. Fried, ed., *Readings in Anthropology,* II. New York: Thomas Y. Crowell Company.

Pomeroy, W. J. 1970. *American Neo-Colonialism: its Emergence in the Philippines and Asia.* New York: International Publishing Company.

———. 1973. *American Made Tragedy: Neo-Colonialism and Dictatorship in the Philippines.* New York: International Publishers Co., Inc.

Popper, K. P. 1959. *The Logic of Scientific Discovery.* Rev. ed. New York: Harper Row, Publishers.

———. 1972. *Objective Knowledge: An Evolutionary Approach.* London: Oxford University Press.

Pospisil, L. 1963a. *Kapauku Papuan Economy.* New Haven, Conn.: Yale University Press.

———. 1963b. *The Kapauku Papuans of West New Guinea.* New York: Holt, Rinehart and Winston.

———. 1968. Law and Order. In J. A. Clifton, ed., *Introduction to Cultural Anthropology.* Boston: Houghton Mifflin Company.

Postal, P. M. 1972. The Best Theory. In E. S. Peters, ed., *Goals in Linguistic Theory.* Englewood Cliffs, N.J.: Prentice-Hall, Inc.

Potter, J. M., M. N. Diaz, and G. M. Foster, eds. 1967. *Peasant Society: A Reader.* Boston: Little, Brown and Company.

Powell, H. A. 1960. Competitive Leadership in Trobriand Political Organization. *Journal of the Royal Anthropological Institute* 90:118-145.

———. 1968. Correspondence: Virgin Birth. *Man* 3:651-652.

———. 1969a. Genealogy, Residence and Kinship in Kiriwina. *Man* 4(2):177-202.

———. 1969b. Territory, Hierarchy and Kinship in Kiriwina. *Man* 4(4):580-604.

Premack, A. J., and D. Premack. 1972. Teaching Language to an Ape. *Scientific American* 227:92-99.

Premack, D. 1971. Language in Chimpanzee? *Science* 172:808-822.

Primbram, K. H. 1967. The New Neurology and the Biology of Emotion: A Structural Approach. *American Psychologist* 22:830-838.

———. 1971. *Languages of the Brain.* Englewood Cliffs, N.J.: Prentice-Hall, Inc.

Price, B. J. 1971. Prehispanic Irrigation Agriculture in Nuclear America. *Latin American Research Review* 6(3):3-60. (Reprinted in abridged form in M. Fried, ed., 1973. *Explorations in Anthropology.* New York: Thomas Y. Crowell Company.)

Price, R. 1973. *Maroon Societies.* Garden City, N.Y. Doubleday & Company, Inc.

Radcliffe-Brown, A. R. 1913. Three Tribes of Western Australia. *Journal of the Royal Anthropological Institute.* 43:143-194.

———. 1922. *The Andaman Islanders.* Cambridge: Cambridge University Press.

———. 1930. The Social Organization of Australian Tribes. *Oceania* 1:34-63.

———. 1950. Introduction. In A. Radcliffe-Brown and C. D. Forde, eds., *African Systems of Kinship and Marriage.* London: Oxford University Press.

———. 1951. The Comparative Method in Social Anthropology. *Journal of the Royal Anthropological Institute* 81:15-22.

———. 1952. *Structure and Function in Primitive Society.* London: Cohen and West.

Rappaport, R. 1967. Ritual Regulation of Environmental Relations among a New Guinea People. *Ethnology* 6:17-30.

———. 1968. *Pigs for the Ancestors: Ritual in the Ecology of a New Guinea People.* New Haven, Conn.: Yale University Press.

———. 1970. Sanctity and Adaptation. *Io,* Winter (Special Oecology Issue):46-70.

———. 1971a. Ritual, Sanctity, and Cybernetics. *American Anthropologist* 73:59-76.

———. 1971b. The Sacred in Human Evolution. *Annual Review of Ecology and Systematics* 2:22-44. Palo Alto: Annual Reviews Press.

———. 1971c. The Flow of Energy in an Agricultural Society. *Scientific American,* September. (Page references are to reprinting in J. G. Jorgenson, ed. 1972. *Biology and Culture in Modern Perspective.* San Francisco: W. H. Freeman and Co., Publishers.)

———. 1971d. Nature, Culture, and Ecological Anthropology. In H. Shapiro, ed., *Man, Culture and Society.* London: Oxford University Press.

Rasmussen, K. 1922. *Grønlandsagen.* Berlin.

Rattray, R. S. 1923. *Ashanti.* Oxford: Clarendon Press.

Redfield, M. P., ed. 1962. *Human Nature and the Study of Society: The Papers of Robert Redfield,* Vol. I. Chicago: University of Chicago Press.

Redfield, R. 1953. *The Primitive World and Its Transformations.* Ithaca, N.Y.: Cornell University Press.

———. 1955. *The Little Community.* Chicago: University of Chicago Press.

———. 1956. *Peasant Society and Culture.* Chicago: University of Chicago Press.

———, R. Linton, and M. J. Herskovits. 1936. A Memorandum on Acculturation. *American Anthropologist* 38:149-152.

Reed, N. 1965. *The Caste War of Yucatan.* Stanford, Calif.: Stanford University Press.

Renfrew, C. 1971. Carbon 14 and the Prehistory of Europe. *Scientific American* 225:63-72.

————. 1973. *Before Civilization: The Radiocarbon Revolution and Prehistoric Europe.* London: Jonathan Cape, Ltd.

Rey, P.-P. 1971. *Colonialisme, Néo-Colonialisme et Transition au Capitalisme.* Paris: Maspero.

————. 1973. Las Alliances de Classes: sur L'Articulation des Modes de Production. Suivi du *Materialisme Historique et Luttes de Classes.* Paris: Maspero.

Reynolds, P. C. 1968. Evolution of Primate Vocal-Auditory Communications Systems. *American Anthropologist* 70:300-308.

Reynolds, V. 1967. *The Apes.* New York: E. P. Dutton & Co., Inc.

Richards, A. I. 1950. Some Types of Family Structure amongst the Central Bantu. In A. R. Radcliffe-Brown and C. D. Forde, eds., *African Systems of Kinship and Marriage.* London: Oxford University Press.

Riley, C. L., J. C. Kelley, C. W. Pennington, and R. L. Rands, eds. 1971. *Man Across the Sea: Problems of Pre-Columbian Contacts.* Austin: University of Texas Press.

Rivers, W. H. R. 1906. *The Todas.* New York: The Macmillan Company.

Robbins, L. 1935. The Subject Matter of Economics. In *An Essay on the Nature and Significance of Economic Science.* London: Macmillan & Co., Ltd.

Roberts, J. M., and B. Sutton-Smith. 1962. Child Training and Game Involvement. *Ethnology* 1:166-185.

Robinson, M. 1962. Complementary Filiation and Marriage in the Trobriand Islands. In M. Fortes, ed., *Marriage in Tribal Societies.* Cambridge Papers in Social Anthropology, 3. London: Cambridge University Press.

Rohlen, T. 1974. *For Harmony and Strength: Japanese White-Collar Organization in Anthropological Perspective.* Berkeley: University of California Press.

Romney, A. K., and P. Epling. 1958. A Simplified Model of Kariera Kinship. *American Anthropologist* 60:59-74.

Rosaldo, M. Z. 1974. Woman, Culture and Society: A Theoretical Overview. In M. Z. Rosaldo and L. Lamphere, eds., *Woman, Culture and Society.* Stanford, Calif.: Stanford University Press.

————, and L. Lamphere. 1974. *Woman, Culture, and Society,* Stanford, Calif.: Stanford University Press.

Rosch, E. 1974. Universals and Cultural Specifics in Human Categorization. In R. Breslin, W. Lonner, and S. Bochner, eds., *Cross-cultural Perspectives on Learning.* New York: Russell Sage Foundation.

Rowe, W. L. 1973. Caste, Kinship and Association in Urban India. In A. Southall, ed., *Urban Anthropology.* London: Oxford University Press.

Rowell, T. E. 1966. Forest-living Baboons in Uganda. *Journal of Zoology* 149:344-364.

Rowley, C. D. 1970-1971. *Aboriginal Policy and Practice.* Vol. 1: The Destruction of Aboriginal Society; Vol. 2: Outcasts in White Australia; Vol. 3: The Remote Aborigines. Canberra: Australian National University Press.

Rowthorn, R. E. 1974. Neo-Classicism, Neo-Ricardianism and Marxism, *New Left Review* no. 86:63-87.

Rubel, A. J., and H. J. Kupferer. 1968. Perspectives on the Atomistic-Type Society—Introduction. *Human Organization,* 189-190.

Rubel, P. 1969. Herd Composition and Social Structure: On Building Models of Nomadic Pastoral Societies. *Man* (N.S.) 4:268-273.

Rubin, J. 1968. *National Bilingualism in Paraguay.* Janua Linguarum, Series Practica 60. The Hague: Mouton and Company.

Sackett, J. R. 1968. Method and Theory of Upper Paleolithic Archeology in Southwestern France. In L. R. and S. Binford, eds., *New Perspectives in Archeology.* Chicago: Aldine Publishing Co.

Sacks, K. 1974. Engels Revisited: Women, the Organization of Production, and Private Property. In M. Rosaldo and L. Lamphere, eds., *Women in Culture and Society.* Stanford, Calif.: Stanford University Press.

Sade, D. S. 1968. Inhibition of Son-Mother Mating among Free-Ranging Rhesus Monkeys. In J. H. Masserman, ed., *Animal and Human.* Scientific Proceedings of the American Academy of Psychoanalysis 7:18-38.

Sahagun, B. De. 1951. *The Florentine Codex: General History of the Things of New Spain.* Trans. by A. J. P. Anderson and C. E. Dibble. Santa Fe, N.M.: Museum of New Mexico.

Sahlins, M. 1958. *Social Stratification in Polynesia.* Seattle: University of Washington Press.

———. 1960. Evolution: Specific and General. in M. Sahlins and E. Service, eds., *Evolution and Culture.* Ann Arbor: University of Michigan Press.

———. 1961. The Segmentary Lineage: An Organization of Predatory Expansion. *American Anthropologist* 63:322-343.

———. 1963. Poor Man, Rich Man, Big Man, Chief: Political Types in Melanesia and Polynesia. *Comparative Studies in Society and History* 5:285-300.

———. 1965. On the Sociology of Primitive Exchange. In M. Banton, ed., *The Relevance of Models in Social Anthropology.* ASA Monographs, 1. London: Tavistock.

———. 1971. Economic Anthropology and Anthropological Economics. *Social Science Information* 8(5):13-33.

———. 1972. *Stone Age Economics.* Chicago: Aldine-Atherton, Inc.

———, and E. R. Service, eds. 1960. *Evolution and Culture.* Ann Arbor: University of Michigan Press.

Salisbury, R. F. 1962. *From Stone to Steel: Economic Consequences of a Technological Change in New Guinea.* Melbourne: Melbourne University Press.

———. 1966. Politics and Shell-Money Finance in New Britain. In M. Swartz, V. Turner and A. Tuden, eds., *Political Anthropology.* Chicago: Aldine Publishing Company.

———. 1970. *Vunamami: Economic Transformation in a Traditional Society.* Berkeley: University of California Press.

Sanders, W. T., and B. J. Price. 1968. *Mesoamerica: The Evolution of a Civilization.* New York: Random House, Inc.

Sapir, E. 1949. *Selected Writings of Edward Sapir in Language, Culture and Personality.* D. G. Mandelbaum, ed. Berkeley: University of California Press.

Sarich, V. M. 1970. A Protein Perspective. In J. R. Napier and P. N. Napier, eds., *Old World Monkeys.* New York: Academic Press, Inc.

———. 1971. Human Variation in an Evolutionary Perspective. In P. J. Dolhinow and V. Sarich, eds., *Background for Man: Readings in Physical Anthropology.* Boston: Little, Brown and Company.

Saussure, F. De. 1916. *Cours de Linguistique Générale.* Paris: Payot. (Trans. as *Course in General Linguistics.* 1959. New York: Philosophical Library.)

Schaller, G. B. 1963. *The Mountain Gorilla: Ecology and Behavior.* Chicago: University of Chicago Press.

Schapera, I. 1955. *A Handbook of Tswana Law and Custom.* 2d ed. London: Oxford University Press.

Scheflen, A. E. 1973. *How Behavior Means: Exploring the Contexts of Speech and Meaning; Kinesics, Posture, Setting and Culture.* New York: Gordon and Breach.

Scheffler, H. W. 1970. "The Elementary Structures of Kinship" by C. Lévi-Strauss: A Review Article. *American Anthropologist* 72:251-268.

——. 1971. Dravidian-Iroquois: The Melanesian Evidence. In L. Hiatt and C. Jayarwardena, eds., *Anthropology in Oceania.* Sydney: Angus and Robertson.

——. 1972a. Kinship Semantics. In B. Siegel, ed., *Annual Reviews of Anthropology.* Palo Alto, Calif.: Annual Reviews, Inc.

——. 1972b. Systems of Kin Classification: A Structural Semantic Typology. In P. Reining, ed., *Kinship Studies in the Morgan Centennial Year.* Washington, D.C.: Anthropological Society of Washington.

——. n.d. *Australian System of Kin Classification.* Part 1: *Kariera-Like Systems.* Unpublished MS.

Schlegel, A. 1973. Adolescent Socialization of the Hopi Girl. *Ethnology* 12:449-462.

——. 1974. Review of M. Rosaldo and L. Lamphere, eds., *Women, Culture and Society. Reviews in Anthropology* 1.

Schneider, D. M. 1961. Introduction. In D. Schneider and K. Gough, eds., *Matrilineal Kinship.* Berkeley: University of California Press.

——. 1972. What is Kinship All About? In R. Reining, ed., *Kinship Studies in the Morgan Centennial Year.* Washington, D.C.: Anthropological Society of Washington.

——, and E. K. Gough, eds. 1961. *Matrilineal Kinship.* Berkeley: University of California Press.

Schneider, P., J. Schneider, and E. Hansen. 1972. Modernization and Development: The Role of Regional Elites and Non-Corporate Groups in the European Mediterranean. *Comparative Studies in Society and History.* 14:328-350.

Scholte, B. 1972. Toward a Reflexive and Critical Anthropology. In D. Hymes, ed., *Reinventing Anthropology.* New York: Random House, Inc.

Schwartz, T. 1962. *The Paliau Movement in the Admiralty Islands, 1946-1954.* New York: American Museum of Natural History Occasional Papers, Vol. 49, Part 2.

——. 1963. Systems of Areal Integration: Some considerations based on the Admiralty Islands of Northern Melanesia. *Anthropological Forum* 1:56-97.

Sebeok, T. A. 1968. Goals and Limitations of the Study of Animal Communication. In T. A. Sebeok, ed., *Animal Communication.* Bloomington: Indiana University Press.

Service, E. R. 1962. *Primitive Social Organization: An Evolutionary Perspective.* New York: Random House, Inc.

——. 1966. *The Hunters.* Englewood Cliffs, N.J.: Prentice-Hall, Inc.

——. 1968a. War and our Contemporary Ancestors. In M. Fried et. al. eds., *War: The Anthropology of Armed Conflict and Aggression.* Garden City, N.Y.: Doubleday & Company, Inc.

——. 1968b. The Prime-Mover of Cultural Evolution. *Southwestern Journal of Anthropology* 24(4):396-409.

Shack, W. A. 1973. Urban Ethnicity and the Cultural Process of Urbanization in Ethiopia. In A. Southall, ed., *Urban Anthropology.* London: Oxford University Press.

Shapiro, W. 1970. Local Exogamy and the Wife's Mother in Aboriginal Australia. In R. Berndt, ed., *Australian Aboriginal Anthropology.* Nedlands, Australia: University of Western Australia Press.

Sharp, R. L. 1952. Steel Axes for Stone-Age Australians. *Human Organization* 11:17-22.

Shillinglaw, J. 1870. *Journal of the Rev. Knopwood: Historical Records of Port Phillip.* Melbourne: Government Printer.

Silverman, J. 1967. Shamans and Acute Schizophrenia. *American Anthropologist* 69:21-31.

Sider, K. B. 1967. Affinity and the Role of the Father in the Trobriands. *Southwestern Journal of Anthropology* 23:65-109.

Simonis, Y. 1968. *Claude Lévi-Strauss, ou la Passion de l'Inceste: Introduction au Structuralisme.* Paris: Aubier.

Simons, E. L. 1972. *Primate Evolution: An Introduction to Man's Place in Nature.* New York: The Macmillan Company.

Simpson, G. G. 1966. The Biological Nature of Man. *Science* 152:472-478.

Singer, M., and B. S. Cohn, eds. 1968. *Structure and Change in Indian Society.* Viking Fund Publications in Anthropology, 47. Chicago: Aldine Publishing Company.

Sinha, S. 1967. Caste in India: Its Essential Pattern of Socio-Cultural Integration. In A. De Reuk and J. Knight, eds., *Caste and Race: Comparative Approaches.* London: J. and A. Churchill, Ltd.

Sjoberg, G. 1960. *The Preindustrial City.* New York: The Free Press.

Smith, E. W. 1926. *The Golden Stool: Some Aspects of the Conflict of Cultures in Modern Africa.* London: Holborn Publishing House.

Smith, M. G. 1956. On Segmentary Lineage Systems. *Journal of the Royal Anthropological Institute* 86(2):39-80.

Smith, R. J. 1973. Town and City in Pre-Modern Japan: Small Families, Small Households and Residential Instability. In A. Southall, ed., *Urban Anthropology.* London: Oxford University Press.

Sorensen, A. P., Jr. 1967. Multilingualism in the Northern Amazon. *American Anthropologist* 69(6):670-684.

Southall, A. 1973a. Introduction to *Urban Anthropology.* A. Southall, ed. London: Oxford University Press.

———. 1973b. The Density of Role-Relationships as a Universal Index of Urbanization. In A. Southall, ed., *Urban Anthropology.* London: Oxford University Press.

———, ed. 1973c. *Urban Anthropology: Cross-Cultural Studies of Urbanization.* London: Oxford University Press.

Spencer, R. F., J. D. Jennings, et al. 1965. *The Native Americans.* New York: Harper & Row, Publishers.

Sperry, R. W. 1974. Lateral Specialization in the Surgically Separated Hemispheres. In F. D. Schmitt and F. G. Worden, eds., *The Neurosciences: Third Study Program.* Cambridge, Mass.: MIT Press.

Spicer, E. H. 1961. Yaqui. In E. H. Spicer, ed., *Perspectives in American Indian Culture Change.* Chicago: University of Chicago Press.

———, ed. 1952. *Human Problems in Technological Change: A Casebook.* New York: Russell Sage Foundation.

Spindler, G. D. 1955. *Sociocultural and Psychological Processes in Menomini Acculturation.* Berkeley: University of California Publications in Culture and Society, 5.

———. 1968. Psychocultural Adaptation. In E. Norbeck et al., eds. *The Study of Personality.* New York: Holt, Rinehart and Winston.

———. 1973. *Burgbach: Urbanization and Identity in a German Village.* New York: Holt, Rinehart and Winston.

———. 1974. Schooling in Schönhausen: A Study of Cultural Transmission and Instrumental Adaptation in an Urbanizing German Village. In G. Spindler, ed., *Educa-*

tion and Cultural Process. New York: Holt, Rinehart and Winston.

Spindler, G. E., and L. S. Spindler. 1971. *Dreamers Without Power: The Menomini Indians.* New York: Holt, Rinehart and Winston.

Spindler, L. S. 1962. *Menomini Women and Culture Change.* American Anthropological Association, Memoir 91. *American Anthropologist* 64(1), part 2.

Spiro, M. E. 1966. Religion: Problems of Definition and Explanation. In M. Banton, ed., *Anthropological Approaches to the Study of Religion.* ASA Monographs, 3. London: Tavistock Publications.

Spradley, J. P. 1972a. *Culture and Cognition: Rules, Maps, and Plans.* San Francisco: Chandler Publishing Company.

———. 1972b. Foundations of Cultural Knowledge. In J. P. Spradley, ed., *Culture and Cognition: Rules, Maps, and Plans.* pp. 3-40. San Francisco: Chandler Publishing Company.

Stack, C. B. 1974. *All Our Kin: Strategies for Survival in a Black Community.* New York: Harper & Row, Publishers.

Stanner, W. E. H. 1956. The Dreaming. In T. A. G. Hungerford, ed., *Australian Signpost.* Melbourne: F. W. Chesire.

———. 1963. On Aboriginal Religion. *Oceania Monographs,* no. 2. Sydney.

———. 1965. Religion, Totemism and Symbolism. In R. M. and C. H. Berndt, eds., *Aboriginal Man in Australia.* Sydney: Angus and Robertson.

———. 1973. Fictions, Nettles and Freedoms. *Search* 4(4):104-111.

Stavenhagen, R. 1975. *Social Classes in Agrarian Societies.* Garden City, New York: Doubleday & Company, Inc. (Anchor Book).

Steward, J. H. 1938. Basin-Plateau Aboriginal Sociopolitical Groups. *Bureau of American Ethnology Bulletin* 120. Washington, D.C.: Government Printing Office.

———. 1949. Cultural Causality and Law: A Trial Formulation of the Development of Early Civilizations. *American Anthropologist* 51:1-27.

———, ed. 1955a. *Irrigation Civilizations: A Comparative Study.* Social Science Monograph 1. Washington, D.C.: Pan American Union.

———. 1955b. *Theory of Culture Change.* Urbana: University of Illinois Press.

Strathern, A. J. 1972. *One Father, One Blood.* Canberra: Australian National University Press.

Suzuki, A. 1969. An Ecological Study of Chimpazees in a Savanna Woodland. *Primates* 10:103-148.

Swartz, M. J. 1968a. Introduction to *Local Level Politics.* M. J. Swartz, ed. Chicago: Aldine Publishing Co.

———, ed. 1968b. *Local Level Politics.* Chicago: Aldine Publishing Co.

Swartz, M. J., V. Turner, and A. Tuden, eds. 1966. *Political Anthropology.* Chicago: Aldine Publishing Co.

Talmon, Y. 1962. Pursuit of the Millenium: The Relation Between Religious and Social Change. *Archives Européennes de Sociologie* III: 125-148.

Tambiah, S. J. 1969. The Magical Power of Words. *Man* 3(2): 175-208.

Tawney, R. H. 1926. *Religion and the Rise of Capitalism.* London: John Murray, (Publishers) Ltd.

Teleki, G. 1973. *The Predatory Behavior of Wild Chimpanzees.* Lewisburg, Pa.: Bucknell University Press.

Terray, E. 1972. *Marxism and 'Primitive' Societies.* New York: Monthly Review Press.

Textor, R. B. 1967. *Cross-Cultural Summary.* New Haven, Conn.: Human Relations Area Files Press.

Thrupp, S., ed. 1962. Millennial Dreams in Action: Essays in Comparative Study. *Comparative Studies in Society and History,* Supplement No. 2. The Hague: Mouton. (Reprinted in 1970 as *Millennial Dreams in Action: Studies in Revolutionary Religious Movements.* New York: Schocken Books, Inc.)

Thurwald, R. 1916. *Bánaro Society: Social Organization and Kinship System of a Tribe in the Interior of New Guinea.* American Anthropological Association Memoir 3, no. 2. Lancaster, Pa.: New Era Printing Company.

Tiger, L. 1969. *Men in Groups.* New York: Random House, Inc.

Tinker, H. 1974. *A New System of Slavery: The Export of Indian Labour Overseas, 1830-1920.* Oxford: Oxford University Press.

Tipps, D. C. 1973. Modernization and Comparative Study of Society. *Comparative Studies in Society and History* 15:199-226.

Trigger, B. 1971. Archaeology and Ecology. *World Archaeology* 2:321-326.

———. 1972. Determinants of Urban Growth in Pre-Industrial Societies. In P. J. Ucko, R. Tringham and G. W. Dimbleby, eds., *Man, Settlement and Urbanism.* London: Gerald Duckworth & Co., Ltd.

Turnbull, C. M. 1961. *The Forest People: A Study of the Pygmies of the Congo.* New York: Simon & Schuster, Inc.

Turner, V. 1957. *Schism and Continuity in an African Society.* New York: Humanities Press, Inc. (Reprinted 1972.)

———. 1964. Betwixt and Between: The Liminal Period in Rites de Passage. In J. Helm, ed., *Proceedings of the 1964 Annual Spring Meeting of the American Ethnological Society.* Seattle: University of Washington Press.

———. 1966. Colour Classification in Ndembu Ritual. In M. Banton, ed., *Anthropological Approaches to the Study of Religion.* ASA Monographs, 3. London: Tavistock Publications.

———. 1967. *The Forest of Symbols: Studies in Ndembu Ritual.* Ithaca, N.Y.: Cornell University Press.

———. 1968a. Mukanda: The Politics of a Non-Political Ritual. In M. J. Swartz, ed., *Local Level Politics.* Chicago: Aldine Publishing Company.

———. 1968b. *The Drums of Affliction: A Study of Religious Processes among the Ndembu of Zambia.* Oxford: Clarendon Press.

Tuttle, R. H. 1969. Knuckle-walking and the Problem of Human Origins. *Science* 166:953-961.

Tyler, S. ed. 1969. *Cognitive Anthropology.* New York: Holt, Rinehart and Winston.

Tylor, E. B. 1871. *Primitive Culture: Researches into the Development of Mythology, Philosophy, Religion, Art and Custom.* London: John Murray, (Publishers) Ltd.

———. 1889. On a Method of Investigating the Development of Institutions; applied to Laws of Marriage and Descent. *Journal of the Royal Anthropological Institute* 18:245-269.

Uberoi, J. P. Singh. 1962. *Politics of the Kula Ring.* Manchester, England: University of Manchester Press.

Ucko, P. J., and A. Rosenfeld. 1967. *Palaeolithic Cave Art.* London: Weidenfeld and Nicolson.

Udall, L. 1969. *Me and Mine: The Life Story of Helen Sekaquaptewa.* Tucson: University of Arizona Press.

Valentine, C. A. 1968. *Culture and Poverty: Critique and Counter-Proposals.* Chicago: University of Chicago Press.

———, and B. Valentine. 1971. *Anthropological Interpretations of Black Culture.*

Reading, Mass.: Addison-Wesley Modules in Anthropology.

Van Baal, J. 1966. *Dema: Description and Analysis of Culture* (South New Guinea). The Hague: Martinius Nijhoff.

Van Gennep, A. 1909. *Les Rites de Passage.* Paris: Librairie Critique Emile Nourry. (Trans. as *The Rites of Passage.* 1960. London: Routledge & Kegan Paul Ltd.)

Van Lawick-Goodall, J. 1968a. The Behavior of Free-Living Chimpanzees in the Gombe Stream Reserve. *Animal Behavior Monographs* 1:161-311.

———. 1968b. Expressive Movements and Communications in Chimpanzees. In P. Jay, ed., *Primates: Studies in Adaptation and Variability.* New York: Holt, Rinehart and Winston, Inc.

———. 1971. Some Aspects of Mother-Infant Relationships in a Group of Wild Chimpanzees. In H. R. Schaffer, ed., *The Origin of Human Social Relations.* London and New York: Academic Press, Inc.

Van Velsen, J. 1967. The Extended-case Method and Situational Analysis. In A. L. Epstein, ed., *The Craft of Social Anthropology.* London: Tavistock Publications. Pp. 129-149.

Van Zantwijk, R. A. M. 1967. *Servants of the Saints: The Social and Cultural Identity of a Tarascan Community in Mexico.* Assen, Holland: Van Gorcum.

Vayda, A. P. 1961. Expansion and Warfare among Swidden Agriculturalists. *American Anthropologist* 63:346-358.

———. 1968. Primitive Warfare. *International Encyclopedia of Social Science* 16:468-472. New York: The Macmillan Company.

———. 1969. An Ecological Approach to Cultural Anthropology. *Bucknell Review* 17:112-119.

———, and Rappaport, R. 1968. Ecology, Cultural and Noncultural. In J. A. Clifton, ed., *Introduction to Cultural Anthropology.* Boston: Houghton Mifflin Company.

Vogt, E. Z. 1965. Structural and Conceptual Replication in Zinacantan Culture. *American Anthropologist* 67:342-353.

———. 1969. *Zinacantan: A Maya Community in the Highlands of Chiapas.* Cambridge, Mass.: Harvard University Press.

———. 1970. *The Zinacantecos of Mexico: A Modern Maya Way of Life.* New York: Holt, Rinehart and Winston, Inc.

Waddington, C. H., ed. 1968. *Towards a Theoretical Biology,* Vol. I: Prolegomena. Chicago: Aldine Publishing Company.

———, ed. 1969. *Towards a Theoretical Biology,* Vol. II: Sketches. Chicago: Aldine Press.

———, ed. 1970. *Toward a Theoretical Biology,* Vol. III. Chicago: Aldine Press.

———, ed. 1973. *Towards a Theoretical Biology,* Vol. IV: Essays. Chicago: Aldine Publishing Company.

Wahrhaftig, A. L., and R. K. Thomas. 1972. Renaissance and Repression: The Oklahoma Cherokee. In H. M. Bahr, B. A. Chadwick, and R. C. Day, eds., *Native Americans Today: Sociological Perspectives.* New York: Harper & Row, Publishers.

Wallace, A. F. C. 1952. *The Modal Personality of the Tuscarora Indians as Revealed by the Rorschach Test.* Bureau of American Ethnology Bulletin 150. Washington, D.C.: U.S. Government Printing Office.

———. 1956. Revitalization Movements. *American Anthropologist* 58:264-281.

———. 1960. Mental Illness, Biology and Culture. In F. L. K. Hsu, ed., *Psychological Anthropology.* Homewood, Ill: Dorsey Press.

———. 1970. *Culture and Personality.* 2d ed. New York: Random House, Inc.

Warner, W. L. 1937. *A Black Civilization.* New York: Harper & Row, Publishers. (Rev. ed. 1958.)

Washburn, S. 1972. Human Evolution. In T. Dobzhansky, M. K. Hecht, W. C. Steere, eds. *Evolutionary Biology,* Vol. 6. New York: Appleton-Century-Crofts.

———. 1973. Primate Field Studies and Social Science. In L. Nader and T. Maretzki, eds., *Cultural Illness and Health: Essays in Human Adaptation.* Anthropological Studies 9.

———, and R. S. Harding. 1970. Evolution of Primate Behavior. In F. O. Schmitt, ed. *The Neurosciences: Second Study Program.* New York: Rockefeller University Press.

———, and C. S. Lancaster. 1968. The Evolution of Hunting. In R. B. Lee and I. De Vore, eds., *Man the Hunter.* Chicago: Aldine Publishing Company.

———, and S. C. Strum. 1972. Concluding Comments. In S. Washburn and P. Dolhinow, eds. *Perspectives on Human Evolution,* 2. New York: Holt, Rinehart and Winston.

Weber, M. 1956. *The Protestant Ethic and the Spirit of Capitalism.* New York: Charles Scribner's Sons.

Webster, H. 1932. *Primitive Secret Societies.* Rev. ed. New York: The Macmillan Company.

Wedgewood, C. 1930. The Nature and Function of Secret Societies. *Oceania,* 129-145.

Weiner, A. 1974. *Women of Value: The Main Road of Exchange in Kiriwina, Trobriand Islands.* Unpublished Ph.D. Dissertation, Bryn Mawr College. (Quoted with Dr. Weiner's permission. Forthcoming as a book, University of Texas Press, Austin.)

White, D. R., G. P. Murdock, and R. Scaglion. 1971. Natchez Class and Rank Reconsidered. *Ethnology* 10(4):369-388.

Whiting, B. B., ed. 1963. *Six Cultures: Studies of Child Rearing.* New York: John Wiley & Sons, Inc.

Whiting, J. W. M. 1964. Effects of Climate on Certain Cultural Practices. In W. Goodenough, ed. *Explorations in Cultural Anthropology.* New York: McGraw-Hill, Inc.

Whorf, B. L. 1956. *Language, Thought and Reality: Selected Writings of B. L. Whorf.* J. B. Carroll, ed. Cambridge, Mass., and New York: MIT Press and John Wiley & Sons, Inc.

Whyte, W. F. 1955. *Street Corner Society: The Social Structure of an Italian Slum.* Rev. ed. Chicago: University of Chicago Press.

Wilbert, J. 1972. *Survivors of Eldorado: Four Indian Cultures of South America.* New York: Praeger Publishers, Inc.

Williams, E. 1944. *Capitalism and Slavery.* Chapel Hill, N.C.: University of North Carolina Press.

———. 1966. *British Historians and the West Indies.* London: Andre Deutsch.

Williams, F. E. 1923. *The Vailala Madness and the Destruction of Native Ceremonies in the Gulf Division.* Territory of Papua Anthropological Reports, 4. Port Moresby, New Guinea.

Williamson, K. 1962. Changes in the Marriage System of the Okrika Ijo. *Africa* 32:53-60.

Wilson, A. C., and V. M. Sarich. 1969. A Molecular Time Scale for Human Evolution. *Proceedings of the National Academy of Science* 63:1088-1093.

Wilson, P. 1969. Virgin Birth: A Comment. *Man* (n.s.) 4(2):287-290.

———. 1972. *Crab Antics: The Social Anthropology of English-speaking Negro Societies of the Caribbean.* New Haven, Conn.: Yale University Press.

Wittfogel, K. A. 1955. Developmental Aspects of Hydraulic Societies. In J. Steward, ed.

Irrigation Civilizations: A Comparative Study. Washington, D.C.: Pan American Union.

———. 1957. *Oriental Despotism: A Study in Total Power.* New Haven, Conn.: Yale University Press.

Wolf, A. D. 1966. Childhood Association, Sexual Attraction, and the Incest Taboo: A Chinese Case. *American Anthropologist* 68:883-898.

———. 1970. Childhood Association and Sexual Attraction: A Further Test of the Westermarck Hypothesis. *American Anthropologist* 72:503-515.

Wolf, E. R. 1957. Closed Corporate Peasant Communities in Mesoamerica and Central Java. *Southwestern Journal of Anthropology* 13:1-18.

———. 1958. The Virgin of Guadalupe: A Mexican National Symbol. *Journal of American Folklore* 71:34-39.

———. 1959. *Sons of the Shaking Earth.* Chicago: University of Chicago Press.

———. 1966a. *Peasants.* Englewood Cliffs, N.J.: Prentice-Hall, Inc.

———. 1966b. Kinship, Friendship, and Patron-Client Relations in Complex Societies. In M. Banton, ed. *The Social Anthropology of Complex Societies.* New York: Praeger Publishers, Inc.

———. 1969a. *Peasant Wars of the Twentieth Century.* New York: Harper & Row, Publishers.

———. 1969b. On Peasant Rebellions. *International Social Science Journal* 21(2):286-294.

Wolpert, L. 1968. The French Flag Problem. In C. H. Waddington, ed. *Towards a Theoretical Biology,* Vol. 1. Chicago: Aldine Publishing Company.

Worsley, P. 1957. *The Trumpet Shall Sound: A Study of "Cargo" Cults in Melanesia.* London: MacGibbon and Kee. (2d ed. 1968. New York: Schocken Books, Inc.)

Wynne-Edwards, V. C. 1962. *Animal Dispersion in Relation to Social Behaviour.* New York: Hafner Publishing Co., Inc.

Yamey, B. S., and R. Firth, eds. 1964. *Capital, Saving and Credit in Peasant Societies: Studies from Asia, Oceania, the Caribbean and Middle America.* London: George Allen & Unwin Ltd.

Yap, P. M. 1969. The Culture-Bound Reactive Syndromes. In W. Caudill and T. Y. Lin, eds. *Culture and Mental Health Research in Asia and the Pacific.* Honolulu: East-West Center Press.

Yazaki, T. 1963. *The Japanese City: A Sociological Analysis.* Tokyo: Japan Publications.

———. 1968. *Social Change and the City in Japan.* Tokyo: Japan Publications.

———. 1973. The History of Urbanization in Japan. In A. Southall, ed. *Urban Anthropology.* London: Oxford University Press.

Young, F. W. 1956. *Initiation Ceremonies: A Cross-Cultural Study of Status Dramatization.* Indianapolis, Ind.: The Bobbs-Merrill Company, Inc.

Zaretzky, E. 1973. Capitalism, the Family and Personal Life. *Socialist Revolution,* January-June. (Reprinted as a bound pamphlet by Loaded Press, Santa Cruz, Calif., 1974.)

Zihlman, A. L., and W. S. Hunter. 1972. A Biomechanical Interpretation of the Pelvis of Australopithecus. *Folia Primatologica.*

INDEXES

NAME INDEX

SUBJECT INDEX

Abnormal behavior, 371-377
Abstraction, culture as, 141-142
Acculturation, 427
Acheulean tools, 32, 34, 36
Action groups, 232, 241-242, 264, 271
Adaptive radiation, 18, 97, 104, 108, 207
Adaptive system(s), cultures as, 207; pastoralism as, 97, 105-106, 116-120; shifting cultivation as, 109-116
Adolescence, 233
Adoption, 240-241, 258, 262, 297
Aegyptopithecus, 21, 22
Affinal kinship, 93, 241, 261, 278-282
Affluent society, "first," 88
Africa, agriculture in, spread of, 106-107; apartheid, 11, 345, 476-477; independence movements, 447-448; legal systems, 379; missionaries in, 430, 460; pidgin language, 457-458; religions, 386, 391; residence patterns, 259; slave trade, 430, 450, 457-458; technology, 106, 107
Age, cultural treatment of, 232-235
Age sets, 235, 301-304
Aggression, channeling of, 369; displaced, 369, 419-420; human, 51-52, 69, 186-187, 198-199, 364-365; phallic, 199; in primates, 44, 46, 47, 372; *see also* Warfare
Agnatic (patrilineal) descent, 244-253, 264-265, 270, 277-278, 284, 295
Agricultural involution, 494
Agriculture, dry farming, 99; East Asian origin, 102-103; irrigation, 99, 101, 104-106, 122, 127-129; Near East origin, 98-101; New World origin, 101-102; pastoralism, 97, 105-106, 116-120; plow, 107; spread of, 84, 85, 103-108; swidden cultivation, 106, 109-116, 128, 256, 262, 263, 313
Algorithms, linguistic, 170
Alliance for Progress, 535
Ambivalence, 193-196, 235, 521
American Fur Company, 463
Amity, axiom of, 241
Anasazi culture, 107
Ancestor worship, 386, 460
Ancestors, 243-245, 392-398
Andaman Islanders, 349, 402, 448
Andean civilizations, 129-130
Animals, communication in, 45, 52-58, 166, 170; domestication of, 97, 99, 101, 102, 104-106, 112; species, relations between, 48-49; *see also* Primates
Animatism, 94, 386

Animism, 94, 133, 386, 436
Anthropological linguistics, 3
Anthropology, applied, 526, 531-535; and colonialism, 429-433, 527-531; cultural, use of term, 3, 138; decolonization of, 537-542; development studies, 534-537; economic, 307-338; as field of knowledge, 2-4; fieldwork and, 8-14; linguistic implications for, 156-163; physical, 2, 17-73, 76; reasons for studying, 227; and science, 4-8; social, 3, 8, 76; subfields of, 2-4; symbolic, 163; and Third World, 526-545; urban, 506-516; women and, 517-525; and world survival, 542-545
Apartheid, 11, 345, 476-477
Apes (*see* Primates)
Applied anthropology, 526, 531-535
Arapaho Indians, 464-465
Arapesh (New Guinea), 441-442, 518, 519, 545
Archaeology, new approaches to, 74-76; prehistoric, 3, 75
Archaeomagnetic dating, 75
Archaic cultures, 83-85, 107
Art, 124, 127, 128, 130, 131, 138, 169, 177, 191, 208, 216, 424; cave, 80-81; primary process of, 425
Ashanti (West Africa), 447, 472
Assiniboin Indians, 352, 446, 449
Astronomy, 128, 131
Aurignacian culture, 78-80
Australian Aborigines, 1, 68, 70, 84-86; "Coranderrk rebellion," 469-471; kinship system, 288-290; legal process, 383; marriage rules, 289-290; physical decimation of populations, 445-446; political organization, 93, 349; religion, 94, 95, 390, 391; technology and adaptation, 75, 87-90, 440-441; warfare, 366-368
Australopithecines, 23-29, 41, 42, 50
Australopithecus africanus, 24-26
Australopithecus robustus, 24-26
Austronesians, 104
Avoidance relationships, 374-375, 409
Axiom of amity, 241
Aymara (South America), 186-187
Aztecs (Mexico), 129, 178, 343-344, 447, 452-453, 498

Banaro (New Guinea), 237-238
Bands, patrilocal, 90, 91, 296; social organization, 242-243
Bantu peoples, 107, 433
Barter, Trobriand, 325-326, 336